CLOVER

COLLECTOR'S EDITION

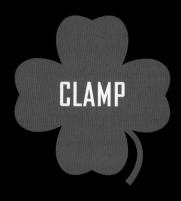

CLAMP

CLOVER: Collector's Edition copyright © 1997-1999 CLAMP·Shigatsu Tsuitachi Co., Ltd. / Kodansha Ltd.
©Haruhiko Shono/Inside Out with GADGET
English translation copyright © 2020 CLAMP·Shigatsu Tsuitachi Co., Ltd. / Kodansha Ltd.
©Haruhiko Shono/Inside Out with GADGET

All rights reserved.

Published in the United States by Kodansha Comics, an imprint of Kodansha USA Publishing, LLC, New York.

Publication rights for this English edition arranged through Kodansha Ltd., Tokyo.

First published in Japan in 1997-1999 by Kodansha Ltd., Tokyo as *CLOVER*, volumes 1-4.

ISBN 978-1-64651-020-7

Printed in China.

www.kodanshacomics.com

9 8 7 6 5 4 3 2 1
Translation: Ray Yoshimoto
Additional translation: Karen McGillicuddy
Lettering: Scott O. Brown
Editing: Vanessa Tenazas
Kodansha Comics edition cover design by Phil Balsman

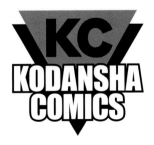

Publisher: Kiichiro Sugawara
Managing editor: Maya Rosewood
Vice president of marketing & publicity: Naho Yamada

Director of publishing services: Ben Applegate
Associate director of operations: Stephen Pakula
Publishing services managing editor: Noelle Webster
Assistant production managers: Emi Lotto, Angela Zurlo

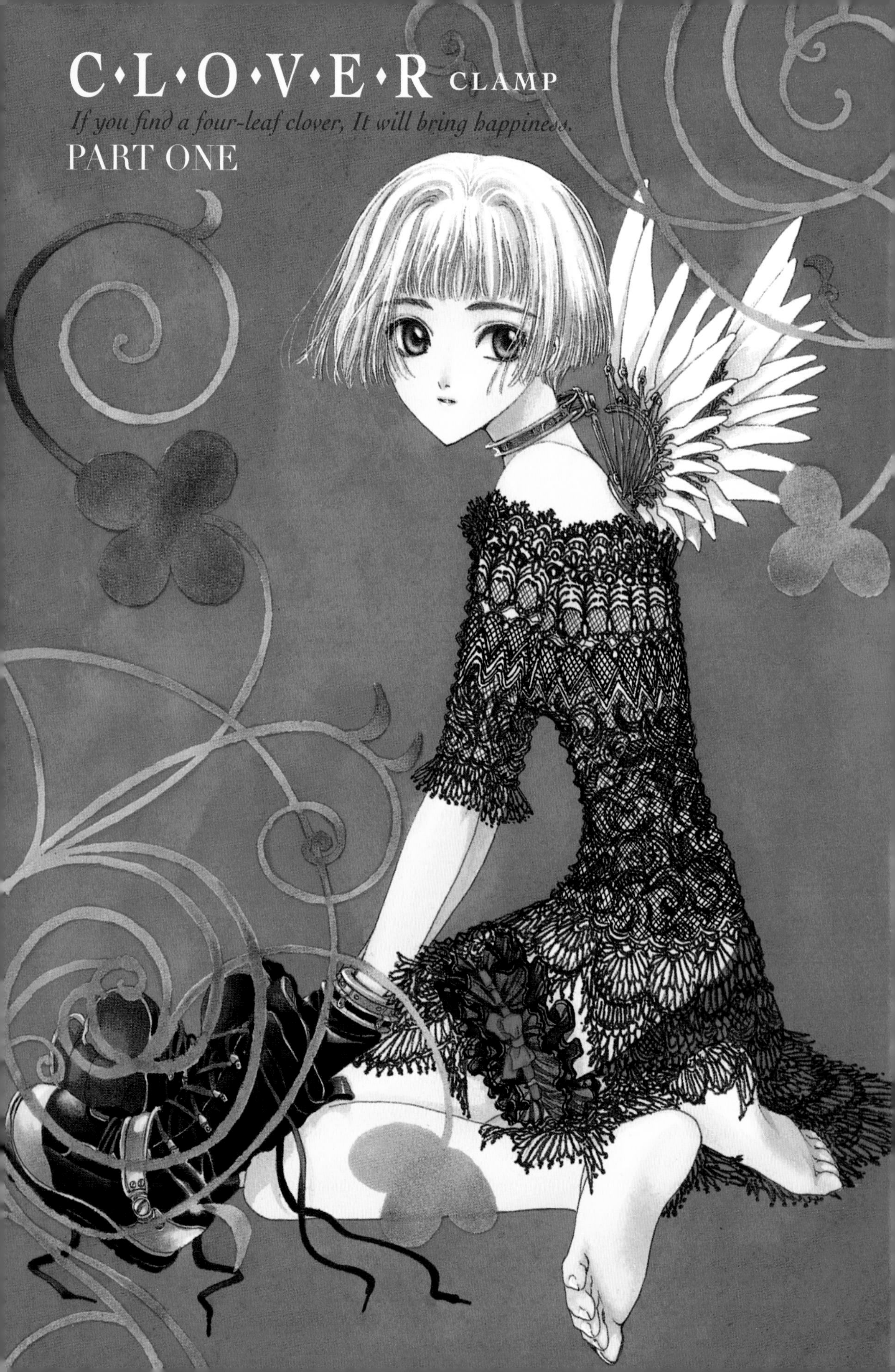
C·L·O·V·E·R CLAMP
If you find a four-leaf clover, It will bring happiness.
PART ONE

I wish for happiness
I seek happiness

To find happiness with you
To be your happiness

So take me
Somewhere far away
To a true Elsewhere
Please take me

An unbreakable spell
A never-ending kiss
An endless dream
Eternal happiness

Take me away
I wish for happiness

The birds sing a song
In a foreign tongue
In a place where wings
Are not enough

A place I cannot reach alone

So take me
To a true Elsewhere

Soaked feathers
Fingers locked
The warmth of skin
Two hearts

Take me away
I seek happiness

I don't want your past
I seek your present

Retrace my broken future

Please take me

To happiness

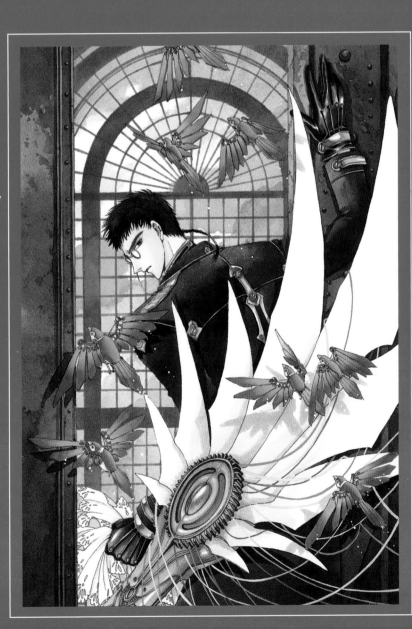

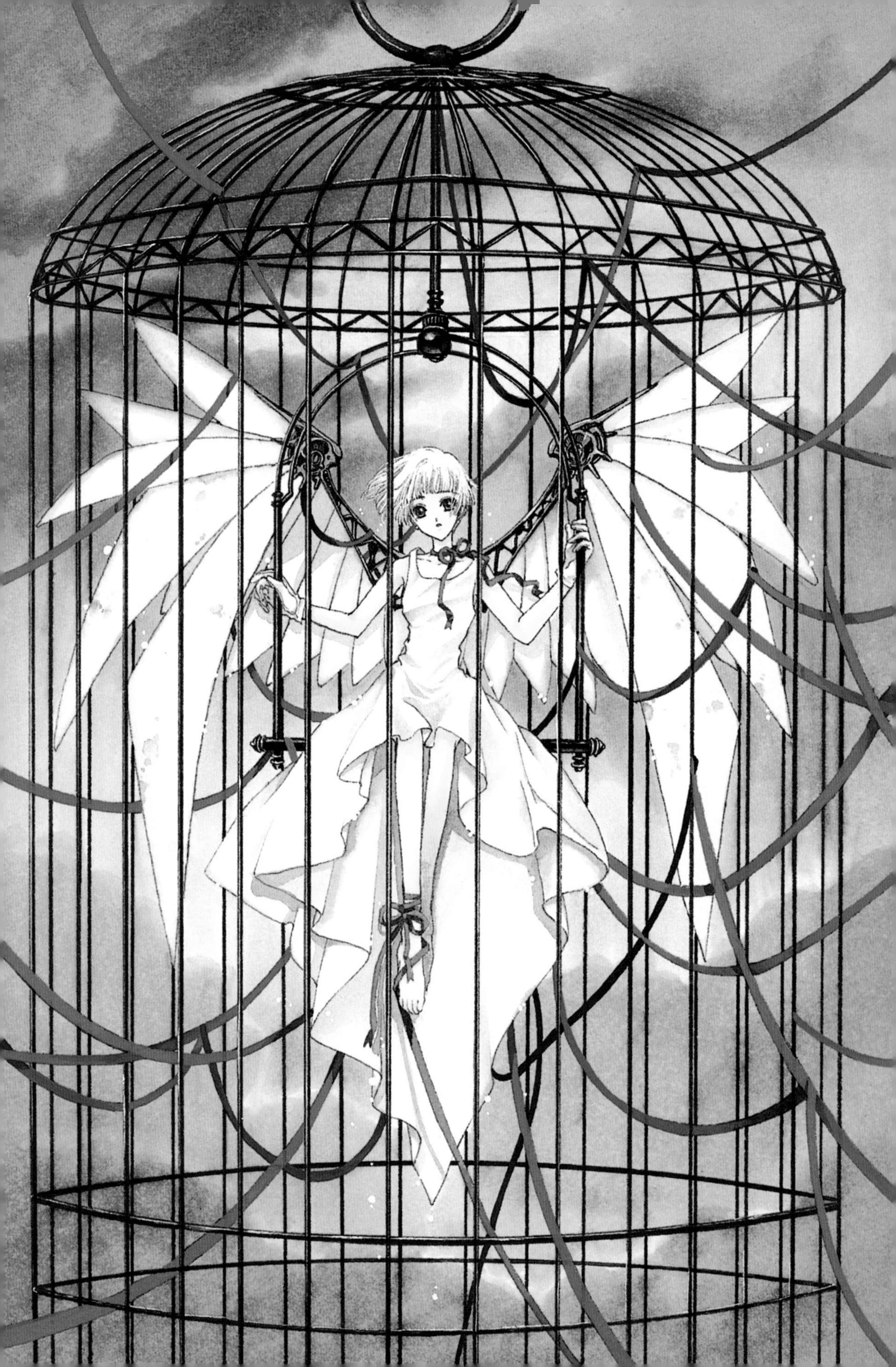

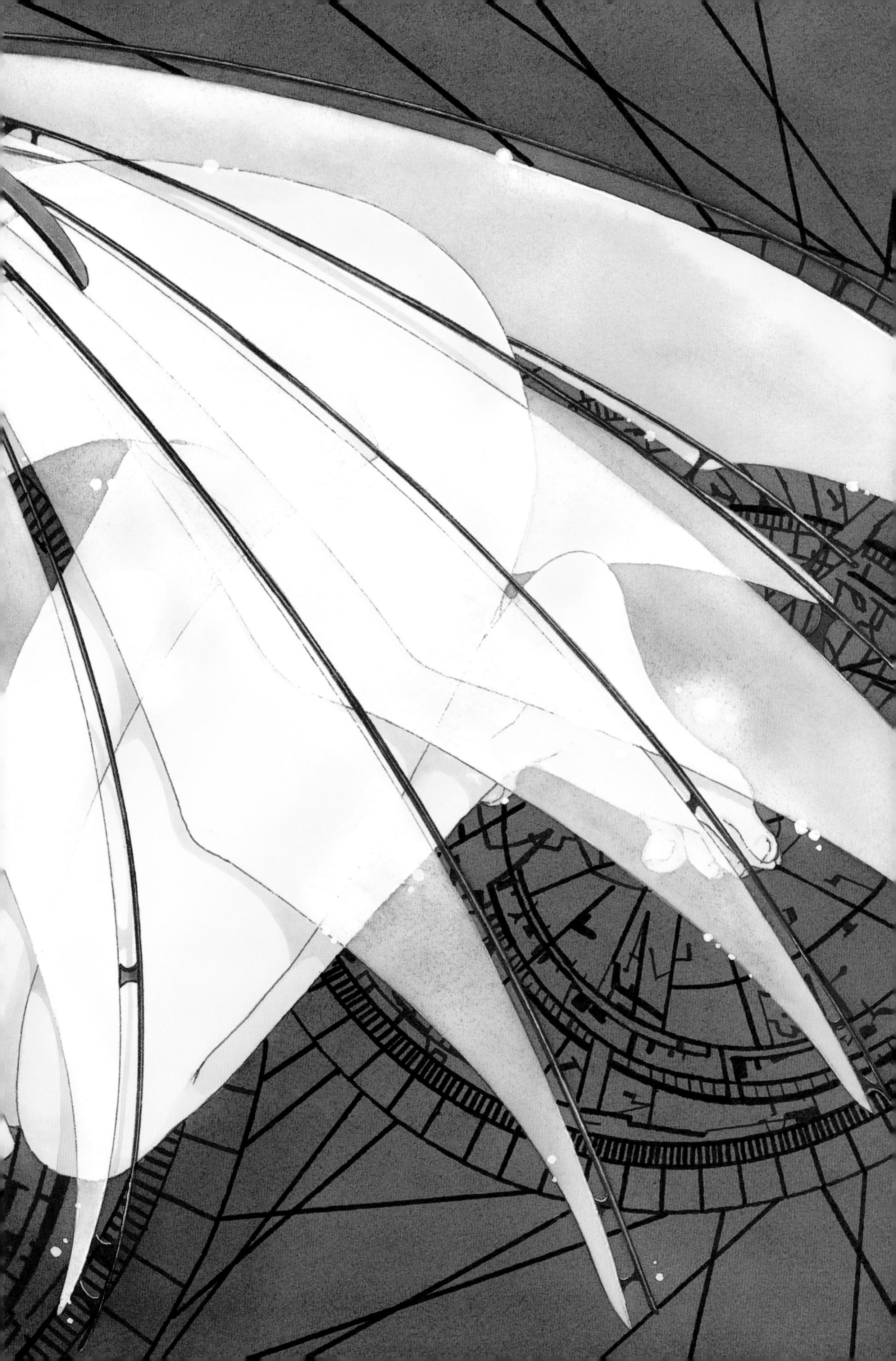

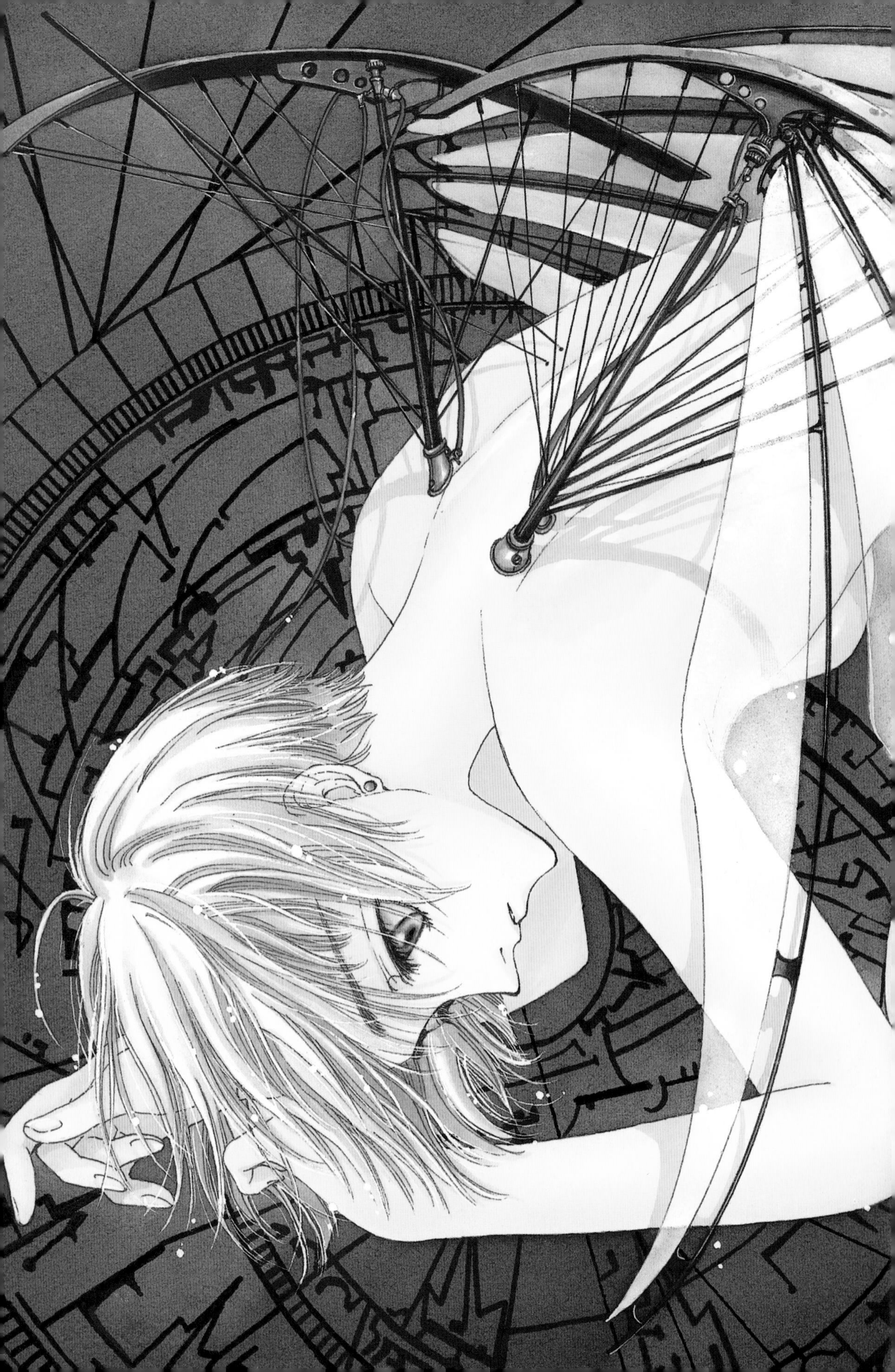

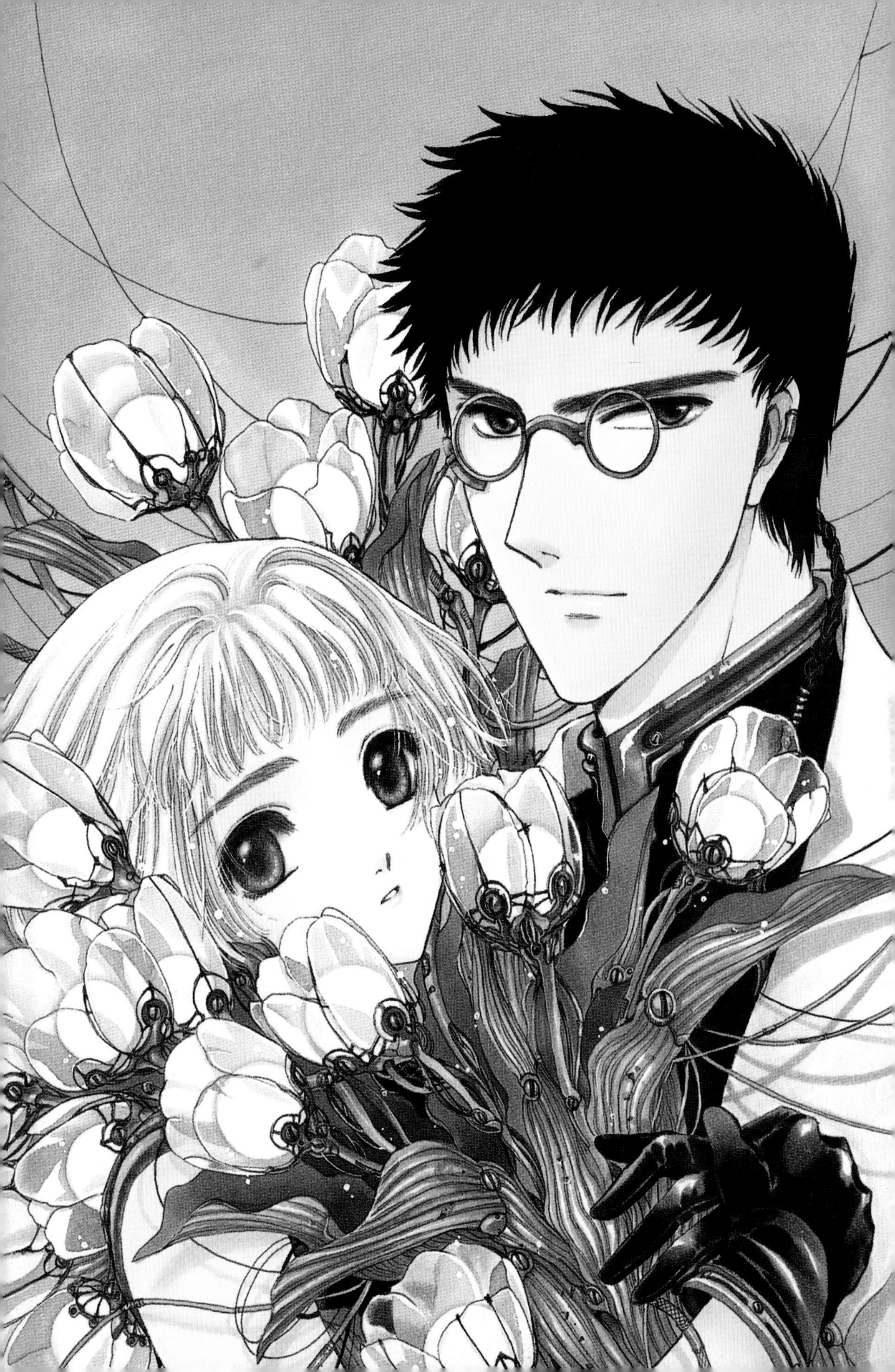

If you find a
four-leaf clover
It will bring you
happiness

But
Don't tell anyone

Where the clovers
Bloom white flowers

Or how many leaves
From its stem extend

A four-leaf clover

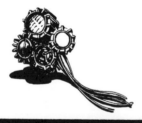

I only want your happiness
But I cannot be yours

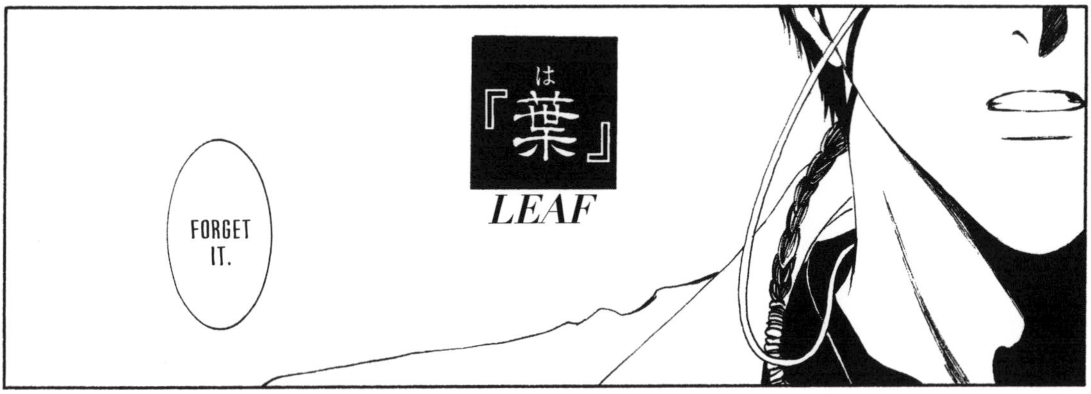
は
『葉』
LEAF
FORGET IT.

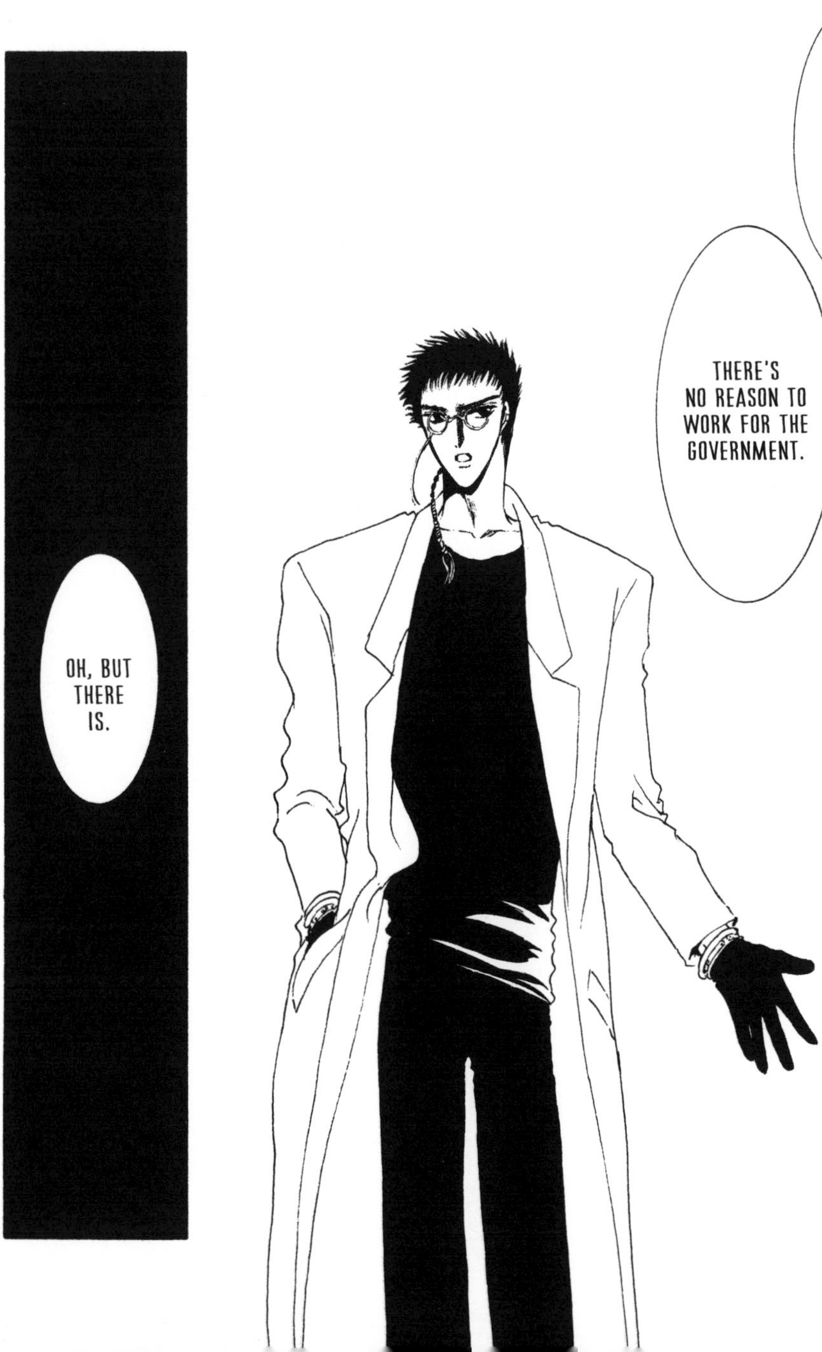
I'M A CIVILIAN NOW.
THERE'S NO REASON TO WORK FOR THE GOVERNMENT.
OH, BUT THERE IS.

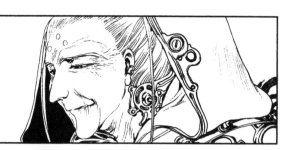

WHEN YOU WERE COURT-MARTIALED, HOW MANY TIMES DO YOU THINK WE PULLED STRINGS FOR YOU?
I NEVER ASKED FOR ANY FAVORS.
WE CAN ALWAYS HAVE THE INVESTIGATION REOPENED.
IS THAT A THREAT?
DO YOU FEEL THREATENED BECAUSE YOU HAVE SOMETHING TO HIDE?
OLD LADY...
...OR SHOULD I ADDRESS YOU AS *GENERAL KO*...?
YOU COULD GET ANY AGENT–
KAZUHIKO, I BELIEVE I SAID AFTER YOUR SIXTH COURT-MARTIAL...

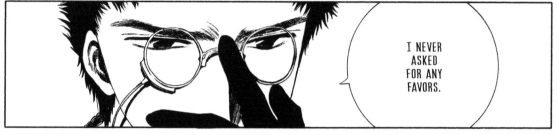

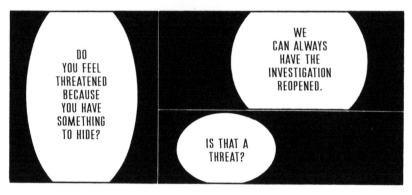

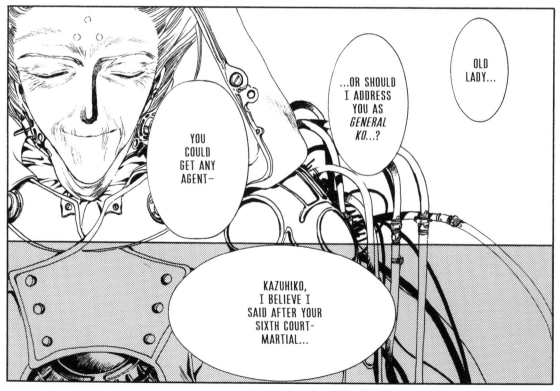

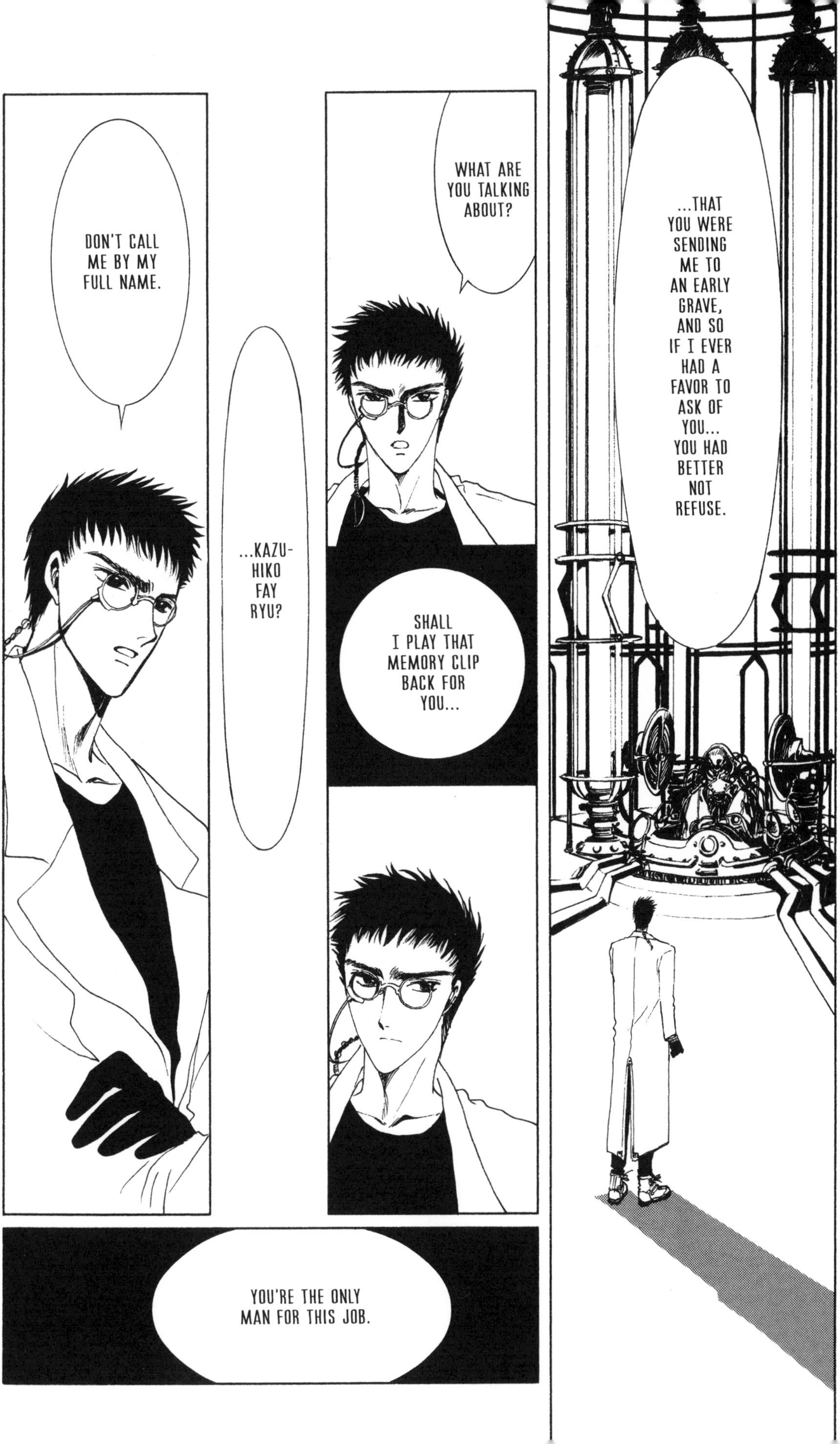
...KAZUHIKO FAY RYU?
DON'T CALL ME BY MY FULL NAME.
WHAT ARE YOU TALKING ABOUT?
SHALL I PLAY THAT MEMORY CLIP BACK FOR YOU...
...THAT YOU WERE SENDING ME TO AN EARLY GRAVE, AND SO IF I EVER HAD A FAVOR TO ASK OF YOU... YOU HAD BETTER NOT REFUSE.
YOU'RE THE ONLY MAN FOR THIS JOB.

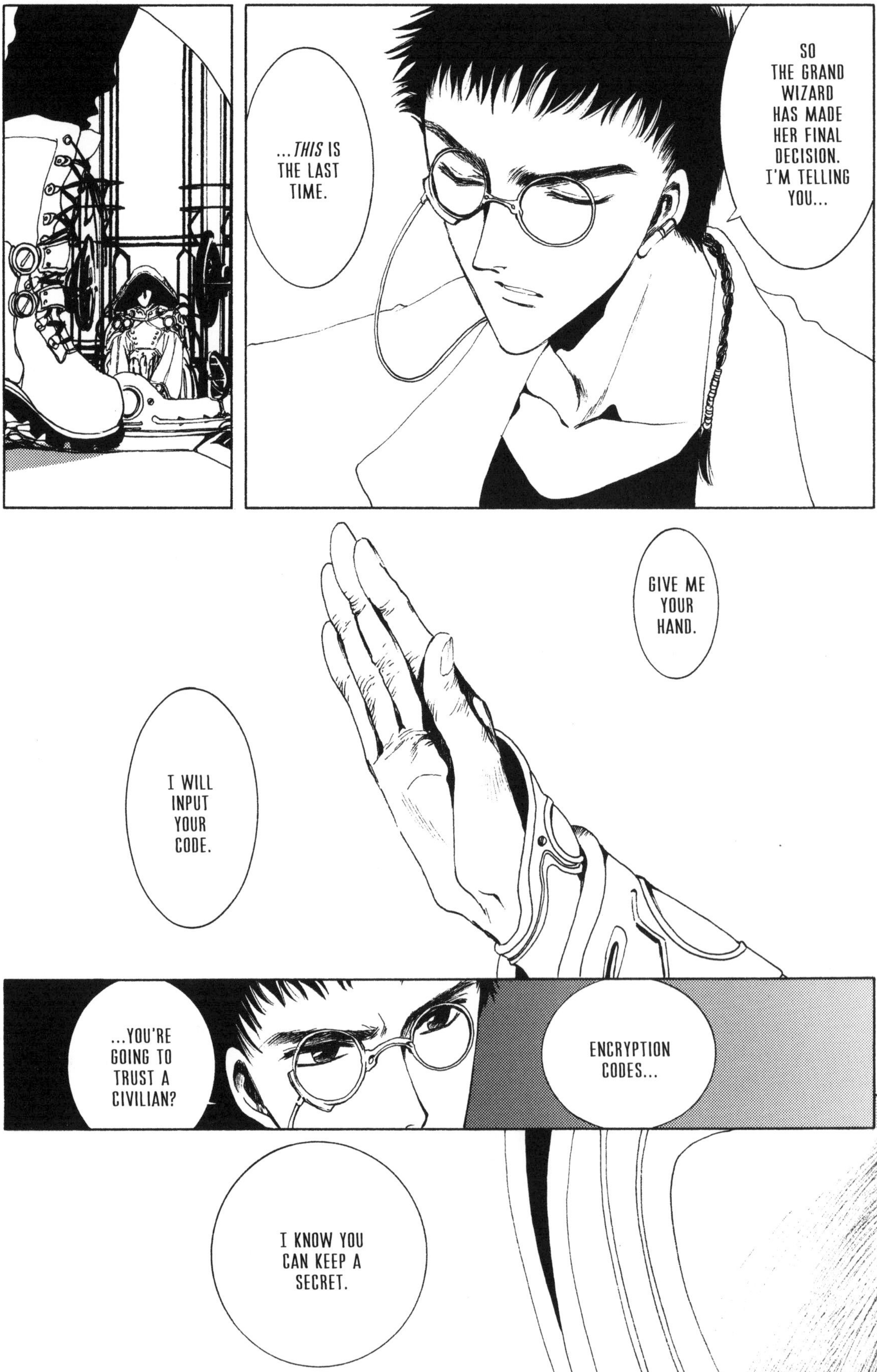
SO THE GRAND WIZARD HAS MADE HER FINAL DECISION. I'M TELLING YOU...
...*THIS* IS THE LAST TIME.
GIVE ME YOUR HAND.
I WILL INPUT YOUR CODE.
ENCRYPTION CODES...
...YOU'RE GOING TO TRUST A CIVILIAN?
I KNOW YOU CAN KEEP A SECRET.

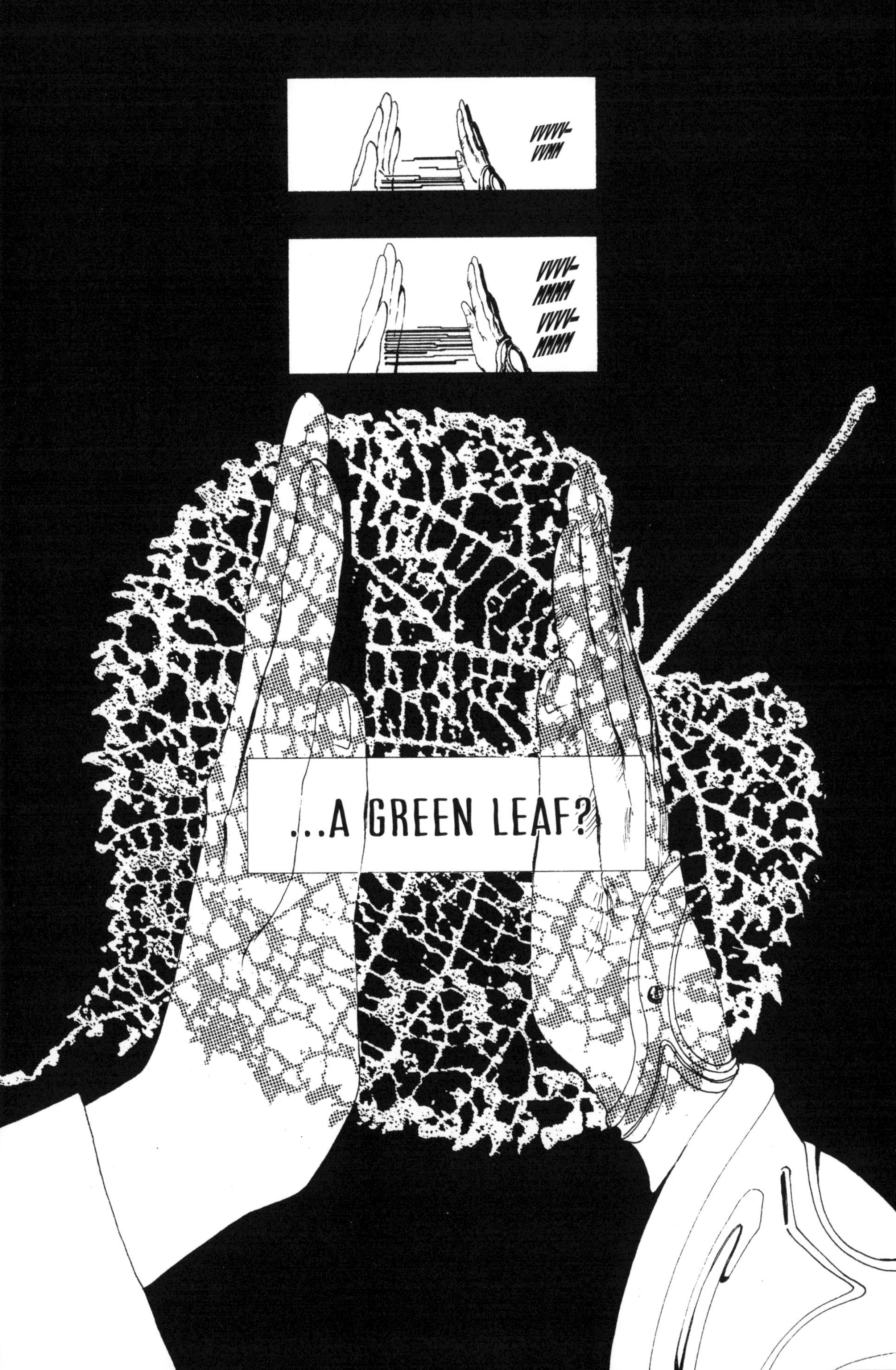
VVVVV-VVMM
VVVV-MMMM
VVVV-MMMM
...A GREEN LEAF?

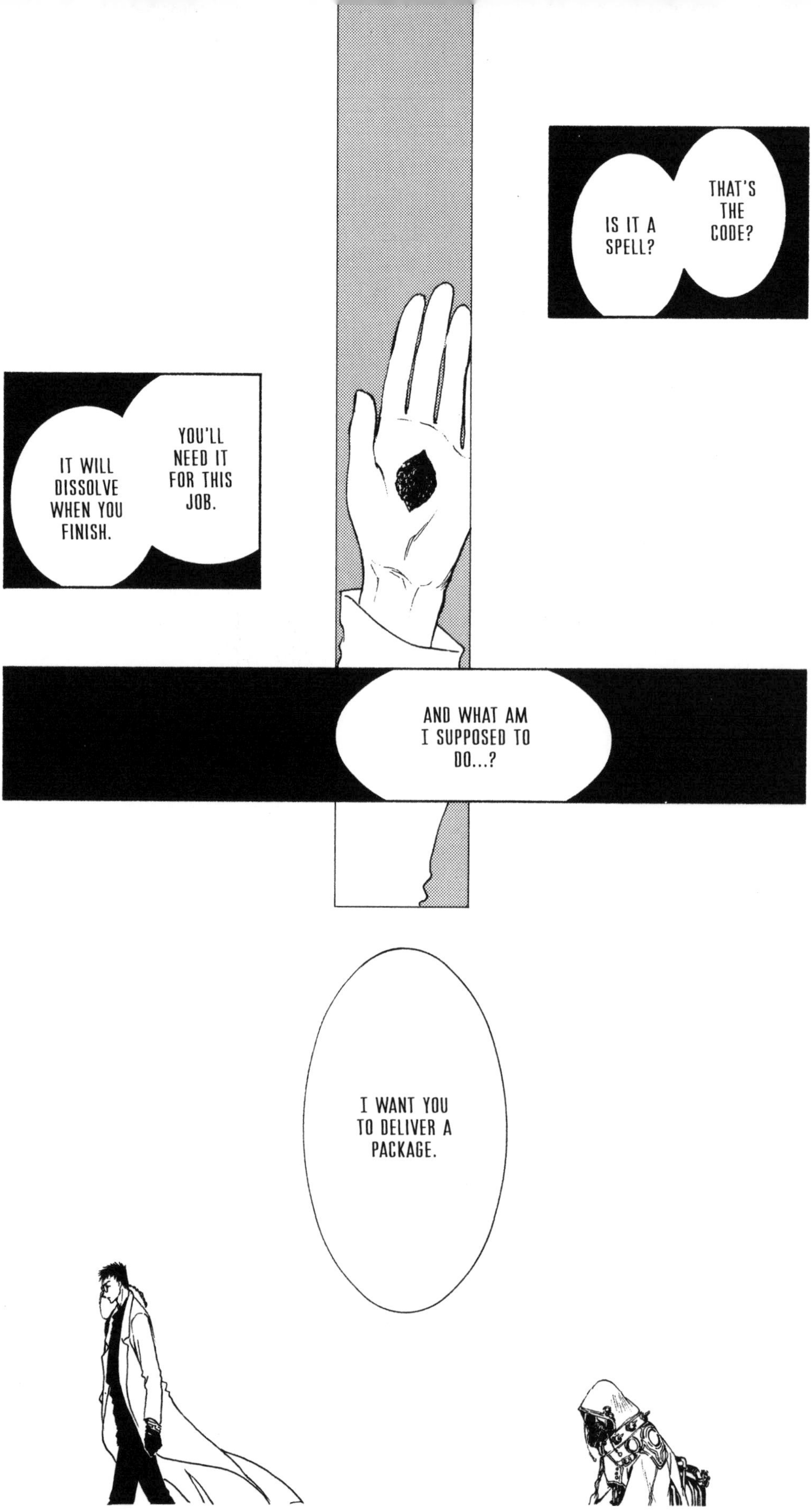
THAT'S THE CODE?
IS IT A SPELL?
YOU'LL NEED IT FOR THIS JOB.
IT WILL DISSOLVE WHEN YOU FINISH.
AND WHAT AM I SUPPOSED TO DO...?
I WANT YOU TO DELIVER A PACKAGE.

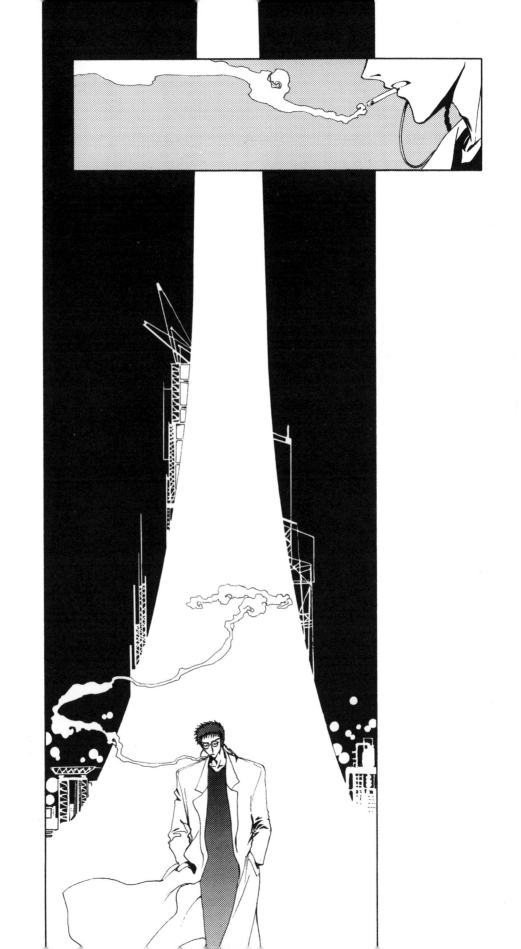

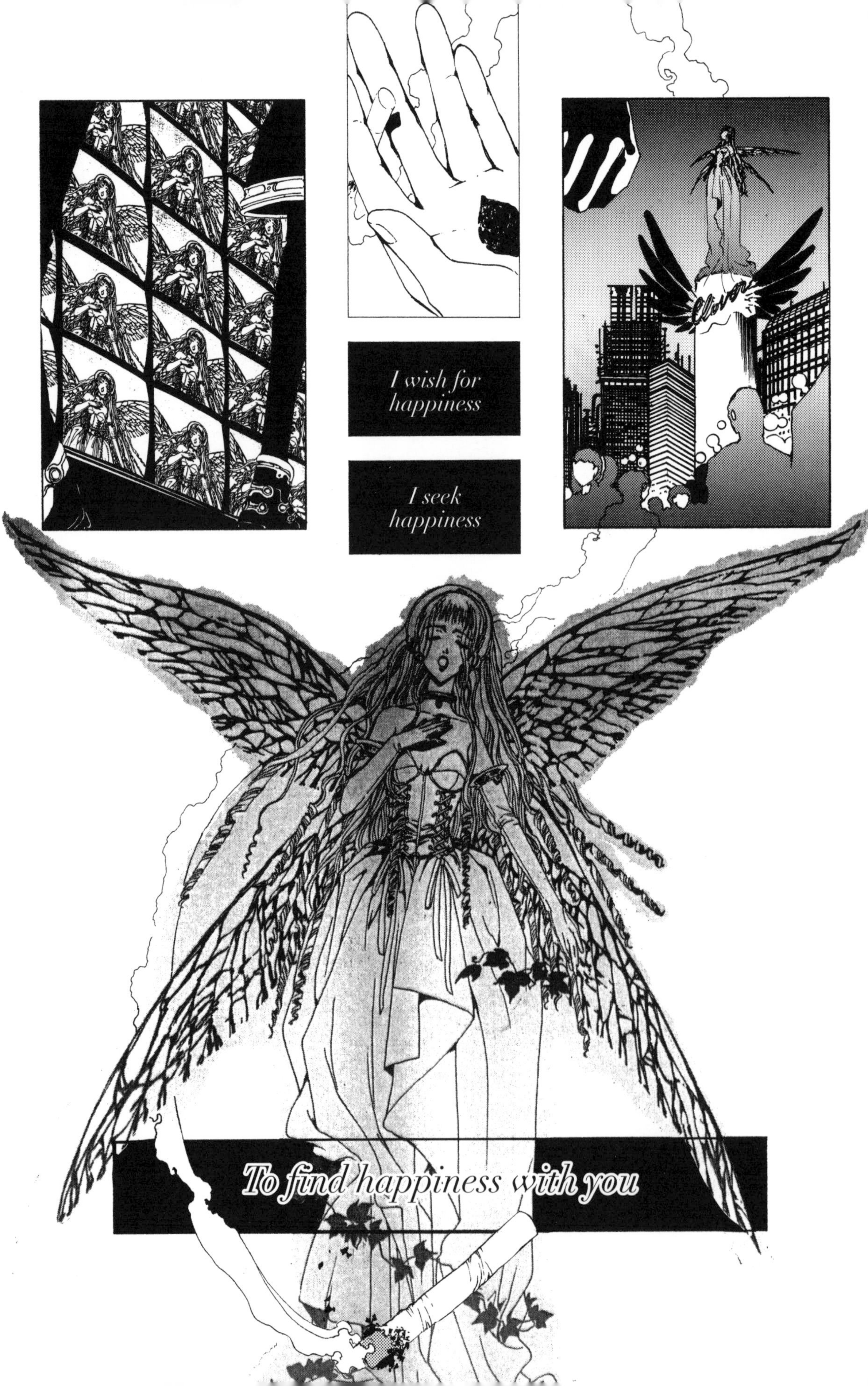
Clover
I wish for happiness
I seek happiness
To find happiness with you

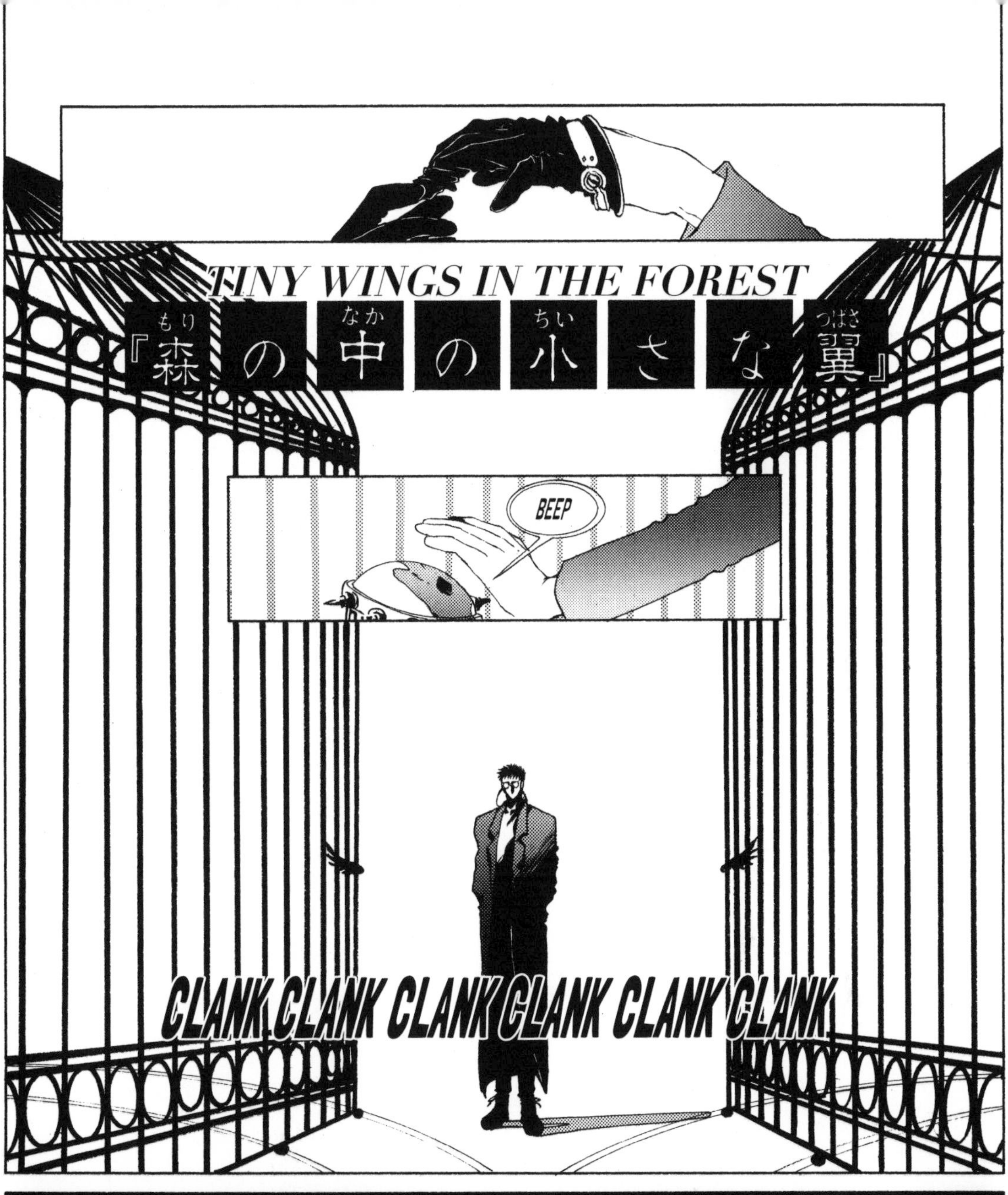
TINY WINGS IN THE FOREST
『森の中の小さな翼』
BEEP
CLANK CLANK CLANK CLANK CLANK CLANK
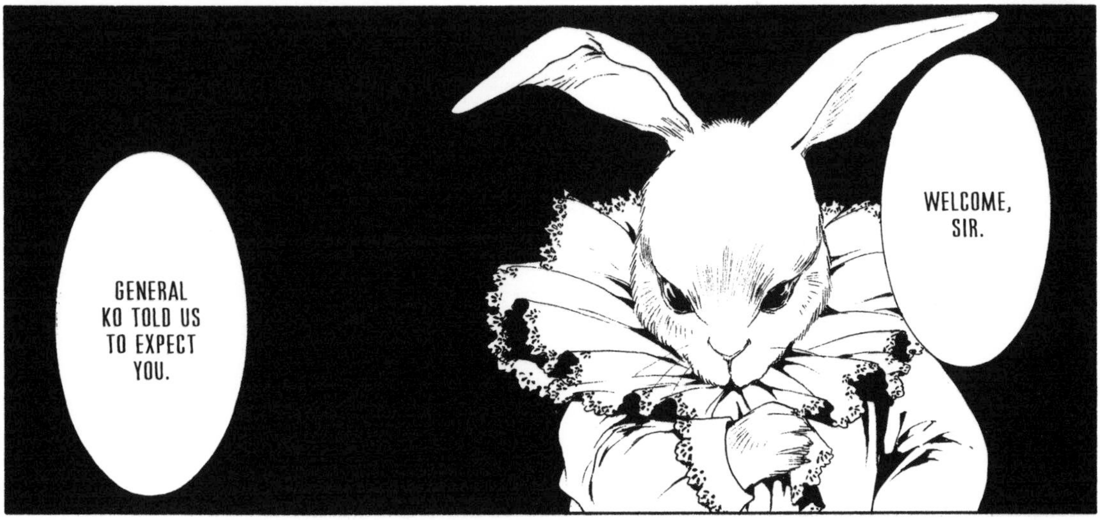
WELCOME, SIR.
GENERAL KO TOLD US TO EXPECT YOU.

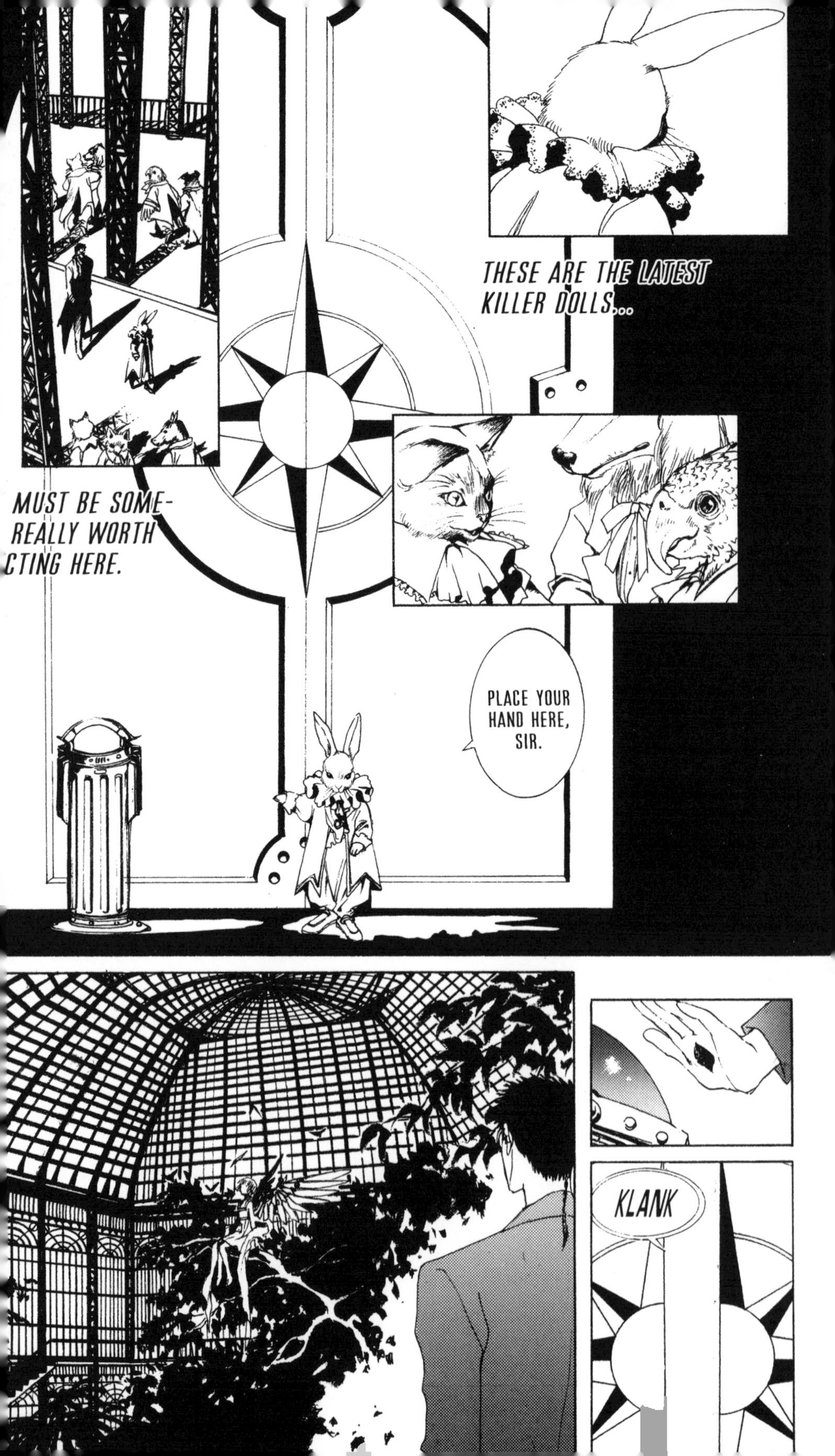
THESE ARE THE LATEST KILLER DOLLS...
MUST BE SOME- REALLY WORTH CTING HERE.
PLACE YOUR HAND HERE, SIR.
KLANK

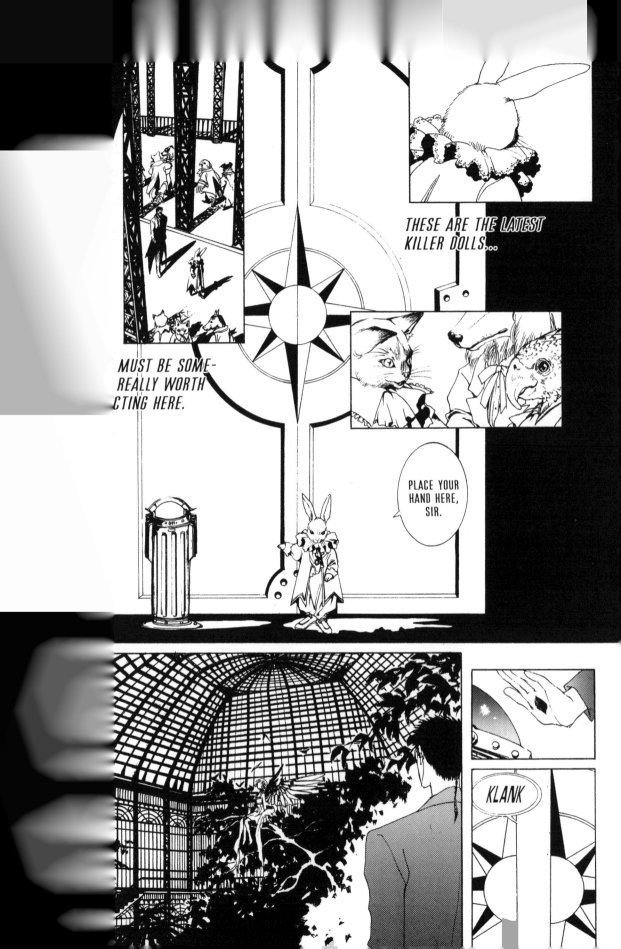

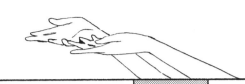

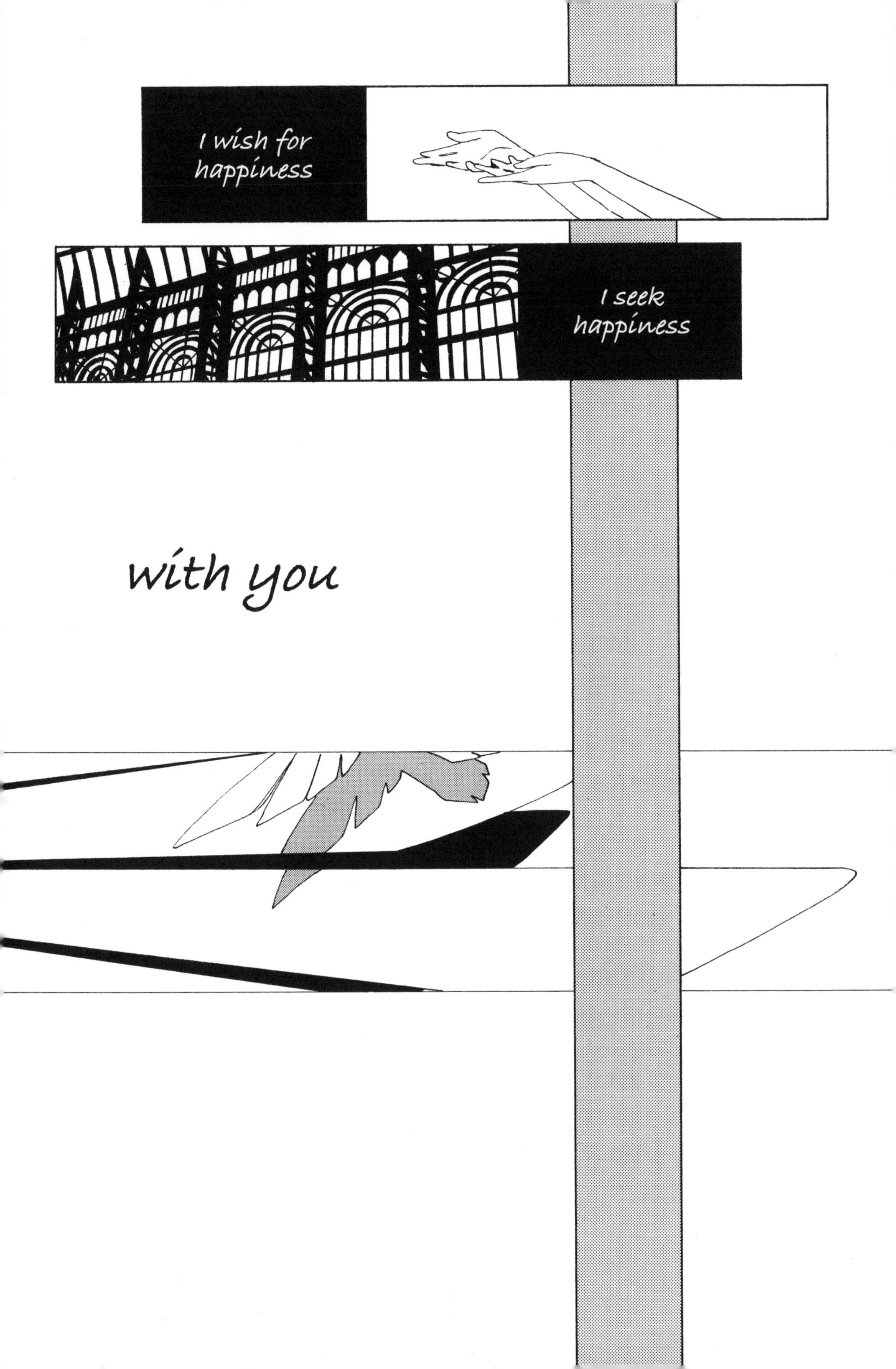

I wish for happiness

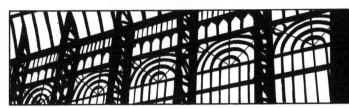

I seek happiness

with you

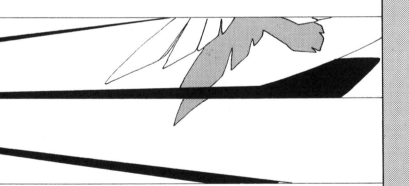

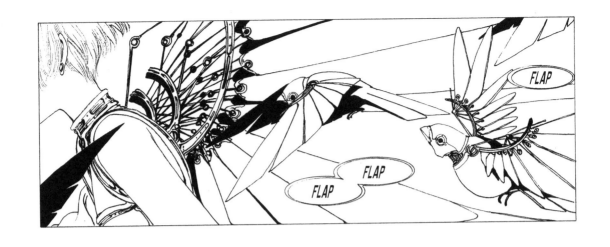

To find happiness

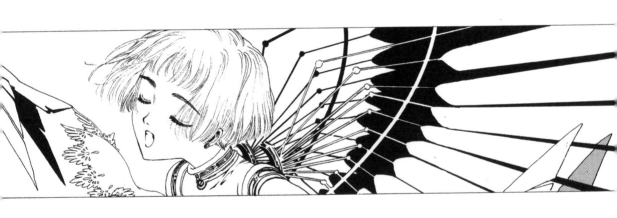

To be your happiness

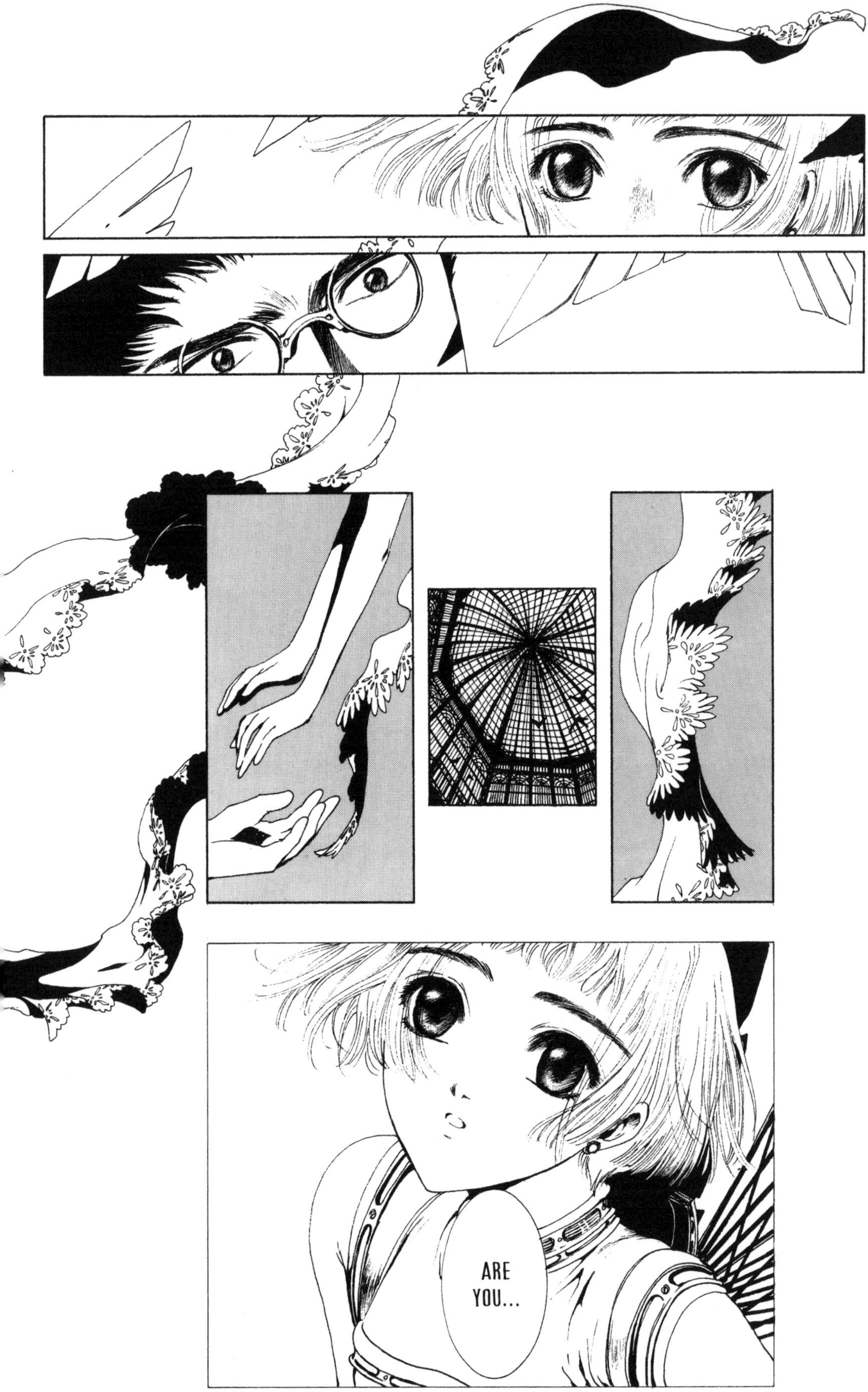
ARE YOU...

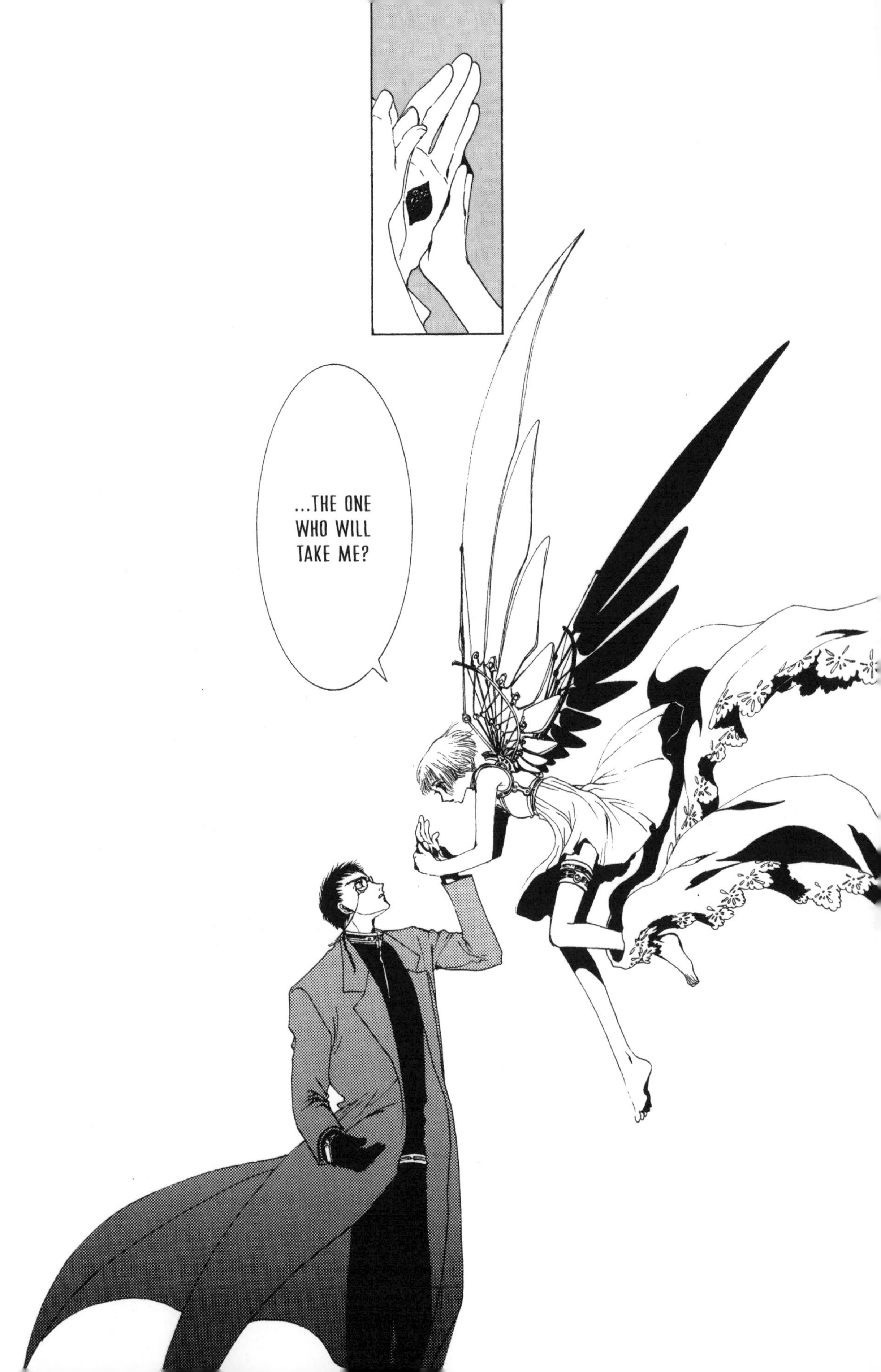
...THE ONE WHO WILL TAKE ME?

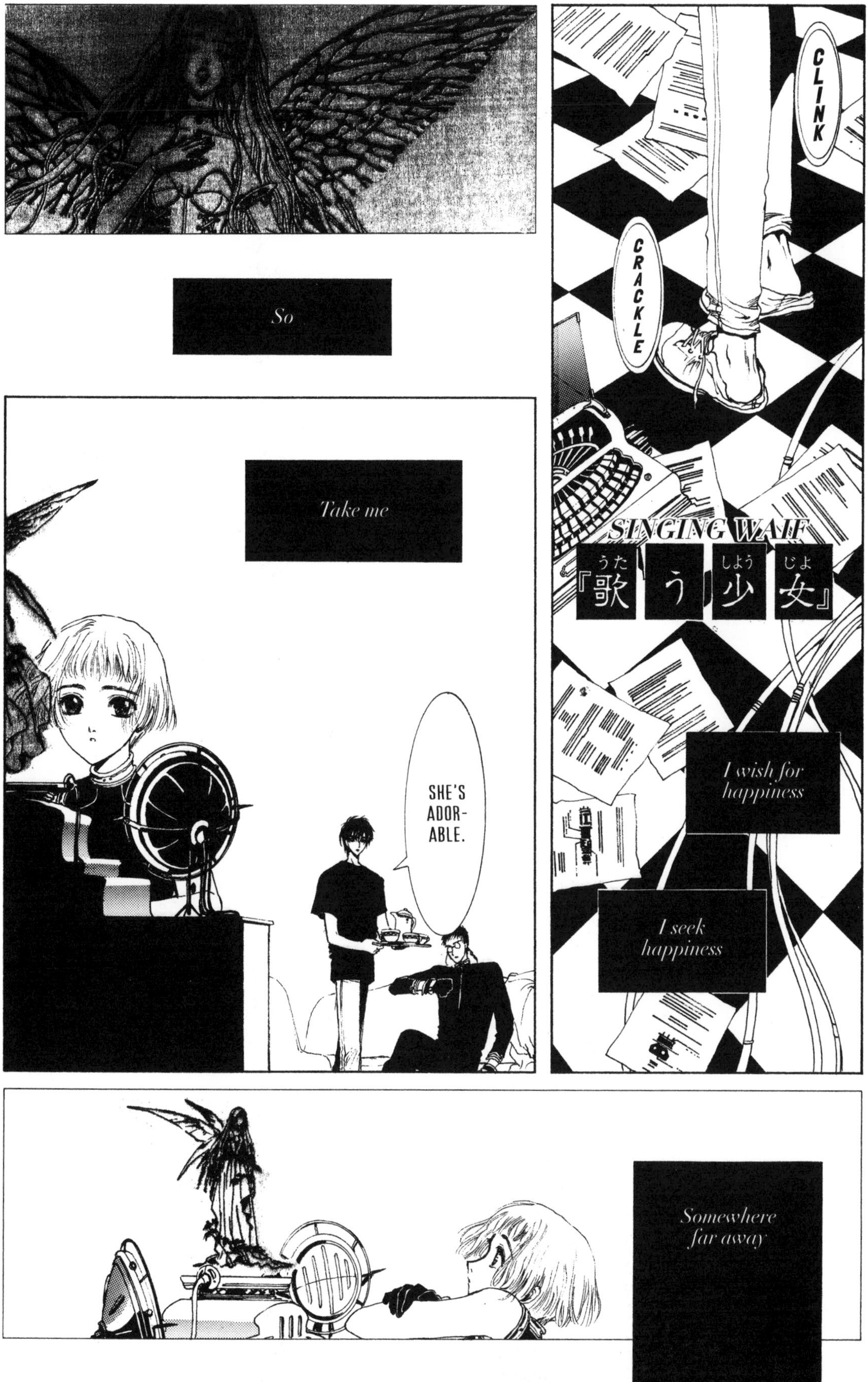
CLINK
CRACKLE
SINGING WAIF
『歌う少女』
I wish for happiness
I seek happiness
So
Take me
SHE'S ADORABLE.
Somewhere far away

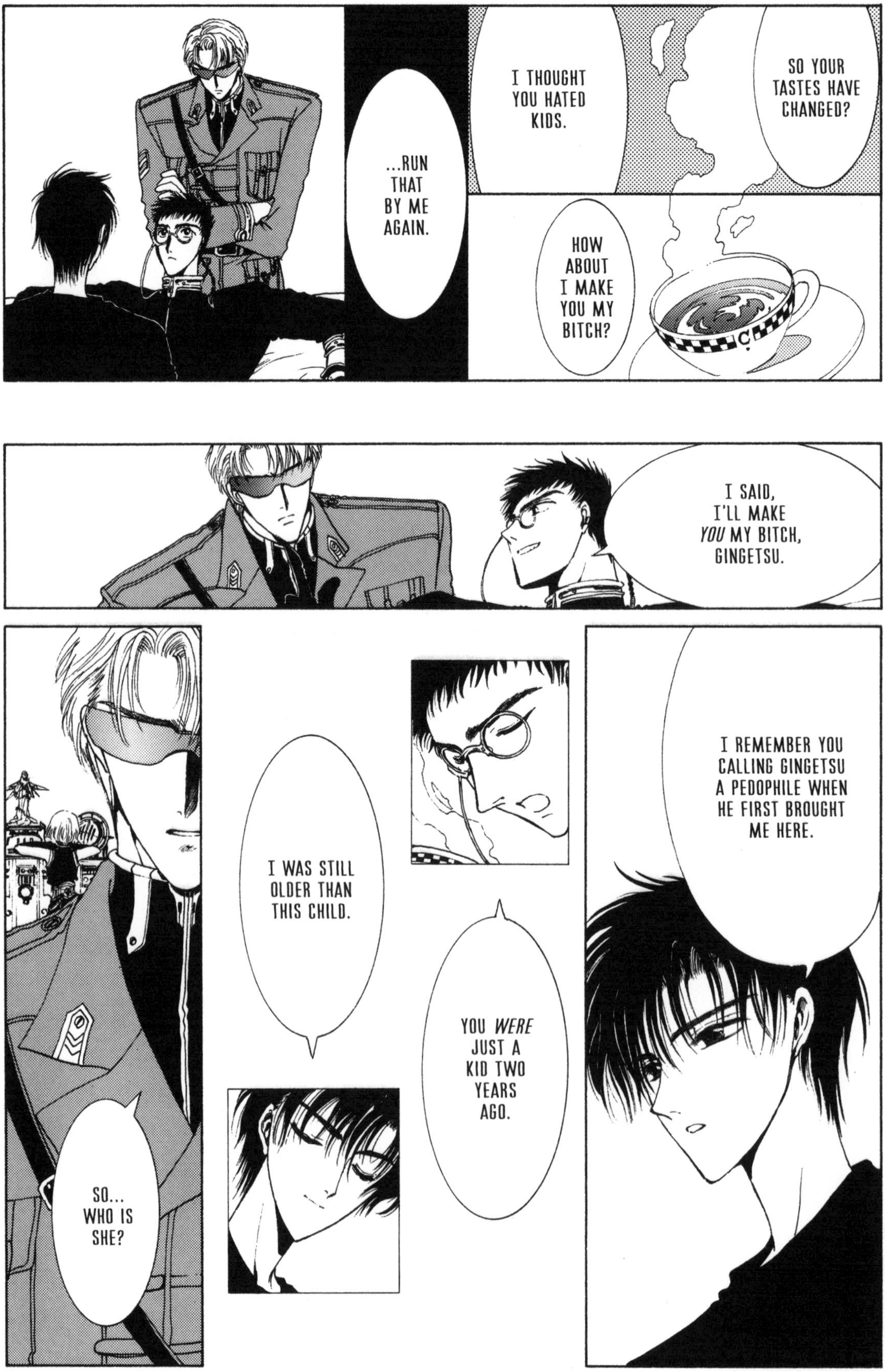
SO YOUR TASTES HAVE CHANGED?
I THOUGHT YOU HATED KIDS.
HOW ABOUT I MAKE YOU MY BITCH?
...RUN THAT BY ME AGAIN.
I SAID, I'LL MAKE *YOU* MY BITCH, GINGETSU.
I REMEMBER YOU CALLING GINGETSU A PEDOPHILE WHEN HE FIRST BROUGHT ME HERE.
YOU *WERE* JUST A KID TWO YEARS AGO.
I WAS STILL OLDER THAN THIS CHILD.
SO... WHO IS SHE?

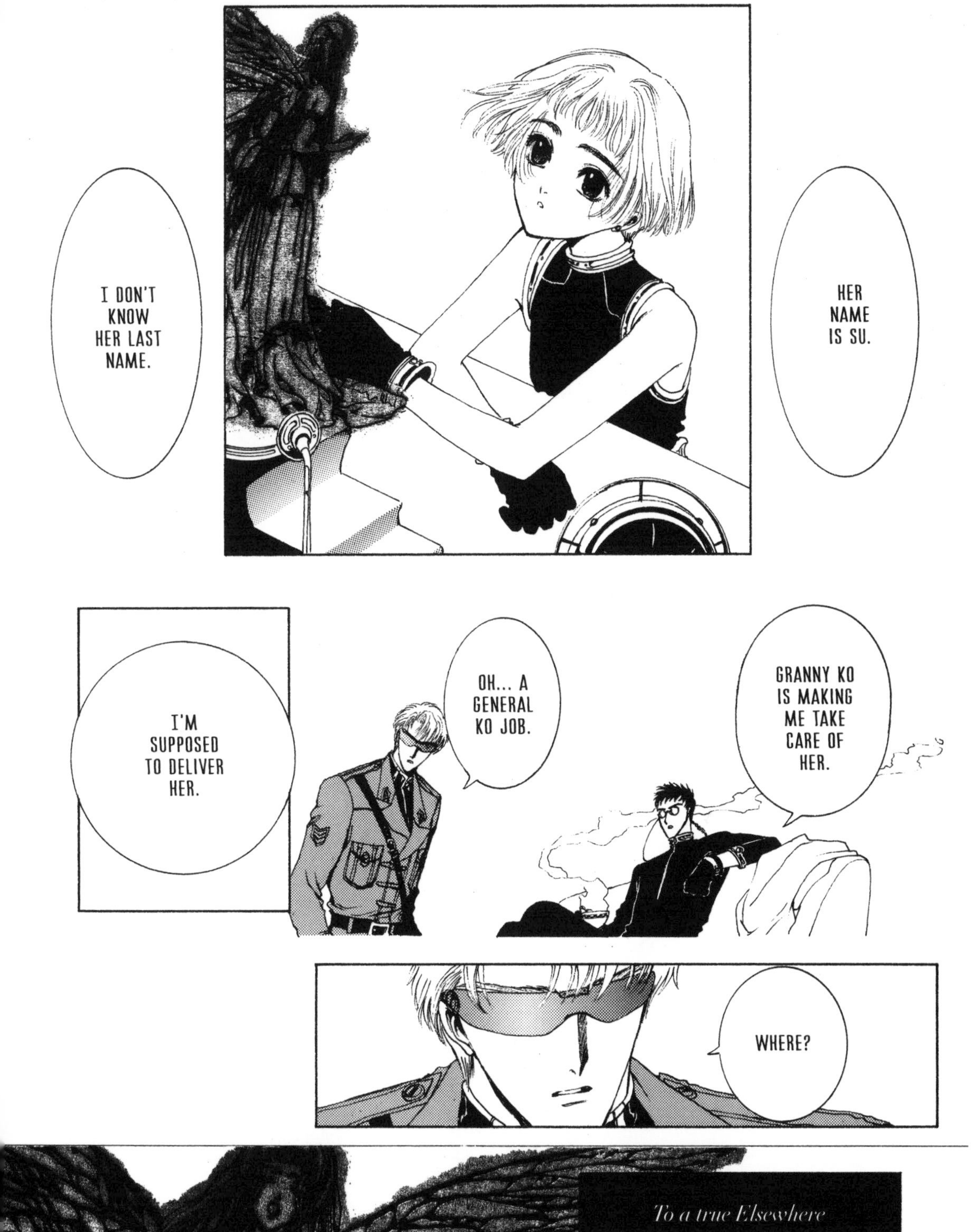
HER NAME IS SU.
I DON'T KNOW HER LAST NAME.
GRANNY KO IS MAKING ME TAKE CARE OF HER.
OH... A GENERAL KO JOB.
I'M SUPPOSED TO DELIVER HER.
WHERE?
To a true Elsewhere
I DON'T KNOW.
BUT *SHE* SEEMS TO.

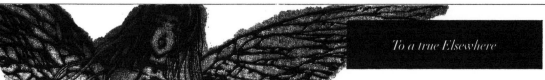

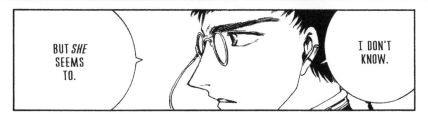

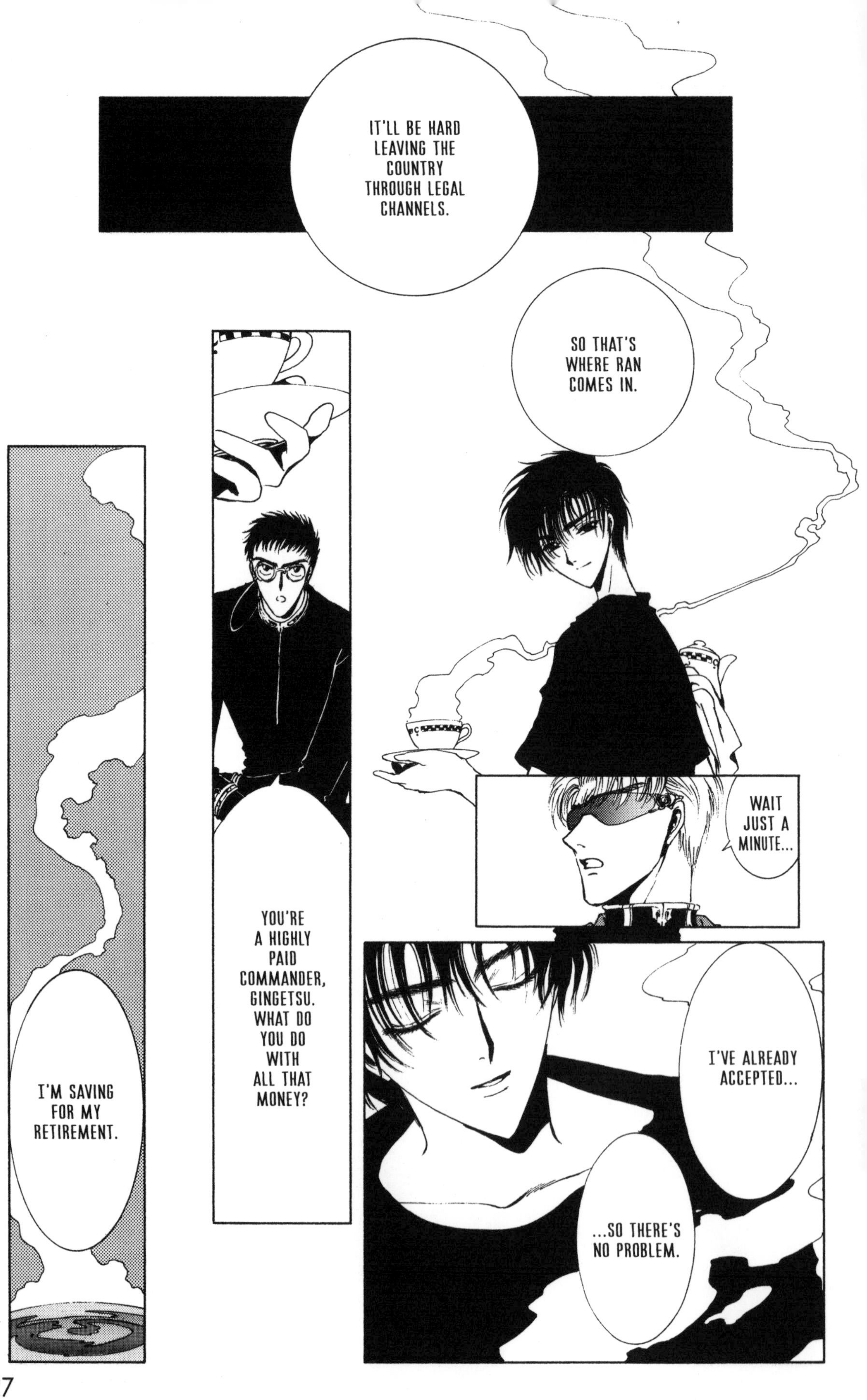
IT'LL BE HARD LEAVING THE COUNTRY THROUGH LEGAL CHANNELS.
SO THAT'S WHERE RAN COMES IN.
WAIT JUST A MINUTE...
I'VE ALREADY ACCEPTED...
...SO THERE'S NO PROBLEM.
YOU'RE A HIGHLY PAID COMMANDER, GINGETSU. WHAT DO YOU DO WITH ALL THAT MONEY?
I'M SAVING FOR MY RETIREMENT.

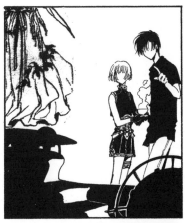

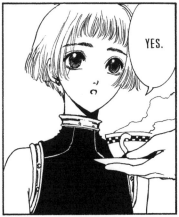

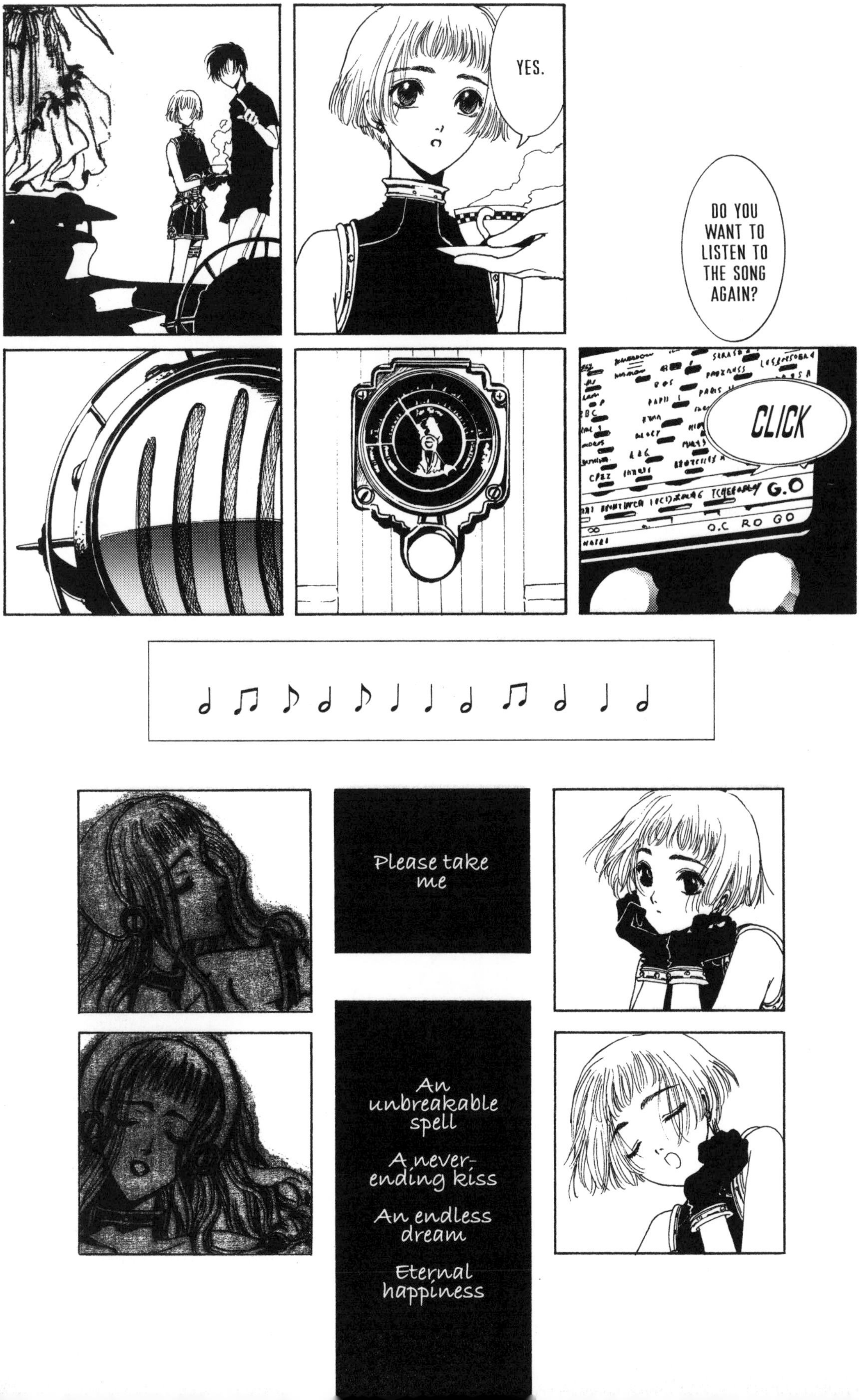

YES.

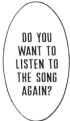

DO YOU WANT TO LISTEN TO THE SONG AGAIN?

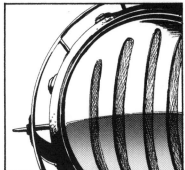

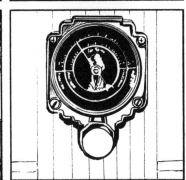

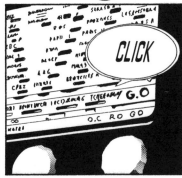

CLICK

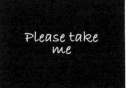

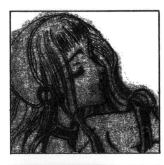

Please take me

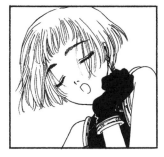

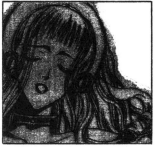

An unbreakable spell

A never-ending kiss

An endless dream

Eternal happiness

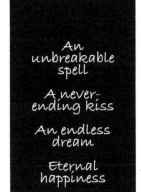

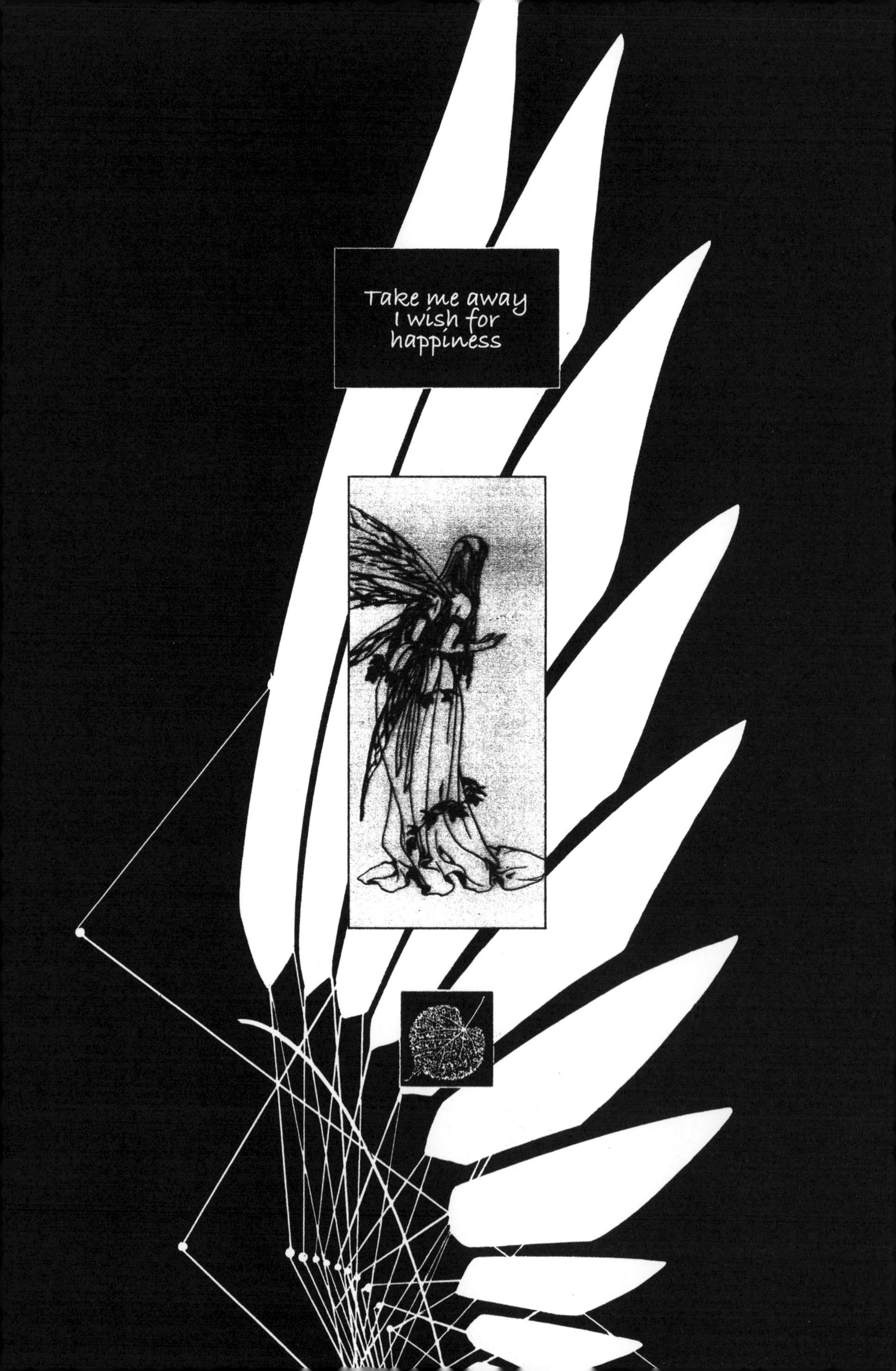
Take me away
I wish for
happiness

WE'RE GOING TO FAIRY PARK.

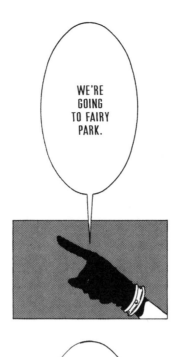

YOU MEAN THAT RUN-DOWN AMUSEMENT PARK?

BIRDCAGE

『鳥籠』

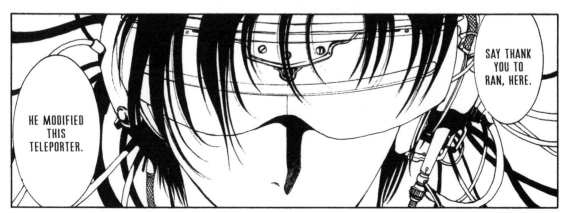

SAY THANK YOU TO RAN, HERE.
HE MODIFIED THIS TELEPORTER.

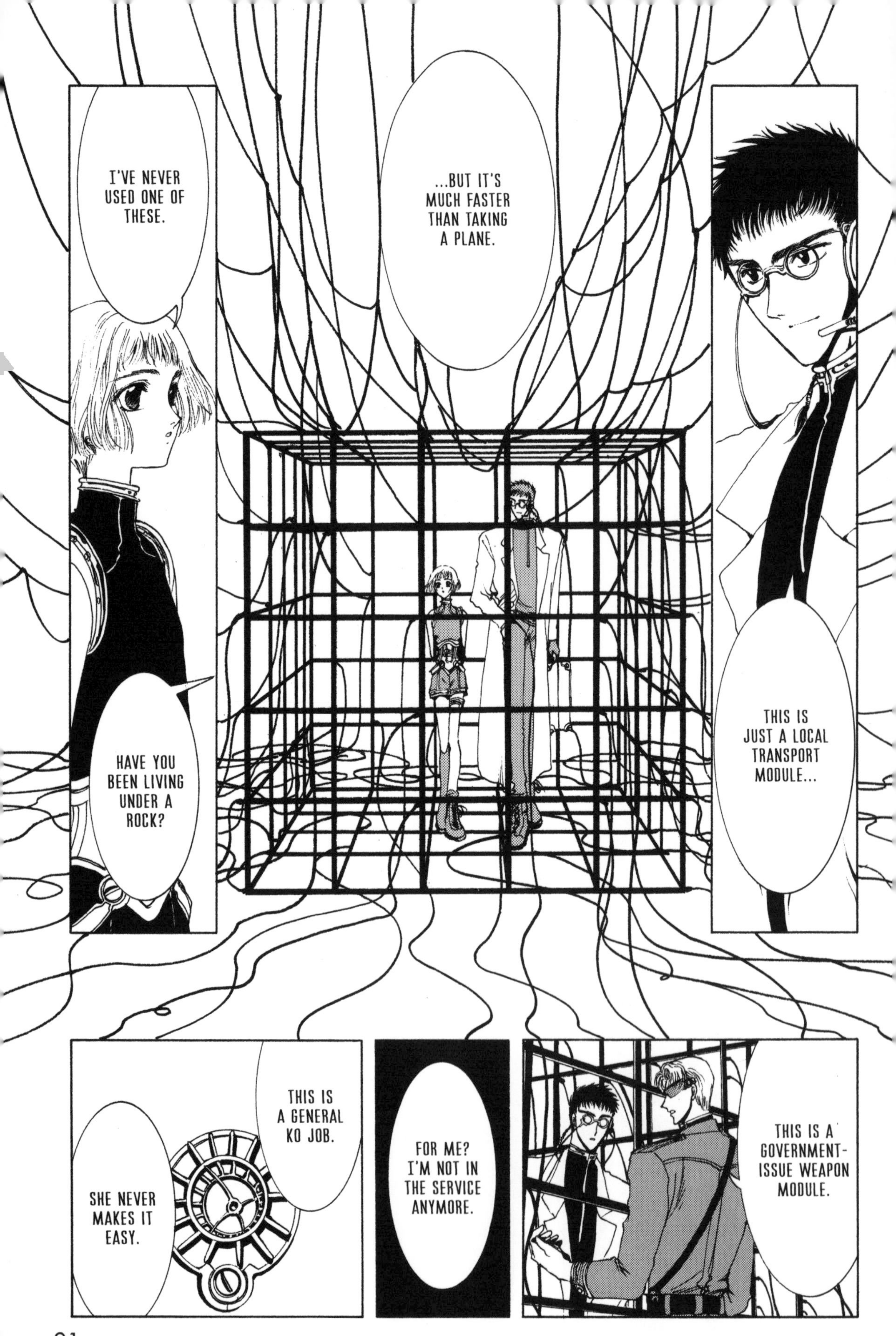
THIS IS JUST A LOCAL TRANSPORT MODULE...
...BUT IT'S MUCH FASTER THAN TAKING A PLANE.
I'VE NEVER USED ONE OF THESE.
HAVE YOU BEEN LIVING UNDER A ROCK?
THIS IS A GOVERNMENT-ISSUE WEAPON MODULE.
FOR ME? I'M NOT IN THE SERVICE ANYMORE.
THIS IS A GENERAL KO JOB.
SHE NEVER MAKES IT EASY.

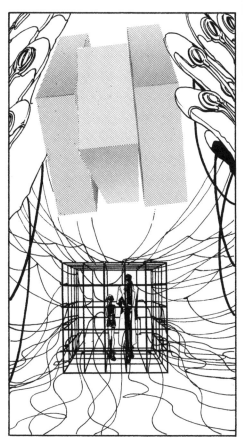

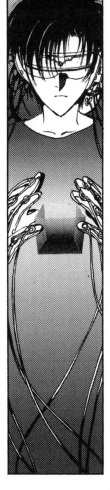

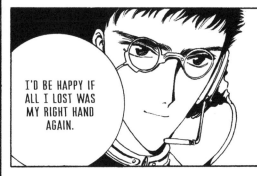

I'D BE HAPPY IF ALL I LOST WAS MY RIGHT HAND AGAIN.

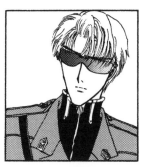

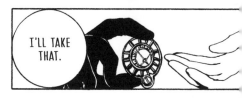

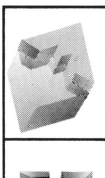

I'LL TAKE THAT.

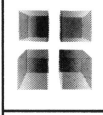

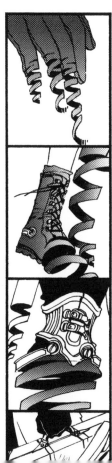

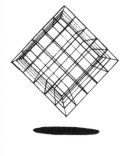

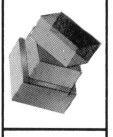

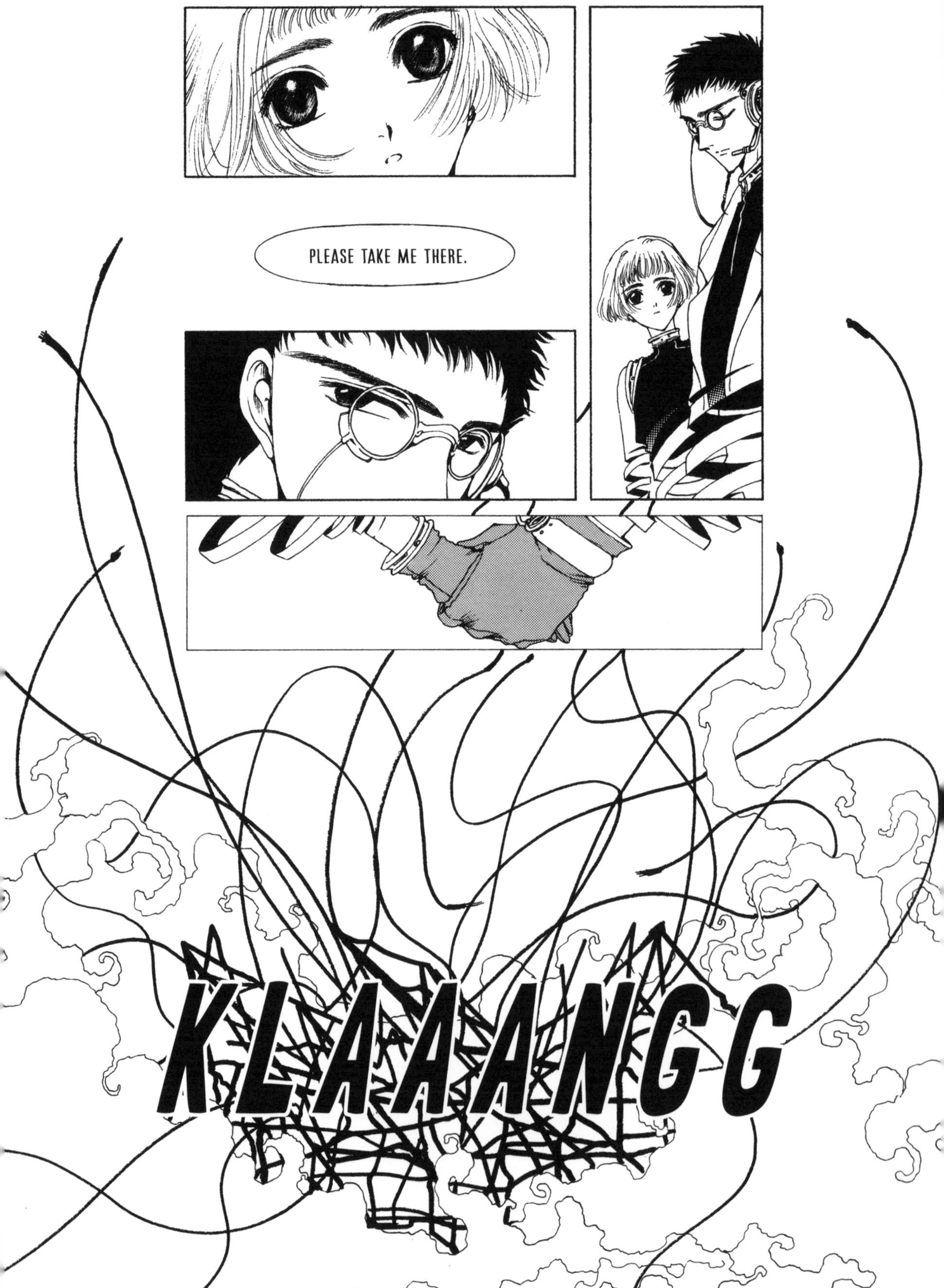
PLEASE TAKE ME THERE.
KLAAANGG

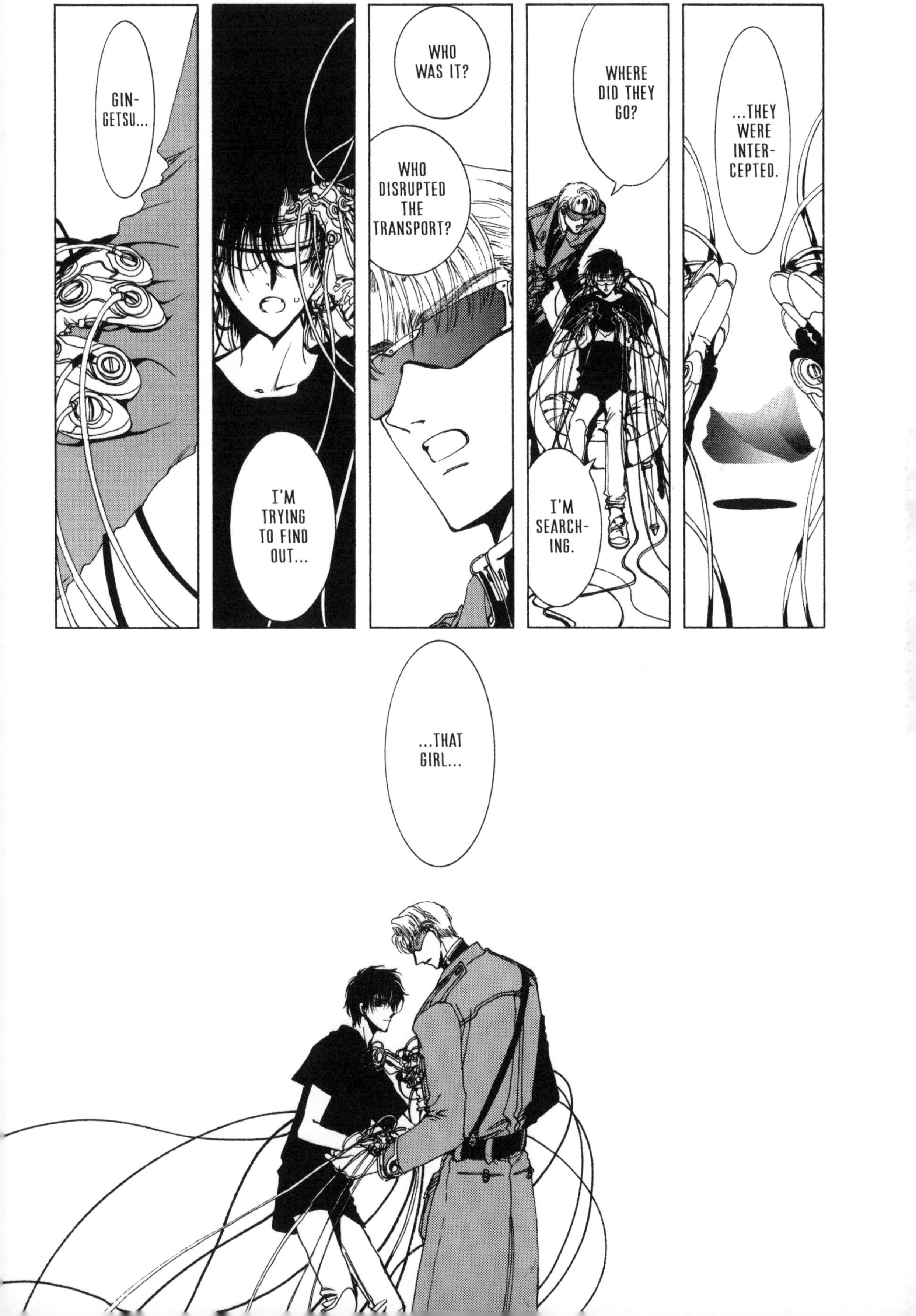
...THEY WERE INTER-CEPTED.
WHERE DID THEY GO?
I'M SEARCH-ING.
WHO WAS IT?
WHO DISRUPTED THE TRANSPORT?
I'M TRYING TO FIND OUT...
GIN-GETSU...
...THAT GIRL...

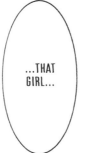

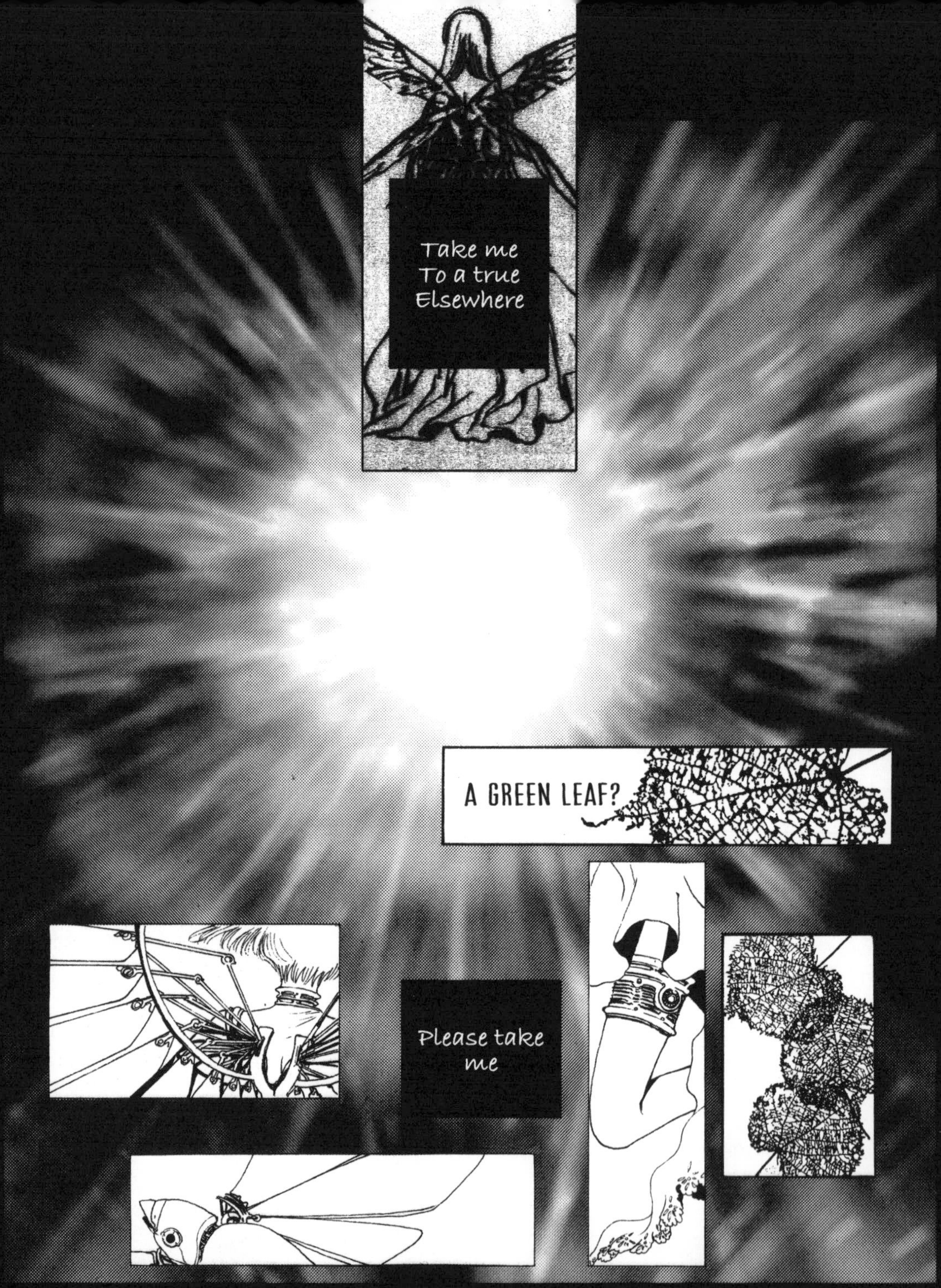
Take me
To a true
Elsewhere
A GREEN LEAF?
Please take
me

An unbreakable spell
A never - ending kiss
An endless dream
Eternal happiness

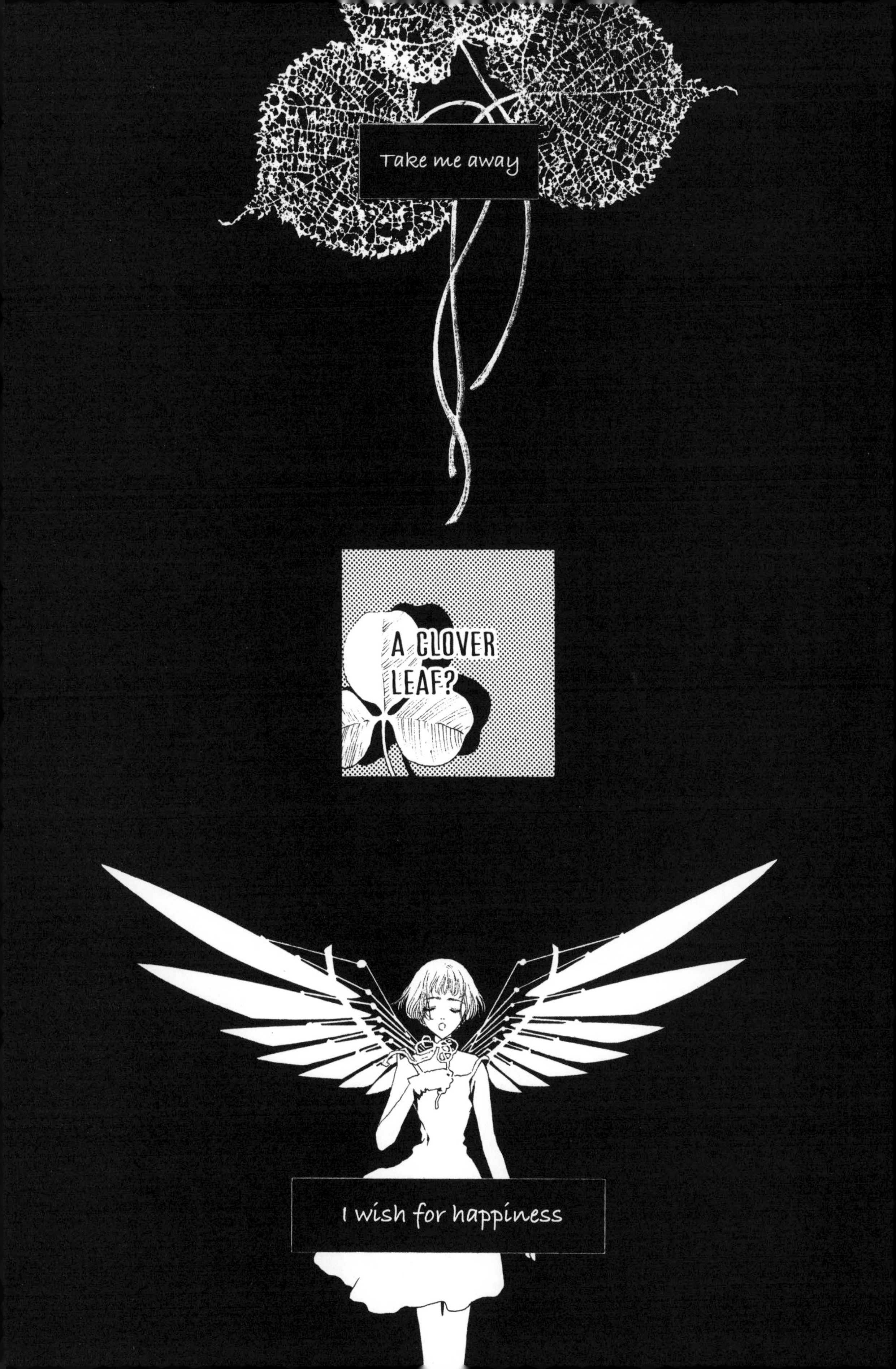
Take me away
A CLOVER LEAF?
I wish for happiness

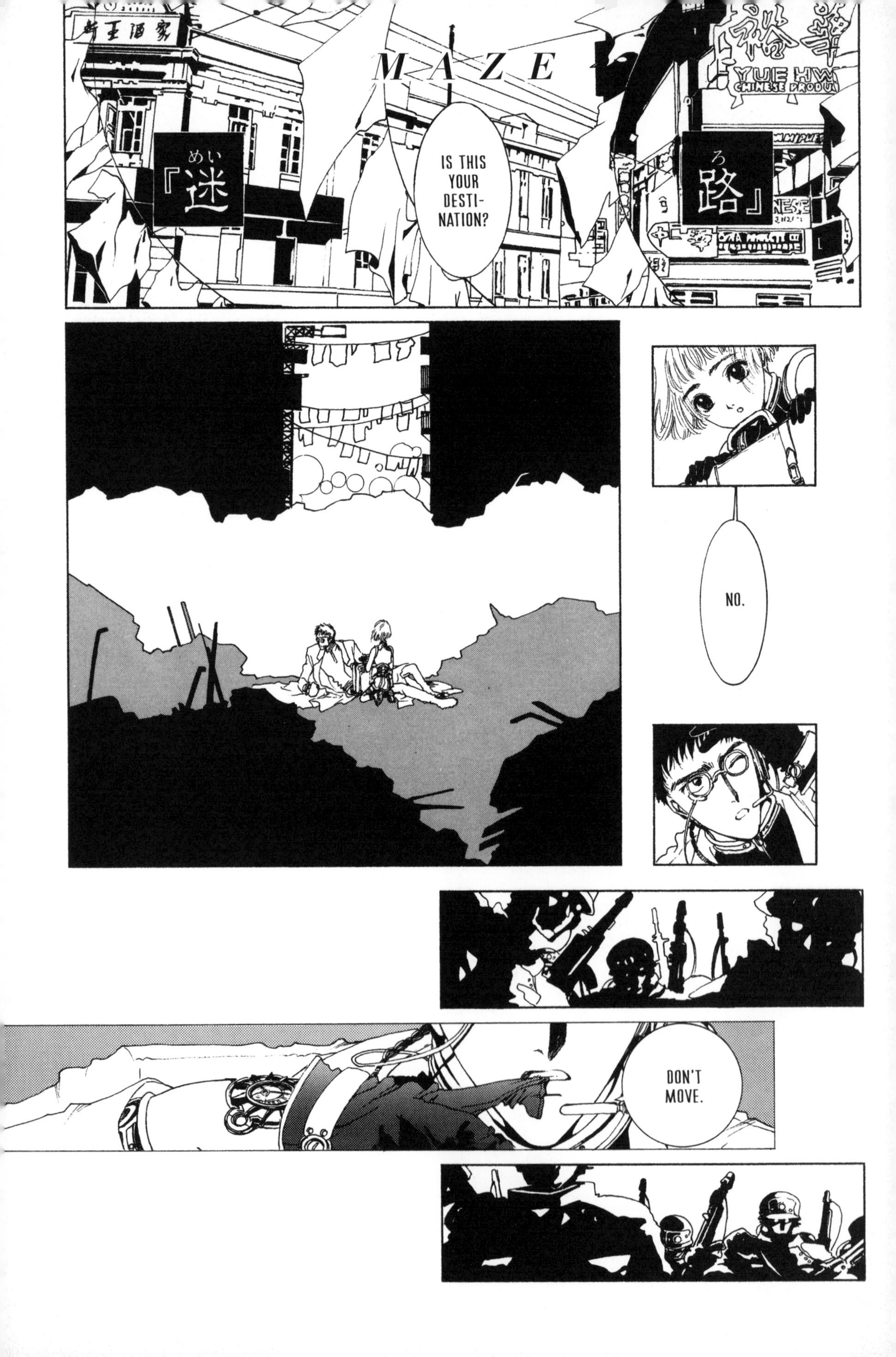
MAZE
『迷路』
めい
ろ
IS THIS YOUR DESTINATION?
NO.
DON'T MOVE.

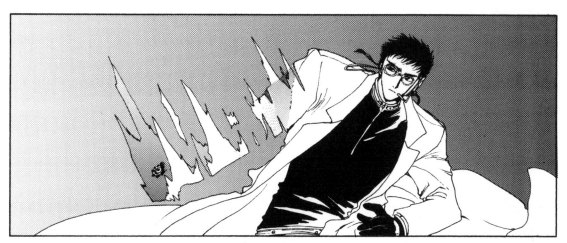

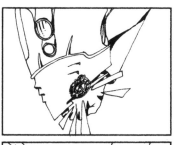

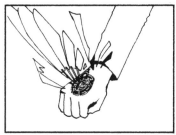

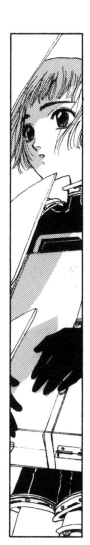

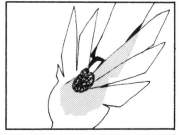

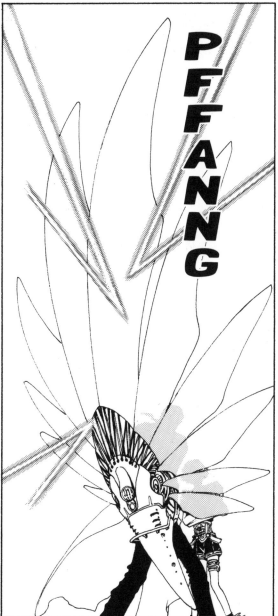

PFFANNG

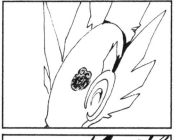

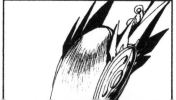

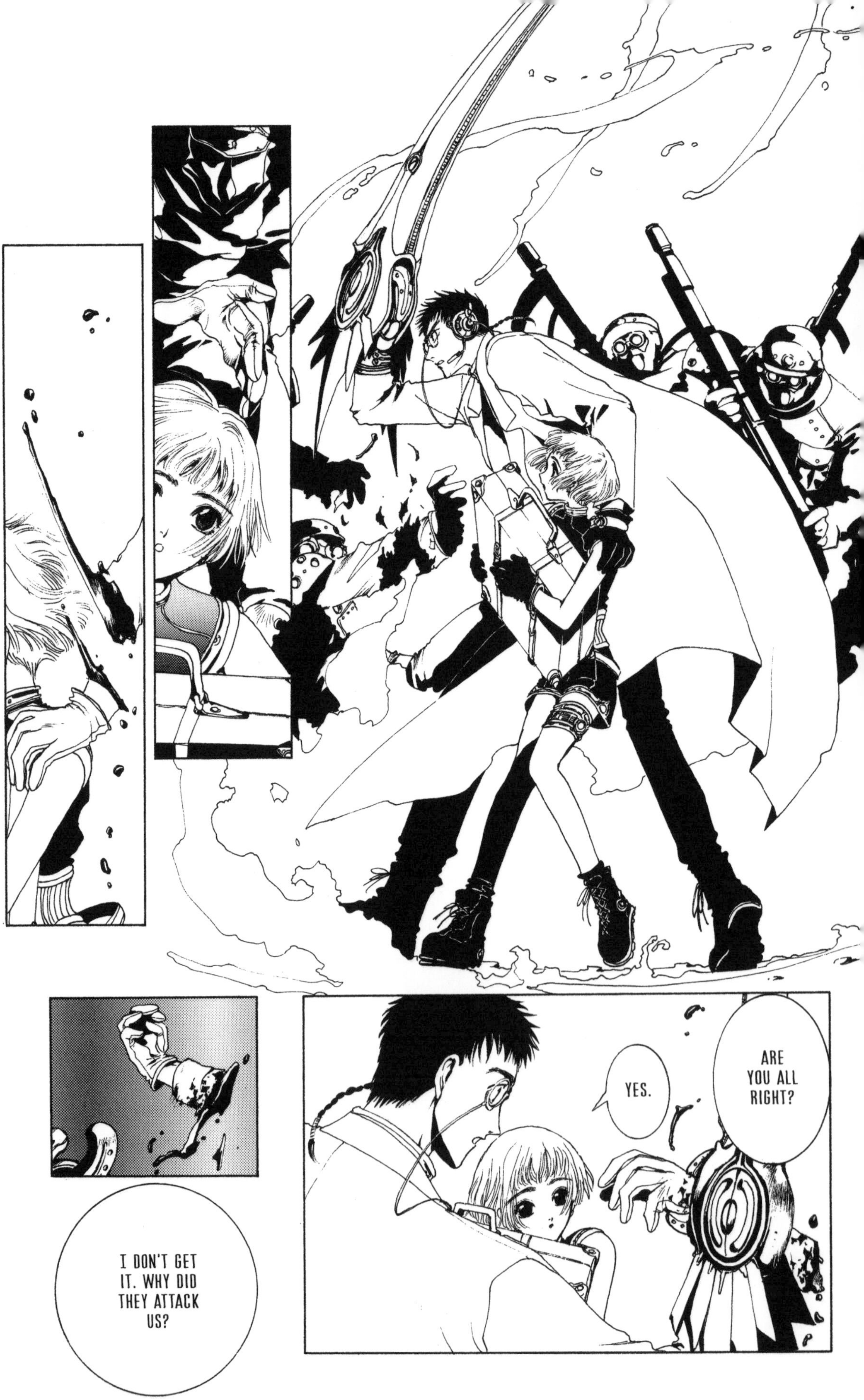
ARE YOU ALL RIGHT?
YES.
I DON'T GET IT. WHY DID THEY ATTACK US?

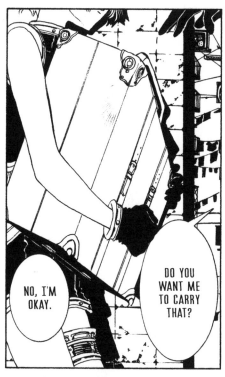

HAHH
HAHH
HAHH
DO YOU WANT ME TO CARRY THAT?
NO, I'M OKAY.
YOUR HAND...
DON'T WORRY.
IT'S ARTIFICIAL.
THESE MILITARY ISSUES ARE TOP QUALITY.
BREEEP BREEEP BREEEP
I CAN'T GET A CLEAR SIGNAL...
TMP

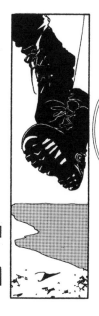

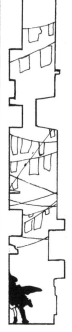

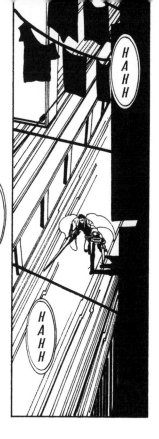

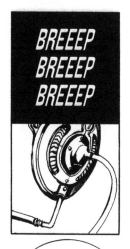

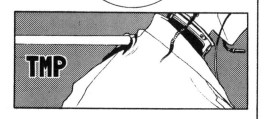

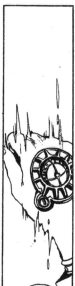

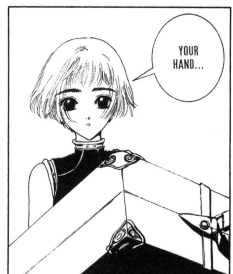

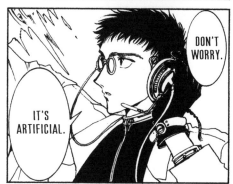

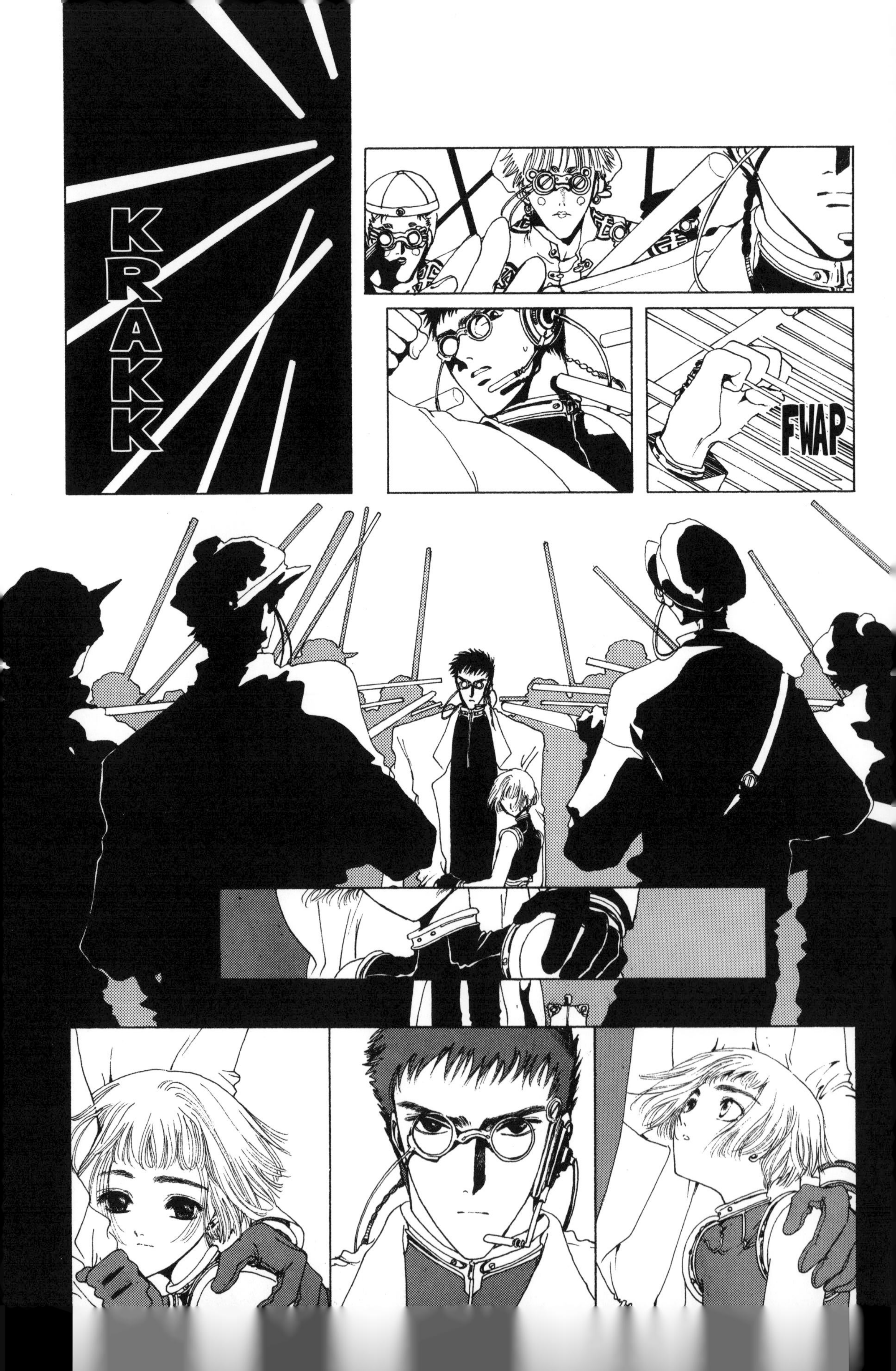
KRAKK
FWAP

CAT

『猫』

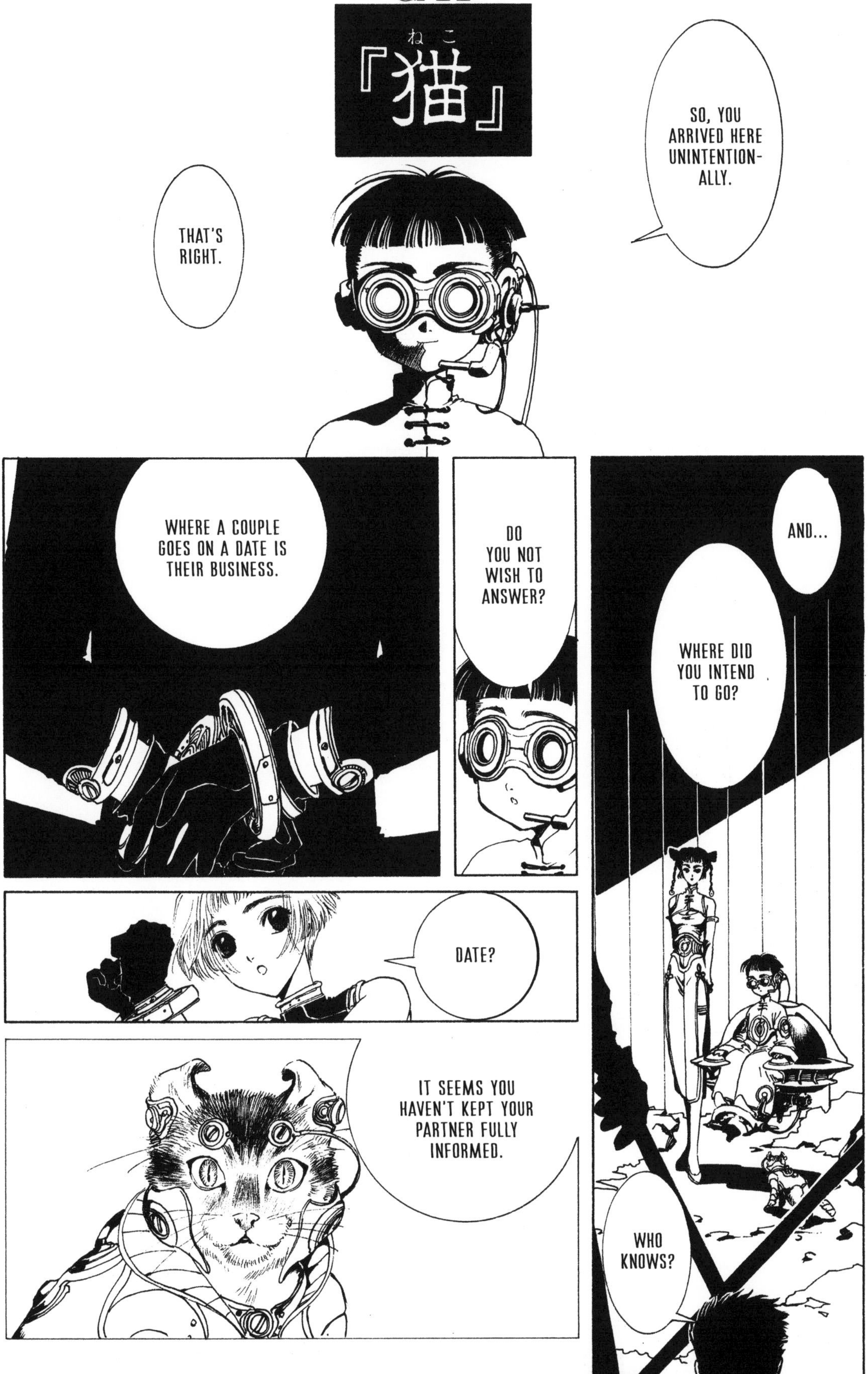
SO, YOU ARRIVED HERE UNINTENTION-ALLY.
THAT'S RIGHT.
AND...
WHERE DID YOU INTEND TO GO?
WHO KNOWS?
DO YOU NOT WISH TO ANSWER?
WHERE A COUPLE GOES ON A DATE IS THEIR BUSINESS.
DATE?
IT SEEMS YOU HAVEN'T KEPT YOUR PARTNER FULLY INFORMED.

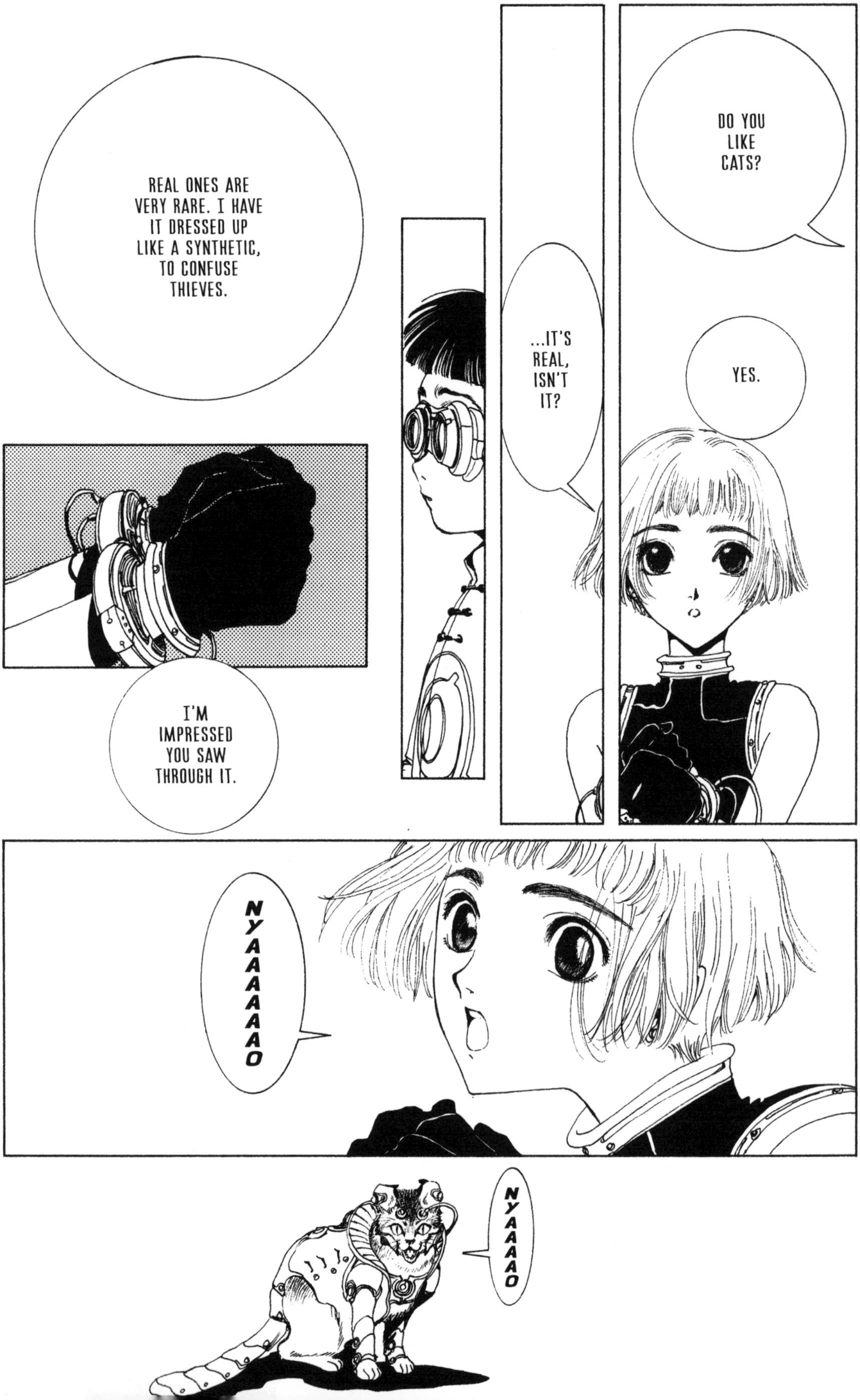
DO YOU LIKE CATS?
YES.
...IT'S REAL, ISN'T IT?
REAL ONES ARE VERY RARE. I HAVE IT DRESSED UP LIKE A SYNTHETIC, TO CONFUSE THIEVES.
I'M IMPRESSED YOU SAW THROUGH IT.
NYAAAAAAAO
NYAAAAO

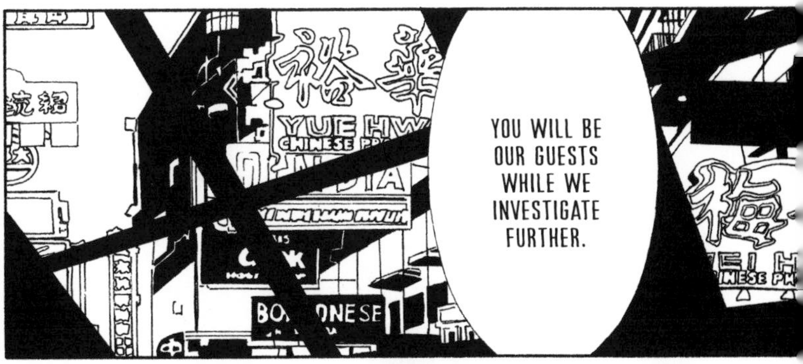
YOU WILL BE OUR GUESTS WHILE WE INVESTIGATE FURTHER.

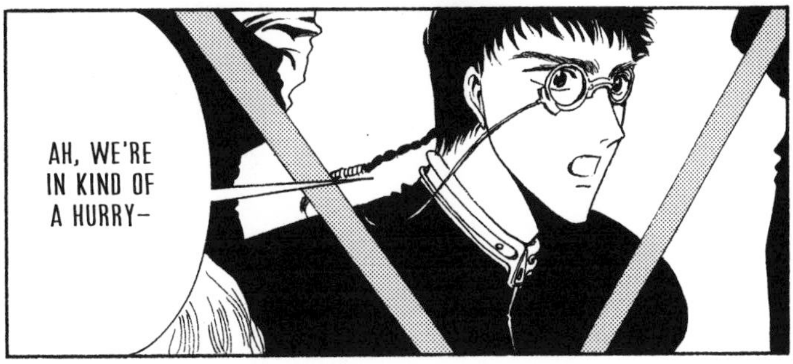
AH, WE'RE IN KIND OF A HURRY–

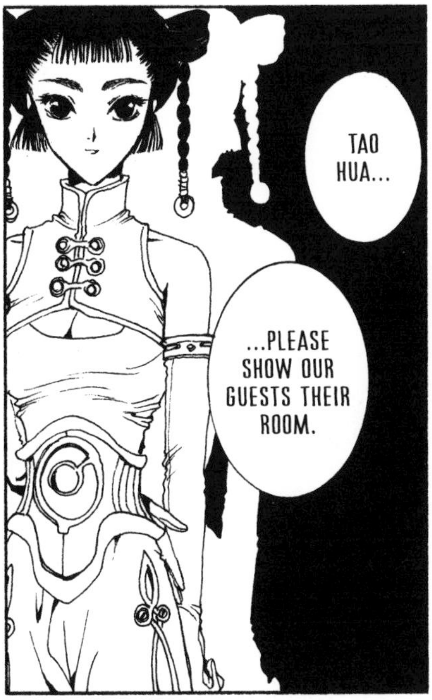
TAO HUA...
...PLEASE SHOW OUR GUESTS THEIR ROOM.

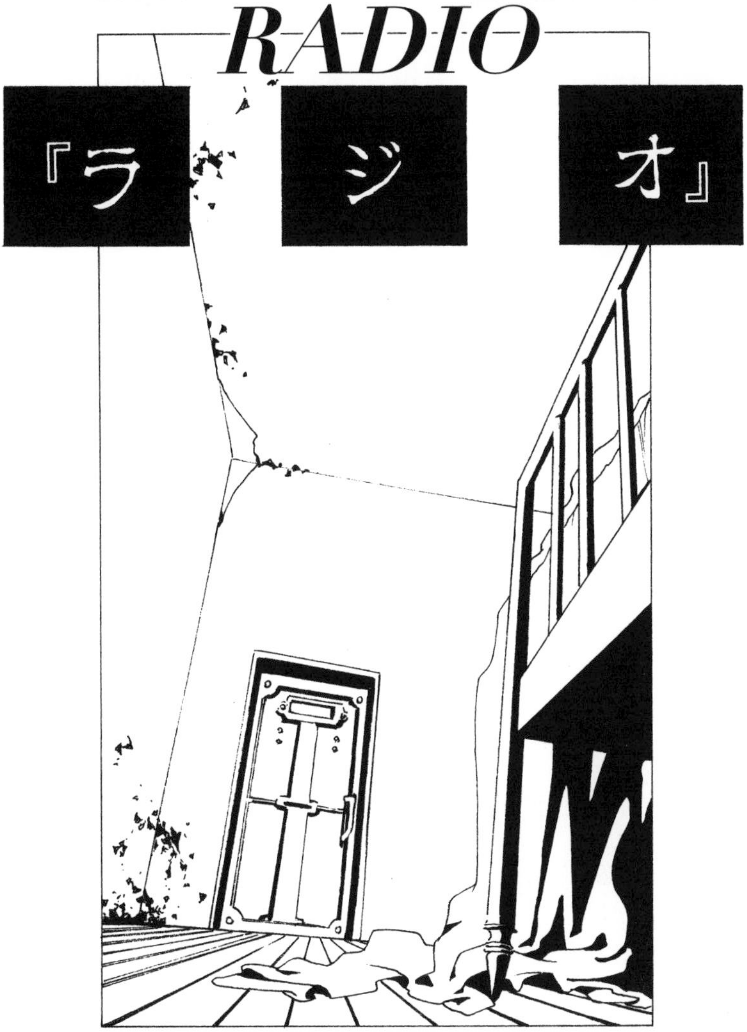
RADIO
『ラジオ』

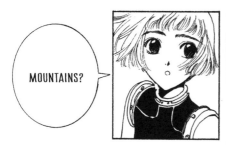

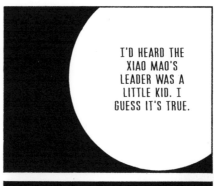

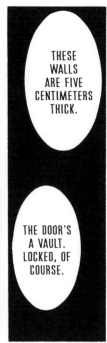

THESE WALLS ARE FIVE CENTIMETERS THICK.
I'D HEARD THE XIAO MAO'S LEADER WAS A LITTLE KID. I GUESS IT'S TRUE.
THE DOOR'S A VAULT. LOCKED, OF COURSE.
IF THESE SO-CALLED "FREEDOM FIGHTERS" HAVE CAUGHT US, WE MUST STILL BE ON THE WRONG SIDE OF THE MOUNTAINS.
MOUNTAINS?
MEANING WE'RE STILL THIS SIDE OF THE BORDER.
YOU REALLY DON'T KNOW ANYTHING, DO YOU?
OH!
I wish for happiness

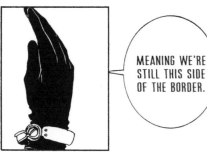

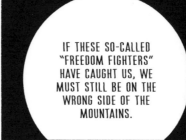

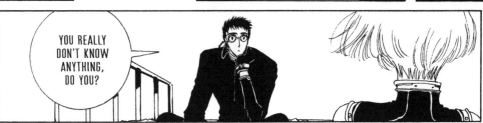

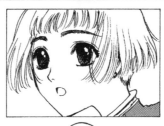

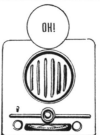

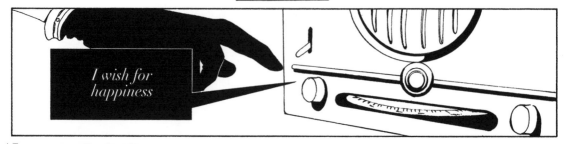

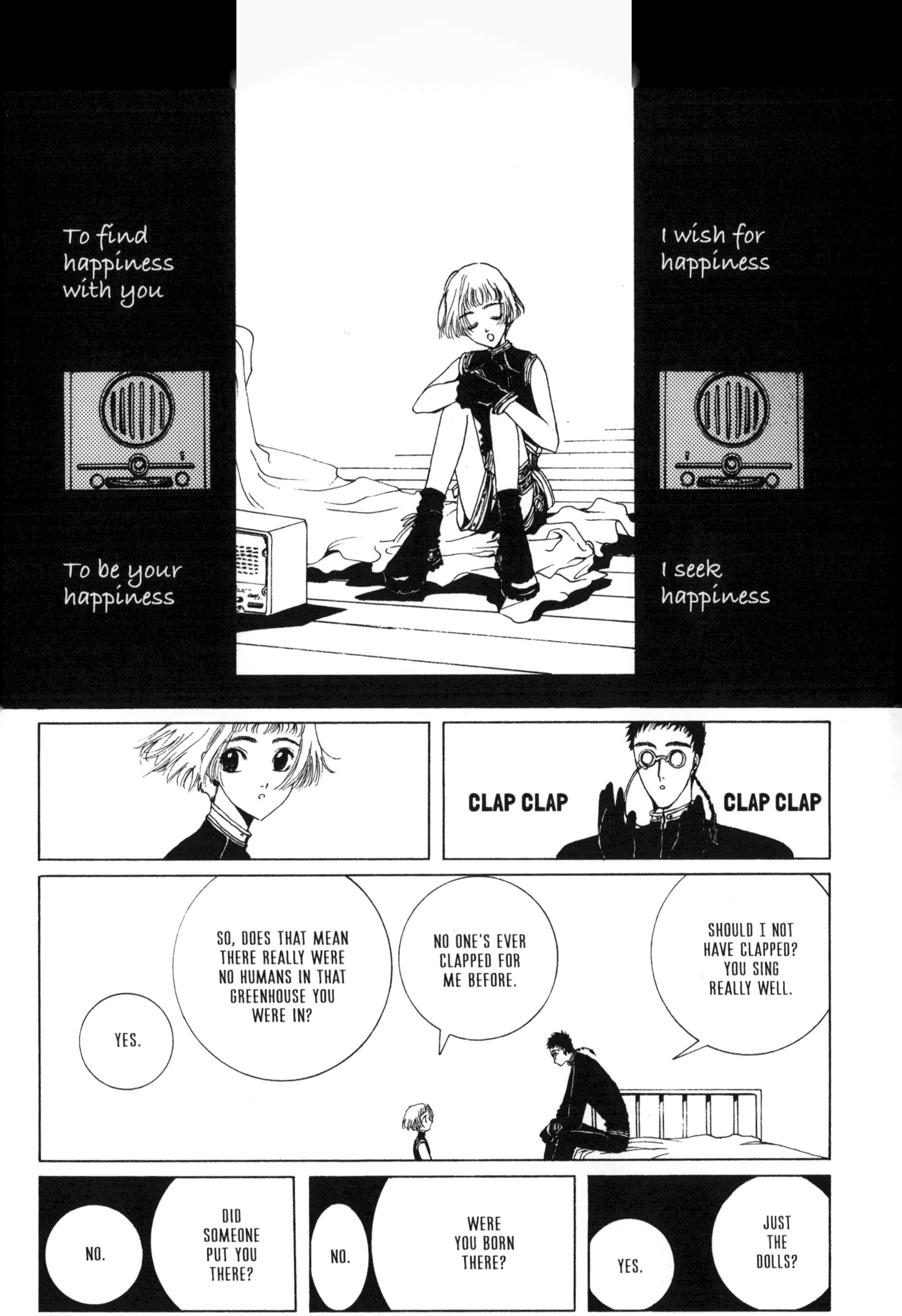
I wish for happiness
I seek happiness
To find happiness with you
To be your happiness
CLAP CLAP
CLAP CLAP
SHOULD I NOT HAVE CLAPPED? YOU SING REALLY WELL.
NO ONE'S EVER CLAPPED FOR ME BEFORE.
SO, DOES THAT MEAN THERE REALLY WERE NO HUMANS IN THAT GREENHOUSE YOU WERE IN?
YES.
JUST THE DOLLS?
YES.
WERE YOU BORN THERE?
NO.
DID SOMEONE PUT YOU THERE?
NO.

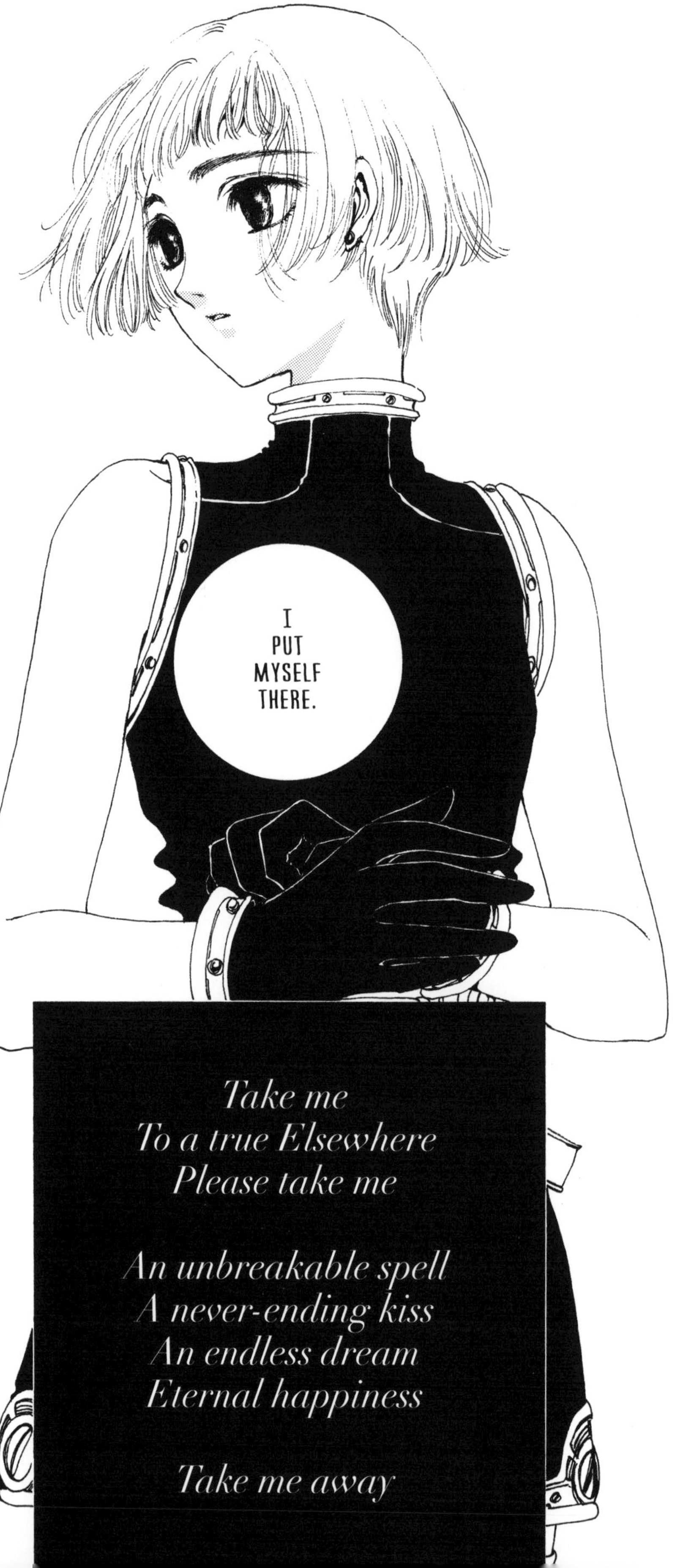
I PUT MYSELF THERE.
Take me
To a true Elsewhere
Please take me
An unbreakable spell
A never-ending kiss
An endless dream
Eternal happiness
Take me away

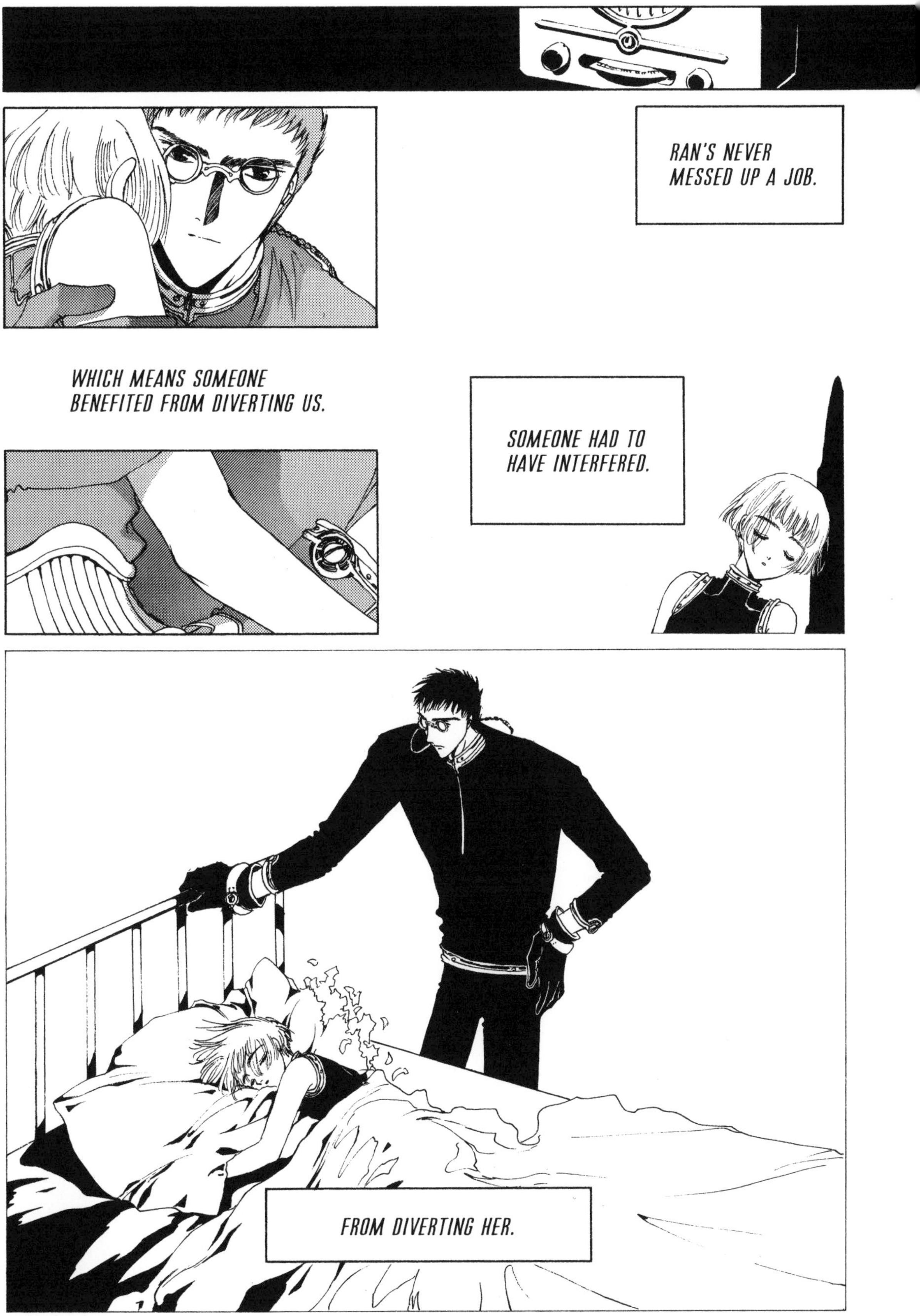
RAN'S NEVER MESSED UP A JOB.
SOMEONE HAD TO HAVE INTERFERED.
WHICH MEANS SOMEONE BENEFITED FROM DIVERTING US.
FROM DIVERTING HER.

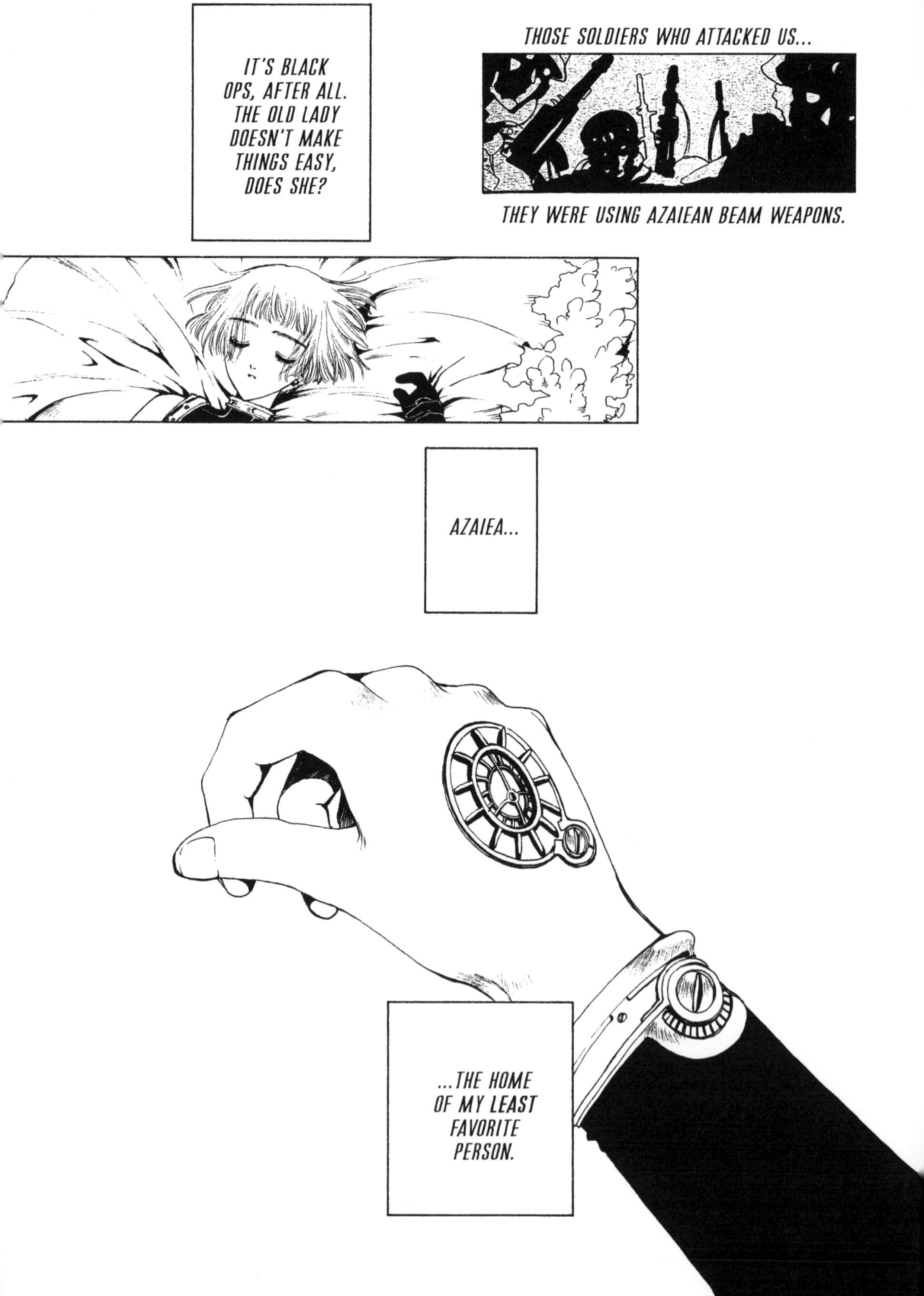
THOSE SOLDIERS WHO ATTACKED US...
THEY WERE USING AZAIEAN BEAM WEAPONS.
IT'S BLACK OPS, AFTER ALL. THE OLD LADY DOESN'T MAKE THINGS EASY, DOES SHE?
AZAIEA...
...THE HOME OF MY LEAST FAVORITE PERSON.

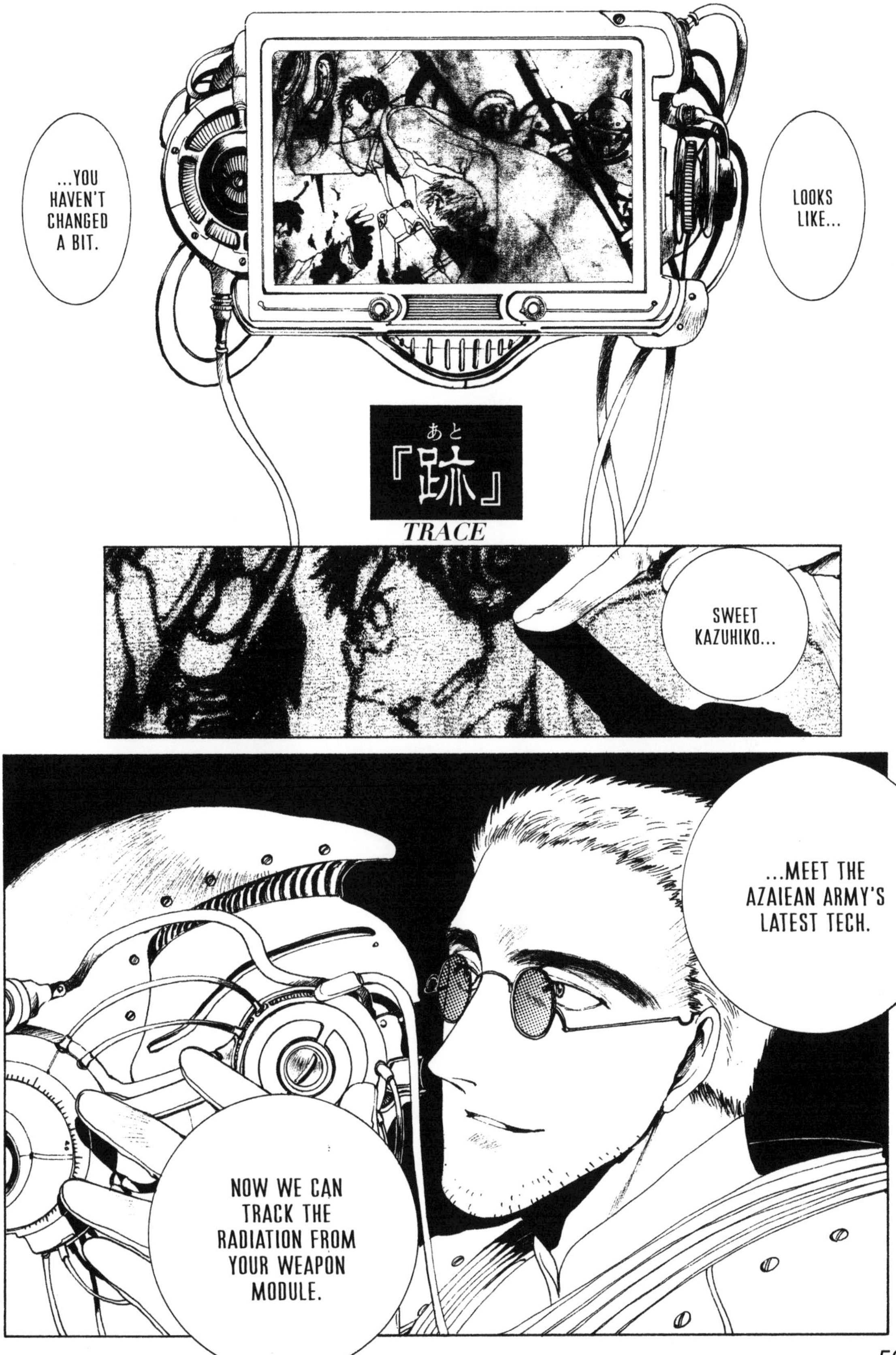
LOOKS LIKE...
...YOU HAVEN'T CHANGED A BIT.
あと
『跡』
TRACE
SWEET KAZUHIKO...
...MEET THE AZAIEAN ARMY'S LATEST TECH.
NOW WE CAN TRACK THE RADIATION FROM YOUR WEAPON MODULE.

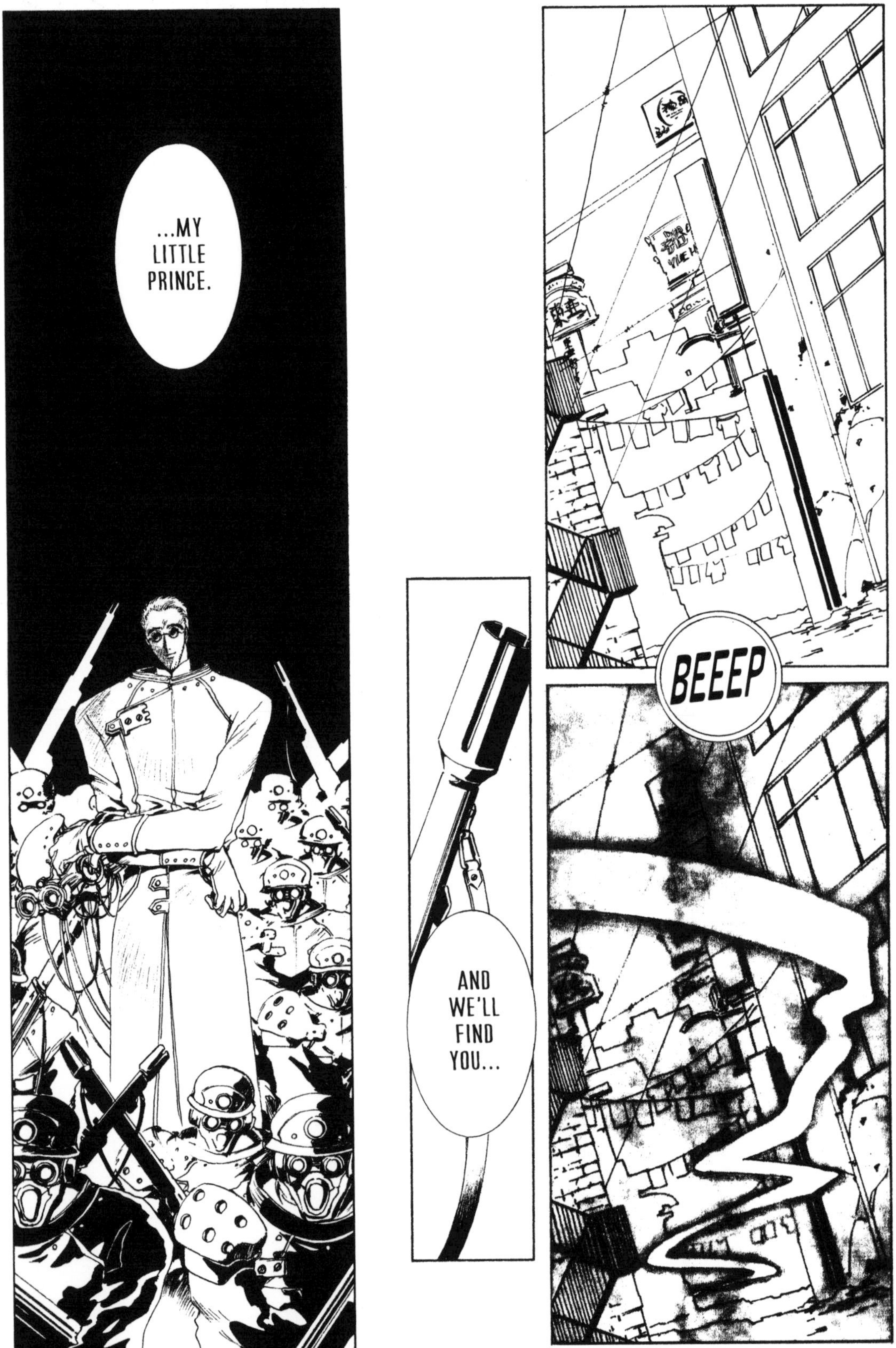
BEEEP
AND WE'LL FIND YOU...
...MY LITTLE PRINCE.

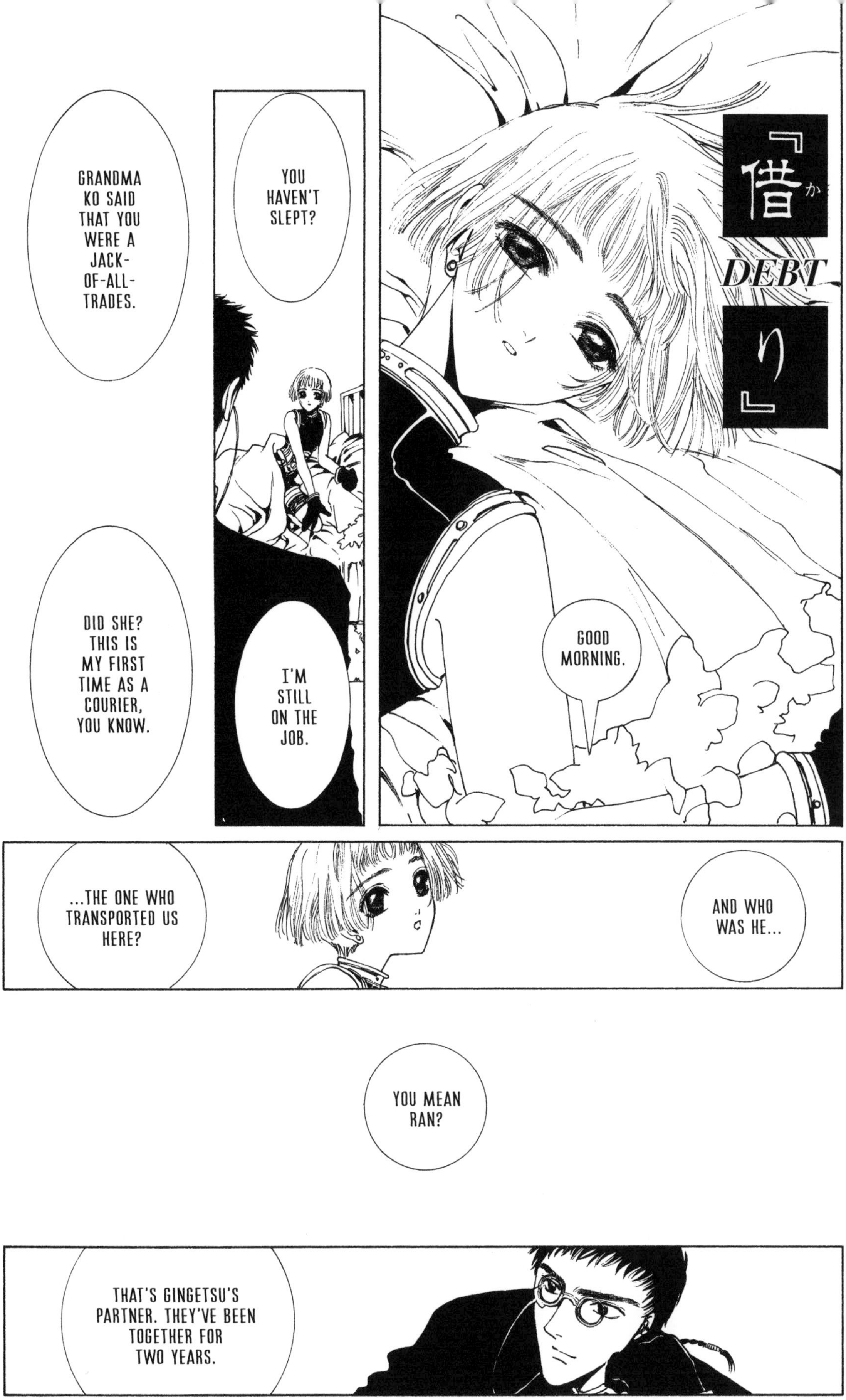
『借り』
DEBT
GOOD MORNING.
YOU HAVEN'T SLEPT?
I'M STILL ON THE JOB.
GRANDMA KO SAID THAT YOU WERE A JACK-OF-ALL-TRADES.
DID SHE? THIS IS MY FIRST TIME AS A COURIER, YOU KNOW.
AND WHO WAS HE...
...THE ONE WHO TRANSPORTED US HERE?
YOU MEAN RAN?
THAT'S GINGETSU'S PARTNER. THEY'VE BEEN TOGETHER FOR TWO YEARS.

TOGETHER...
HOW NICE.

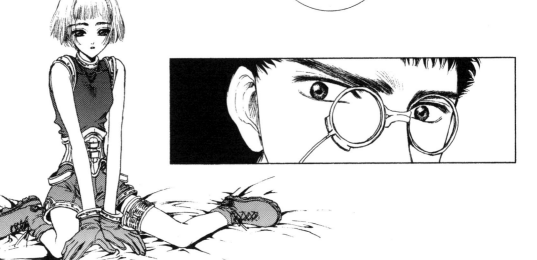

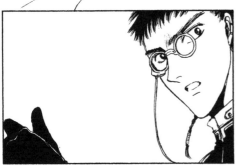

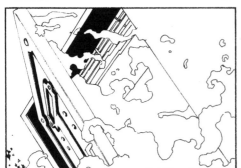

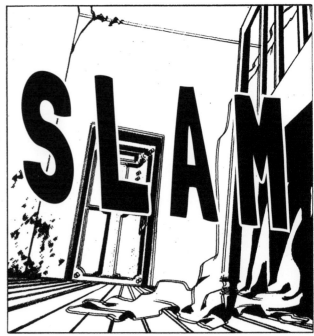

SLAM

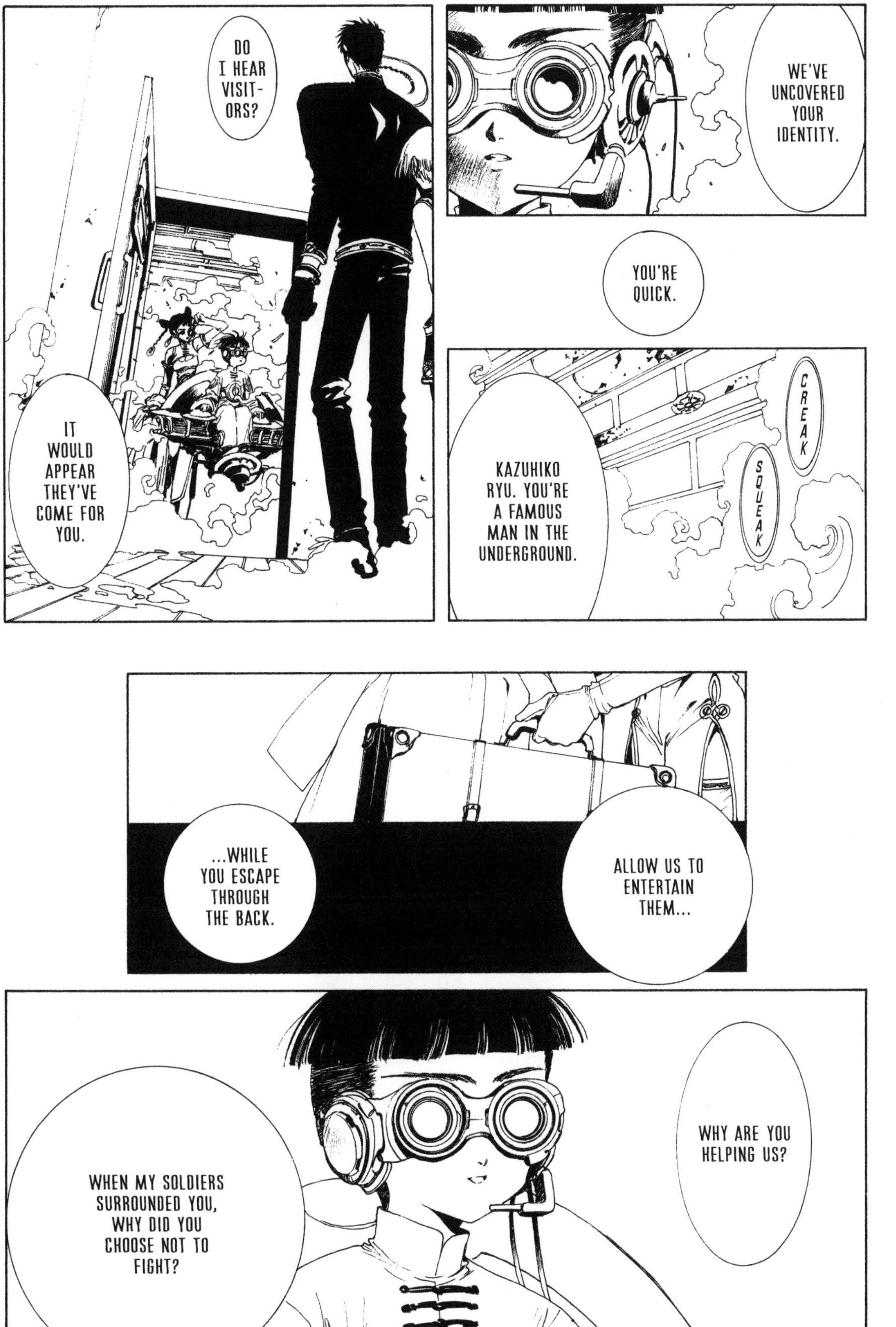
WE'VE UNCOVERED YOUR IDENTITY.
YOU'RE QUICK.
CREAK
SQUEAK
KAZUHIKO RYU. YOU'RE A FAMOUS MAN IN THE UNDERGROUND.
DO I HEAR VISIT- ORS?
IT WOULD APPEAR THEY'VE COME FOR YOU.
ALLOW US TO ENTERTAIN THEM...
...WHILE YOU ESCAPE THROUGH THE BACK.
WHY ARE YOU HELPING US?
WHEN MY SOLDIERS SURROUNDED YOU, WHY DID YOU CHOOSE NOT TO FIGHT?

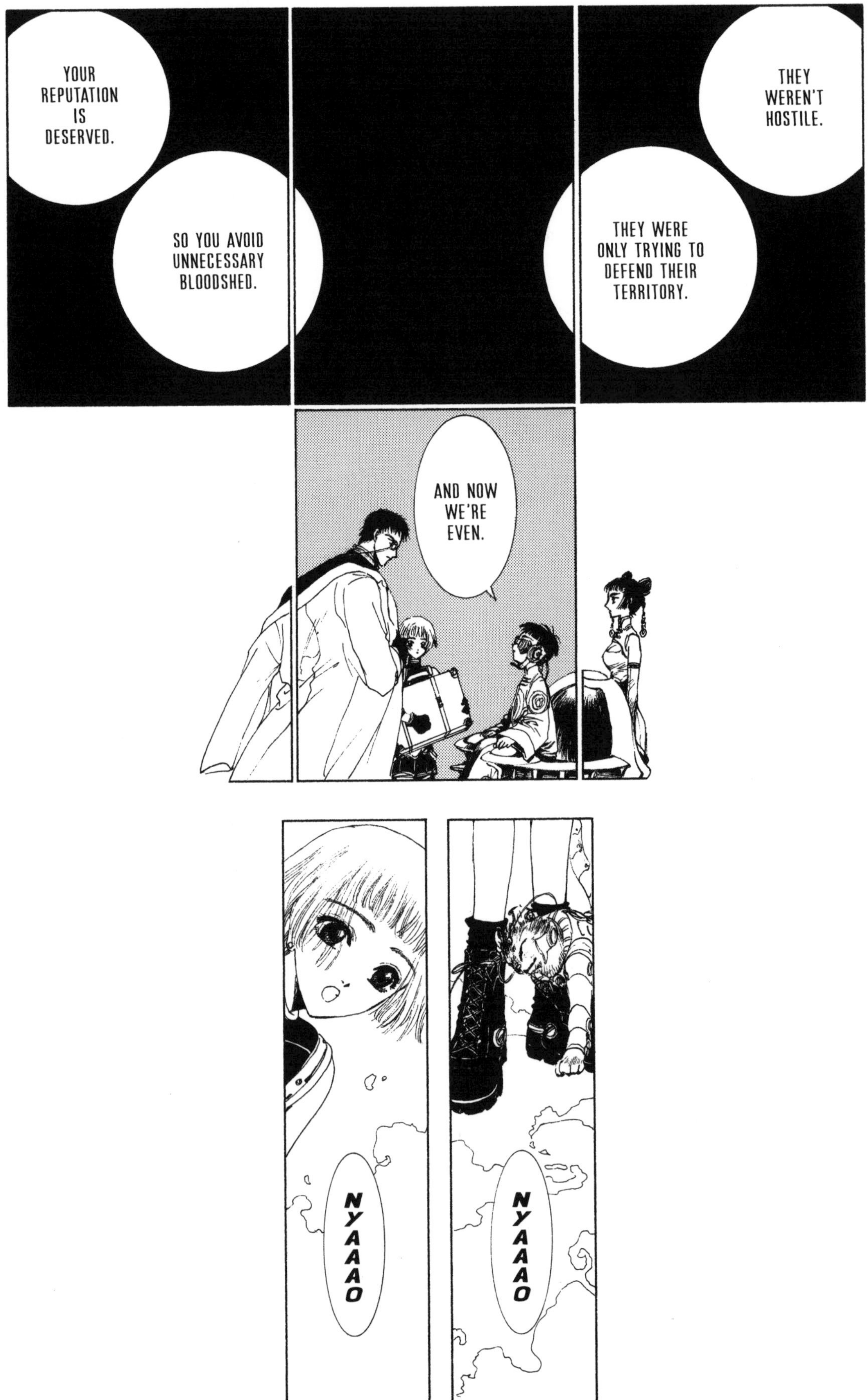
YOUR REPUTATION IS DESERVED.
SO YOU AVOID UNNECESSARY BLOODSHED.
THEY WEREN'T HOSTILE.
THEY WERE ONLY TRYING TO DEFEND THEIR TERRITORY.
AND NOW WE'RE EVEN.
NYAAAO
NYAAAO

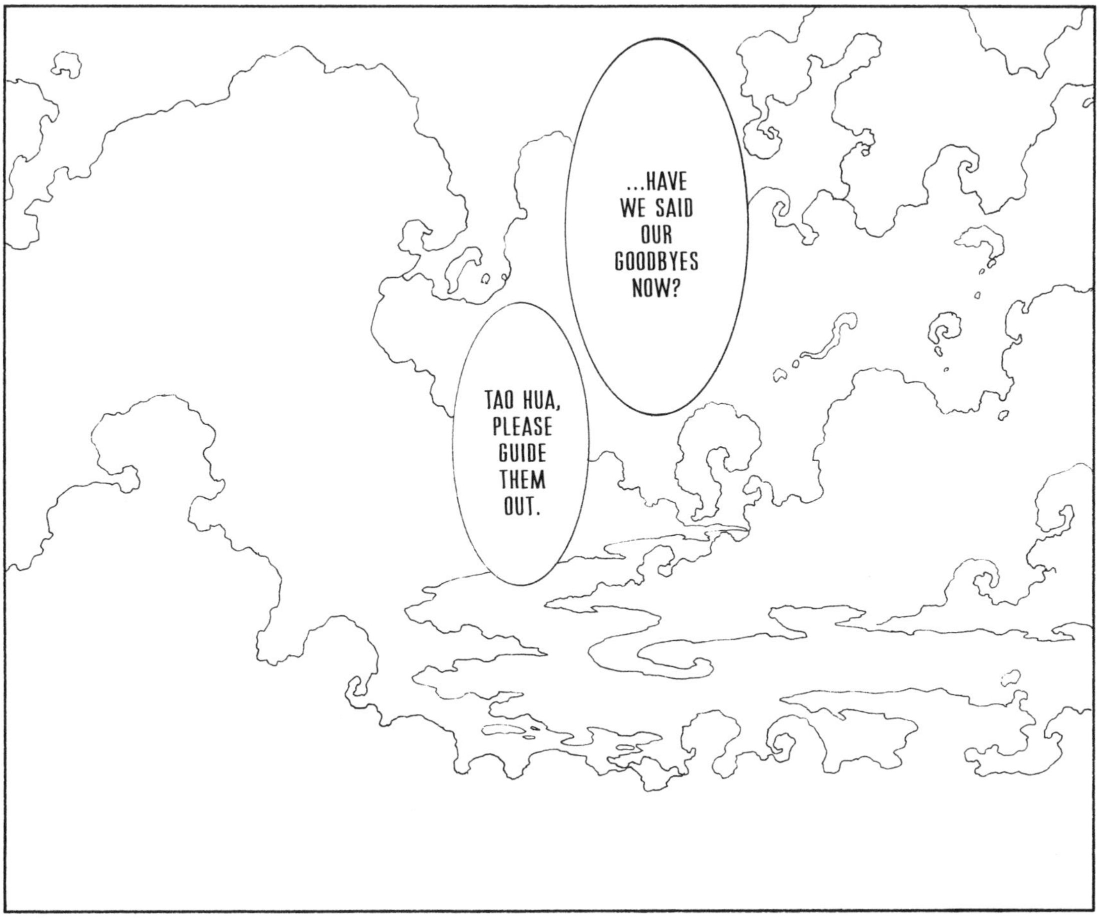
...HAVE WE SAID OUR GOODBYES NOW?
TAO HUA, PLEASE GUIDE THEM OUT.

FLOWER 『花』

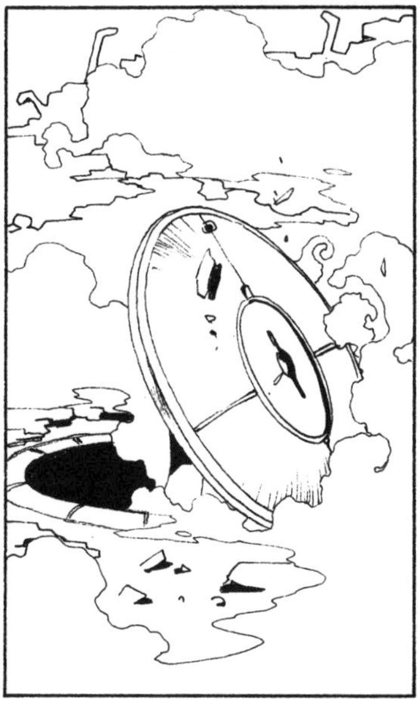
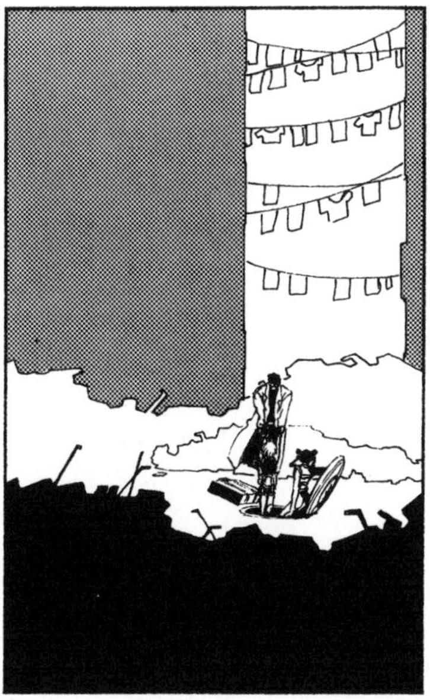
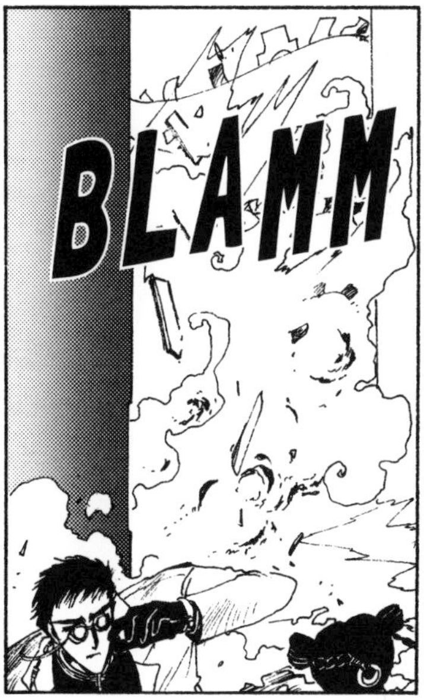
BLAMM

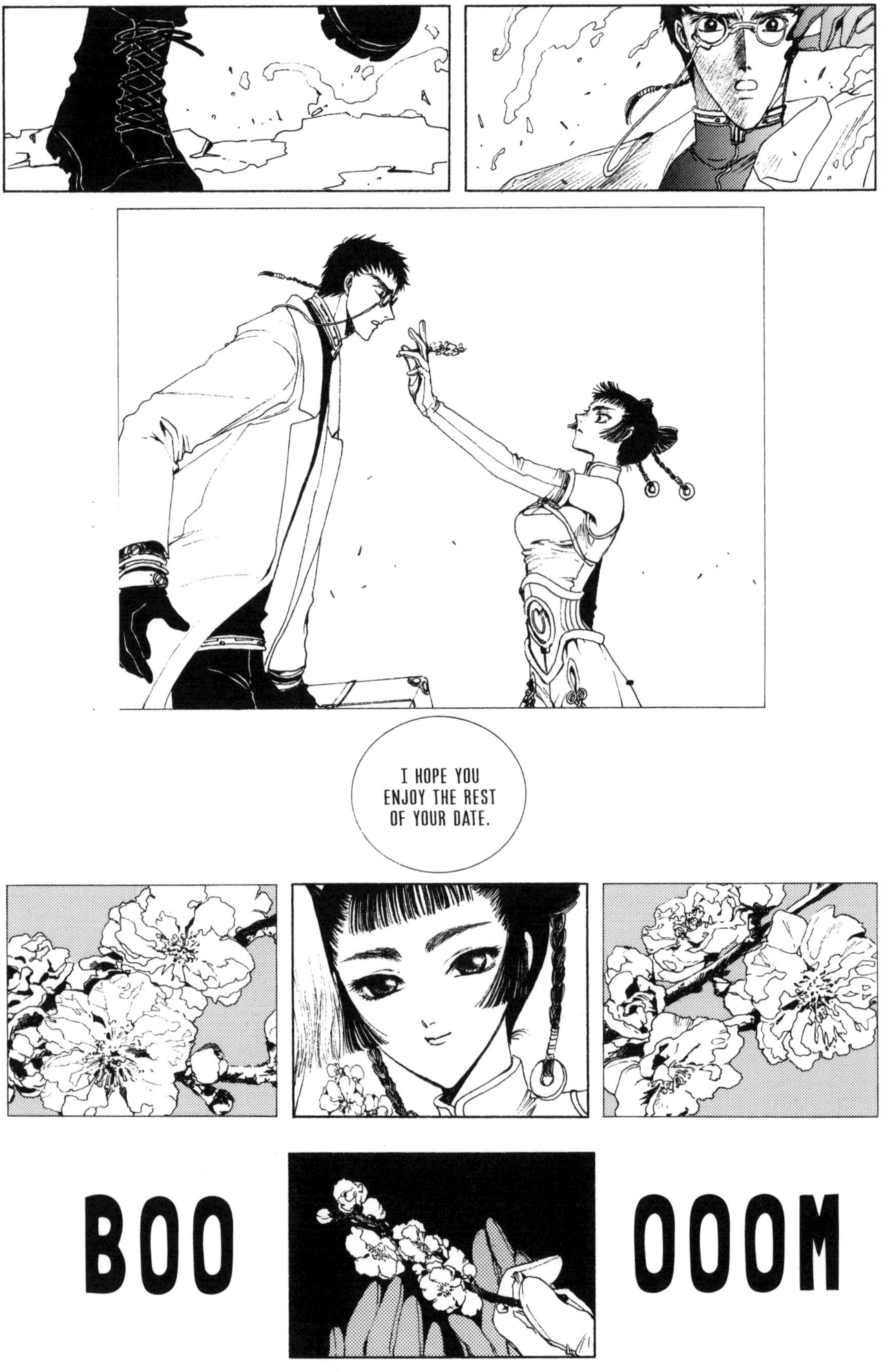
I HOPE YOU ENJOY THE REST OF YOUR DATE.
BOO OOOM

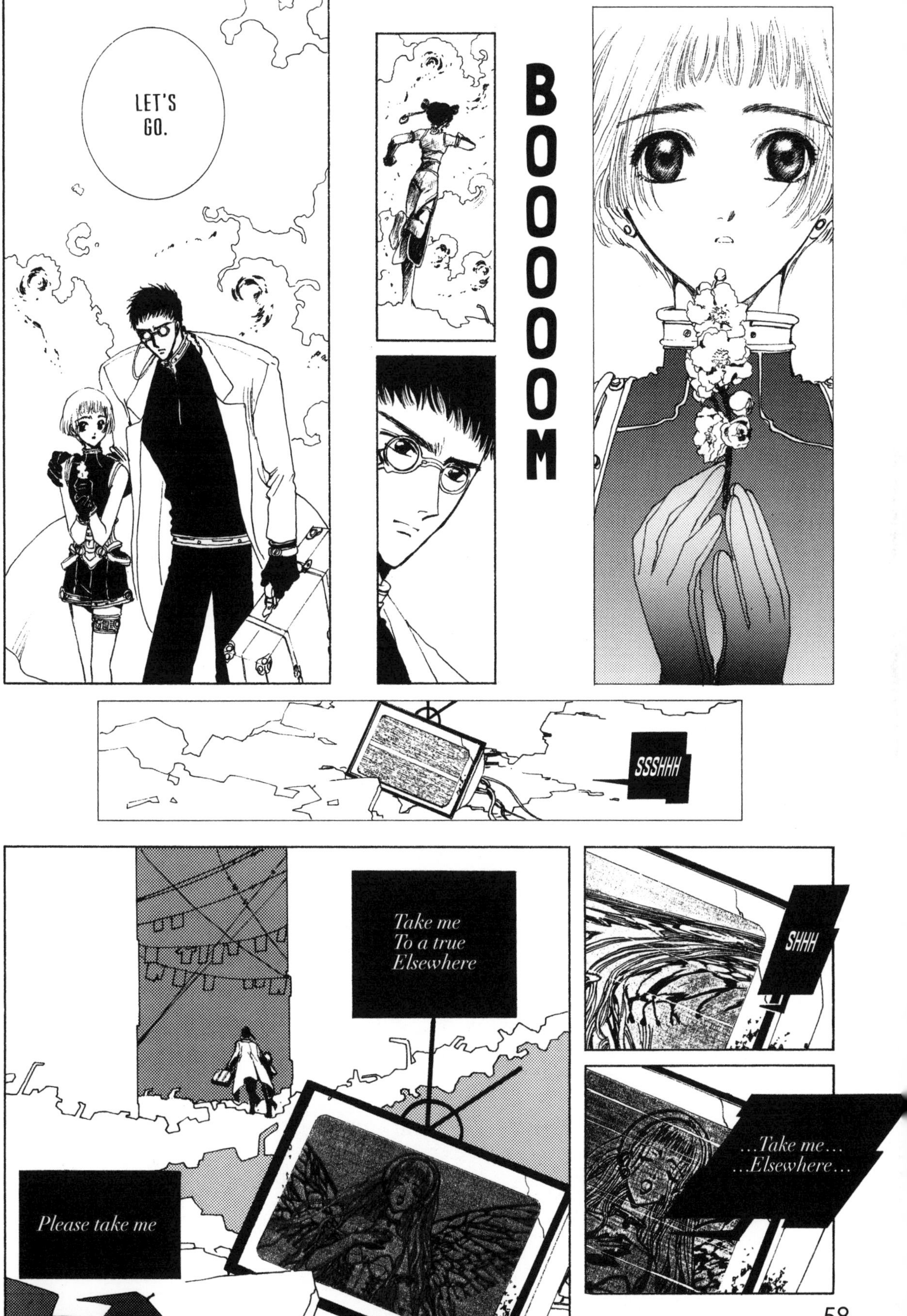
BOOOOOOM
LET'S GO.
SSSHHH
SHHH
…Take me… …Elsewhere…
Take me To a true Elsewhere
Please take me

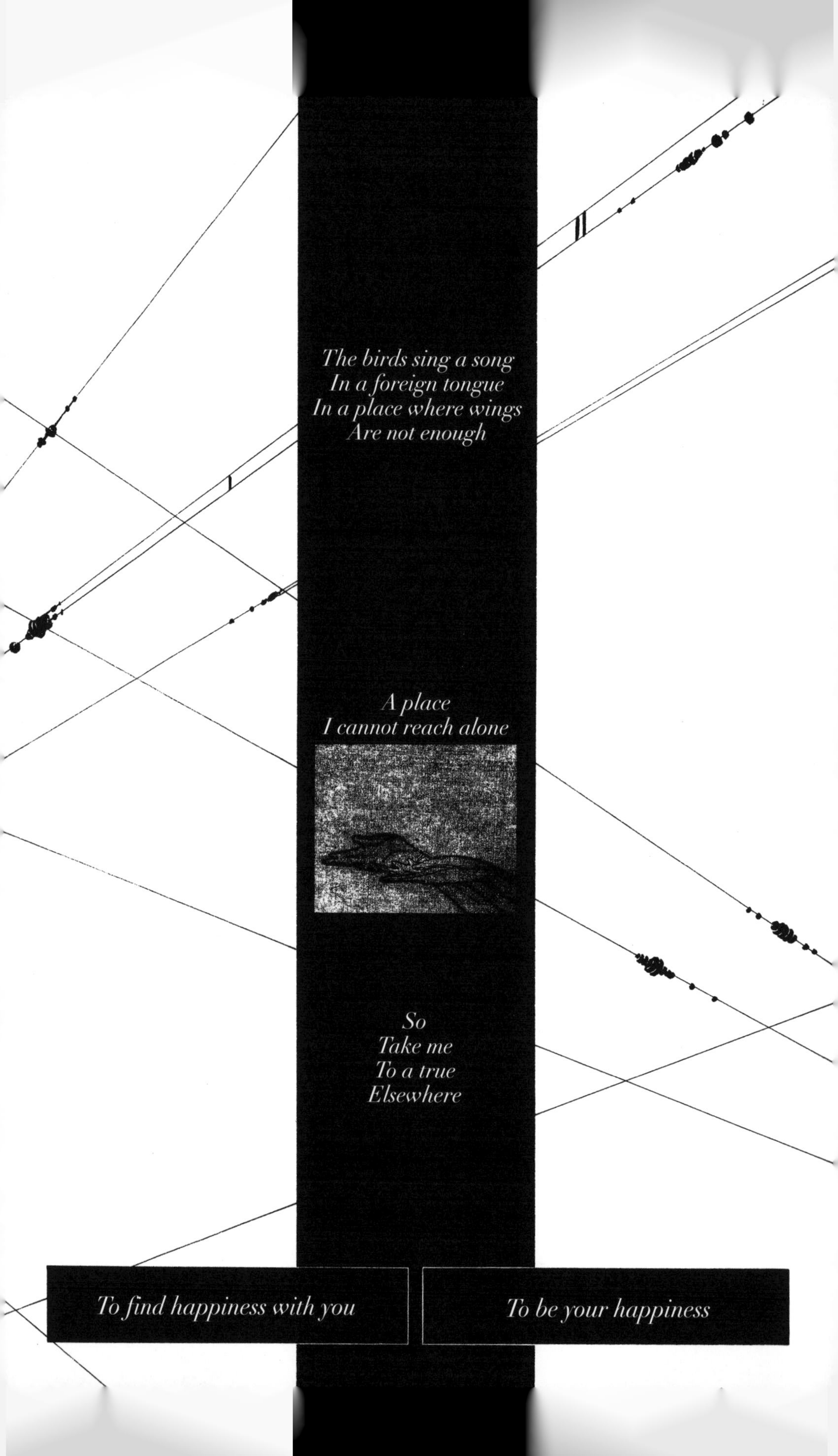
The birds sing a song
In a foreign tongue
In a place where wings
Are not enough
A place
I cannot reach alone
So
Take me
To a true
Elsewhere
To be your happiness
To find happiness with you

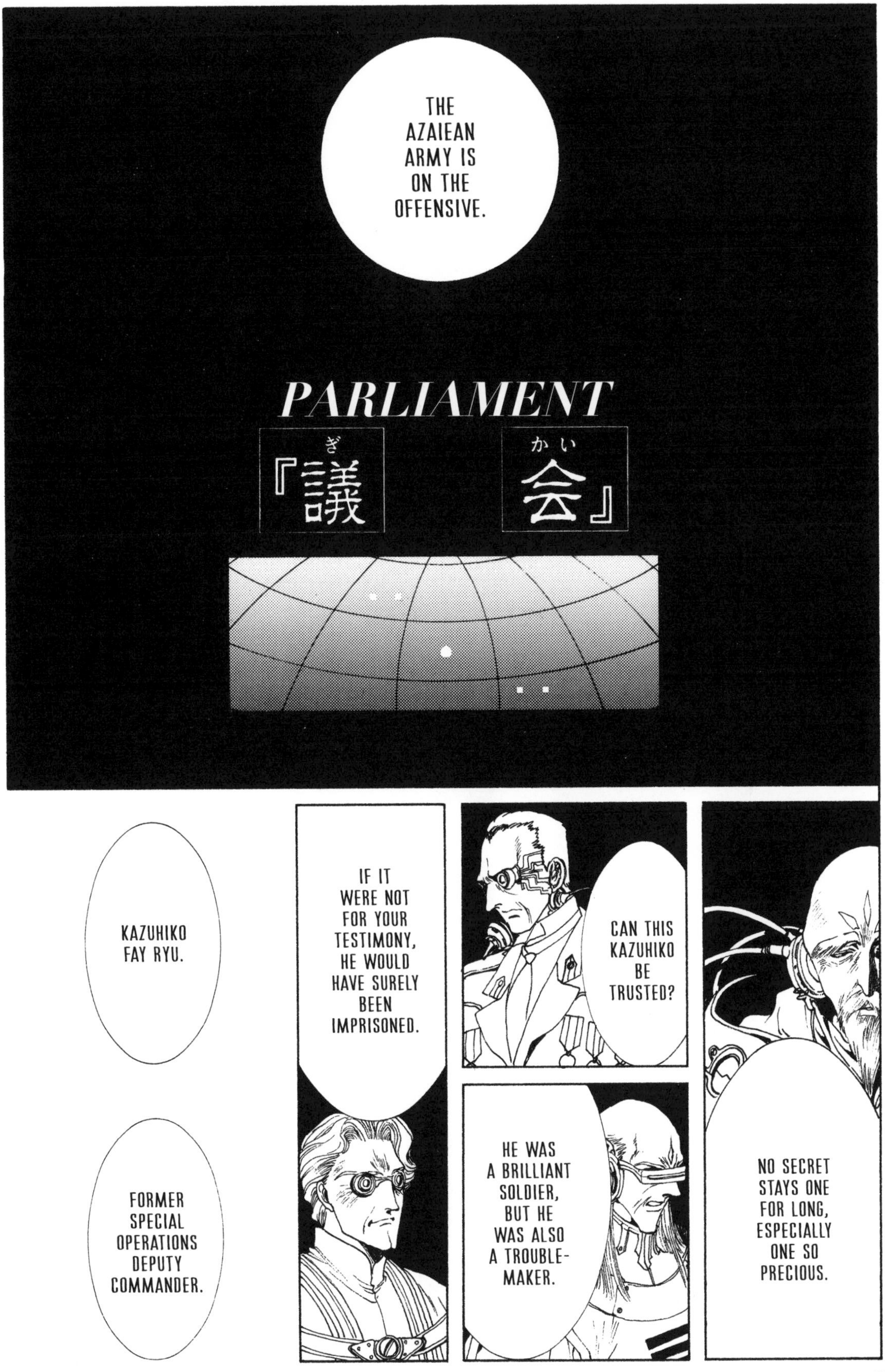
THE AZAIEAN ARMY IS ON THE OFFENSIVE.
PARLIAMENT
『議会』
NO SECRET STAYS ONE FOR LONG, ESPECIALLY ONE SO PRECIOUS.
CAN THIS KAZUHIKO BE TRUSTED?
HE WAS A BRILLIANT SOLDIER, BUT HE WAS ALSO A TROUBLE-MAKER.
IF IT WERE NOT FOR YOUR TESTIMONY, HE WOULD HAVE SURELY BEEN IMPRISONED.
KAZUHIKO FAY RYU.
FORMER SPECIAL OPERATIONS DEPUTY COMMANDER.

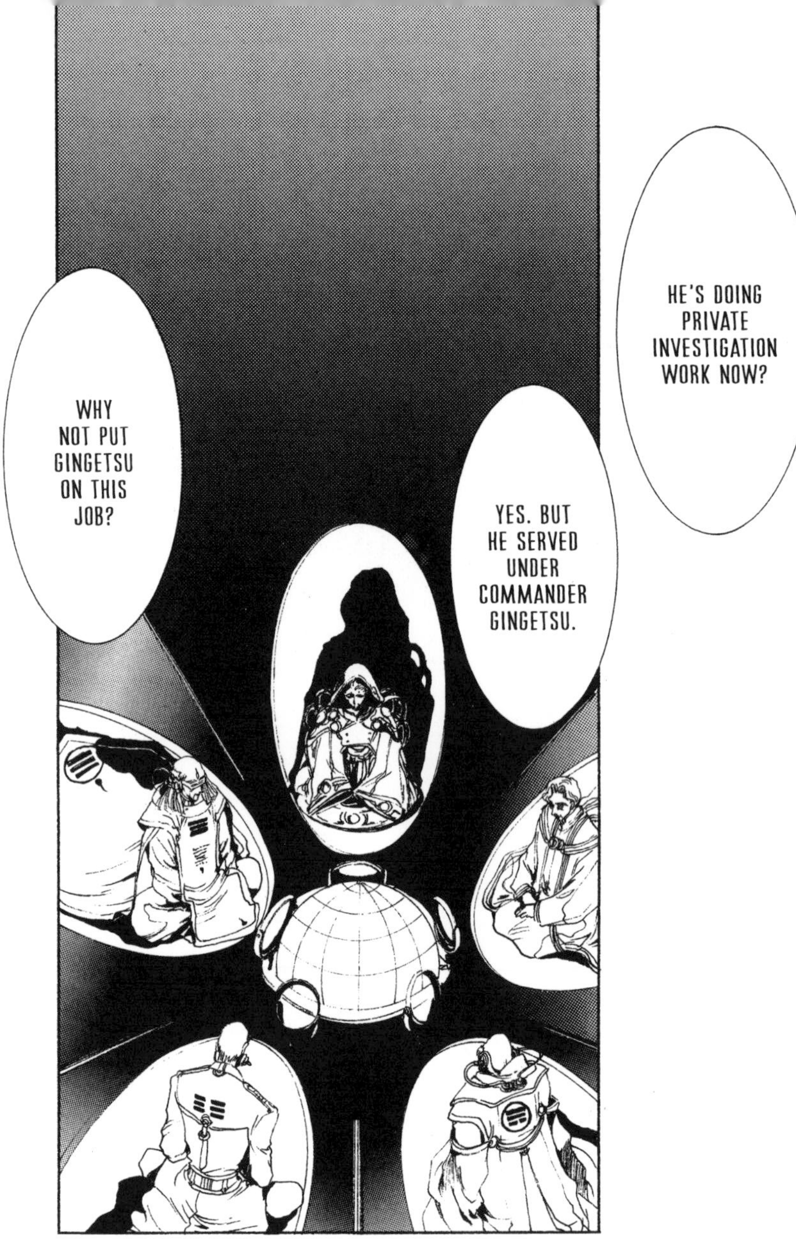
HE'S DOING PRIVATE INVESTIGATION WORK NOW?
YES. BUT HE SERVED UNDER COMMANDER GINGETSU.
WHY NOT PUT GINGETSU ON THIS JOB?
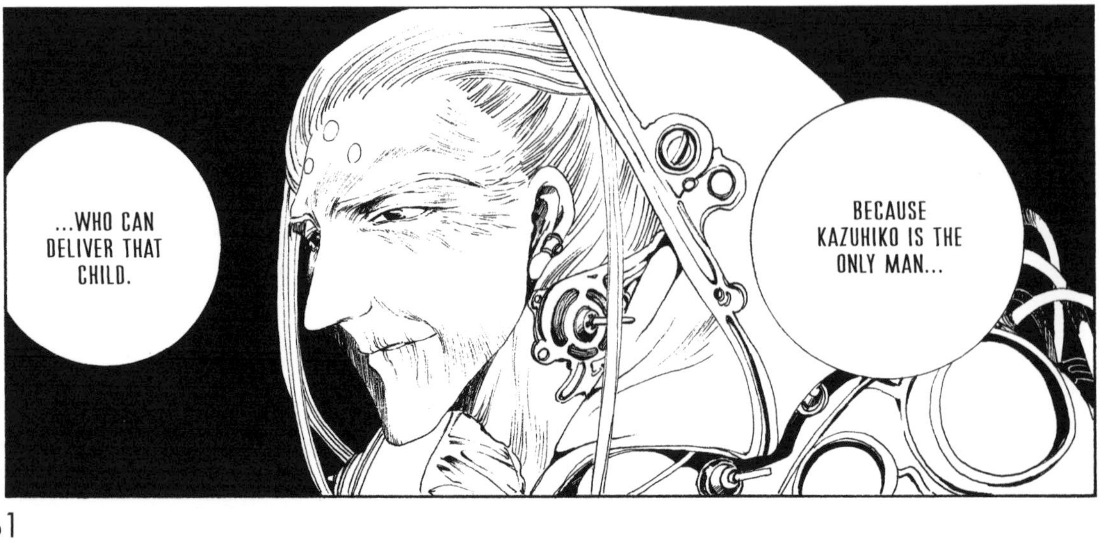
BECAUSE KAZUHIKO IS THE ONLY MAN...
...WHO CAN DELIVER THAT CHILD.

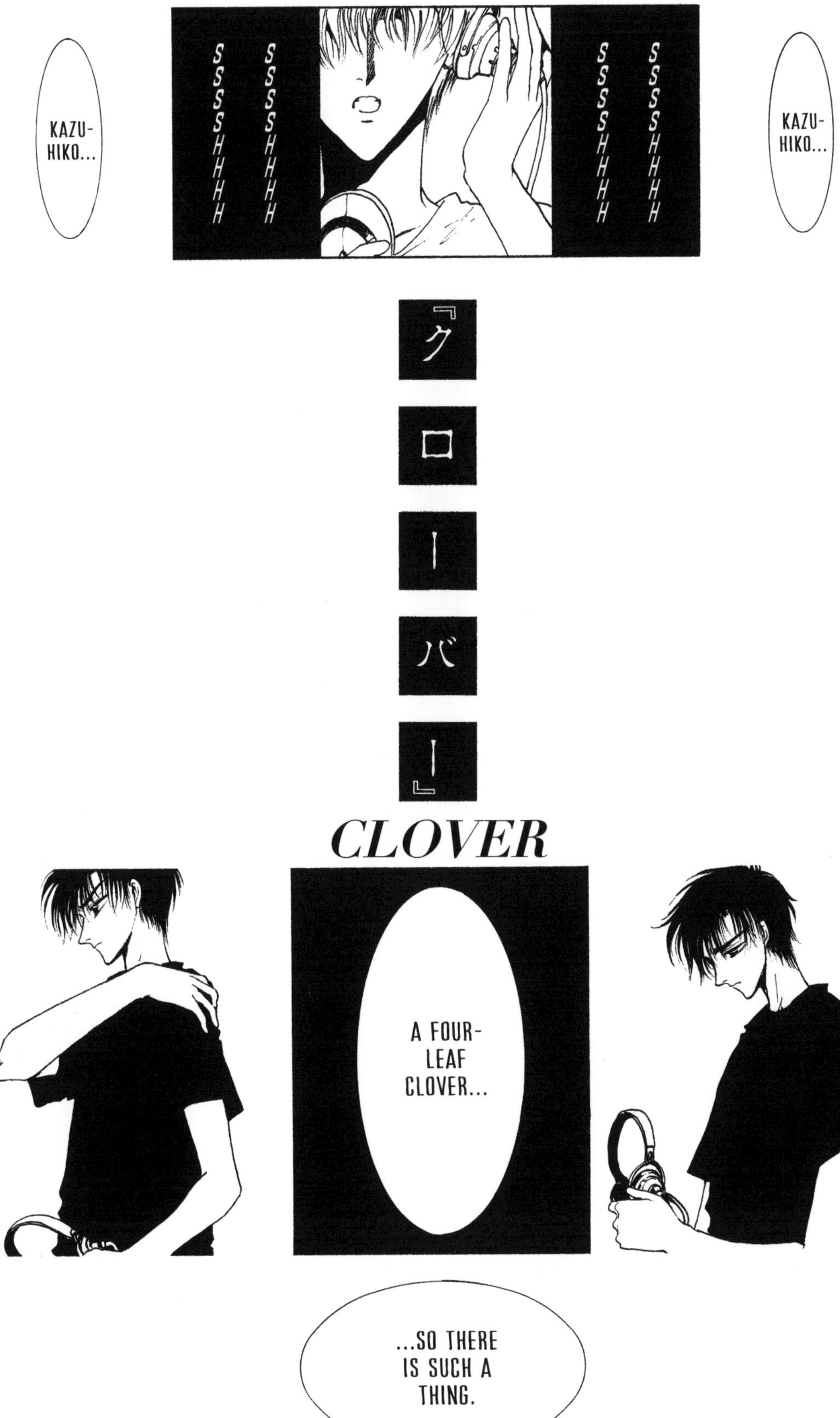
KAZU-HIKO...
SSSSHHHH
SSSSHHHH
SSSSHHHH
SSSSHHHH
KAZU-HIKO...
『クローバー』
CLOVER
A FOUR-LEAF CLOVER...
...SO THERE IS SUCH A THING.

『電話』

TELEPHONE

SSSSHHHH
SSSSHHHH
SSSSHHHH
SSSSHHHH

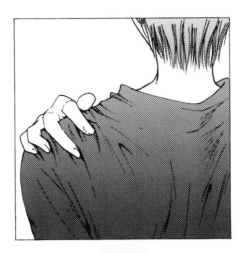

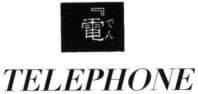

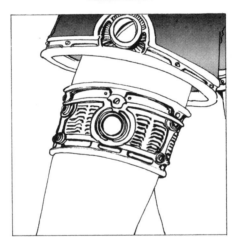

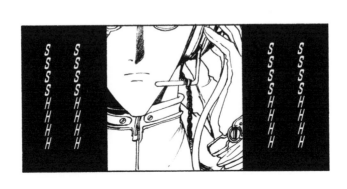

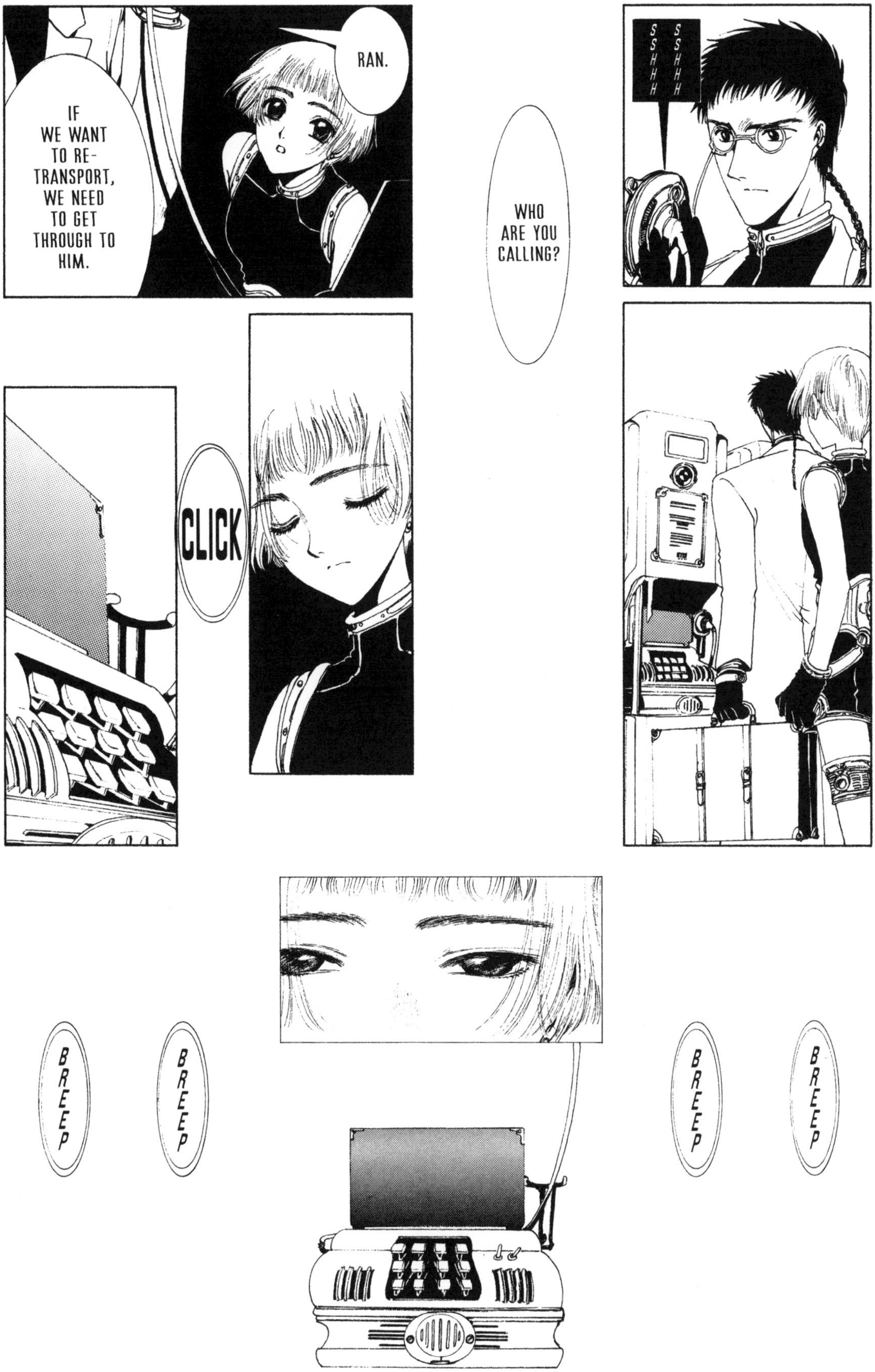
SSHHH SSHHH
WHO ARE YOU CALLING?
RAN.
IF WE WANT TO RE-TRANSPORT, WE NEED TO GET THROUGH TO HIM.
CLICK
BREEP
BREEP
BREEP
BREEP

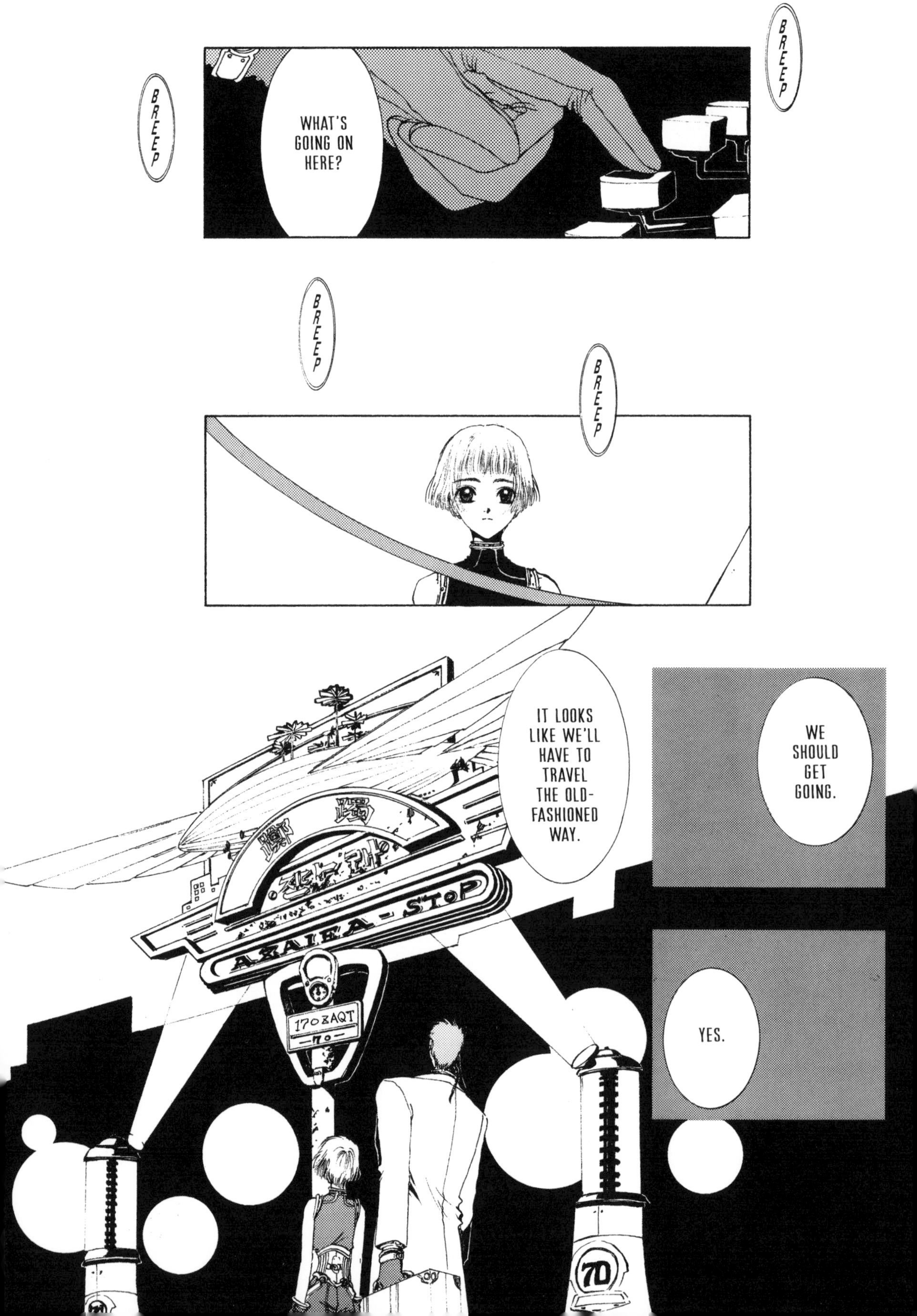
BREEP
WHAT'S GOING ON HERE?
BREEP
BREEP
BREEP
IT LOOKS LIKE WE'LL HAVE TO TRAVEL THE OLD-FASHIONED WAY.
WE SHOULD GET GOING.
YES.

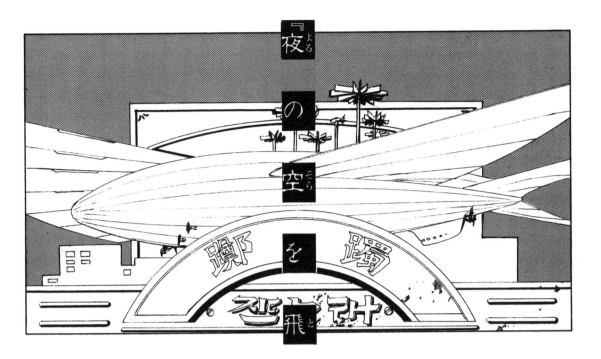

WINGED FISH THAT FLIES THROUGH THE NIGHT

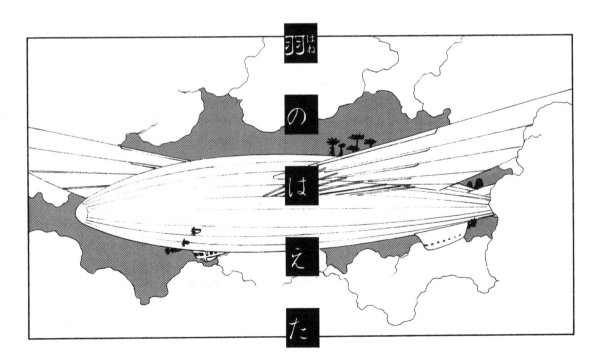

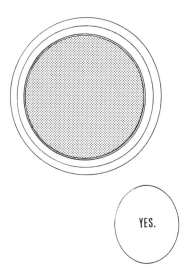

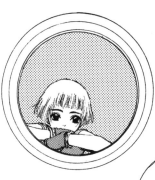

YES.

YOUR FIRST
TIME RIDING
IN ONE OF
THESE?

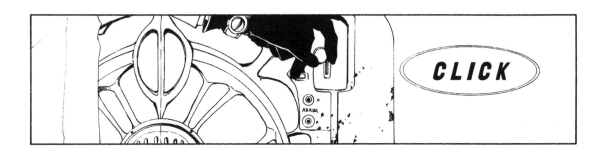

CLICK

*I wish for
happiness*

*I seek
happiness*

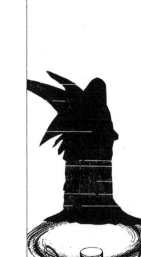

*To find
happiness
with you*

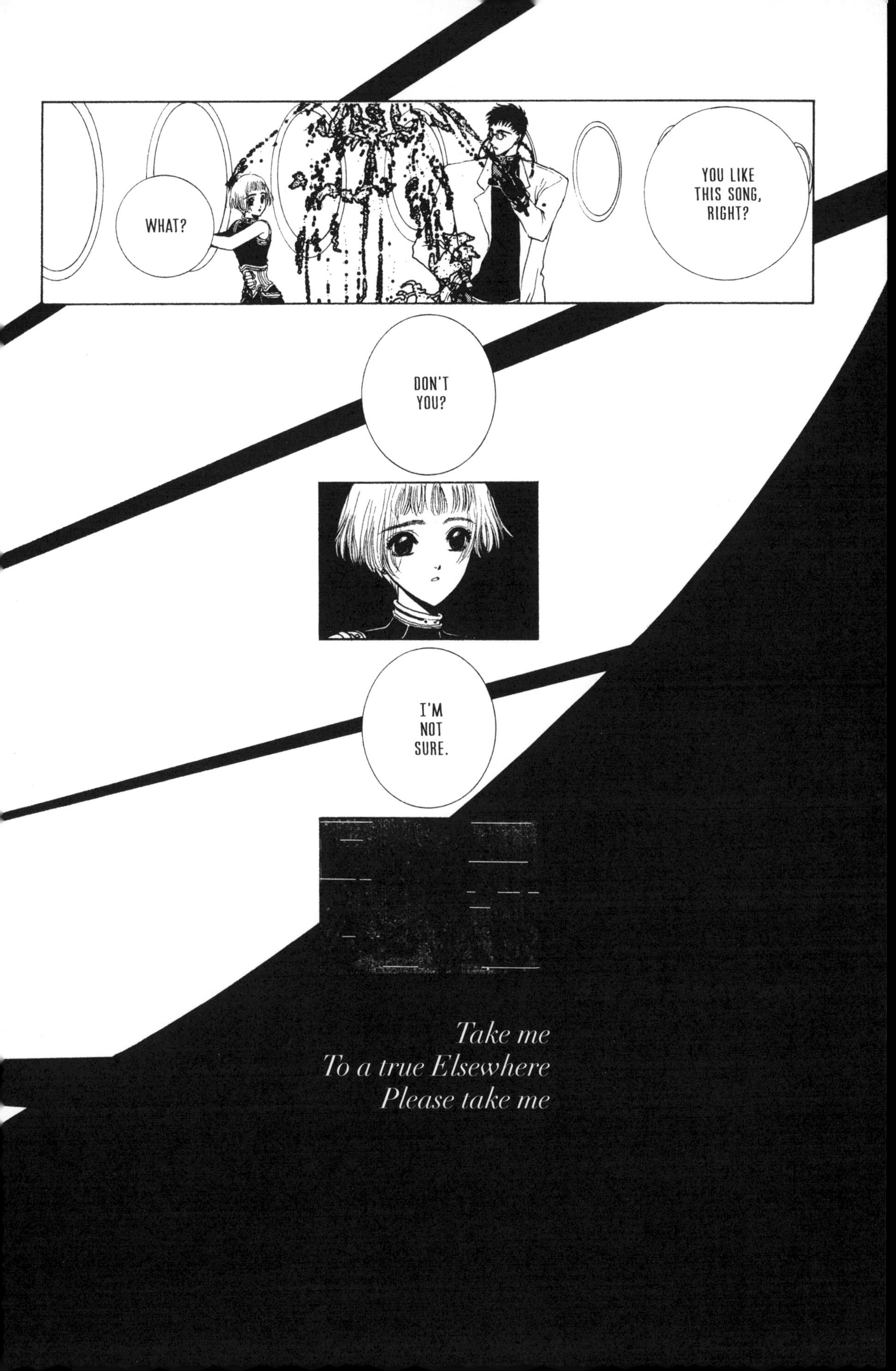

YOU LIKE THIS SONG, RIGHT?
WHAT?
DON'T YOU?
I'M NOT SURE.
Take me
To a true Elsewhere
Please take me

The birds sing a song
In a foreign tongue
In a place where wings
Are not enough
A place
I cannot reach alone

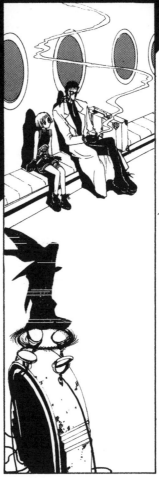

So
Take me
To a true Elsewhere

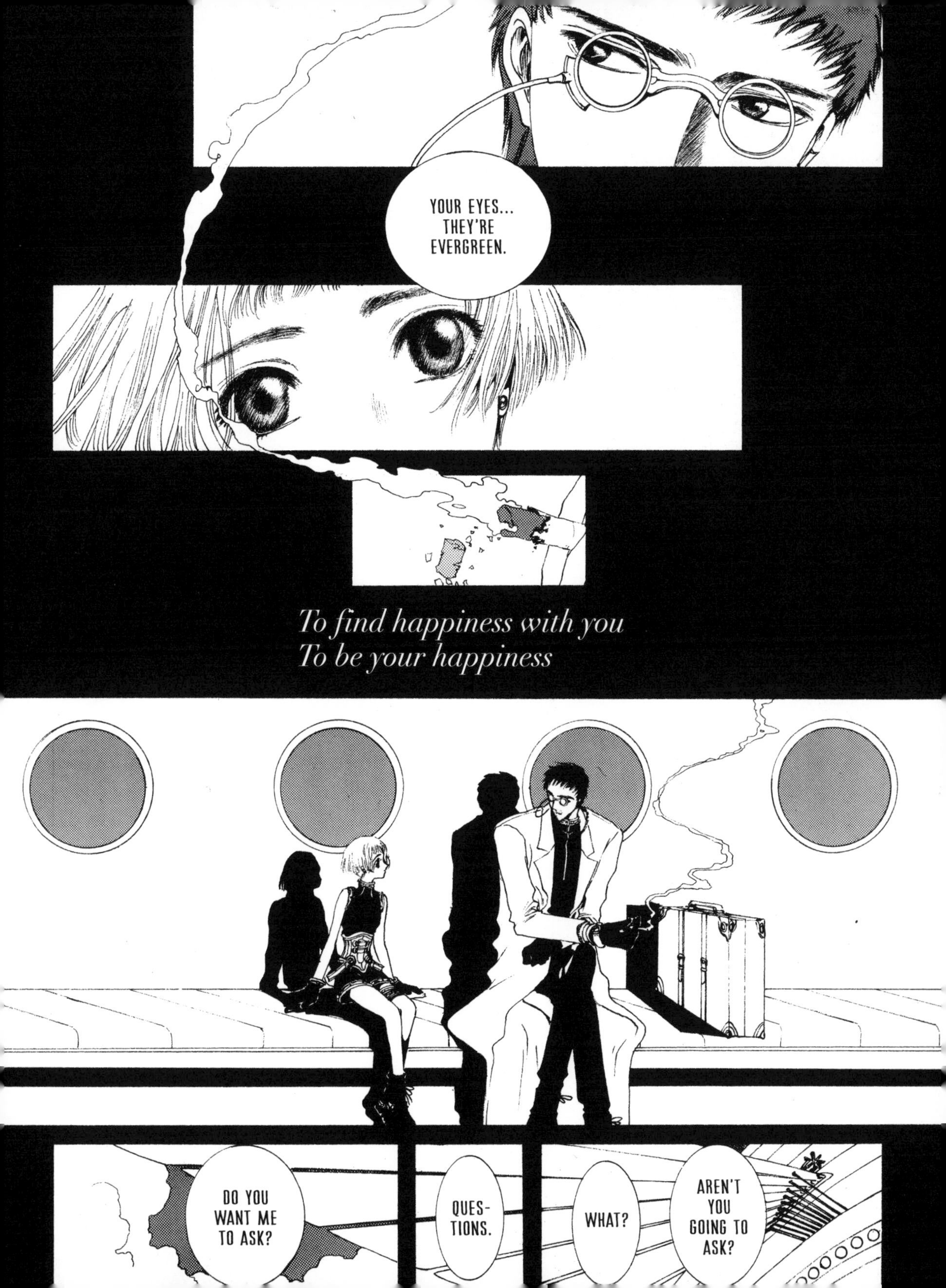
YOUR EYES... THEY'RE EVERGREEN.
To find happiness with you
To be your happiness
AREN'T YOU GOING TO ASK?
WHAT?
QUES-TIONS.
DO YOU WANT ME TO ASK?

NO...

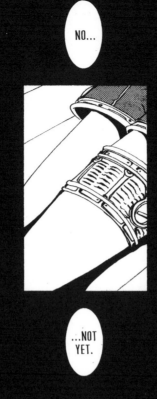

...NOT
YET.

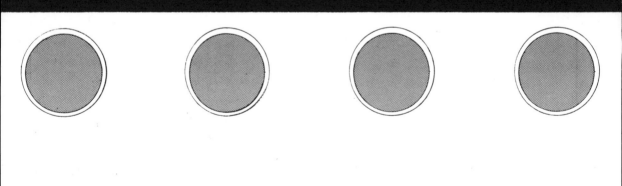

Take me away

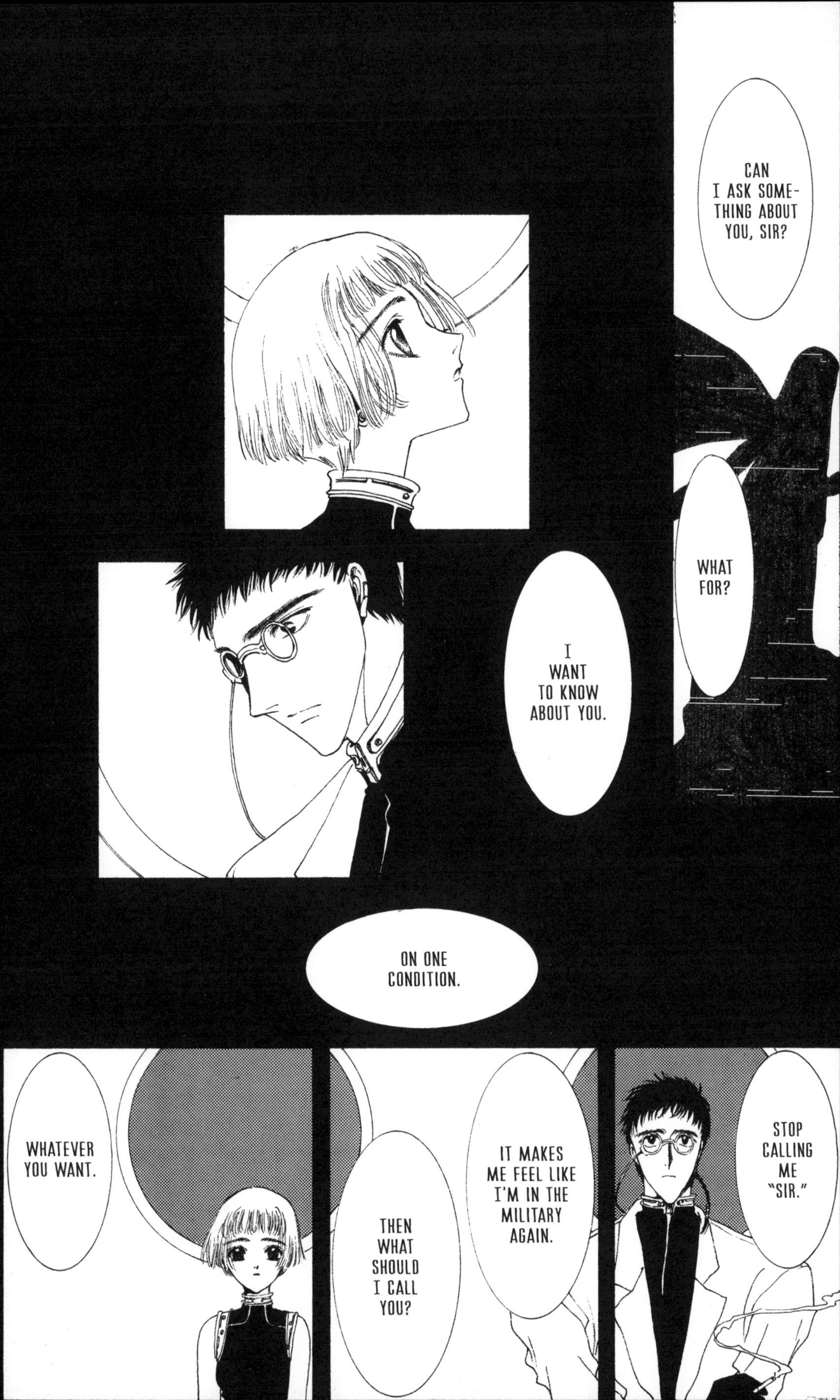
CAN I ASK SOME-THING ABOUT YOU, SIR?
WHAT FOR?
I WANT TO KNOW ABOUT YOU.
ON ONE CONDITION.
STOP CALLING ME "SIR."
IT MAKES ME FEEL LIKE I'M IN THE MILITARY AGAIN.
THEN WHAT SHOULD I CALL YOU?
WHATEVER YOU WANT.

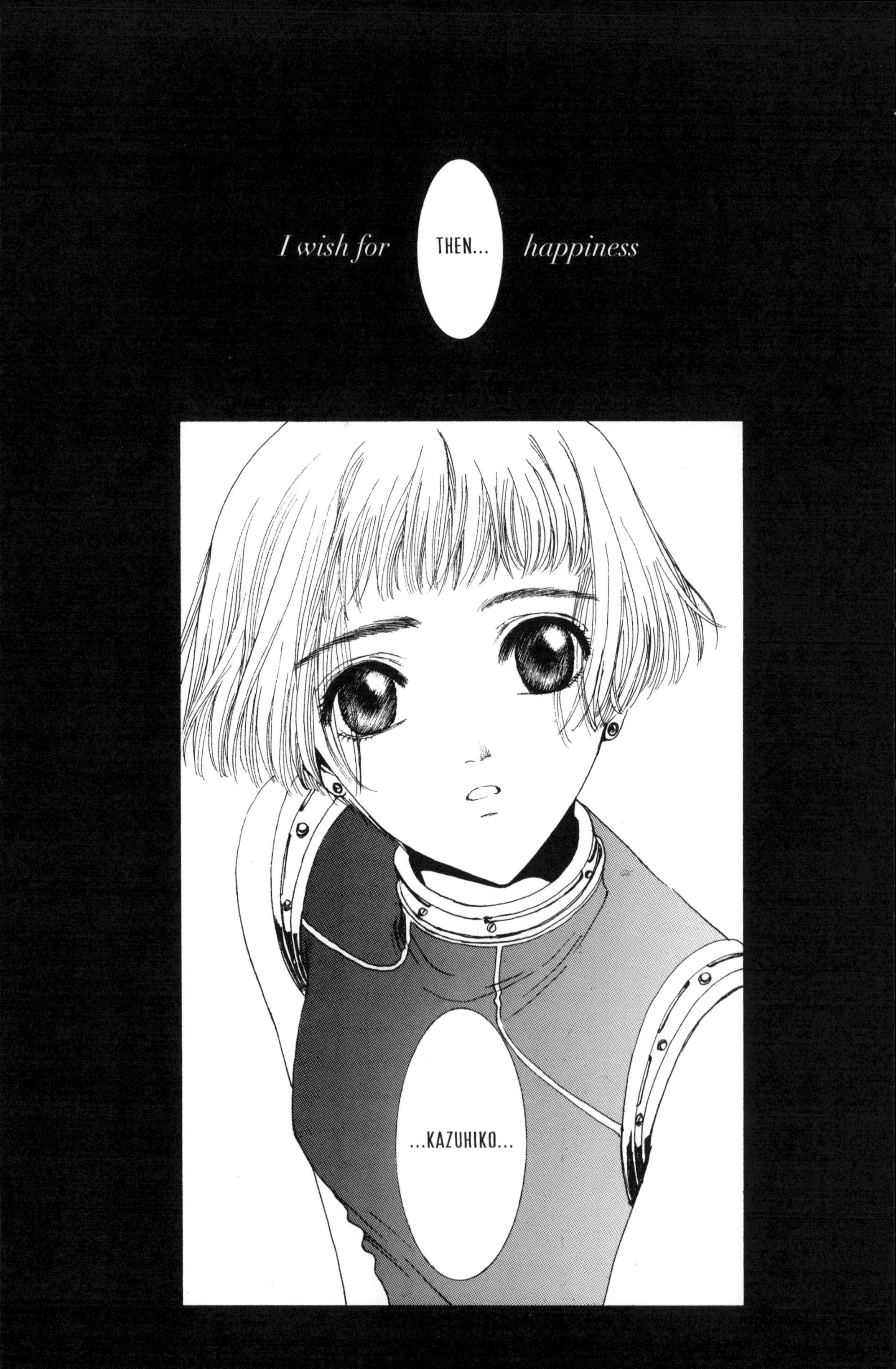

I wish for happiness
THEN...
...KAZUHIKO...

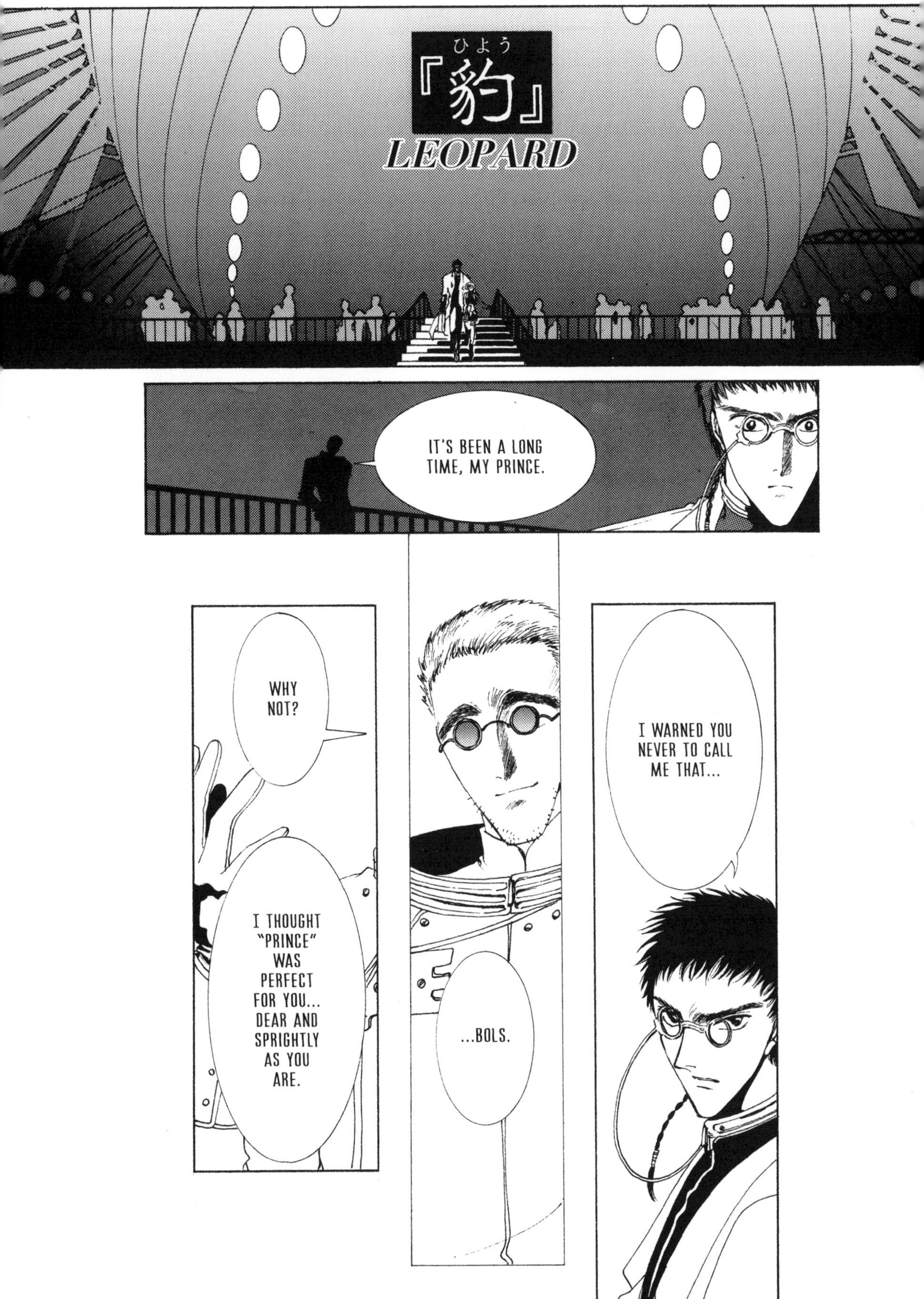
ひよう
『豹』
LEOPARD
IT'S BEEN A LONG TIME, MY PRINCE.
I WARNED YOU NEVER TO CALL ME THAT...
...BOLS.
WHY NOT?
I THOUGHT "PRINCE" WAS PERFECT FOR YOU... DEAR AND SPRIGHTLY AS YOU ARE.

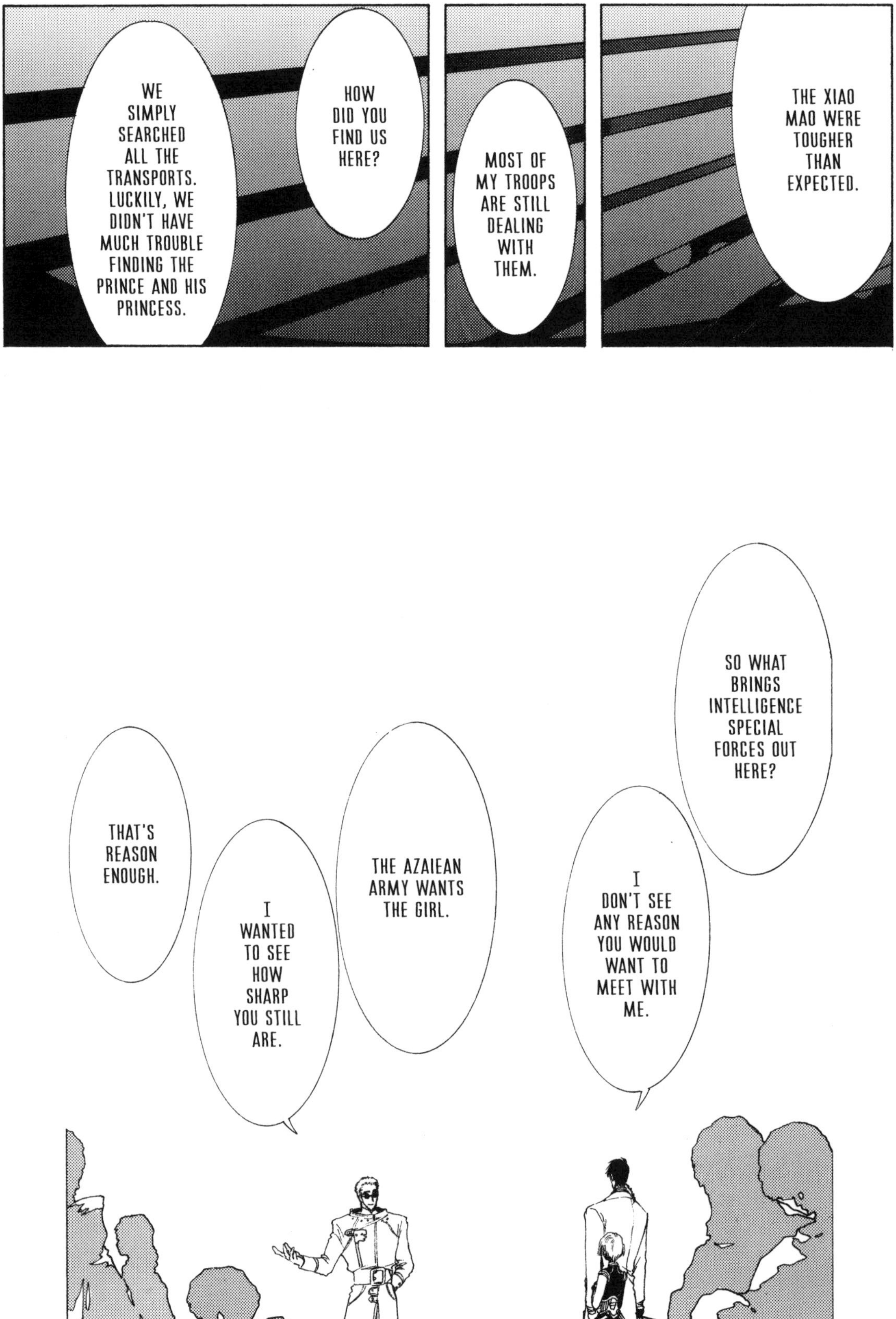
THE XIAO MAO WERE TOUGHER THAN EXPECTED.
MOST OF MY TROOPS ARE STILL DEALING WITH THEM.
HOW DID YOU FIND US HERE?
WE SIMPLY SEARCHED ALL THE TRANSPORTS. LUCKILY, WE DIDN'T HAVE MUCH TROUBLE FINDING THE PRINCE AND HIS PRINCESS.
SO WHAT BRINGS INTELLIGENCE SPECIAL FORCES OUT HERE?
I DON'T SEE ANY REASON YOU WOULD WANT TO MEET WITH ME.
THE AZAIEAN ARMY WANTS THE GIRL.
I WANTED TO SEE HOW SHARP YOU STILL ARE.
THAT'S REASON ENOUGH.

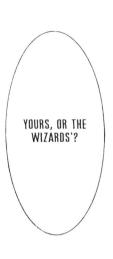

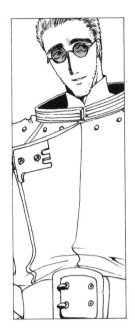

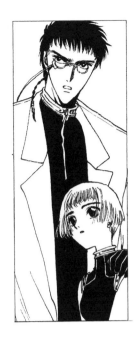

THIS GIRL IS MY RESPONSIBILITY.
YOURS, OR THE WIZARDS'?
I'M SURE THE OLD BUZZARDS OF THE PARLIAMENTARY COUNCIL WOULD BE THRILLED TO HEAR YOU CALL THEM "THE WIZARDS."
BUT I HEAR THOSE RELICS CONTROL MOST OF THE UNDERGROUND THESE DAYS.

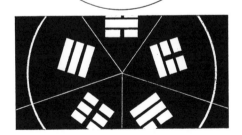

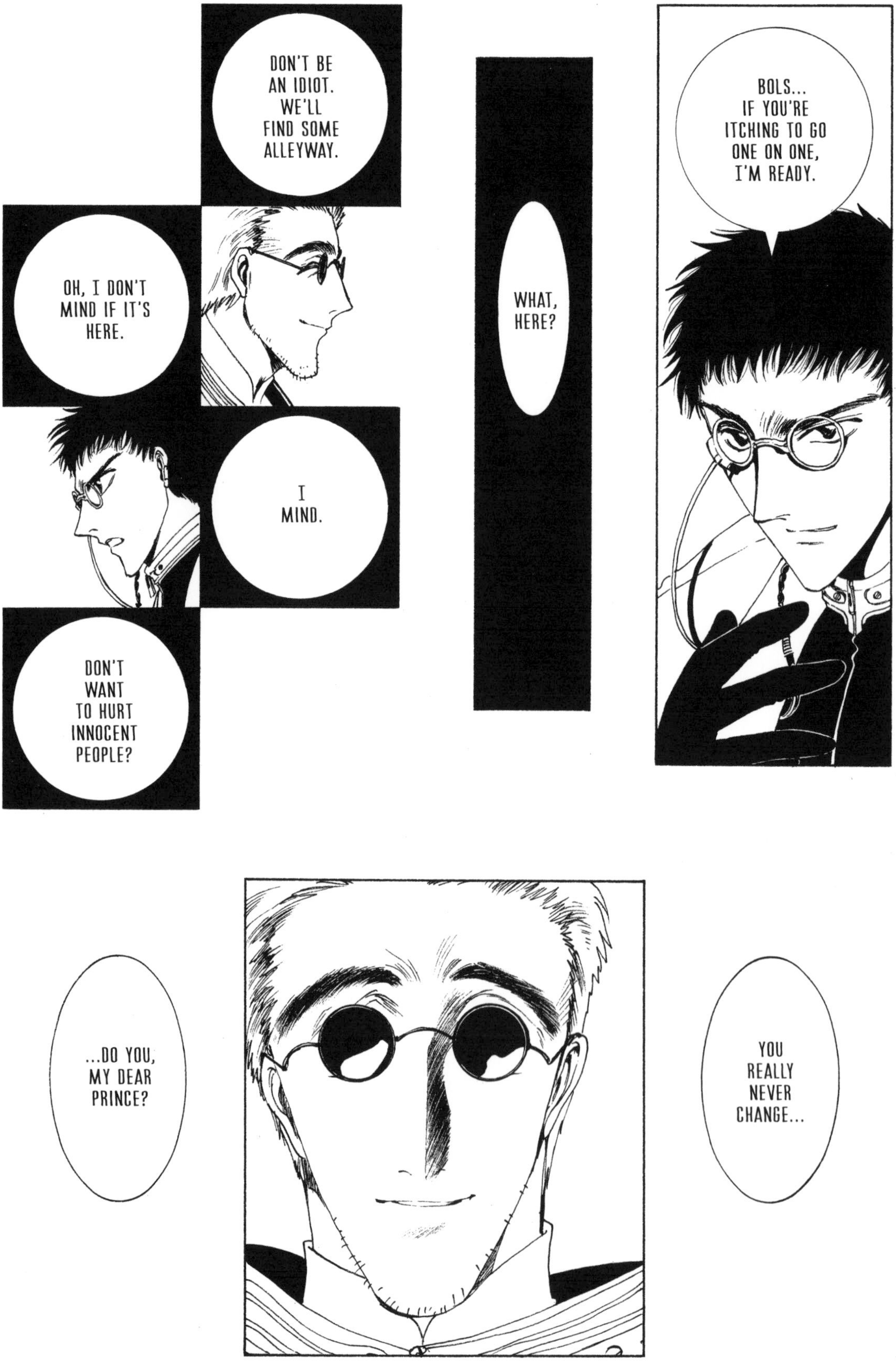
BOLS... IF YOU'RE ITCHING TO GO ONE ON ONE, I'M READY.
WHAT, HERE?
DON'T BE AN IDIOT. WE'LL FIND SOME ALLEYWAY.
OH, I DON'T MIND IF IT'S HERE.
I MIND.
DON'T WANT TO HURT INNOCENT PEOPLE?
YOU REALLY NEVER CHANGE...
...DO YOU, MY DEAR PRINCE?

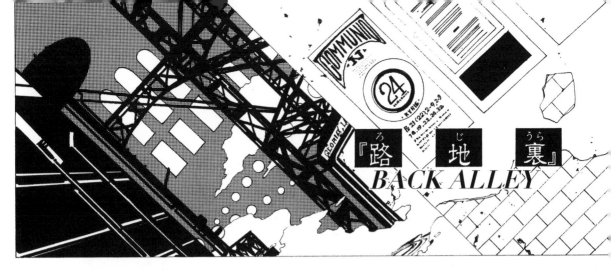

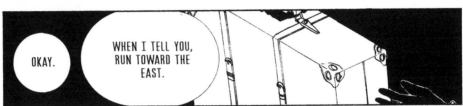

OKAY.

WHEN I TELL YOU, RUN TOWARD THE EAST.

NO MATTER WHAT HAPPENS, YOU RUN.

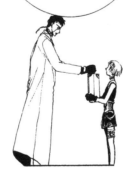

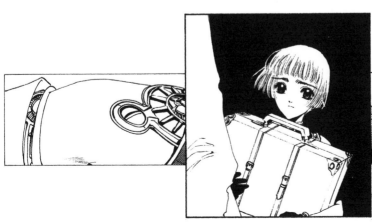

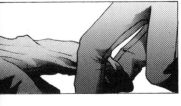

I'M GLAD WE GET TO PLAY TOGETHER AGAIN, KAZUHIKO.
VVVMMM
DON'T TELL ME NO ONE *ELSE* WANTS TO PLAY WITH YOU, BOLS.
VVVMMM
I GUESS EVERYBODY REALLY HATES YOU.

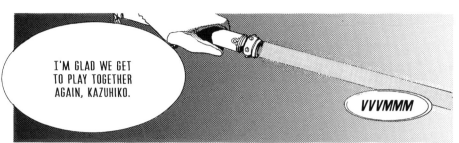

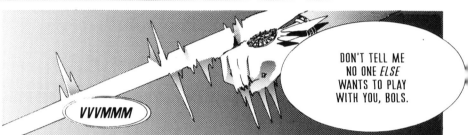

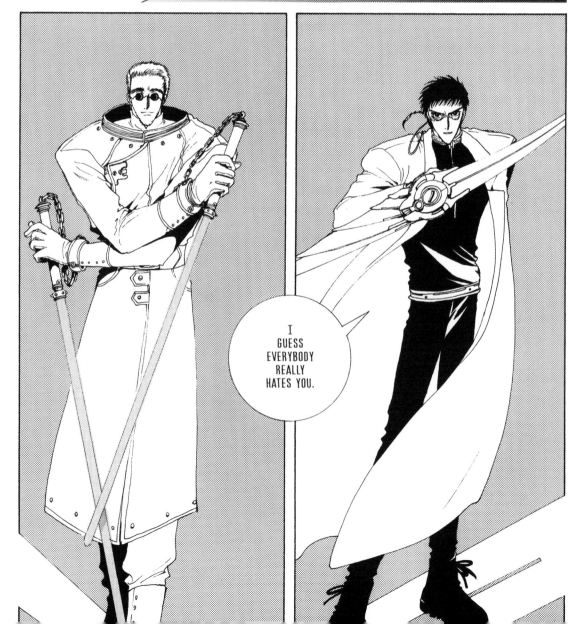

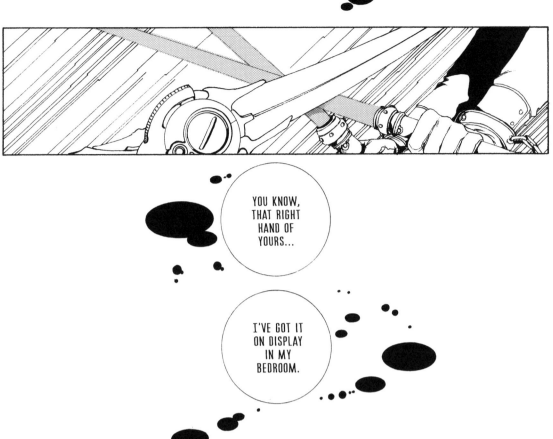

YOU KNOW, THAT RIGHT HAND OF YOURS...
I'VE GOT IT ON DISPLAY IN MY BEDROOM.
IN FACT, I GO TO SLEEP WITH IT EVERY NIGHT...
...DOESN'T THAT MAKE YOU HARD?

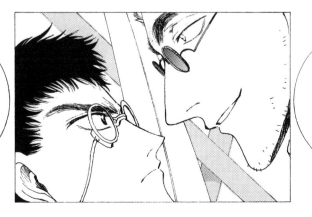

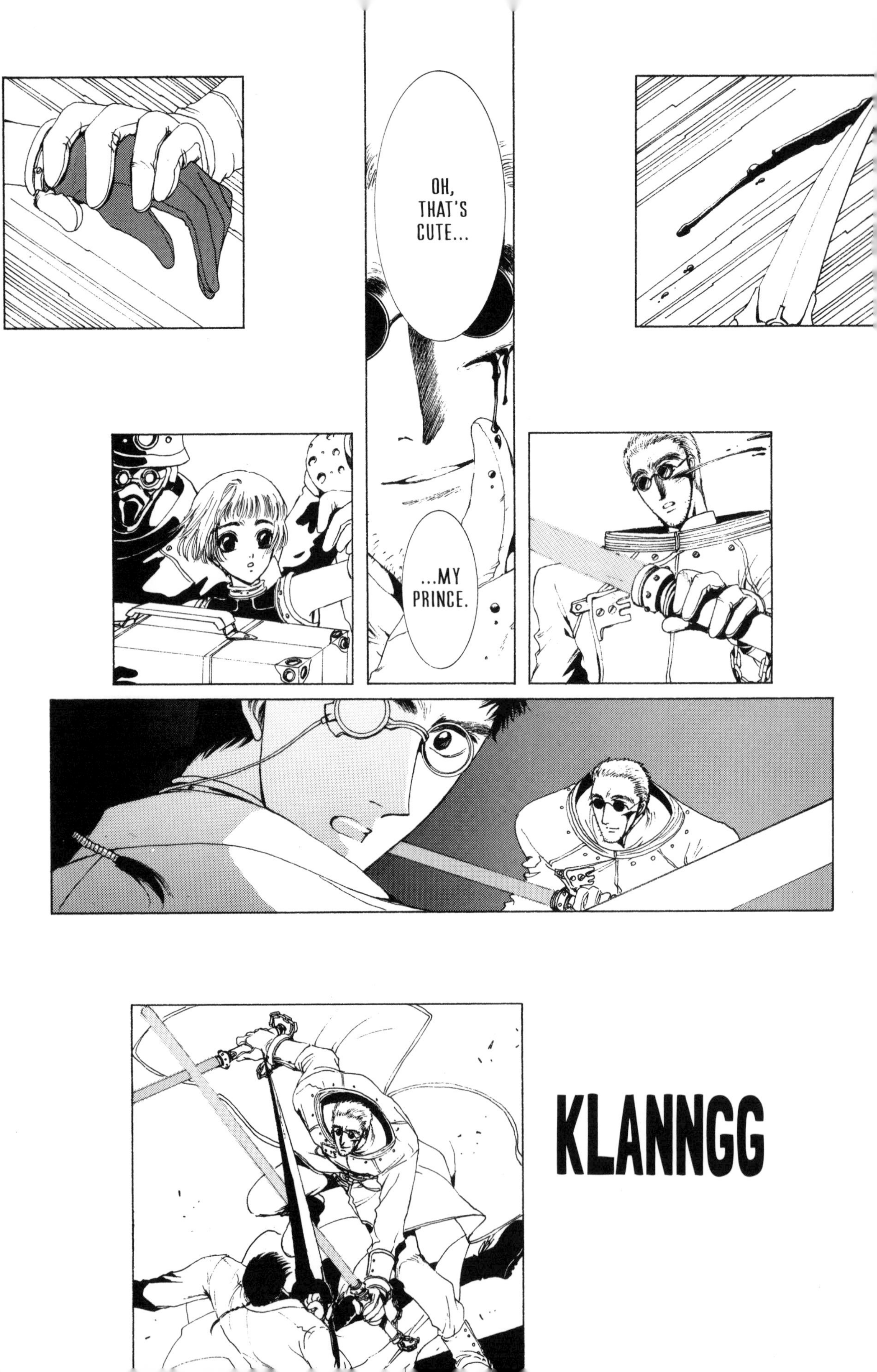
OH, THAT'S CUTE...
...MY PRINCE.
KLANNGG

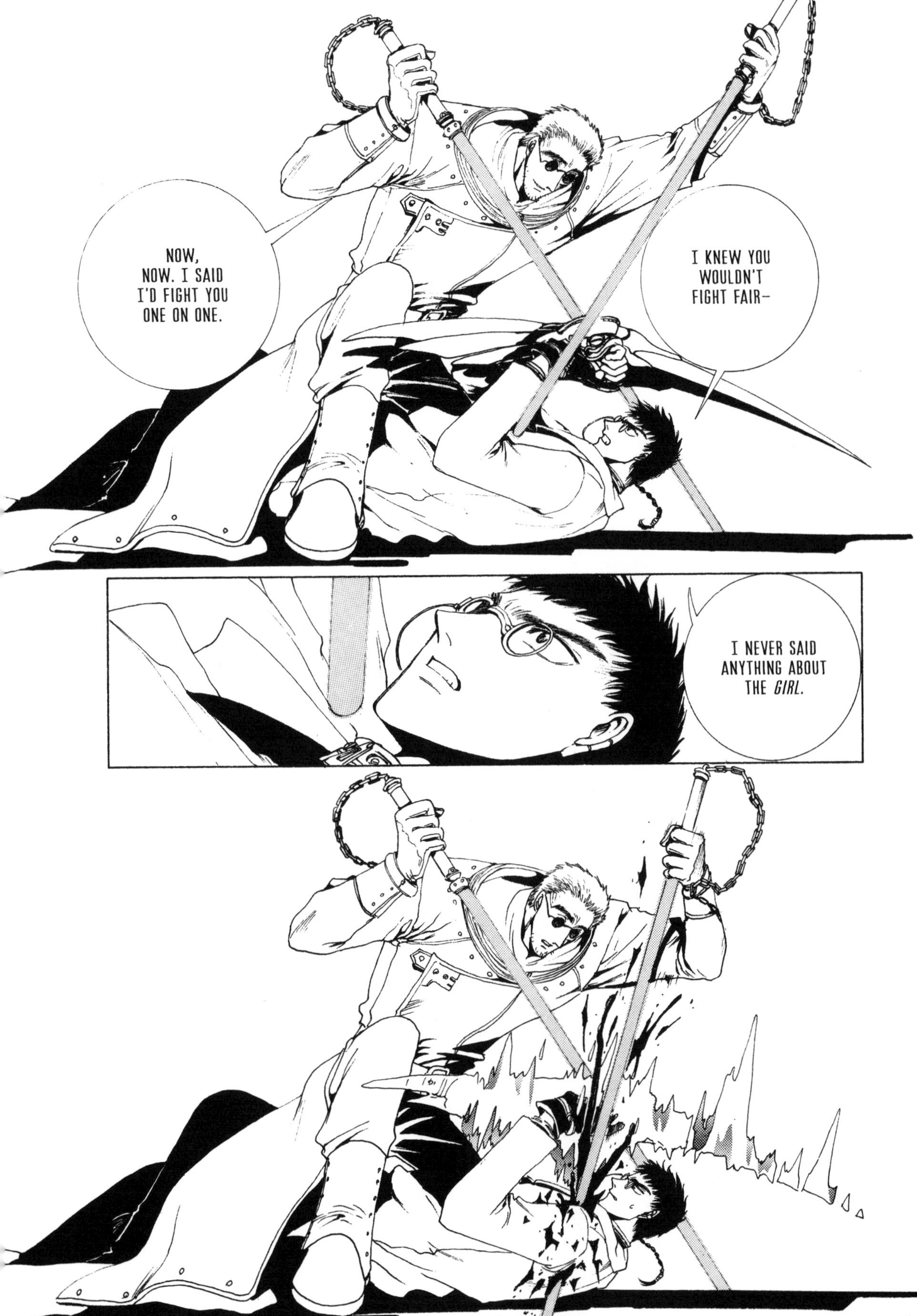
I KNEW YOU WOULDN'T FIGHT FAIR–
NOW, NOW. I SAID I'D FIGHT YOU ONE ON ONE.
I NEVER SAID ANYTHING ABOUT THE *GIRL.*

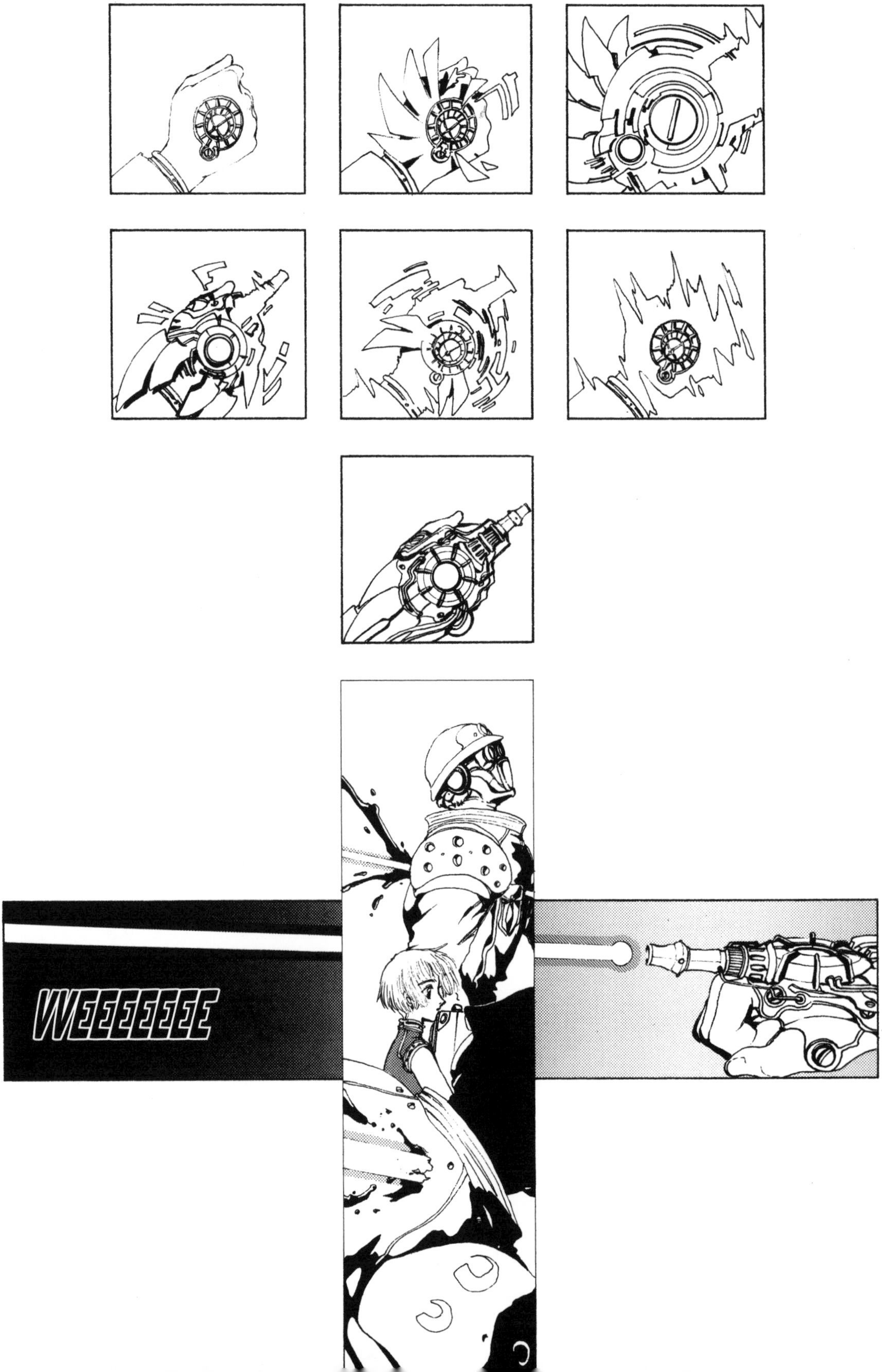
VVEEEEEEEE

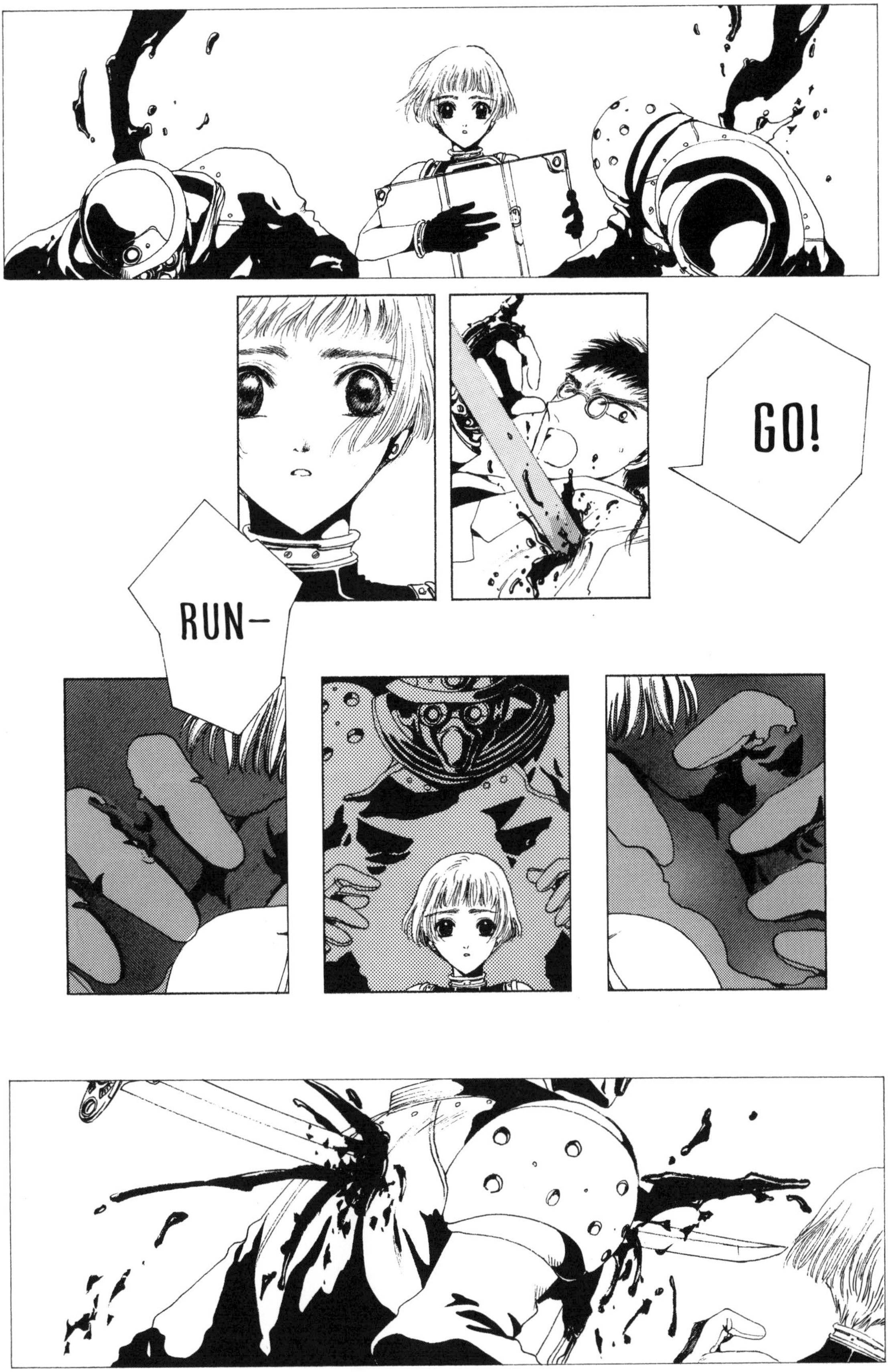
GO!
RUN-

...GIN-GETSU?

『傷(きず)痕(あと)』 SCAR

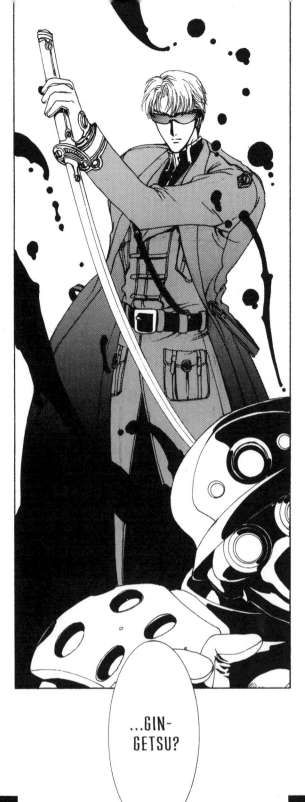

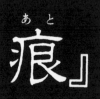

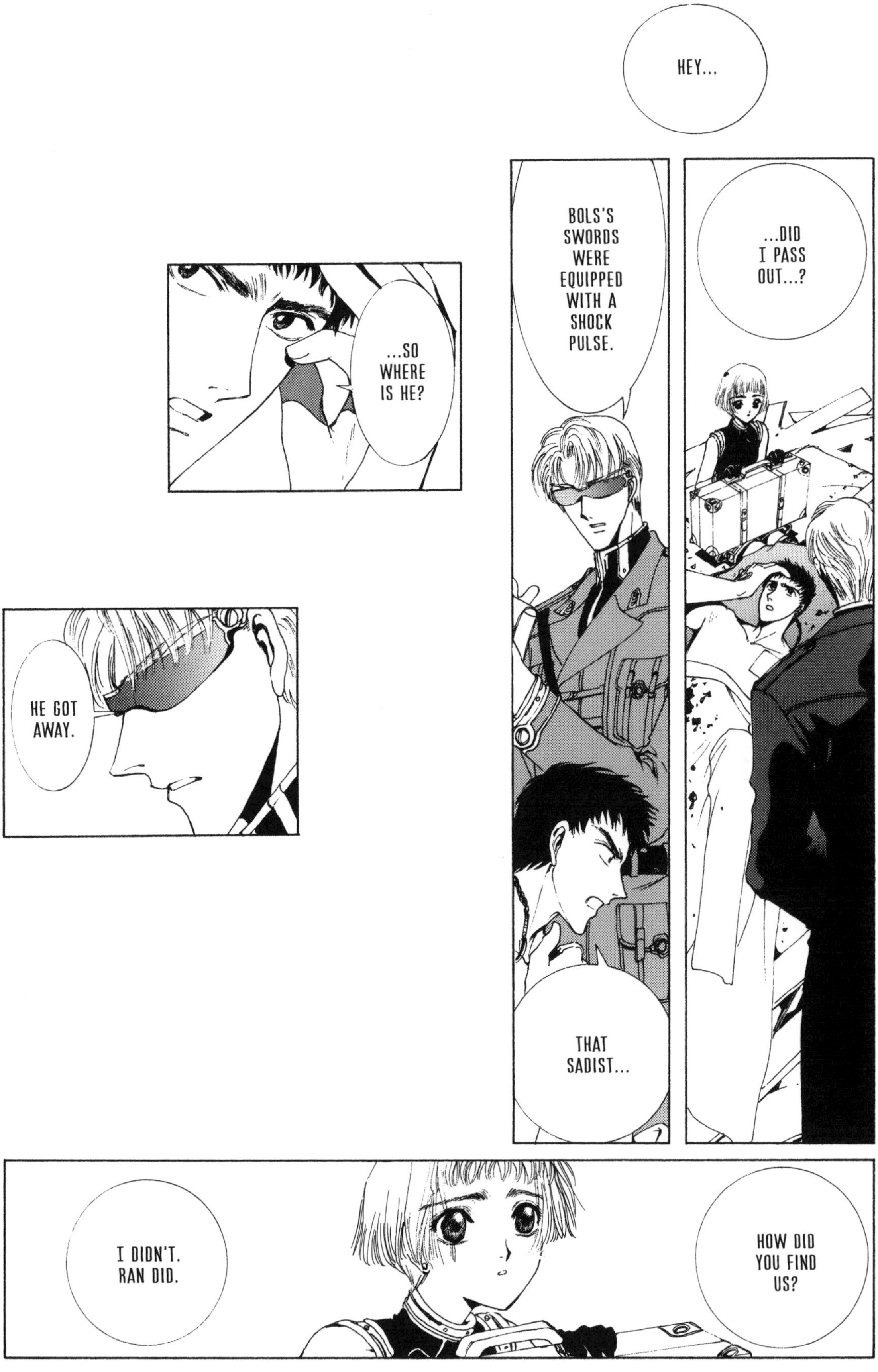
HEY...
...DID I PASS OUT...?
BOLS'S SWORDS WERE EQUIPPED WITH A SHOCK PULSE.
THAT SADIST...
...SO WHERE IS HE?
HE GOT AWAY.
HOW DID YOU FIND US?
I DIDN'T. RAN DID.

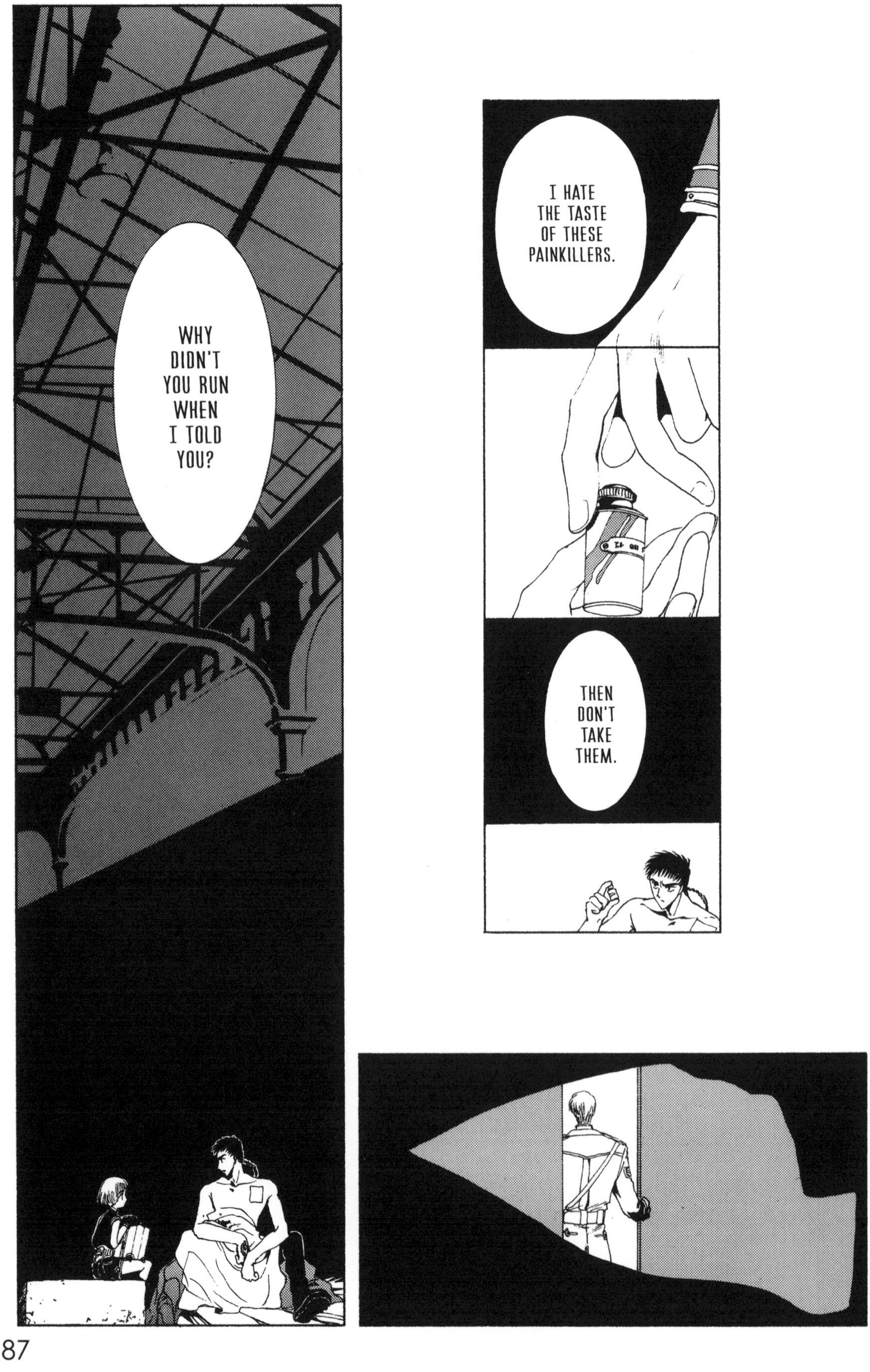
I HATE THE TASTE OF THESE PAINKILLERS.
THEN DON'T TAKE THEM.
WHY DIDN'T YOU RUN WHEN I TOLD YOU?

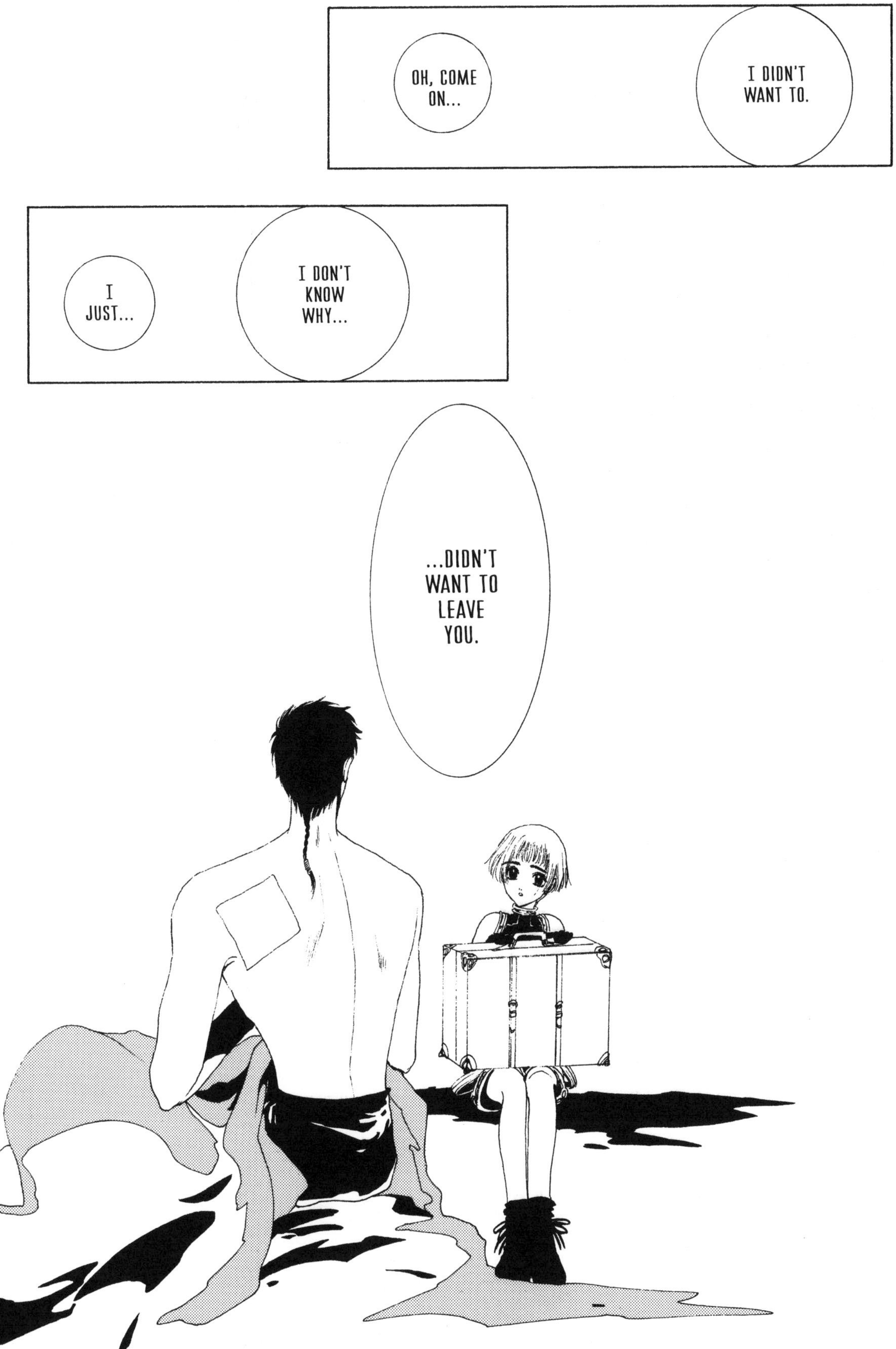
I DIDN'T WANT TO.
OH, COME ON...
I DON'T KNOW WHY...
I JUST...
...DIDN'T WANT TO LEAVE YOU.

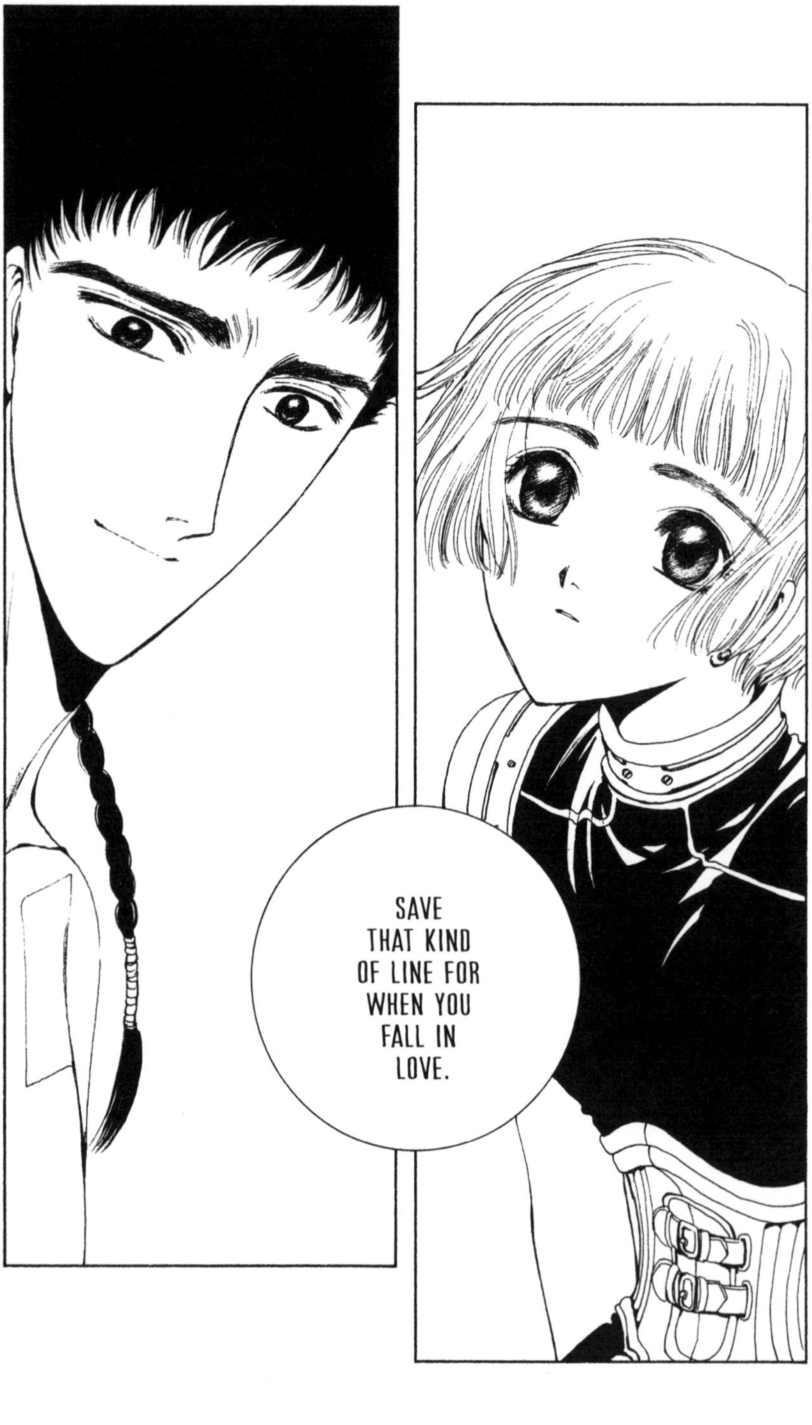
SAVE THAT KIND OF LINE FOR WHEN YOU FALL IN LOVE.

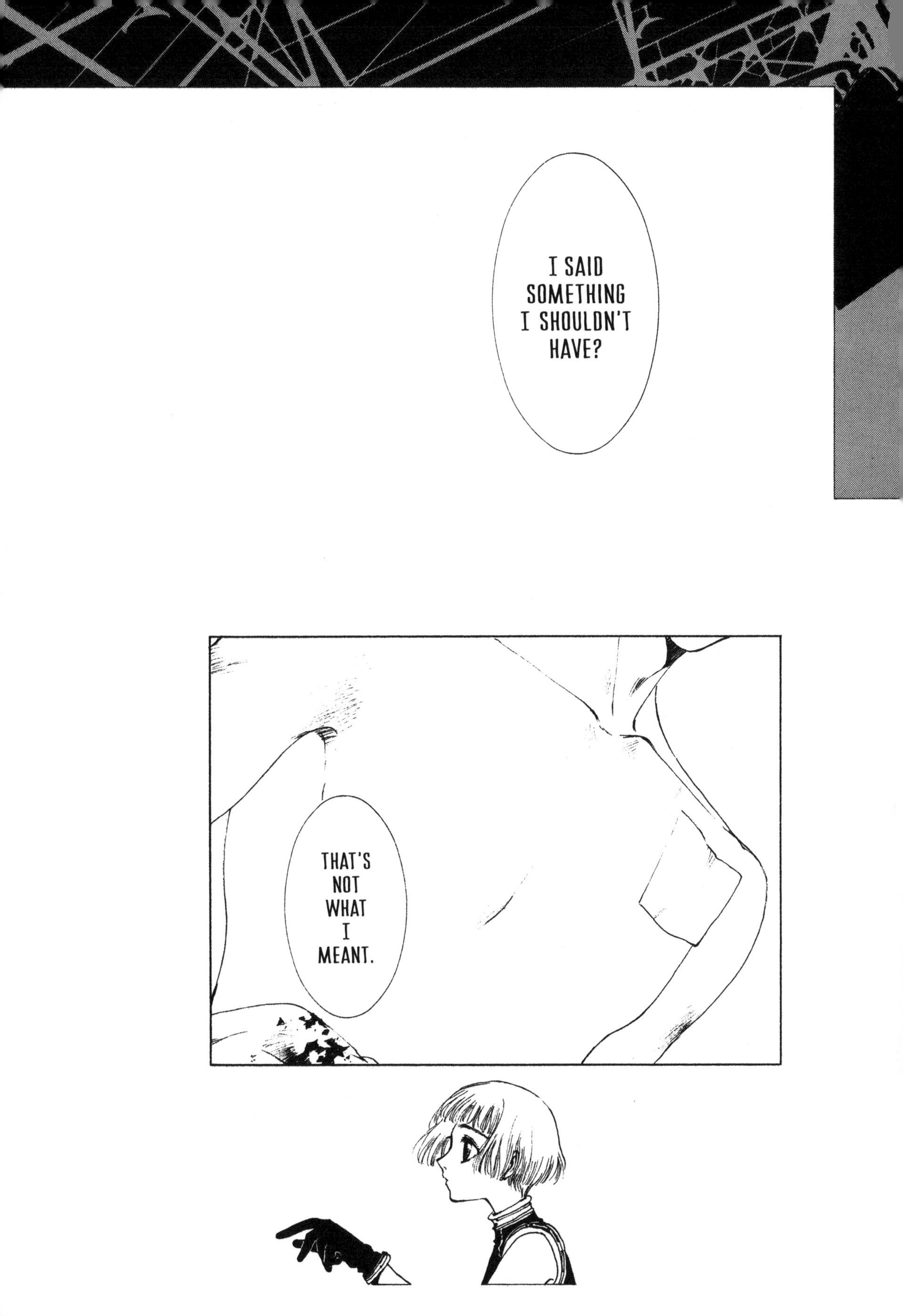
I SAID SOMETHING I SHOULDN'T HAVE?
THAT'S NOT WHAT I MEANT.

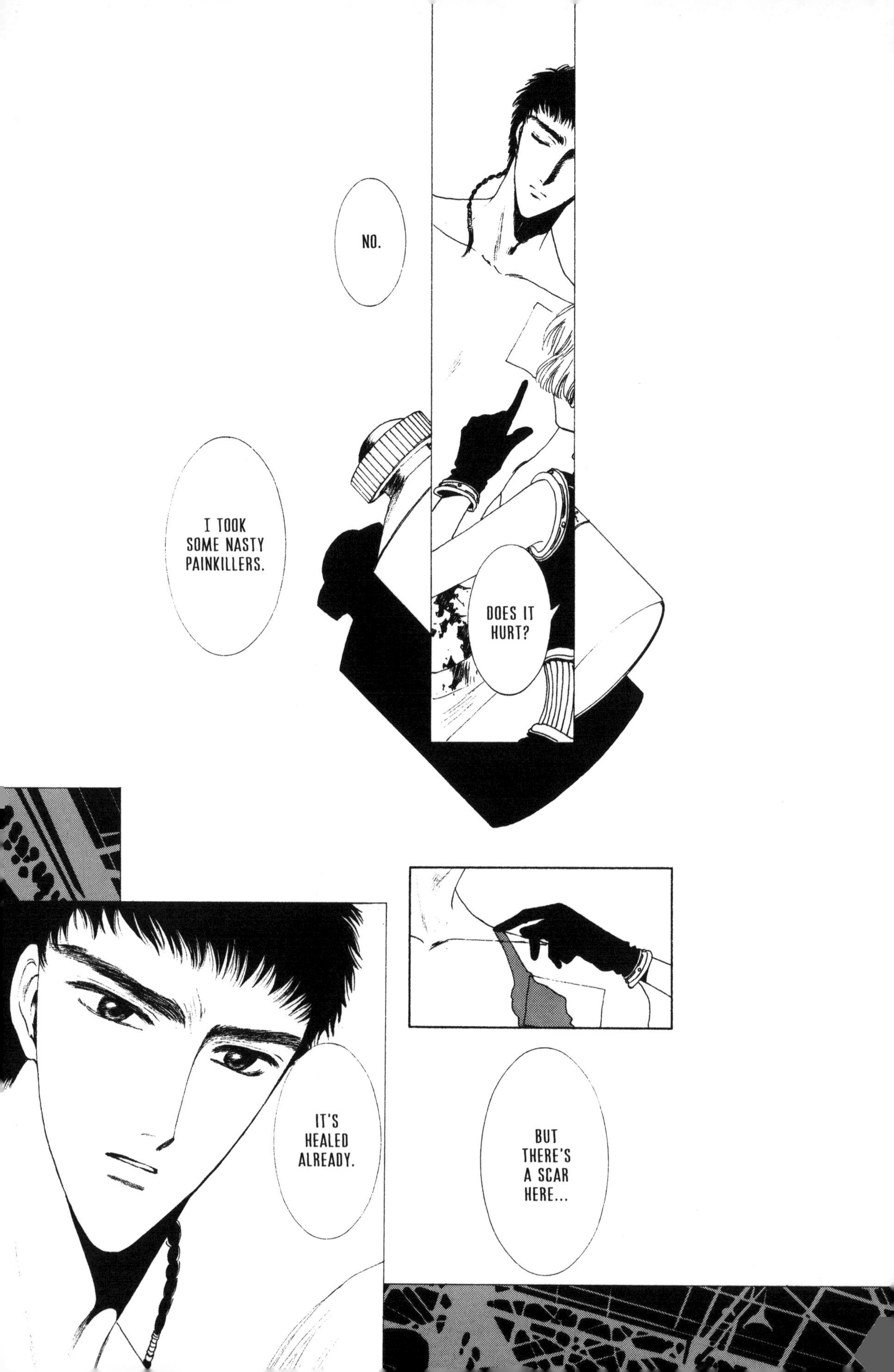
DOES IT HURT?
NO.
I TOOK SOME NASTY PAINKILLERS.
BUT THERE'S A SCAR HERE...
IT'S HEALED ALREADY.

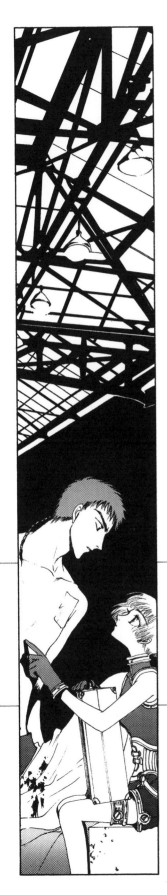

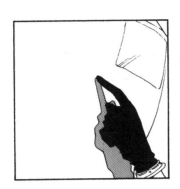

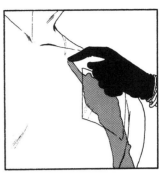

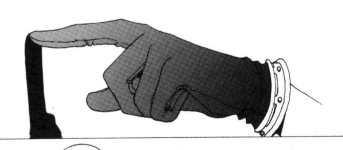

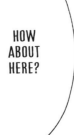

HOW
ABOUT
HERE?

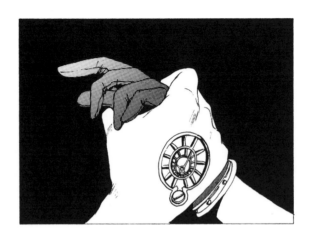

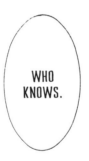

WHO
KNOWS.

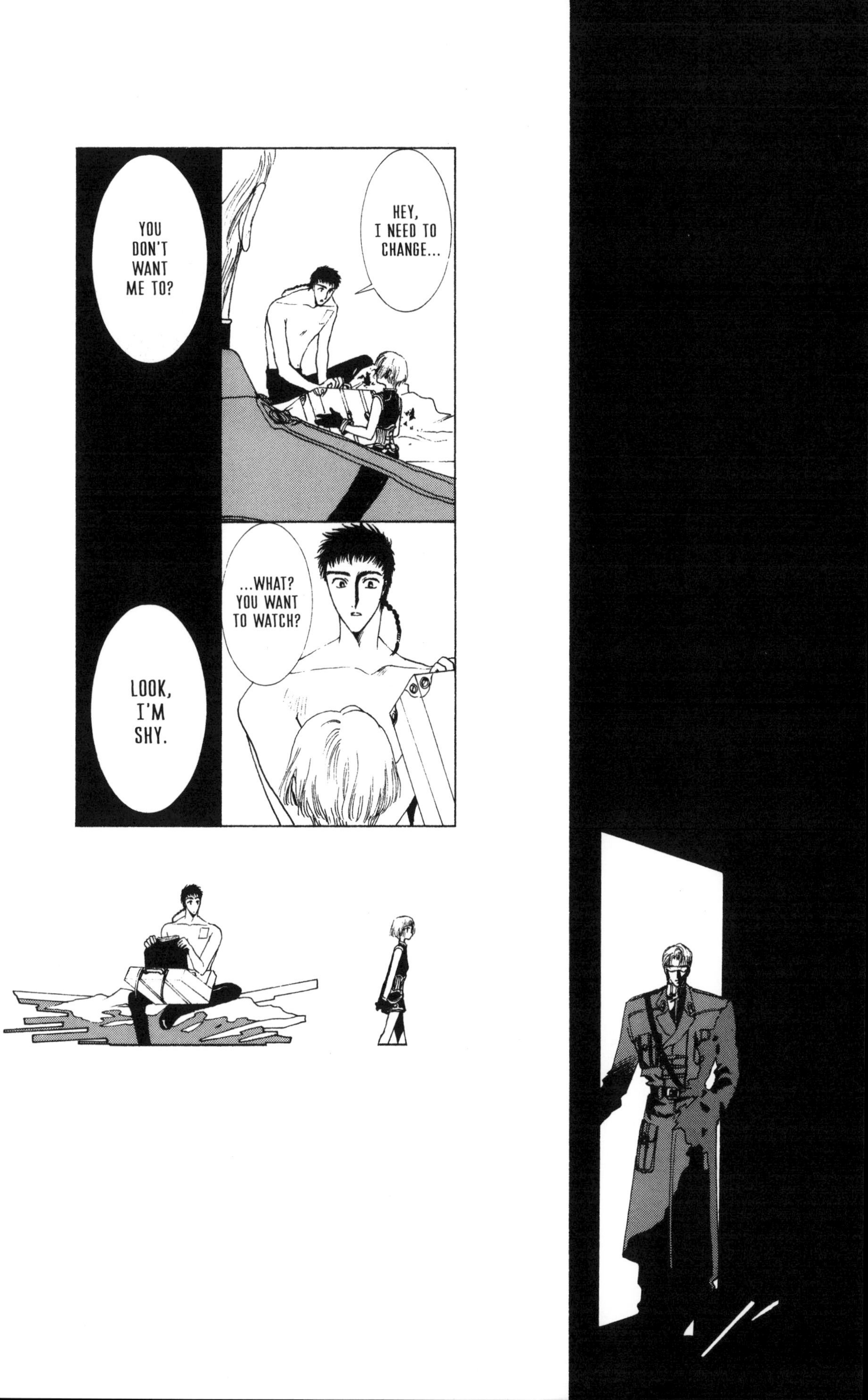
HEY, I NEED TO CHANGE...
YOU DON'T WANT ME TO?
...WHAT? YOU WANT TO WATCH?
LOOK, I'M SHY.

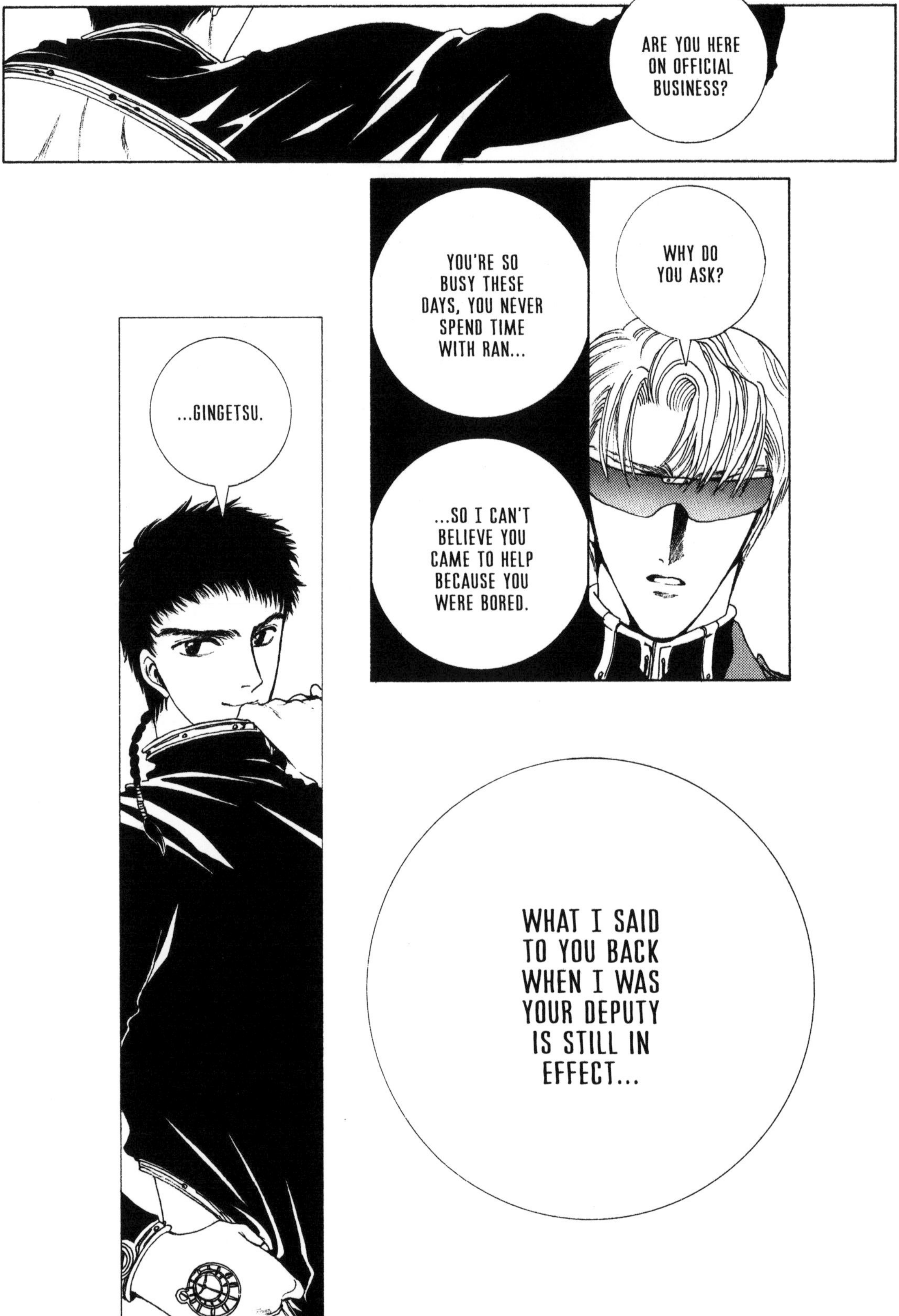
ARE YOU HERE ON OFFICIAL BUSINESS?
WHY DO YOU ASK?
YOU'RE SO BUSY THESE DAYS, YOU NEVER SPEND TIME WITH RAN...
...SO I CAN'T BELIEVE YOU CAME TO HELP BECAUSE YOU WERE BORED.
...GINGETSU.
WHAT I SAID TO YOU BACK WHEN I WAS YOUR DEPUTY IS STILL IN EFFECT...

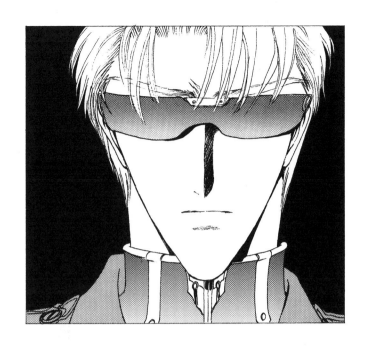

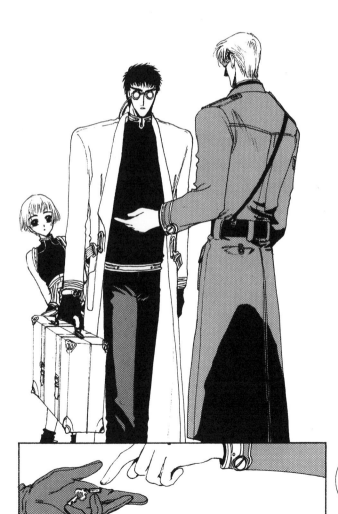

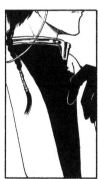

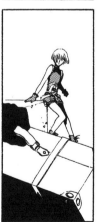

BOLS'S MEN
ARE WATCHING THE
TRANSPORTS... FROM
HERE, YOU DRIVE.

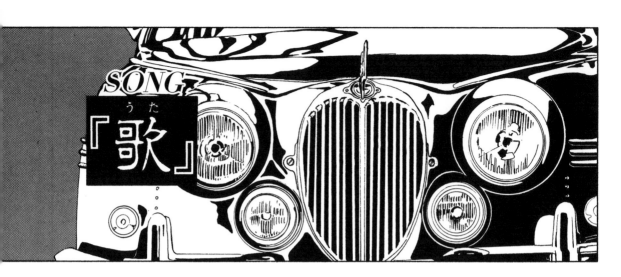

SONG
うた
『歌』
SSHHH
AN EXPLOSION HAS OCCURRED IN THE LUO XIA HONG DISTRICT.
ALL TRAFFIC HAS BEEN DIVERTED.
MUST BE THE XIAO MAO.

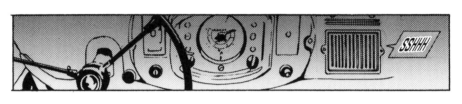

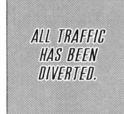

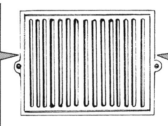

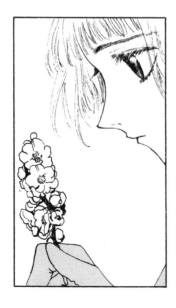

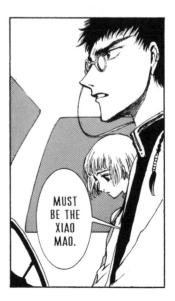

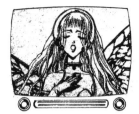

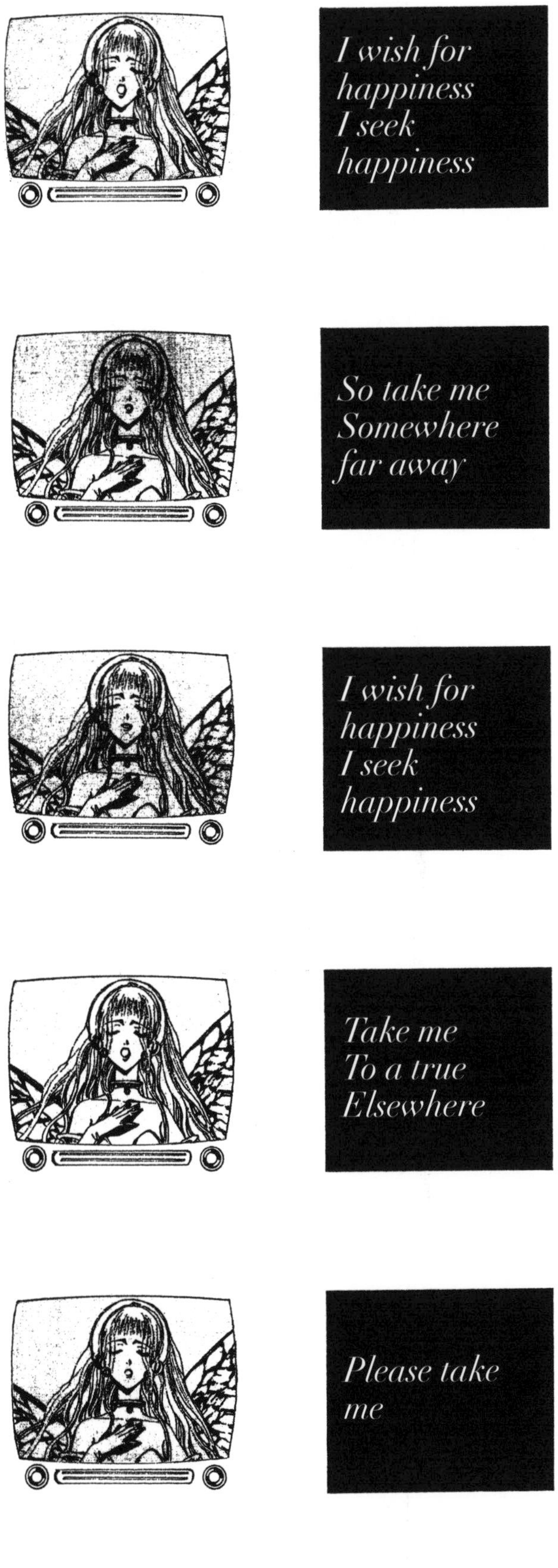

*I wish for
happiness
I seek
happiness*

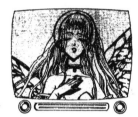

*So take me
Somewhere
far away*

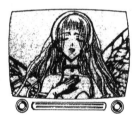

*I wish for
happiness
I seek
happiness*

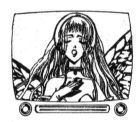

*Take me
To a true
Elsewhere*

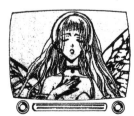

*Please take
me*

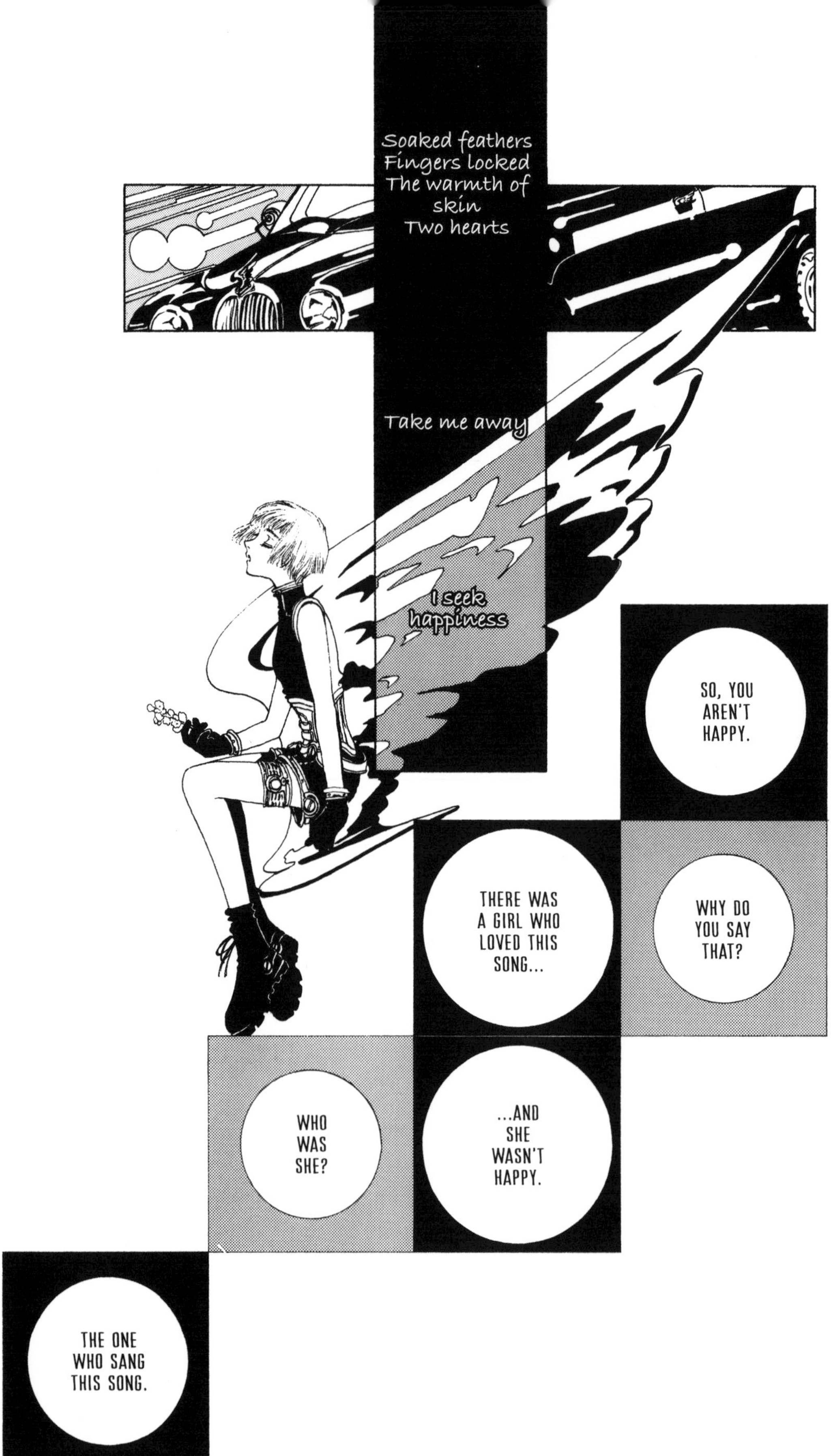
Soaked feathers
Fingers locked
The warmth of skin
Two hearts
Take me away
I seek happiness
SO, YOU AREN'T HAPPY.
WHY DO YOU SAY THAT?
THERE WAS A GIRL WHO LOVED THIS SONG...
...AND SHE WASN'T HAPPY.
WHO WAS SHE?
THE ONE WHO SANG THIS SONG.

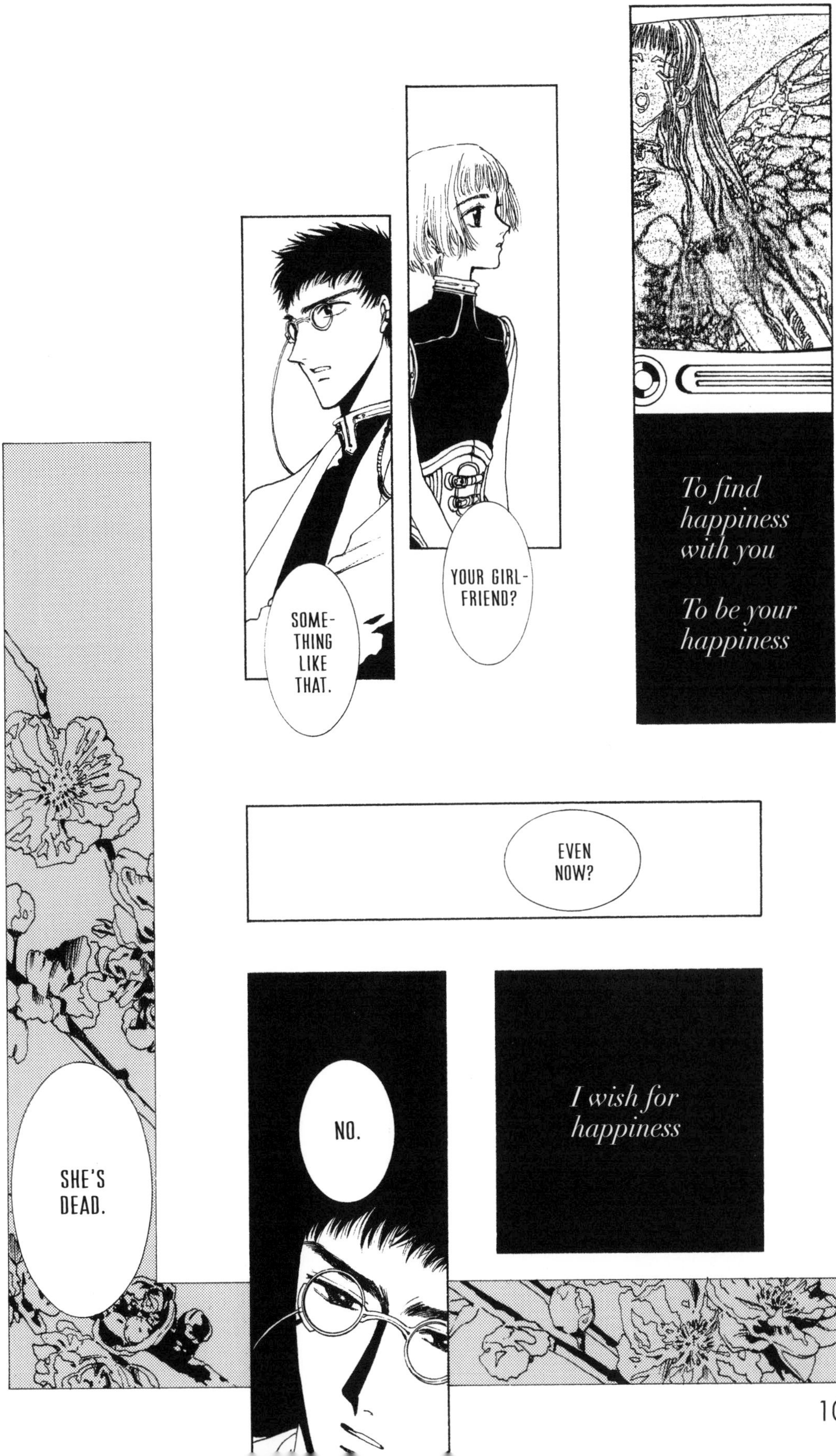
To find happiness with you
To be your happiness
YOUR GIRL-FRIEND?
SOME-THING LIKE THAT.
EVEN NOW?
I wish for happiness
NO.
SHE'S DEAD.

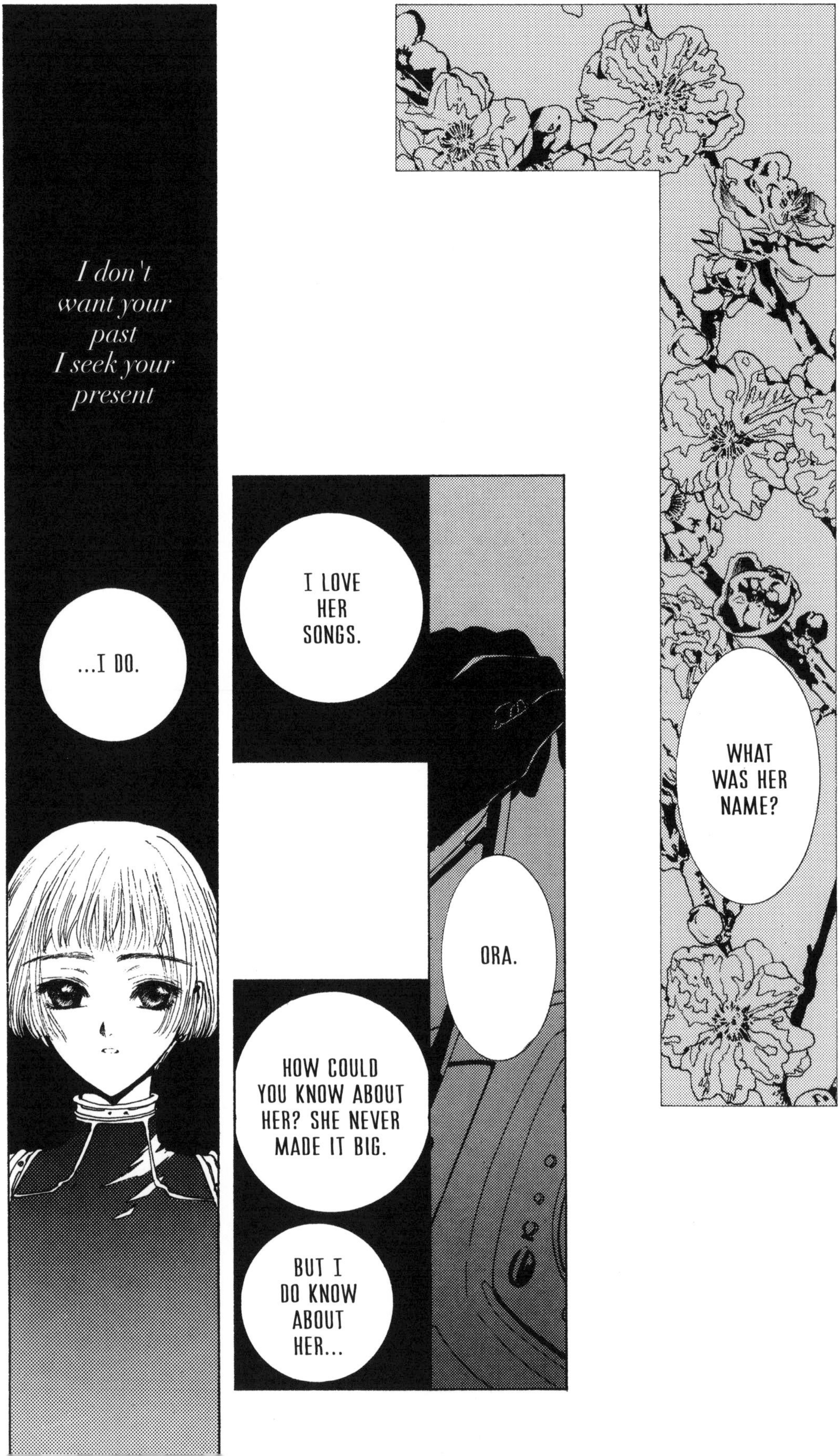
WHAT WAS HER NAME?
I LOVE HER SONGS.
ORA.
HOW COULD YOU KNOW ABOUT HER? SHE NEVER MADE IT BIG.
BUT I DO KNOW ABOUT HER...
I don't want your past I seek your present
...I DO.

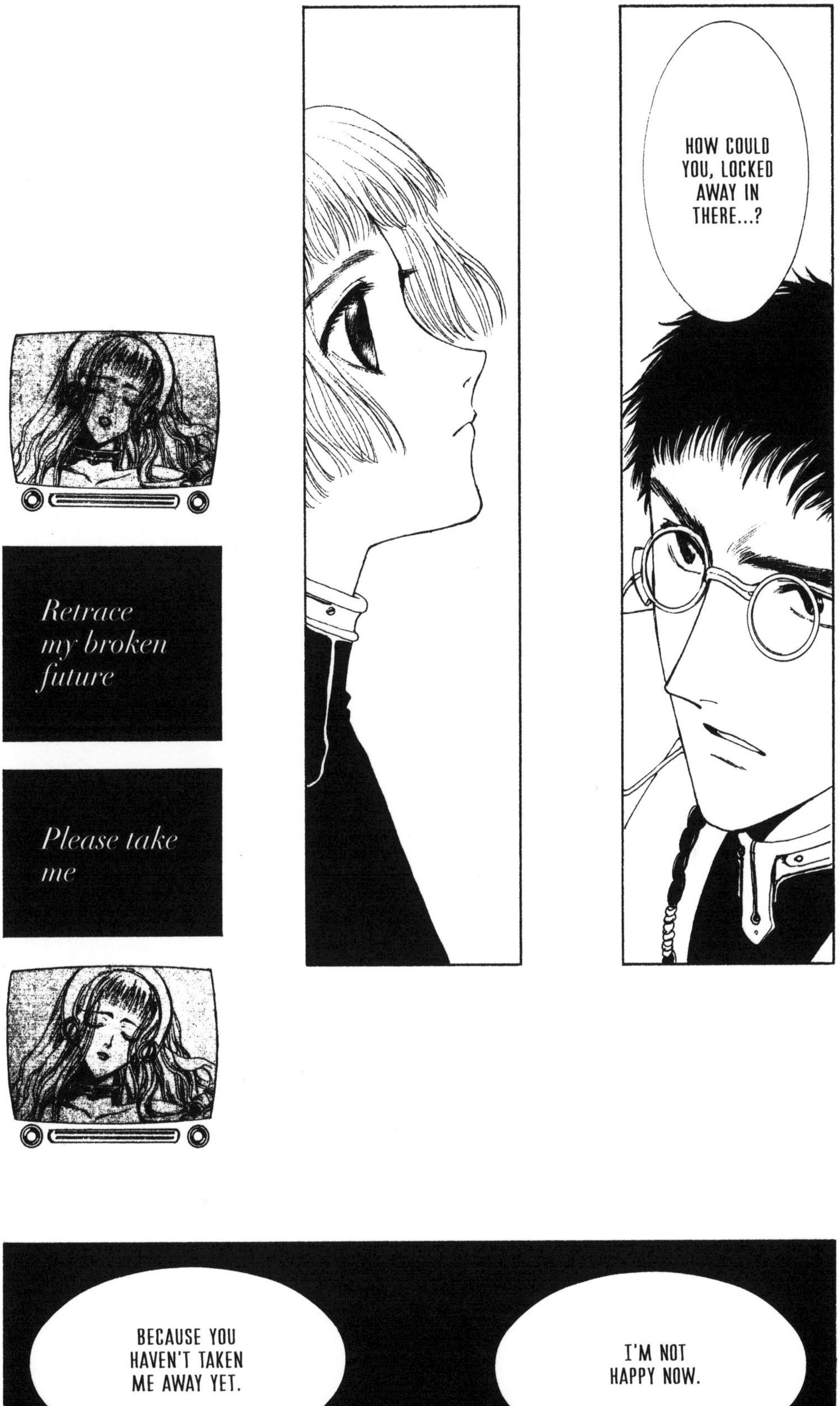
HOW COULD YOU, LOCKED AWAY IN THERE...?
Retrace my broken future
Please take me
I'M NOT HAPPY NOW.
BECAUSE YOU HAVEN'T TAKEN ME AWAY YET.

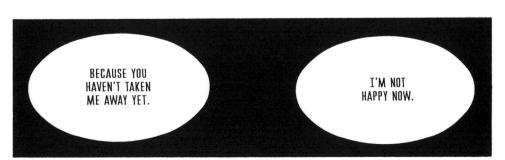

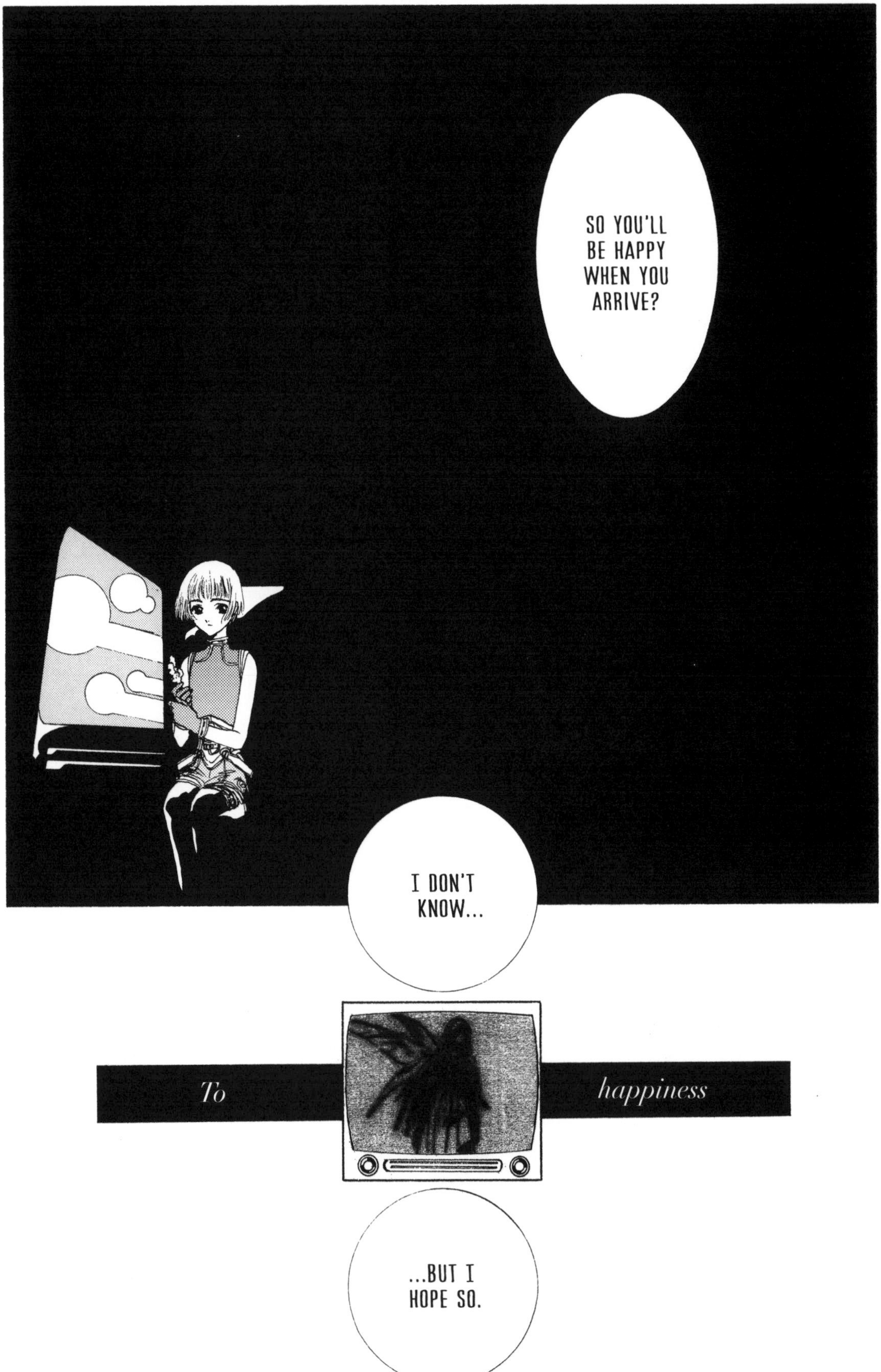
SO YOU'LL BE HAPPY WHEN YOU ARRIVE?
I DON'T KNOW...
To
happiness
...BUT I HOPE SO.

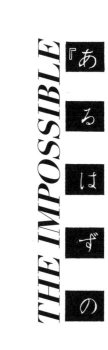

THE IMPOSSIBLE 『あるはずのない』
THEY'VE PROCEEDED IN THE CAR I PREPARED FOR THEM.
AZAIEA ISN'T THE ONLY ONE AFTER THE GIRL.
CONTINUE TO MONITOR THEM.

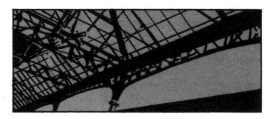

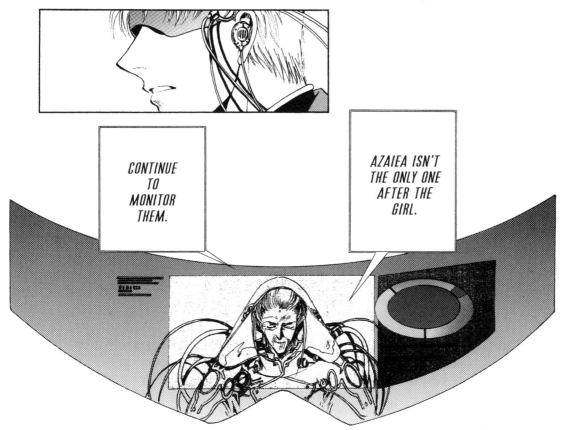

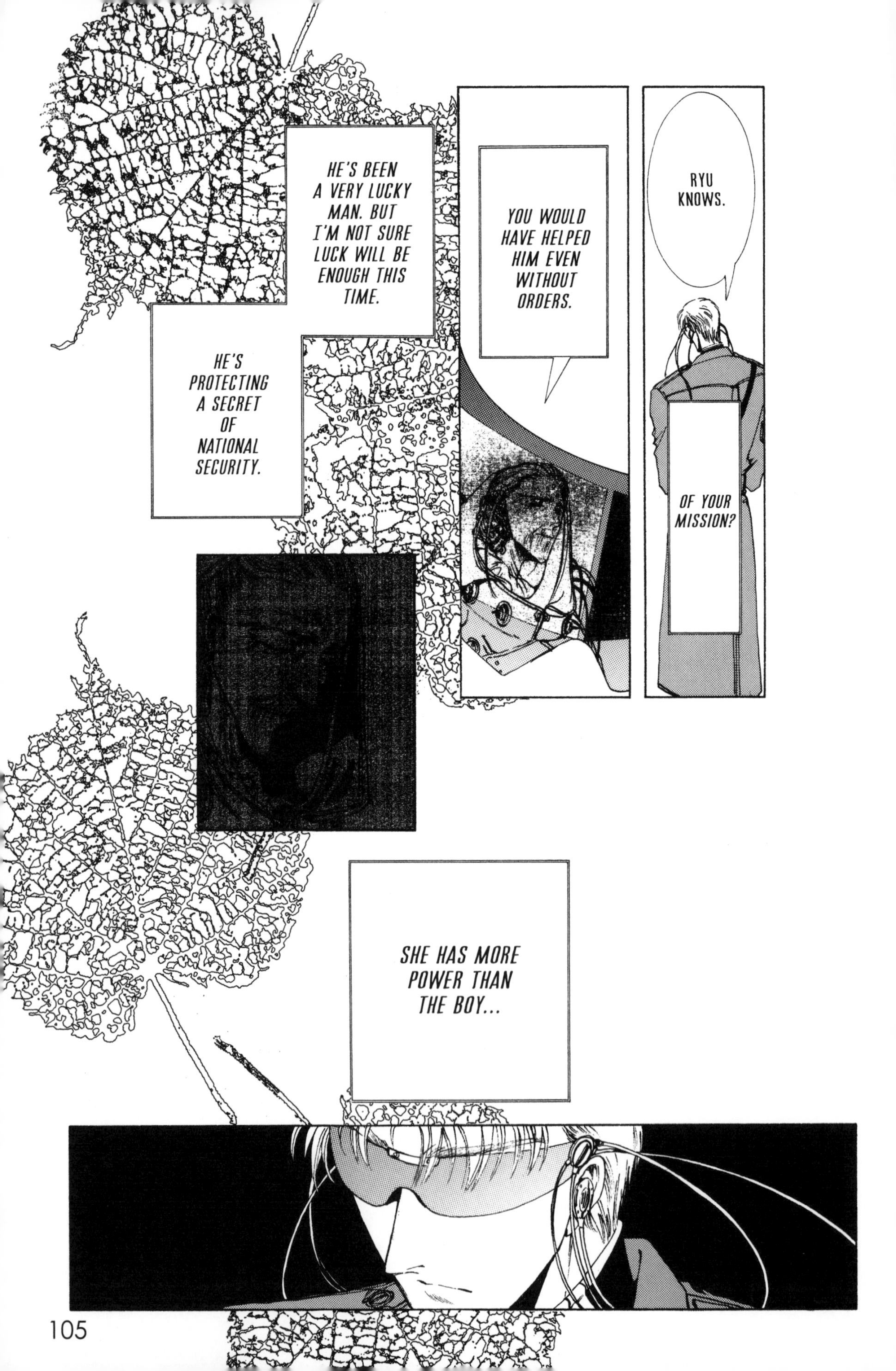
RYU KNOWS.
OF YOUR MISSION?
YOU WOULD HAVE HELPED HIM EVEN WITHOUT ORDERS.
HE'S BEEN A VERY LUCKY MAN. BUT I'M NOT SURE LUCK WILL BE ENOUGH THIS TIME.
HE'S PROTECTING A SECRET OF NATIONAL SECURITY.
SHE HAS MORE POWER THAN THE BOY...

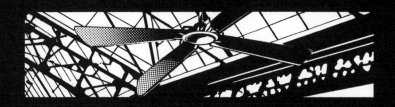

WE NEVER
IMAGINED
IT COULD BE
POSSIBLE, BUT
SHE'S A FOUR-
LEAF CLOVER.

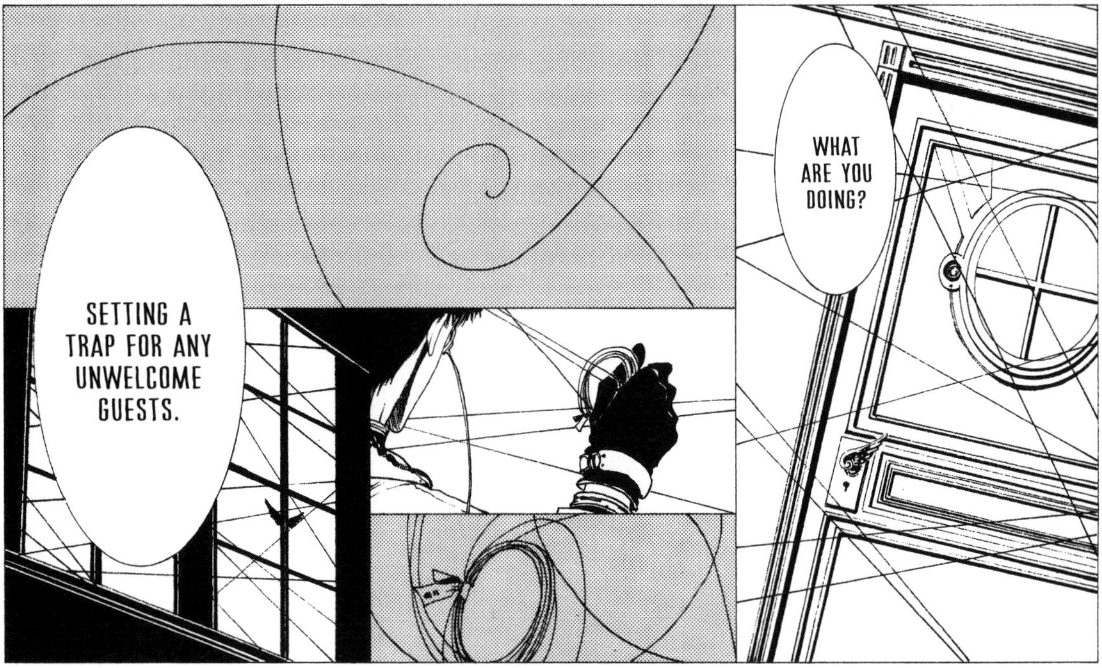
WHAT ARE YOU DOING?
SETTING A TRAP FOR ANY UNWELCOME GUESTS.

GOOD NIGHT
『おやすみ』

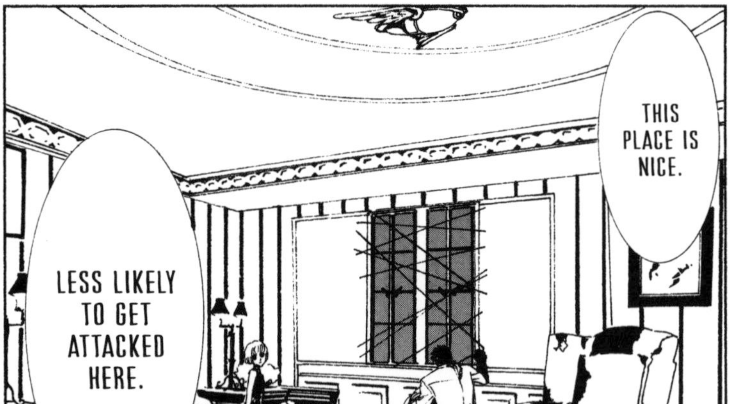
THIS PLACE IS NICE.
LESS LIKELY TO GET ATTACKED HERE.

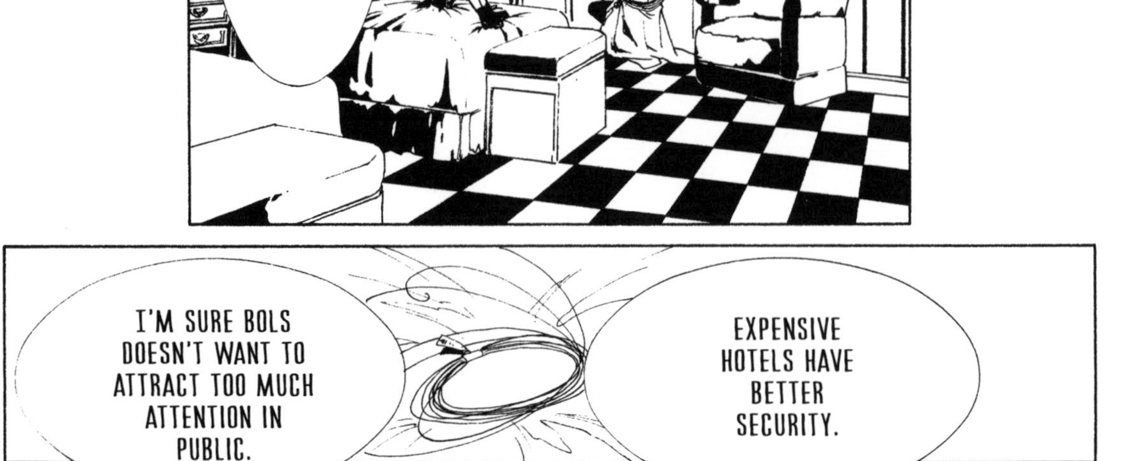
EXPENSIVE HOTELS HAVE BETTER SECURITY.
I'M SURE BOLS DOESN'T WANT TO ATTRACT TOO MUCH ATTENTION IN PUBLIC.

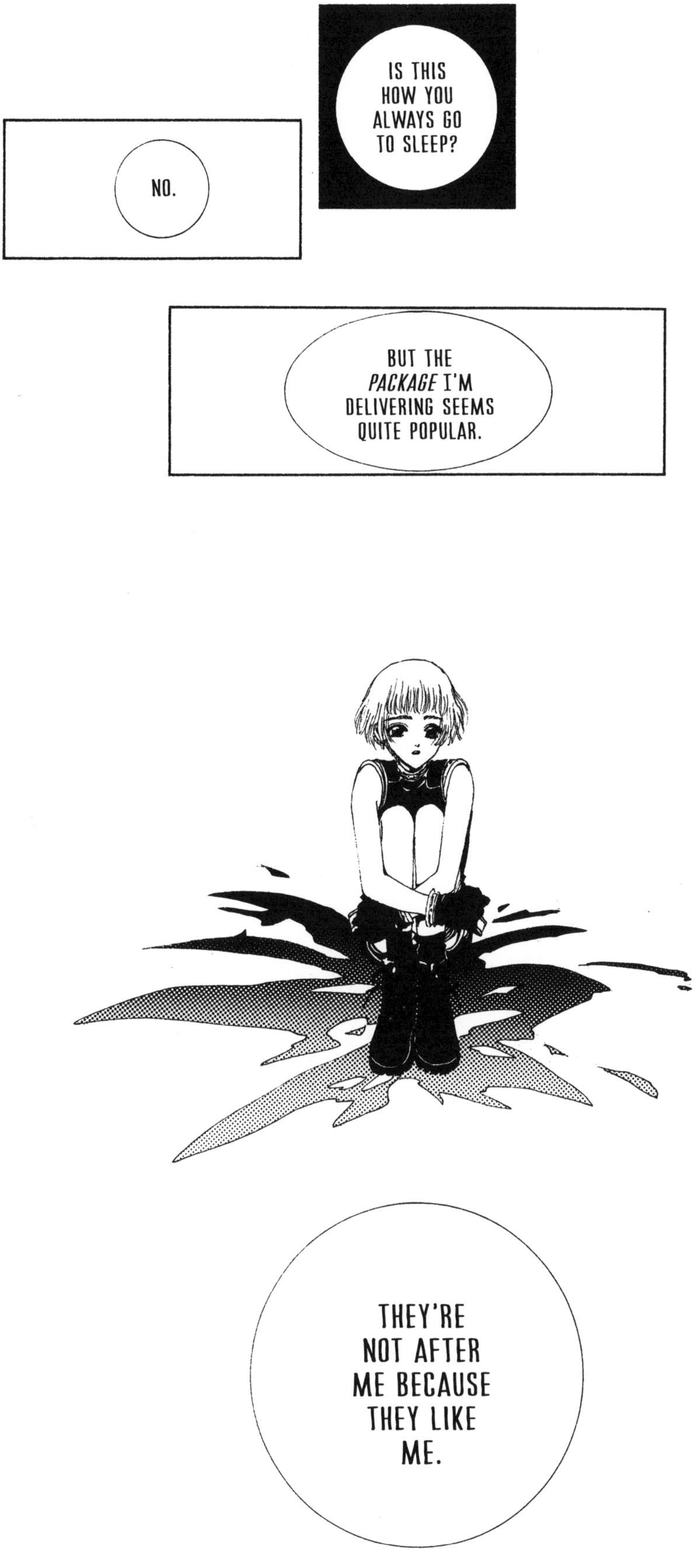
IS THIS HOW YOU ALWAYS GO TO SLEEP?
NO.
BUT THE *PACKAGE* I'M DELIVERING SEEMS QUITE POPULAR.
THEY'RE NOT AFTER ME BECAUSE THEY LIKE ME.

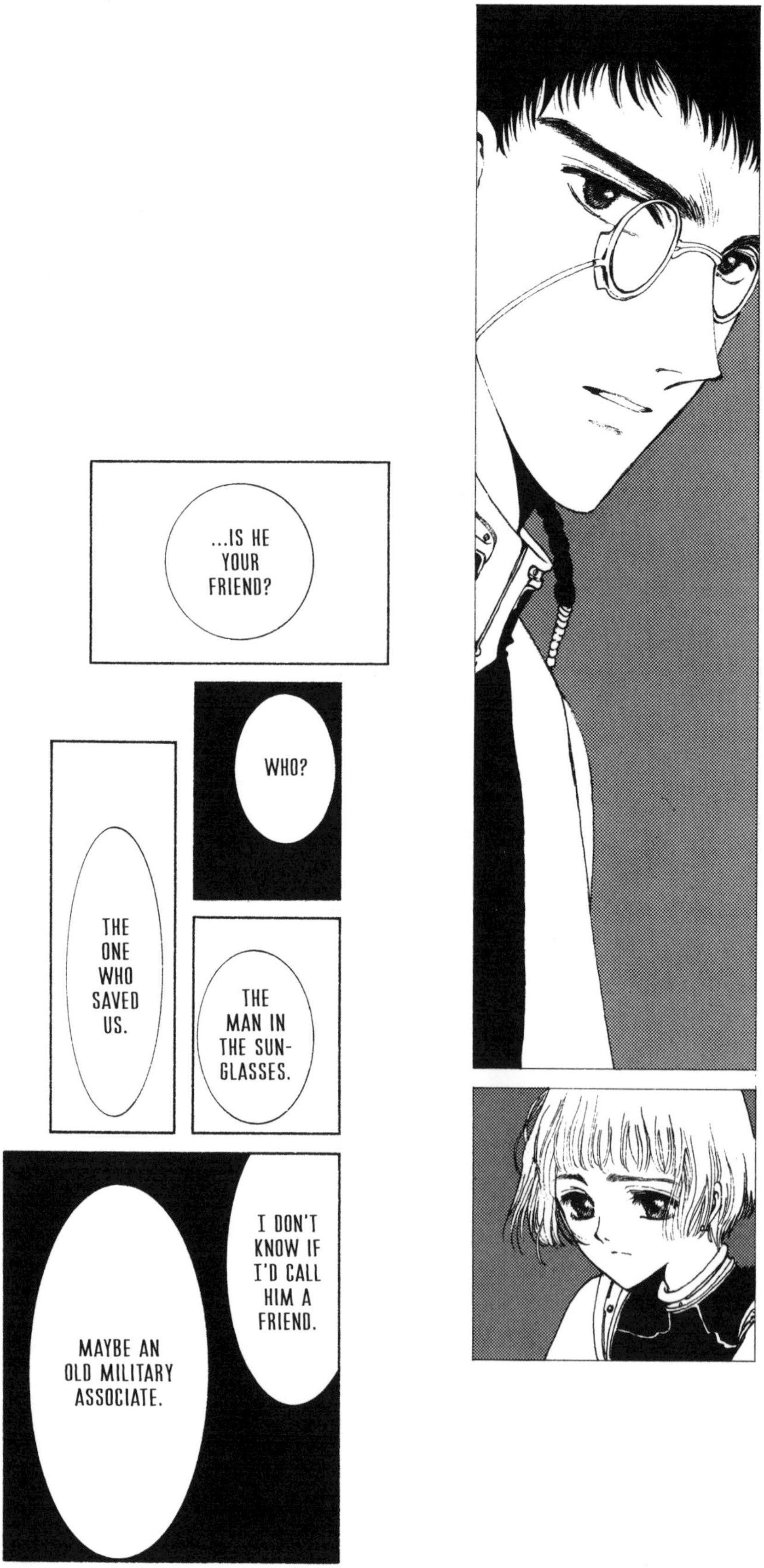
...IS HE YOUR FRIEND?
WHO?
THE MAN IN THE SUN-GLASSES.
THE ONE WHO SAVED US.
I DON'T KNOW IF I'D CALL HIM A FRIEND.
MAYBE AN OLD MILITARY ASSOCIATE.

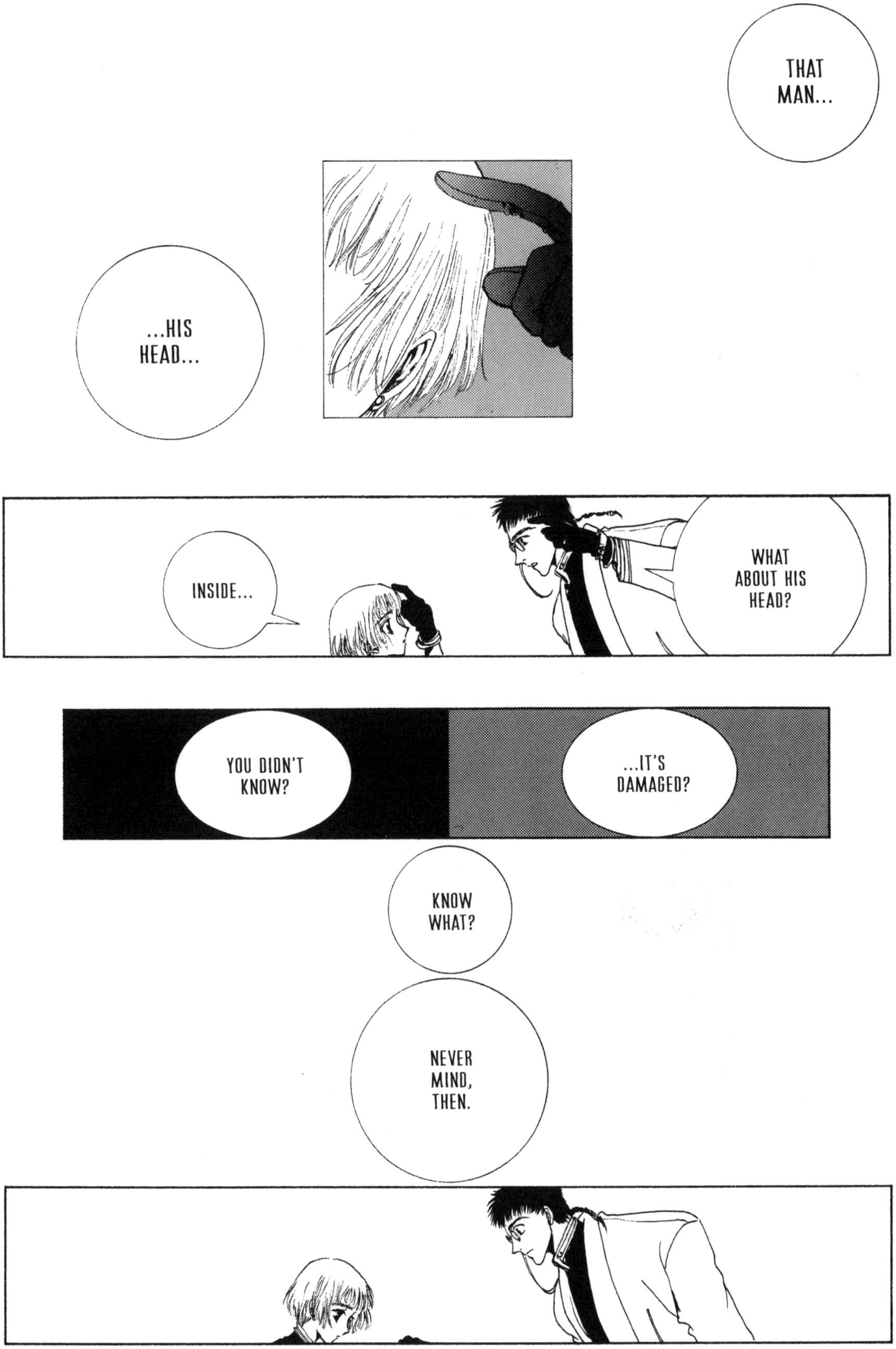
THAT MAN...
...HIS HEAD...
WHAT ABOUT HIS HEAD?
INSIDE...
...IT'S DAMAGED?
YOU DIDN'T KNOW?
KNOW WHAT?
NEVER MIND, THEN.

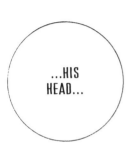

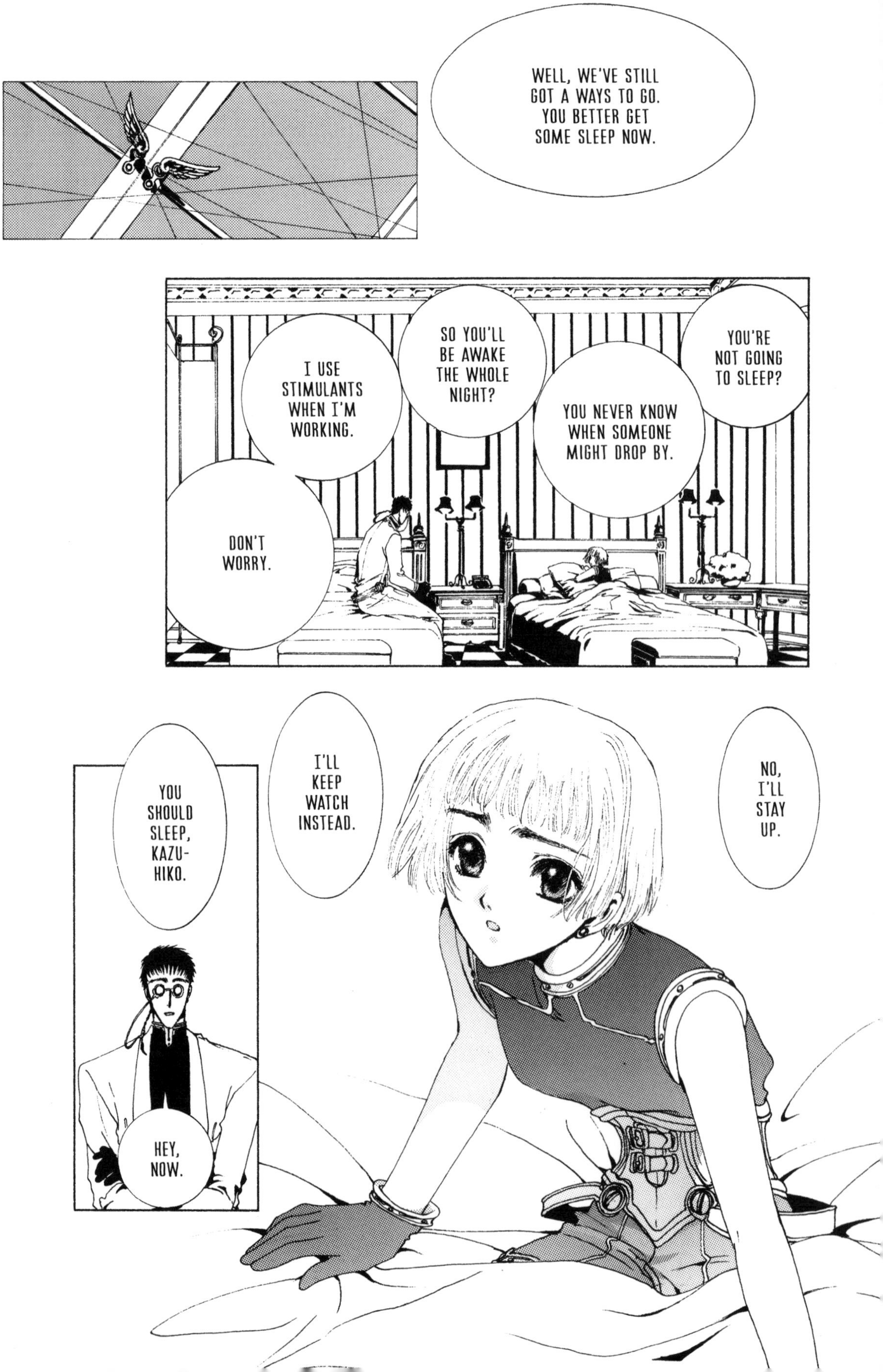
WELL, WE'VE STILL GOT A WAYS TO GO. YOU BETTER GET SOME SLEEP NOW.
YOU'RE NOT GOING TO SLEEP?
YOU NEVER KNOW WHEN SOMEONE MIGHT DROP BY.
SO YOU'LL BE AWAKE THE WHOLE NIGHT?
I USE STIMULANTS WHEN I'M WORKING.
DON'T WORRY.
NO, I'LL STAY UP.
I'LL KEEP WATCH INSTEAD.
YOU SHOULD SLEEP, KAZU-HIKO.
HEY, NOW.

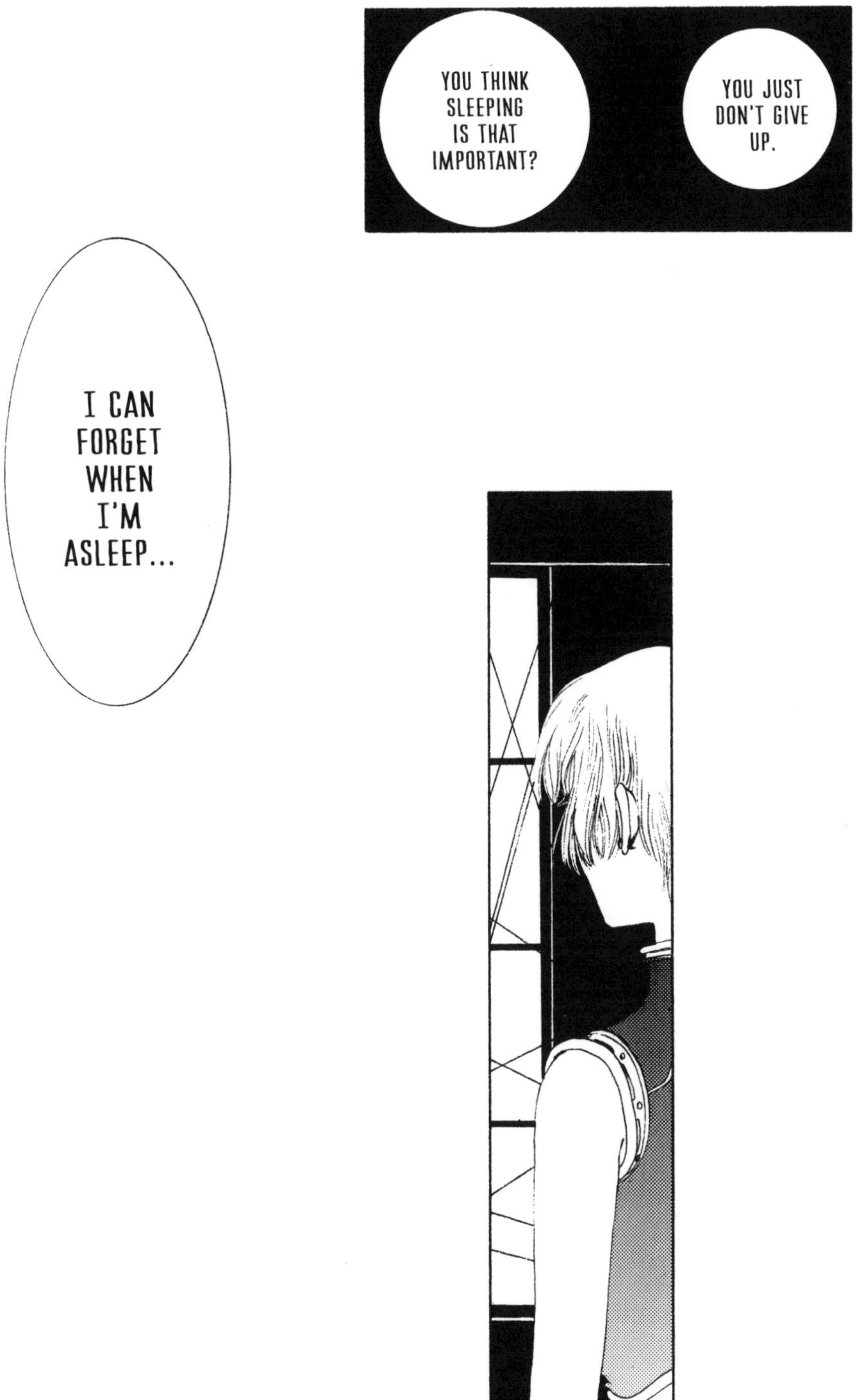
YOU JUST DON'T GIVE UP.
YOU THINK SLEEPING IS THAT IMPORTANT?
I CAN FORGET WHEN I'M ASLEEP...

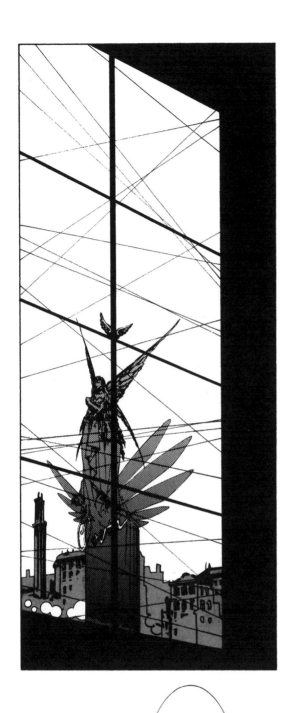

...FORGET
I'M
ALONE.

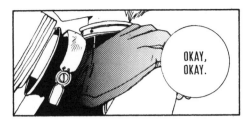

OKAY, OKAY.

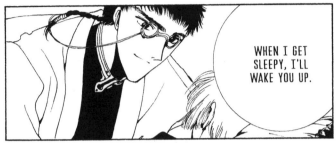

WHEN I GET SLEEPY, I'LL WAKE YOU UP.

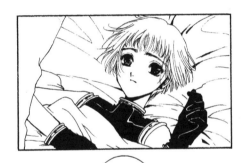

WHEN ORA DIED, WERE YOU SAD?

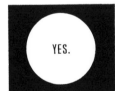

YES.

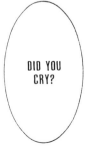

DID YOU CRY?

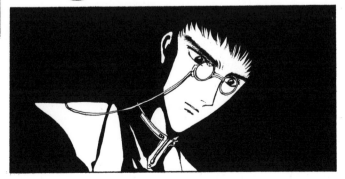

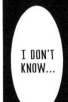

I DON'T KNOW...

WHEN I DIE, NOBODY WILL CRY FOR ME.
WHY?
BECAUSE I'M ALONE.

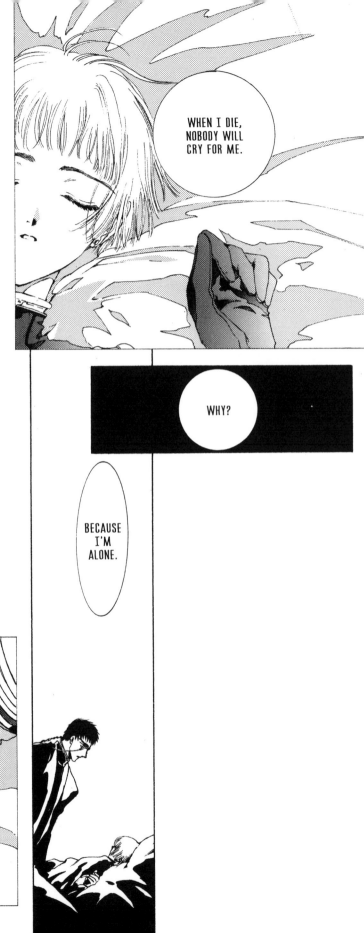

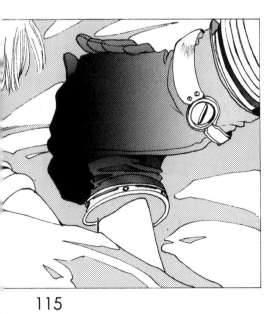

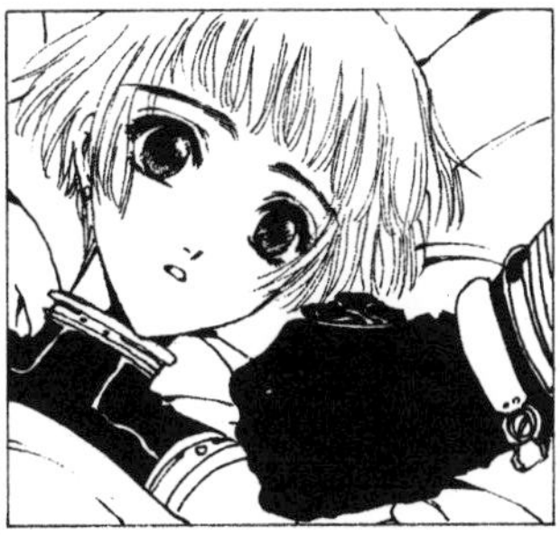

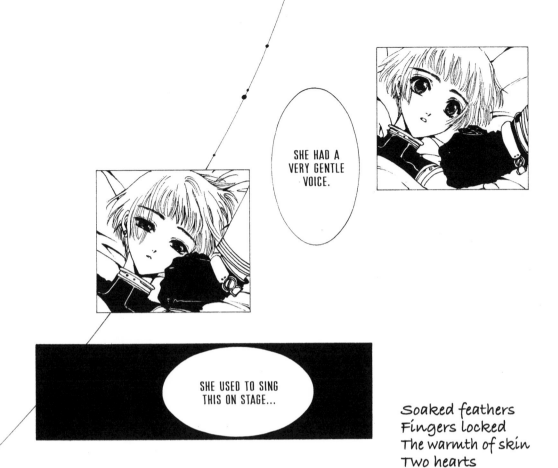

SHE HAD A VERY GENTLE VOICE.

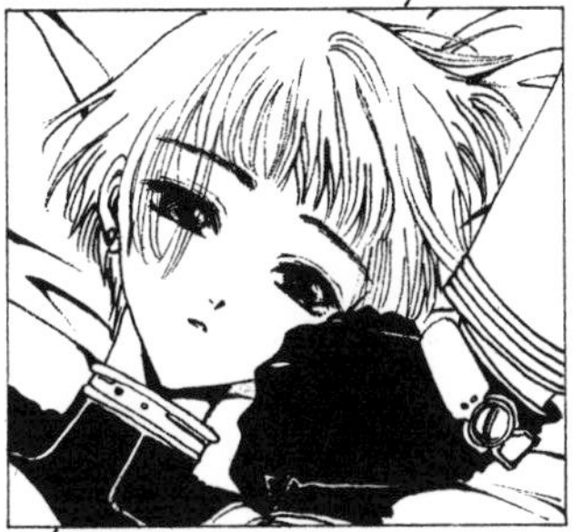

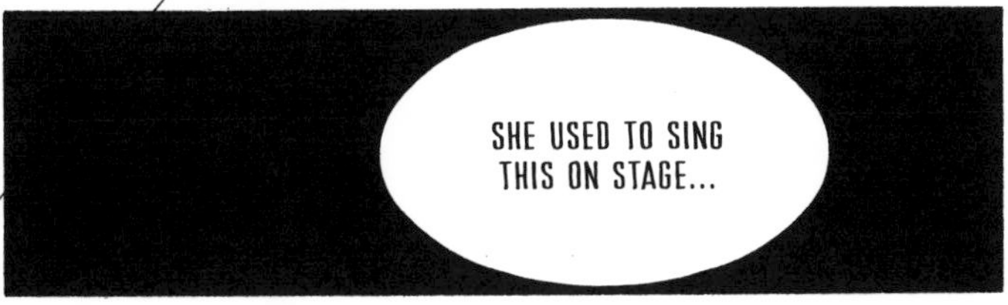
SHE USED TO SING THIS ON STAGE...

Soaked feathers
Fingers locked
The warmth of skin
Two hearts

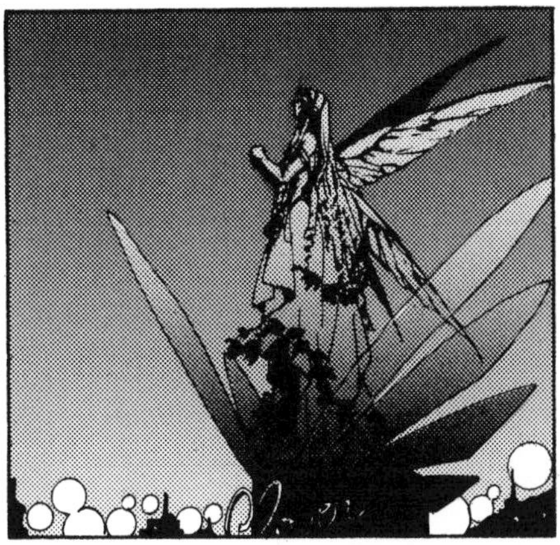

Take me away
I seek
happiness

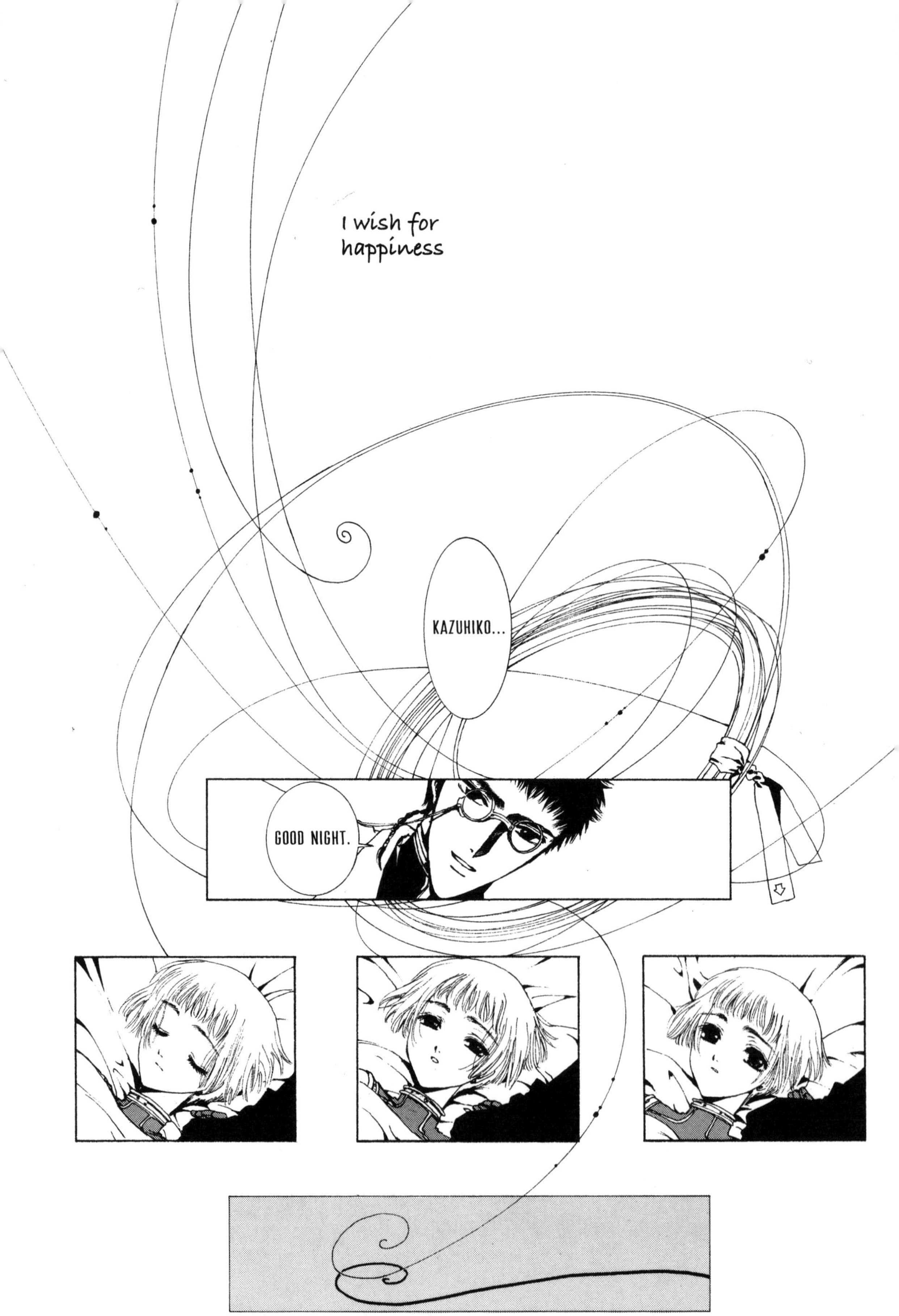
I wish for happiness
KAZUHIKO...
GOOD NIGHT.

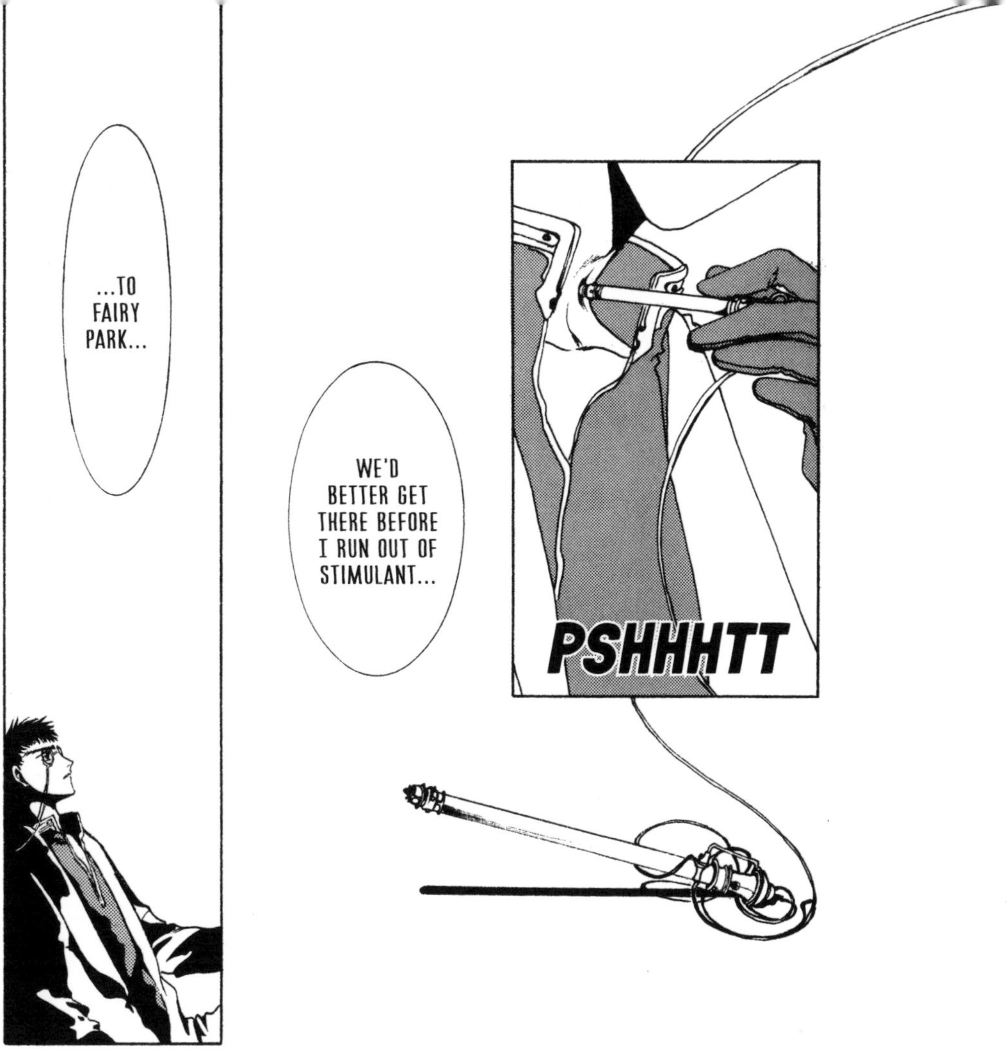
PSHHHTT
WE'D BETTER GET THERE BEFORE I RUN OUT OF STIMULANT...
...TO FAIRY PARK...

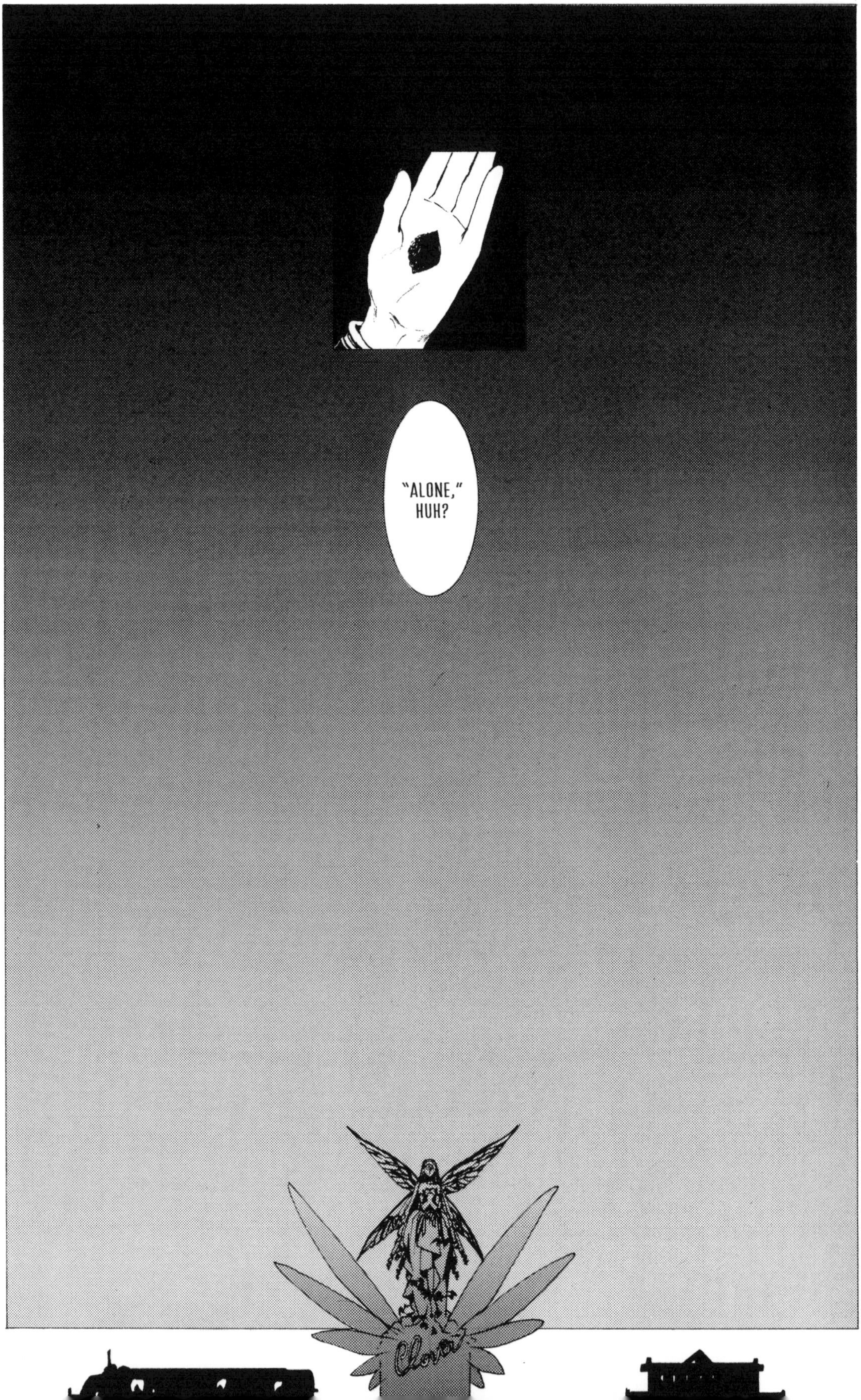
"ALONE," HUH?

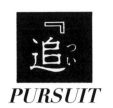

『追跡』
PURSUIT

AH, GINGETSU.
I WAS THINKING THAT KAZUHIKO JUST *MIGHT* BE A DECOY.
BUT IF COMMANDER GINGETSU OF SPECIAL OPERATIONS IS HERE...
...THEN IT MUST BE THE REAL THING.

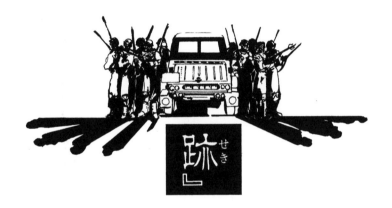

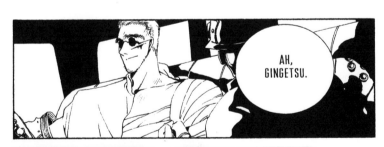

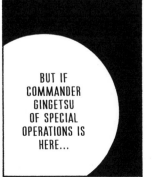

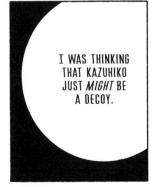

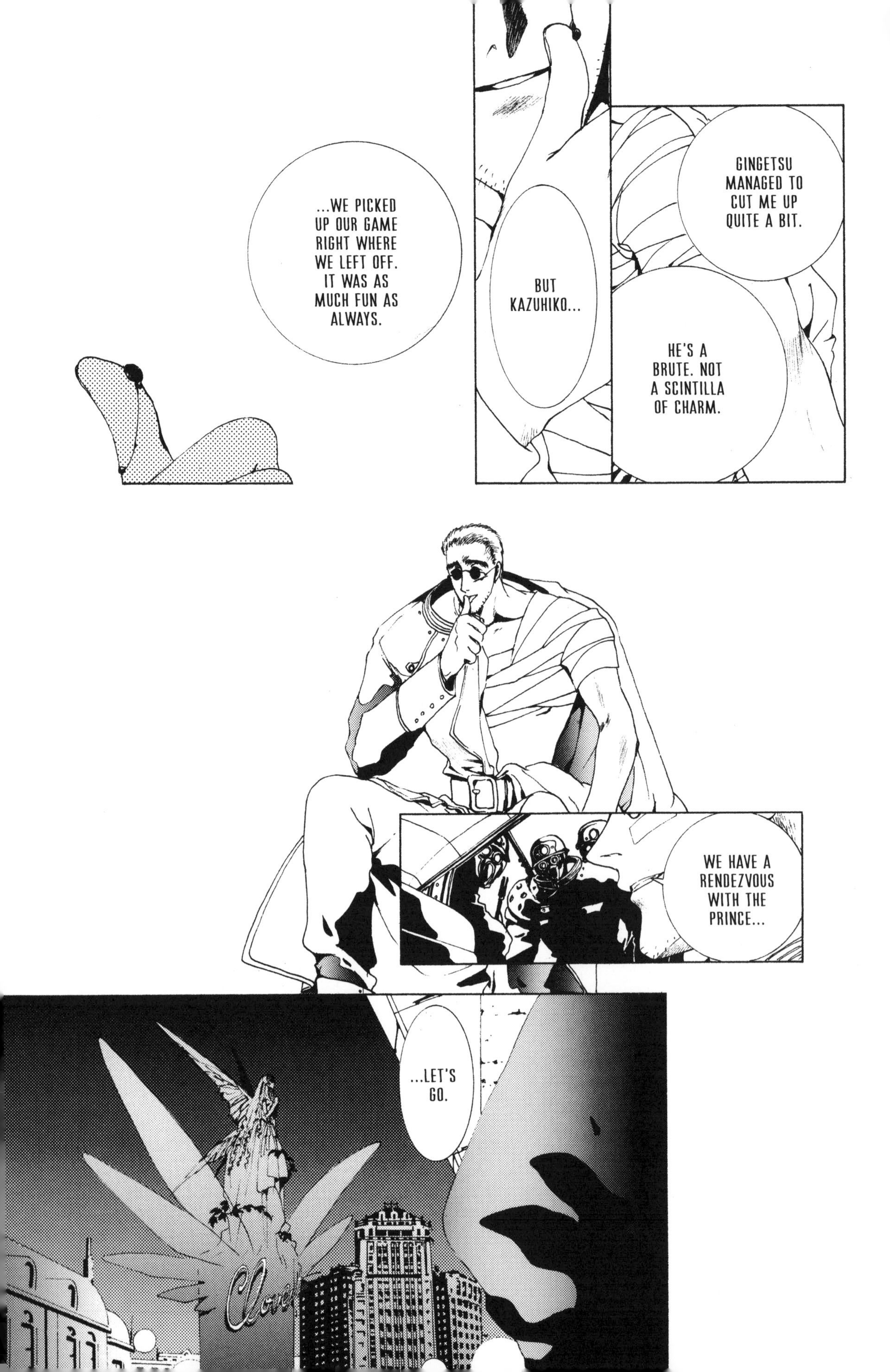
GINGETSU MANAGED TO CUT ME UP QUITE A BIT.
HE'S A BRUTE. NOT A SCINTILLA OF CHARM.
BUT KAZUHIKO...
...WE PICKED UP OUR GAME RIGHT WHERE WE LEFT OFF. IT WAS AS MUCH FUN AS ALWAYS.
WE HAVE A RENDEZVOUS WITH THE PRINCE...
...LET'S GO.
Clover

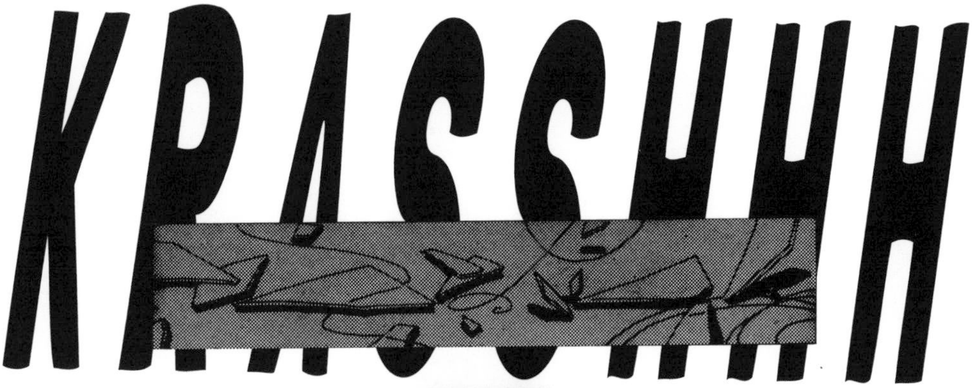
KRASSHH

『羽根』

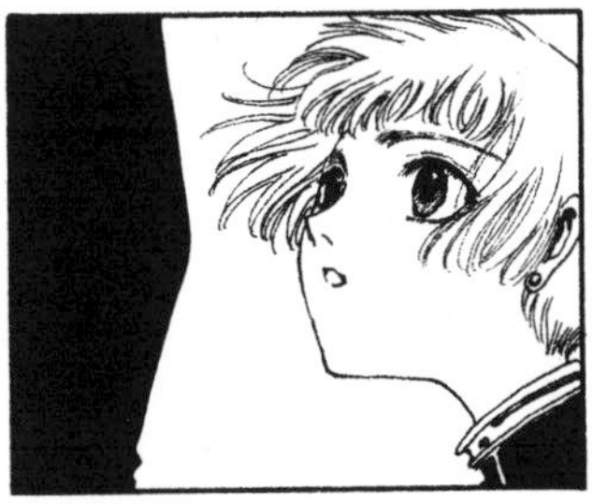

FEATHERS

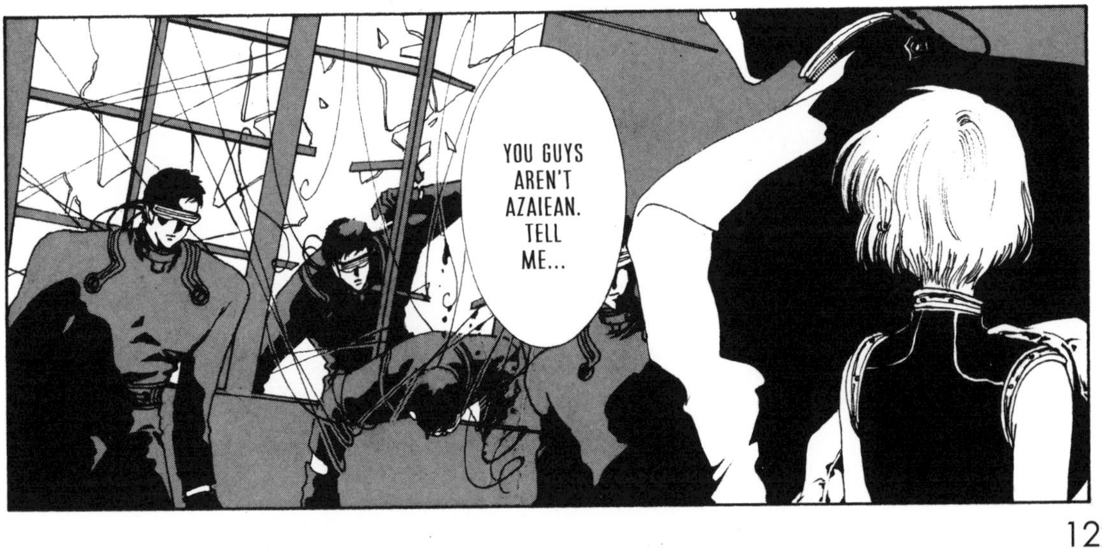
YOU GUYS AREN'T AZAIEAN. TELL ME...

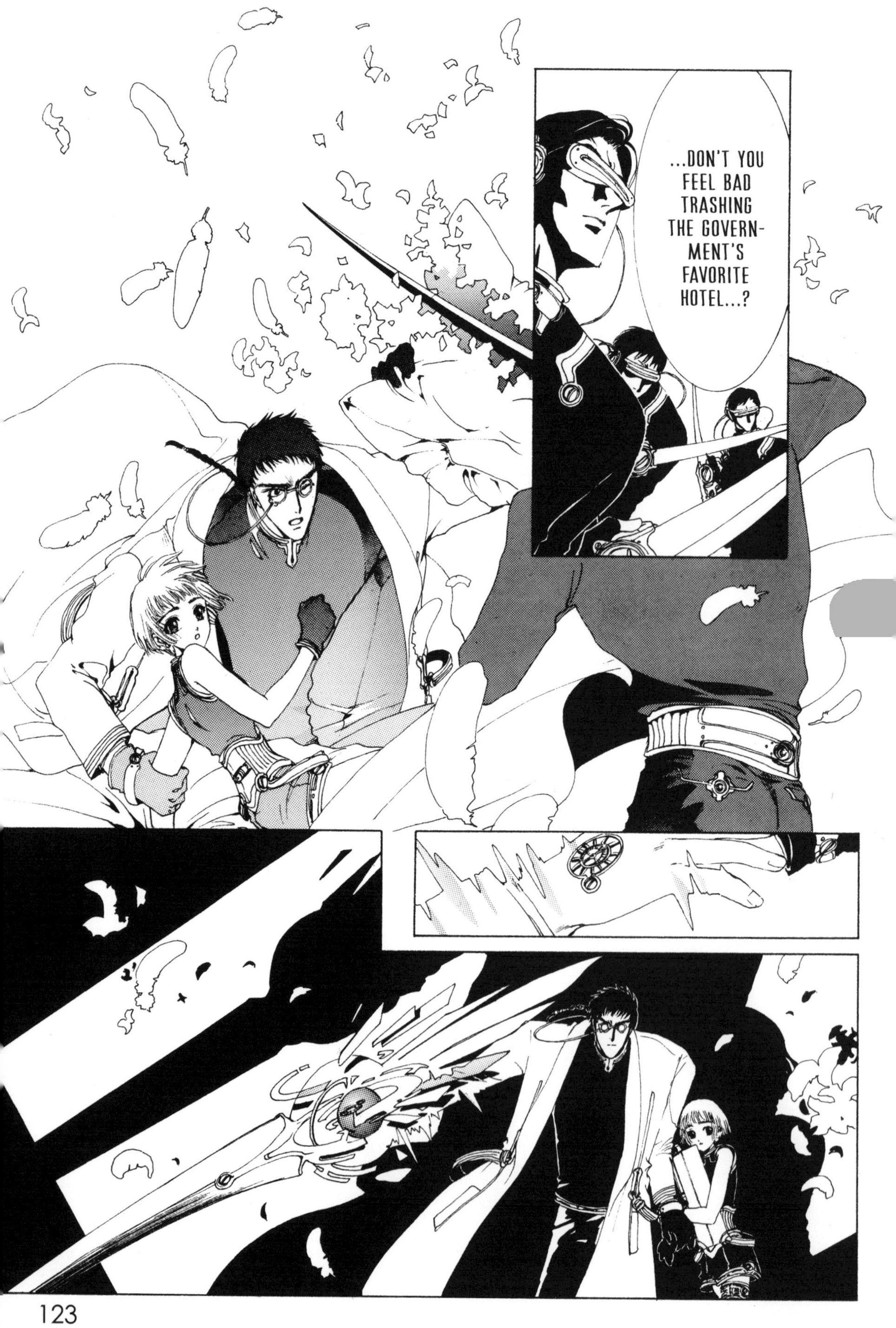
...DON'T YOU FEEL BAD TRASHING THE GOVERN-MENT'S FAVORITE HOTEL...?

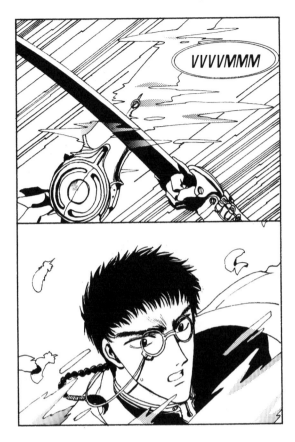

VVVVMMM

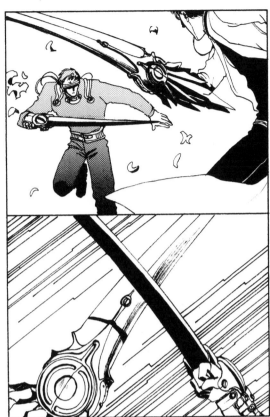

SLLL

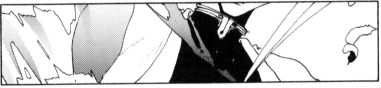

SHH

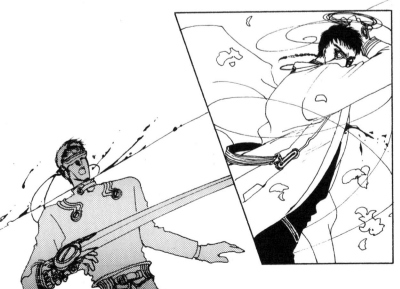

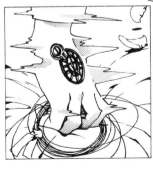

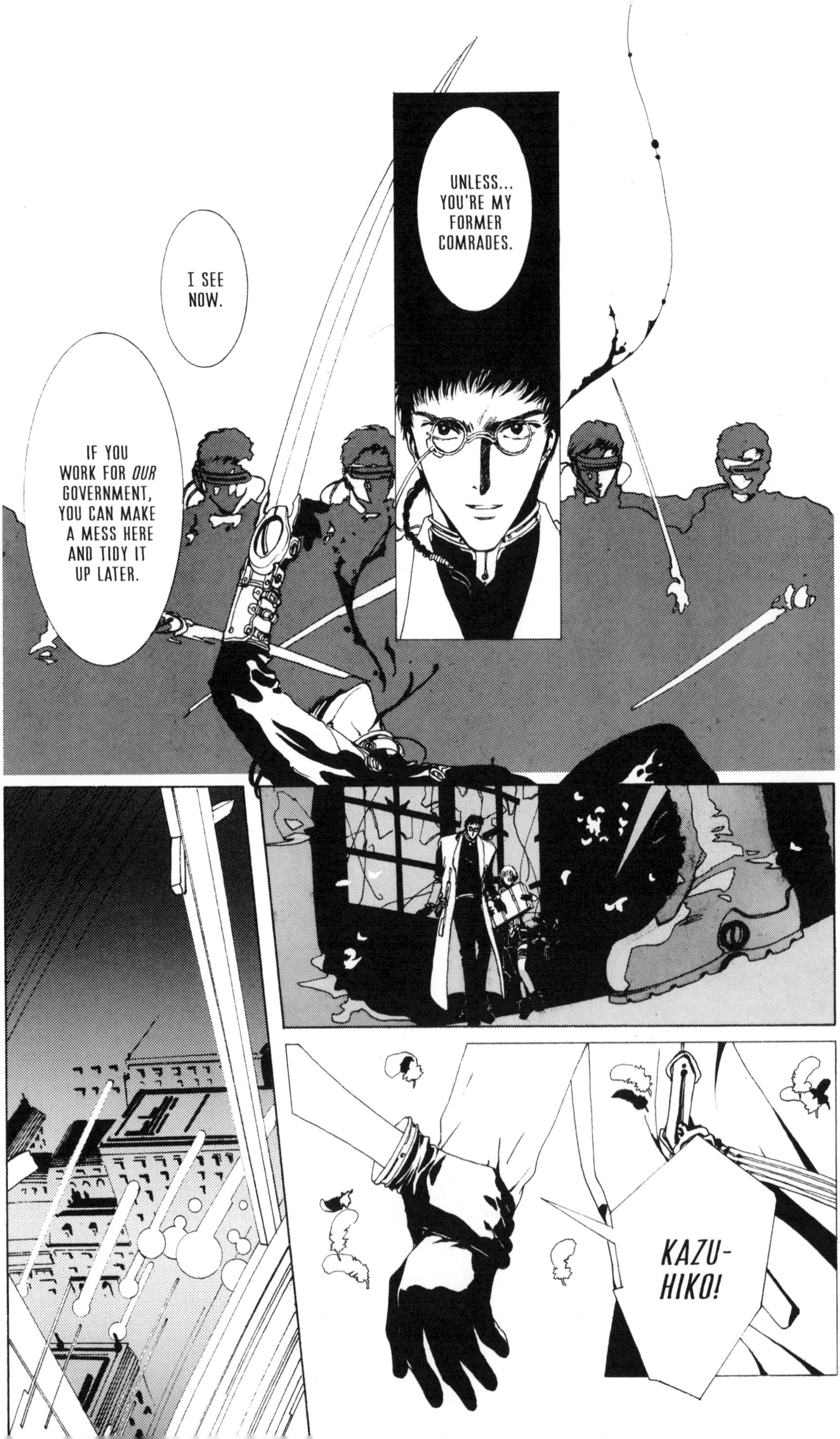
IF YOU WORK FOR *OUR* GOVERNMENT, YOU CAN MAKE A MESS HERE AND TIDY IT UP LATER.
I SEE NOW.
UNLESS... YOU'RE MY FORMER COMRADES.
KAZU-HIKO!

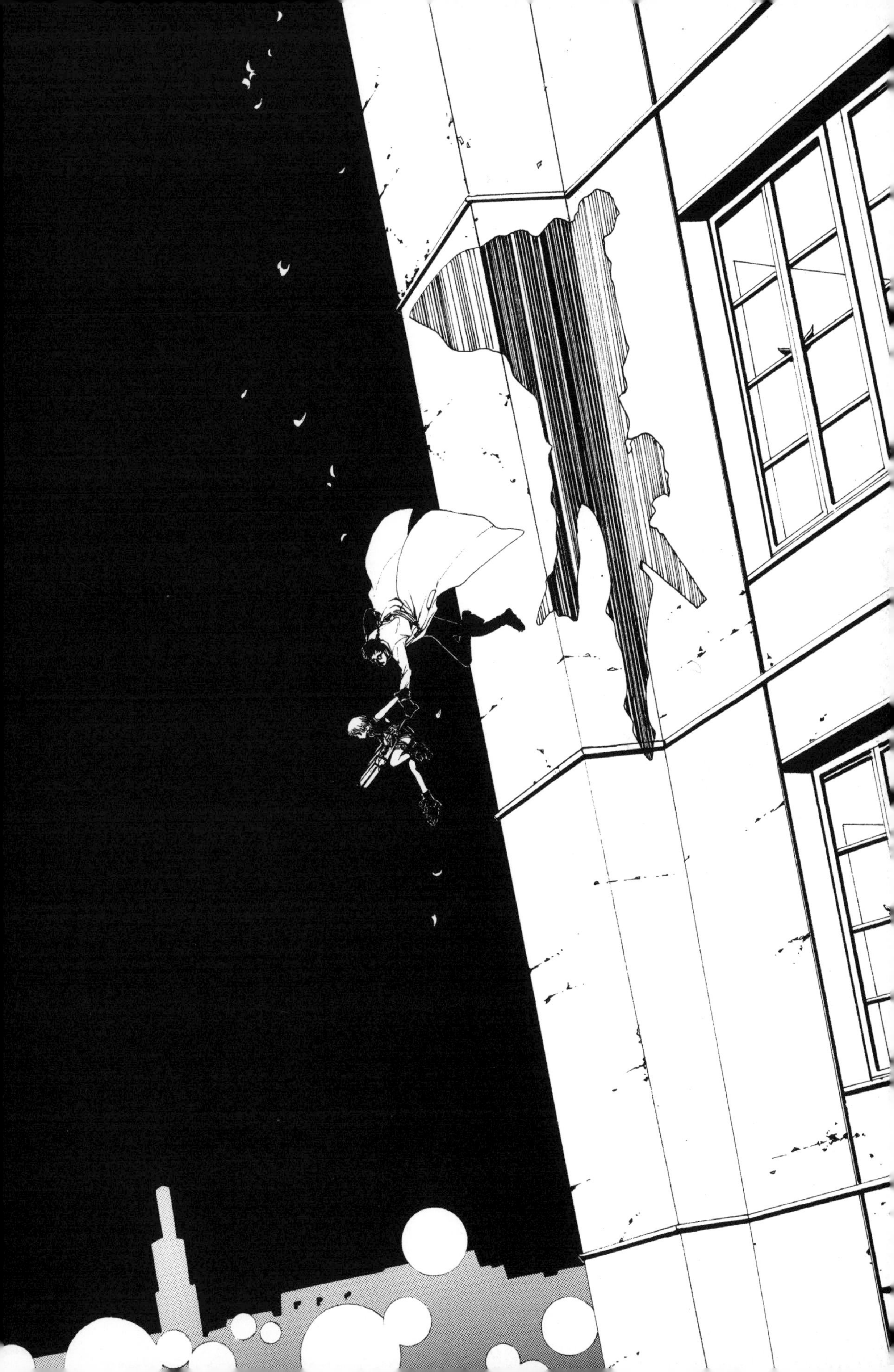

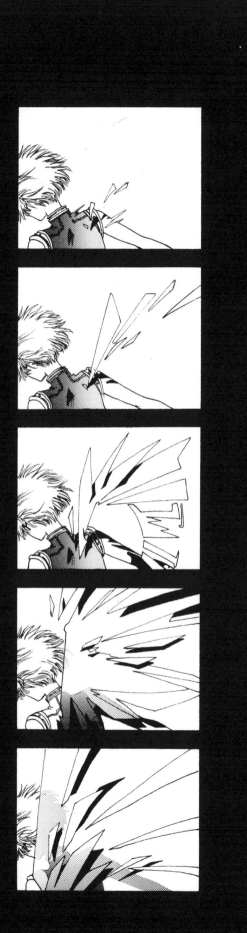

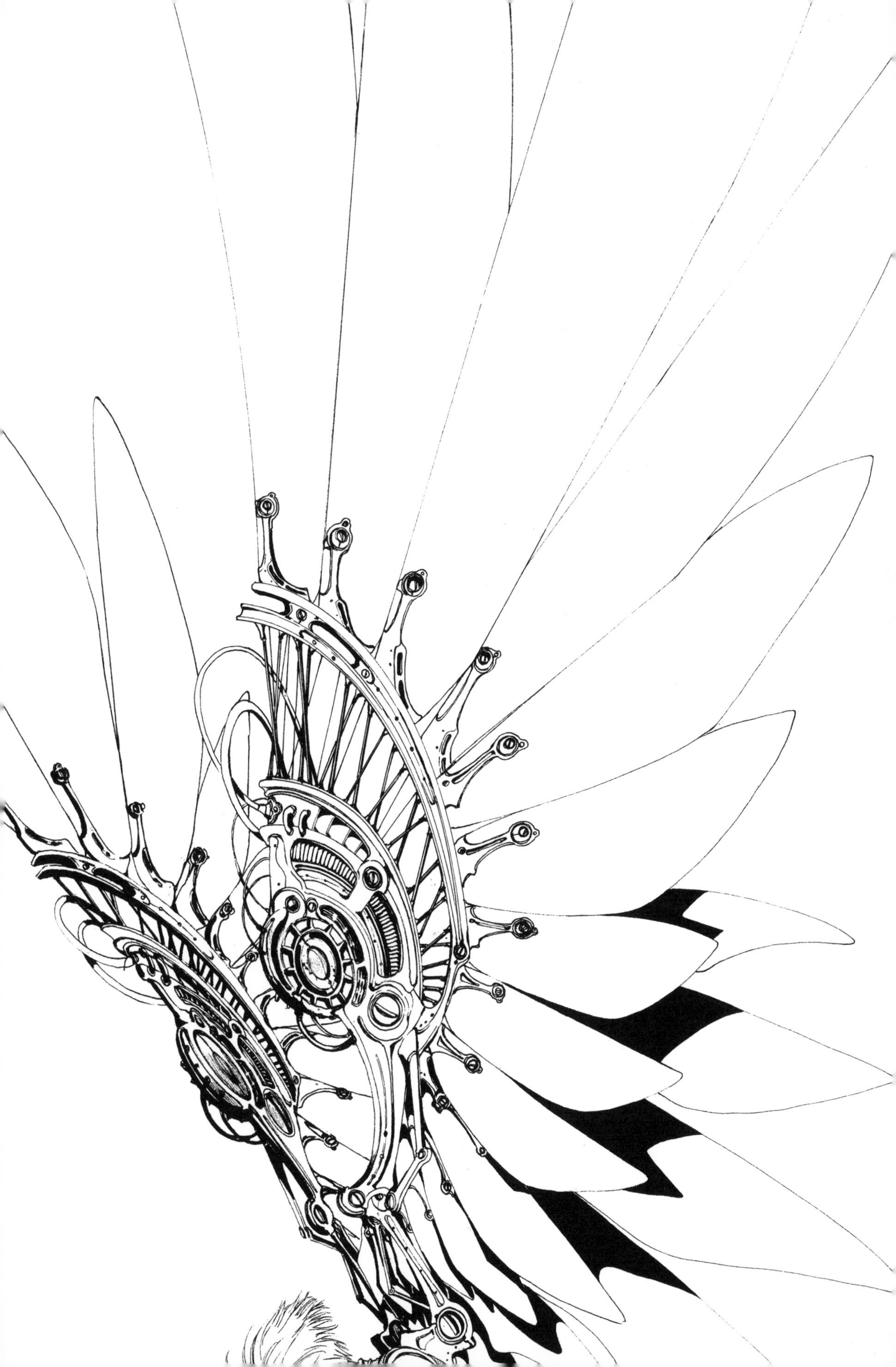

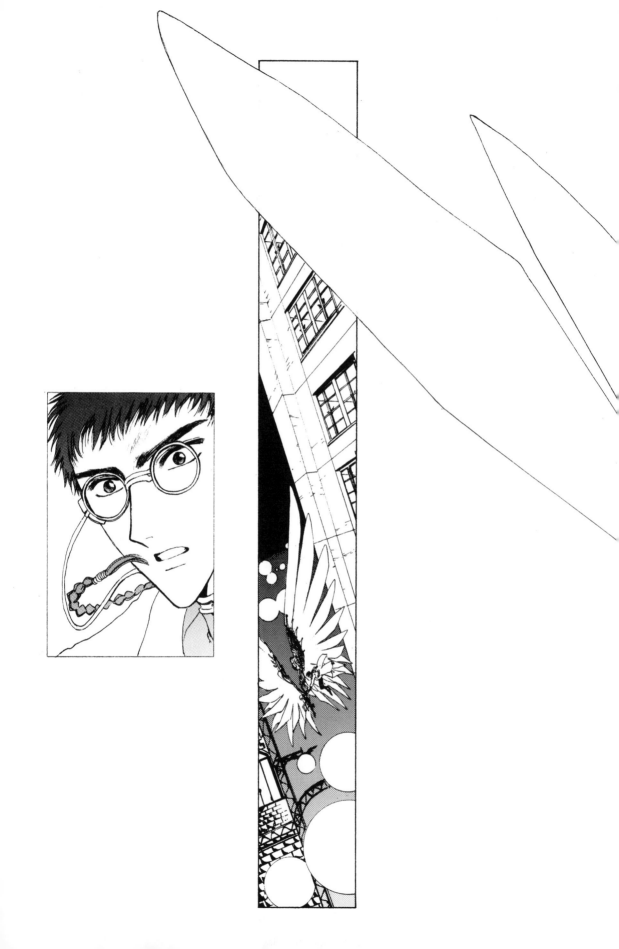

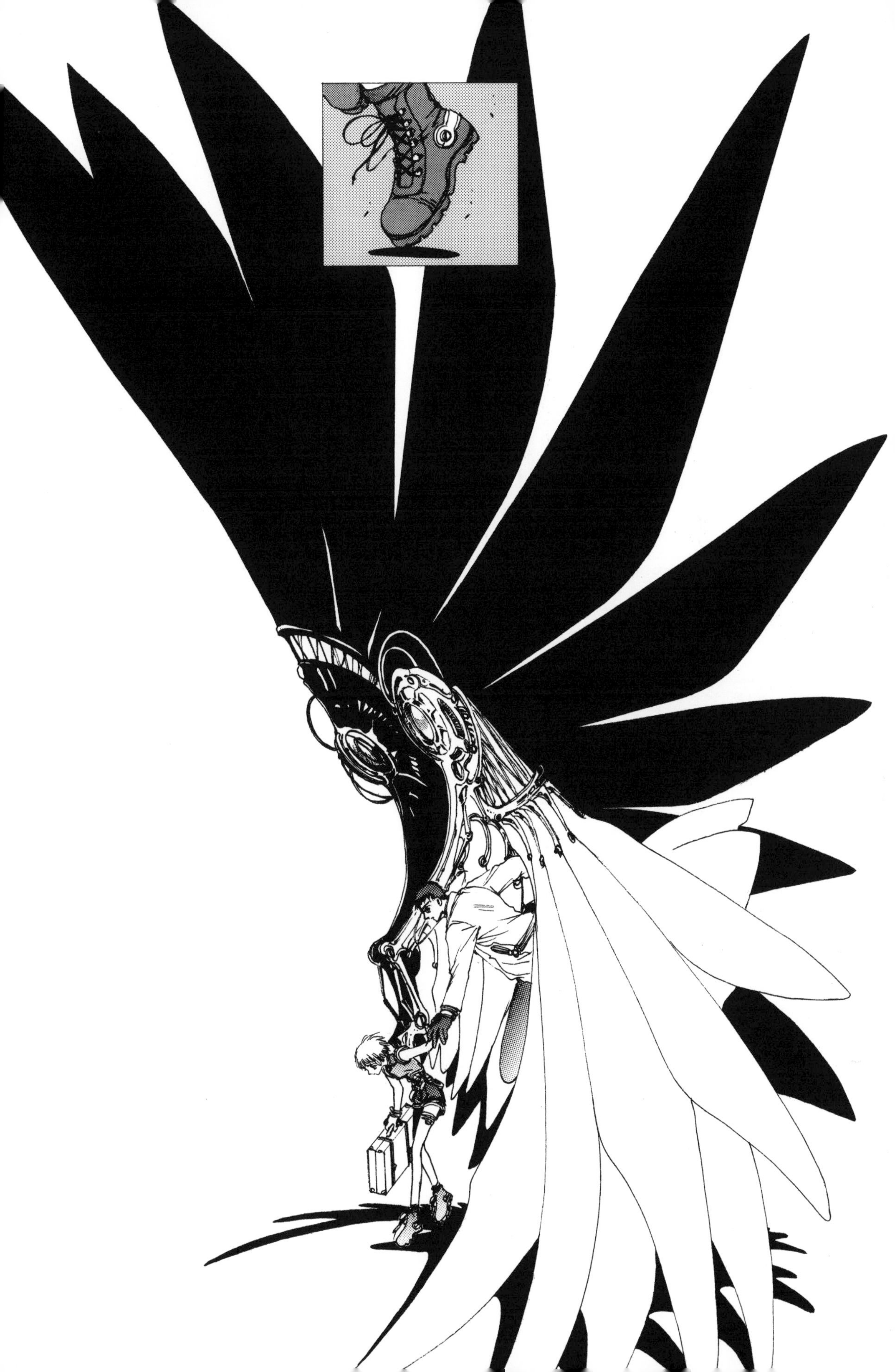

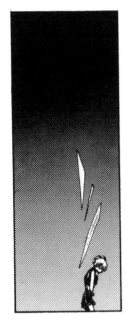
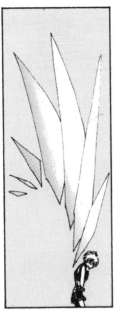
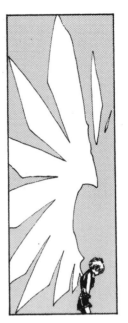
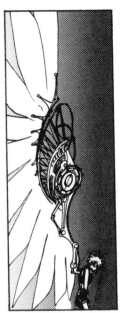

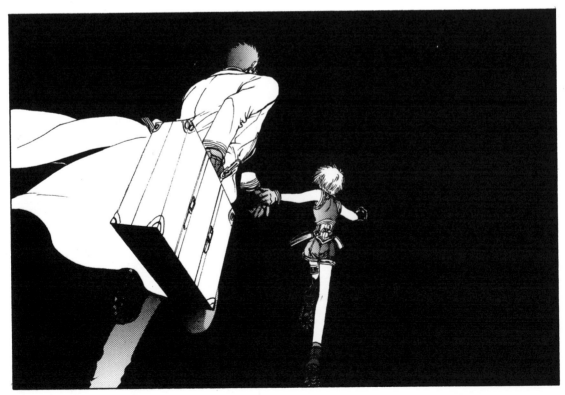

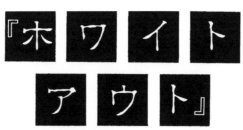

『ホワイトアウト』

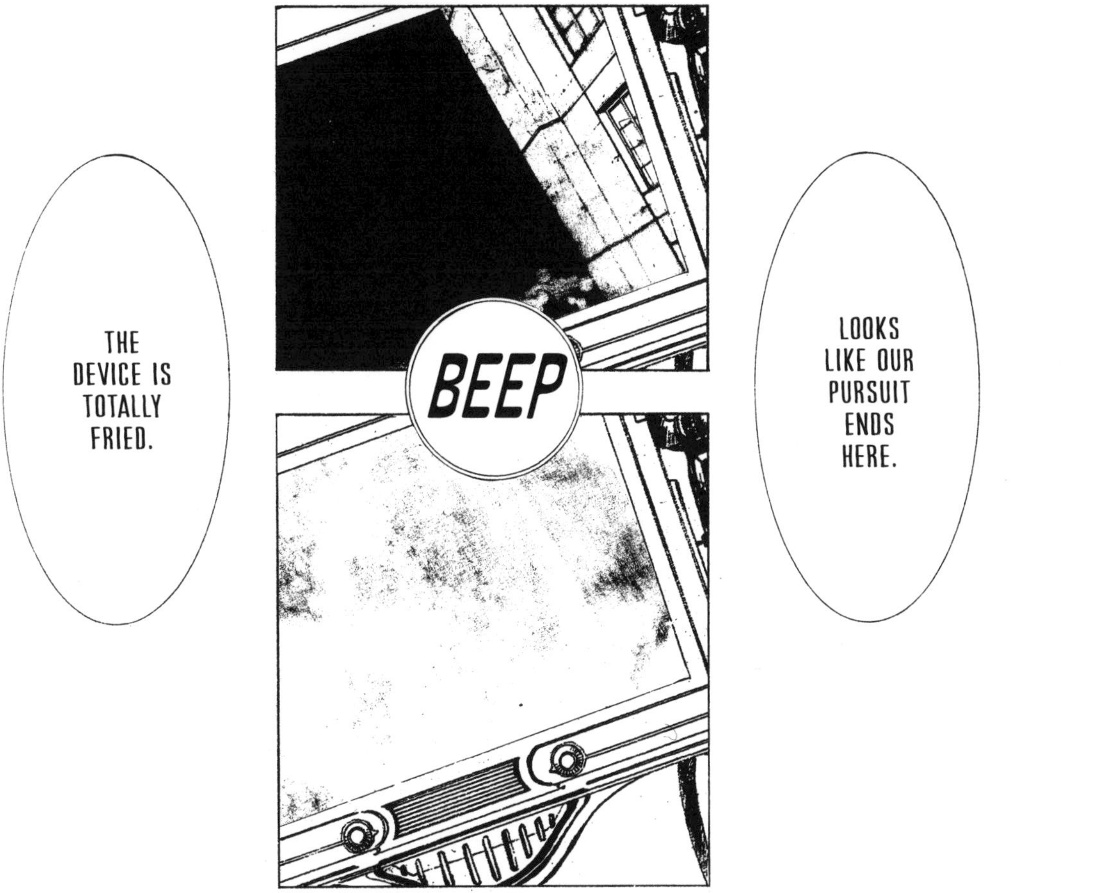
BEEP
LOOKS LIKE OUR PURSUIT ENDS HERE.
THE DEVICE IS TOTALLY FRIED.

WHITEOUT

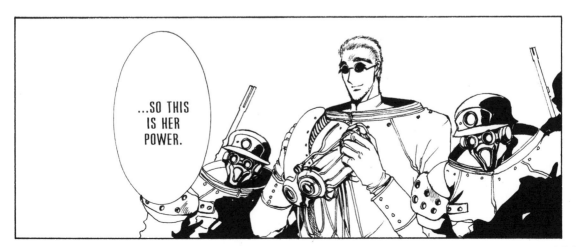

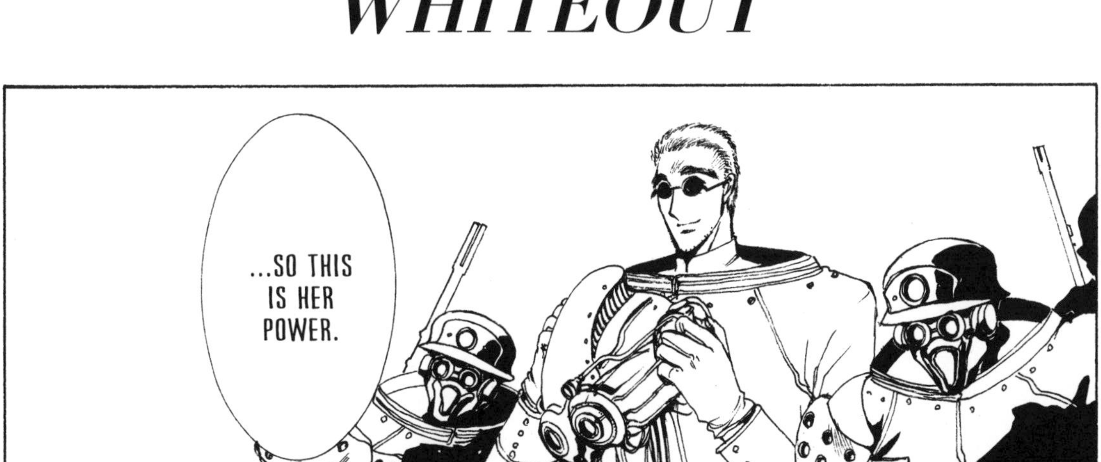
...SO THIS IS HER POWER.

JUST LIKE ME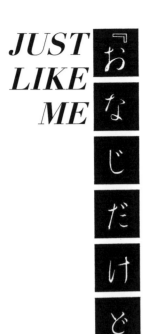

RAN.

RAN!

BZZZT

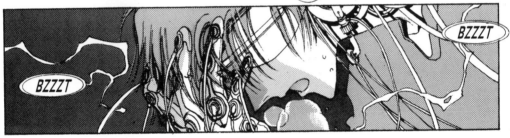

BZZZT

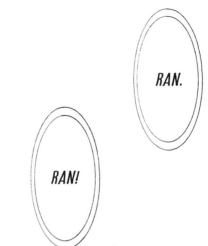

KLIK!

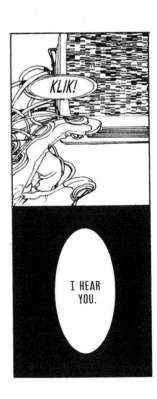

THE TRACKING DEVICE ON RYU'S WEAPON MODULE SEEMS TO HAVE MALFUNCTIONED.

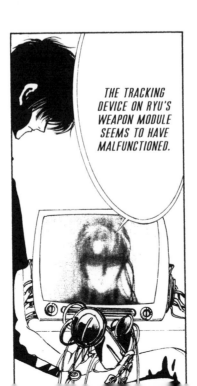

BUT NOT THE SAME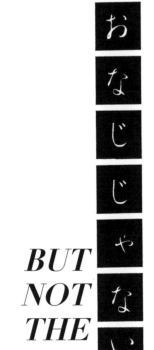

I HEAR YOU.

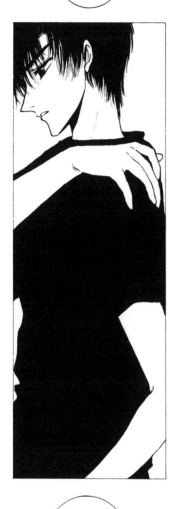

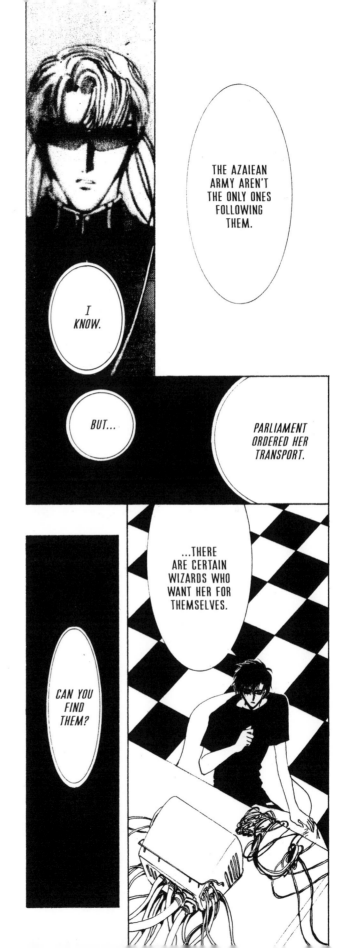

I WILL.

THE AZAIEAN ARMY AREN'T THE ONLY ONES FOLLOWING THEM.

I KNOW.

BUT...

PARLIAMENT ORDERED HER TRANSPORT.

...THERE ARE CERTAIN WIZARDS WHO WANT HER FOR THEMSELVES.

CAN YOU FIND THEM?

SHE'S A CLOVER... JUST LIKE ME.

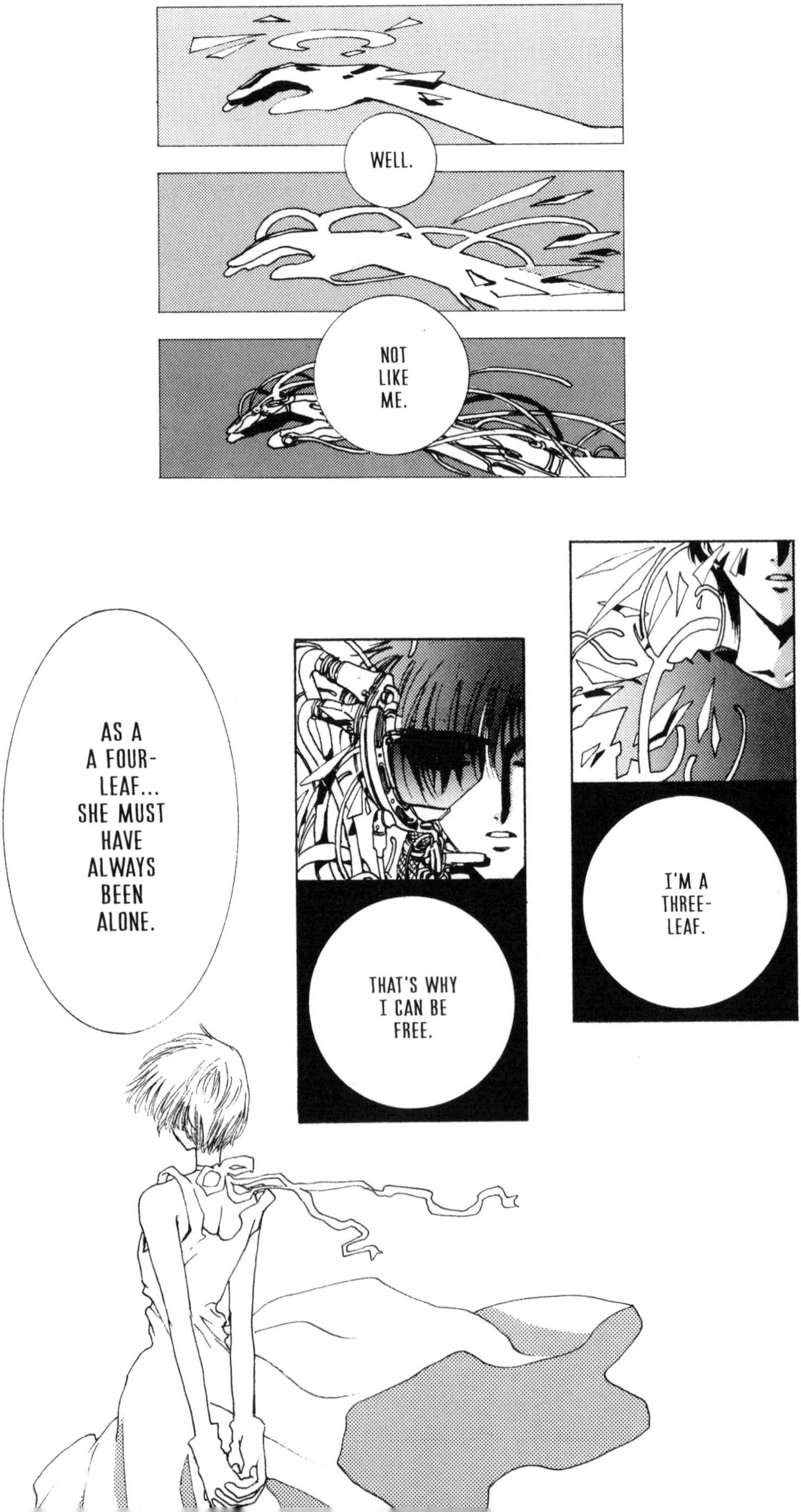
WELL.
NOT LIKE ME.
I'M A THREE-LEAF.
THAT'S WHY I CAN BE FREE.
AS A A FOUR-LEAF... SHE MUST HAVE ALWAYS BEEN ALONE.

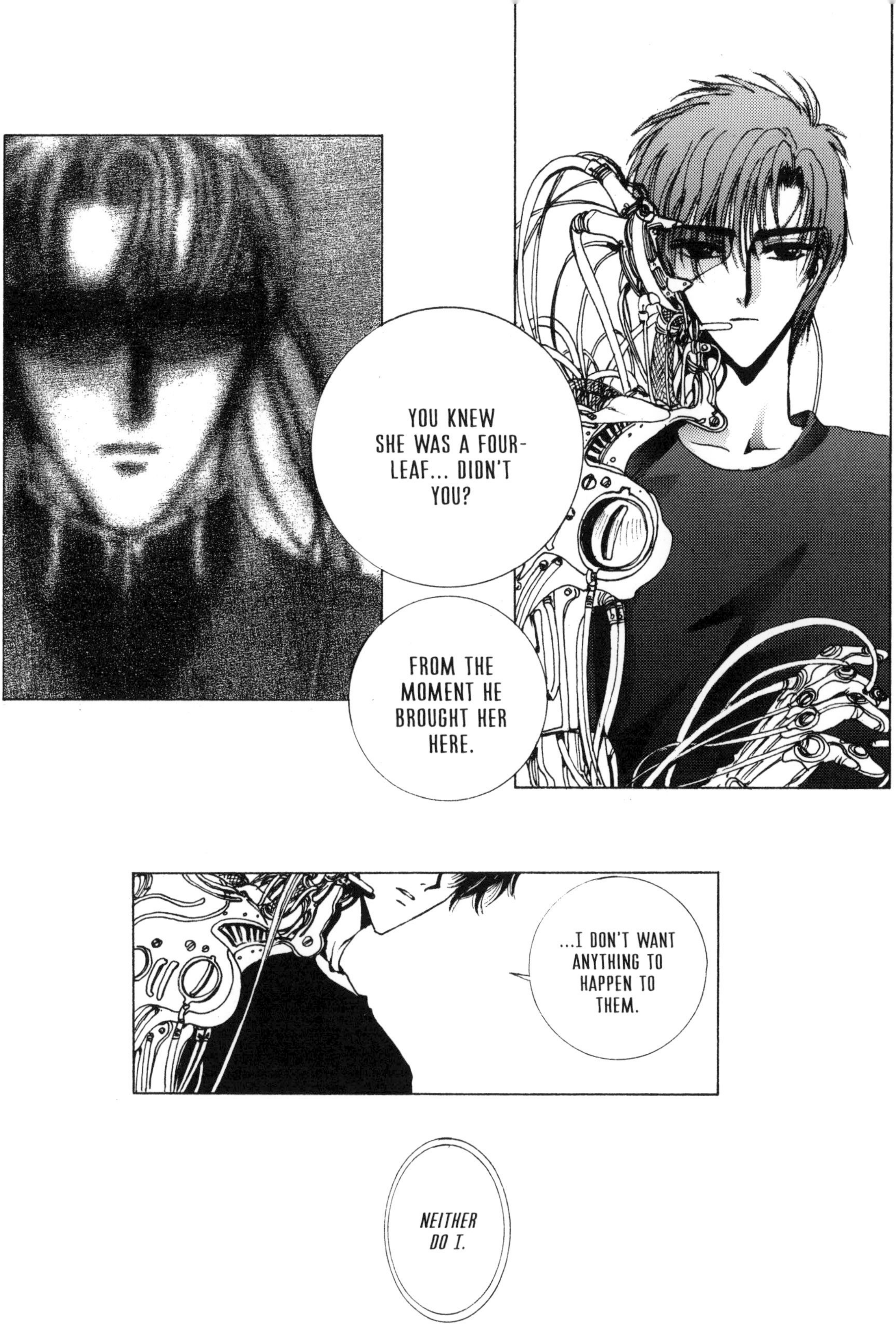
YOU KNEW SHE WAS A FOUR-LEAF... DIDN'T YOU?
FROM THE MOMENT HE BROUGHT HER HERE.
...I DON'T WANT ANYTHING TO HAPPEN TO THEM.
NEITHER DO I.

NIGHT

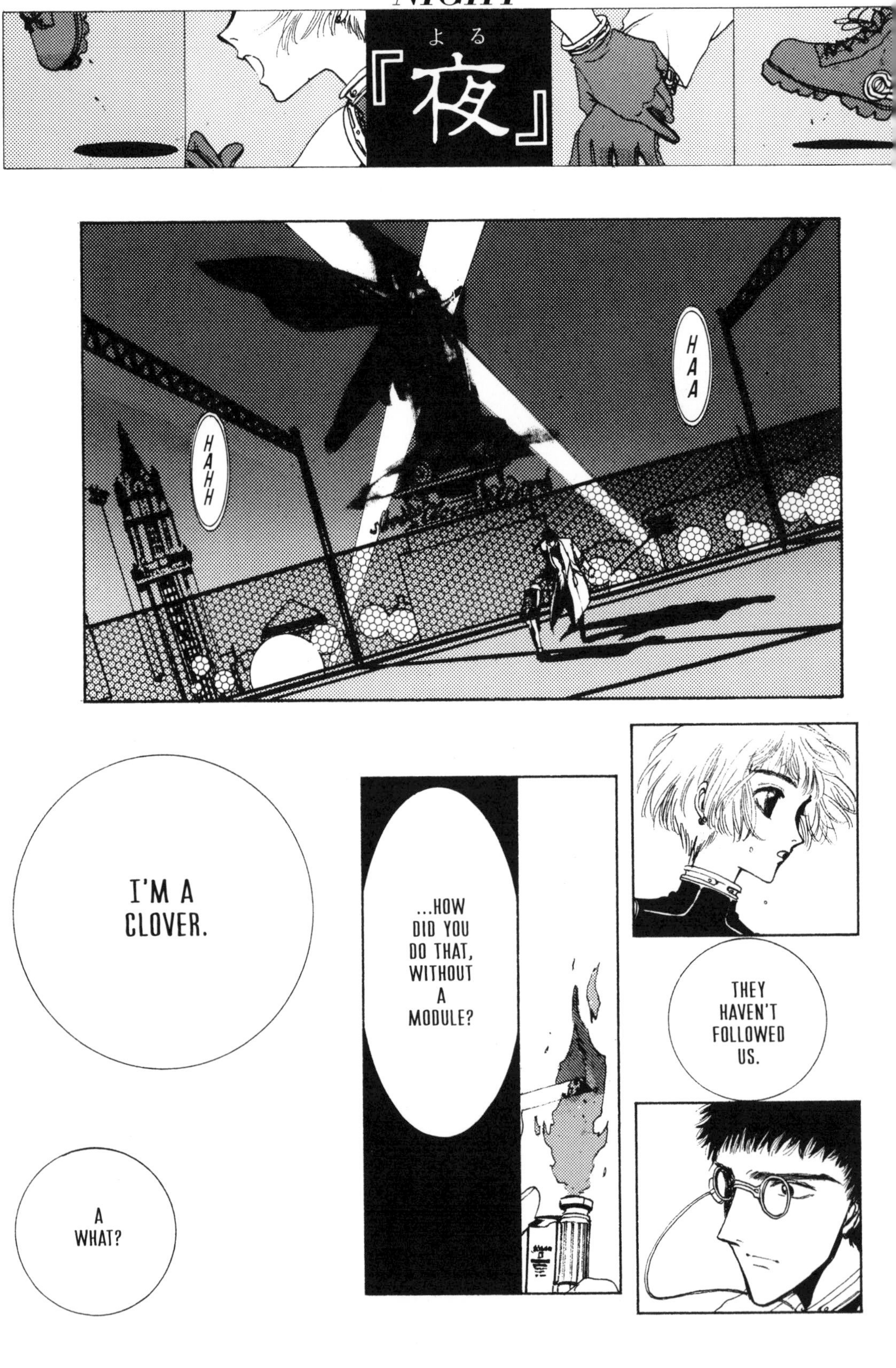
よる
『夜』
HAA
HAHH
THEY HAVEN'T FOLLOWED US.
...HOW DID YOU DO THAT, WITHOUT A MODULE?
I'M A CLOVER.
A WHAT?

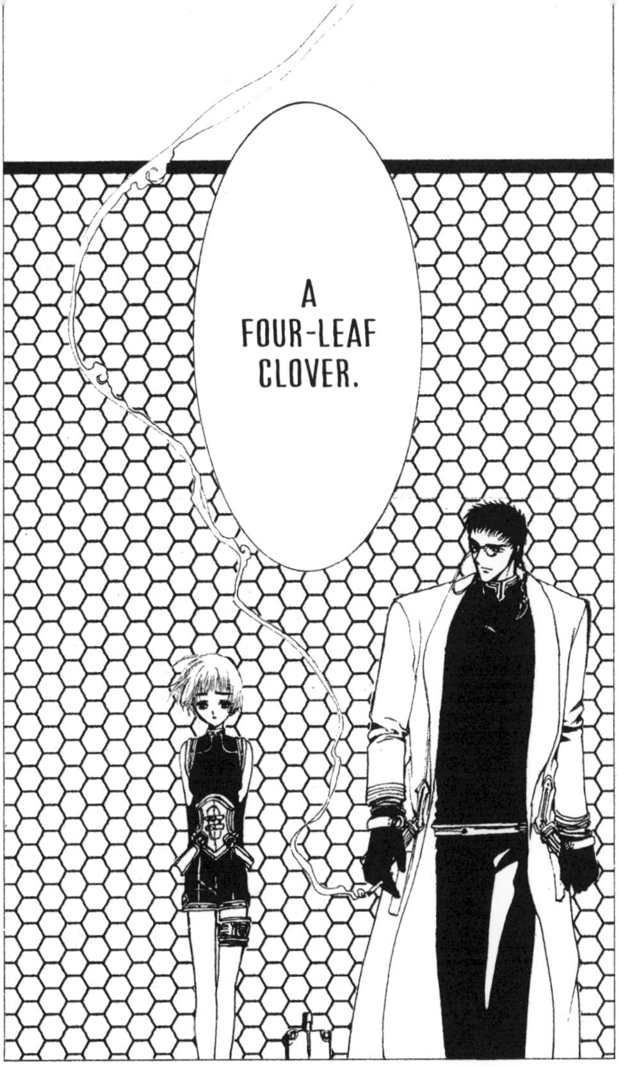
A FOUR-LEAF CLOVER.

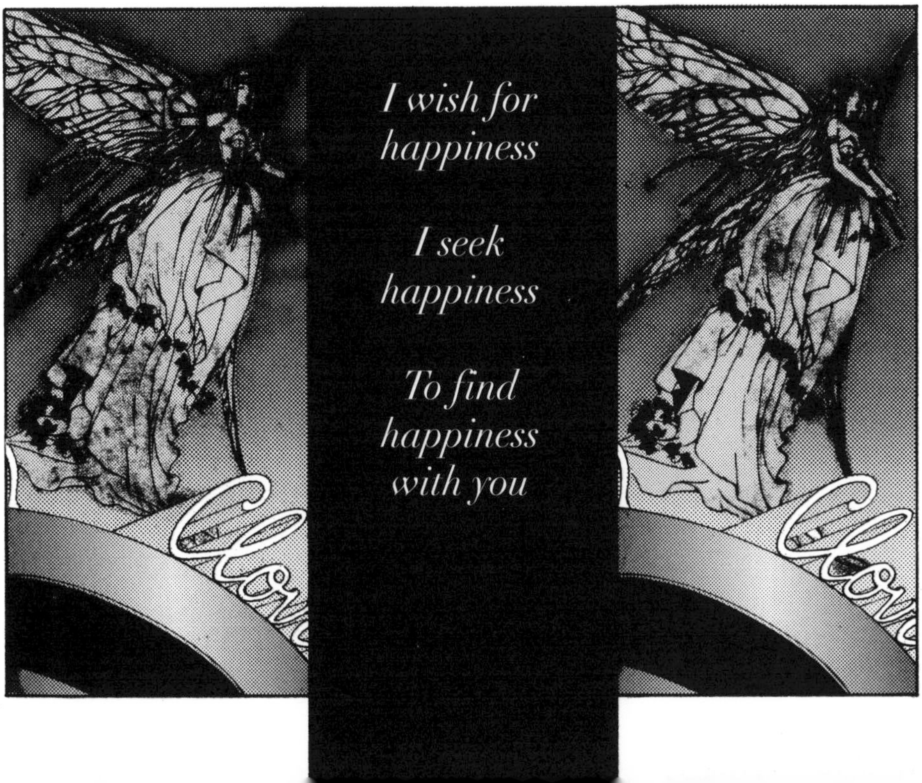
I wish for happiness
I seek happiness
To find happiness with you

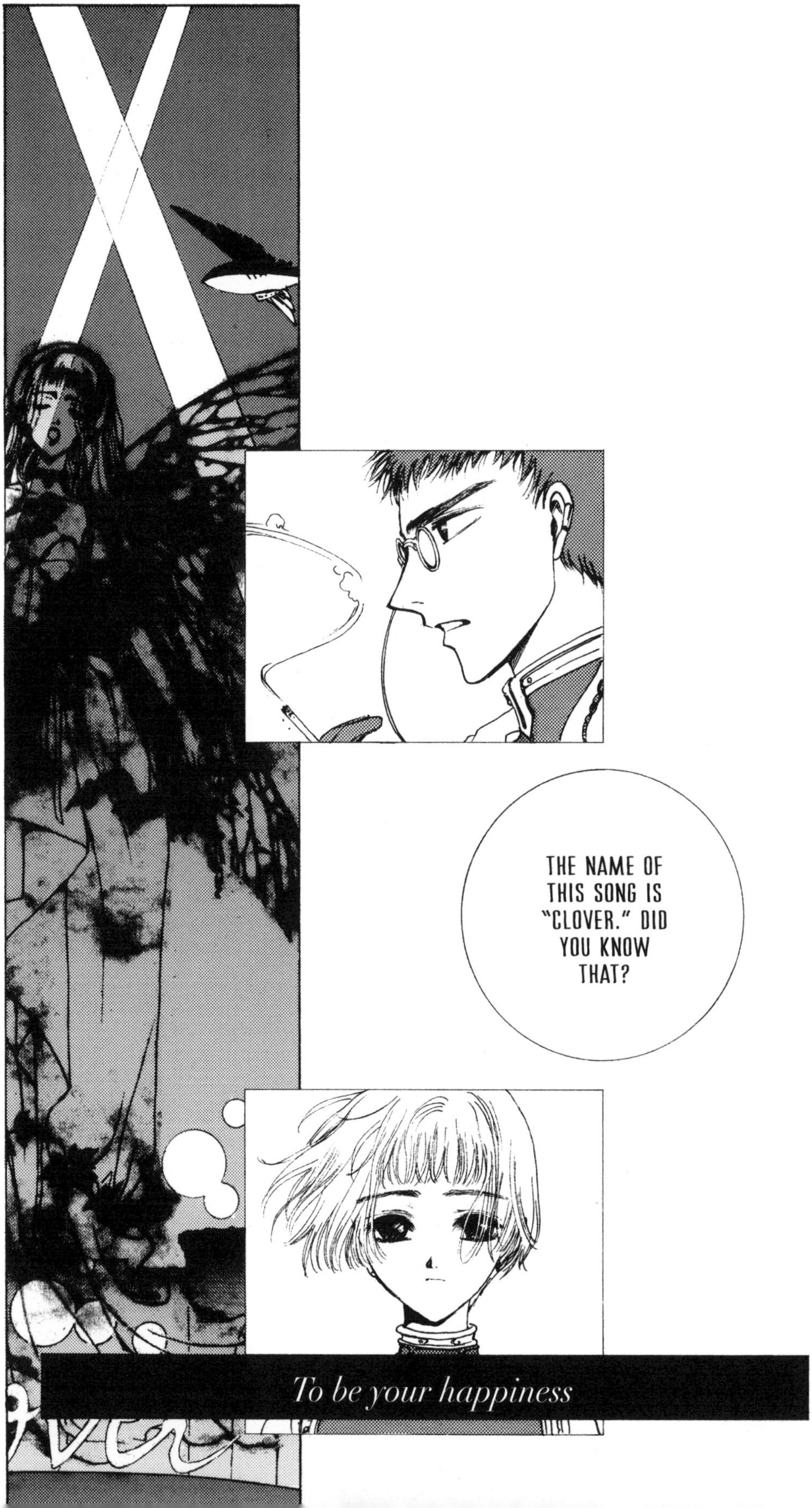
THE NAME OF THIS SONG IS "CLOVER." DID YOU KNOW THAT?
To be your happiness

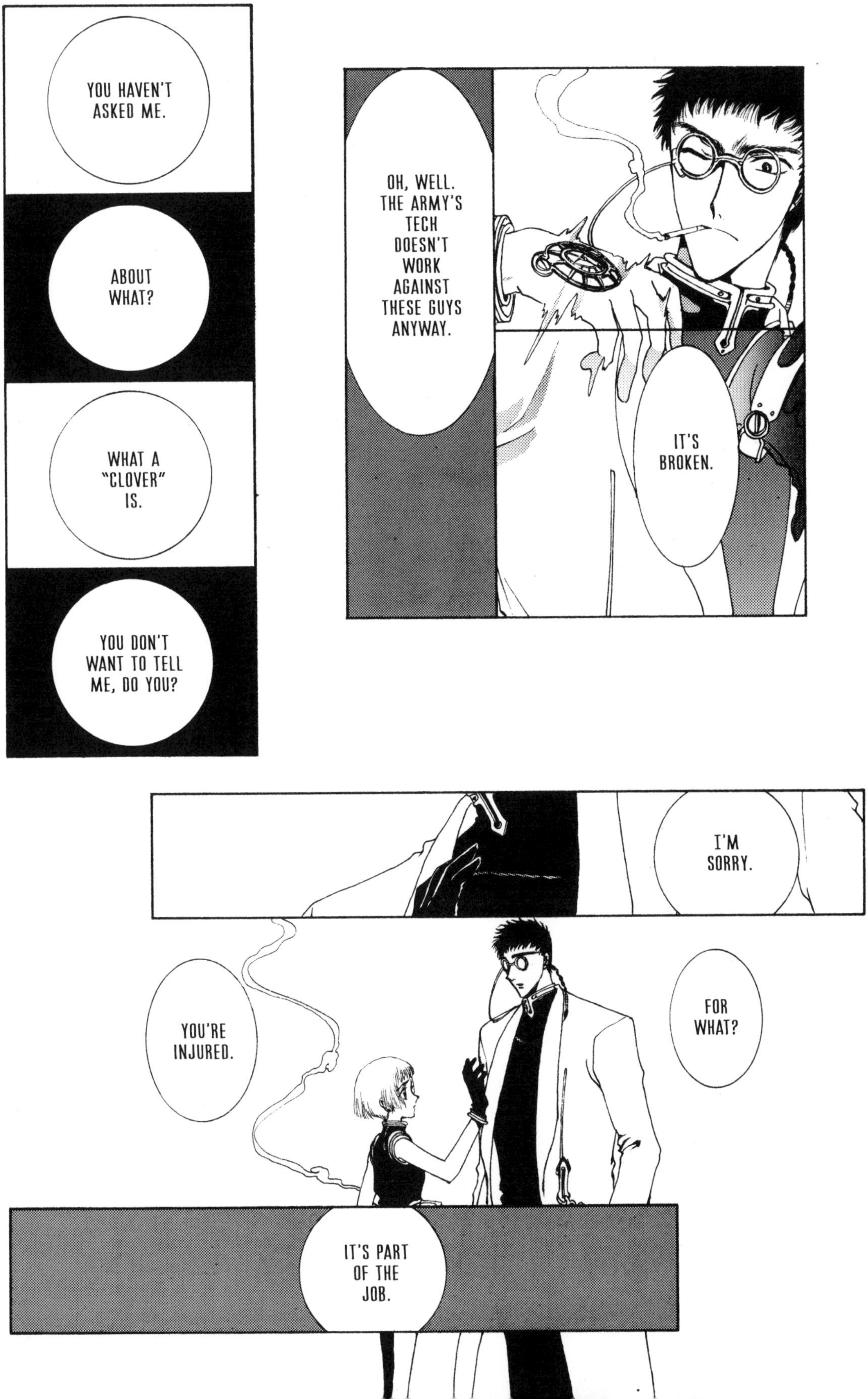
IT'S BROKEN.
OH, WELL. THE ARMY'S TECH DOESN'T WORK AGAINST THESE GUYS ANYWAY.
YOU HAVEN'T ASKED ME.
ABOUT WHAT?
WHAT A "CLOVER" IS.
YOU DON'T WANT TO TELL ME, DO YOU?
I'M SORRY.
FOR WHAT?
YOU'RE INJURED.
IT'S PART OF THE JOB.

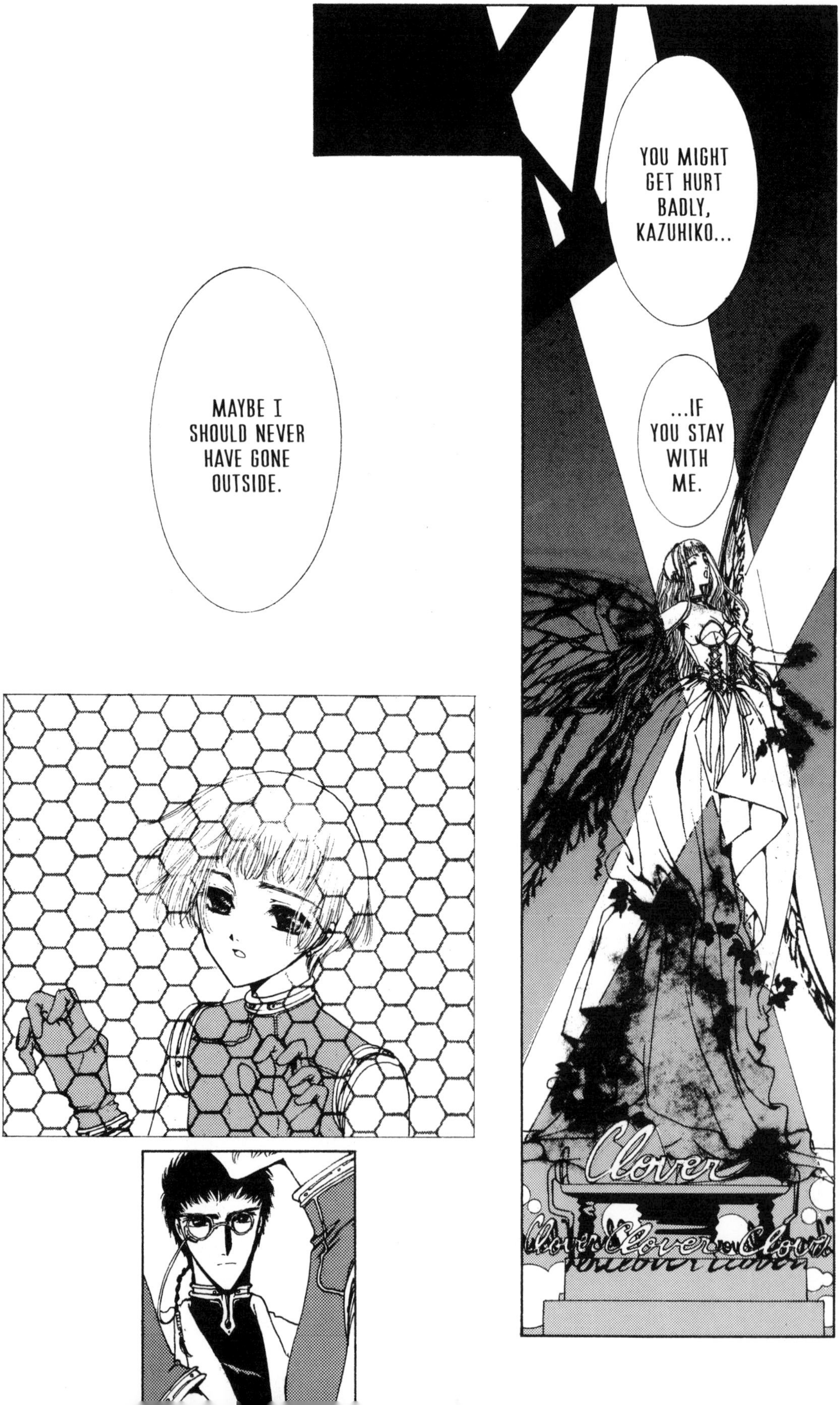
YOU MIGHT GET HURT BADLY, KAZUHIKO...
...IF YOU STAY WITH ME.
Clover
MAYBE I SHOULD NEVER HAVE GONE OUTSIDE.

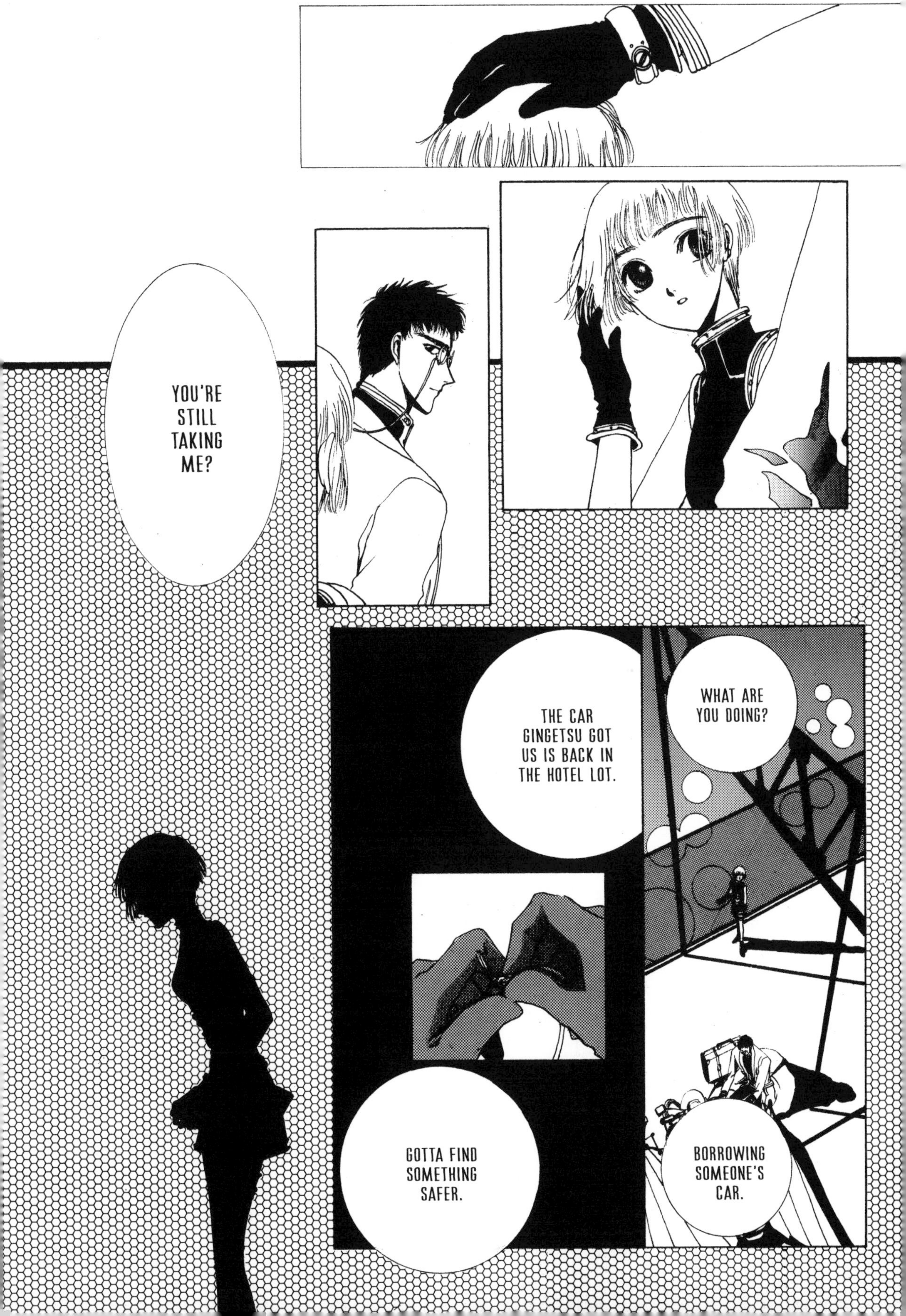
YOU'RE STILL TAKING ME?
WHAT ARE YOU DOING?
BORROWING SOMEONE'S CAR.
THE CAR GINGETSU GOT US IS BACK IN THE HOTEL LOT.
GOTTA FIND SOMETHING SAFER.

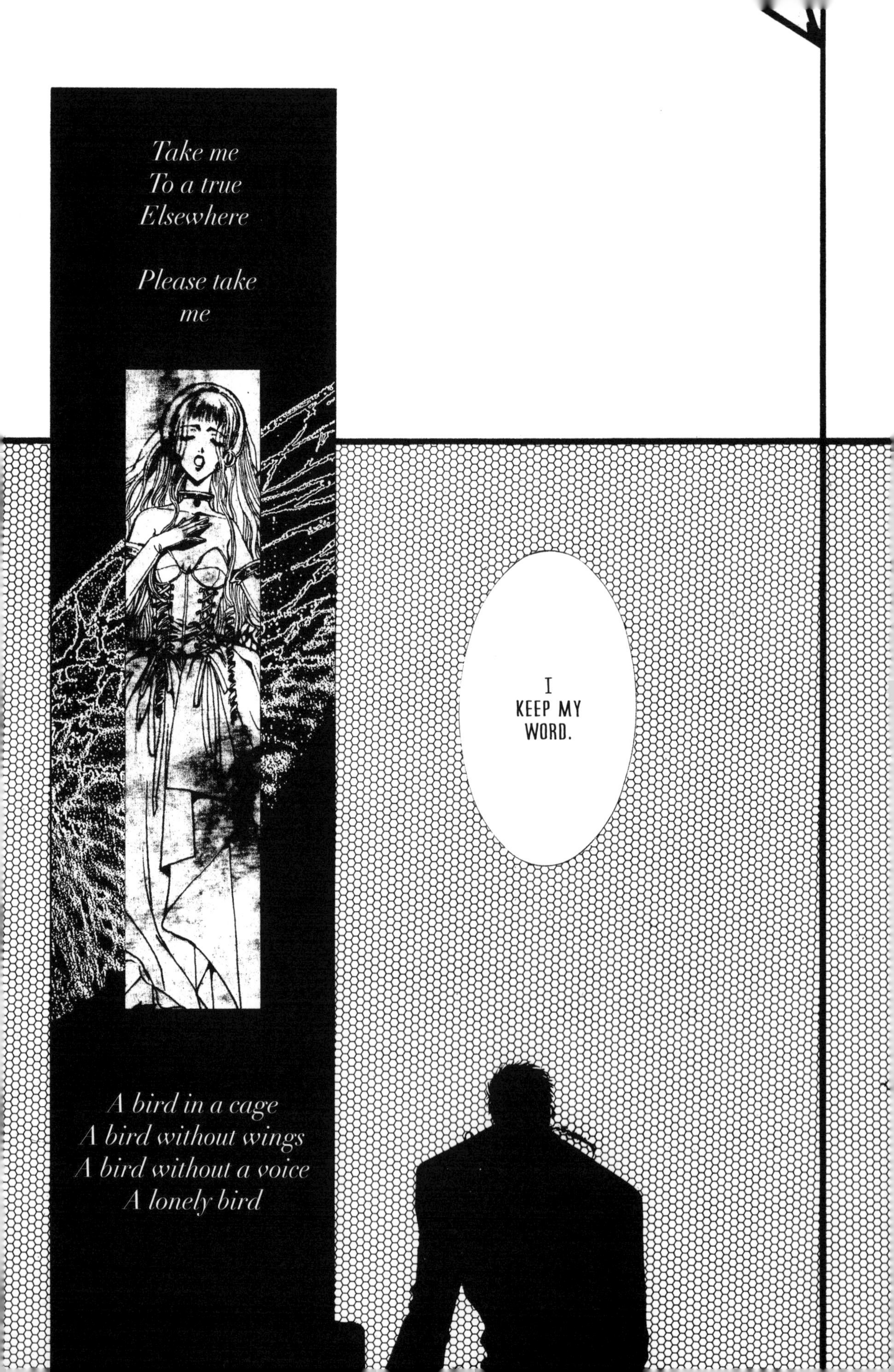
I KEEP MY WORD.
Take me
To a true
Elsewhere
Please take
me
A bird in a cage
A bird without wings
A bird without a voice
A lonely bird

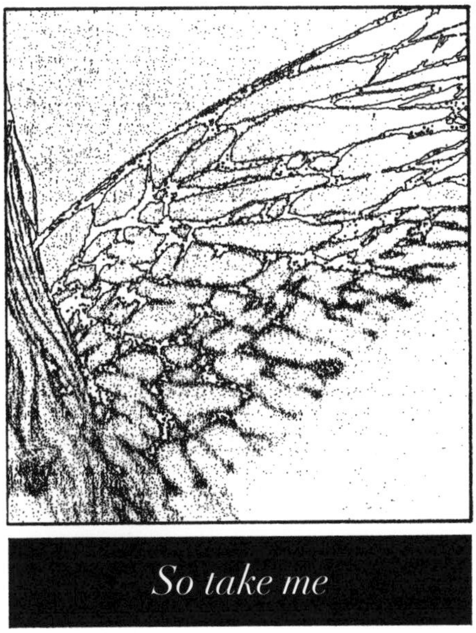
So take me

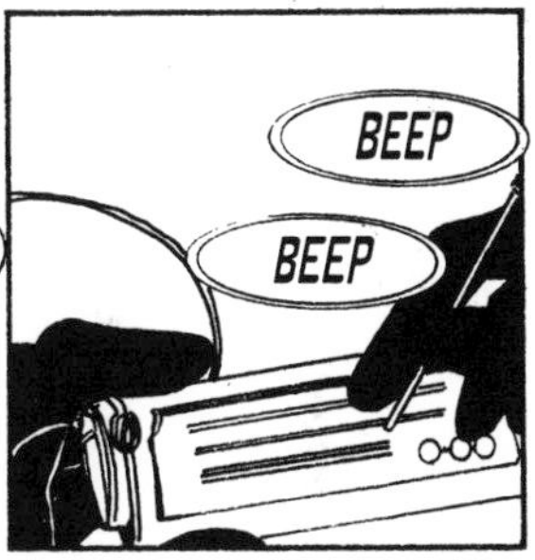
BEEP
BEEP

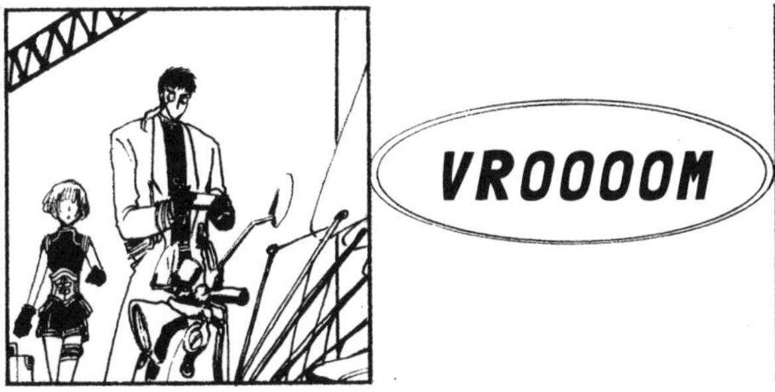
VROOOOM

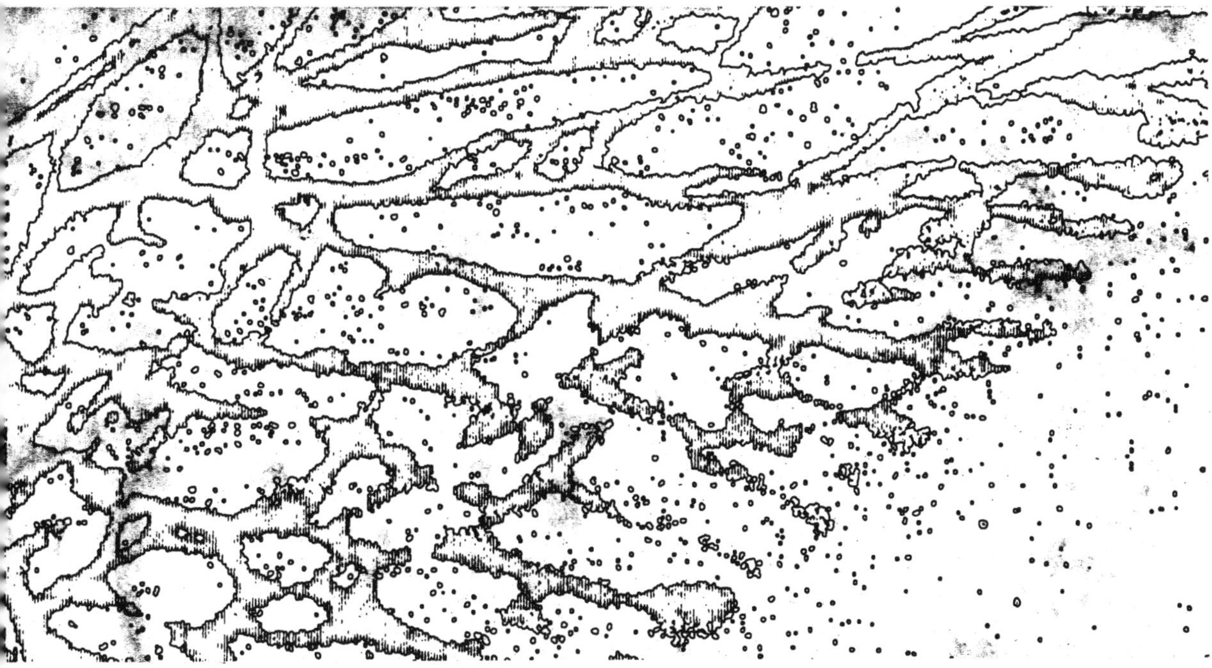

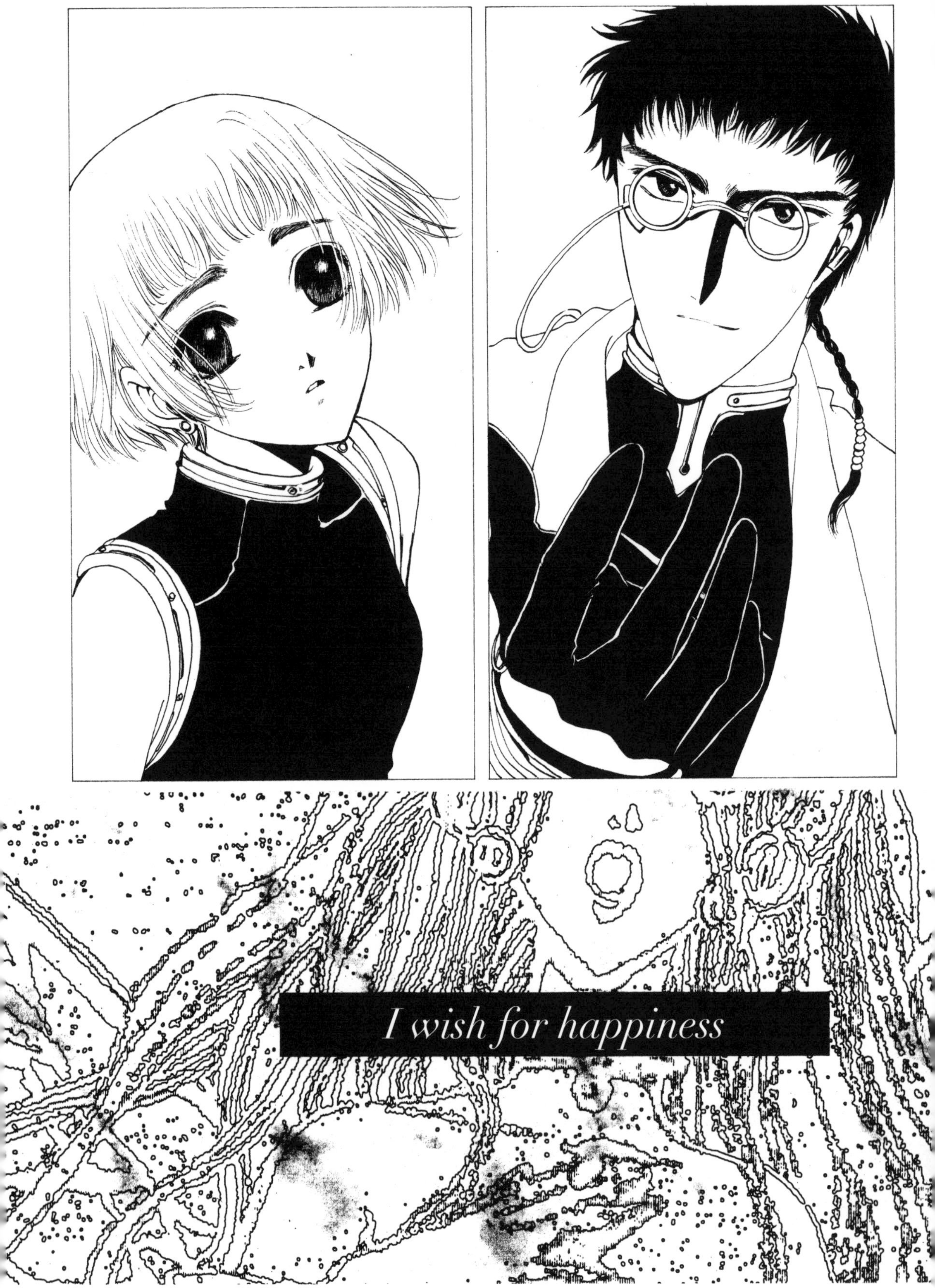
I wish for happiness

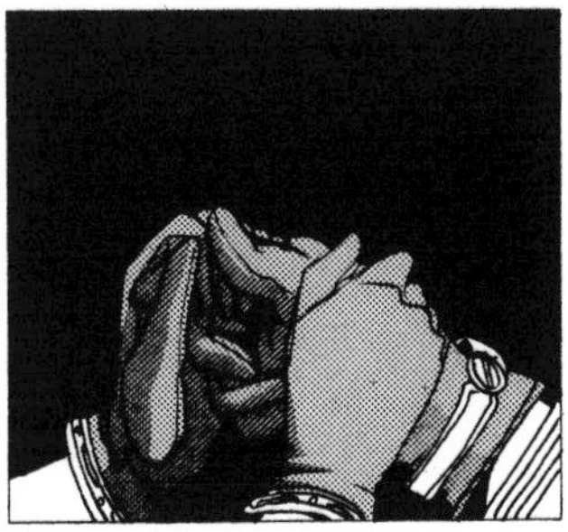

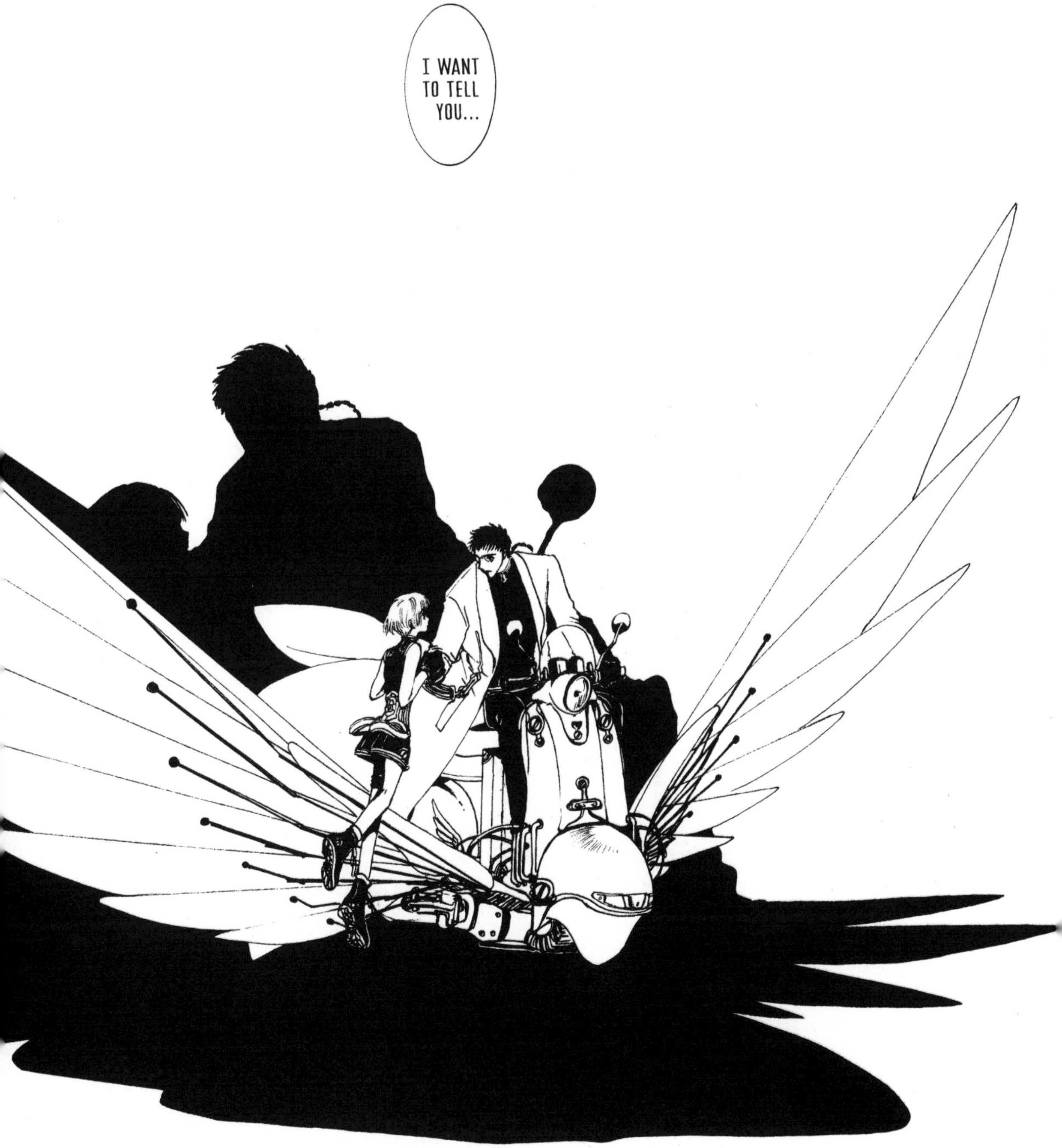
I WANT TO TELL YOU...

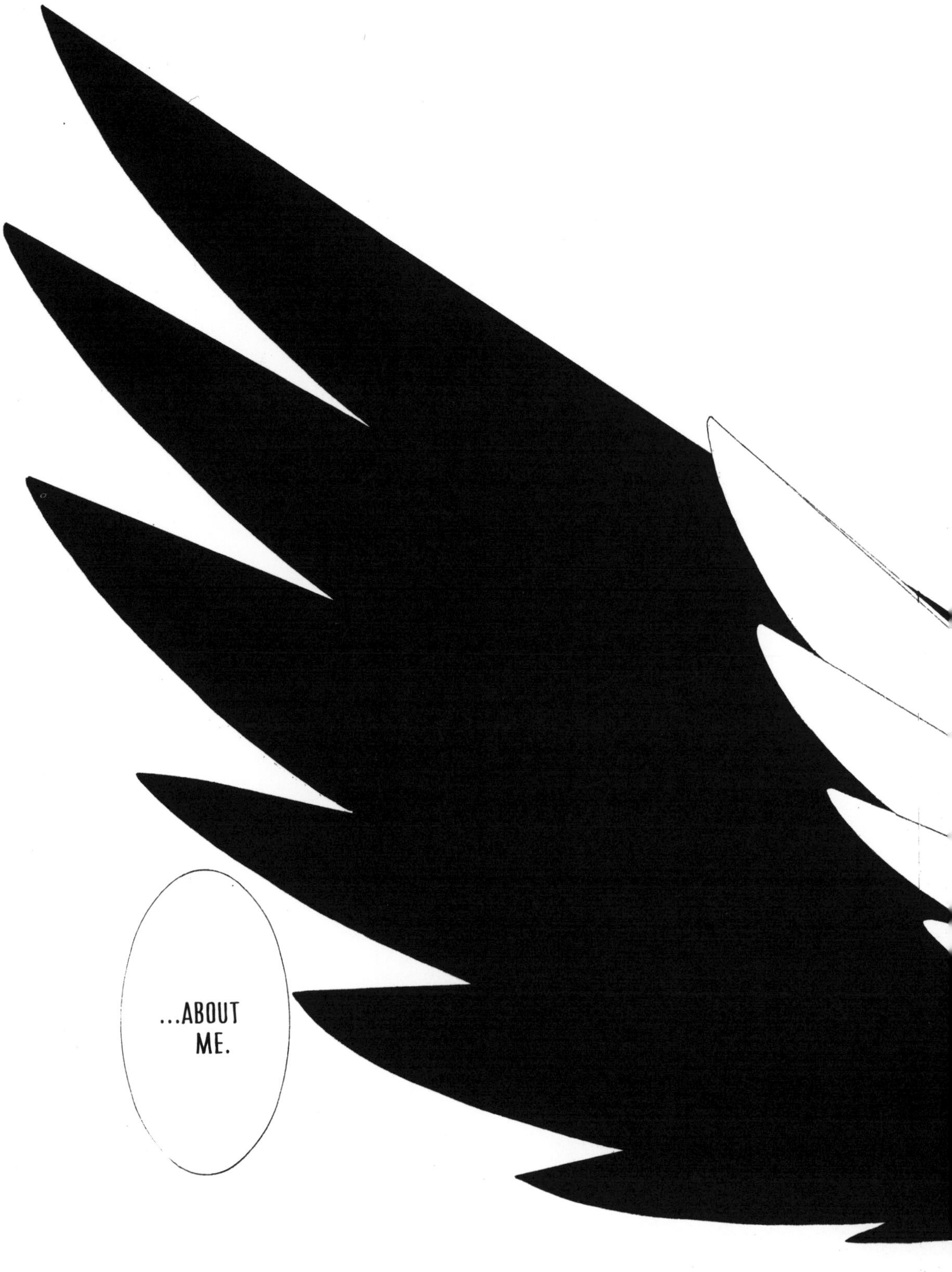
...ABOUT ME.

ABOUT ME 『わたしのこと』

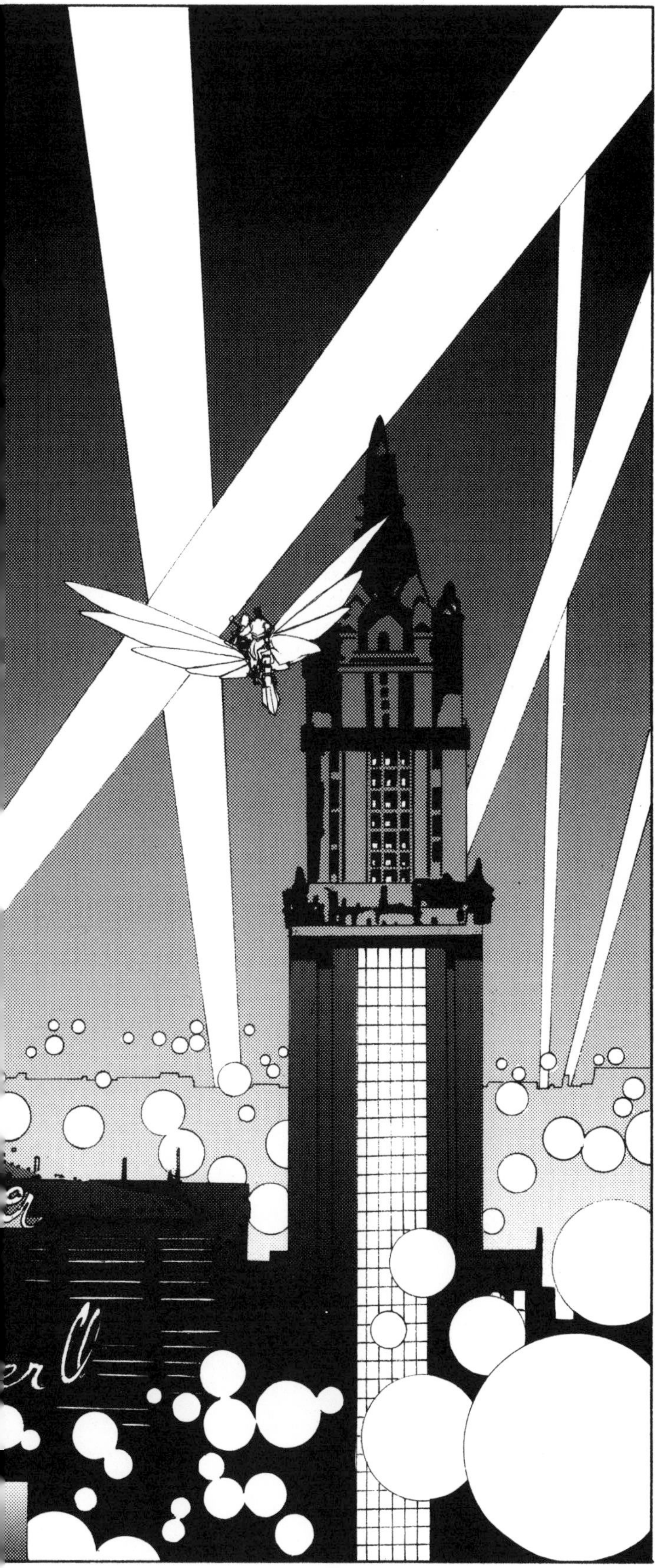

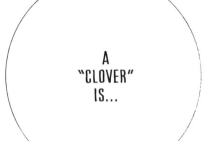

A
"CLOVER"
IS...

...A CHILD WHO
CAN USE MAGIC.

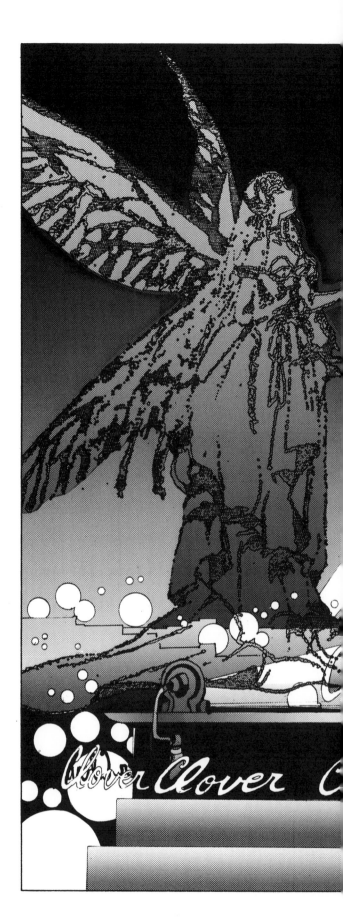

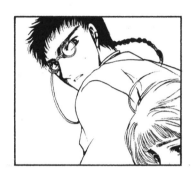

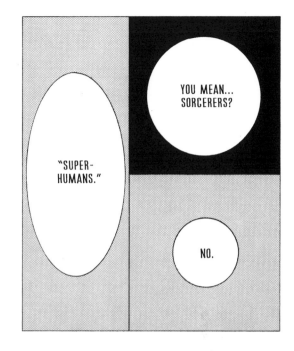

"SUPER-HUMANS."

YOU MEAN... SORCERERS?

NO.

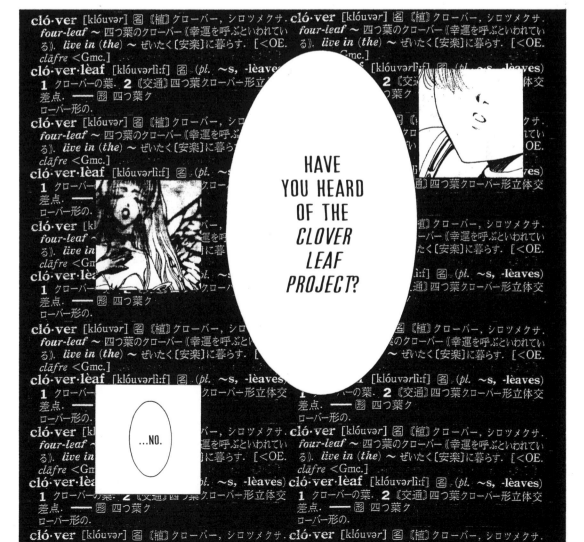

HAVE YOU HEARD OF THE *CLOVER LEAF PROJECT?*

...NO.

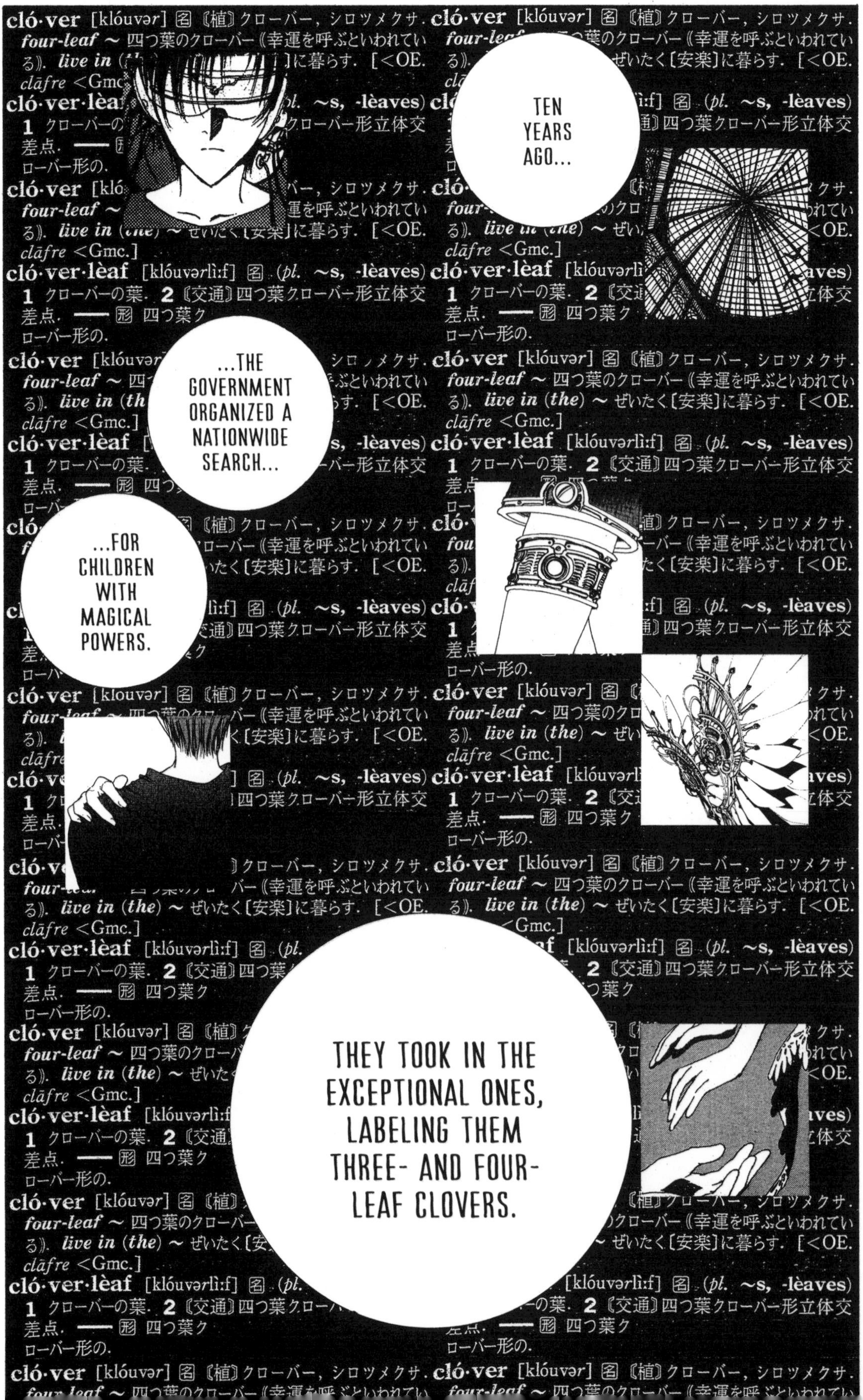
TEN YEARS AGO...
...THE GOVERNMENT ORGANIZED A NATIONWIDE SEARCH...
...FOR CHILDREN WITH MAGICAL POWERS.
THEY TOOK IN THE EXCEPTIONAL ONES, LABELING THEM THREE- AND FOUR-LEAF CLOVERS.

I BET THE ARMY WAS INVOLVED, TOO.
HOW MANY DID THEY FIND?

THERE WERE THREE THREE-LEAFS AT FIRST.
ONE DIED, SO THERE ARE TWO LEFT.

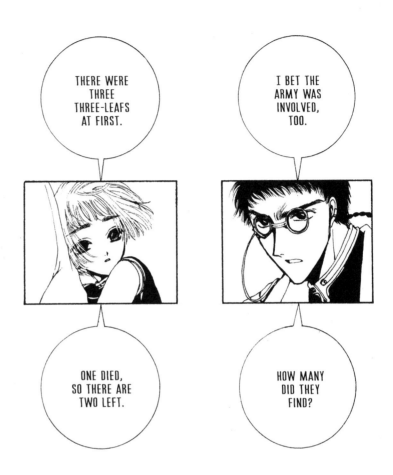

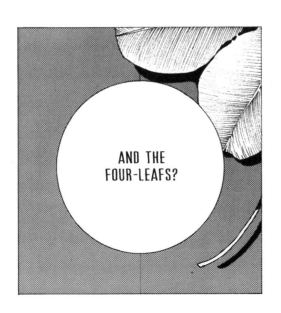

AND THE FOUR-LEAFS?

JUST
ME.

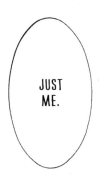

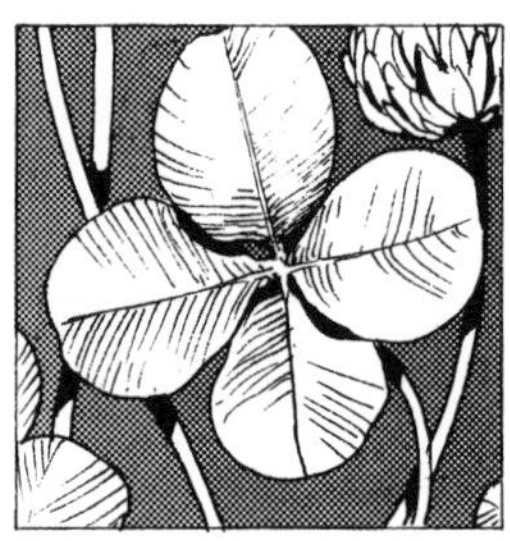

THEY TOLD
ME THAT'S
WHY I HAD
TO BE
ALONE.

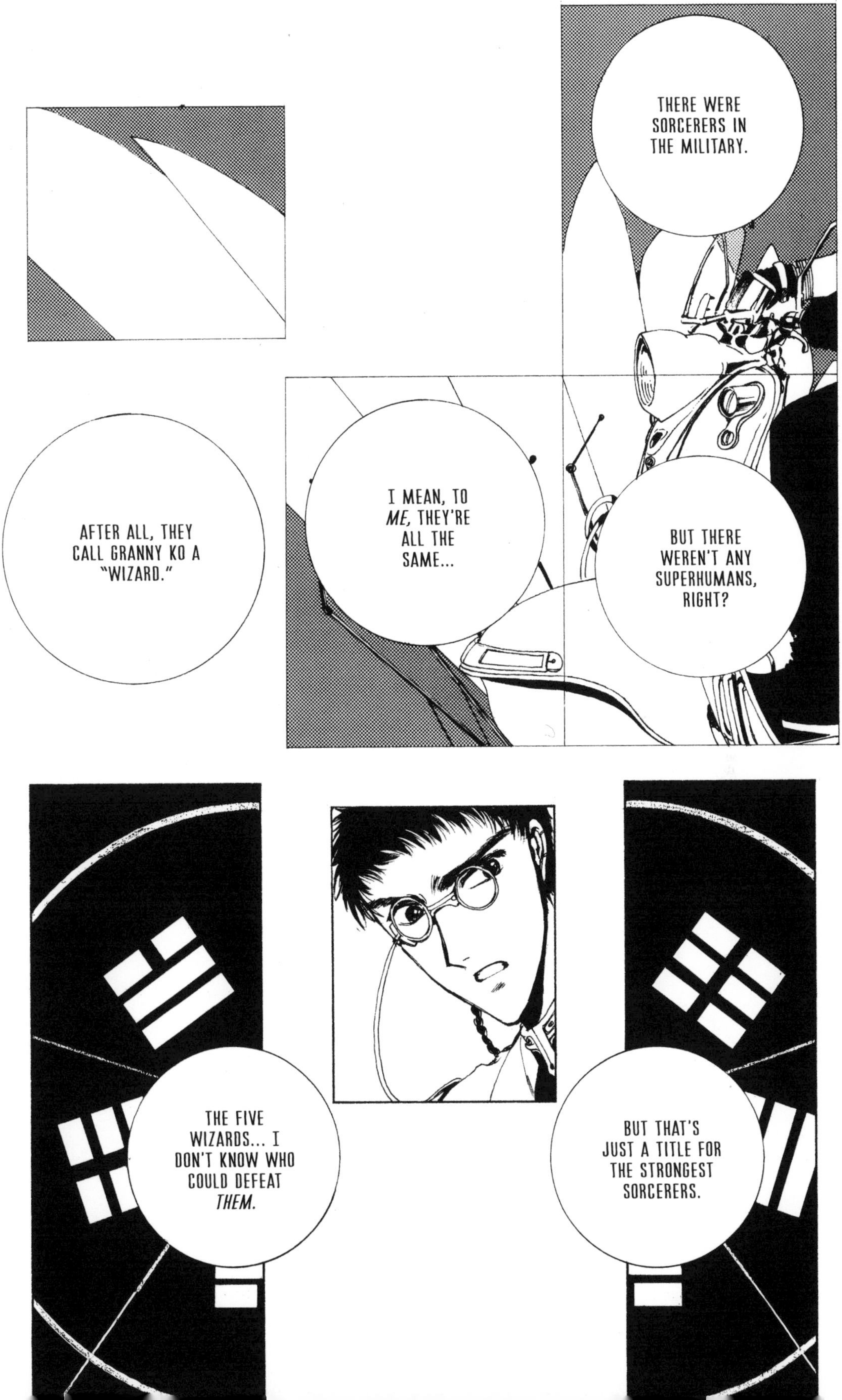
THERE WERE SORCERERS IN THE MILITARY.
BUT THERE WEREN'T ANY SUPERHUMANS, RIGHT?
I MEAN, TO *ME,* THEY'RE ALL THE SAME...
AFTER ALL, THEY CALL GRANNY KO A "WIZARD."
BUT THAT'S JUST A TITLE FOR THE STRONGEST SORCERERS.
THE FIVE WIZARDS... I DON'T KNOW WHO COULD DEFEAT *THEM.*

IT WOULD TAKE ALL FIVE TO EVEN HOPE TO WIN AGAINST A THREE-LEAF CLOVER.

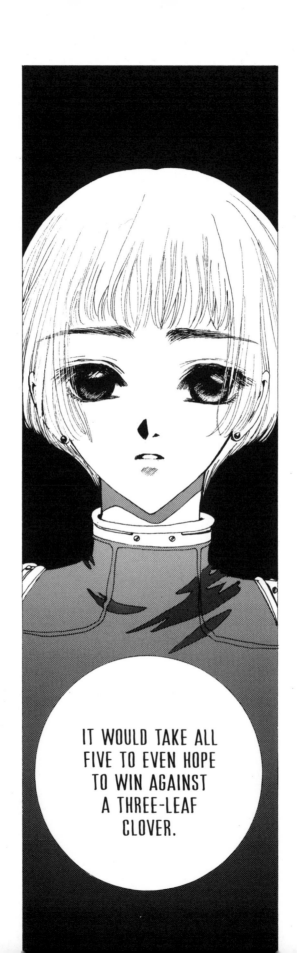

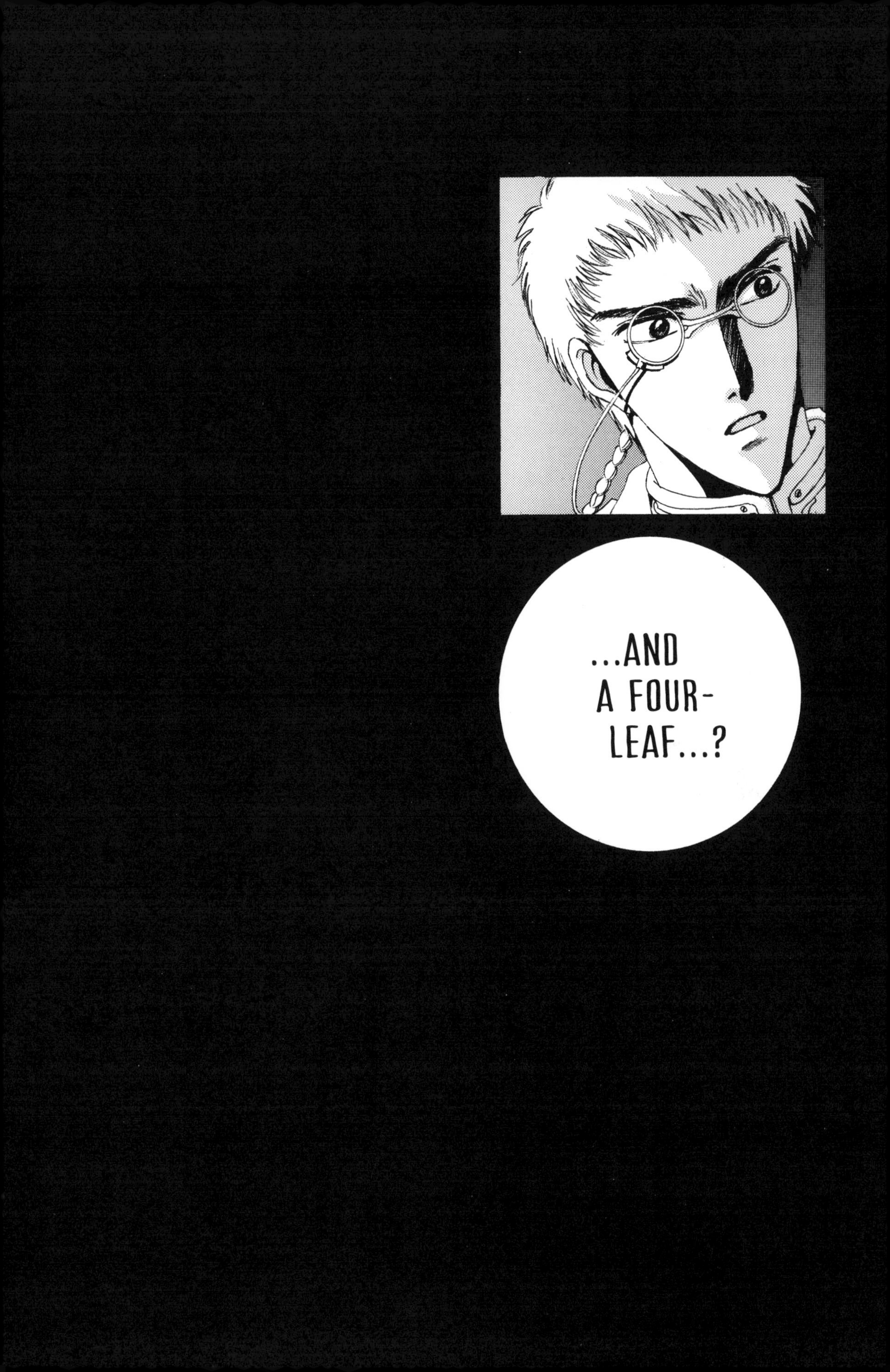
...AND A FOUR-LEAF...?

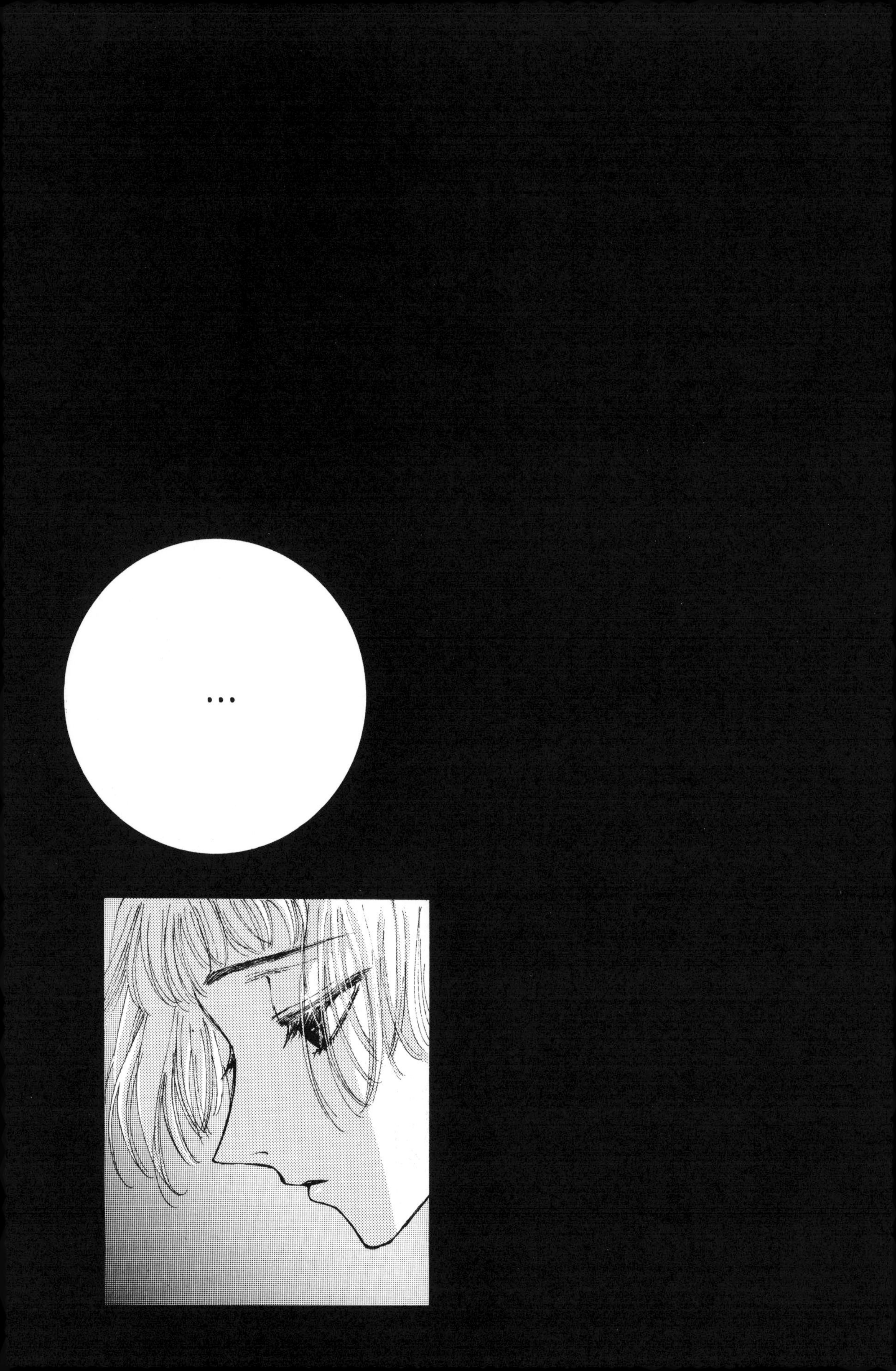
...

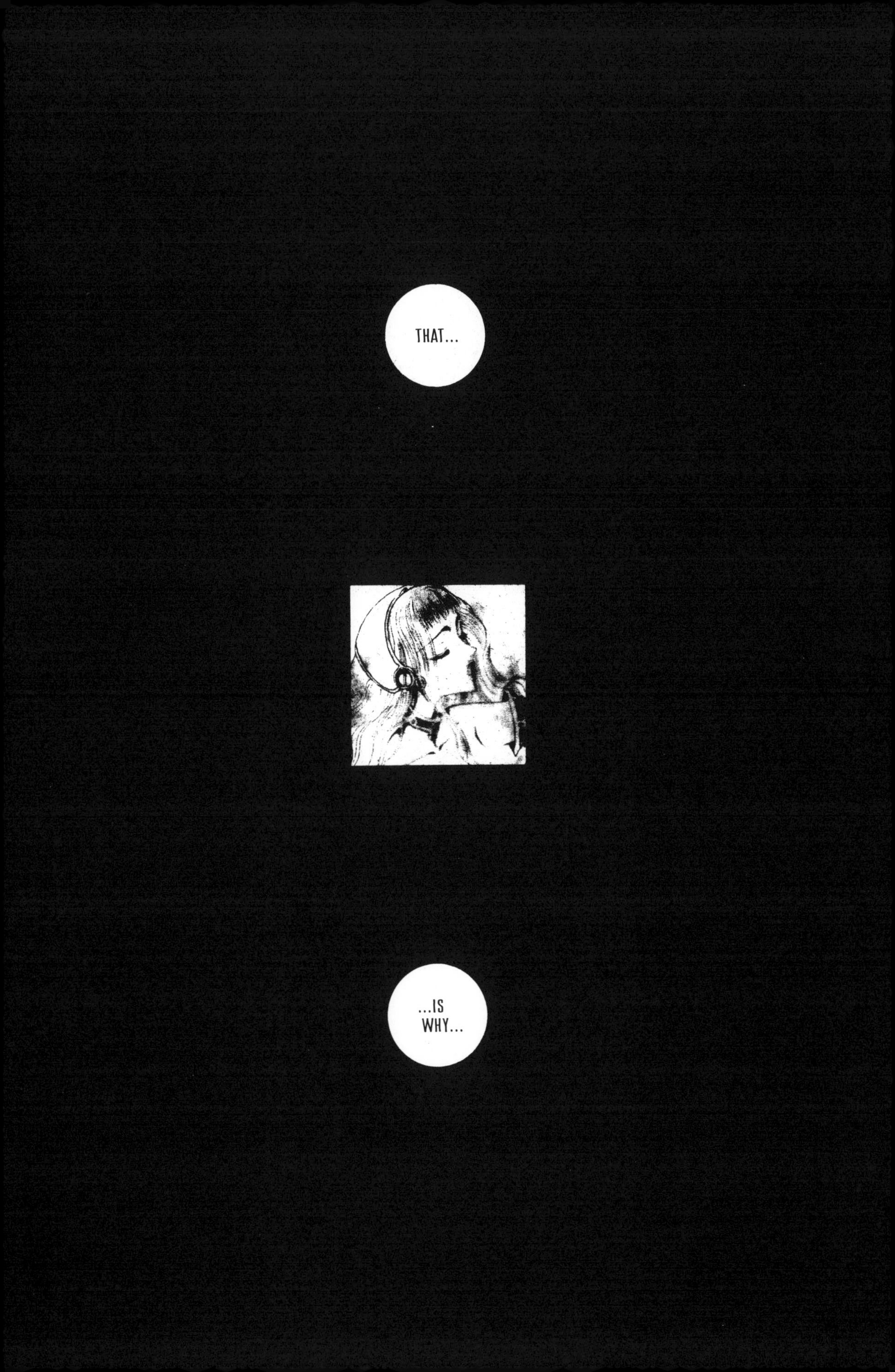
THAT...
...IS WHY...

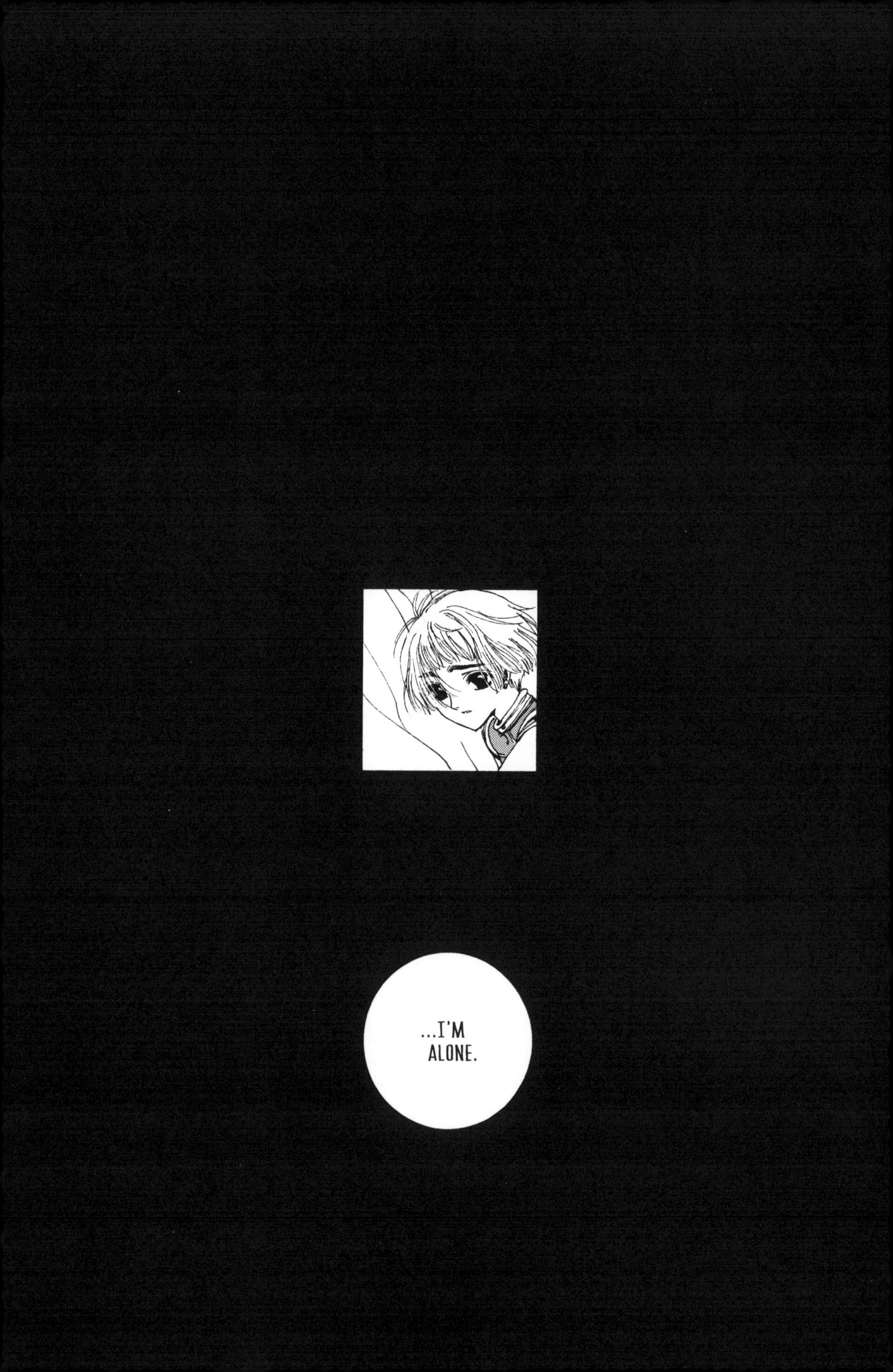
...I'M ALONE.

MEMORY

『記憶』

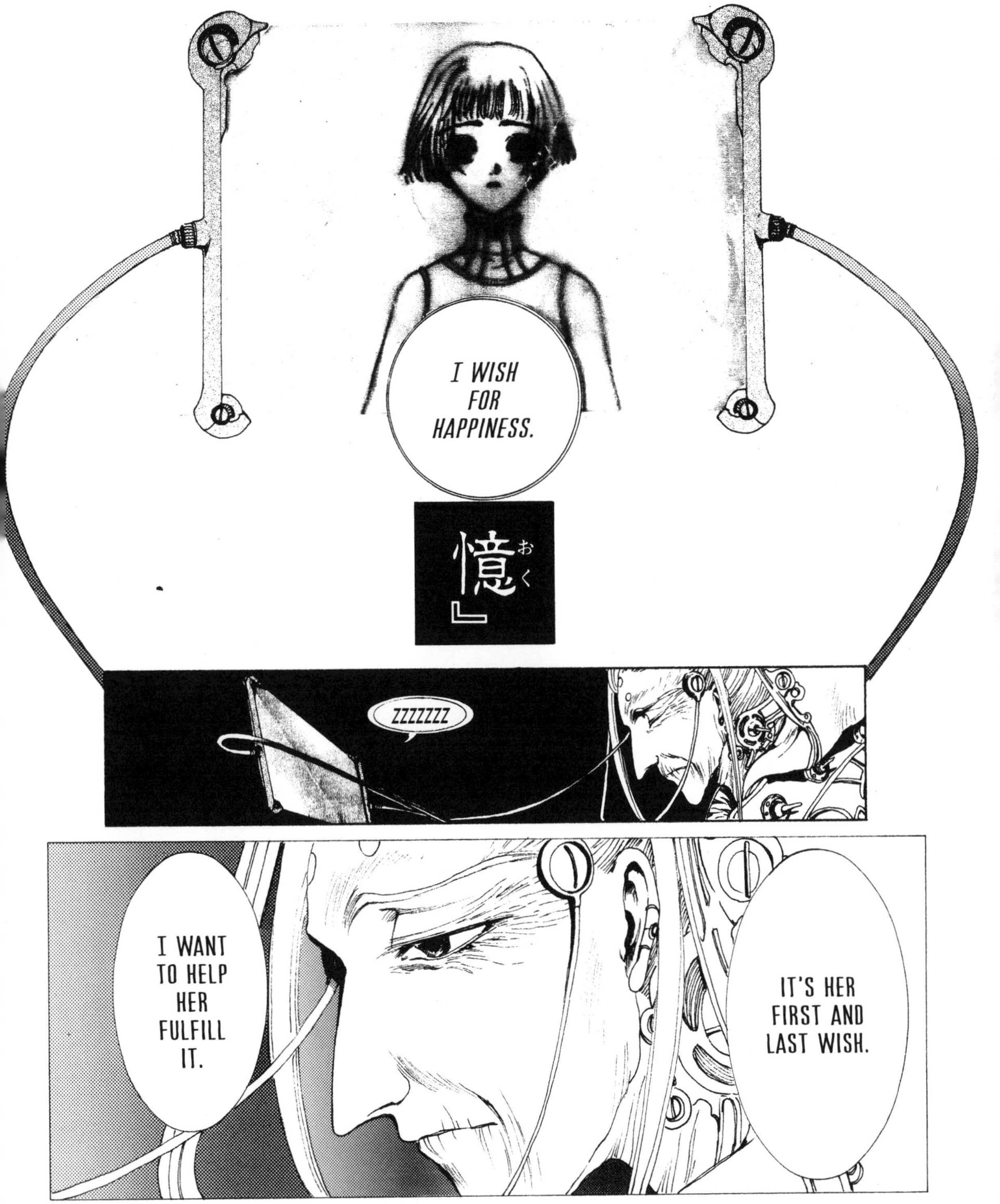

I WISH FOR HAPPINESS.
ZZZZZZZ
IT'S HER FIRST AND LAST WISH.
I WANT TO HELP HER FULFILL IT.

『移動装置』

VEHICLE

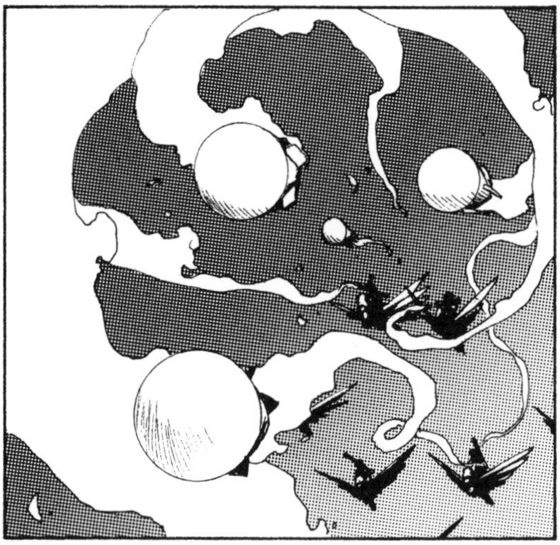

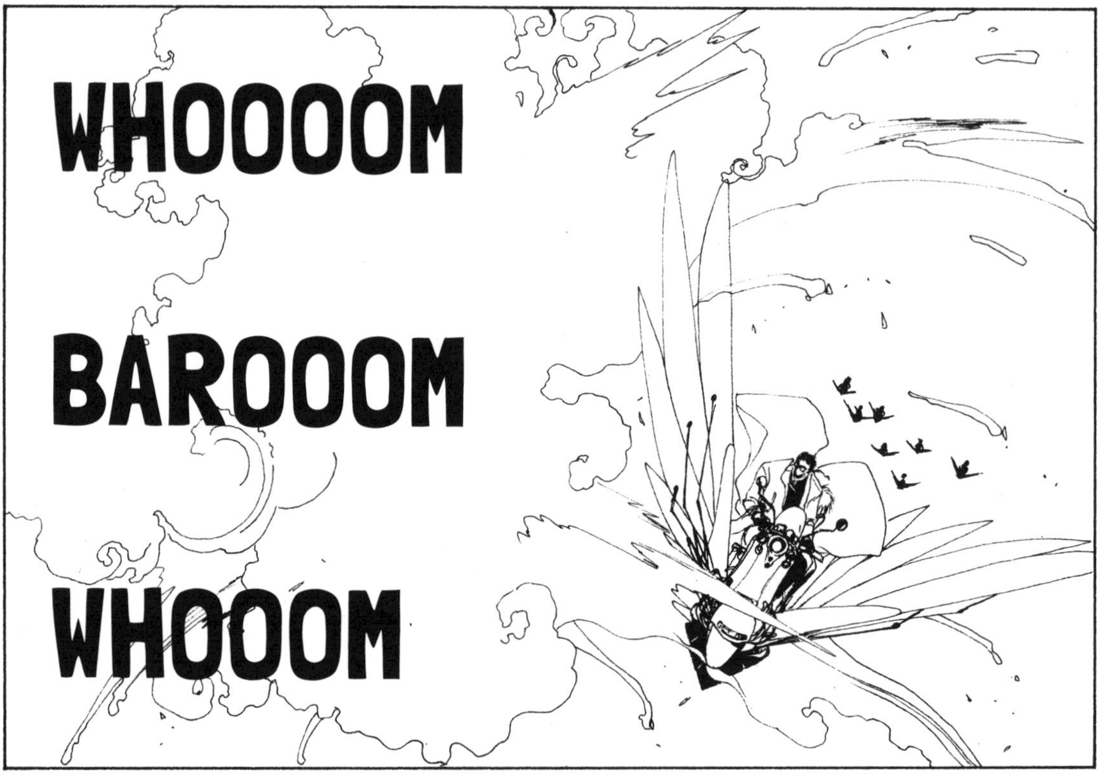
WHOOOOM
BAROOOM
WHOOOM

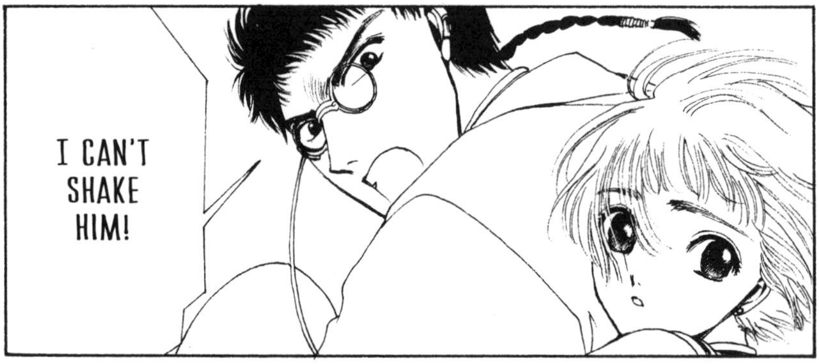
I CAN'T SHAKE HIM!

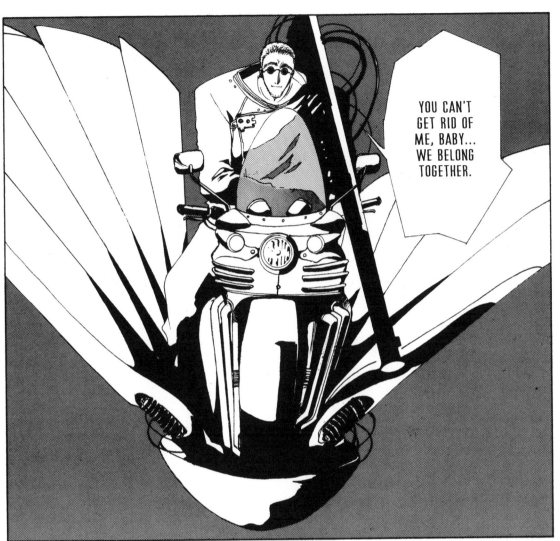

YOU CAN'T GET RID OF ME, BABY... WE BELONG TOGETHER.

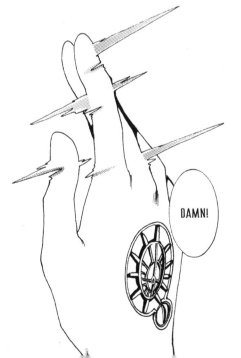

DAMN!

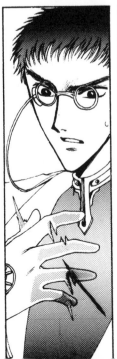

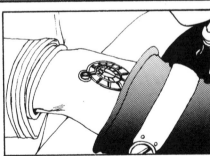

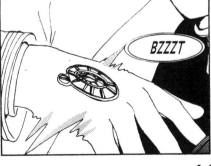

BZZZT

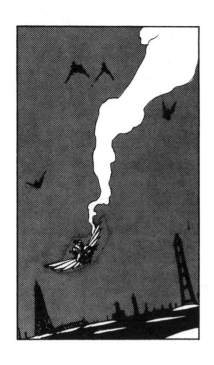

BOOOOM

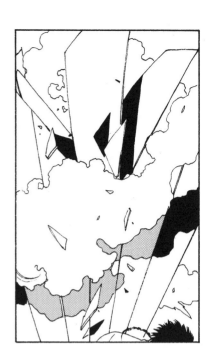

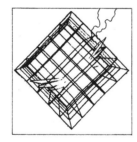

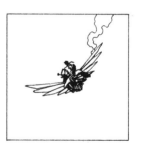

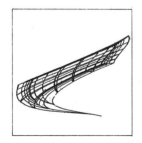

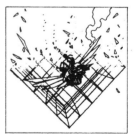

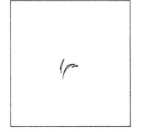

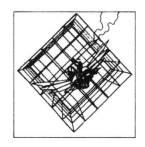

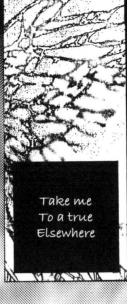

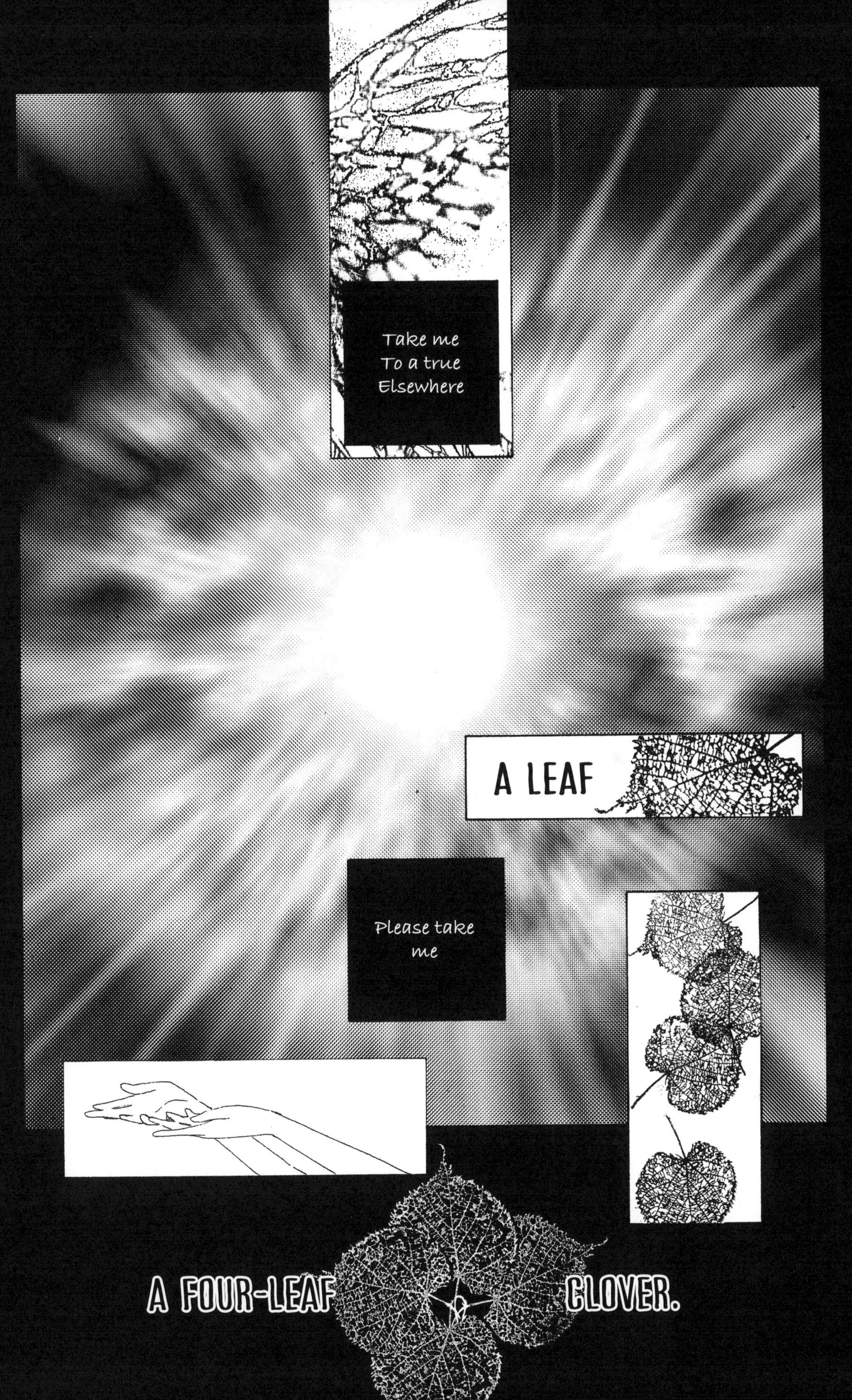

Take me
To a true
Elsewhere

A LEAF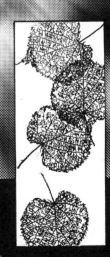

Please take
me

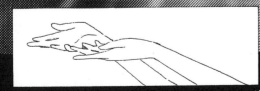

A FOUR-LEAF CLOVER.

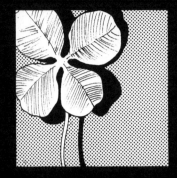

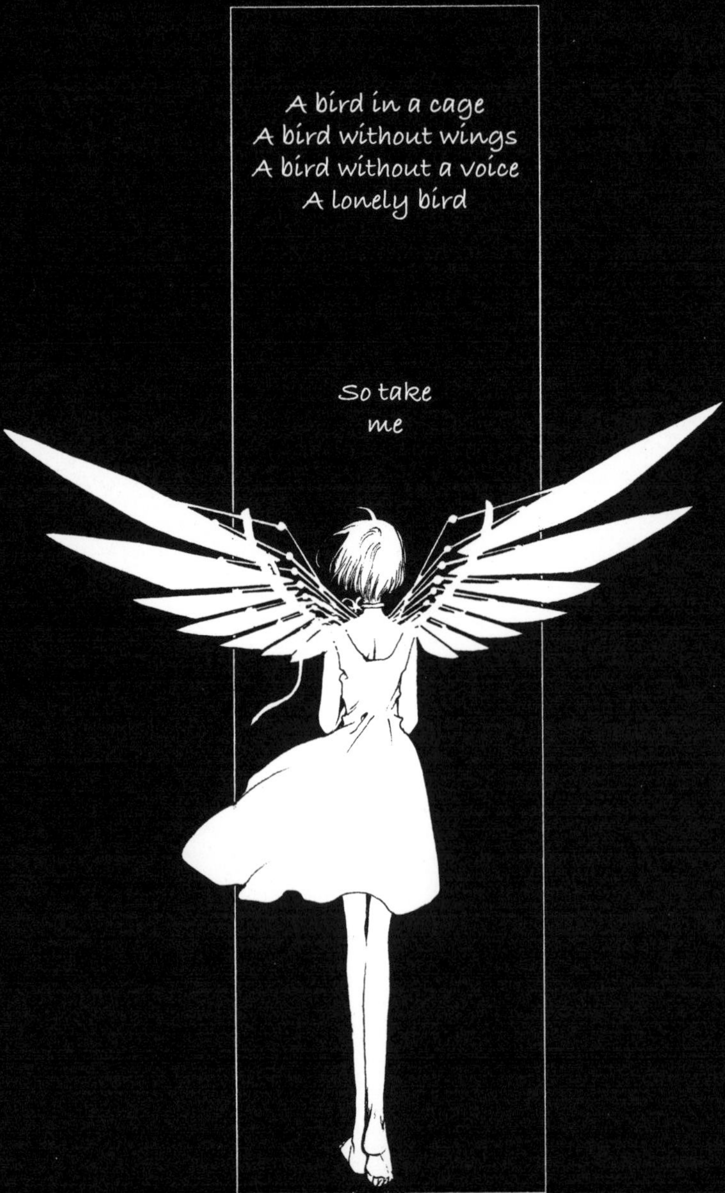

A bird in a cage
A bird without wings
A bird without a voice
A lonely bird

So take
me

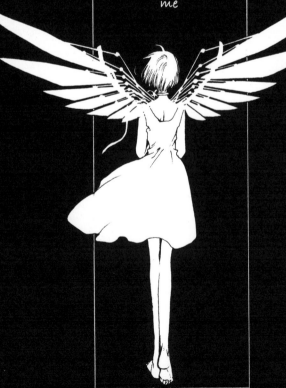

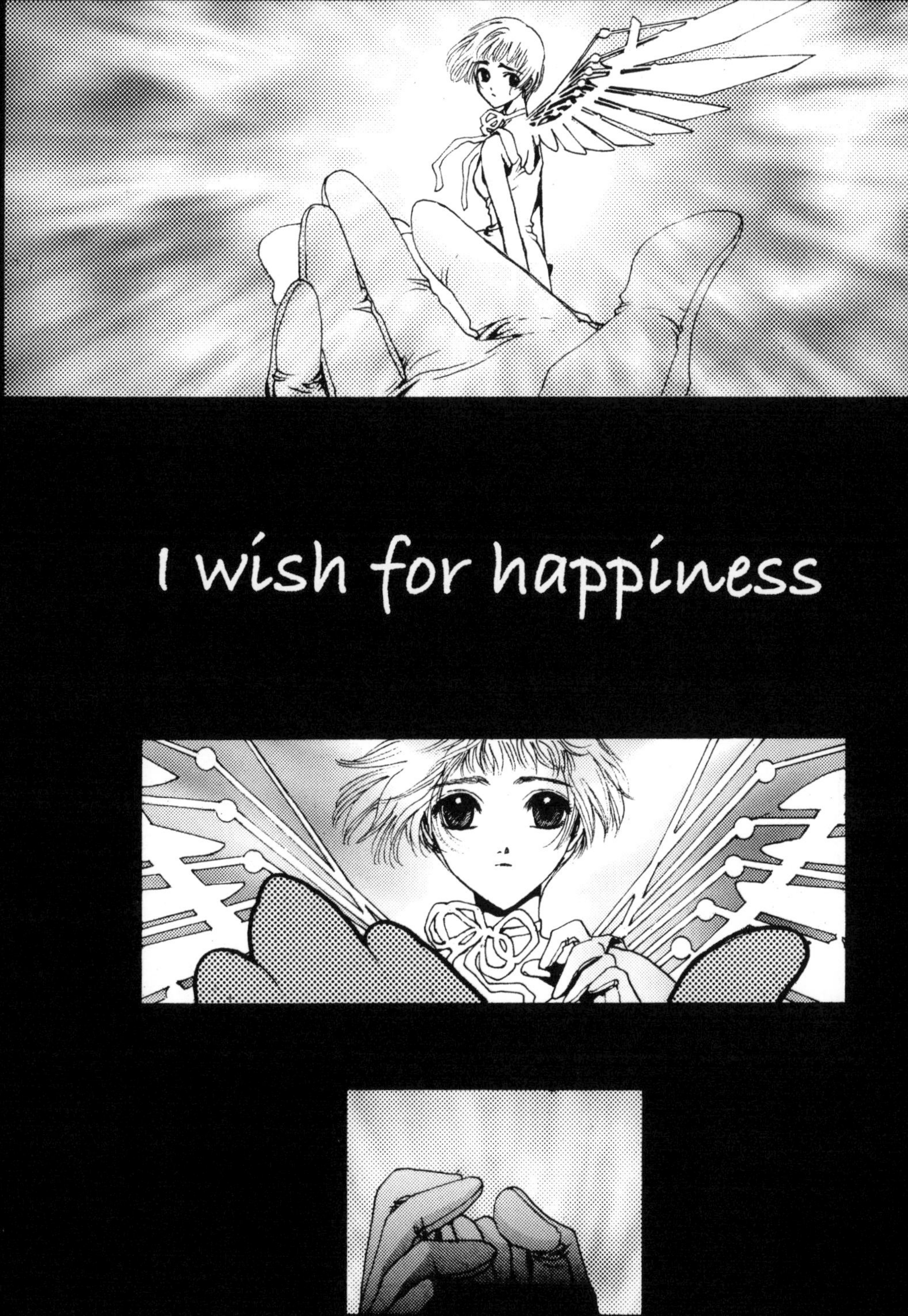
I wish for happiness

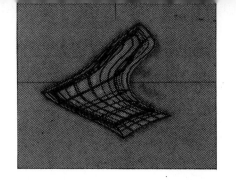

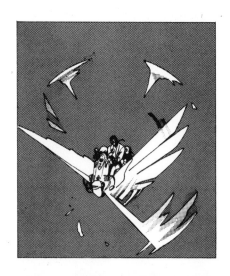

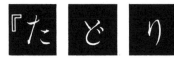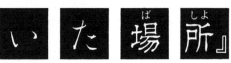

『たどりついた場所』
LANDING SITE

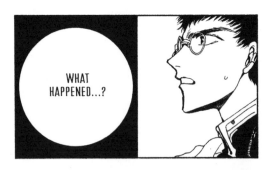

WHAT
HAPPENED...?

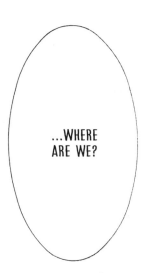

...WHERE
ARE WE?

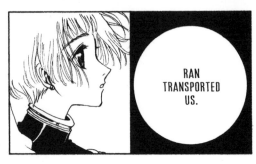

RAN
TRANSPORTED
US.

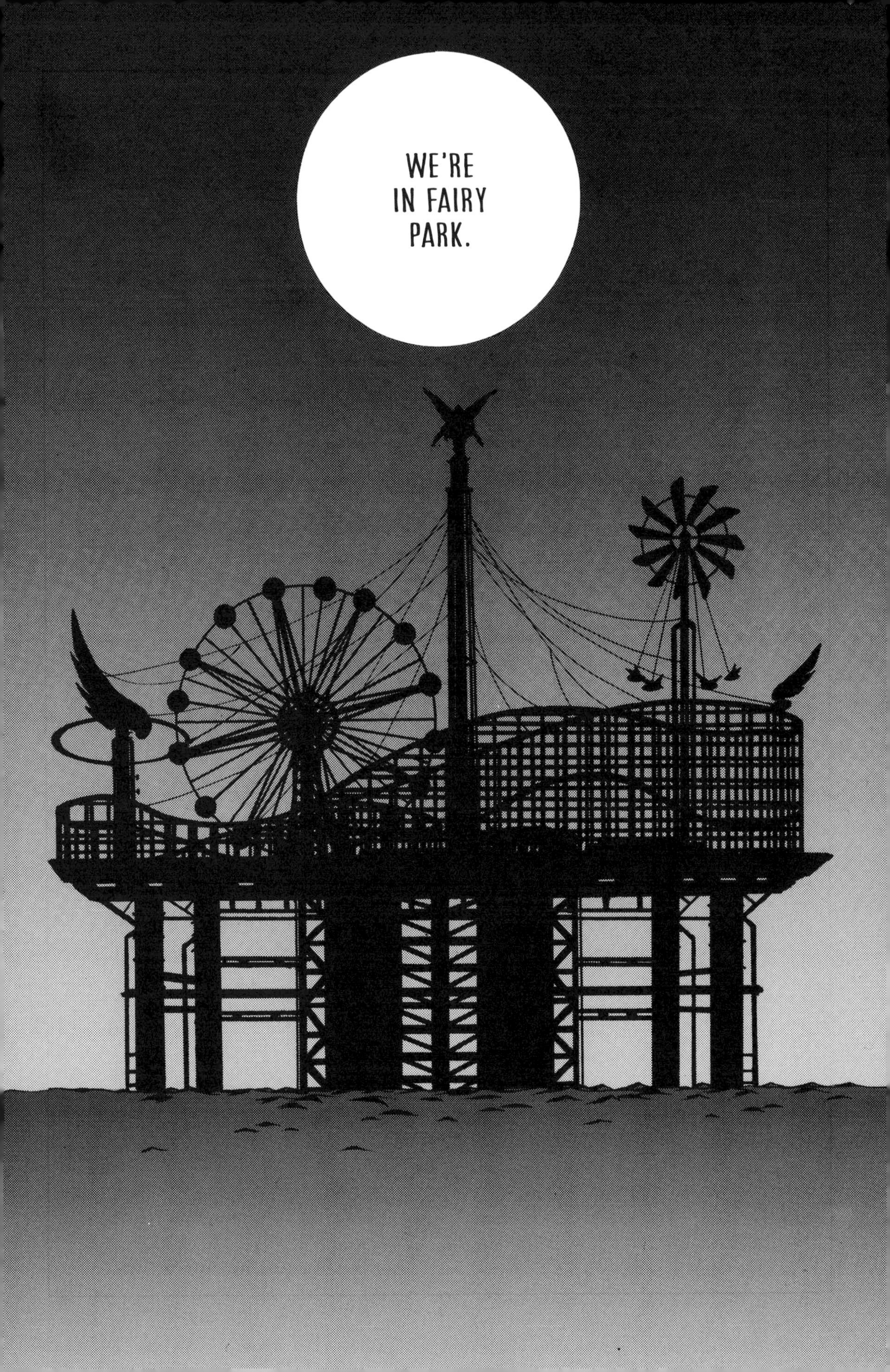
WE'RE IN FAIRY PARK.

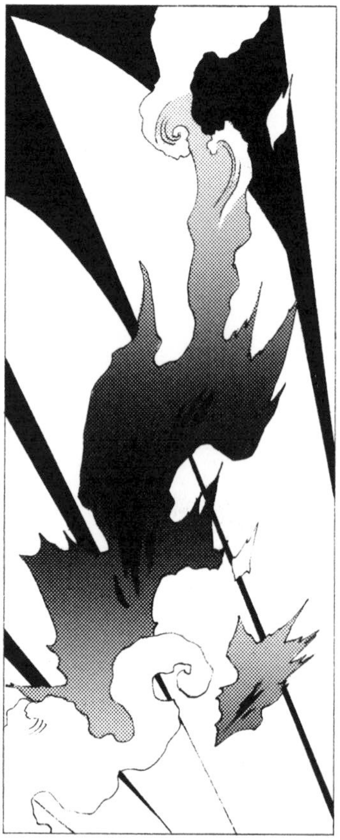
WHMMP

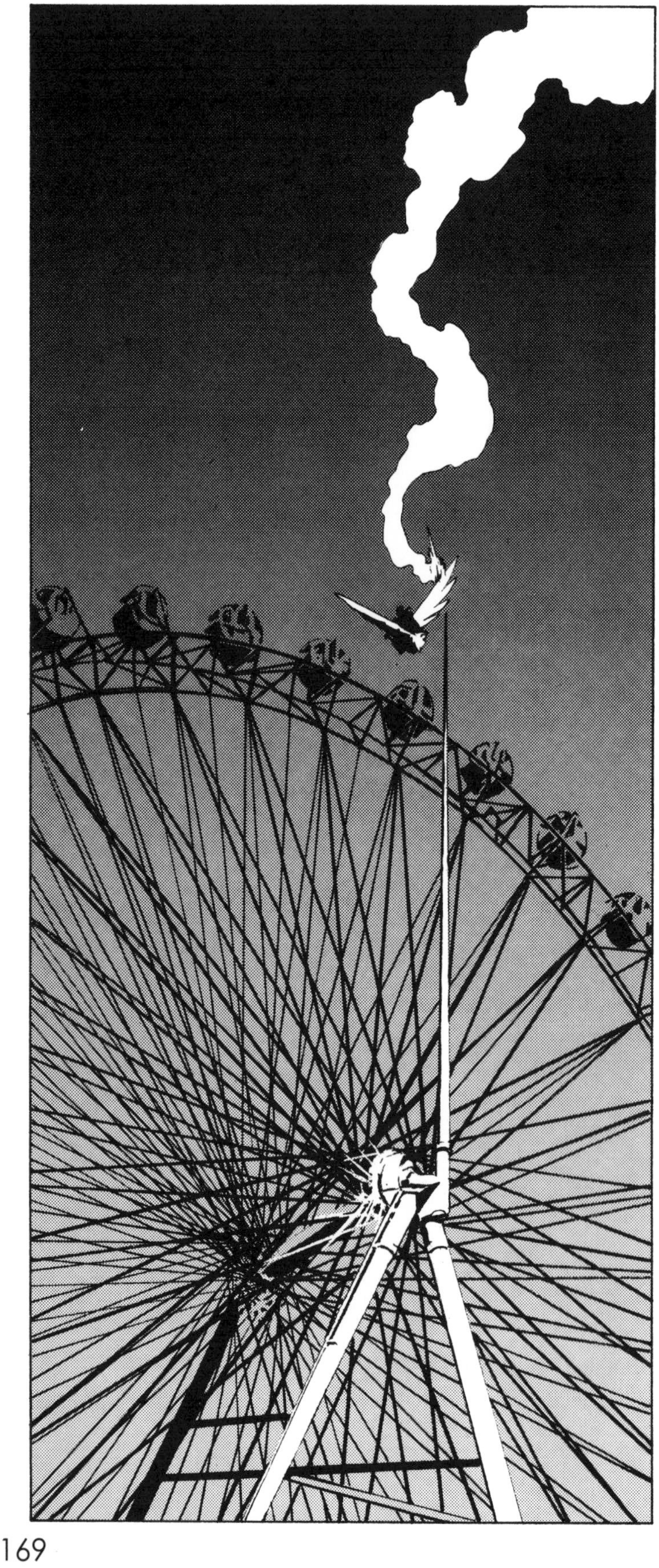

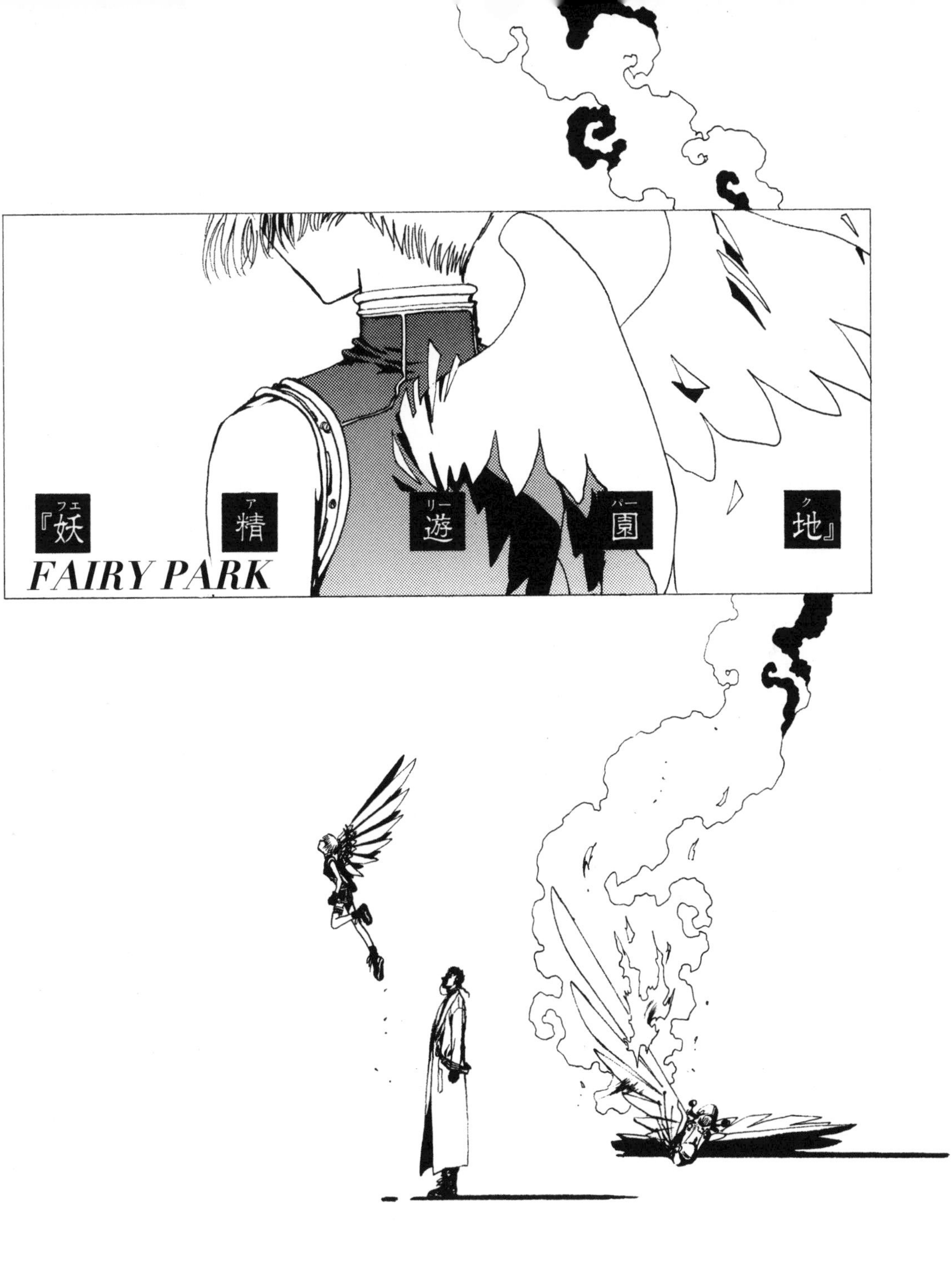
『妖精遊園地』
フェアリーパーク
FAIRY PARK
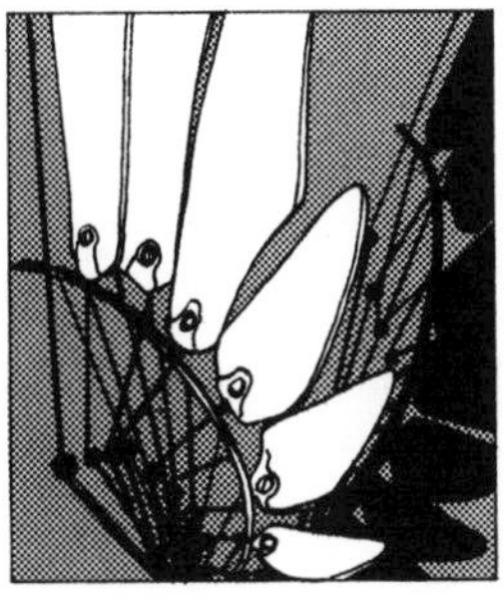

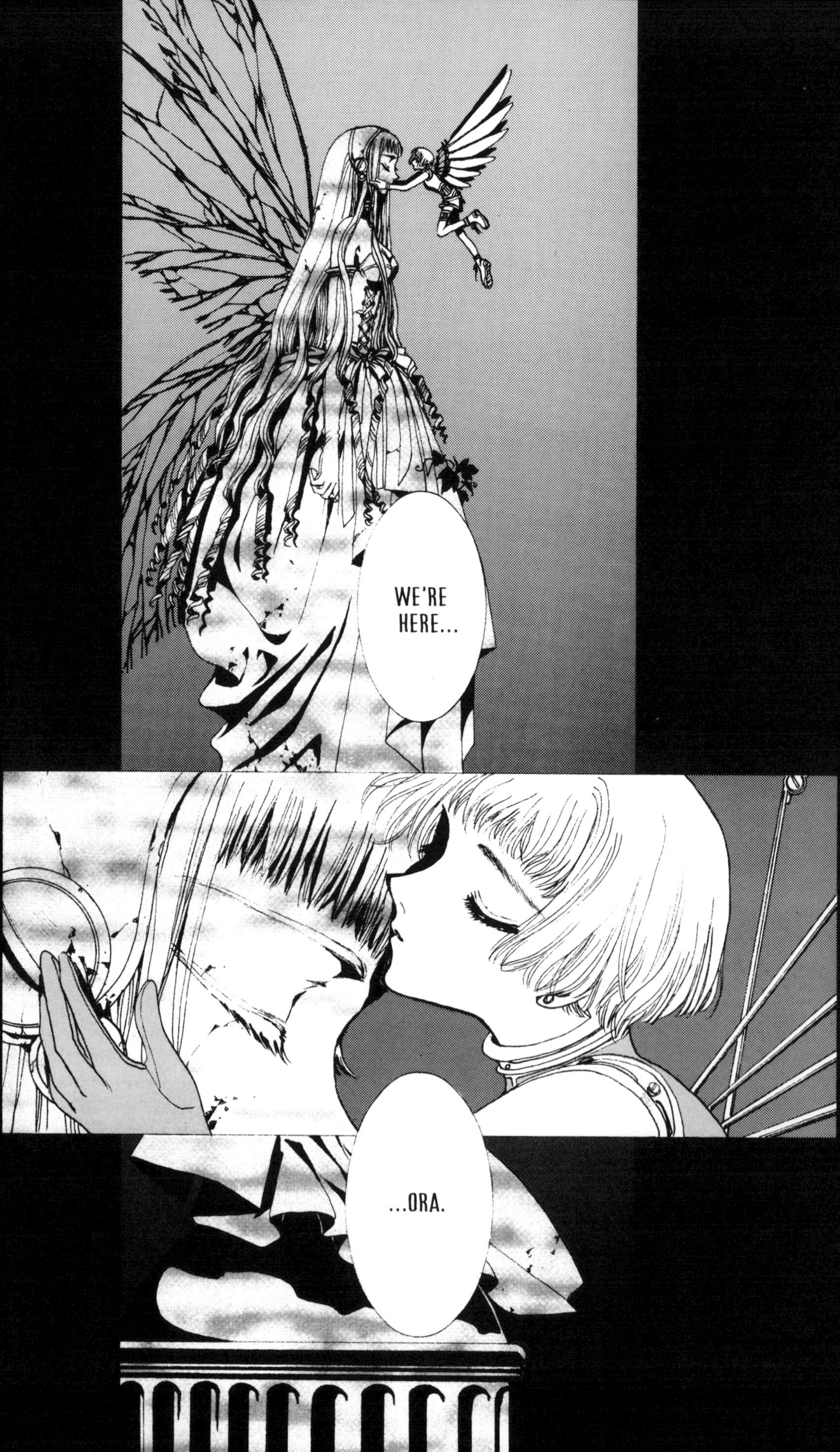
WE'RE HERE...
...ORA.

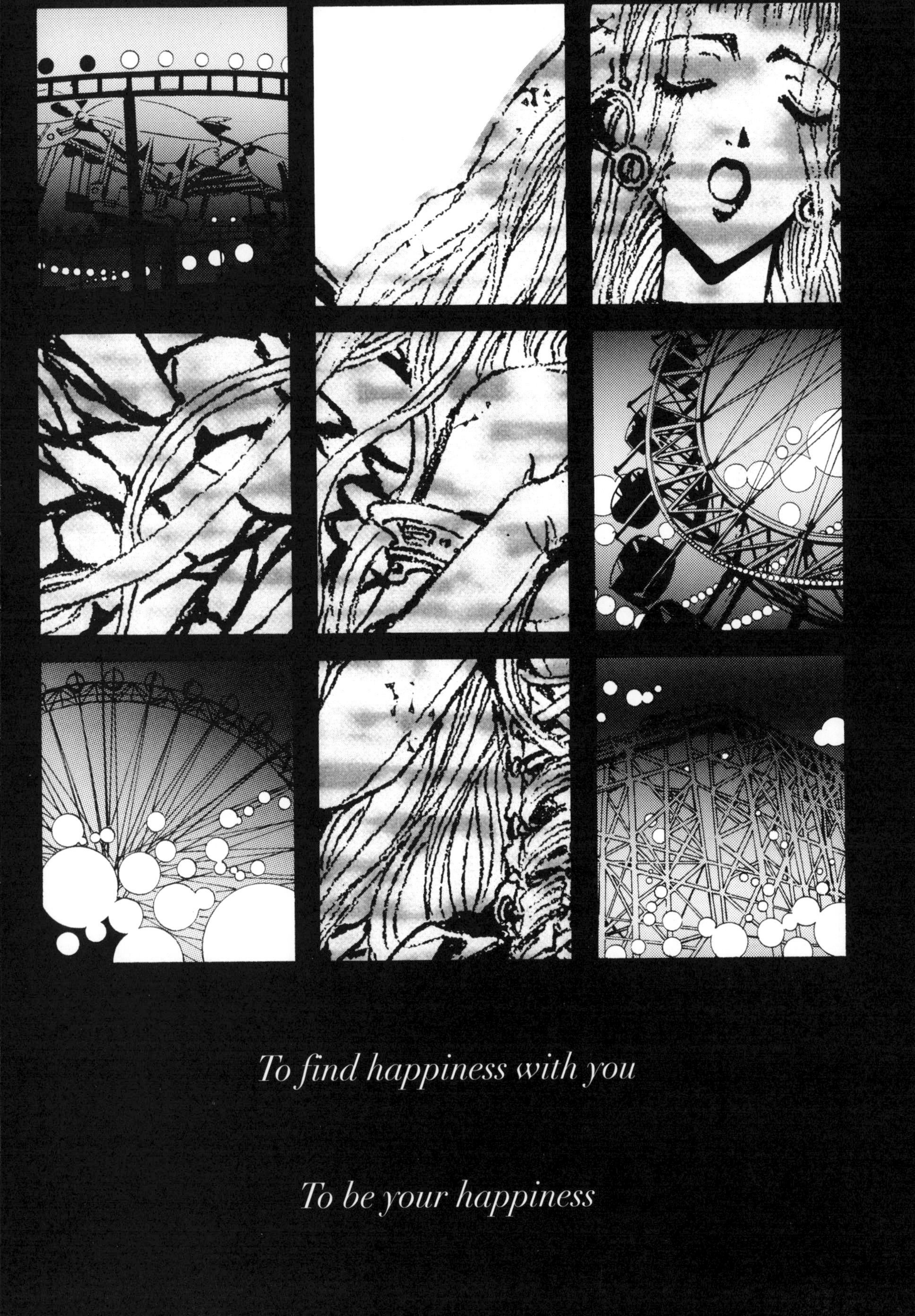

To find happiness with you

To be your happiness

*I'm happy just to
be with you*

Happy just to see your smile

So take me

*To a true
Elsewhere*

Take me away

I seek happiness

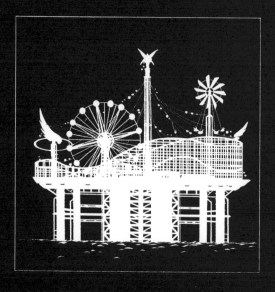

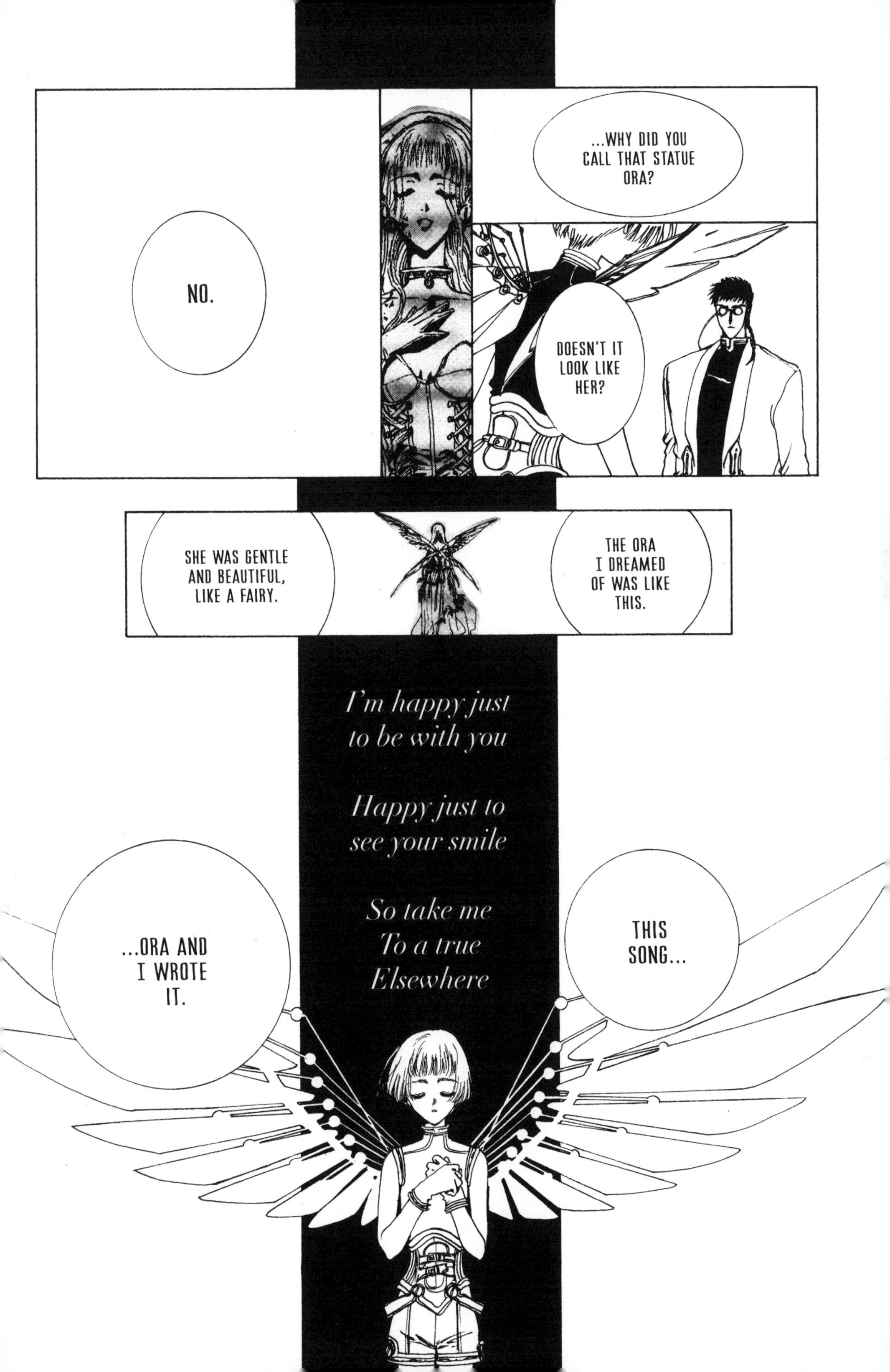
...WHY DID YOU CALL THAT STATUE ORA?
DOESN'T IT LOOK LIKE HER?
NO.
THE ORA I DREAMED OF WAS LIKE THIS.
SHE WAS GENTLE AND BEAUTIFUL, LIKE A FAIRY.
I'm happy just to be with you
Happy just to see your smile
So take me To a true Elsewhere
THIS SONG...
...ORA AND I WROTE IT.

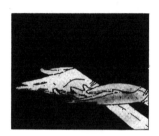

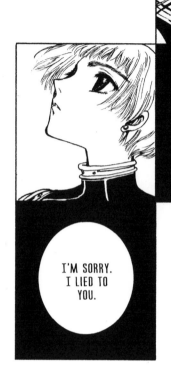

WHAT ARE YOU TALKING ABOUT...?
I'M SORRY. I LIED TO YOU.

I KNEW ORA. I SPOKE WITH HER.

I HEARD HER VOICE, FROM FAR AWAY.

I HEARD HER SINGING IN CONCERT, HER BEAUTIFUL VOICE.

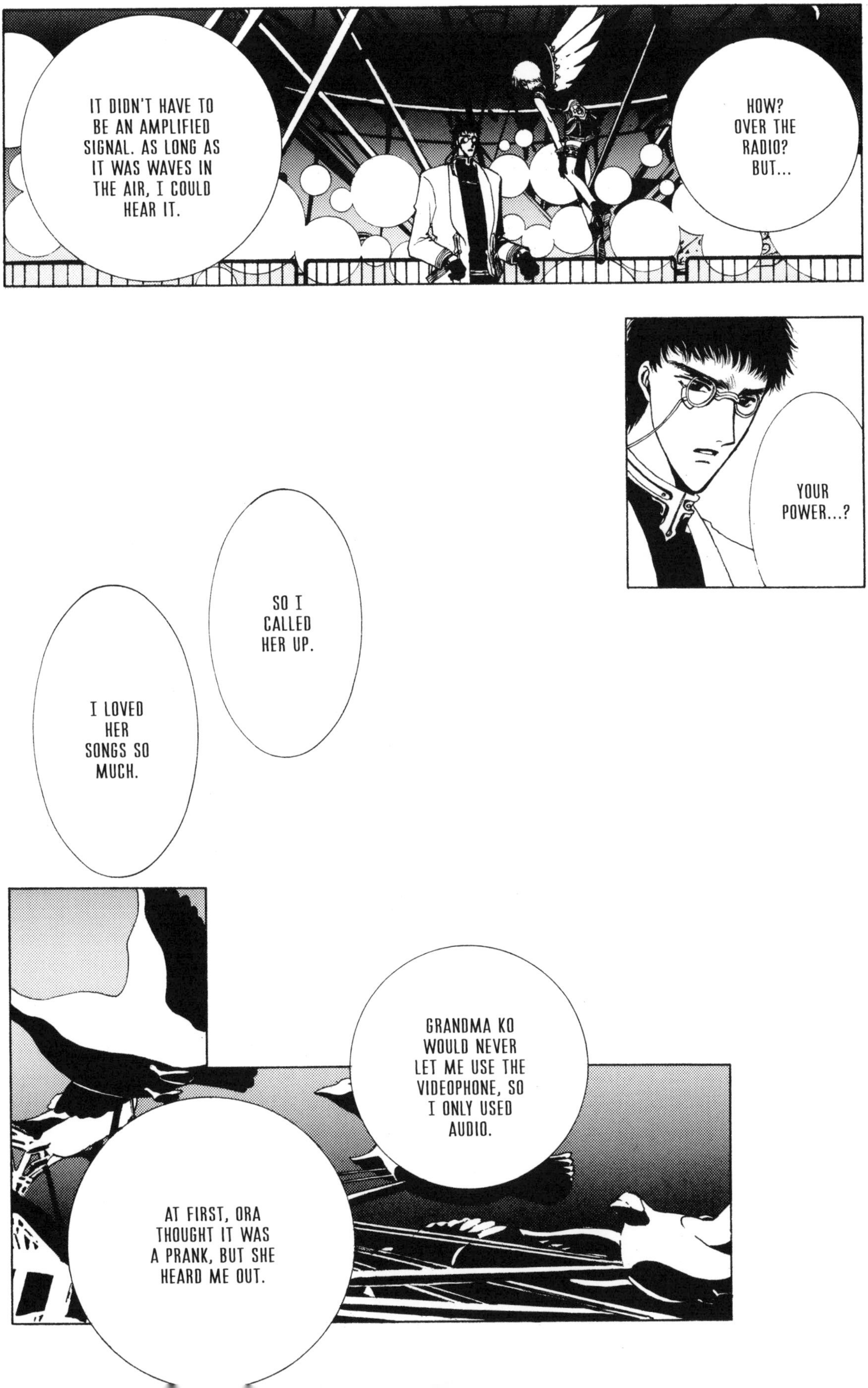

HOW? OVER THE RADIO? BUT...
IT DIDN'T HAVE TO BE AN AMPLIFIED SIGNAL. AS LONG AS IT WAS WAVES IN THE AIR, I COULD HEAR IT.
YOUR POWER...?
SO I CALLED HER UP.
I LOVED HER SONGS SO MUCH.
GRANDMA KO WOULD NEVER LET ME USE THE VIDEOPHONE, SO I ONLY USED AUDIO.
AT FIRST, ORA THOUGHT IT WAS A PRANK, BUT SHE HEARD ME OUT.

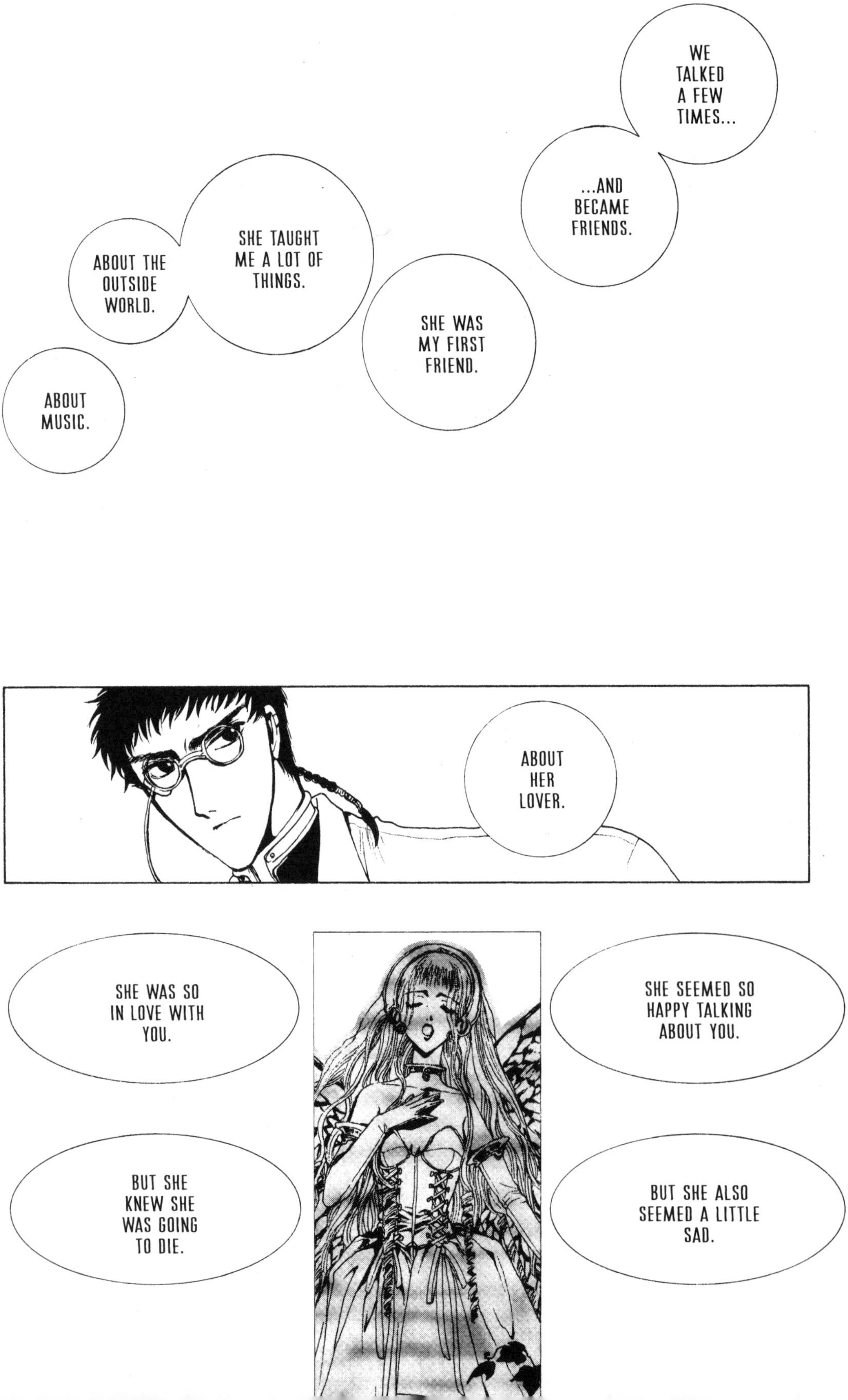
WE TALKED A FEW TIMES...
...AND BECAME FRIENDS.
SHE WAS MY FIRST FRIEND.
SHE TAUGHT ME A LOT OF THINGS.
ABOUT THE OUTSIDE WORLD.
ABOUT MUSIC.
ABOUT HER LOVER.
SHE SEEMED SO HAPPY TALKING ABOUT YOU.
SHE WAS SO IN LOVE WITH YOU.
BUT SHE ALSO SEEMED A LITTLE SAD.
BUT SHE KNEW SHE WAS GOING TO DIE.

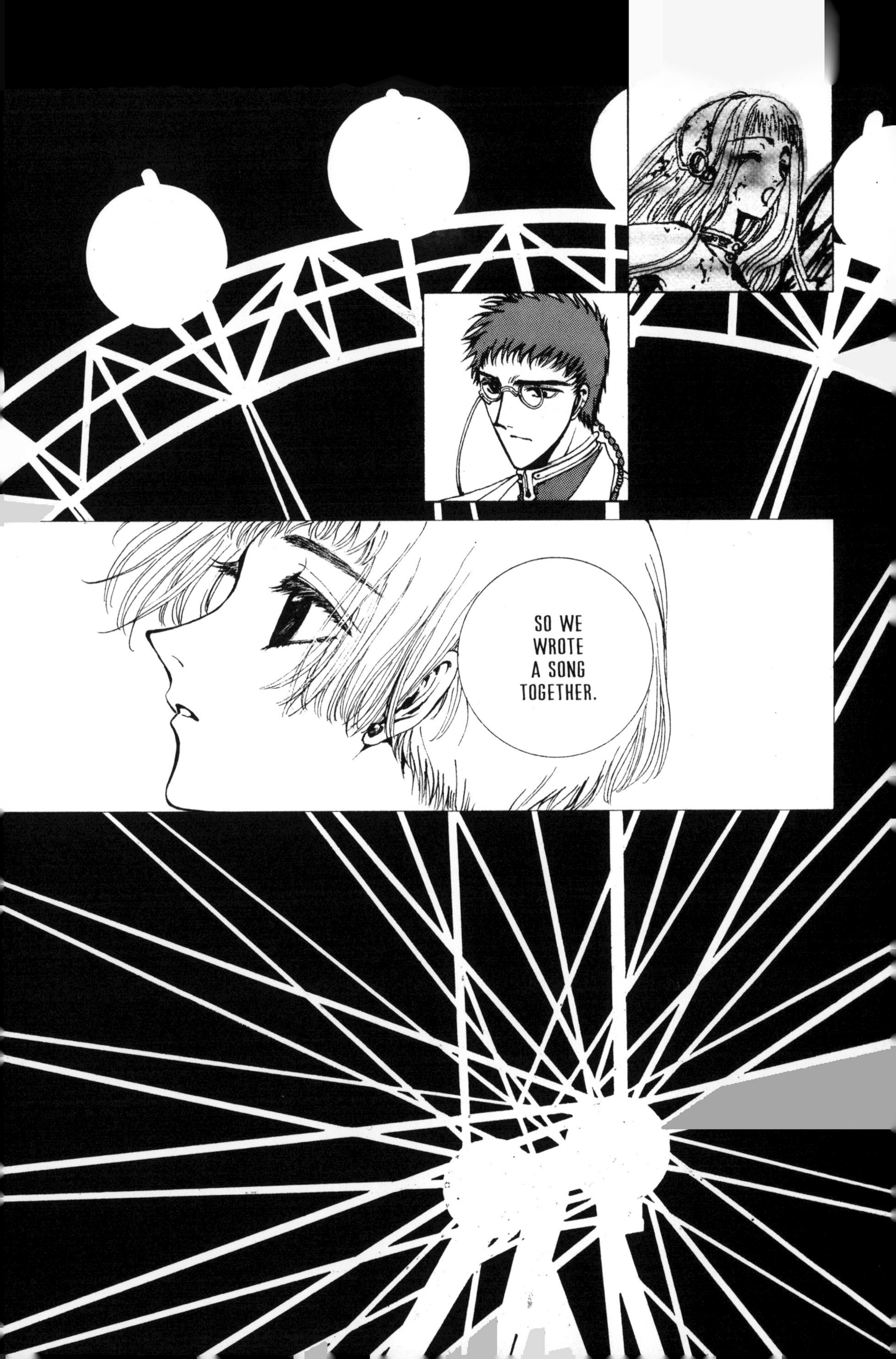
SO WE WROTE A SONG TOGETHER.

I'm happy just to be
with you

Happy just to see
your smile

So take me

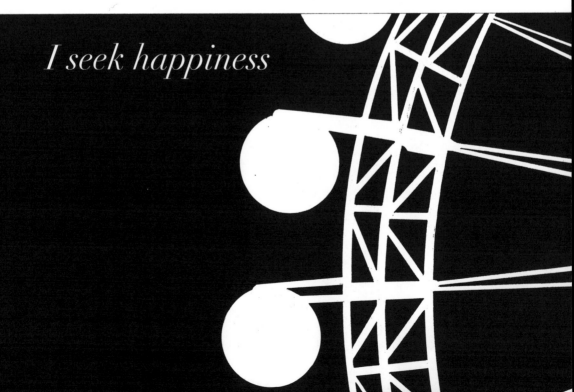

IT WAS CALLED
"CLOVER."

I seek happiness

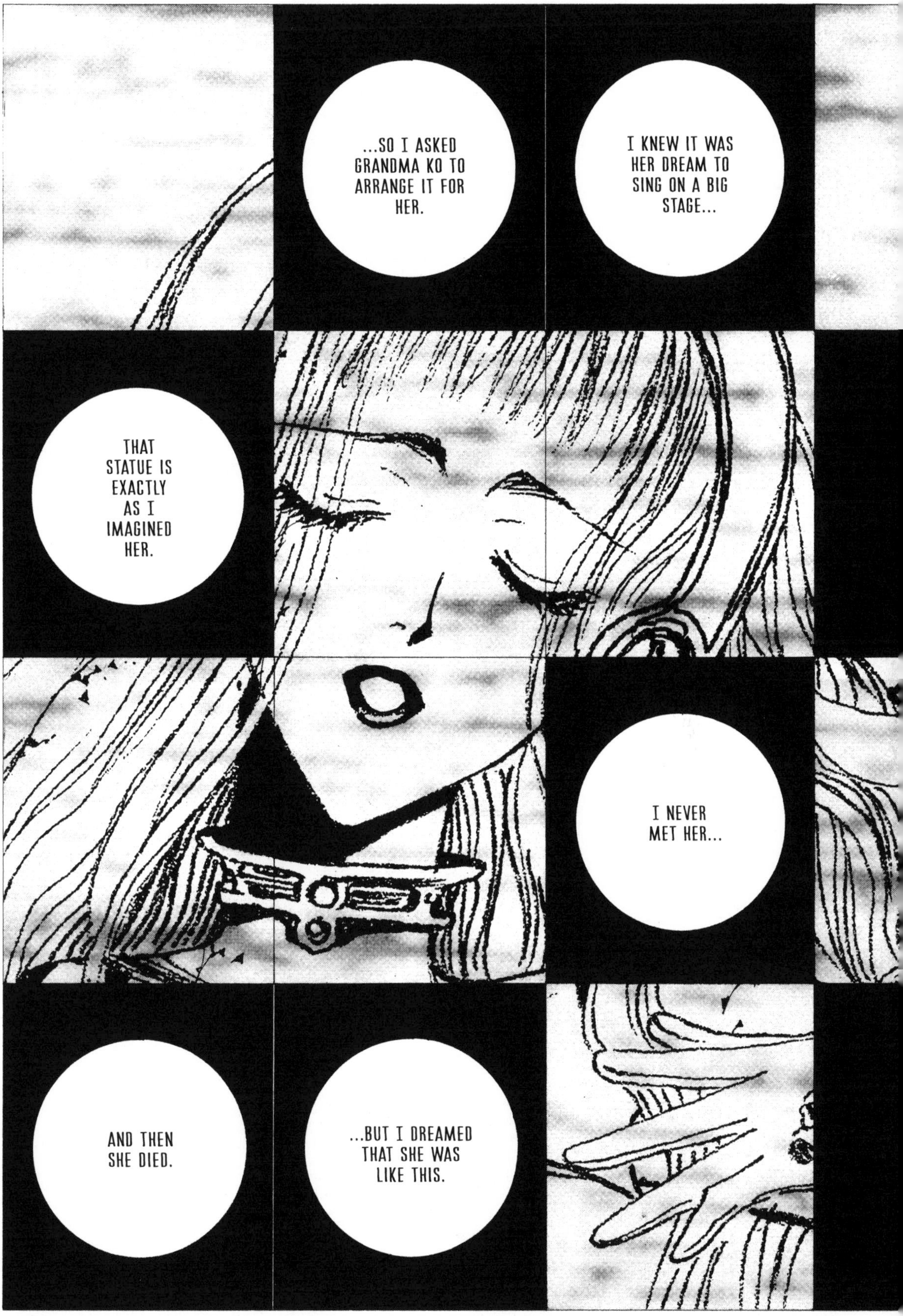
I KNEW IT WAS HER DREAM TO SING ON A BIG STAGE...
...SO I ASKED GRANDMA KO TO ARRANGE IT FOR HER.
THAT STATUE IS EXACTLY AS I IMAGINED HER.
I NEVER MET HER...
...BUT I DREAMED THAT SHE WAS LIKE THIS.
AND THEN SHE DIED.

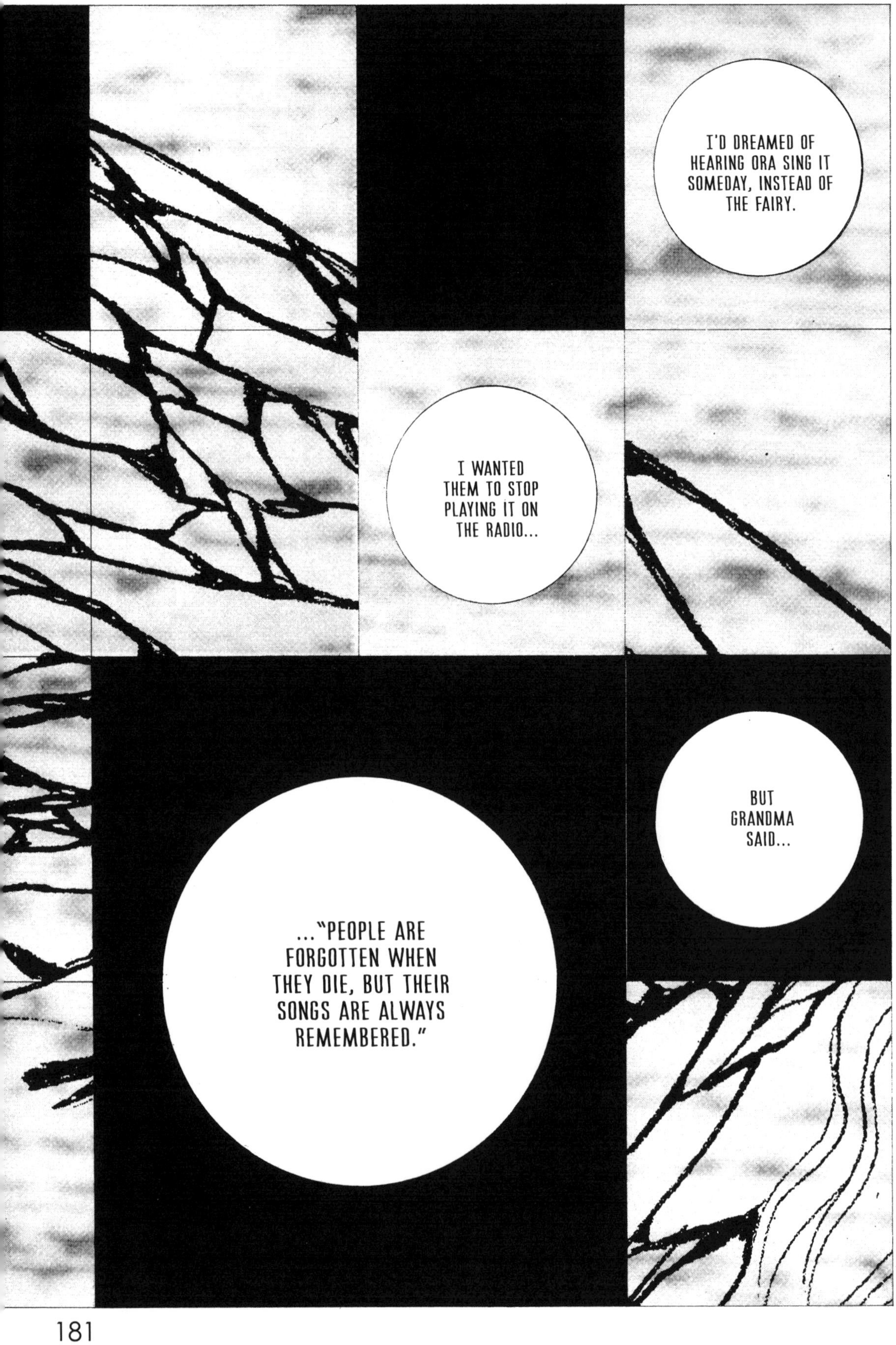
I'D DREAMED OF HEARING ORA SING IT SOMEDAY, INSTEAD OF THE FAIRY.
I WANTED THEM TO STOP PLAYING IT ON THE RADIO...
BUT GRANDMA SAID...
..."PEOPLE ARE FORGOTTEN WHEN THEY DIE, BUT THEIR SONGS ARE ALWAYS REMEMBERED."

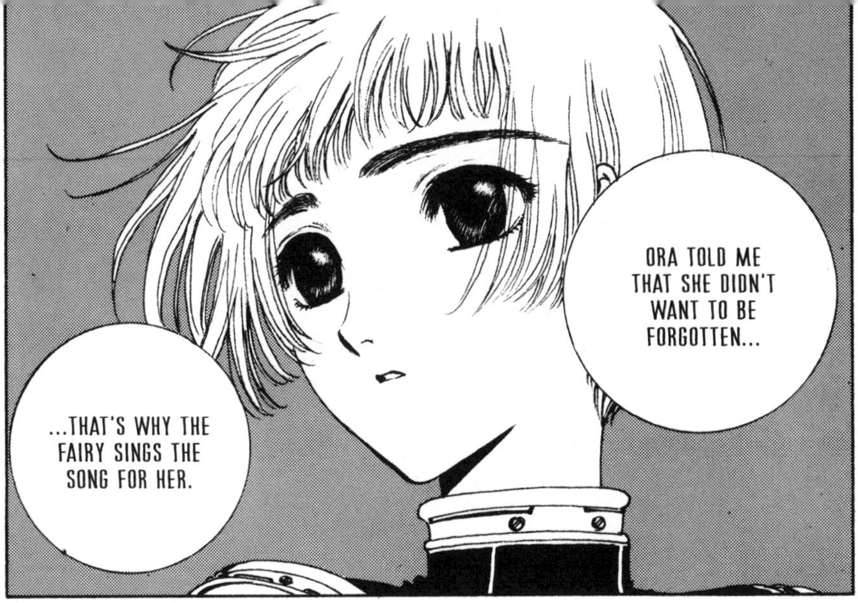
ORA TOLD ME THAT SHE DIDN'T WANT TO BE FORGOTTEN...
...THAT'S WHY THE FAIRY SINGS THE SONG FOR HER.

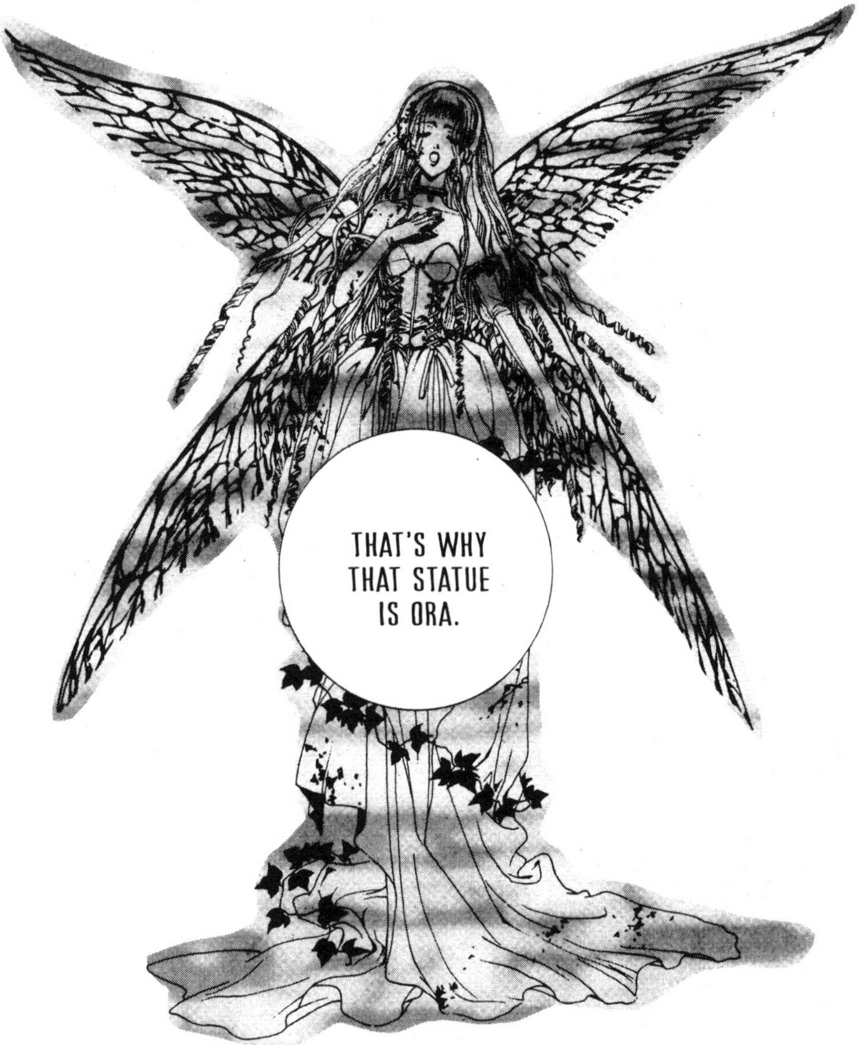
THAT'S WHY THAT STATUE IS ORA.

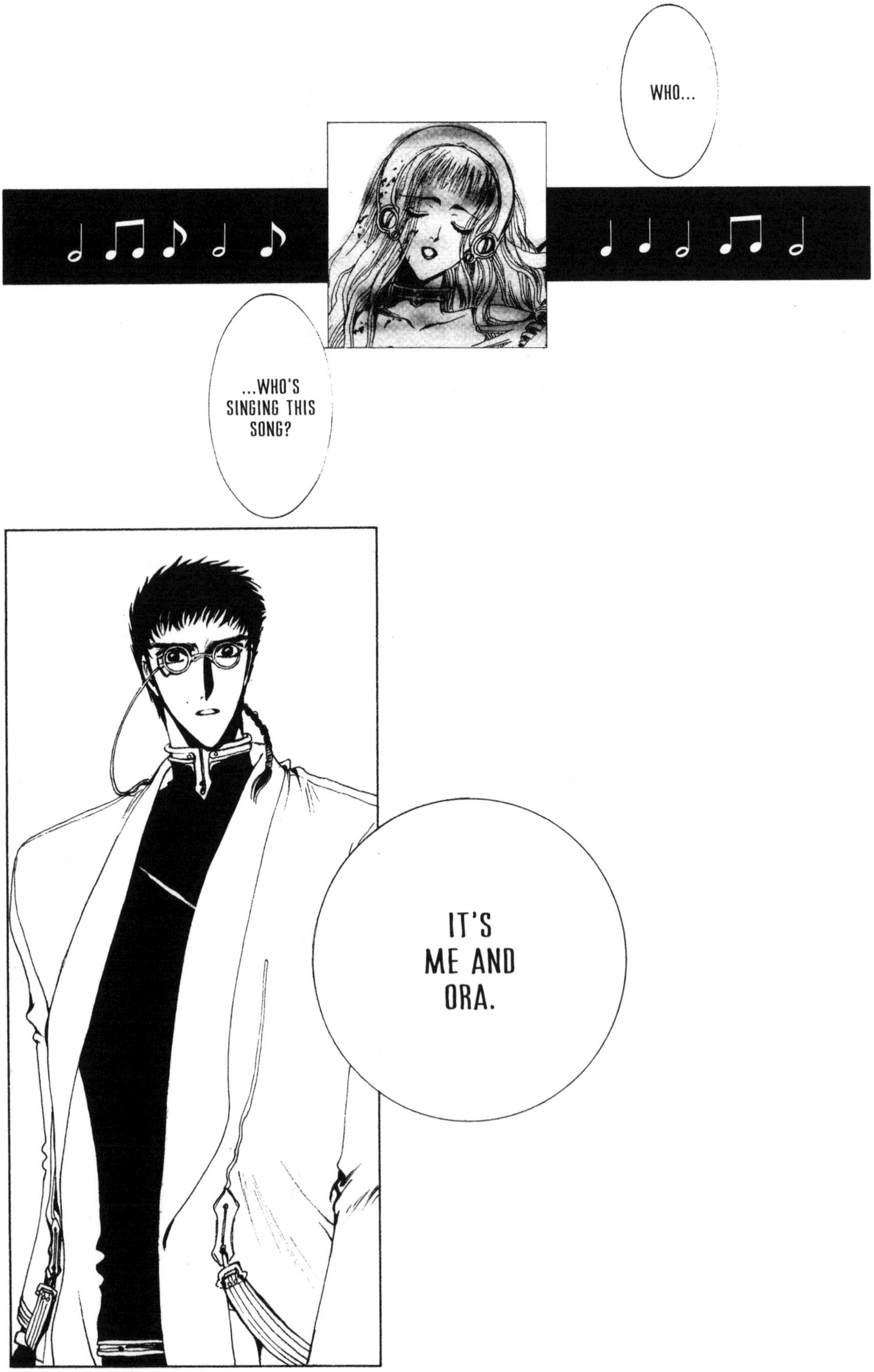
WHO...
...WHO'S SINGING THIS SONG?
IT'S ME AND ORA.

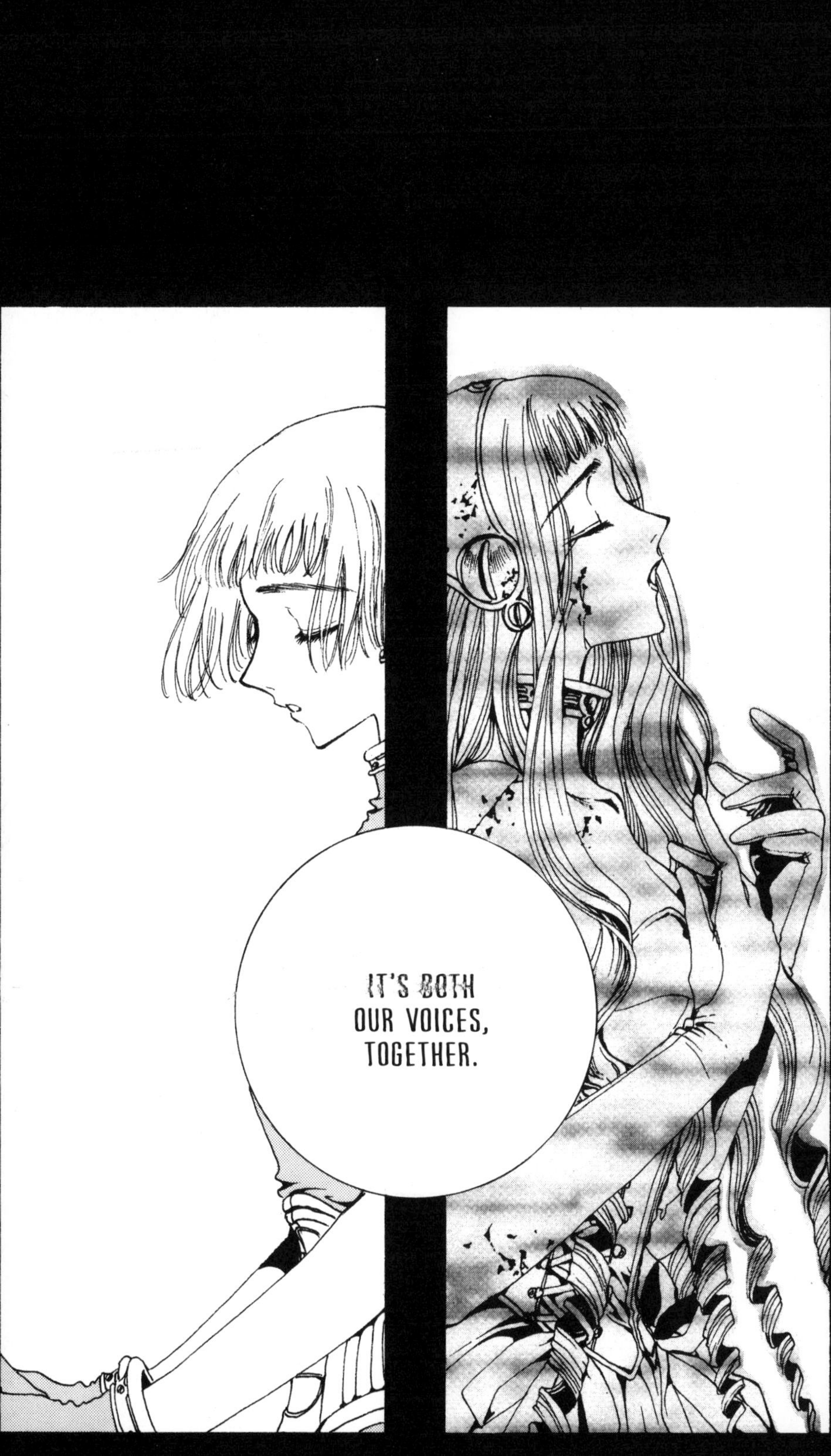
IT'S BOTH
OUR VOICES,
TOGETHER.

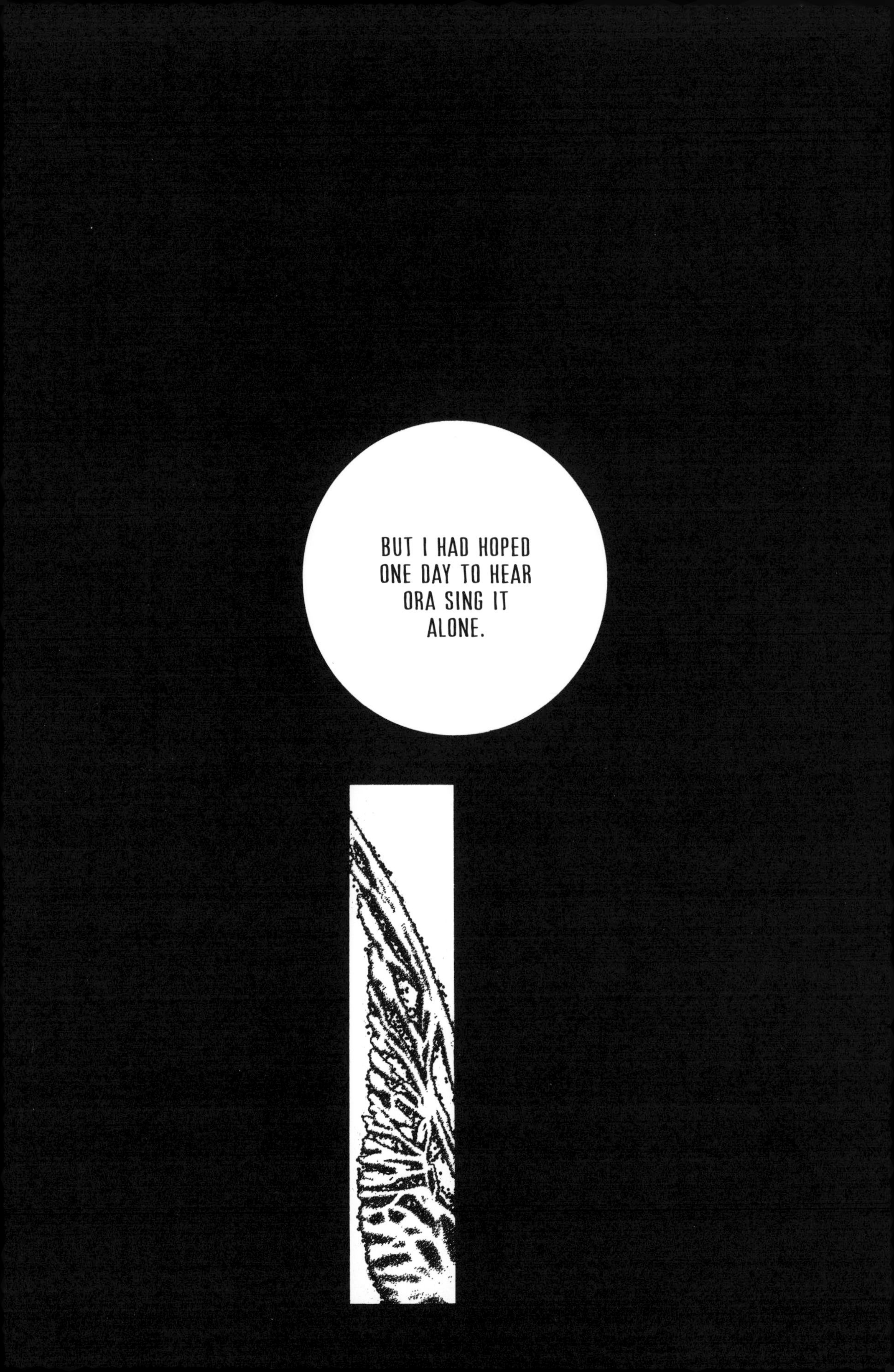
BUT I HAD HOPED ONE DAY TO HEAR ORA SING IT ALONE.

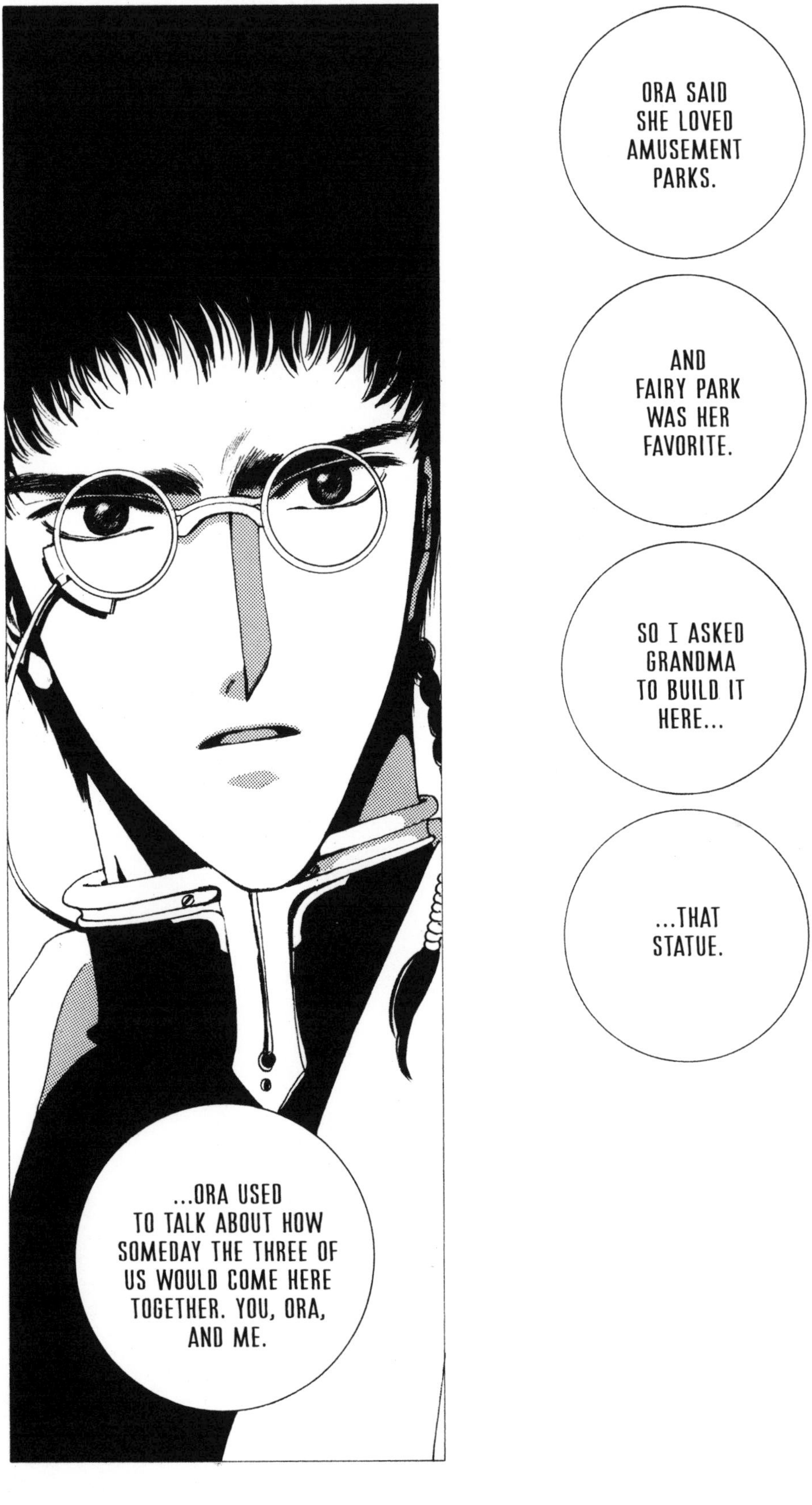
...ORA USED TO TALK ABOUT HOW SOMEDAY THE THREE OF US WOULD COME HERE TOGETHER. YOU, ORA, AND ME.
ORA SAID SHE LOVED AMUSEMENT PARKS.
AND FAIRY PARK WAS HER FAVORITE.
SO I ASKED GRANDMA TO BUILD IT HERE...
...THAT STATUE.

I'm happy just to
be with you

Happy just to see
your smile

So take me
To a true Elsewhere

I seek
happiness

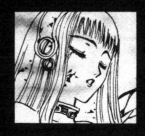

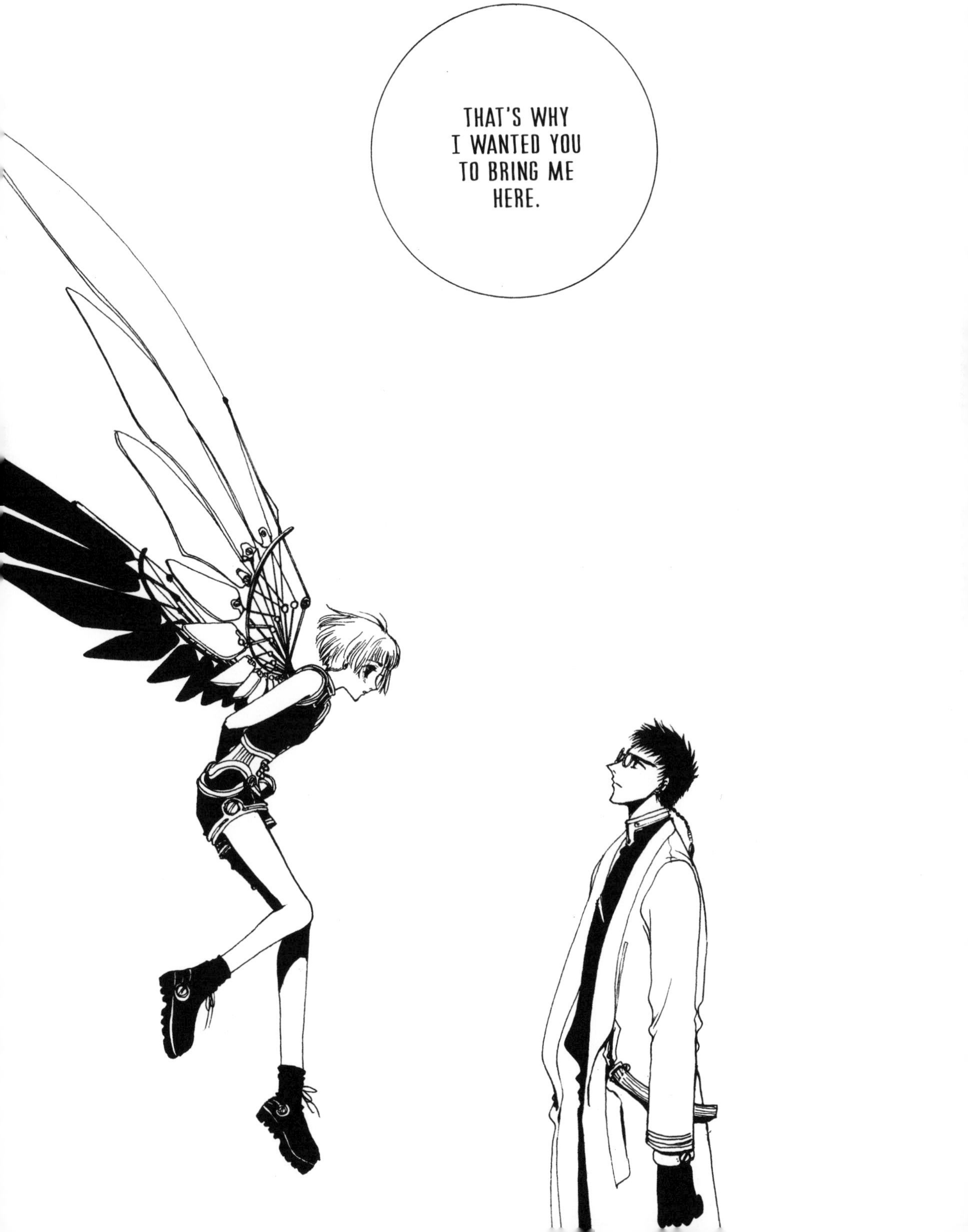
THAT'S WHY I WANTED YOU TO BRING ME HERE.

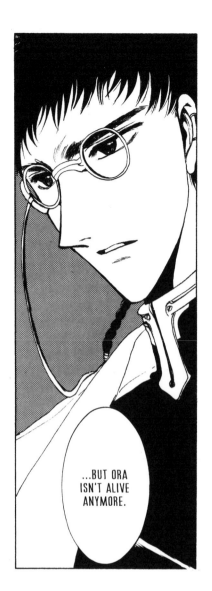

...BUT ORA
ISN'T ALIVE
ANYMORE.

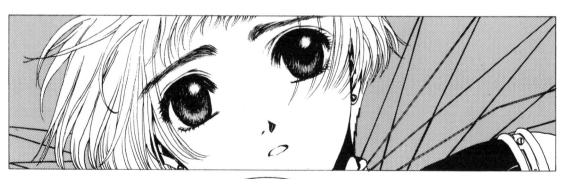

YES,
SHE IS.

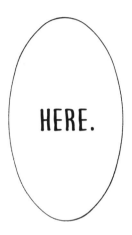

HERE.

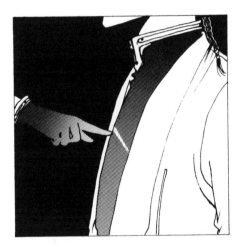

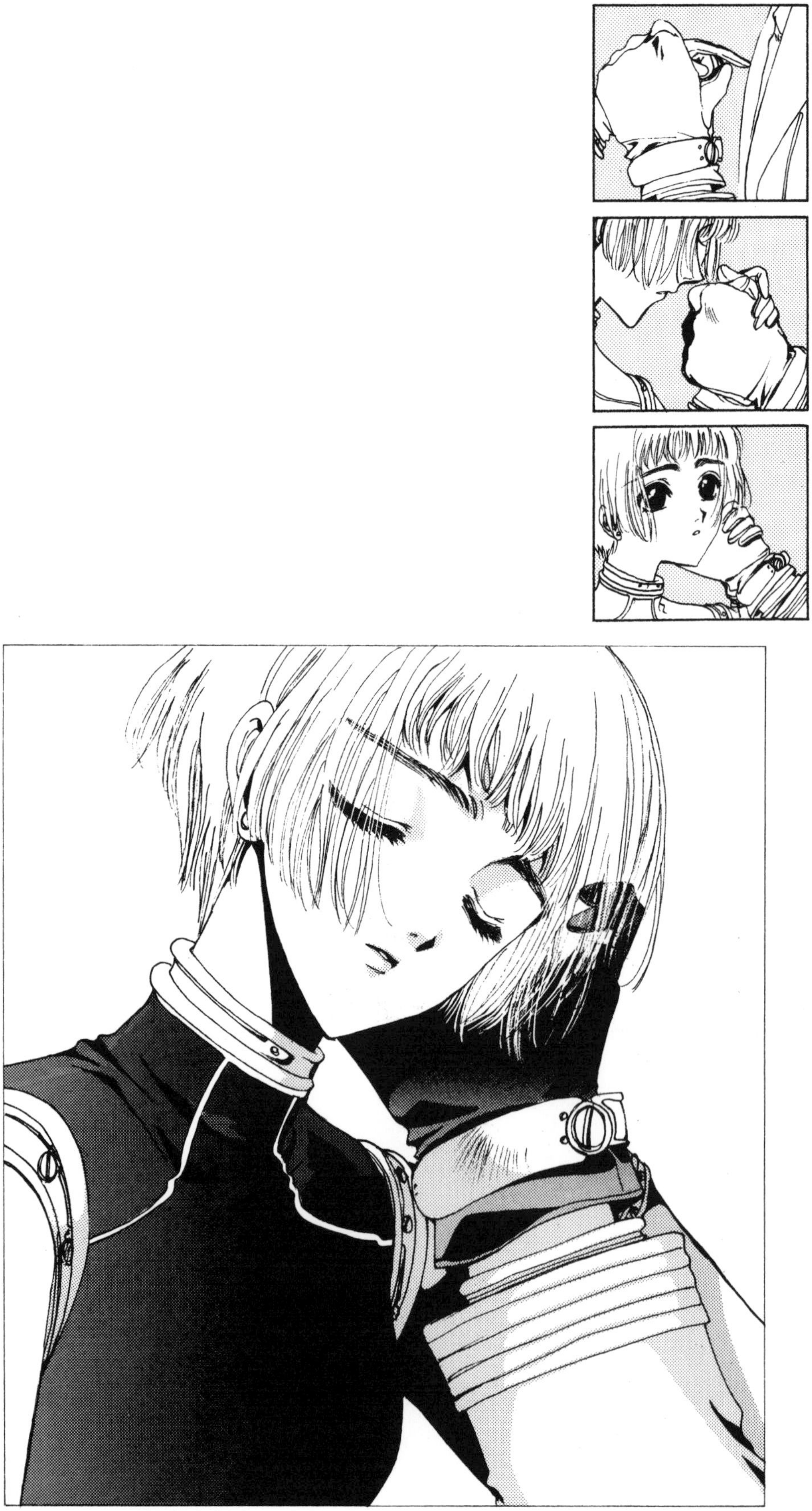

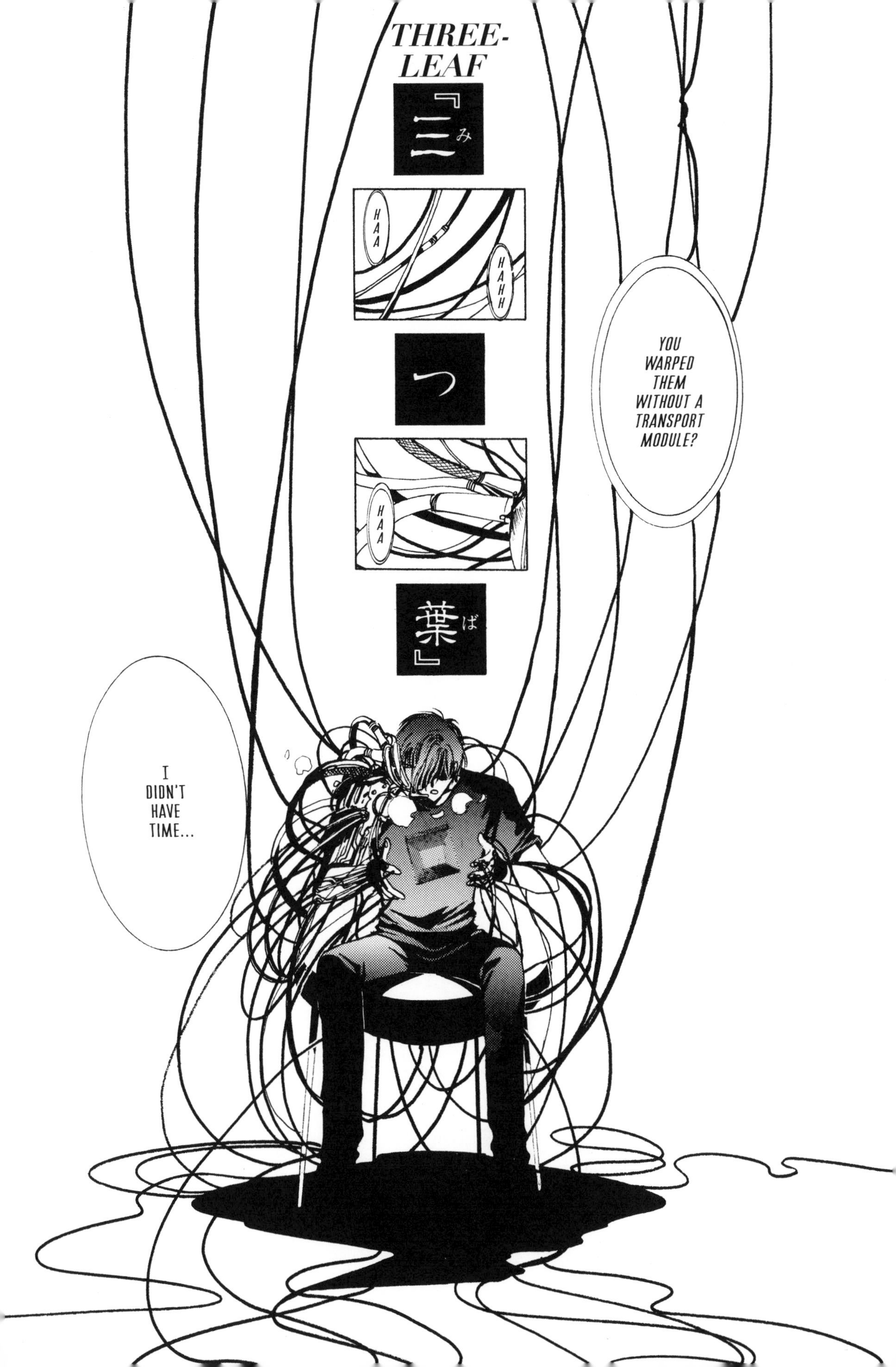
THREE-LEAF
『三つ葉』
HAA
HAHH
HAA
YOU WARPED THEM WITHOUT A TRANSPORT MODULE?
I DIDN'T HAVE TIME...

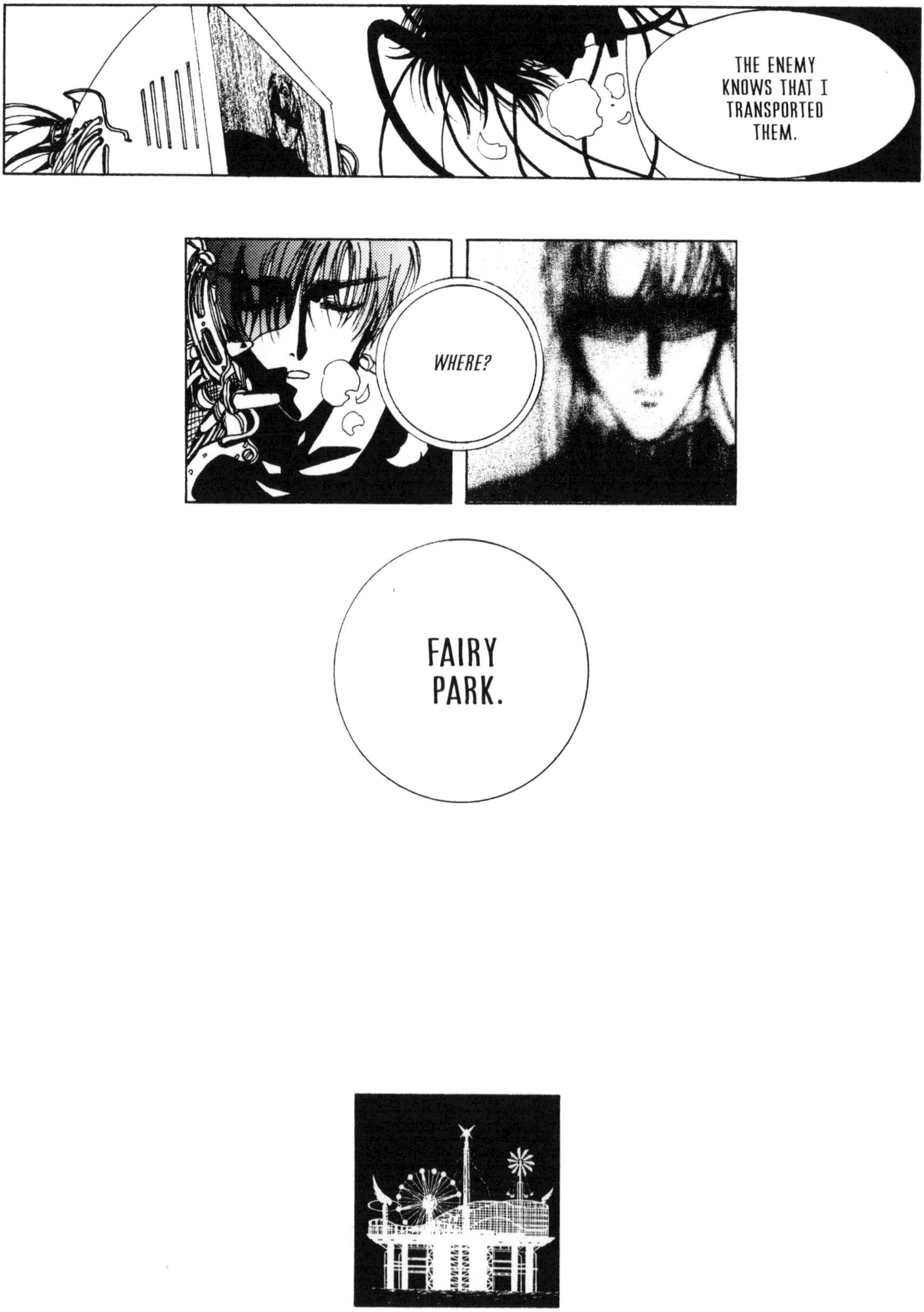
THE ENEMY KNOWS THAT I TRANSPORTED THEM.
WHERE?
FAIRY PARK.

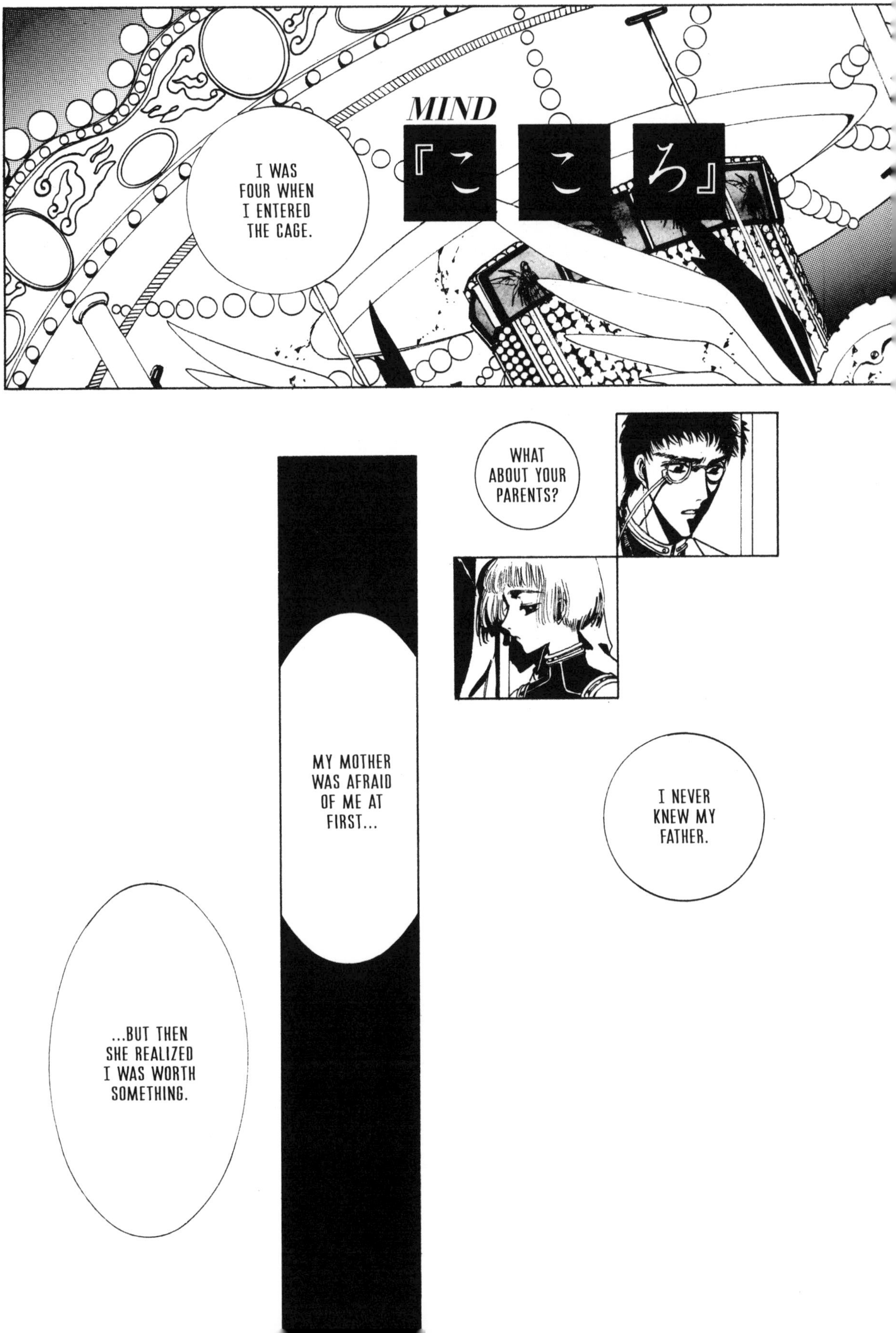
MIND
『こころ』
I WAS FOUR WHEN I ENTERED THE CAGE.
WHAT ABOUT YOUR PARENTS?
I NEVER KNEW MY FATHER.
MY MOTHER WAS AFRAID OF ME AT FIRST...
...BUT THEN SHE REALIZED I WAS WORTH SOMETHING.

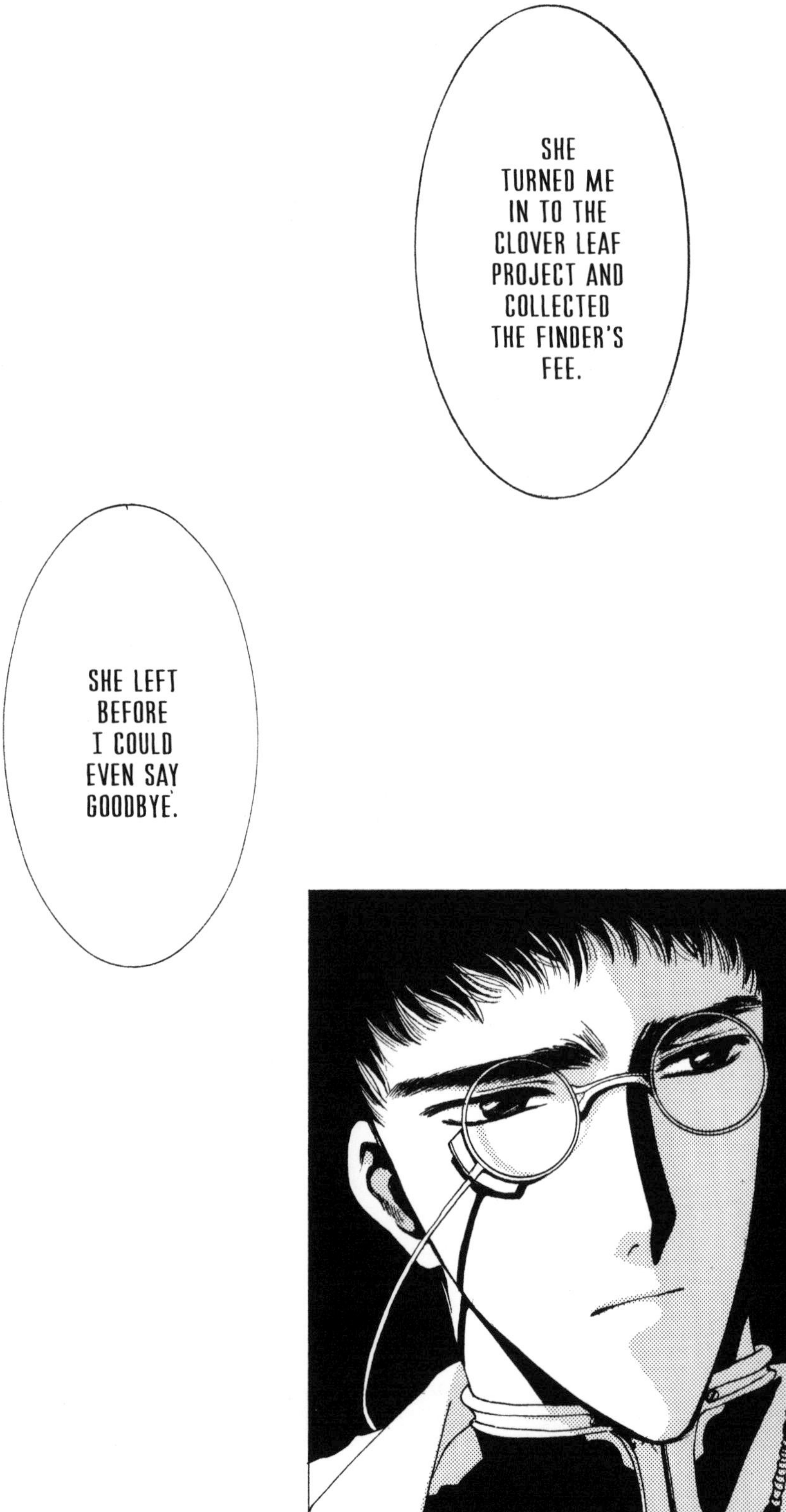
SHE TURNED ME IN TO THE CLOVER LEAF PROJECT AND COLLECTED THE FINDER'S FEE.
SHE LEFT BEFORE I COULD EVEN SAY GOODBYE.

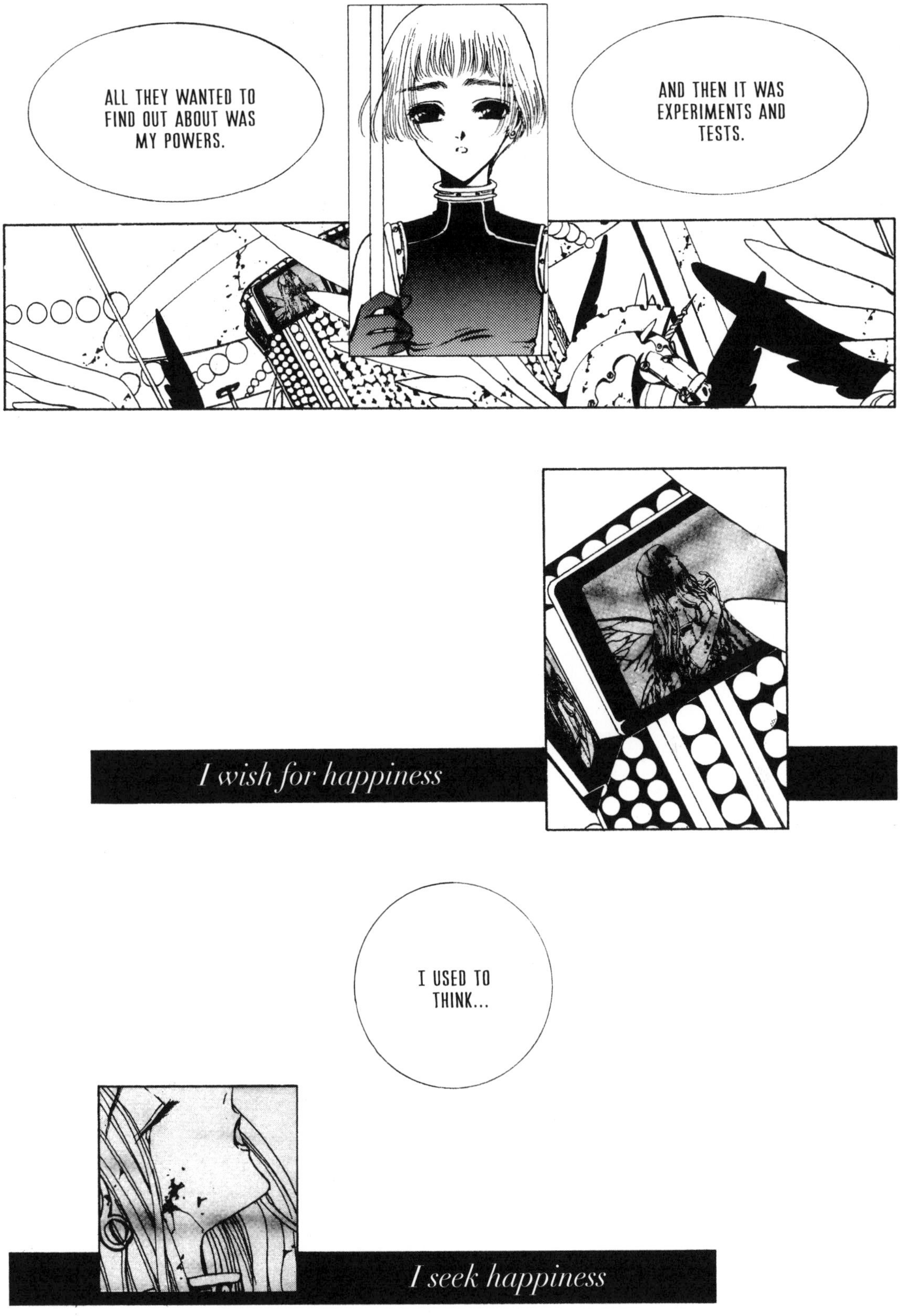
ALL THEY WANTED TO FIND OUT ABOUT WAS MY POWERS.
AND THEN IT WAS EXPERIMENTS AND TESTS.
I wish for happiness
I USED TO THINK...
I seek happiness

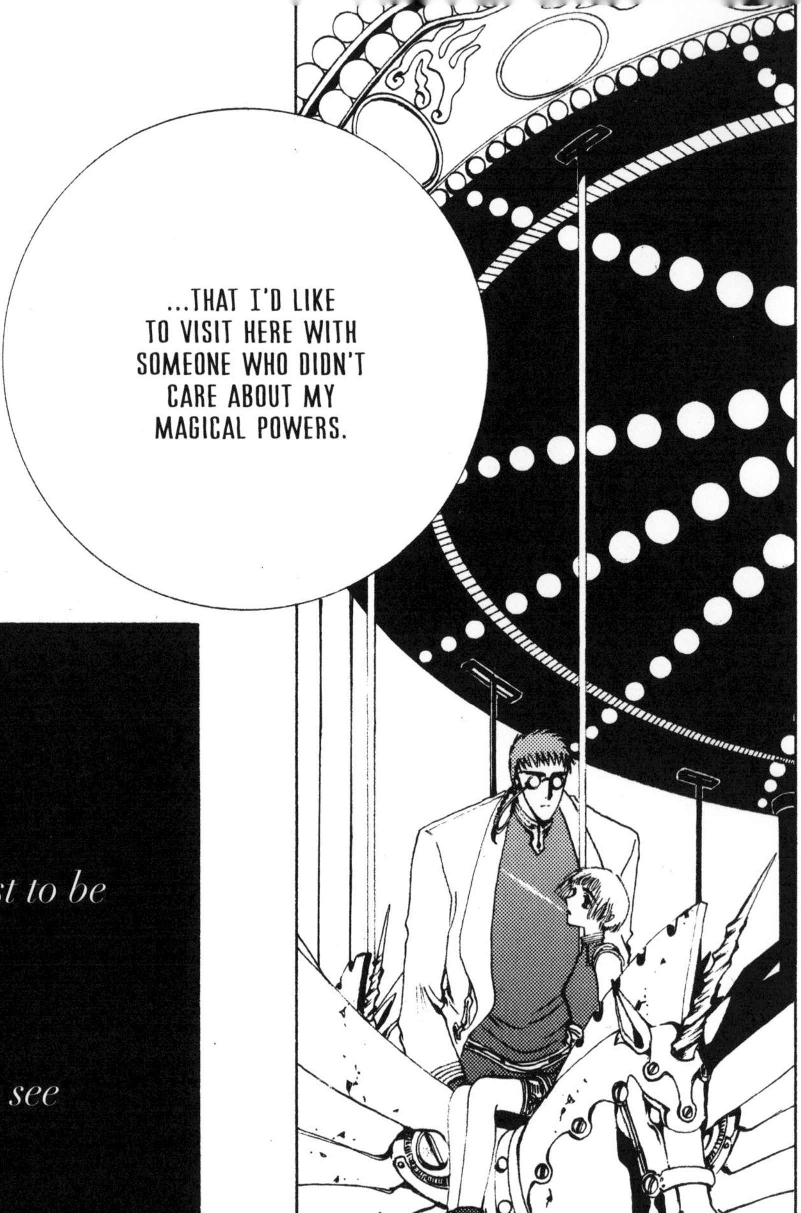
...THAT I'D LIKE TO VISIT HERE WITH SOMEONE WHO DIDN'T CARE ABOUT MY MAGICAL POWERS.

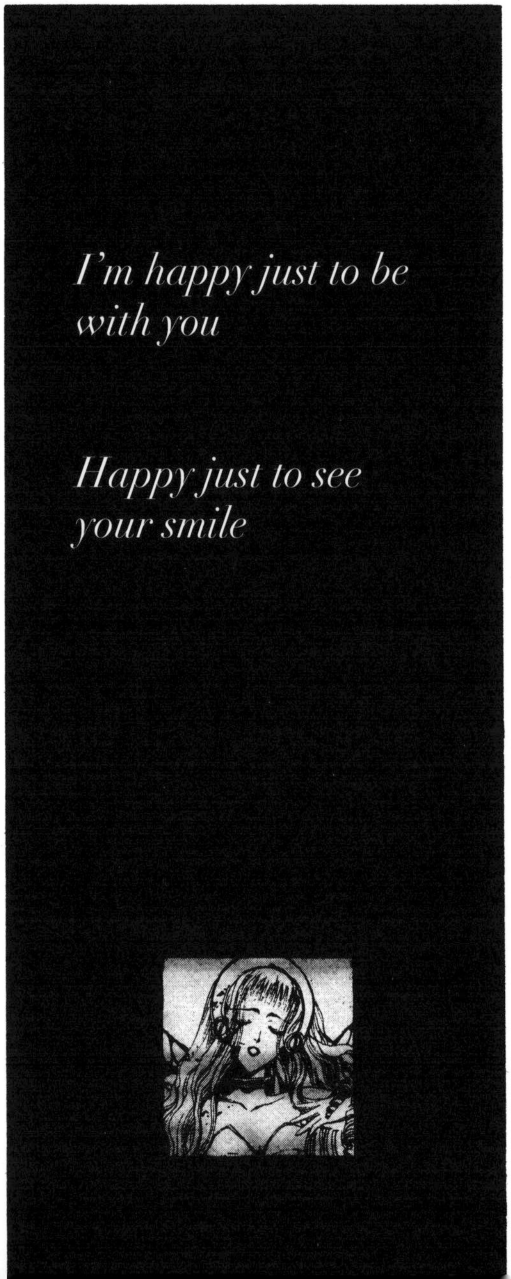
I'm happy just to be with you
Happy just to see your smile

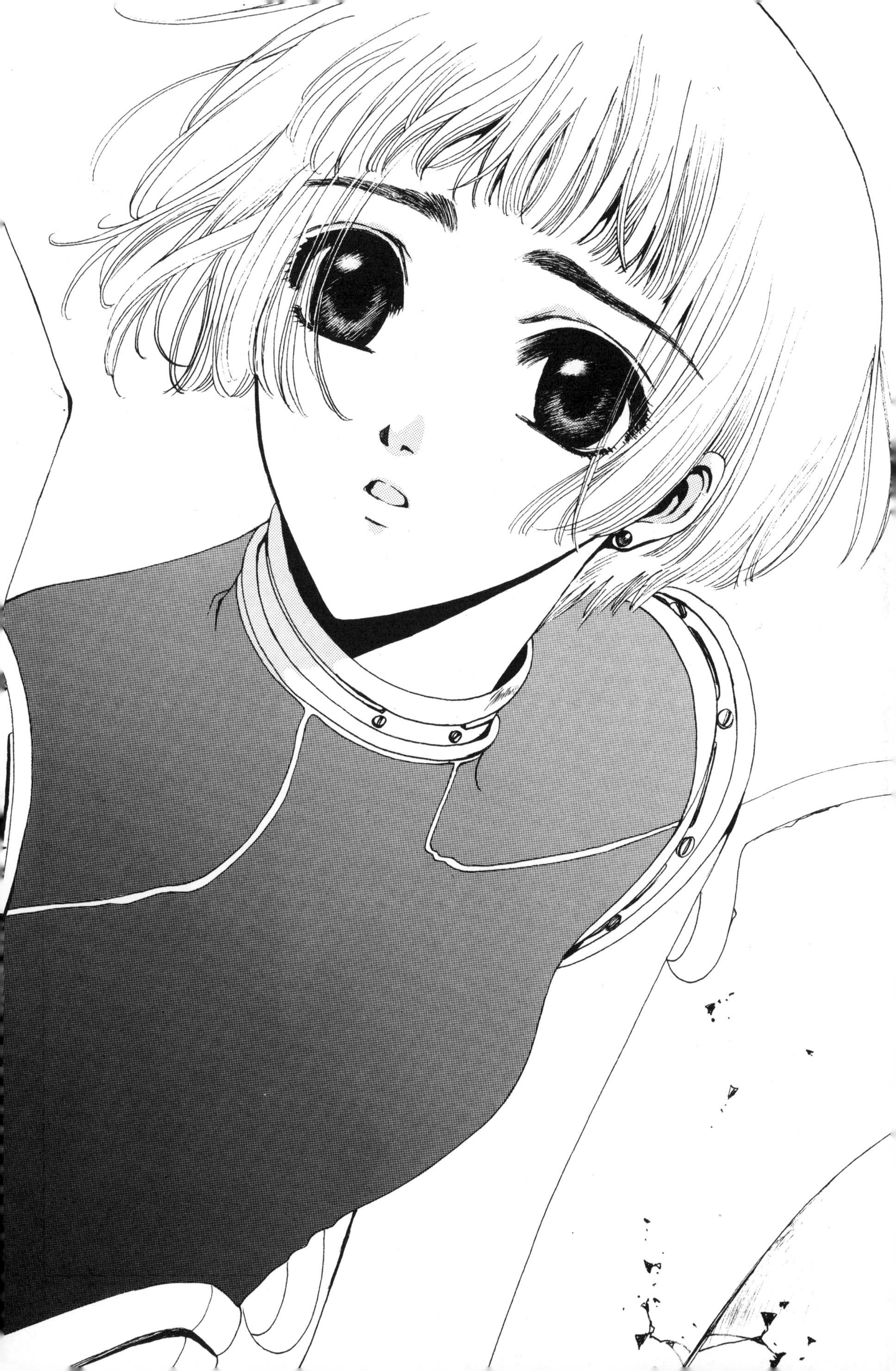

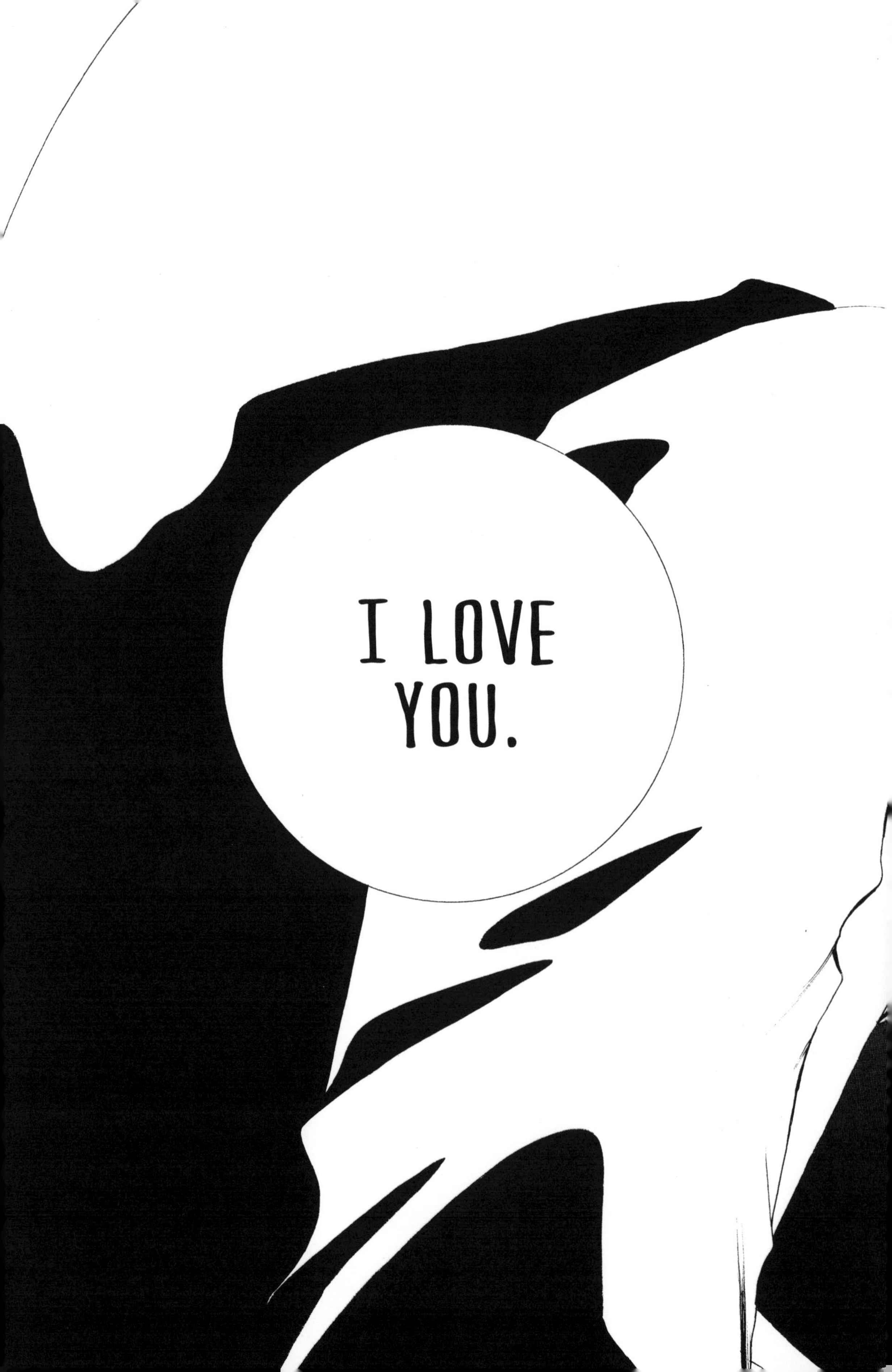
I LOVE YOU.

ORA
TOLD ME
ALL ABOUT
YOU...

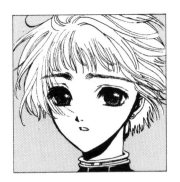

...I ALWAYS
WANTED TO
MEET YOU.

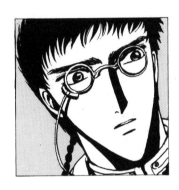

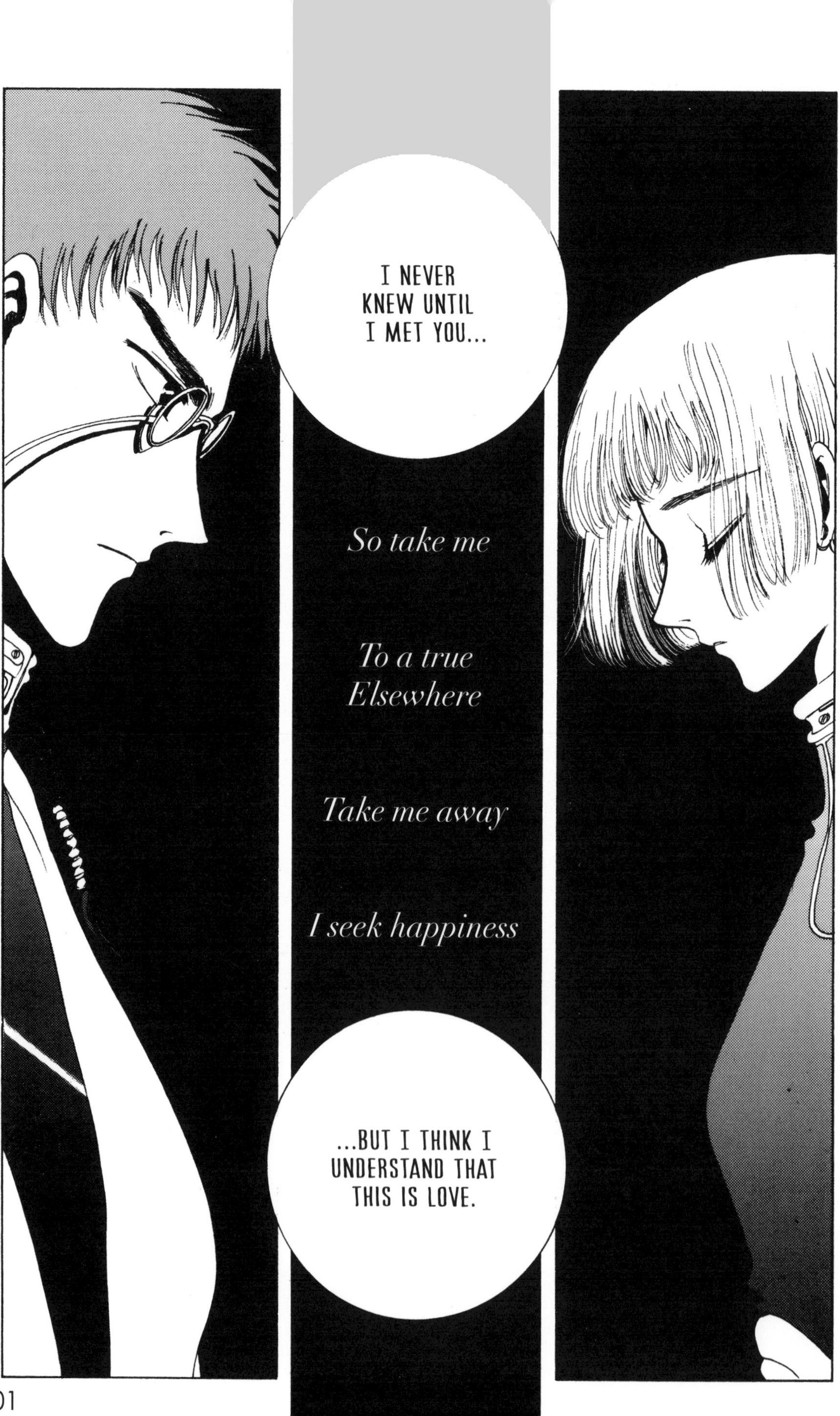
I NEVER KNEW UNTIL I MET YOU...
So take me
To a true Elsewhere
Take me away
I seek happiness
...BUT I THINK I UNDERSTAND THAT THIS IS LOVE.

WINGED STEED

『天(てん)馬(ま)』

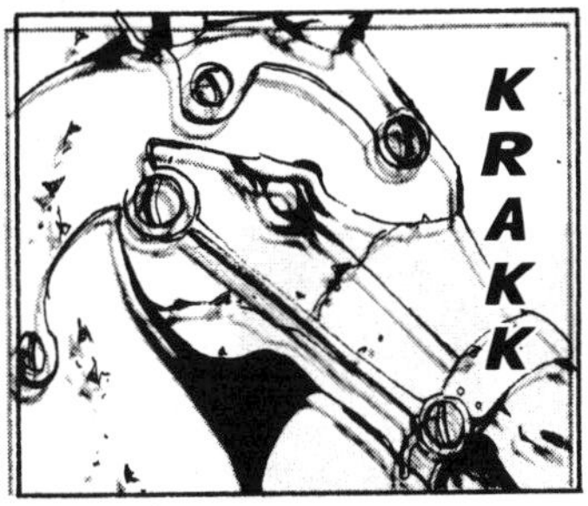
KRAKK

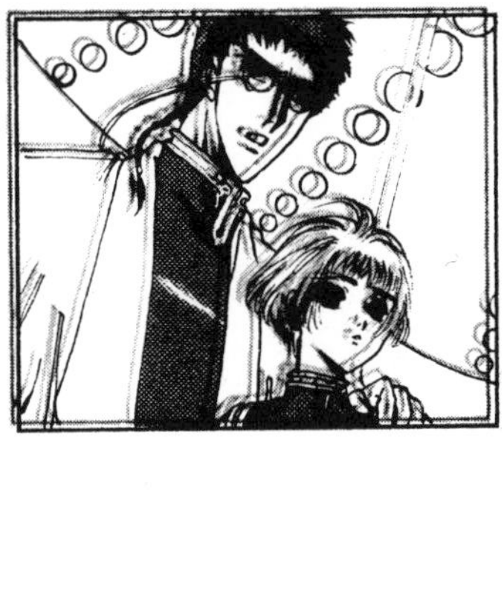

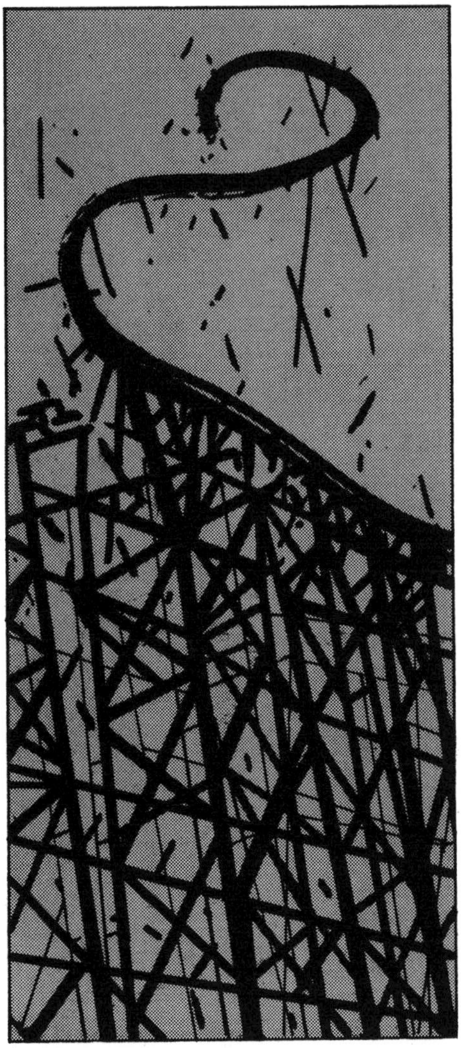
RRRMMMMMBBBLL

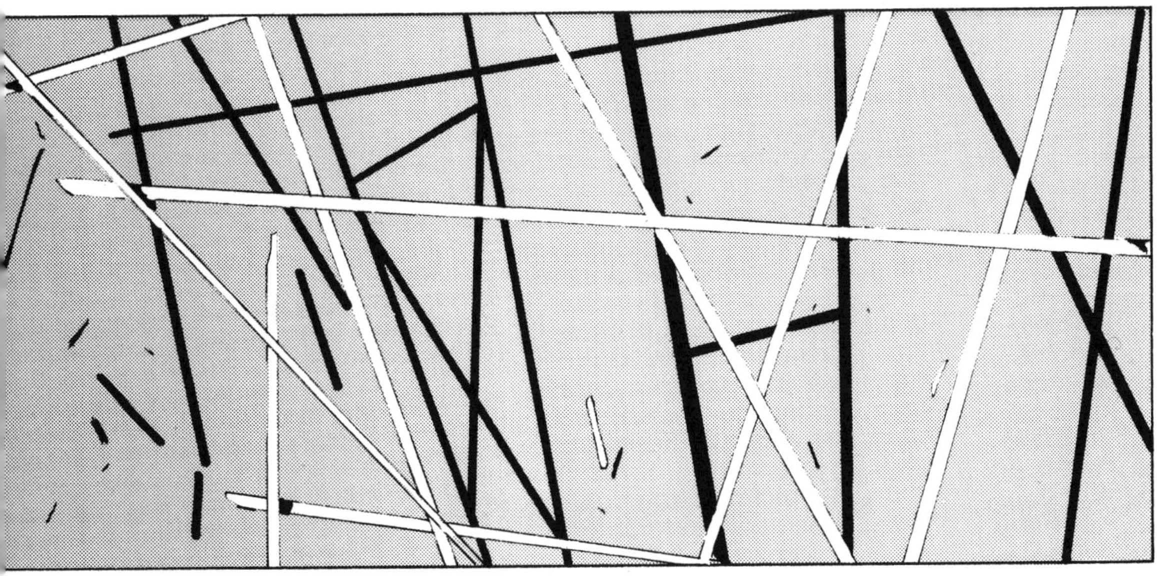

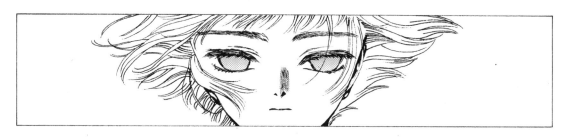

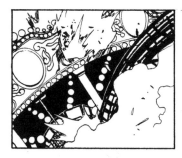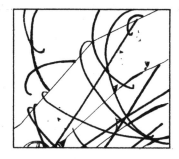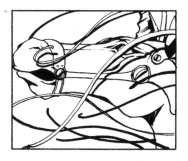

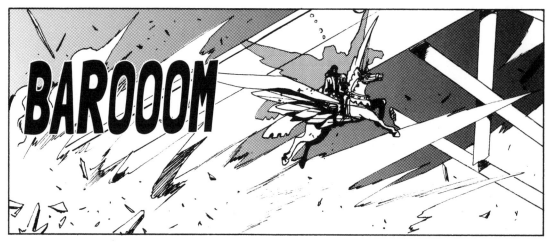

BAROOOM

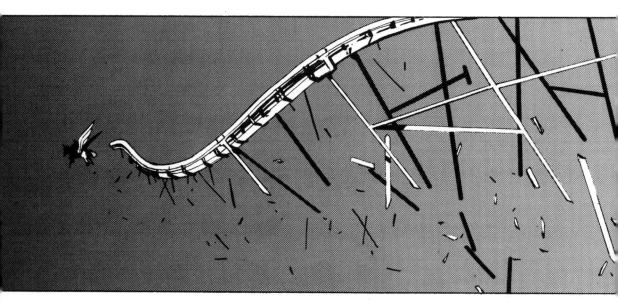

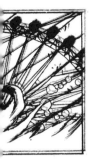
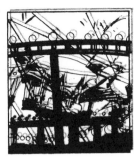
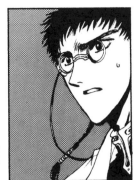
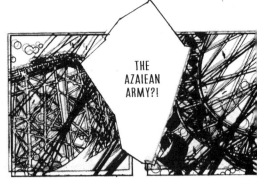

THE AZAIEAN ARMY?!

NO...

...IT'S THE WIZARDS.

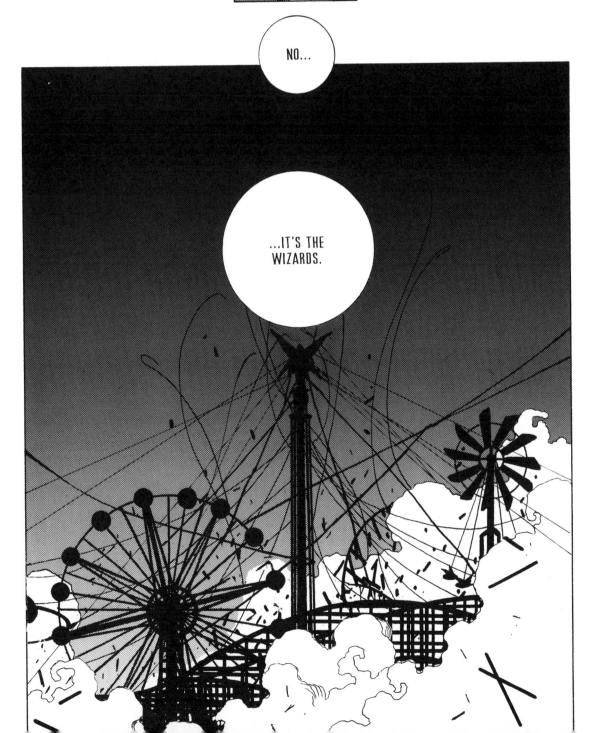

*I wish for happiness
I seek happiness*

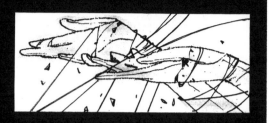

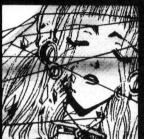

*To find happiness
with you*

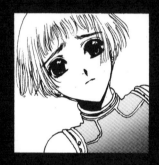

*To be your
happiness*

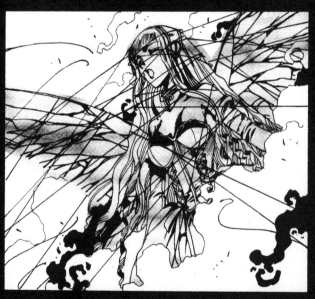

*So take me
To a true Elsewhere*

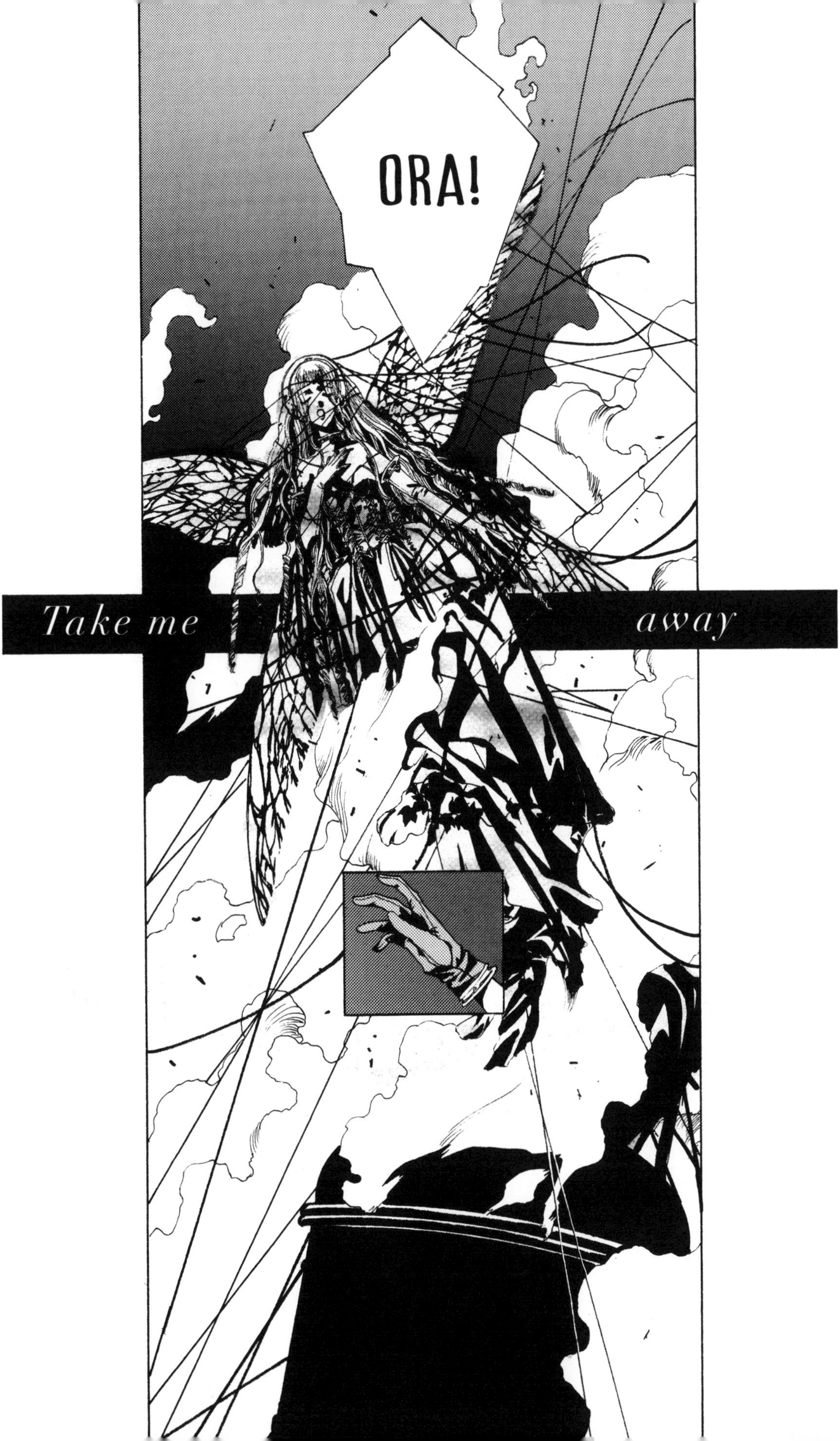
ORA!
Take me away

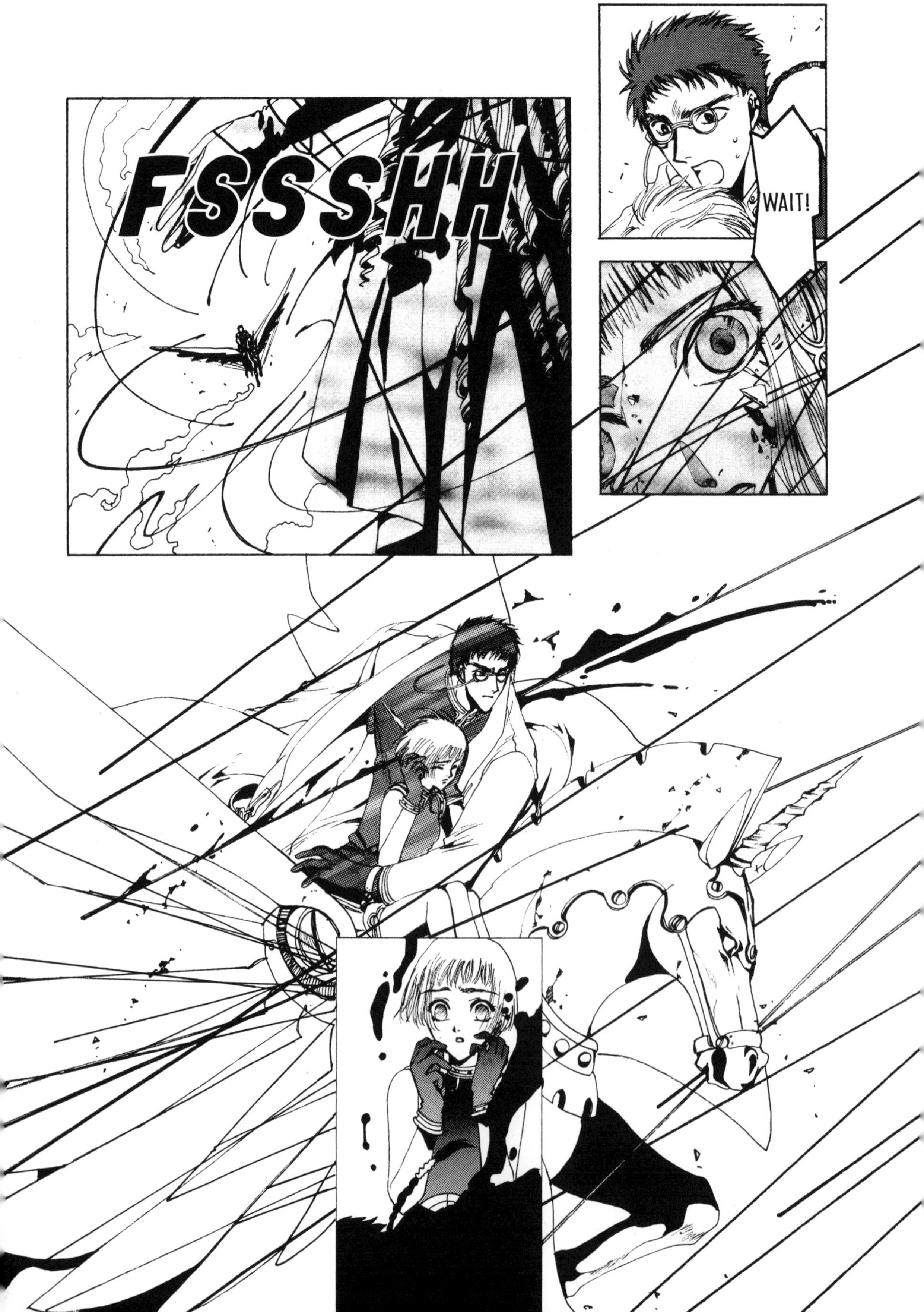
WAIT!
FSSSHH

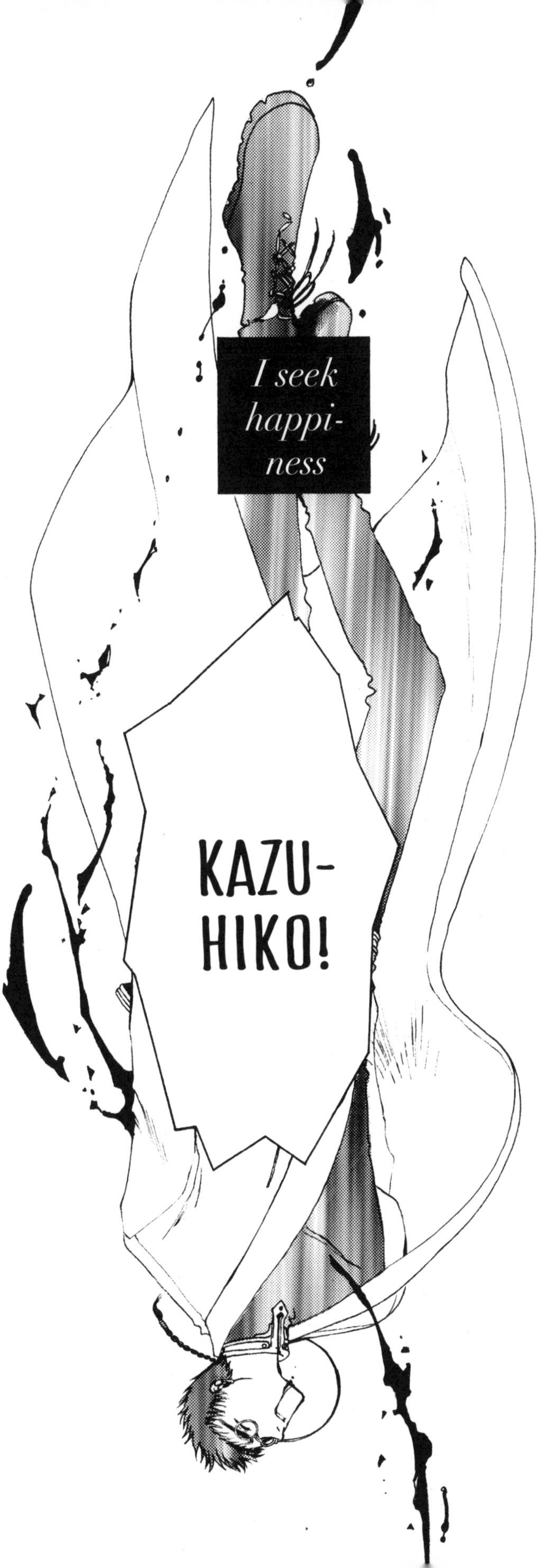
I seek happi-ness
KAZU-HIKO!

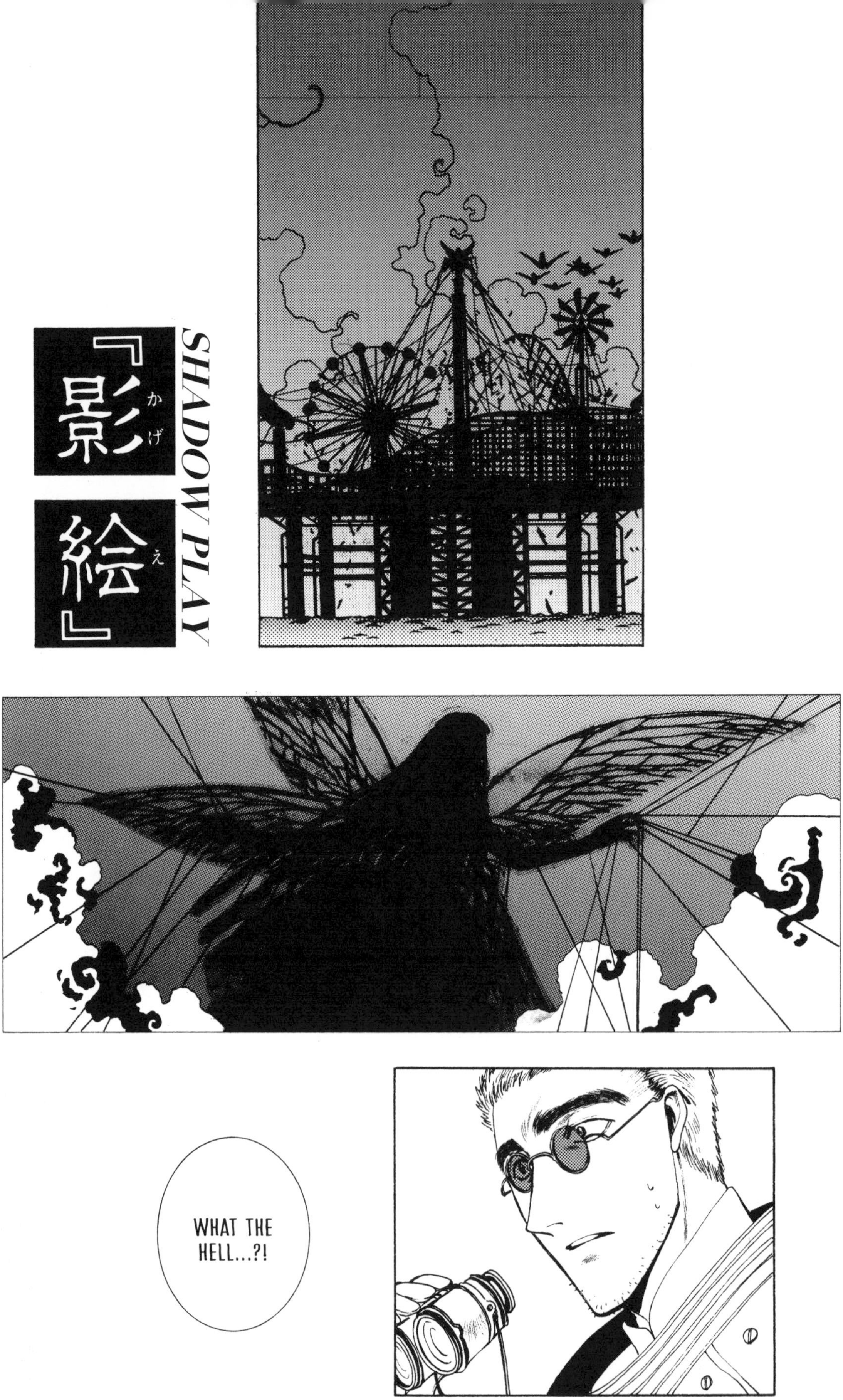
『影(かげ)絵(え)』
SHADOW PLAY
WHAT THE HELL...?!

SHHH
SHHHH
HOMICIDAL
INTENT
『殺意』

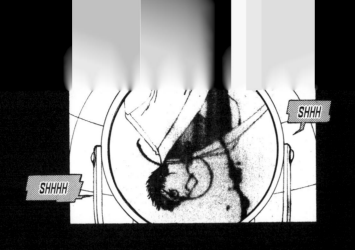

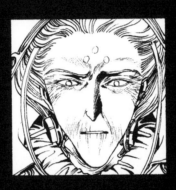

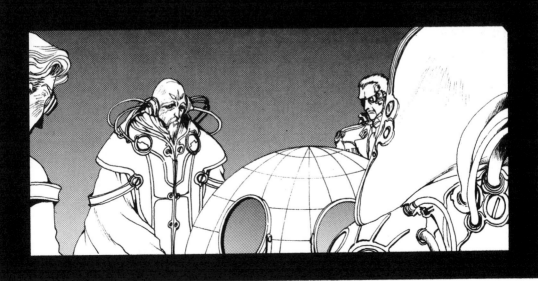

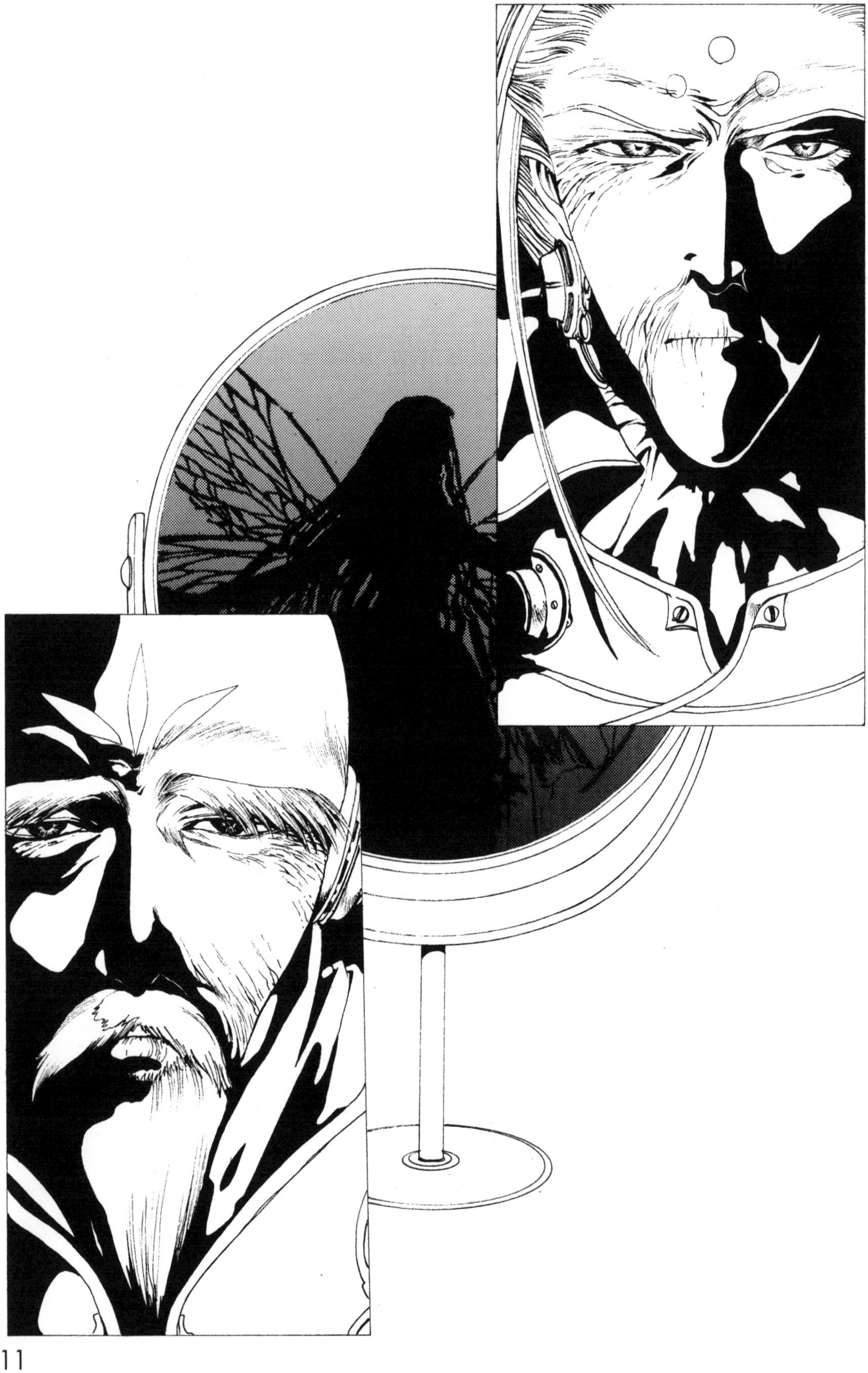

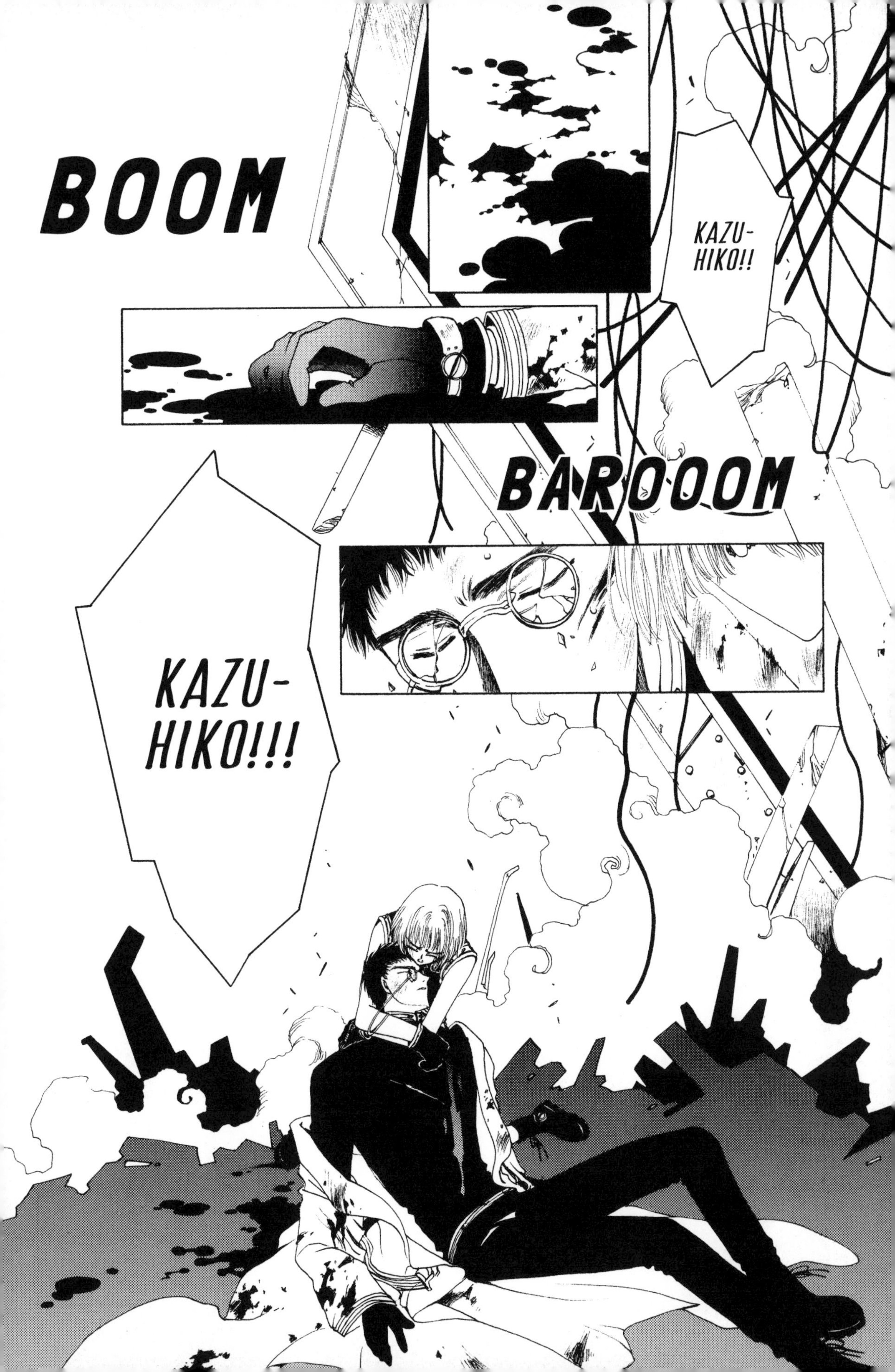
KAZU-HIKO!!
BOOM
BAROOOM
KAZU-HIKO!!!

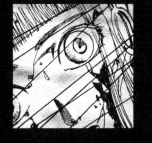

I wish for happiness
I seek happiness

To find happiness with you
To be your happiness

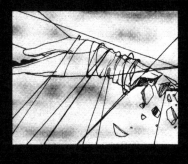

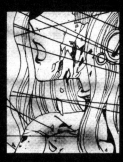

So take me

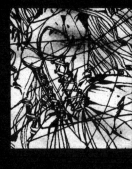

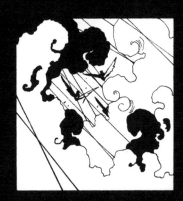

To a true
Elsewhere

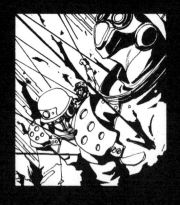

RRMMM 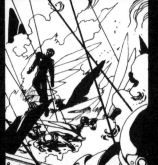 MMMMM

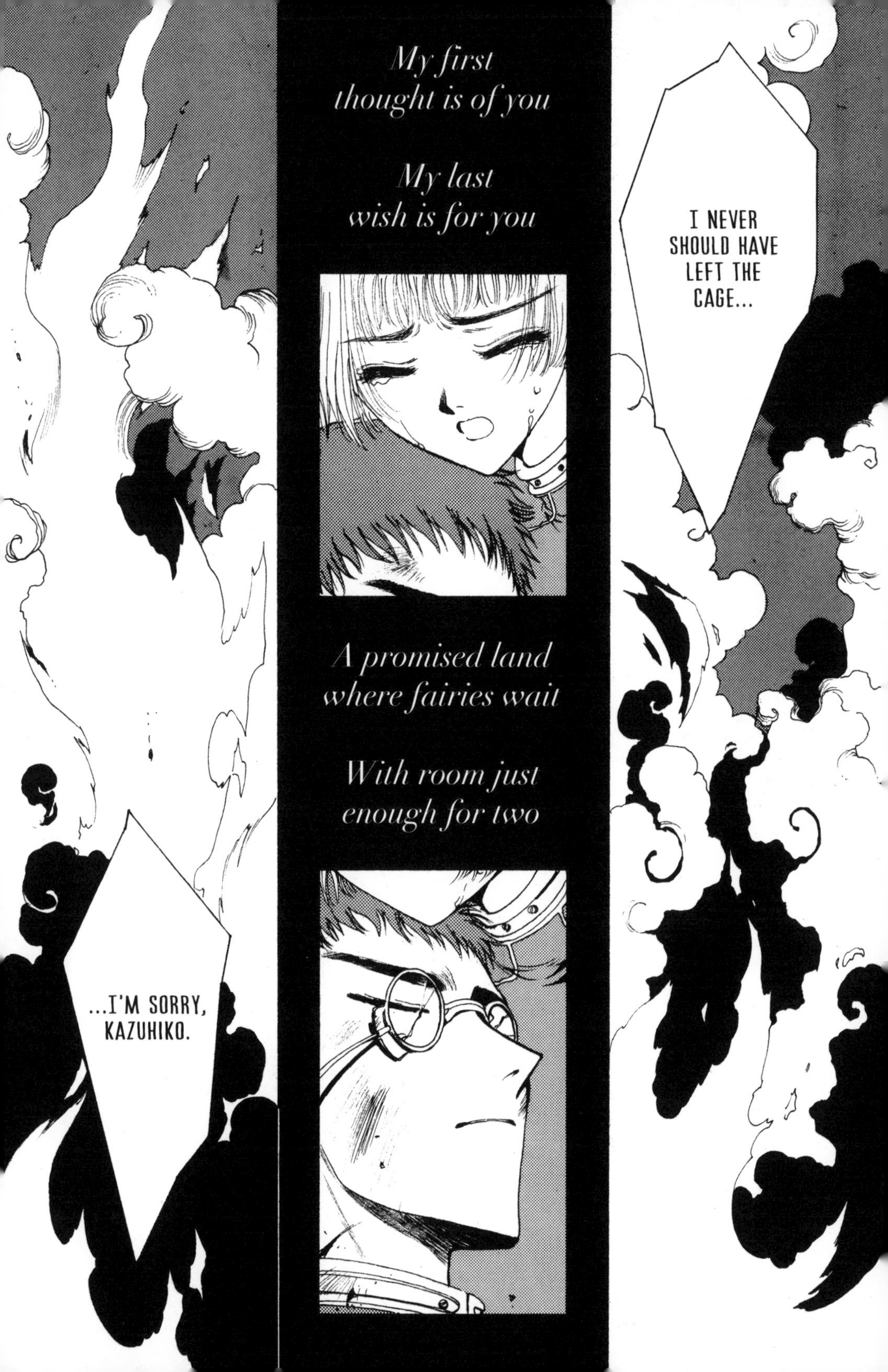
I NEVER SHOULD HAVE LEFT THE CAGE...
My first thought is of you
My last wish is for you
A promised land where fairies wait
With room just enough for two
...I'M SORRY, KAZUHIKO.

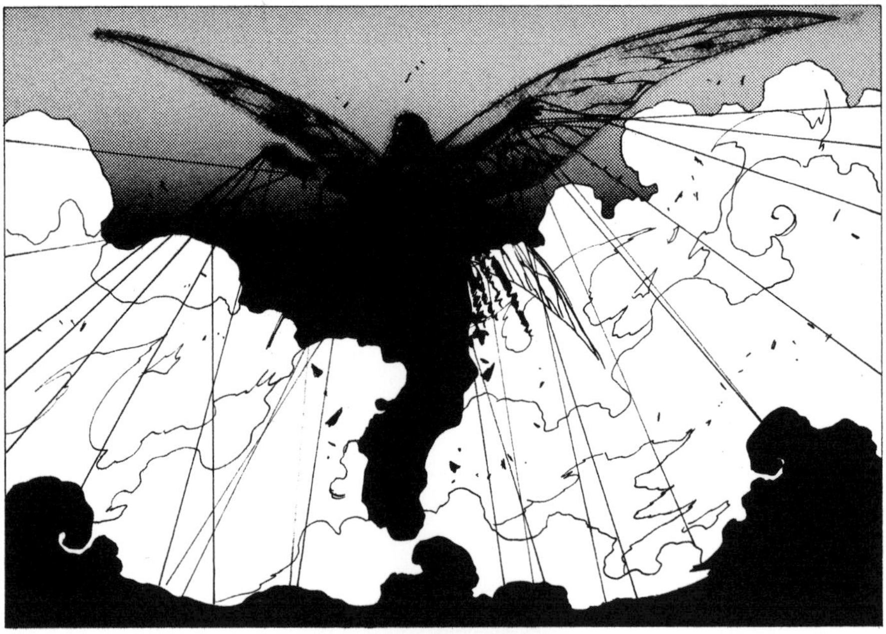

So take me there

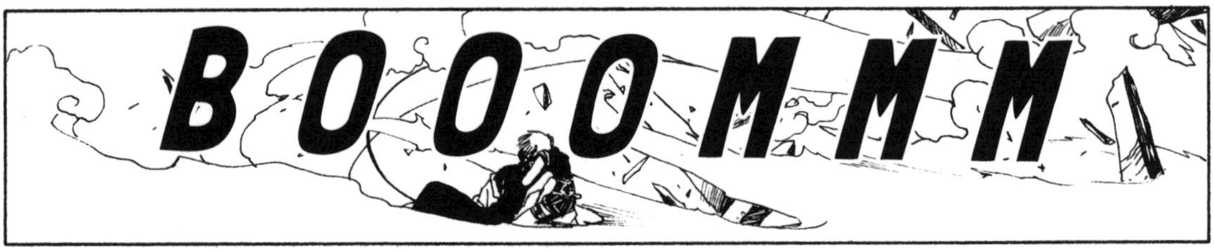
BOOOMMM

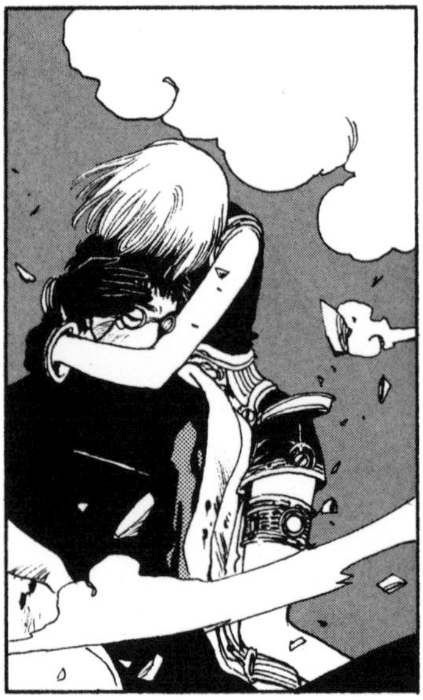

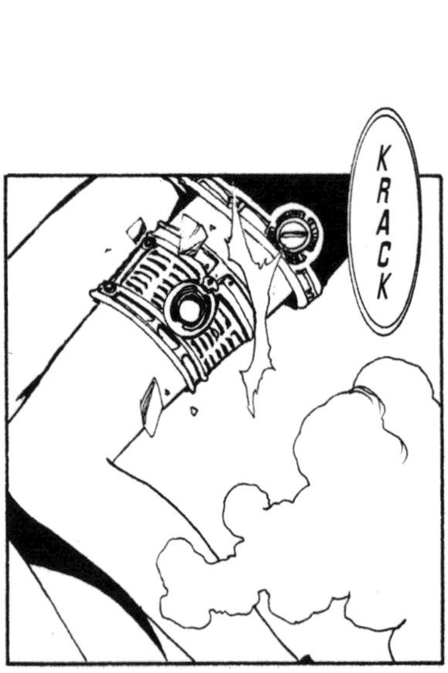
KRACK

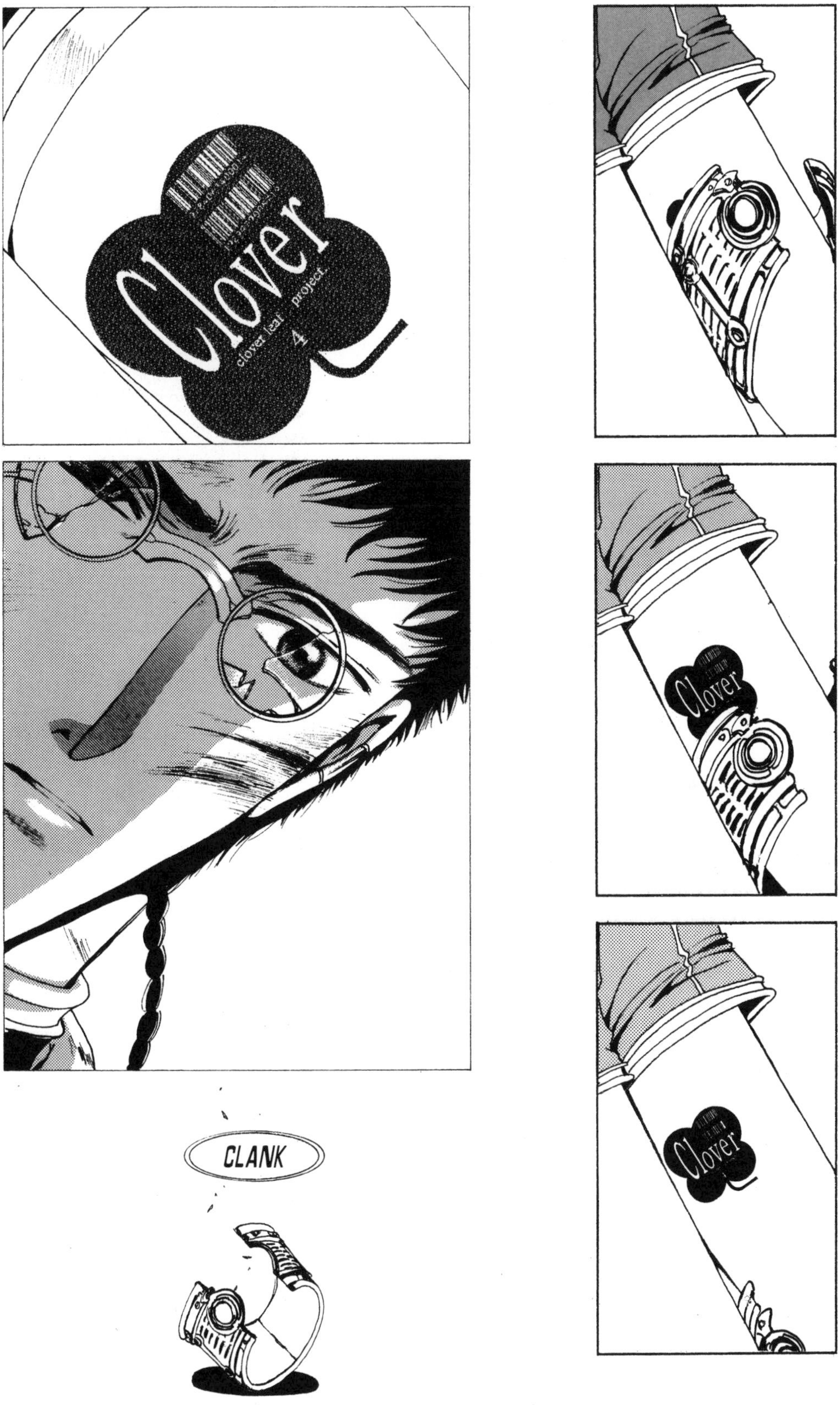

Clover
Clover
Clover
clover leaf project
4
CLANK

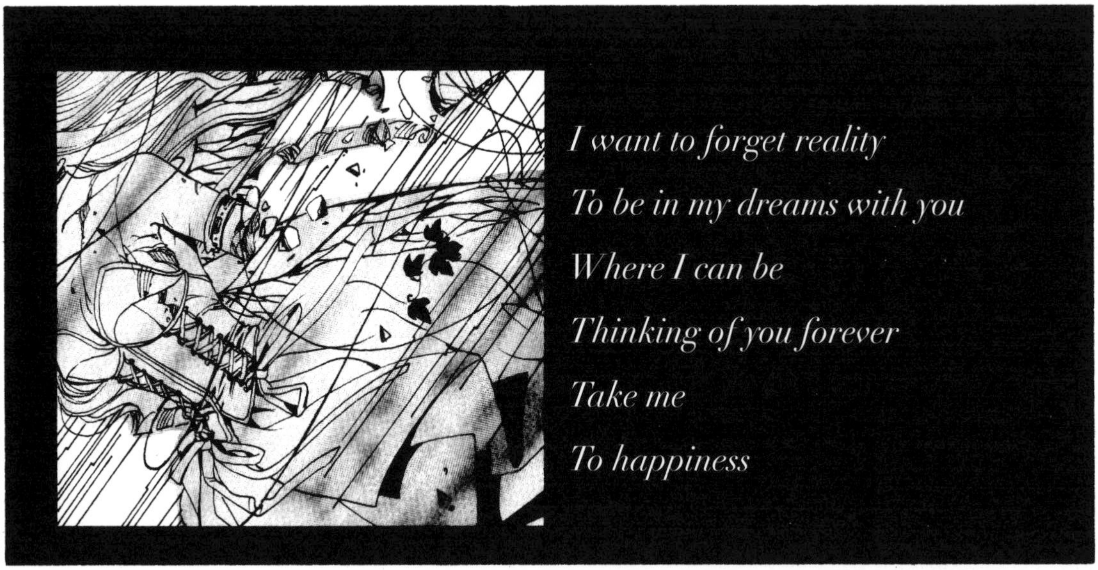
I want to forget reality
To be in my dreams with you
Where I can be
Thinking of you forever
Take me
To happiness

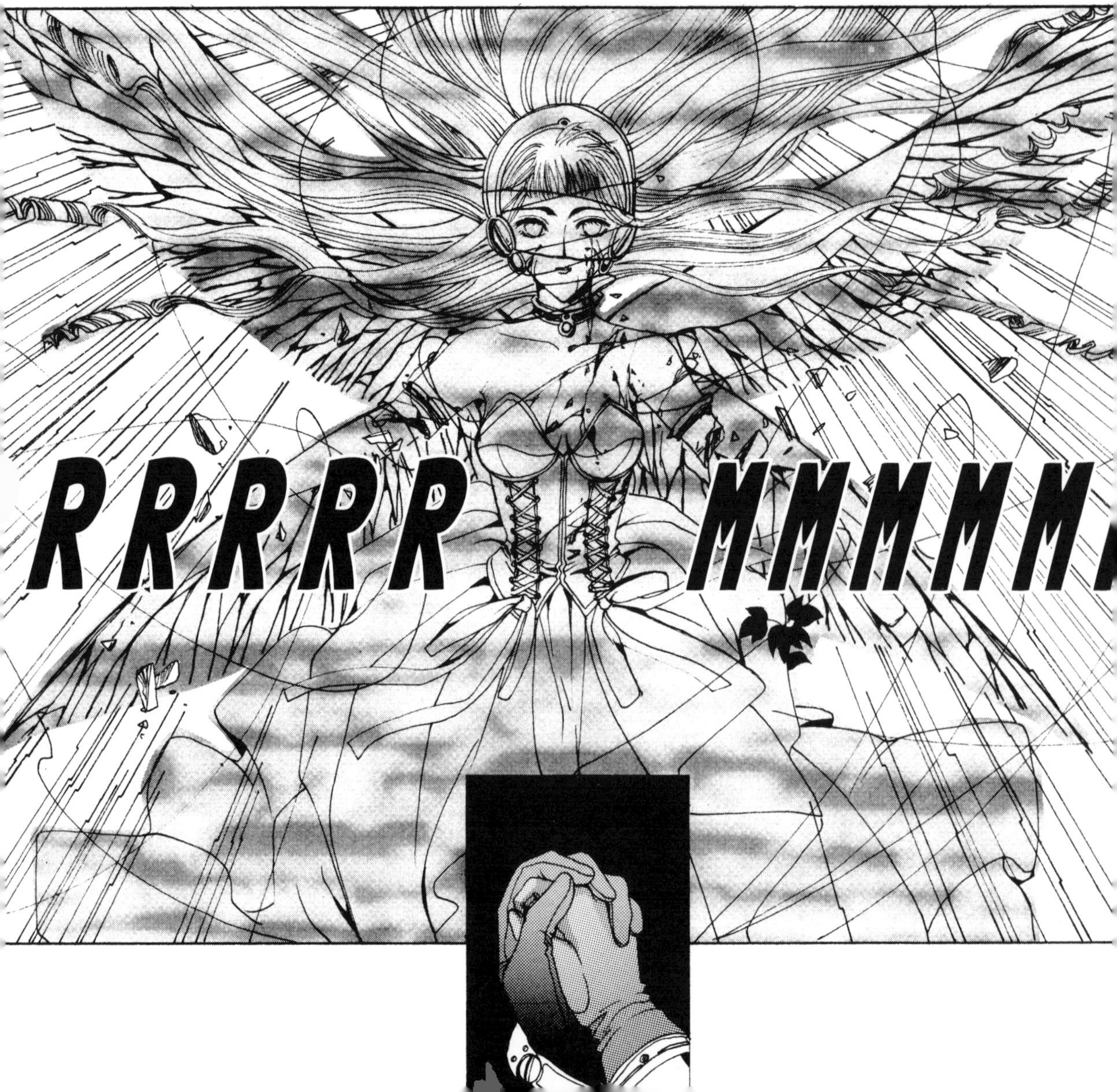
RRRRR MMMMM

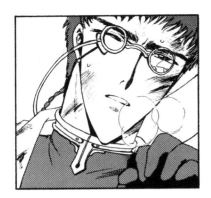
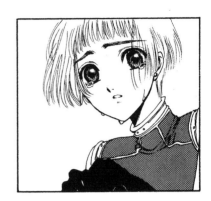

...HELP...
...ME FINISH
THIS.

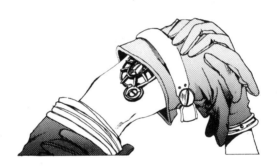

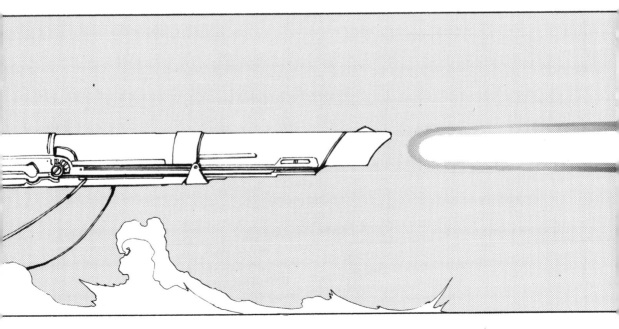

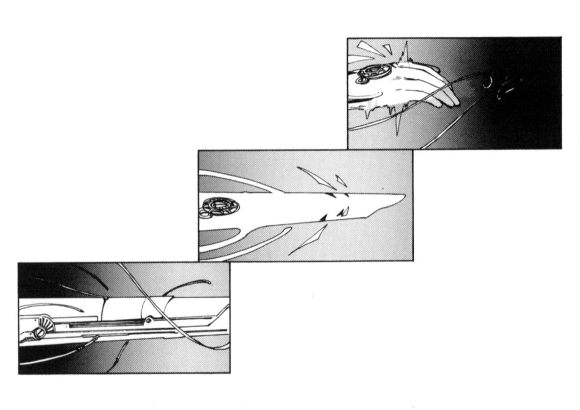

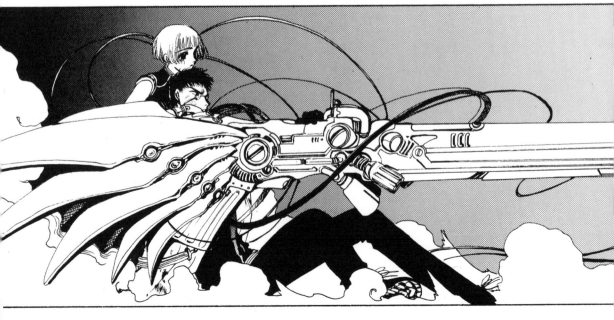

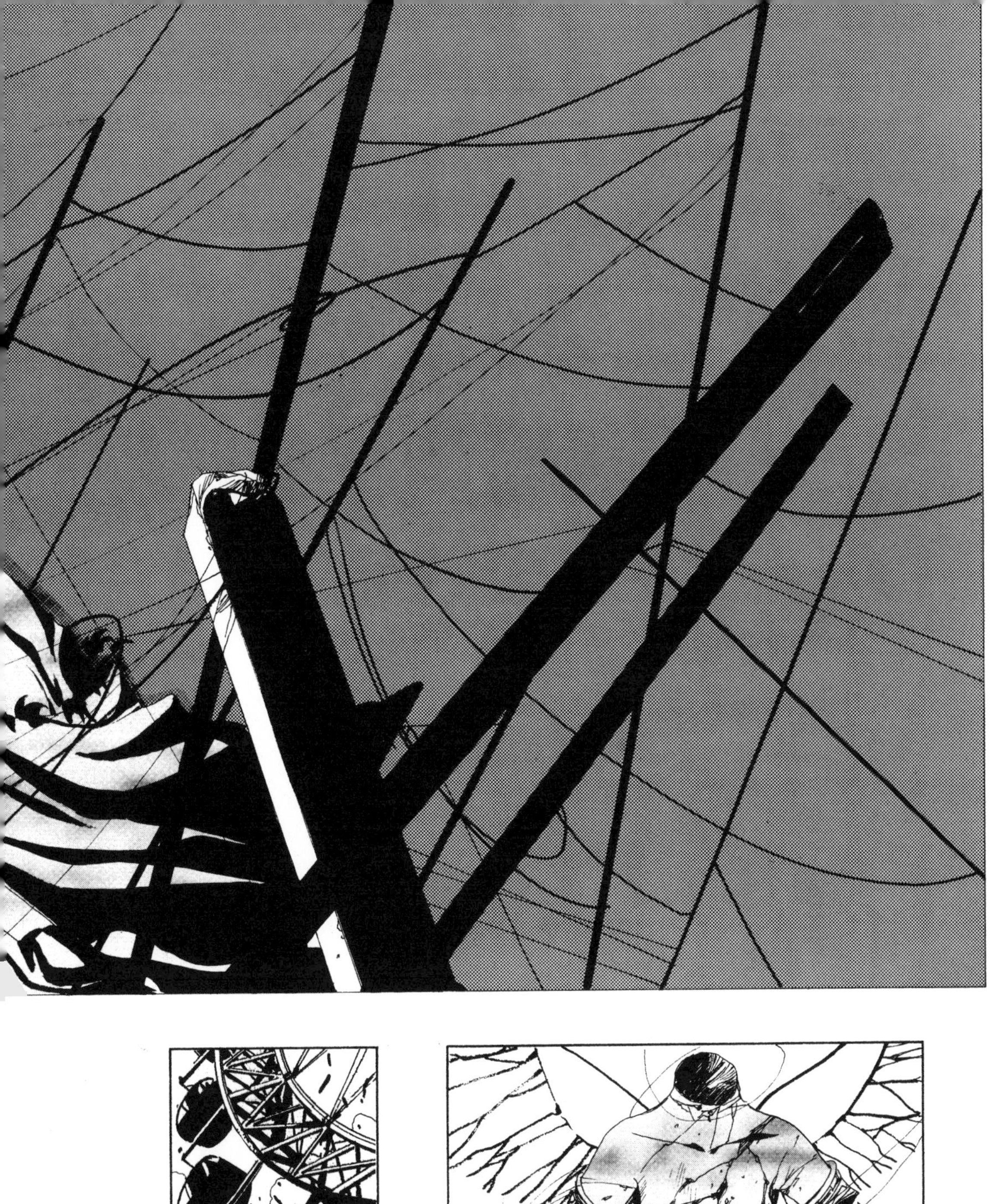
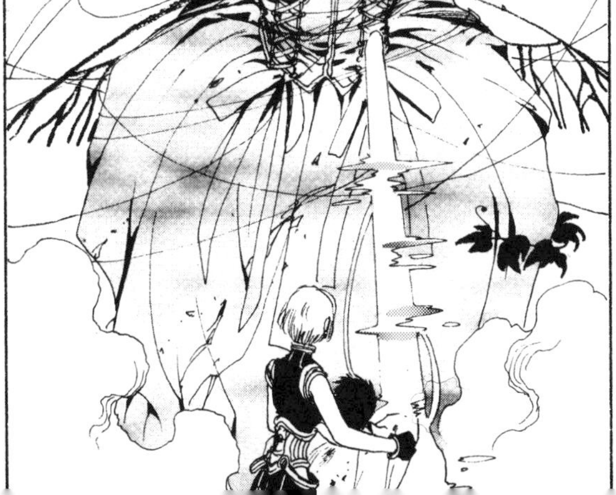
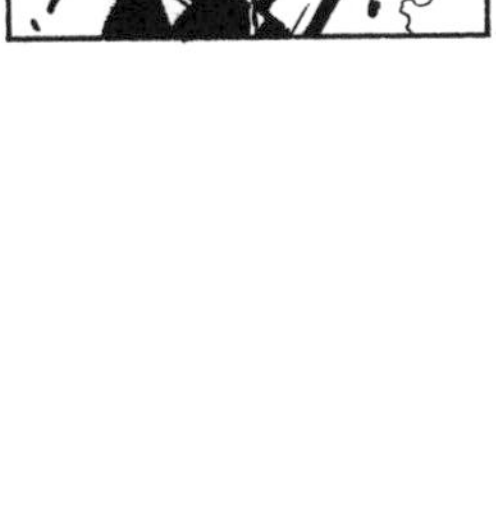

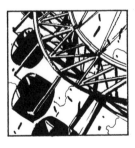

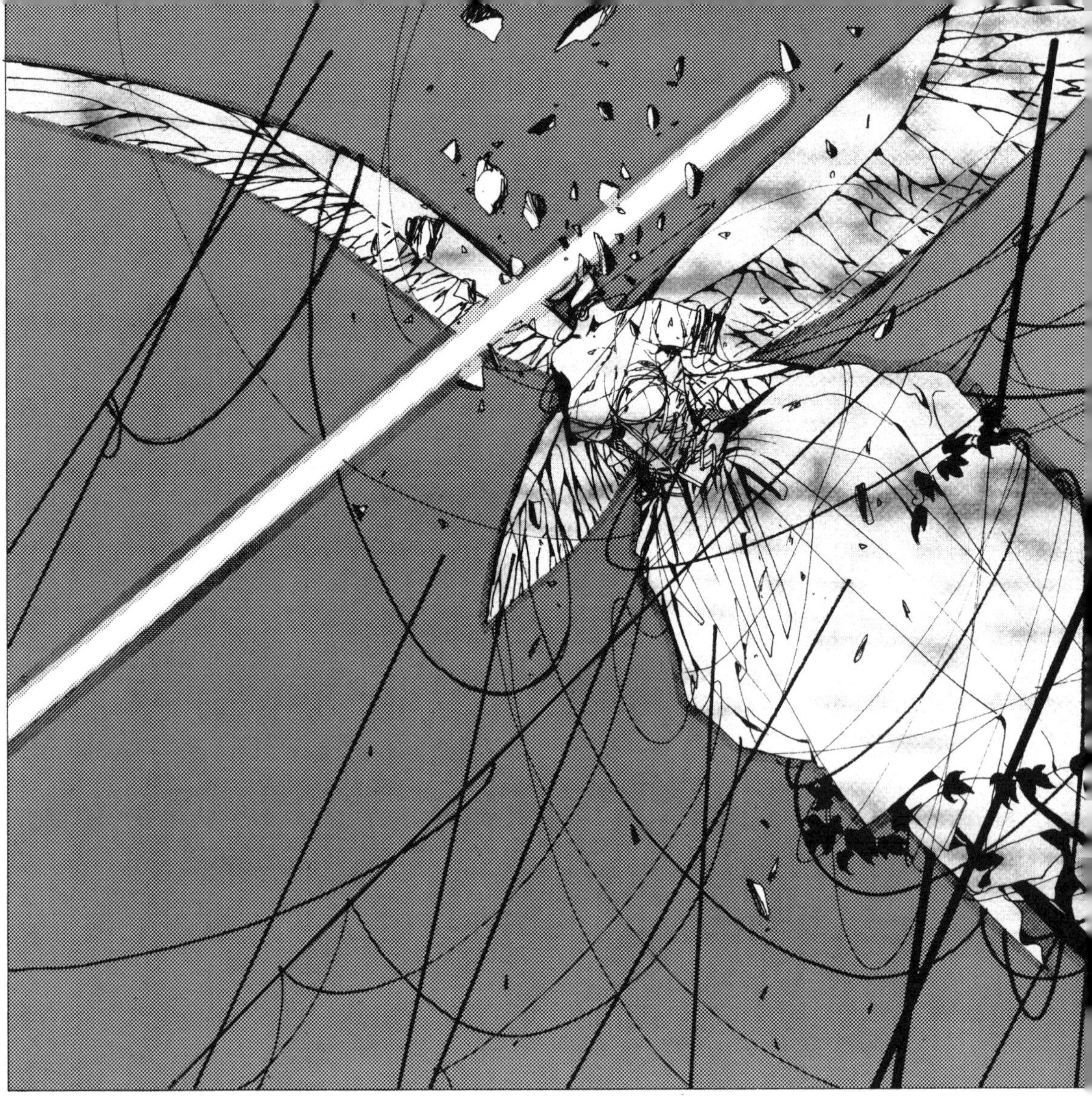
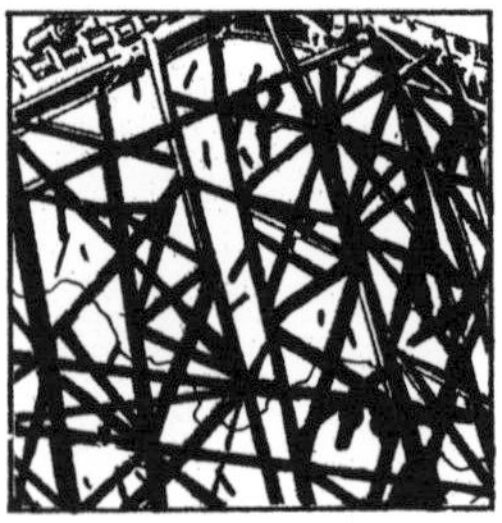
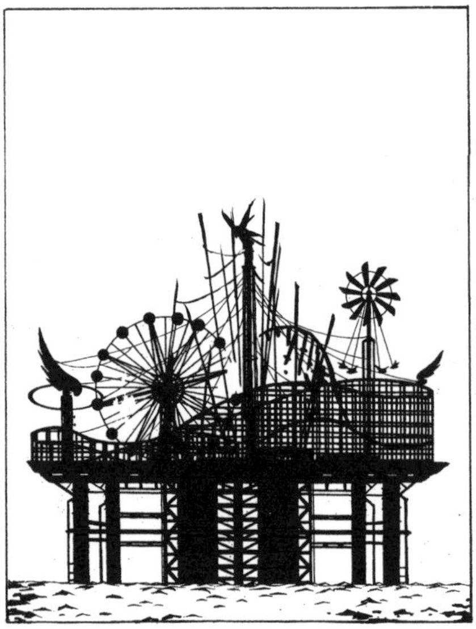

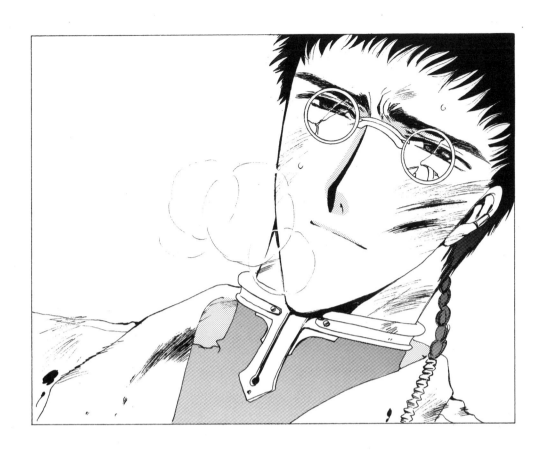

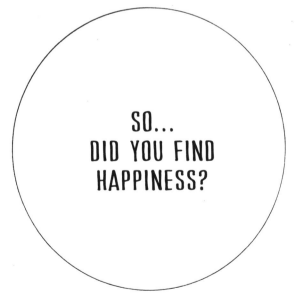

SO...
DID YOU FIND
HAPPINESS?

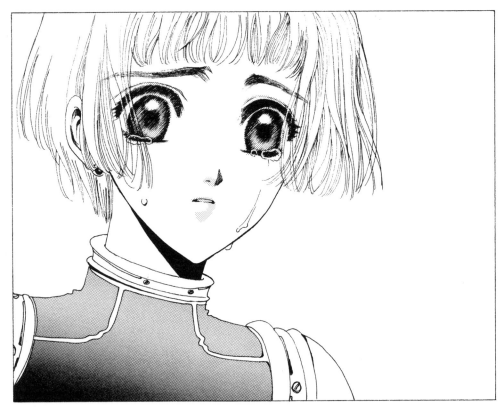

...YES.

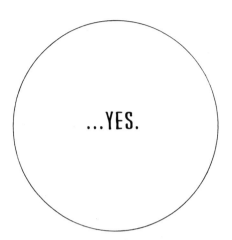

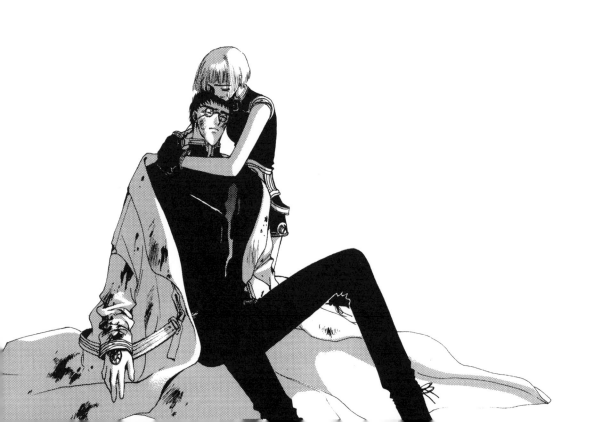

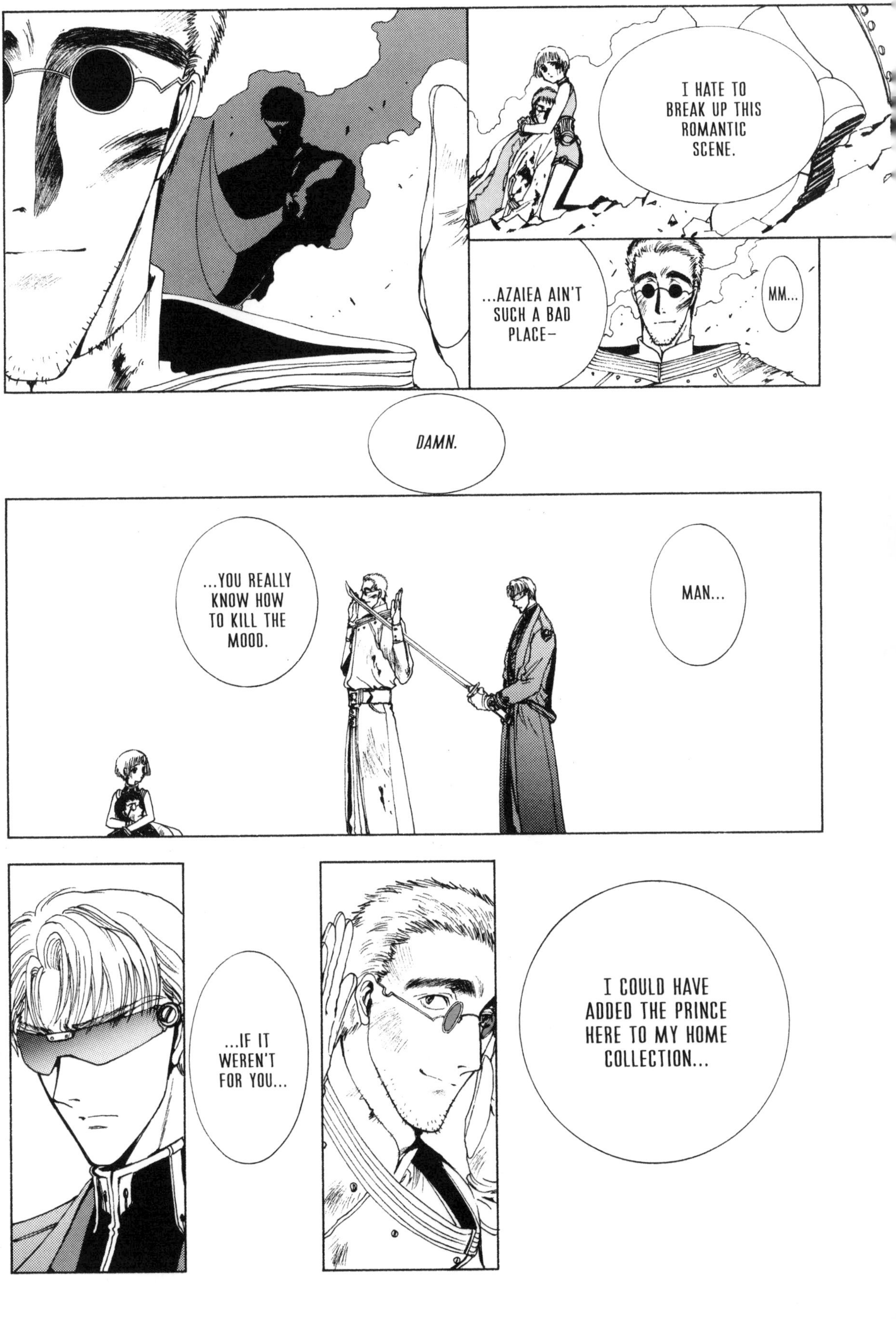
I HATE TO BREAK UP THIS ROMANTIC SCENE.
MM...
...AZAIEA AIN'T SUCH A BAD PLACE–
DAMN.
MAN...
...YOU REALLY KNOW HOW TO KILL THE MOOD.
I COULD HAVE ADDED THE PRINCE HERE TO MY HOME COLLECTION...
...IF IT WEREN'T FOR YOU...

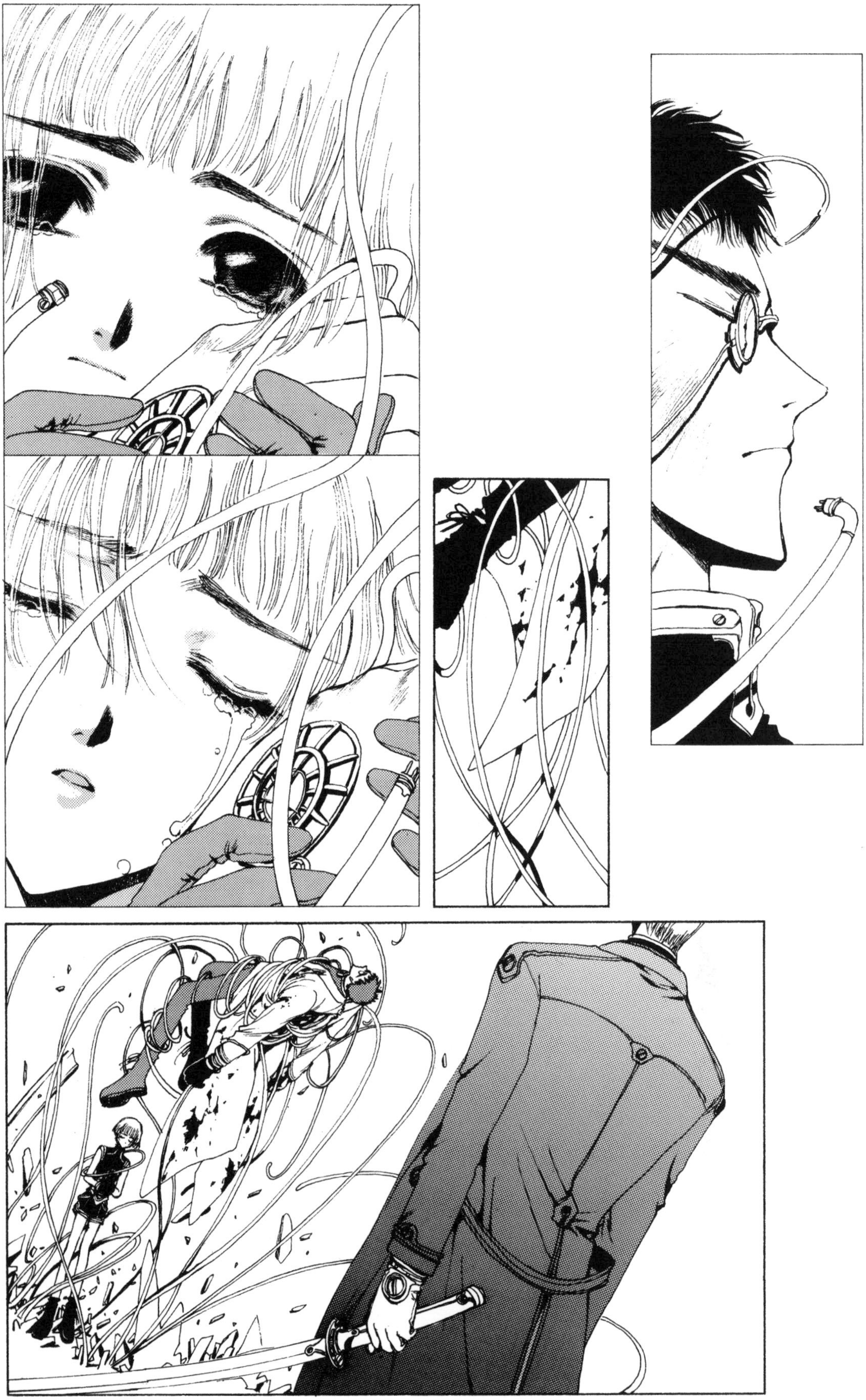

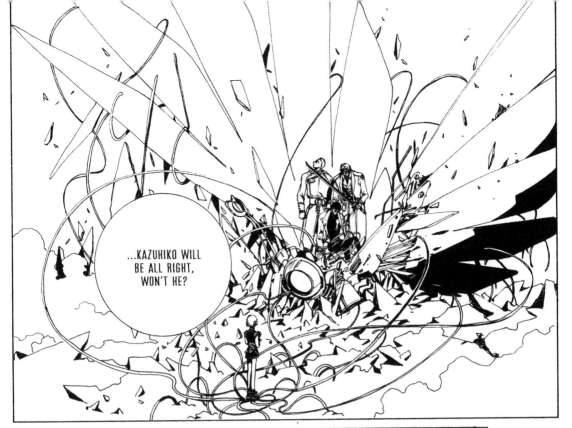

...KAZUHIKO WILL
BE ALL RIGHT,
WON'T HE?

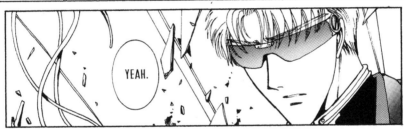

YEAH.

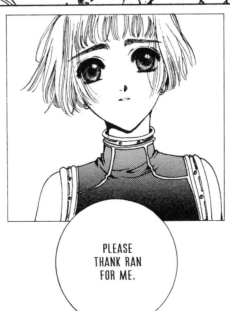

PLEASE
THANK RAN
FOR ME.

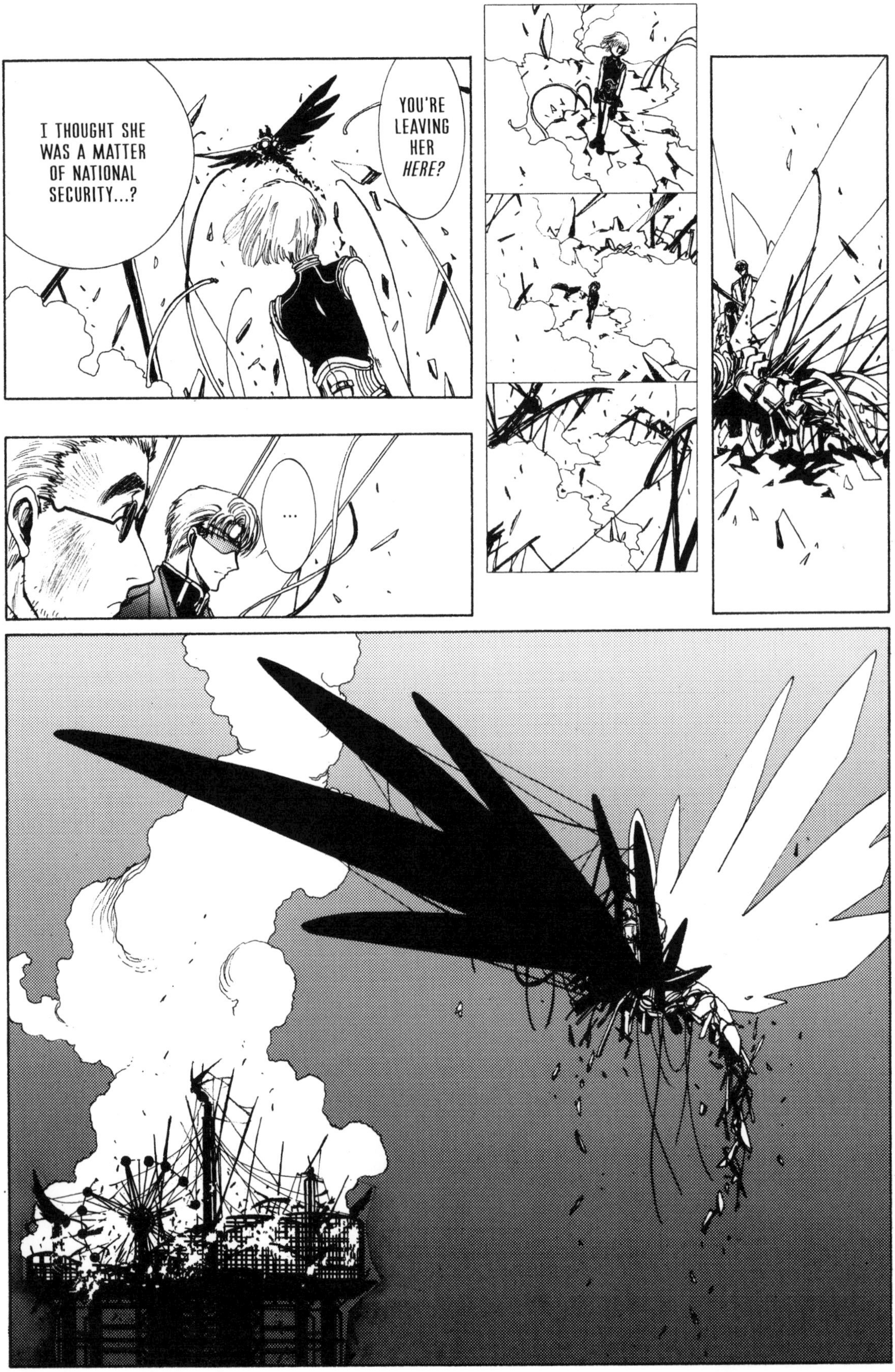
YOU'RE LEAVING HER *HERE?*
I THOUGHT SHE WAS A MATTER OF NATIONAL SECURITY...?
...

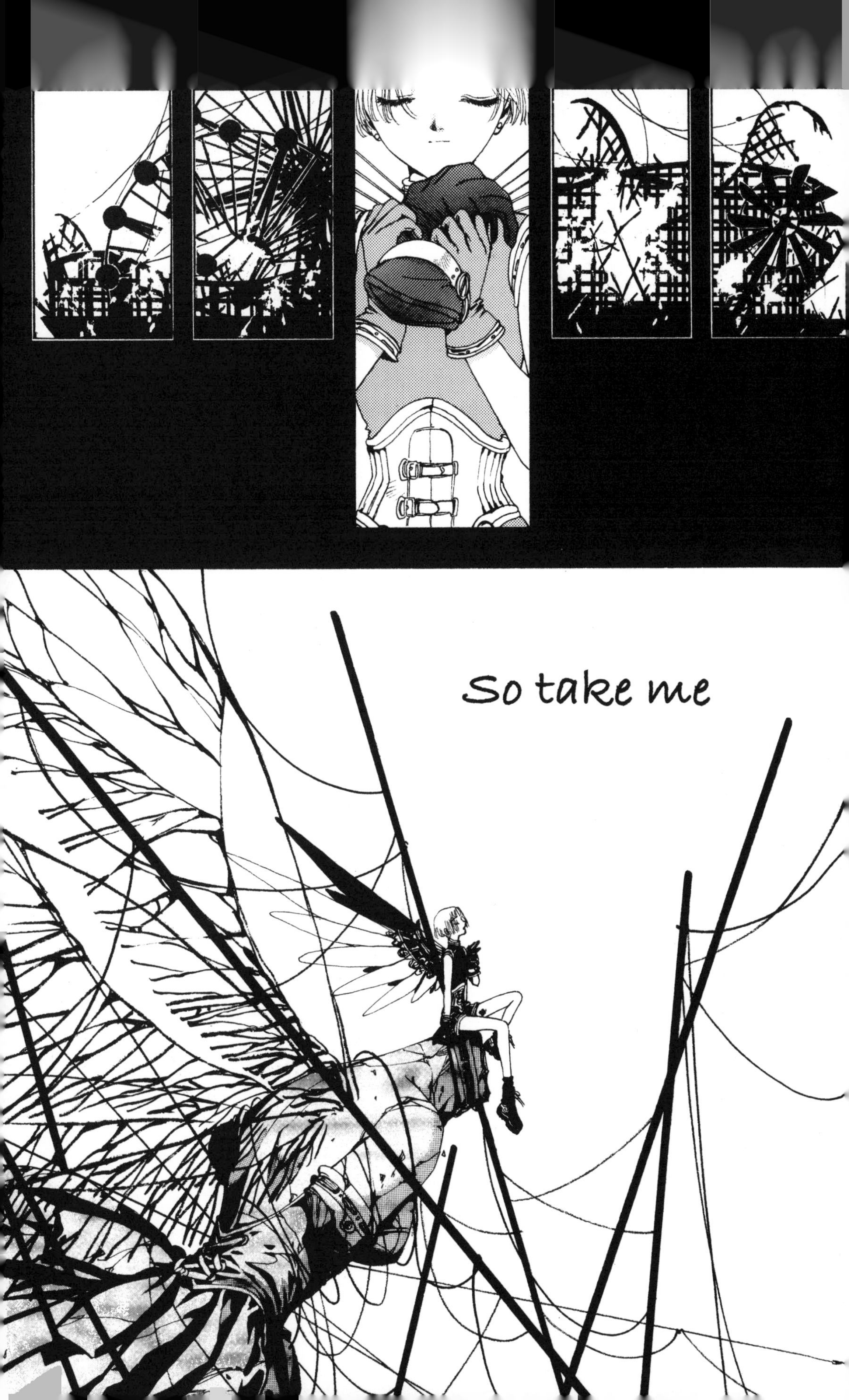
So take me

I wish for happiness
I seek happiness

To find happiness with you
To be your happiness

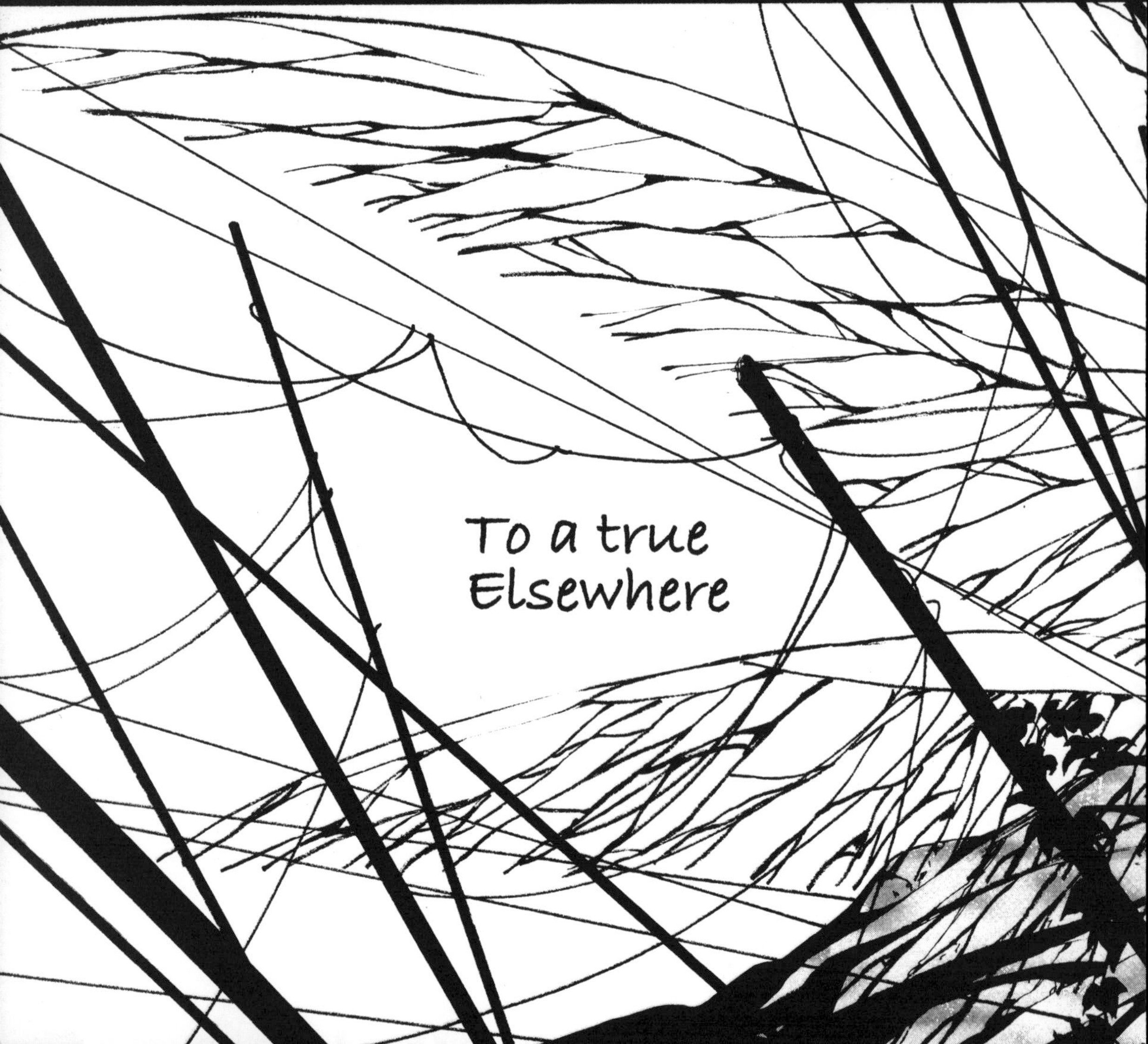
To a true
Elsewhere

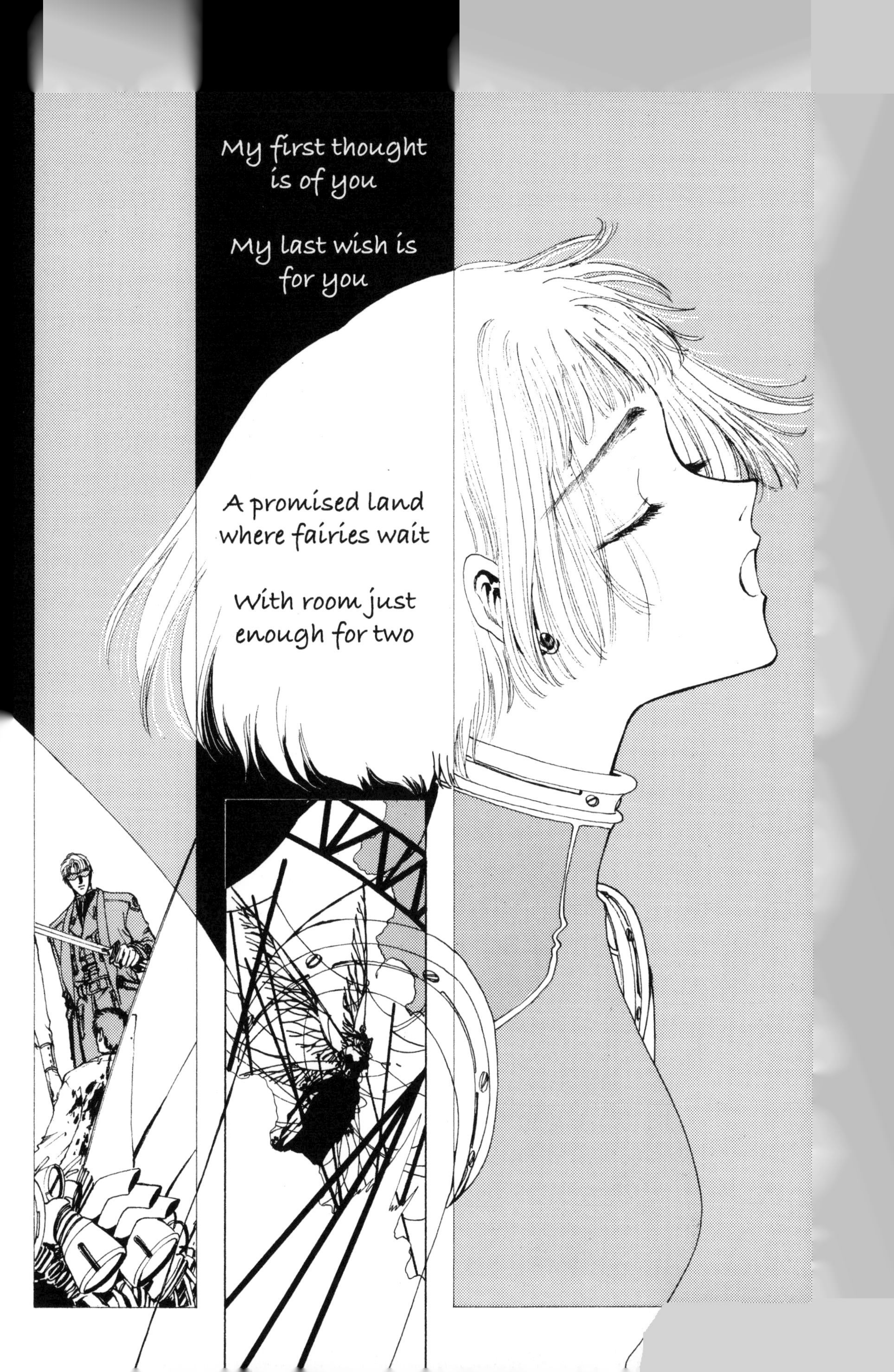
My first thought is of you
My last wish is for you
A promised land where fairies wait
With room just enough for two

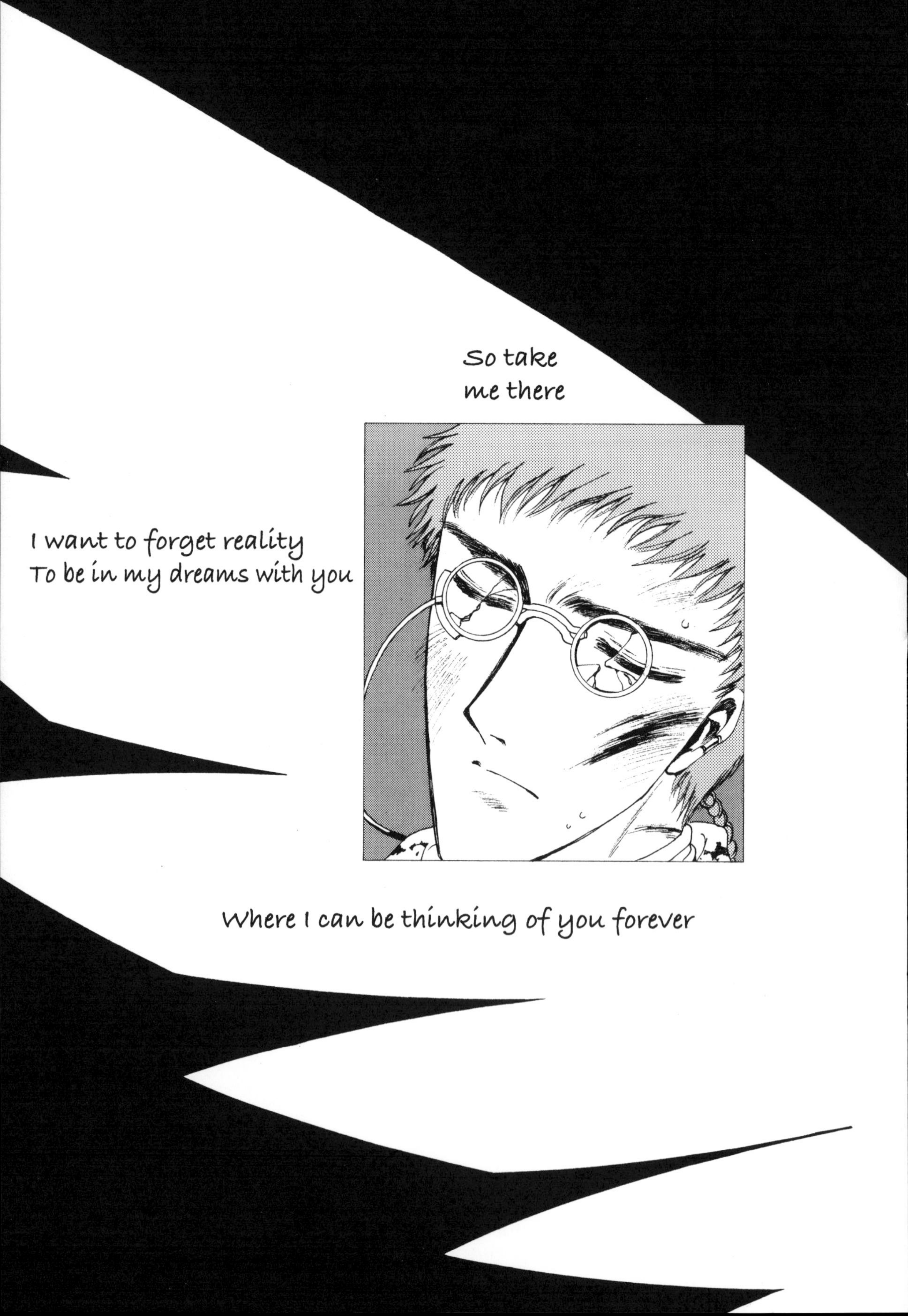
So take me there
I want to forget reality
To be in my dreams with you
Where I can be thinking of you forever

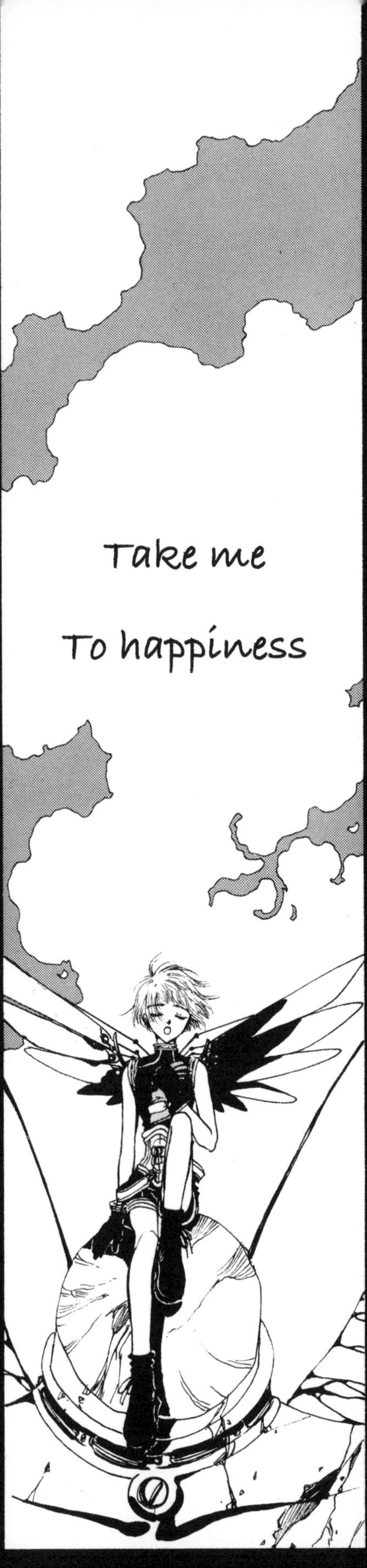
Take me
To happiness

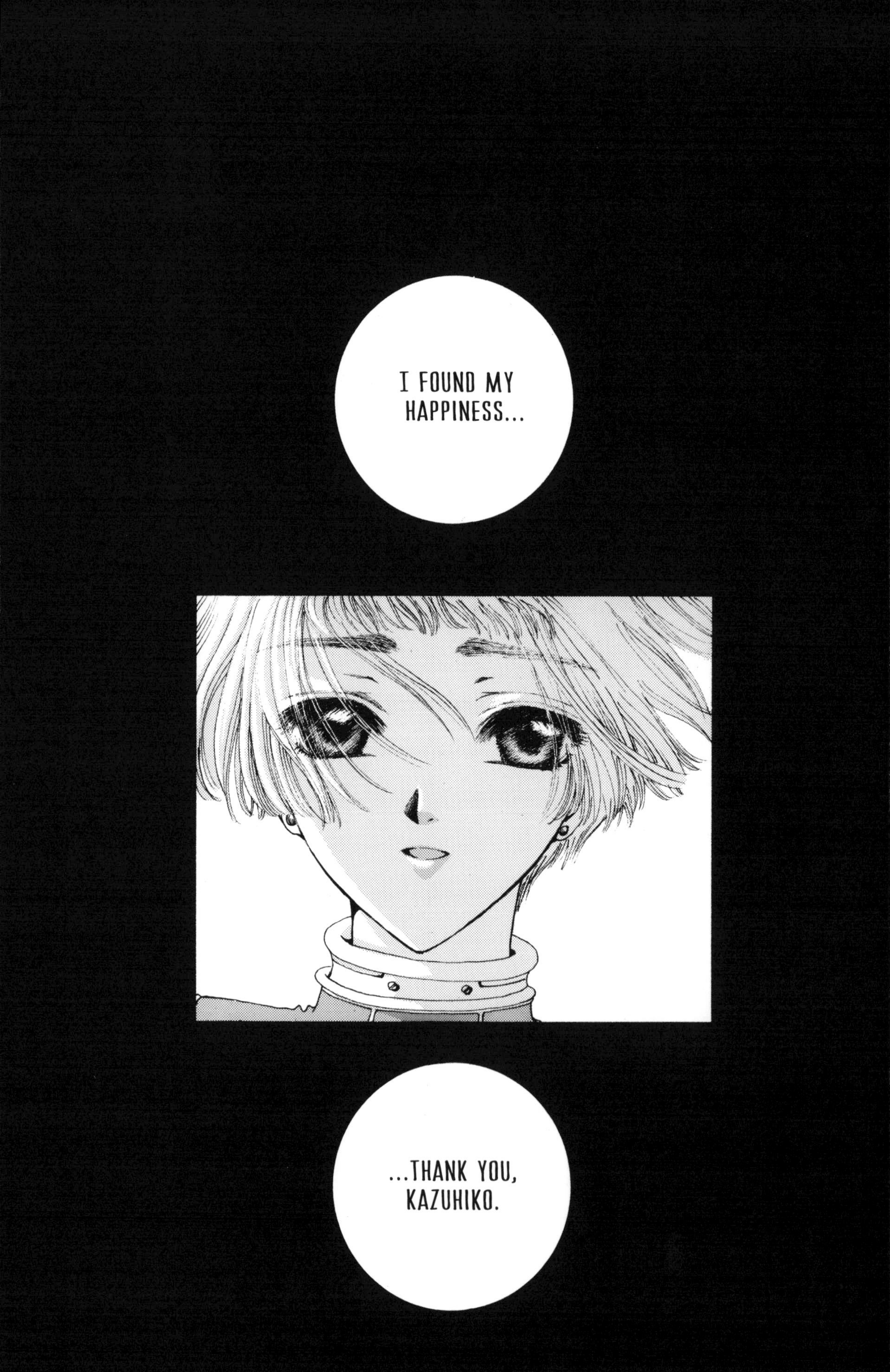
I FOUND MY HAPPINESS...
...THANK YOU, KAZUHIKO.

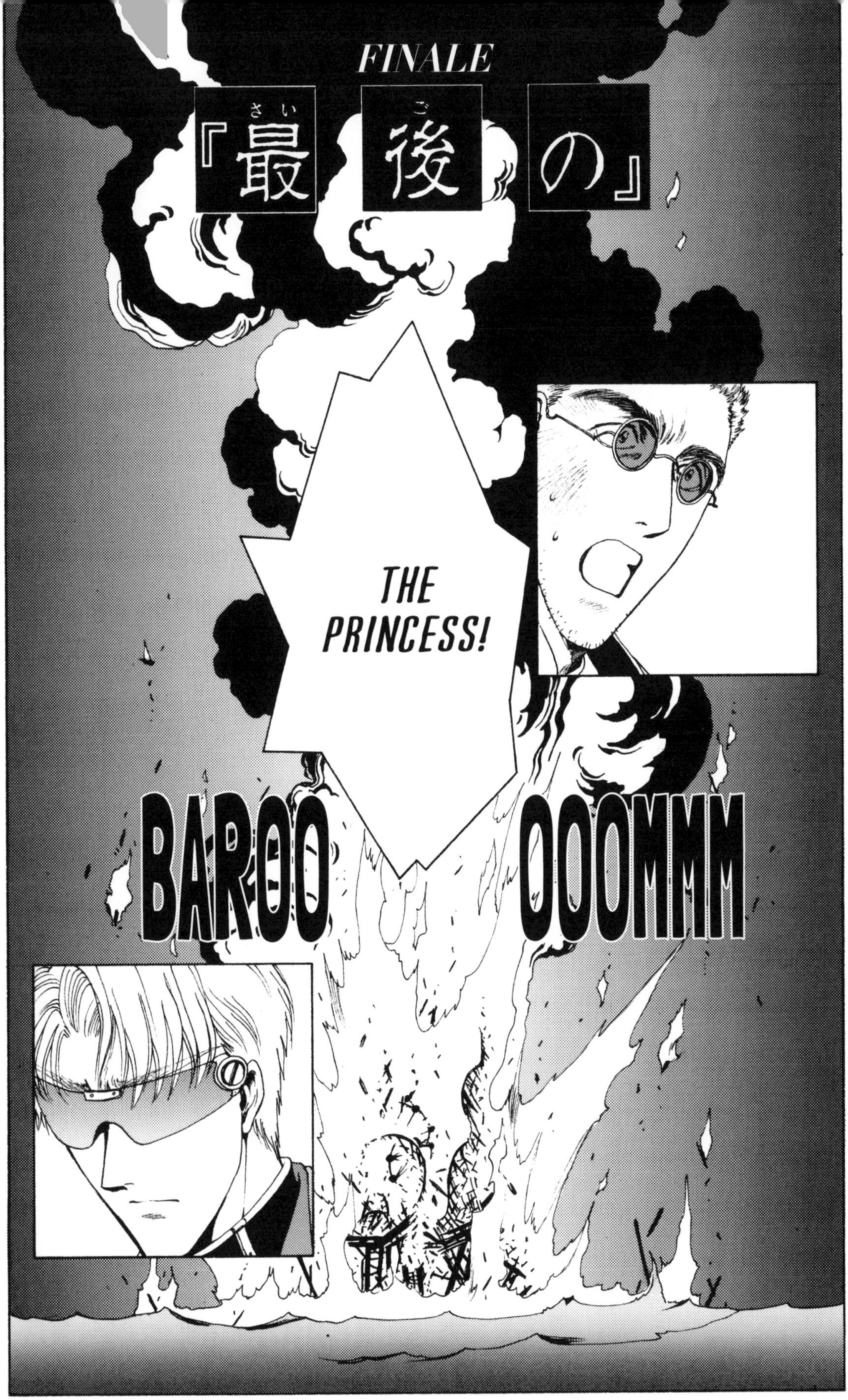
FINALE
『最後の』
THE PRINCESS!
BAROO OOOMMM

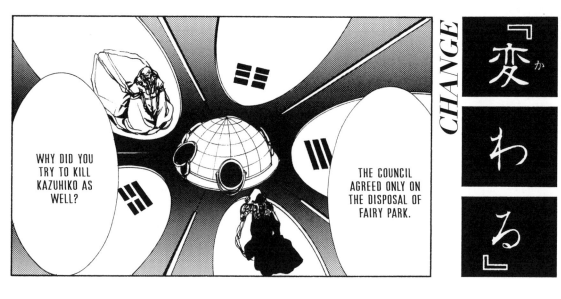

『変わる』 CHANGE

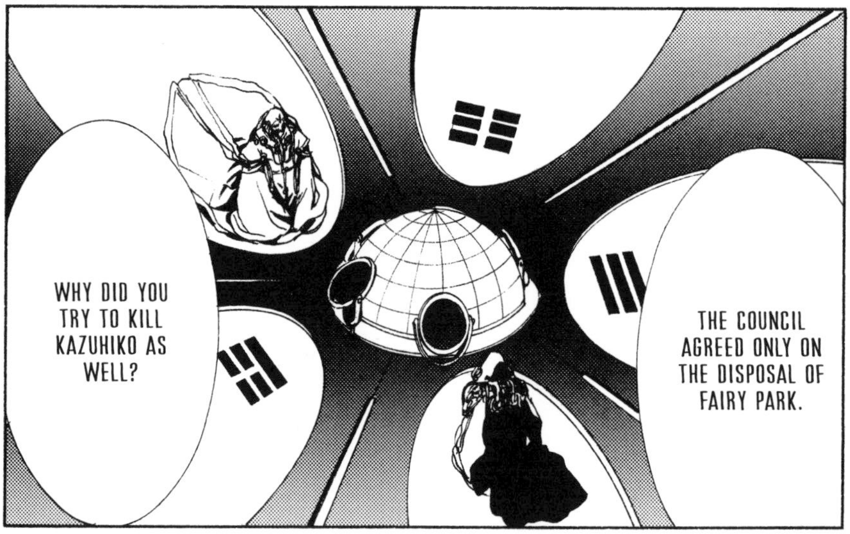
THE COUNCIL AGREED ONLY ON THE DISPOSAL OF FAIRY PARK.
WHY DID YOU TRY TO KILL KAZUHIKO AS WELL?

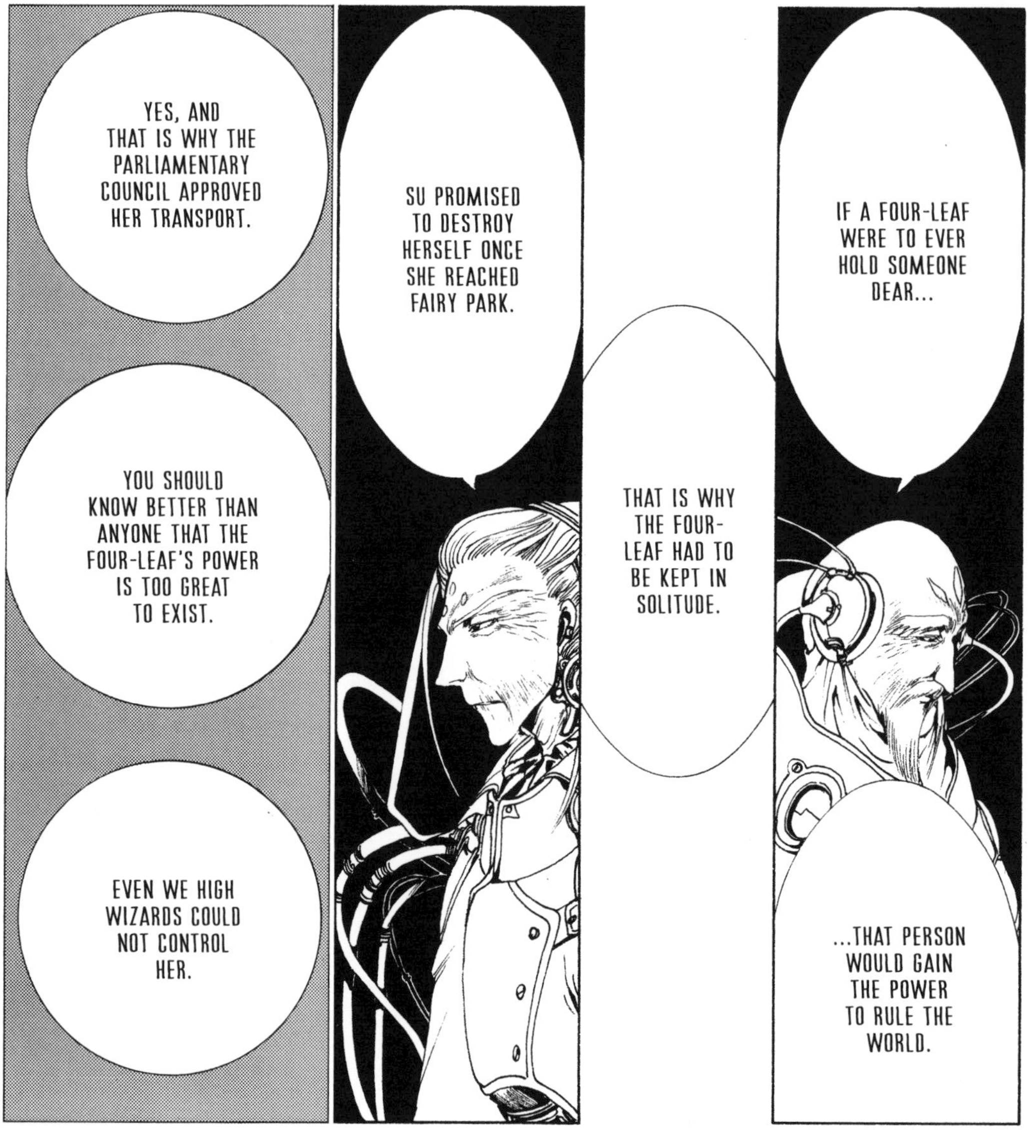
IF A FOUR-LEAF WERE TO EVER HOLD SOMEONE DEAR...
...THAT PERSON WOULD GAIN THE POWER TO RULE THE WORLD.
THAT IS WHY THE FOUR-LEAF HAD TO BE KEPT IN SOLITUDE.
SU PROMISED TO DESTROY HERSELF ONCE SHE REACHED FAIRY PARK.
YES, AND THAT IS WHY THE PARLIAMENTARY COUNCIL APPROVED HER TRANSPORT.
YOU SHOULD KNOW BETTER THAN ANYONE THAT THE FOUR-LEAF'S POWER IS TOO GREAT TO EXIST.
EVEN WE HIGH WIZARDS COULD NOT CONTROL HER.

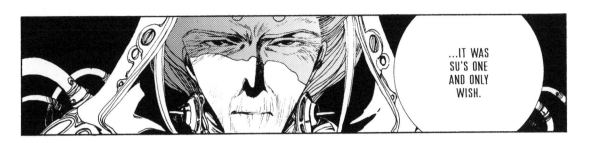

...IT WAS SU'S ONE AND ONLY WISH.
PEOPLE CHANGE THEIR MINDS. ESPECIALLY WHEN THEY GET EMOTIONALLY INVOLVED.
REMEMBER, YOU BROKE THE COUNCIL'S LAW WHEN YOU ALLOWED HER TO COMMUNICATE WITH THAT SINGER.
...I SUPPOSE I'M TO BE COURT-MARTIALED, THEN?
NO.
WHY?
LIKE I SAID, PEOPLE CHANGE THEIR MINDS... WHEN THEY GET EMOTIONALLY INVOLVED.

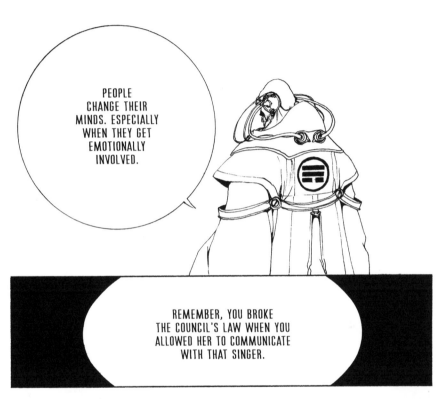

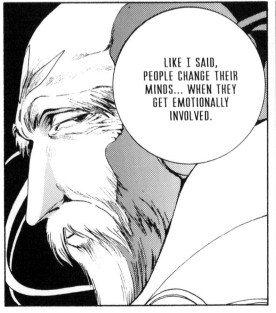

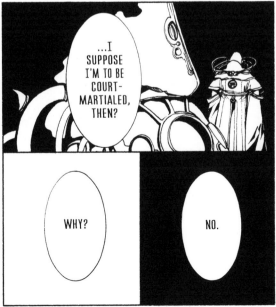

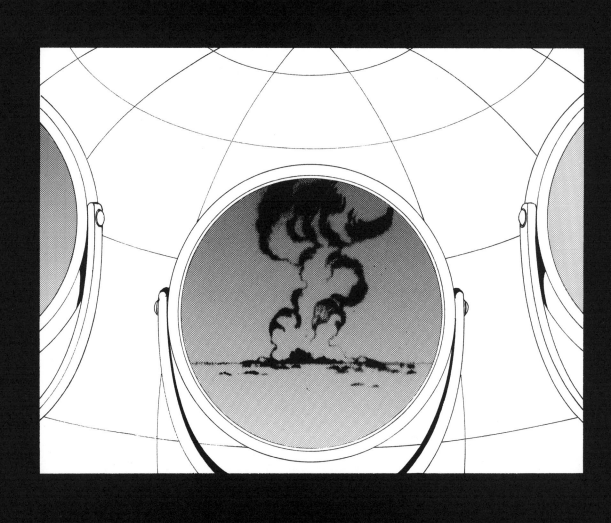

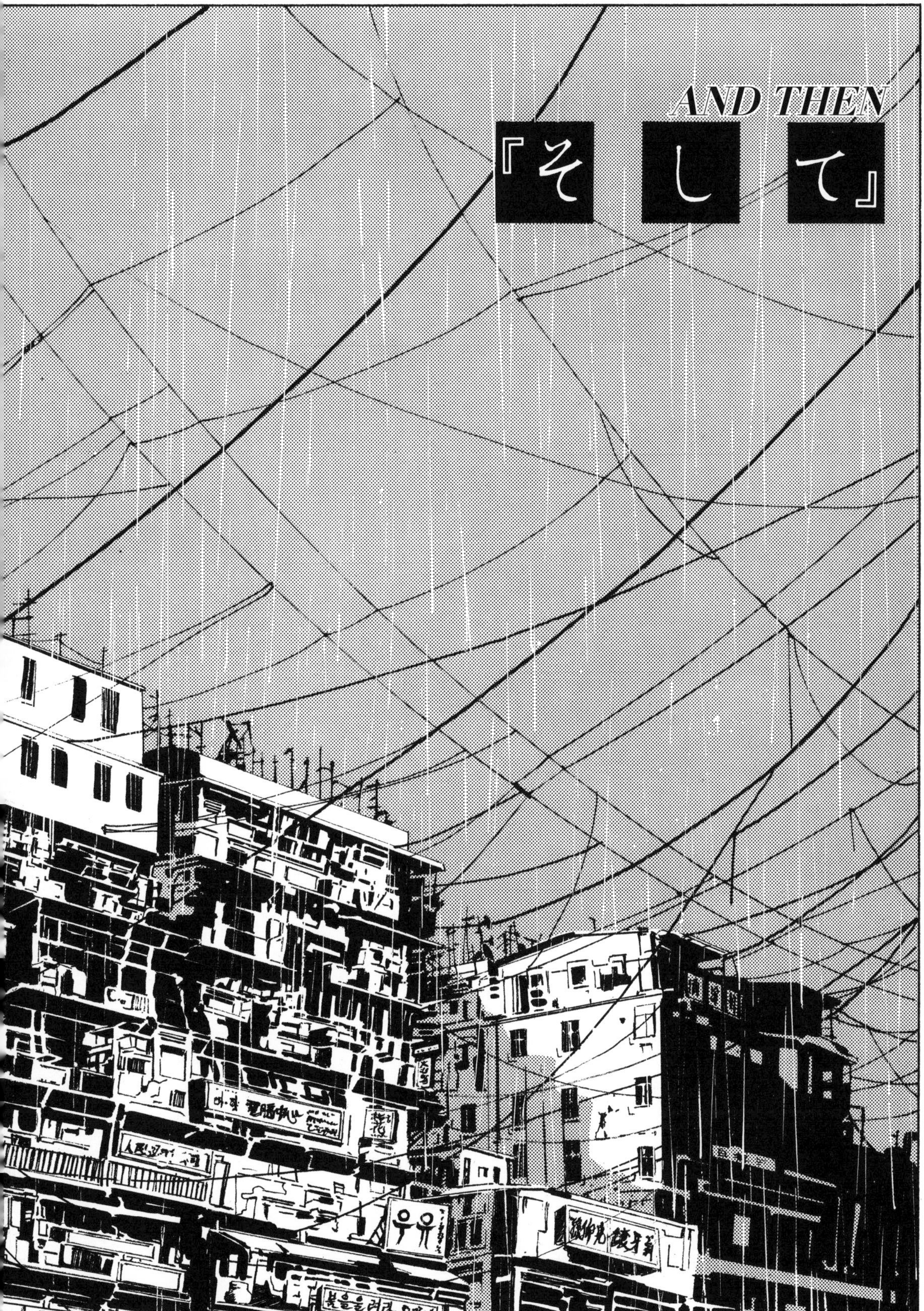
AND THEN
『そして』
우유

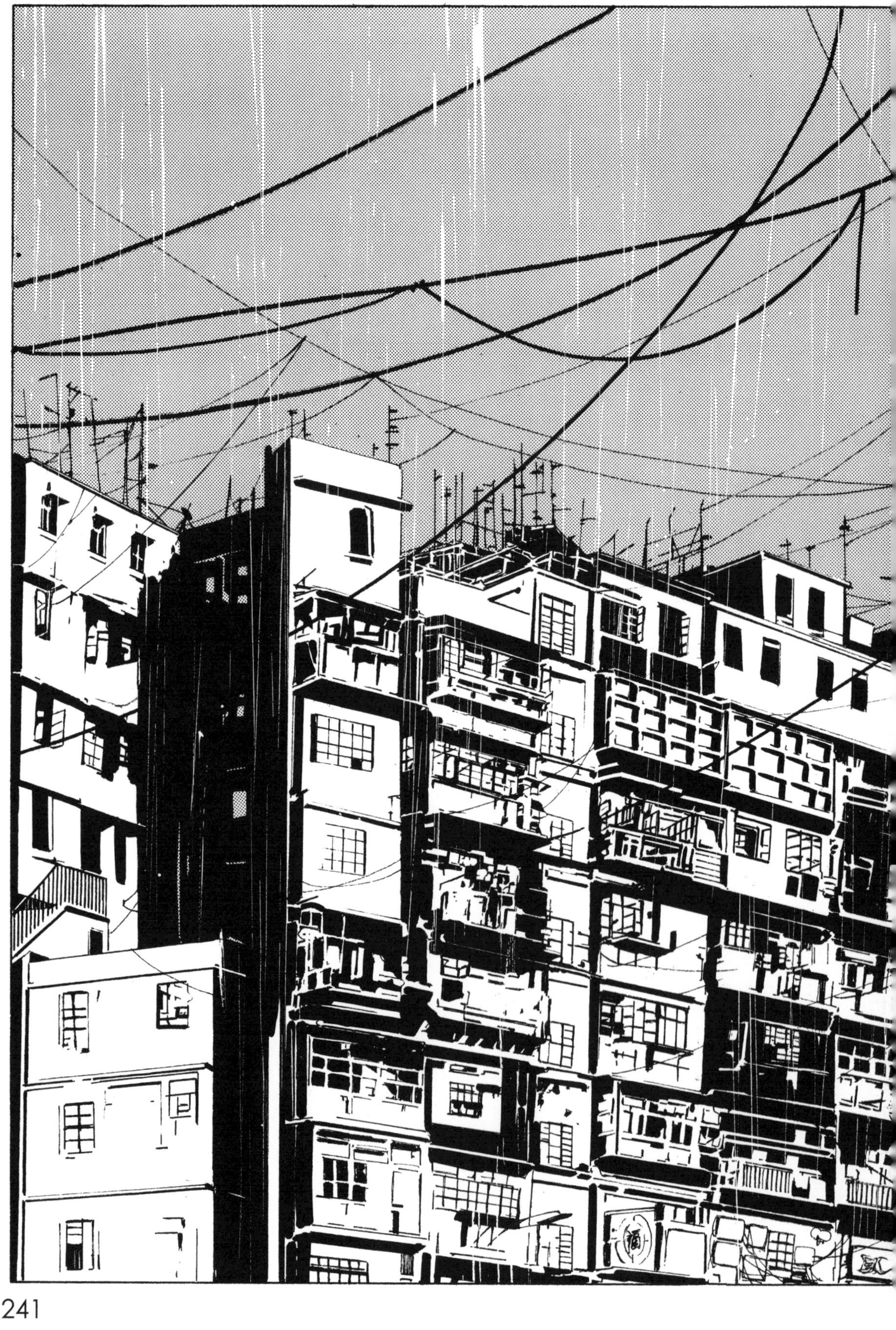

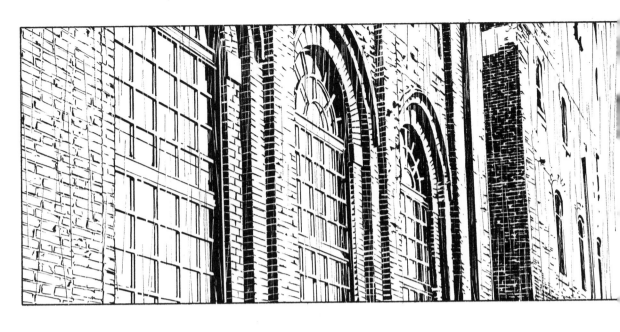

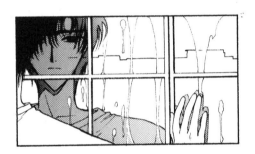

HEART

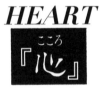

A
FOUR-LEAF
CAN NEVER
BELONG TO
ANYONE.

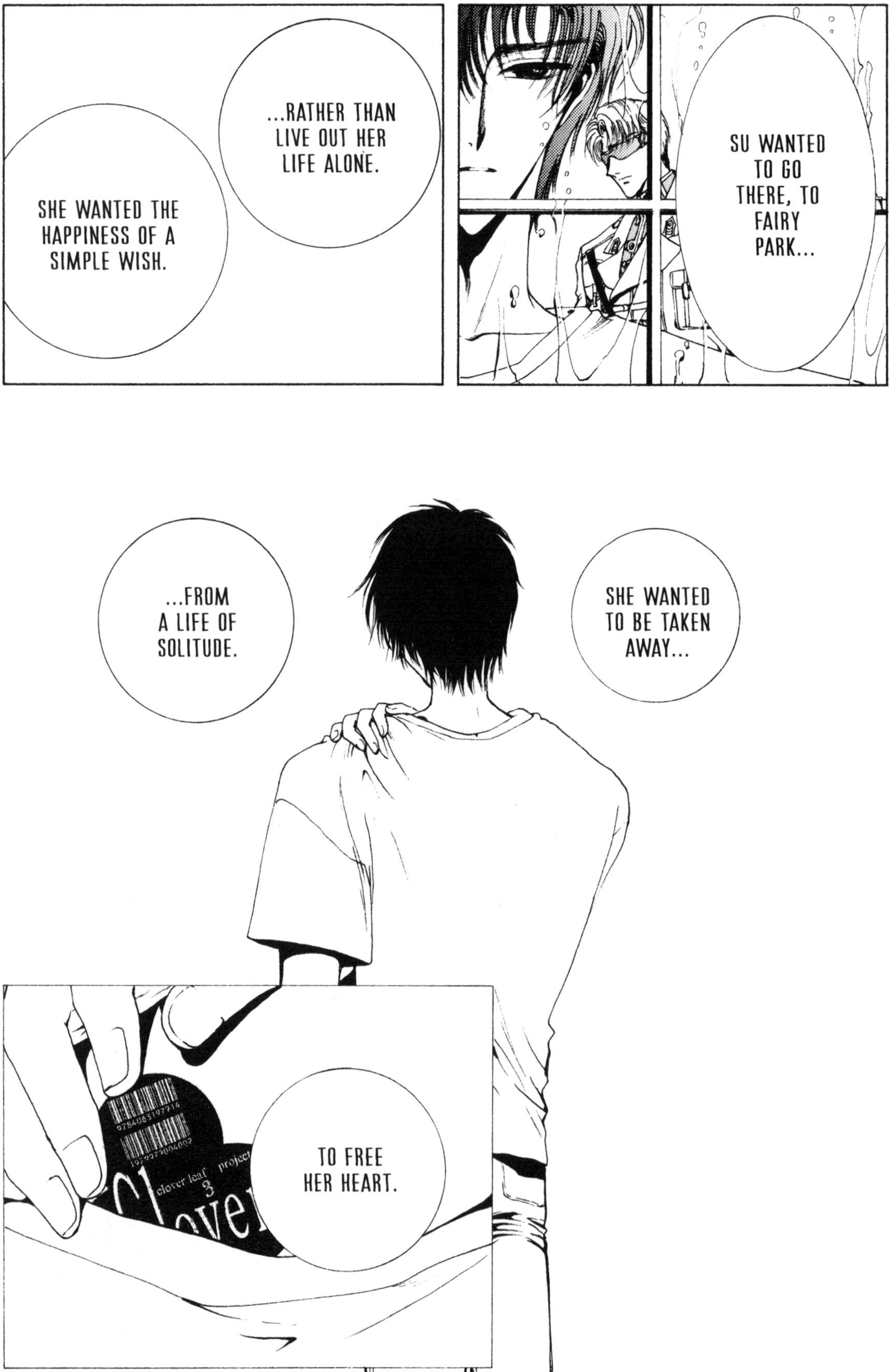
SU WANTED TO GO THERE, TO FAIRY PARK...
SHE WANTED THE HAPPINESS OF A SIMPLE WISH.
...RATHER THAN LIVE OUT HER LIFE ALONE.
SHE WANTED TO BE TAKEN AWAY...
...FROM A LIFE OF SOLITUDE.
TO FREE HER HEART.

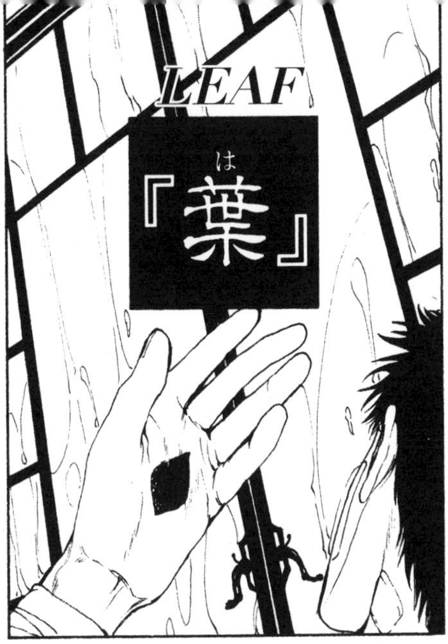
LEAF
『葉』
は

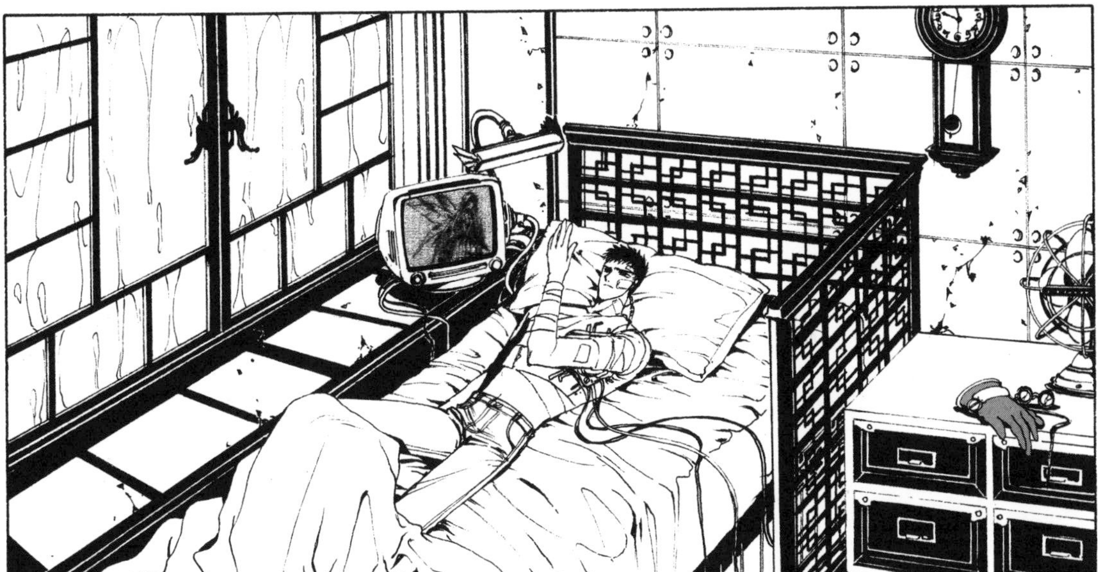

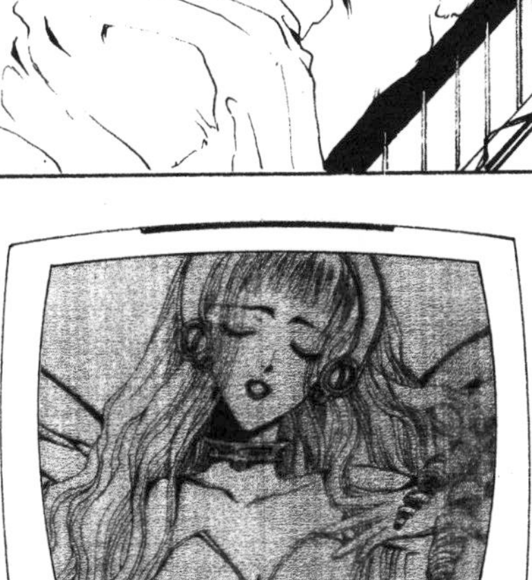

I wish for happiness

I seek happiness

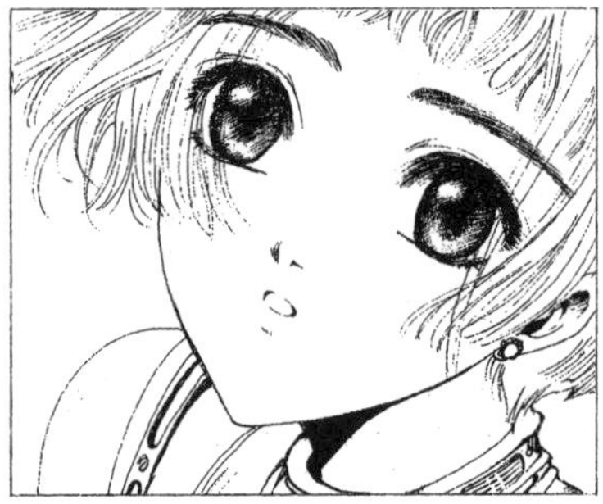

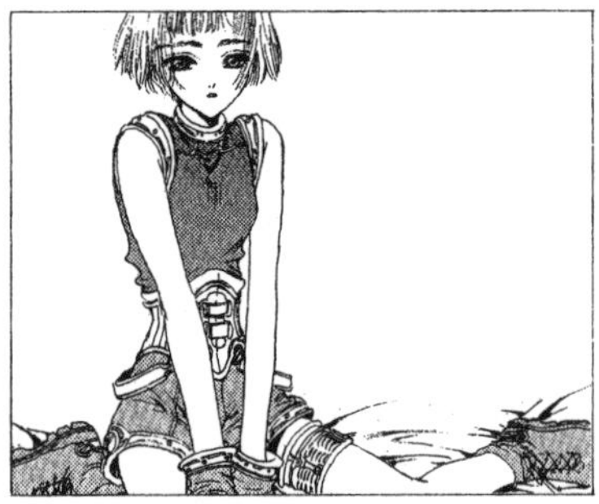

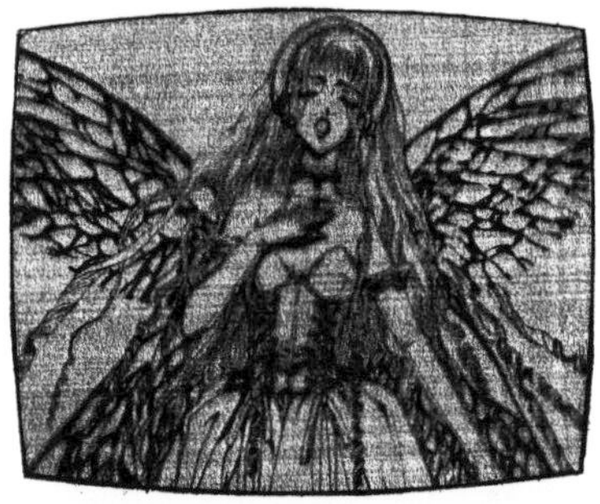

Take me

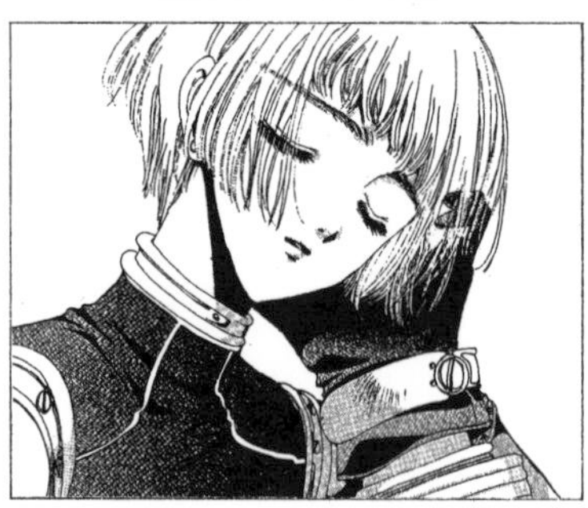

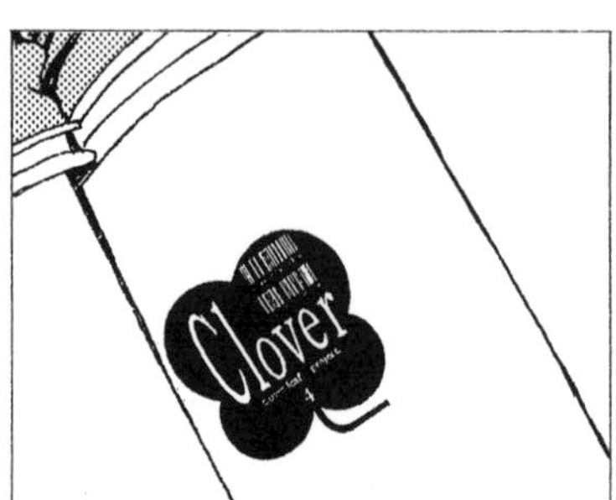
Clover

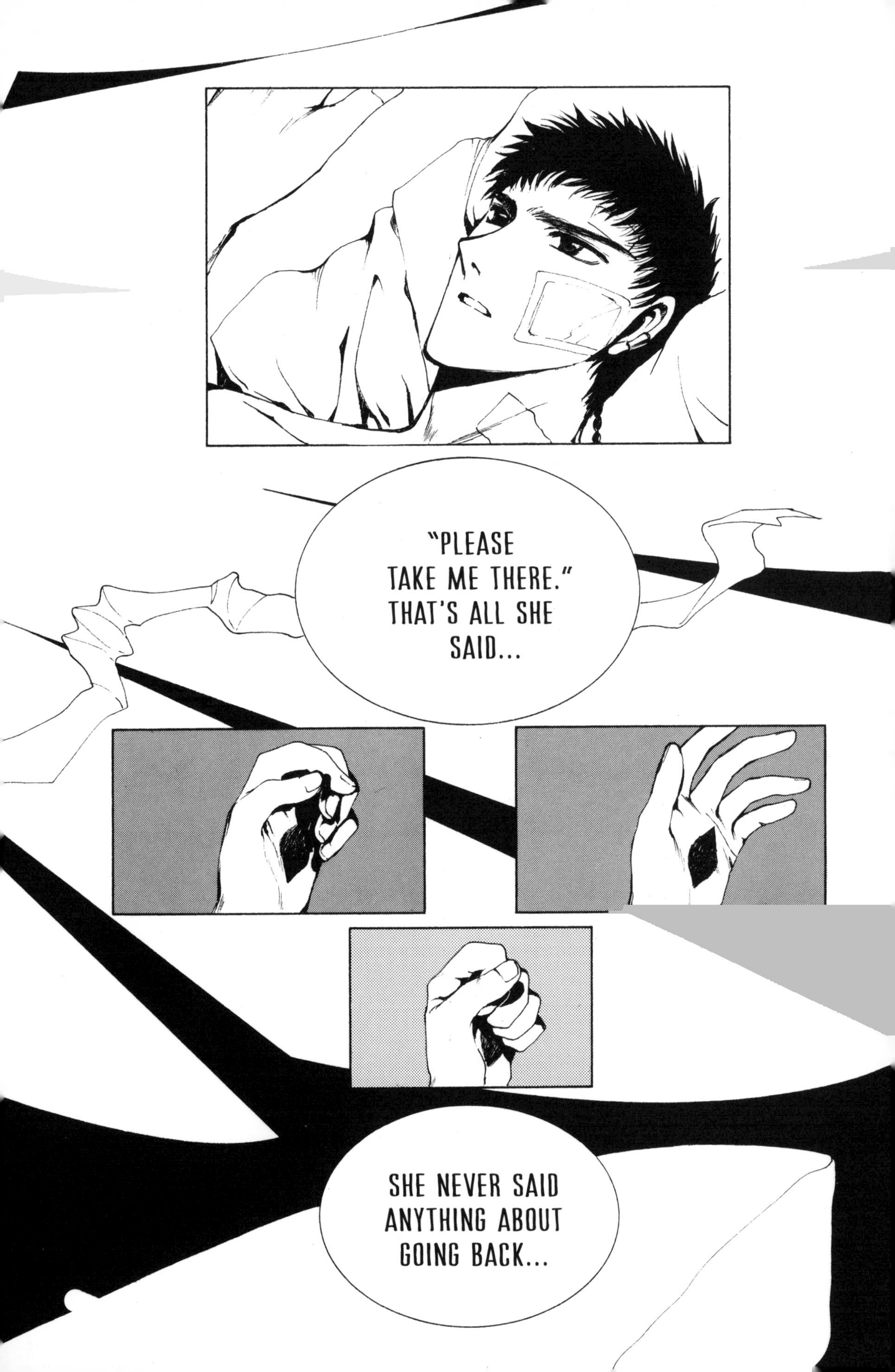
"PLEASE TAKE ME THERE." THAT'S ALL SHE SAID...
SHE NEVER SAID ANYTHING ABOUT GOING BACK...

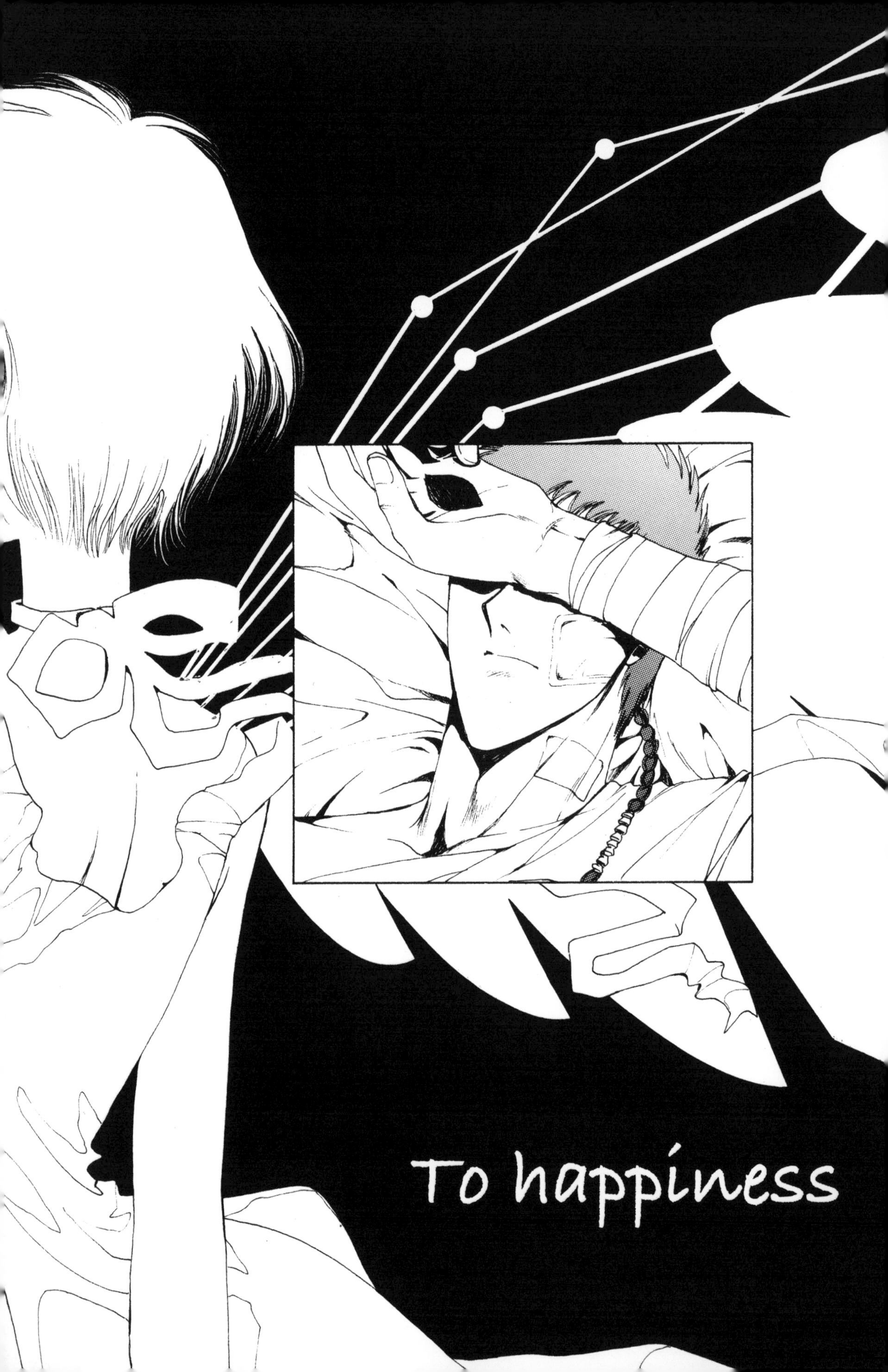
To happiness

I wish for happiness
I seek happiness

To find happiness with you
To be your happiness

Take me
To a true Elsewhere
Please take me

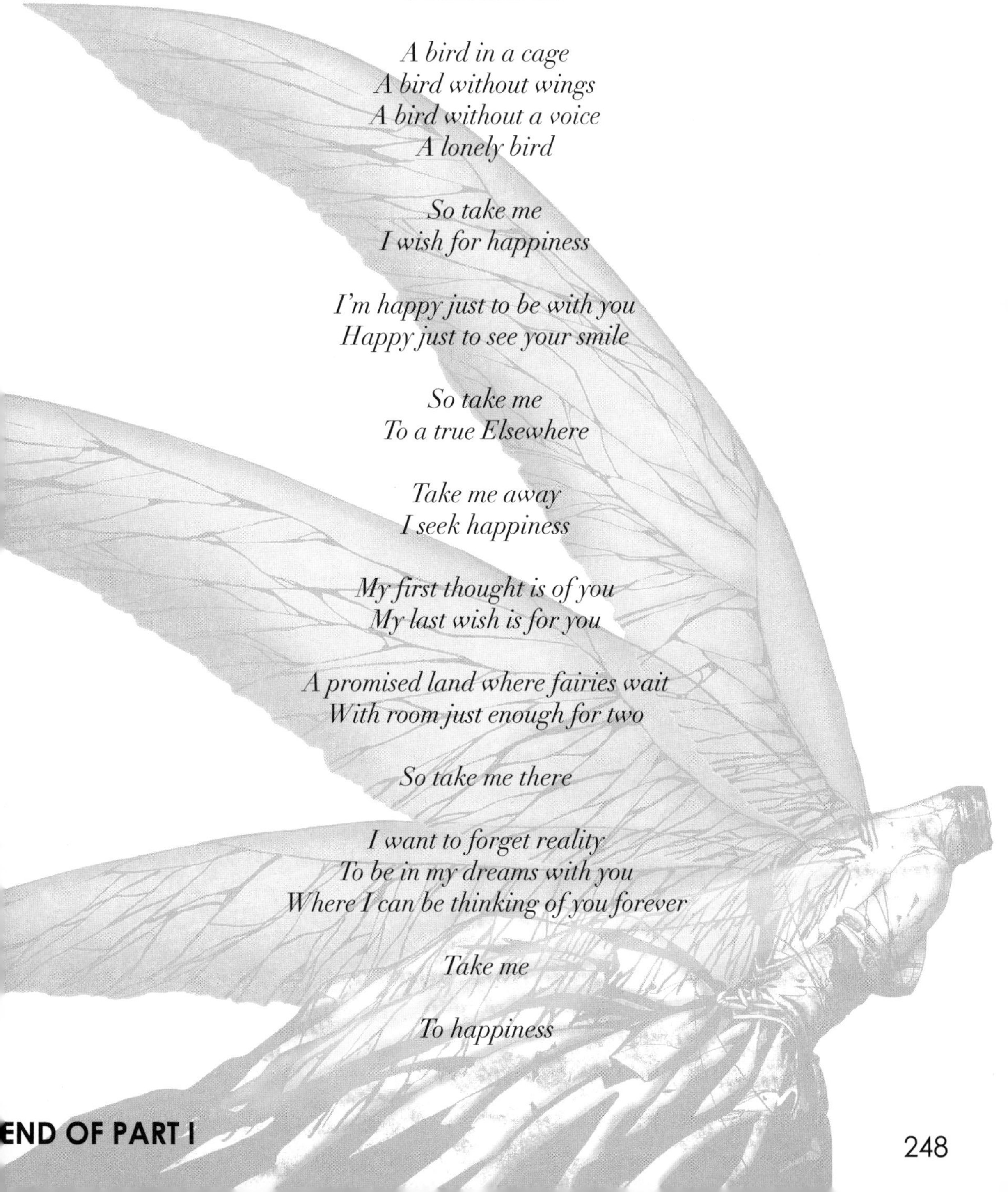

A bird in a cage
A bird without wings
A bird without a voice
A lonely bird

So take me
I wish for happiness

I'm happy just to be with you
Happy just to see your smile

So take me
To a true Elsewhere

Take me away
I seek happiness

My first thought is of you
My last wish is for you

A promised land where fairies wait
With room just enough for two

So take me there

I want to forget reality
To be in my dreams with you
Where I can be thinking of you forever

Take me

To happiness

END OF PART I

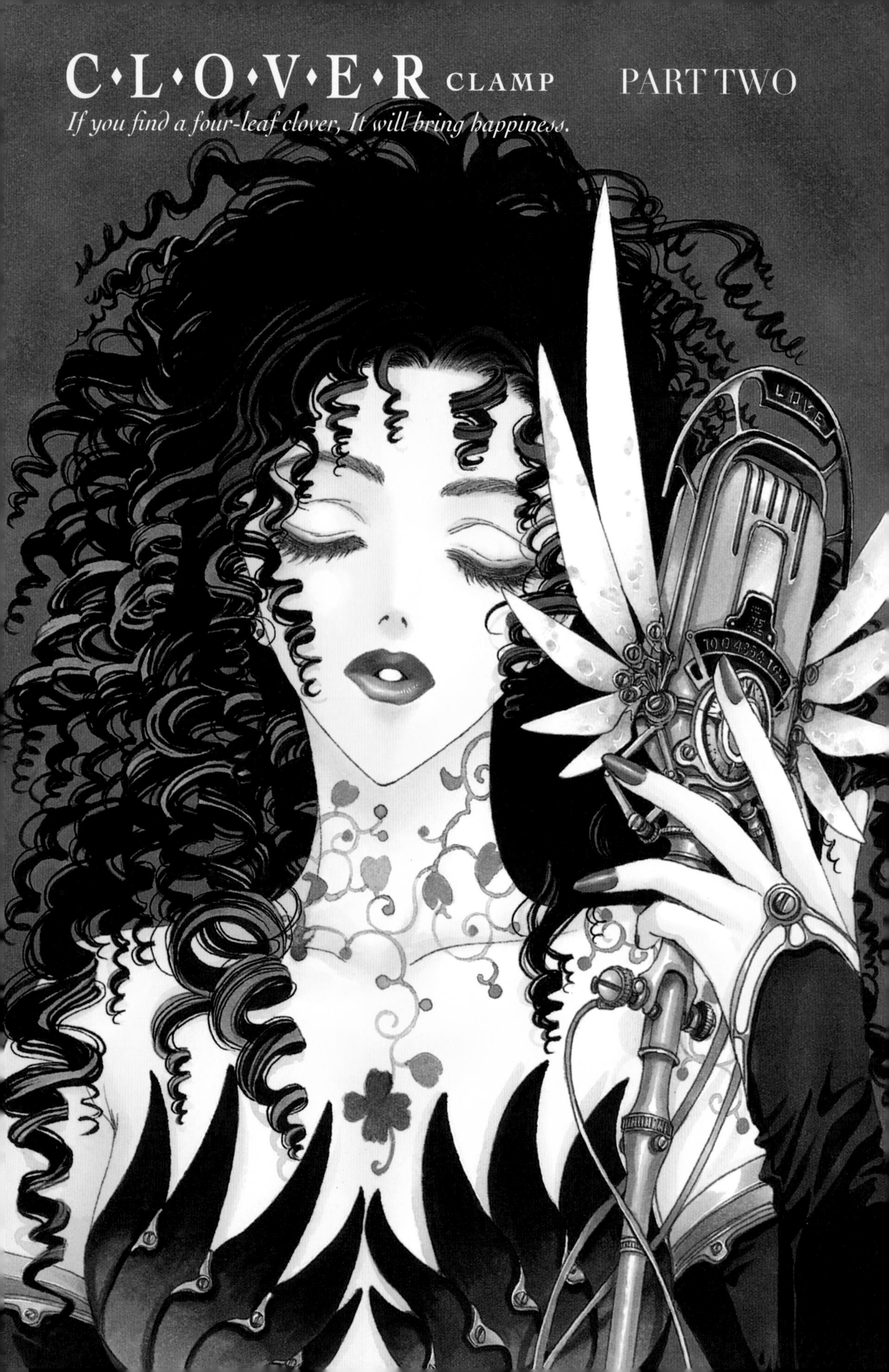
C·L·O·V·E·R CLAMP
PART TWO
If you find a four-leaf clover, It will bring happiness.
LOVE

LOVE
It's my dream

A beautiful dream
Never before seen
A beautiful deceit
Never detected
A beautiful love
That no one can break

LOVE
You might laugh
But it's the most beautiful word

LOVE
You might laugh
But it's the most important
word

Now, come close to me
I'll sing an endless song
God, please show me
The truest love, red deeper
than red

Now, kiss me, hold me
Show me love that's forever
God, please show me
The truest heart, blue lusher
than blue

LOVE
Anyone can say it
But no one knows its true
meaning
Alone, I cannot understand
Together, we will

LOVE
A wonderful soul
Whom everyone admires
A wonderful moment
Which everyone desires
A wonderful romance
That everyone dreams of

LOVE
True love is unmatched

LOVE
You might laugh
But once lost, it never returns

LOVE
You might laugh
But to us, it's the most important word

LOVE
Hear the whisper of the heart, hear its true voice
Listen carefully, where lies true love?
To whom shall you give true love?

LOVE
You might laugh,
But it's the most important word

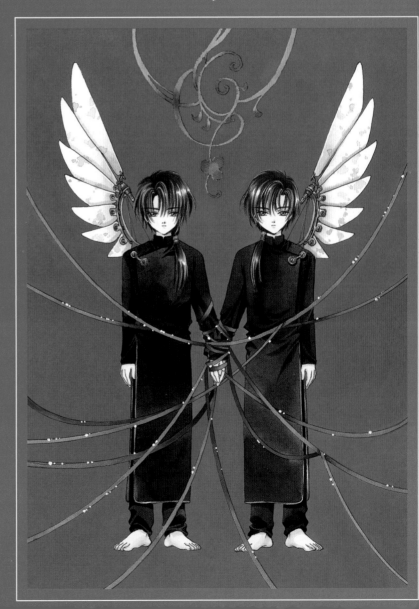

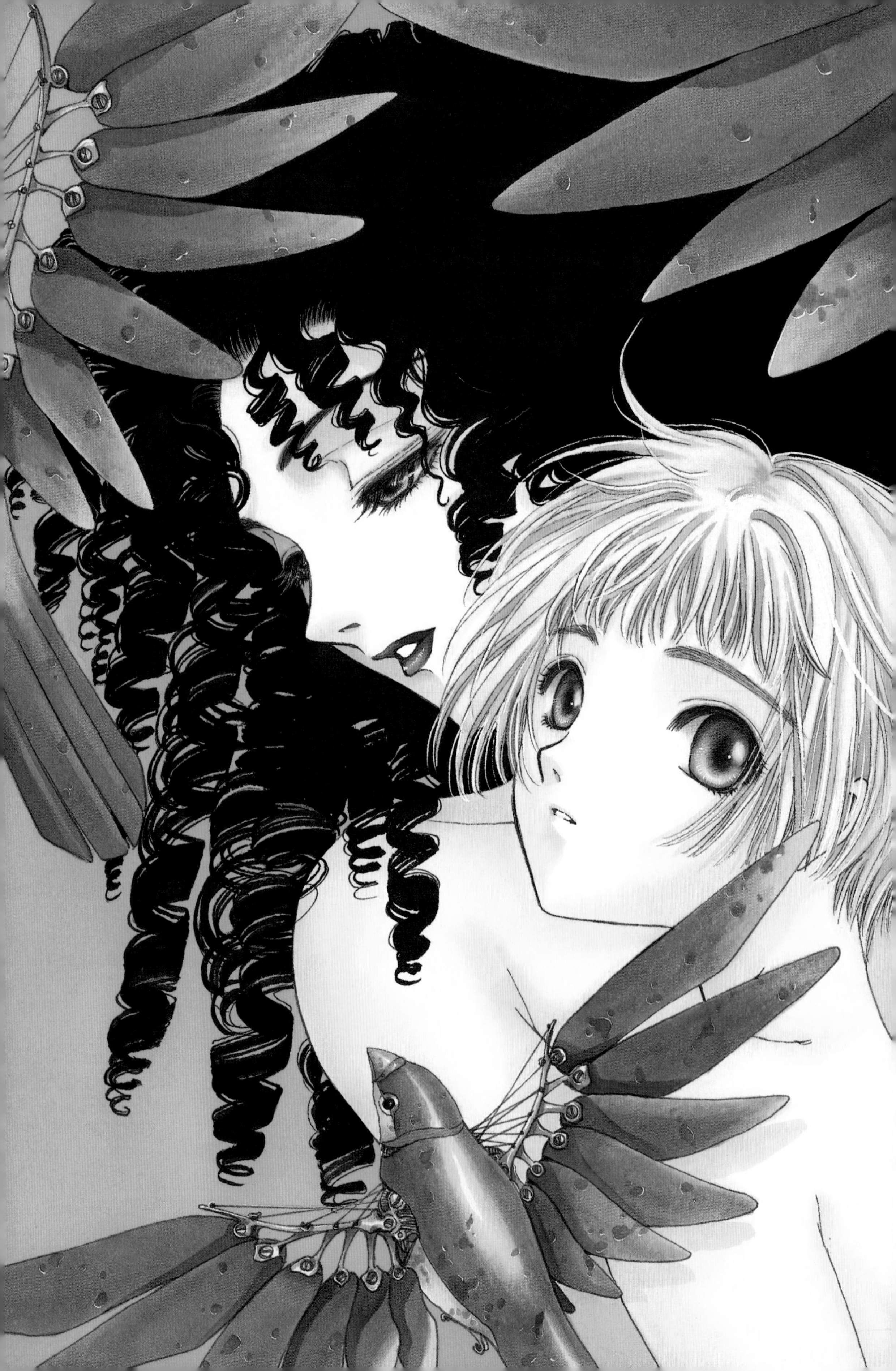

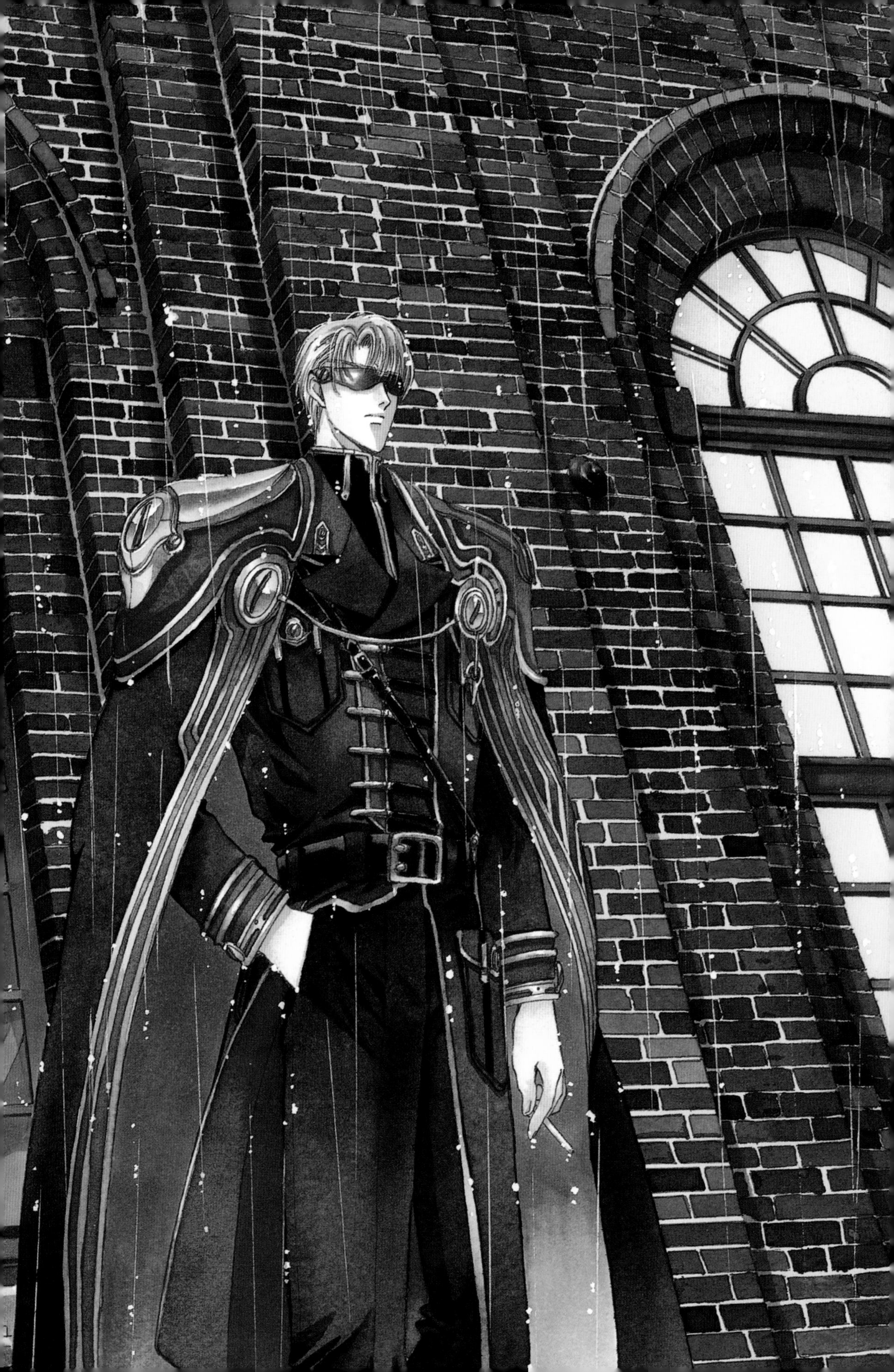

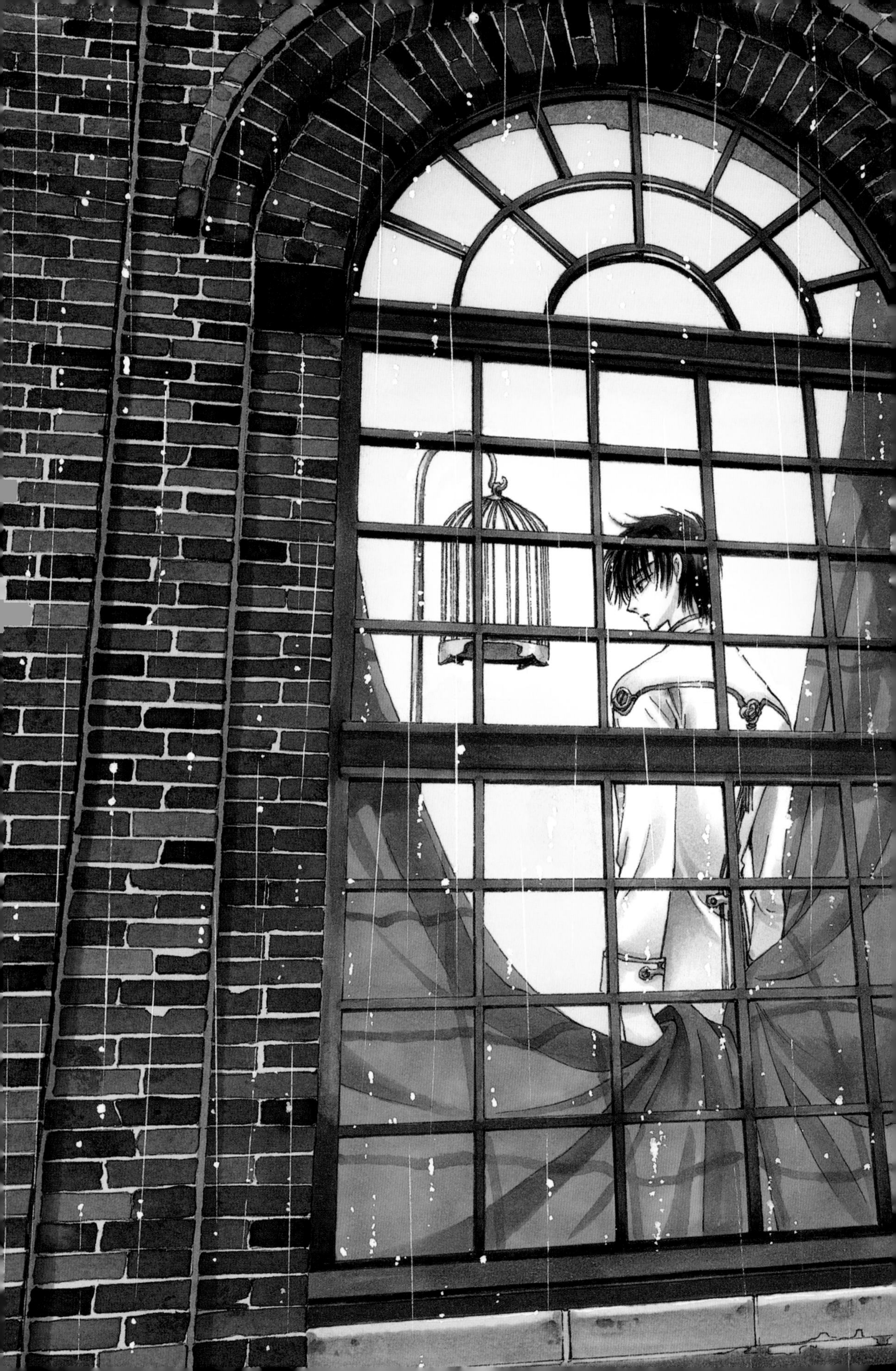

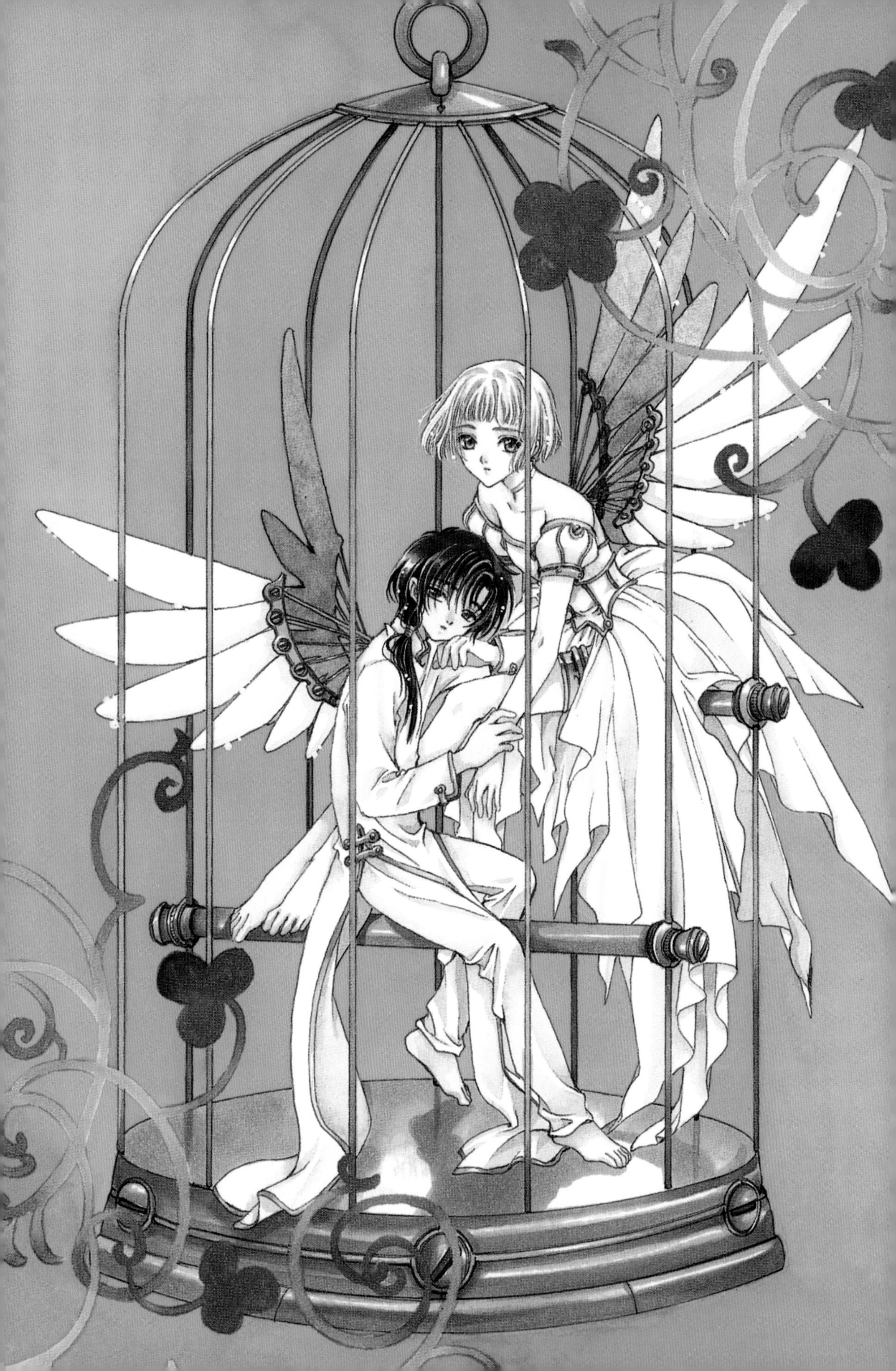

If you find a
four-leaf clover
It will bring you
happiness

But
Don't tell anyone

Where you found
The four-leaf clover

Or how many leaves
From its stem extend

A four-leaf clover

How I wish to make you happy
But I won't be there to see

A FAIRY'S DREAM INSIDE A DREAM

『夢の中の妖精の夢』

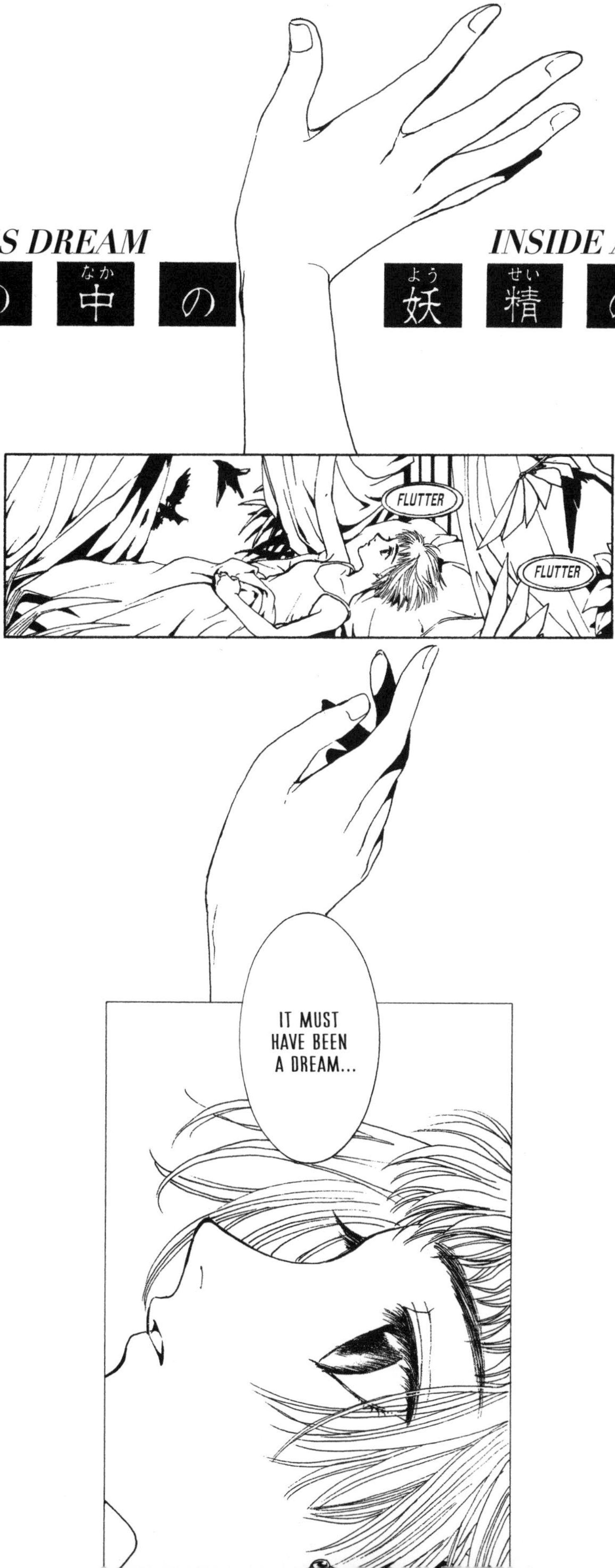
FLUTTER
FLUTTER
IT MUST HAVE BEEN A DREAM...

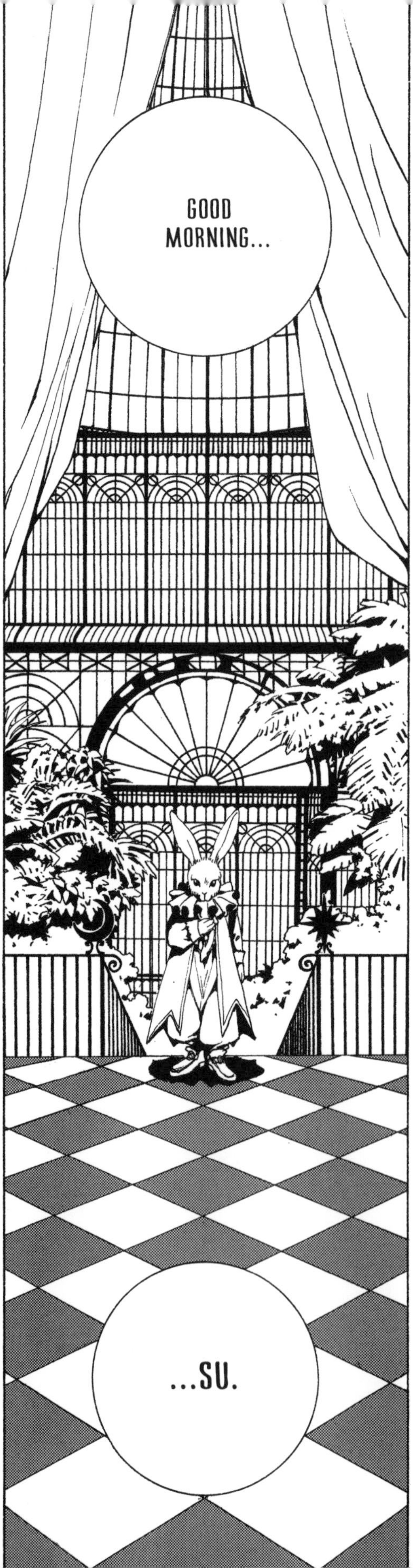
GOOD MORNING...
...SU.

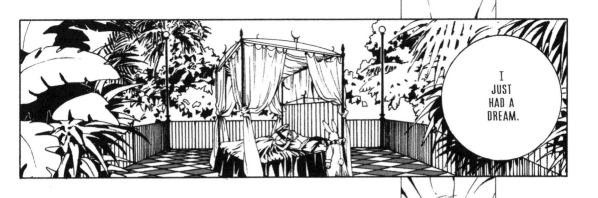

I JUST HAD A DREAM.

A DREAM ABOUT A FAIRY.

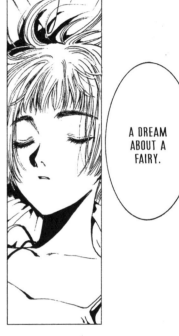

SHE SANG WITH A BEAUTIFUL VOICE.

SHE WAS BEAUTIFUL.

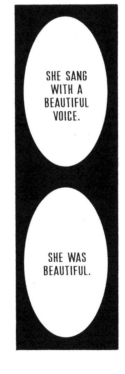

AND I SAW WHAT SHE WAS DREAMING.

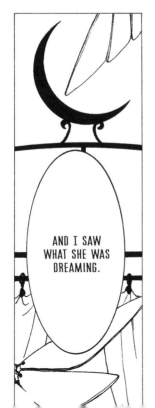

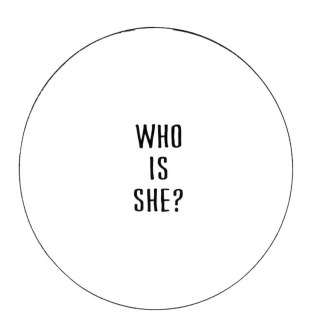

WHO
IS
SHE?

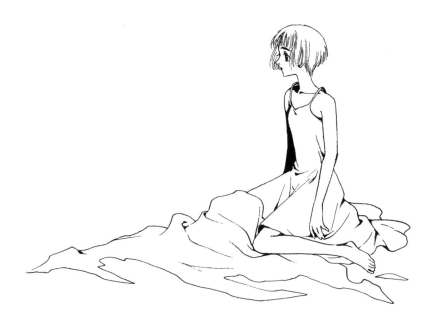

It's my dream

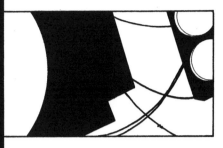

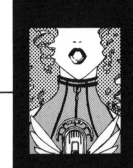

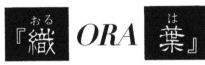

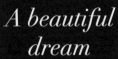
『織 ORA 葉』

A beautiful dream

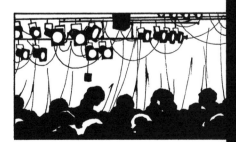

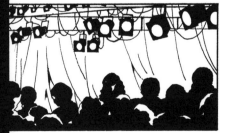

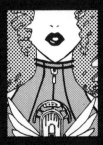

Never before seen

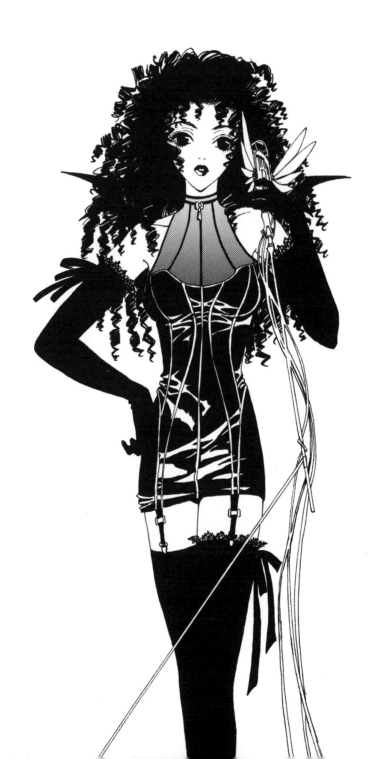

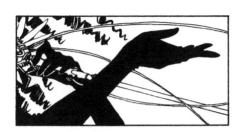

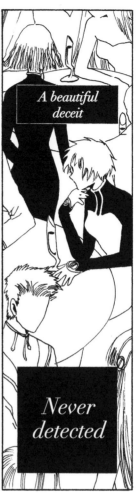

A beautiful deceit
Never detected

A beautiful love

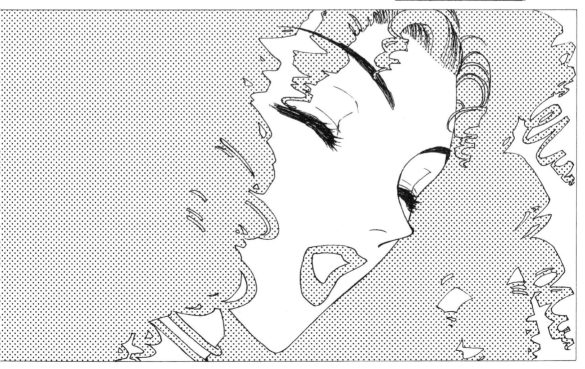

That no one can break

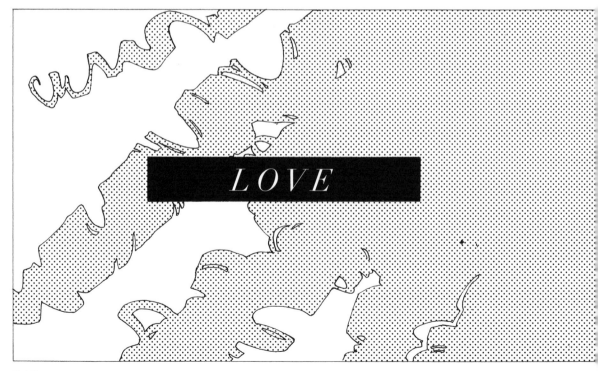

LOVE

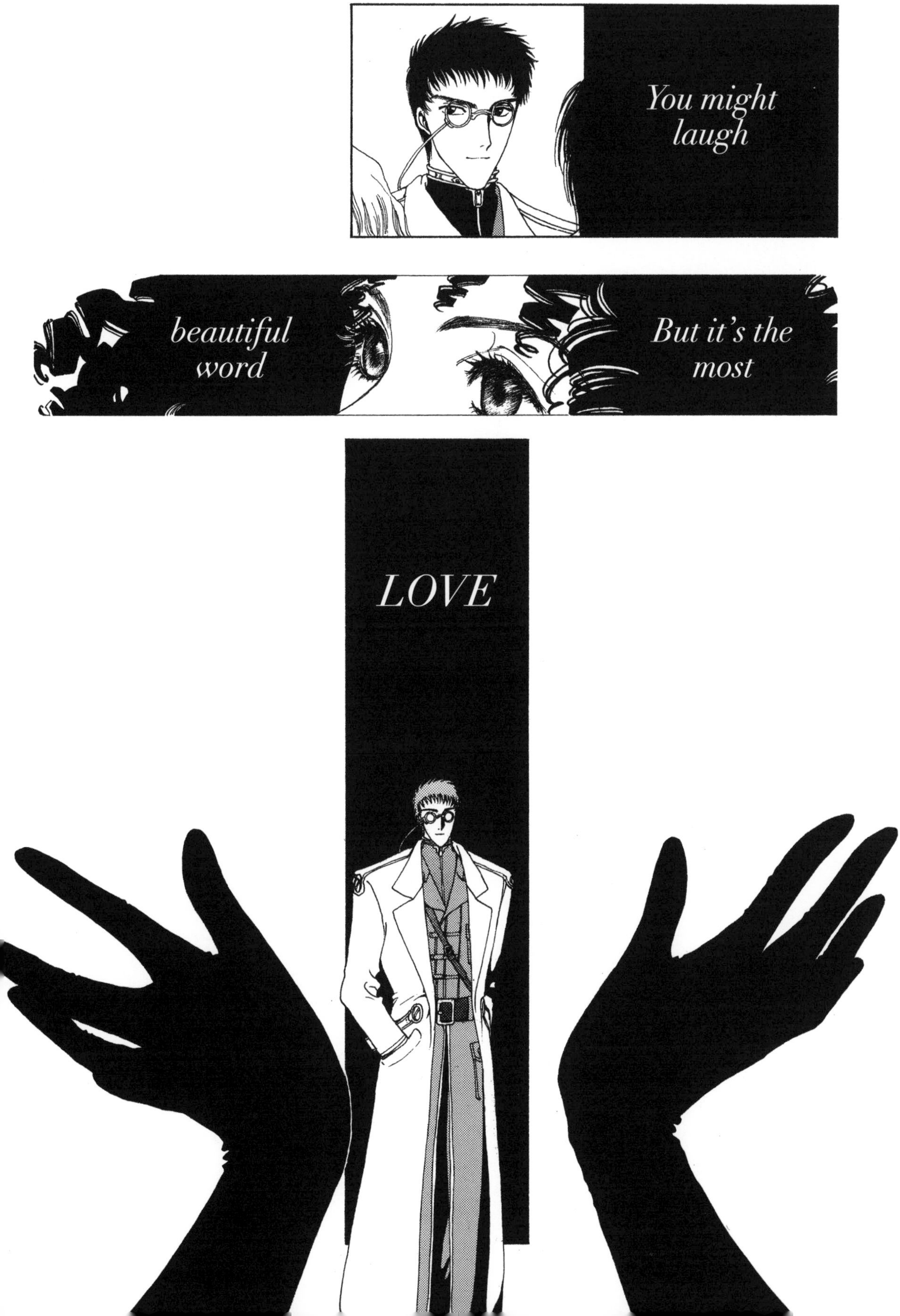
You might laugh
But it's the most
beautiful word
LOVE

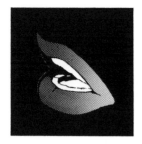

I

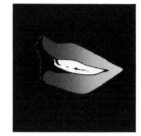

L

o

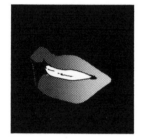

v

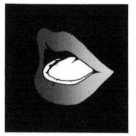

e

You might laugh
But it's the most
important word

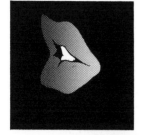

Y

o

u

『楽屋裏の小鳥の巣』 A BIRD'S NEST BACKSTAGE

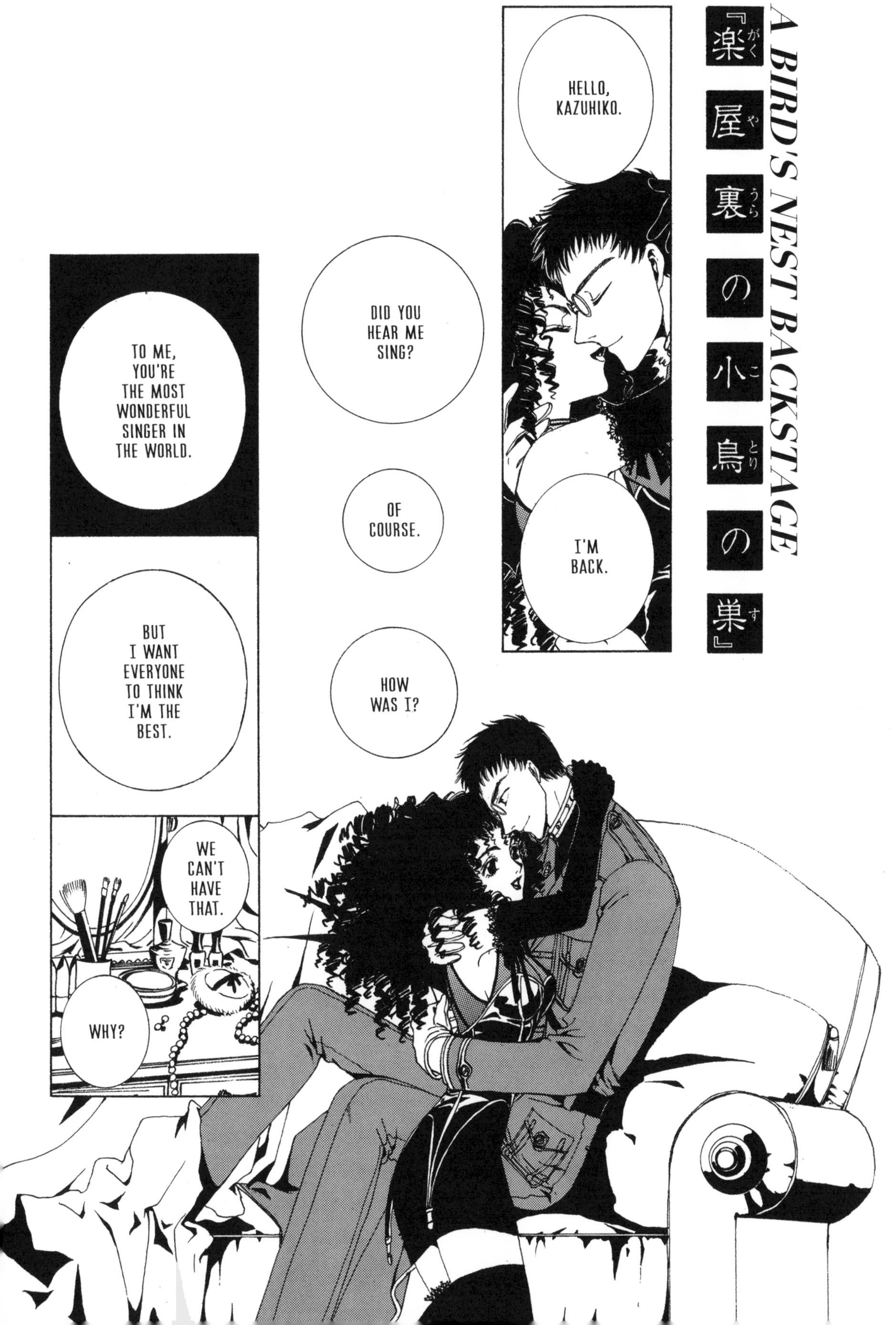
HELLO, KAZUHIKO.
I'M BACK.
DID YOU HEAR ME SING?
OF COURSE.
HOW WAS I?
TO ME, YOU'RE THE MOST WONDERFUL SINGER IN THE WORLD.
BUT I WANT EVERYONE TO THINK I'M THE BEST.
WE CAN'T HAVE THAT.
WHY?

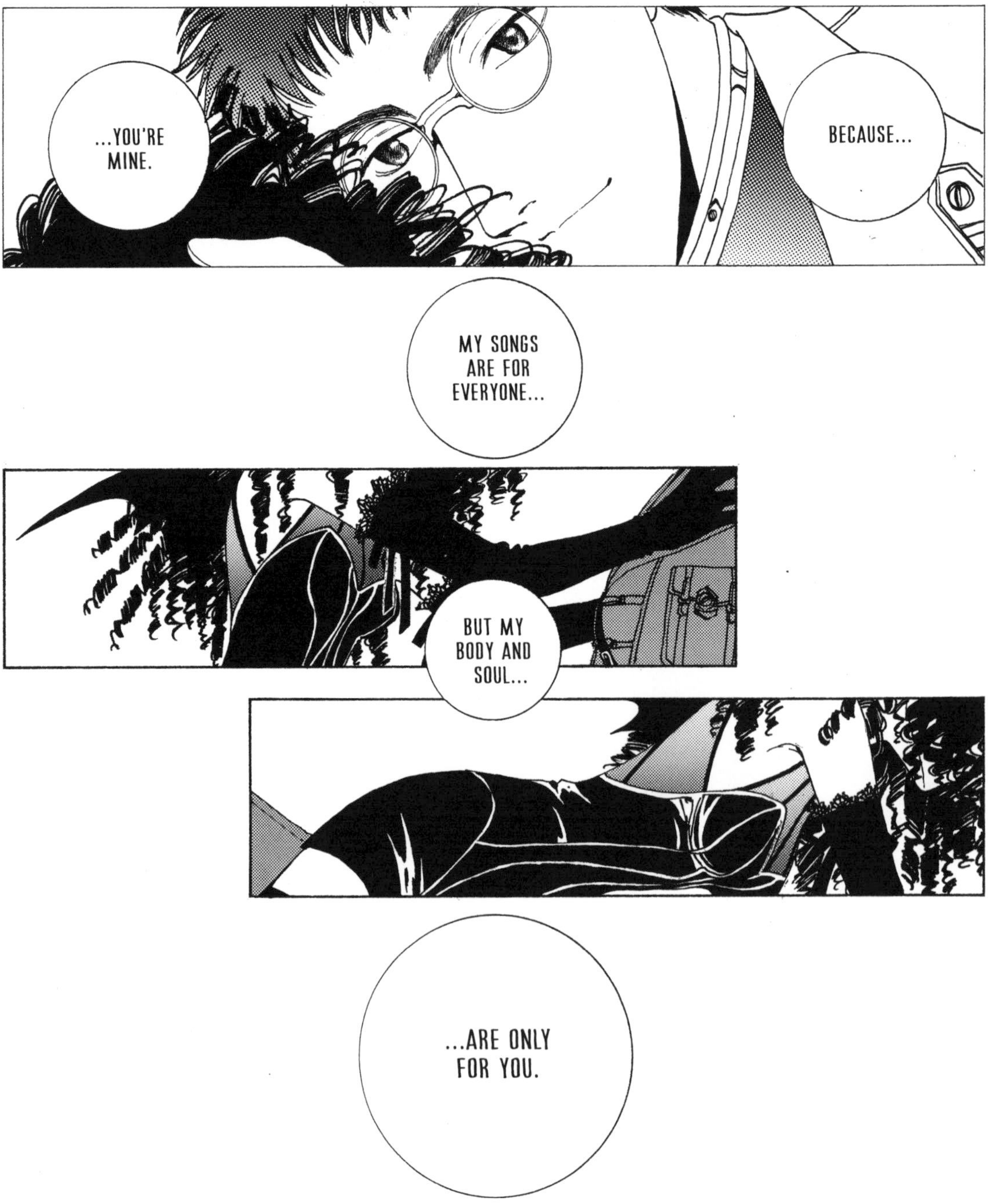
BECAUSE...
...YOU'RE MINE.
MY SONGS ARE FOR EVERYONE...
BUT MY BODY AND SOUL...
...ARE ONLY FOR YOU.

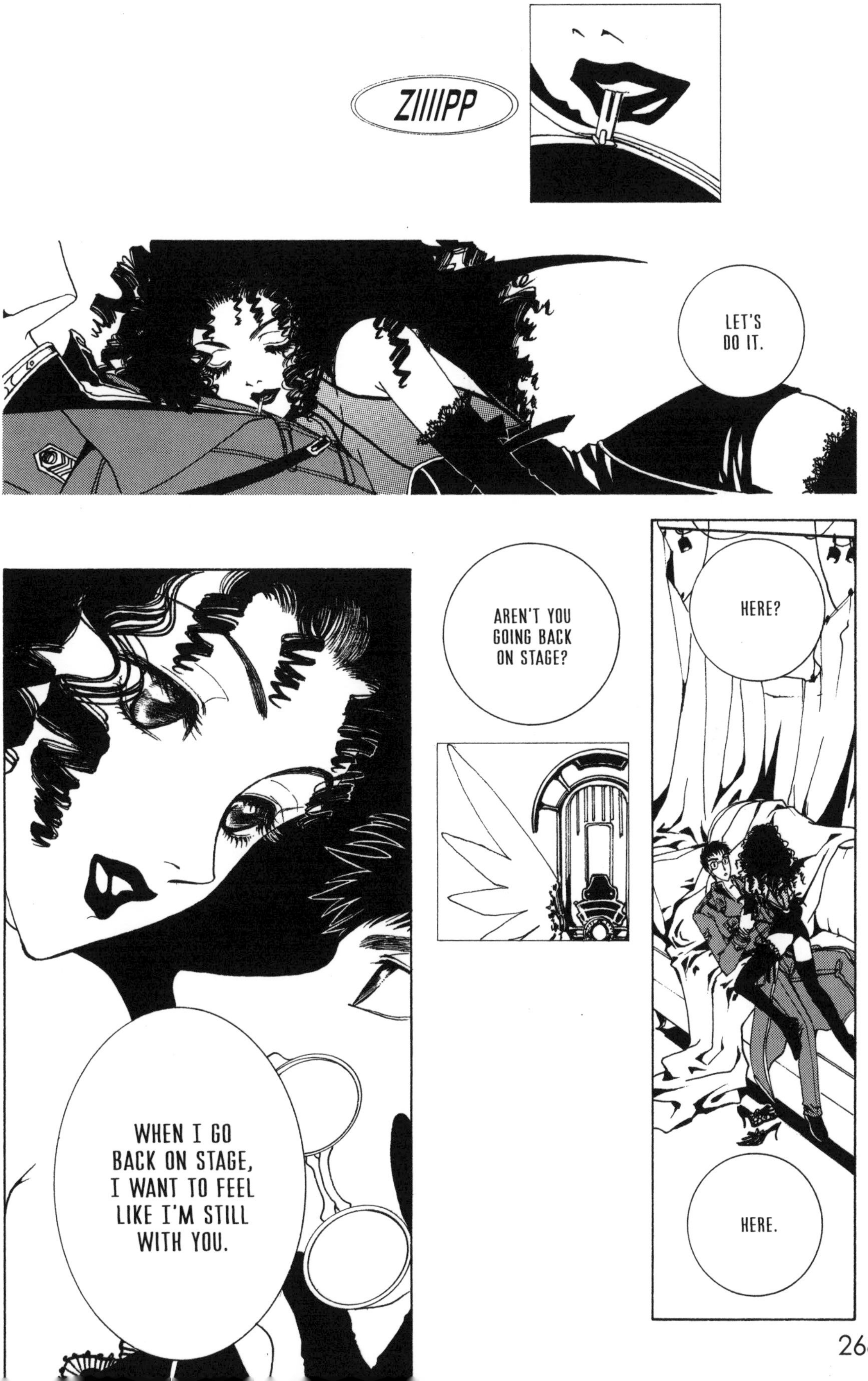
ZIIIIPP
LET'S DO IT.
HERE?
HERE.
AREN'T YOU GOING BACK ON STAGE?
WHEN I GO BACK ON STAGE, I WANT TO FEEL LIKE I'M STILL WITH YOU.

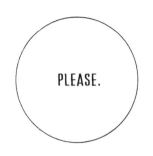

PLEASE.

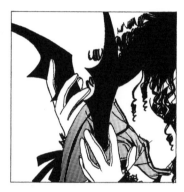

A BIRD'S NEST IN A CAGE

『籠の中の小鳥の巣』

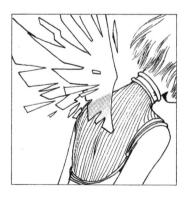

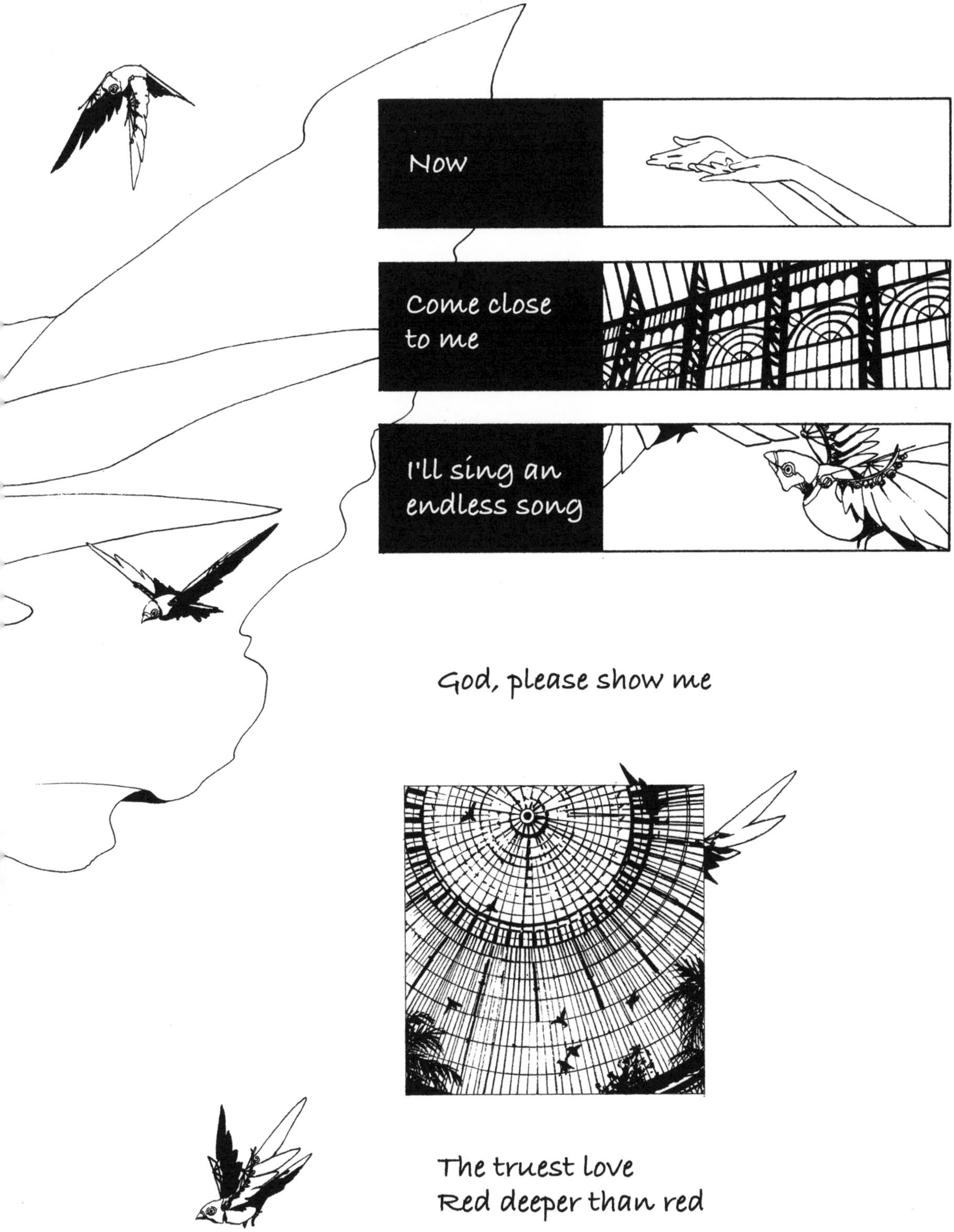
Now
Come close to me
I'll sing an endless song
God, please show me
The truest love
Red deeper than red

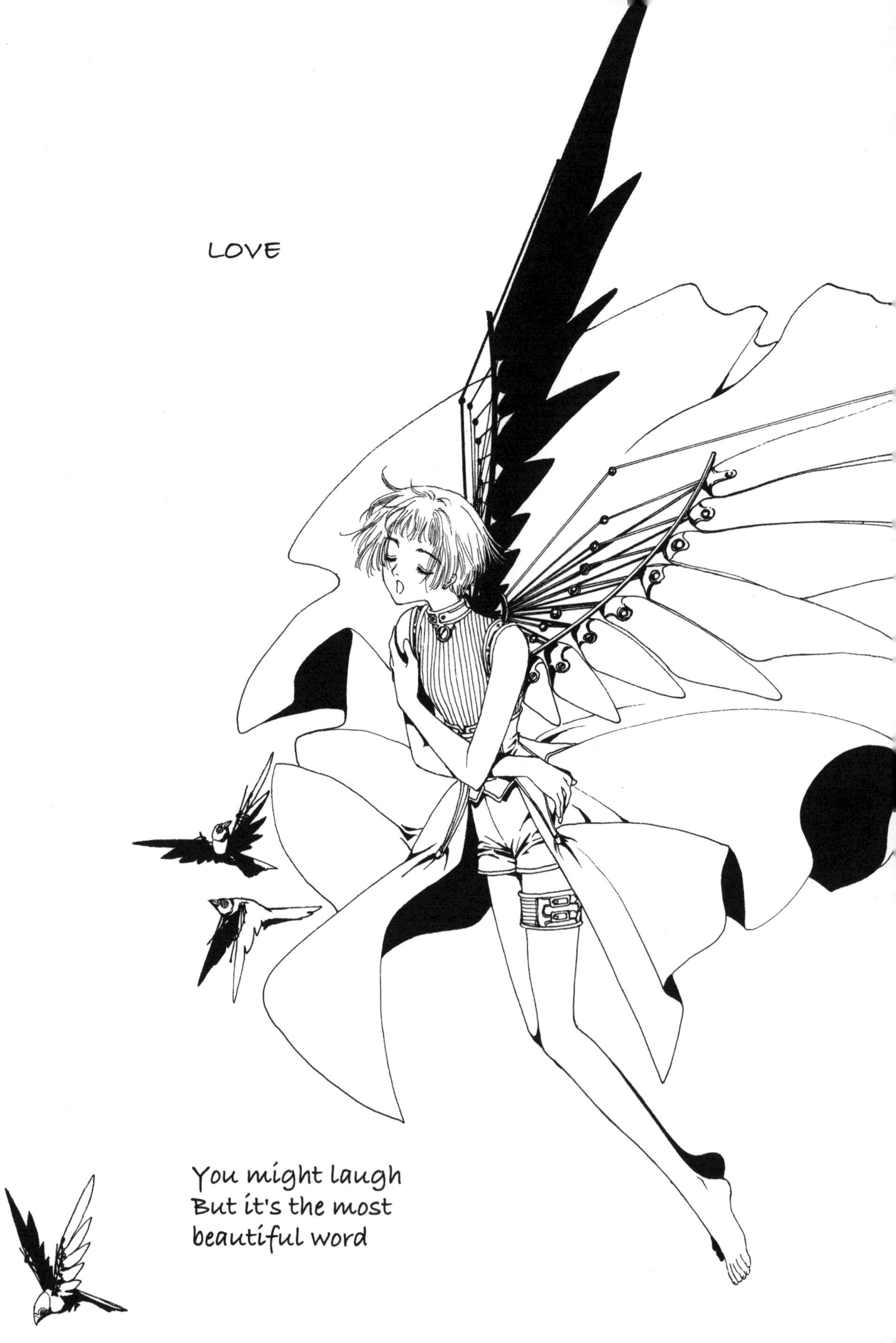
LOVE
You might laugh
But it's the most
beautiful word

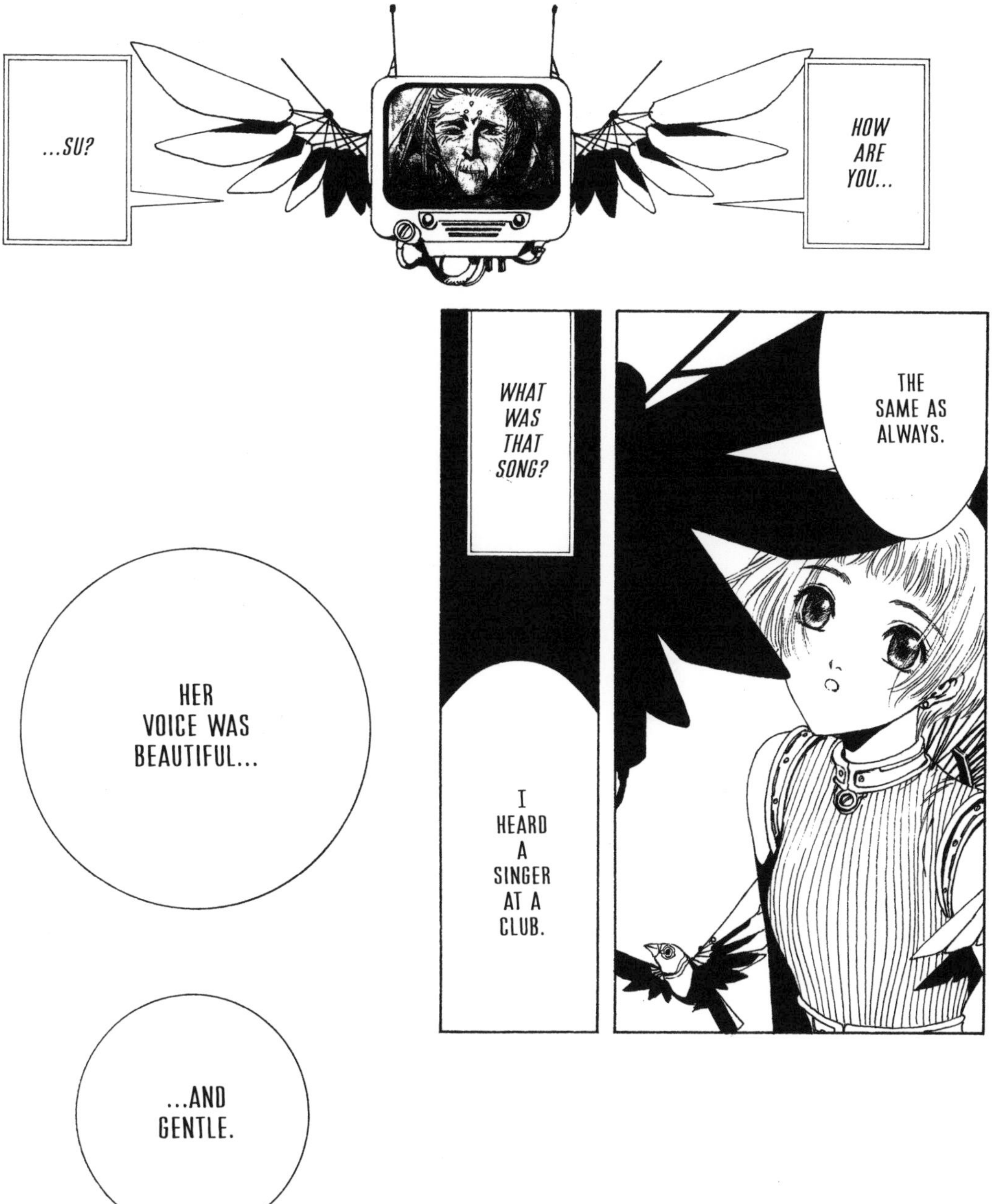
HOW ARE YOU...
...SU?
THE SAME AS ALWAYS.
WHAT WAS THAT SONG?
I HEARD A SINGER AT A CLUB.
HER VOICE WAS BEAUTIFUL...
...AND GENTLE.

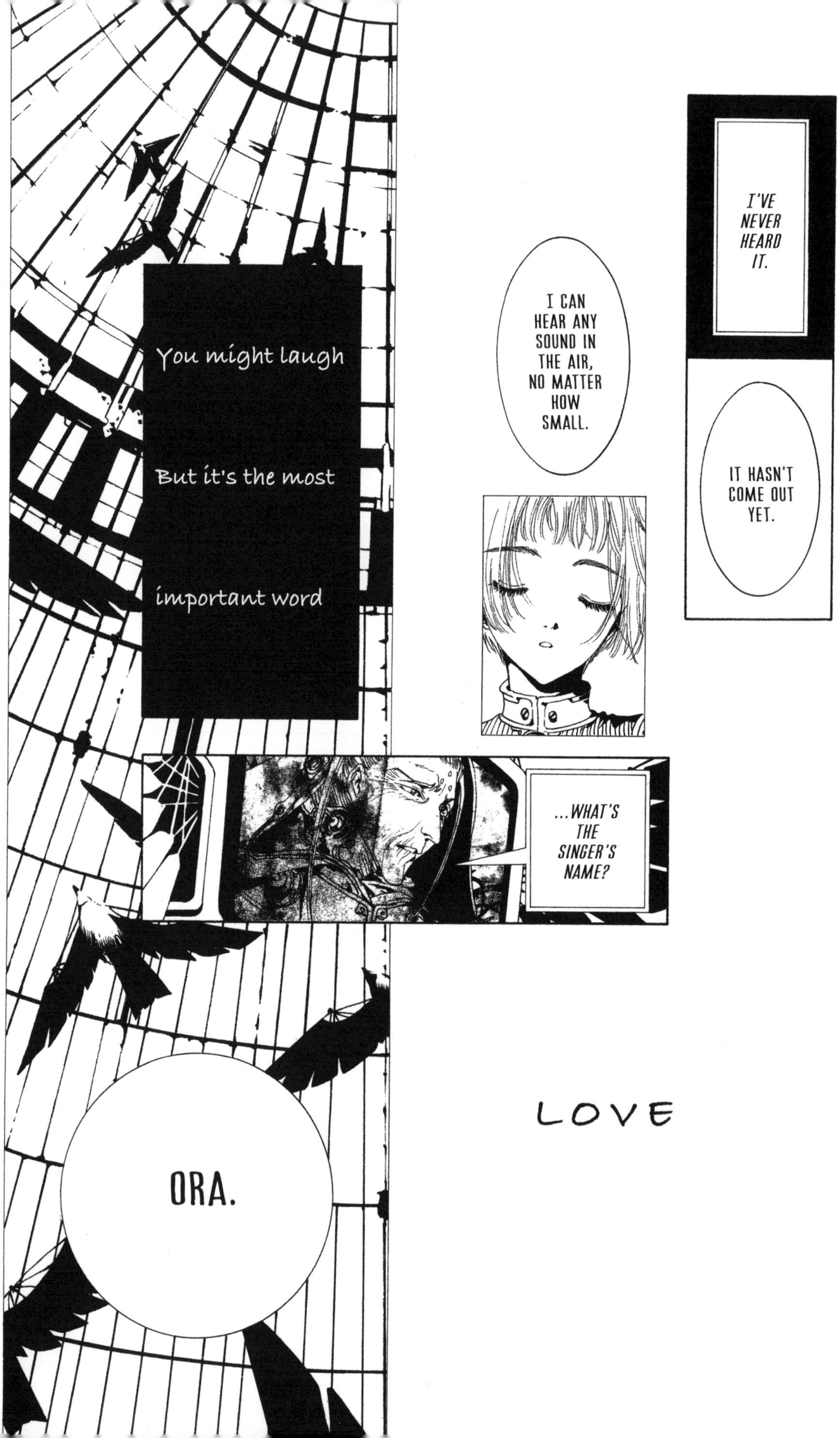
I'VE NEVER HEARD IT.
IT HASN'T COME OUT YET.
I CAN HEAR ANY SOUND IN THE AIR, NO MATTER HOW SMALL.
...WHAT'S THE SINGER'S NAME?
You might laugh
But it's the most
important word
LOVE
ORA.

A FLOWER OF REUNION

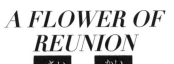

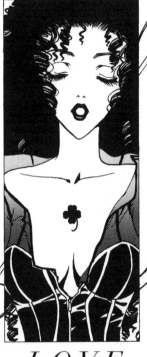

LOVE

*You might laugh
But it's the most
important word*

*Kiss me
Hold me
Show me love
that's forever*

Now

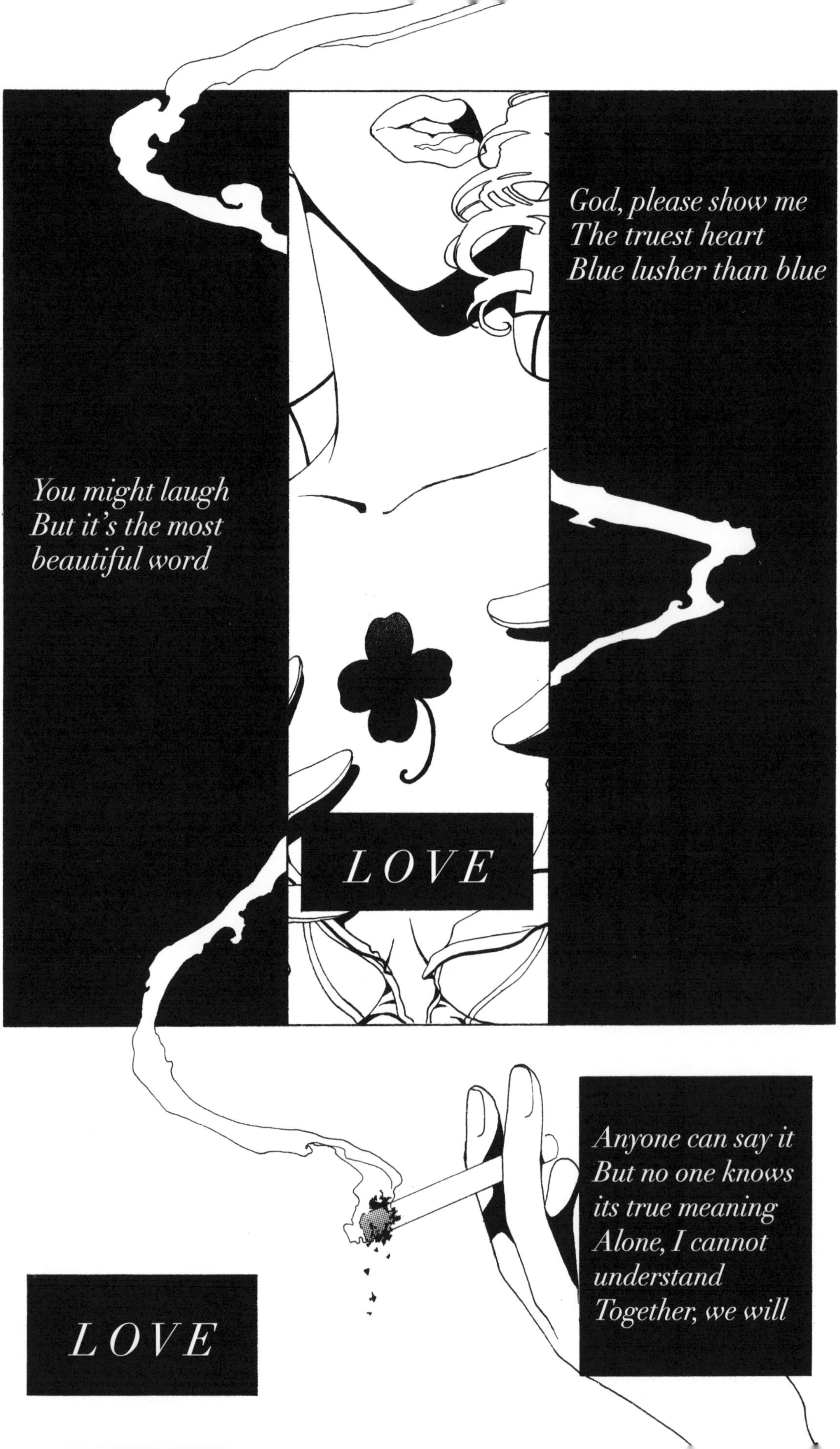
God, please show me
The truest heart
Blue lusher than blue
You might laugh
But it's the most
beautiful word
LOVE
Anyone can say it
But no one knows
its true meaning
Alone, I cannot
understand
Together, we will
LOVE

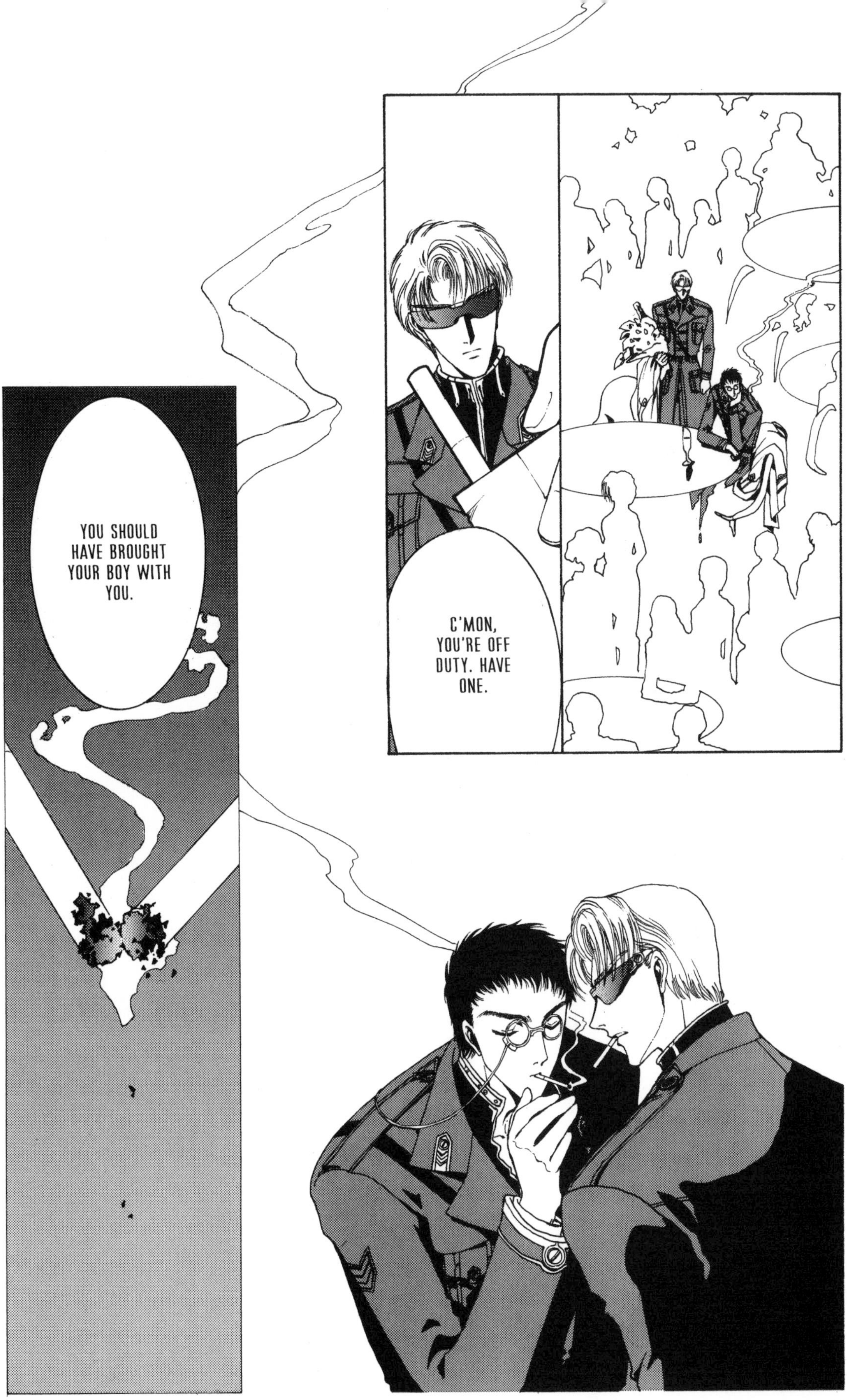
C'MON, YOU'RE OFF DUTY. HAVE ONE.
YOU SHOULD HAVE BROUGHT YOUR BOY WITH YOU.

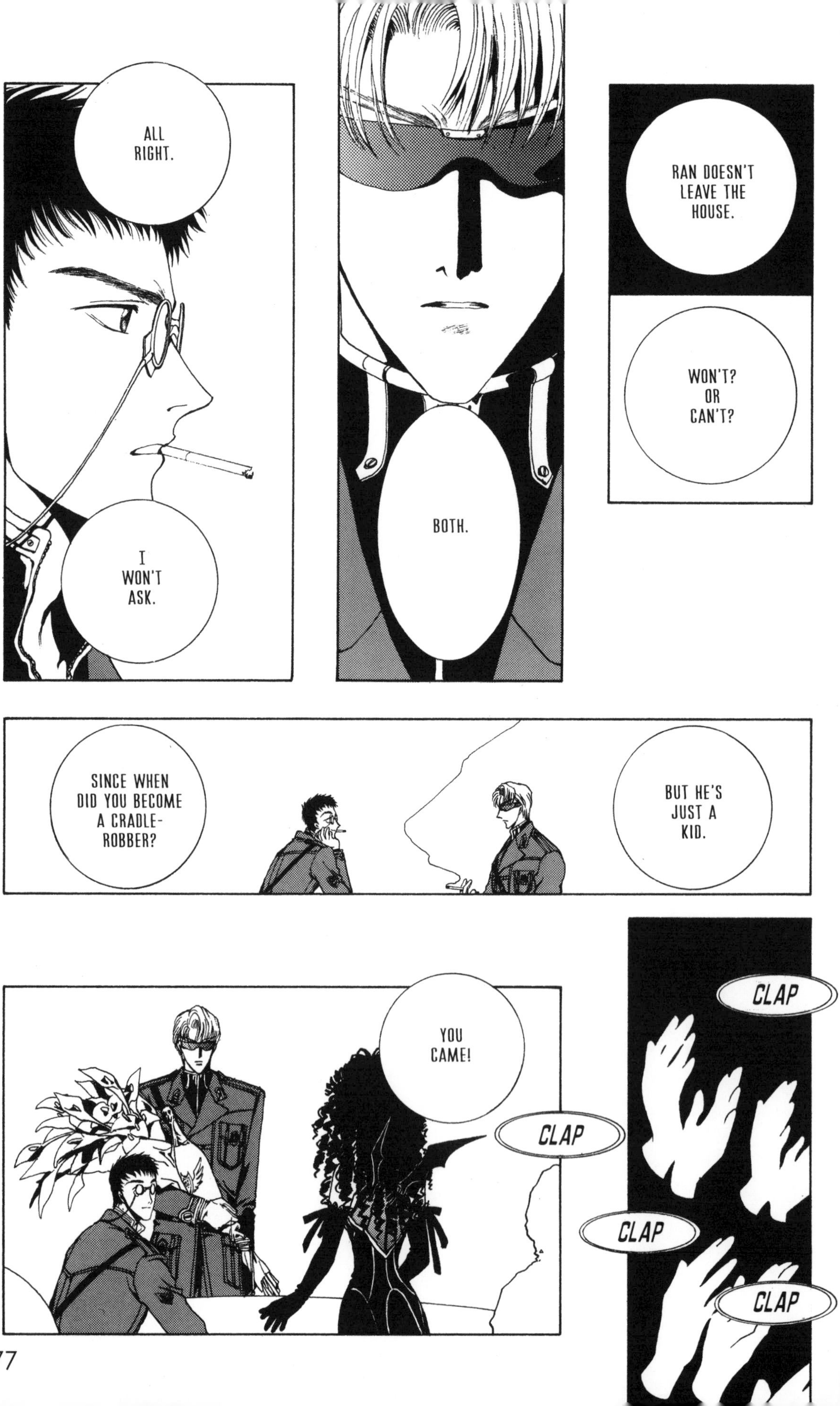
RAN DOESN'T LEAVE THE HOUSE.
WON'T? OR CAN'T?
BOTH.
ALL RIGHT.
I WON'T ASK.
BUT HE'S JUST A KID.
SINCE WHEN DID YOU BECOME A CRADLE-ROBBER?
CLAP
CLAP
CLAP
YOU CAME!
CLAP

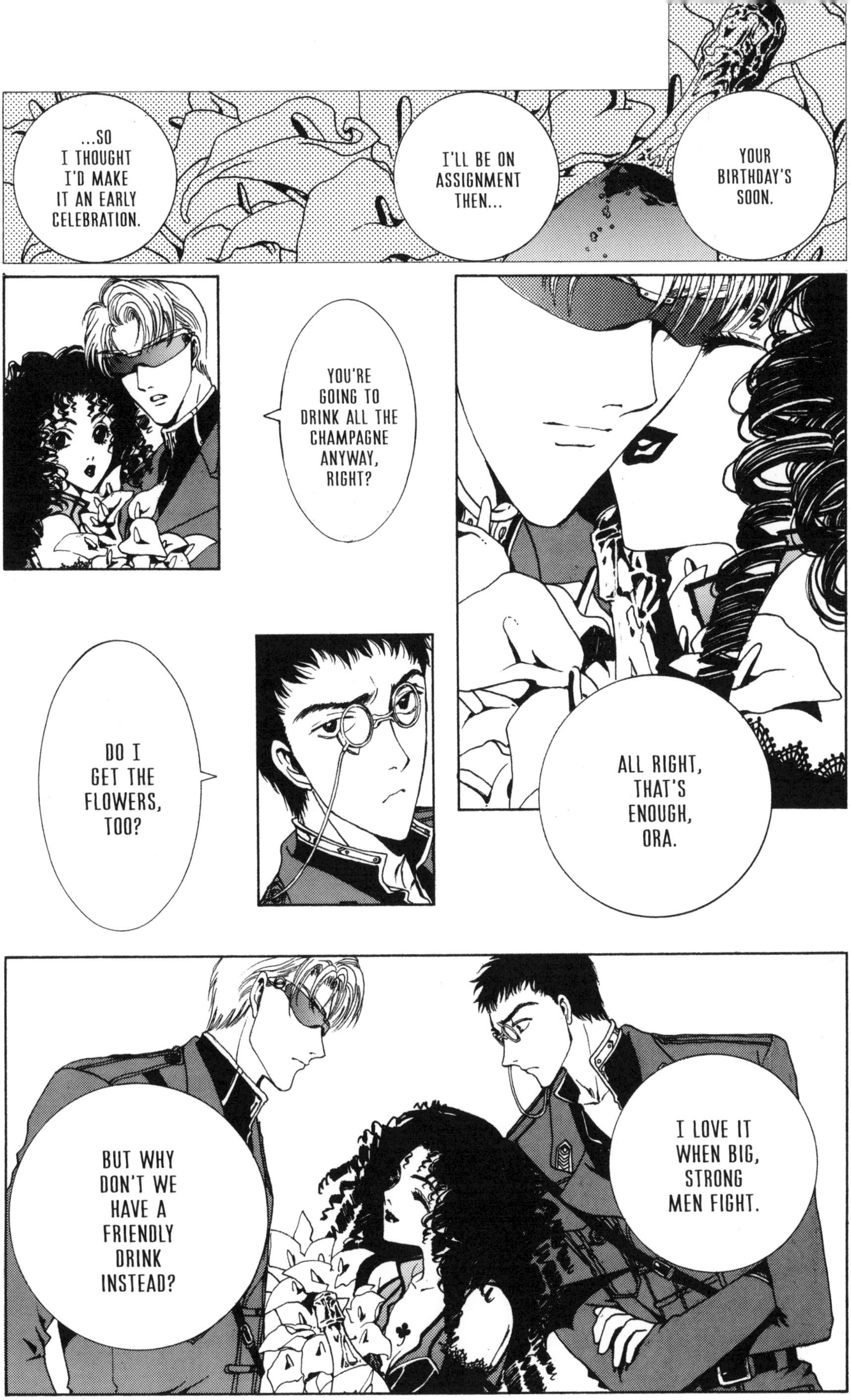
YOUR BIRTHDAY'S SOON.
I'LL BE ON ASSIGNMENT THEN...
...SO I THOUGHT I'D MAKE IT AN EARLY CELEBRATION.
YOU'RE GOING TO DRINK ALL THE CHAMPAGNE ANYWAY, RIGHT?
DO I GET THE FLOWERS, TOO?
ALL RIGHT, THAT'S ENOUGH, ORA.
I LOVE IT WHEN BIG, STRONG MEN FIGHT.
BUT WHY DON'T WE HAVE A FRIENDLY DRINK INSTEAD?

BUG

『虫（むし）

の

目（め）』

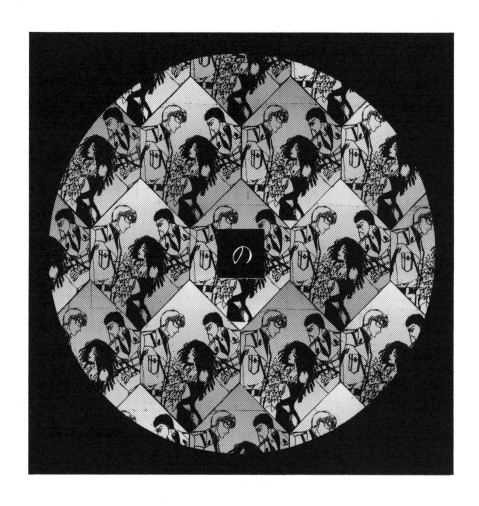

EYE

ALONE

『ひとり』

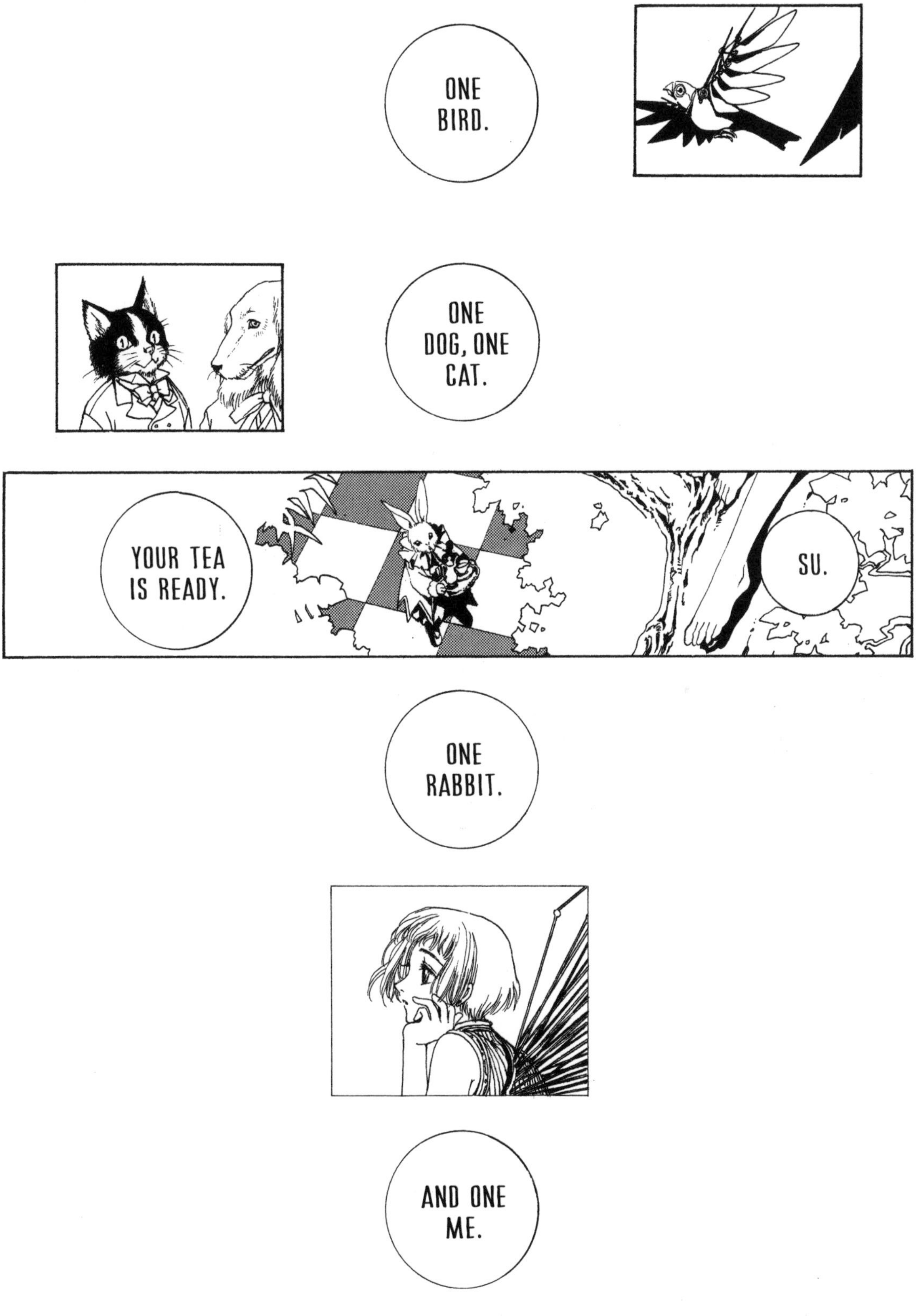
ONE BIRD.
ONE DOG, ONE CAT.
SU.
YOUR TEA IS READY.
ONE RABBIT.
AND ONE ME.

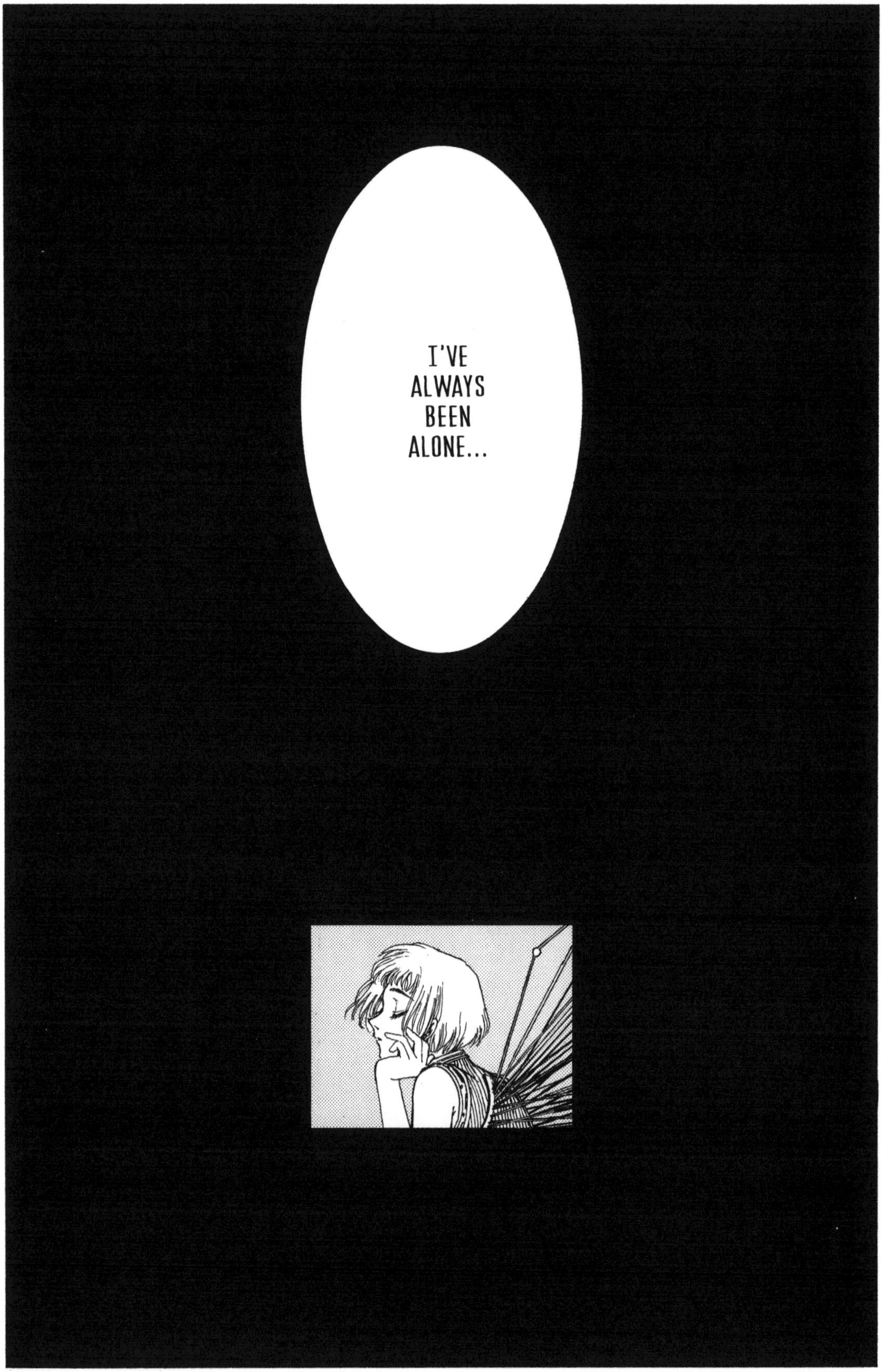
I'VE ALWAYS BEEN ALONE...

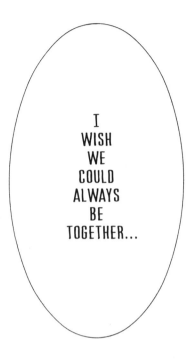

I
WISH
WE
COULD
ALWAYS
BE
TOGETHER...

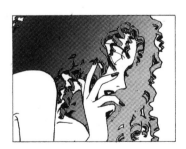

TOGETHER

『ふ　　　た　　　り』

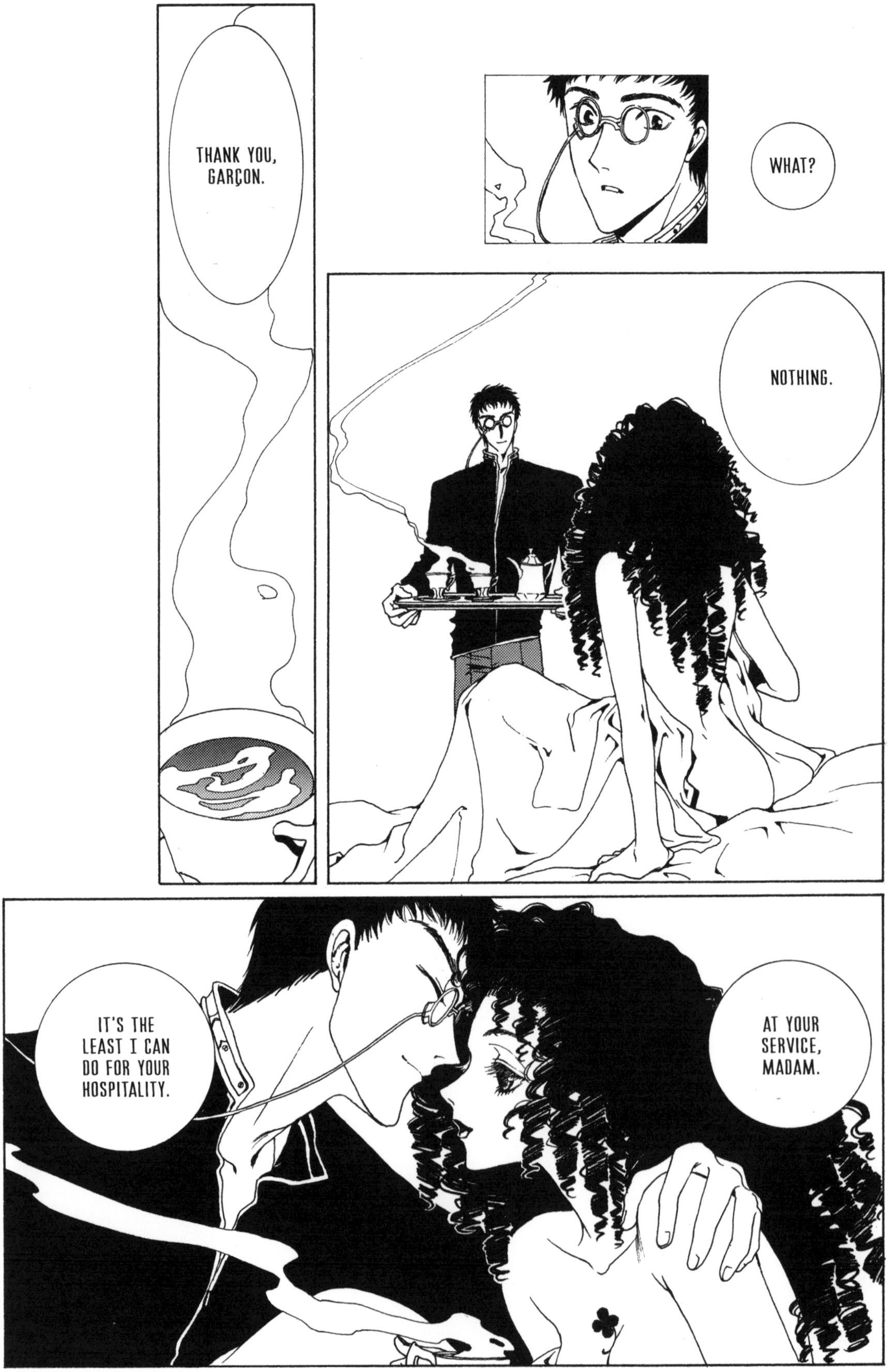
THANK YOU, GARÇON.
WHAT?
NOTHING.
IT'S THE LEAST I CAN DO FOR YOUR HOSPITALITY.
AT YOUR SERVICE, MADAM.

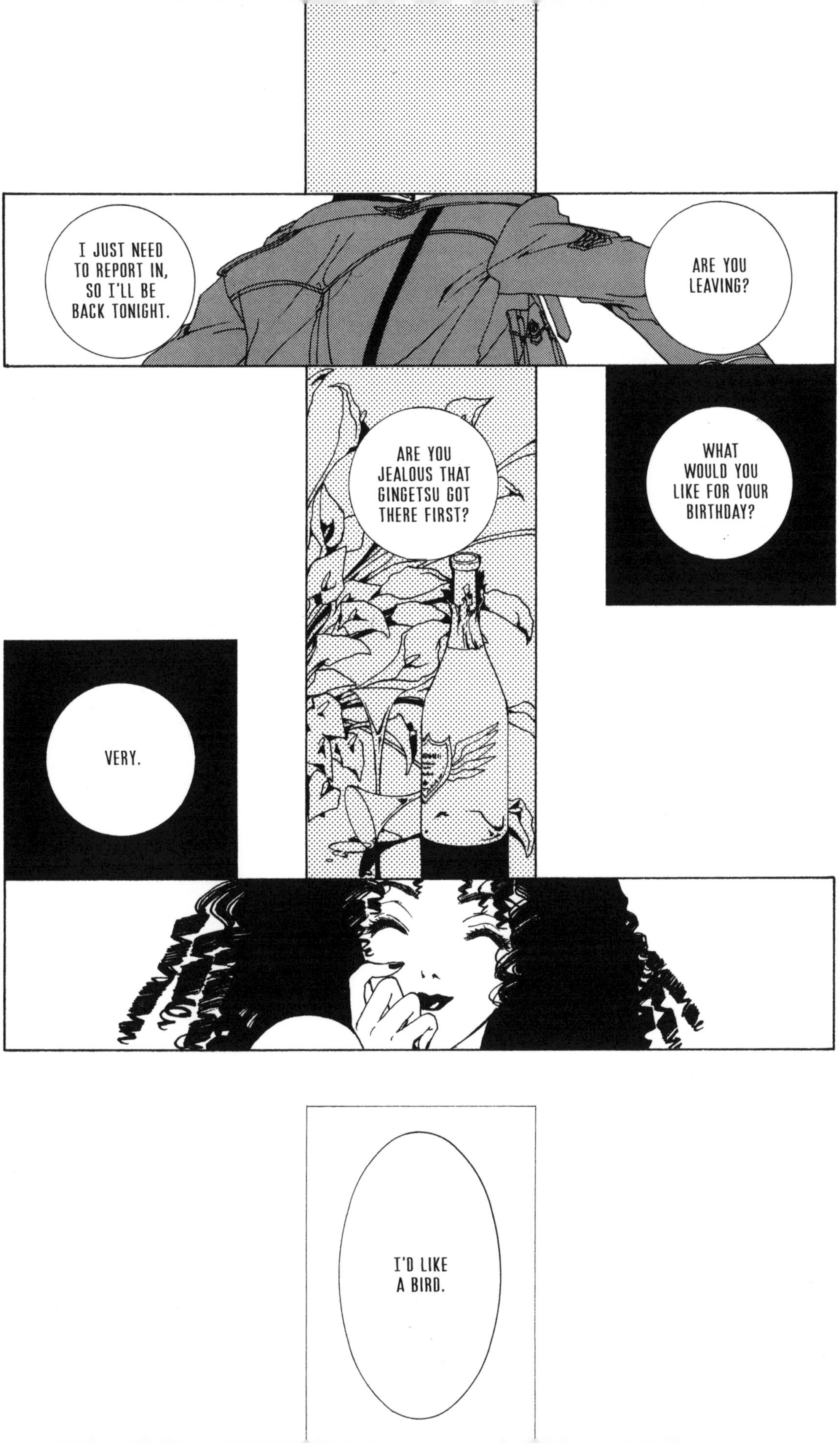
ARE YOU LEAVING?
I JUST NEED TO REPORT IN, SO I'LL BE BACK TONIGHT.
ARE YOU JEALOUS THAT GINGETSU GOT THERE FIRST?
VERY.
WHAT WOULD YOU LIKE FOR YOUR BIRTHDAY?
I'D LIKE A BIRD.

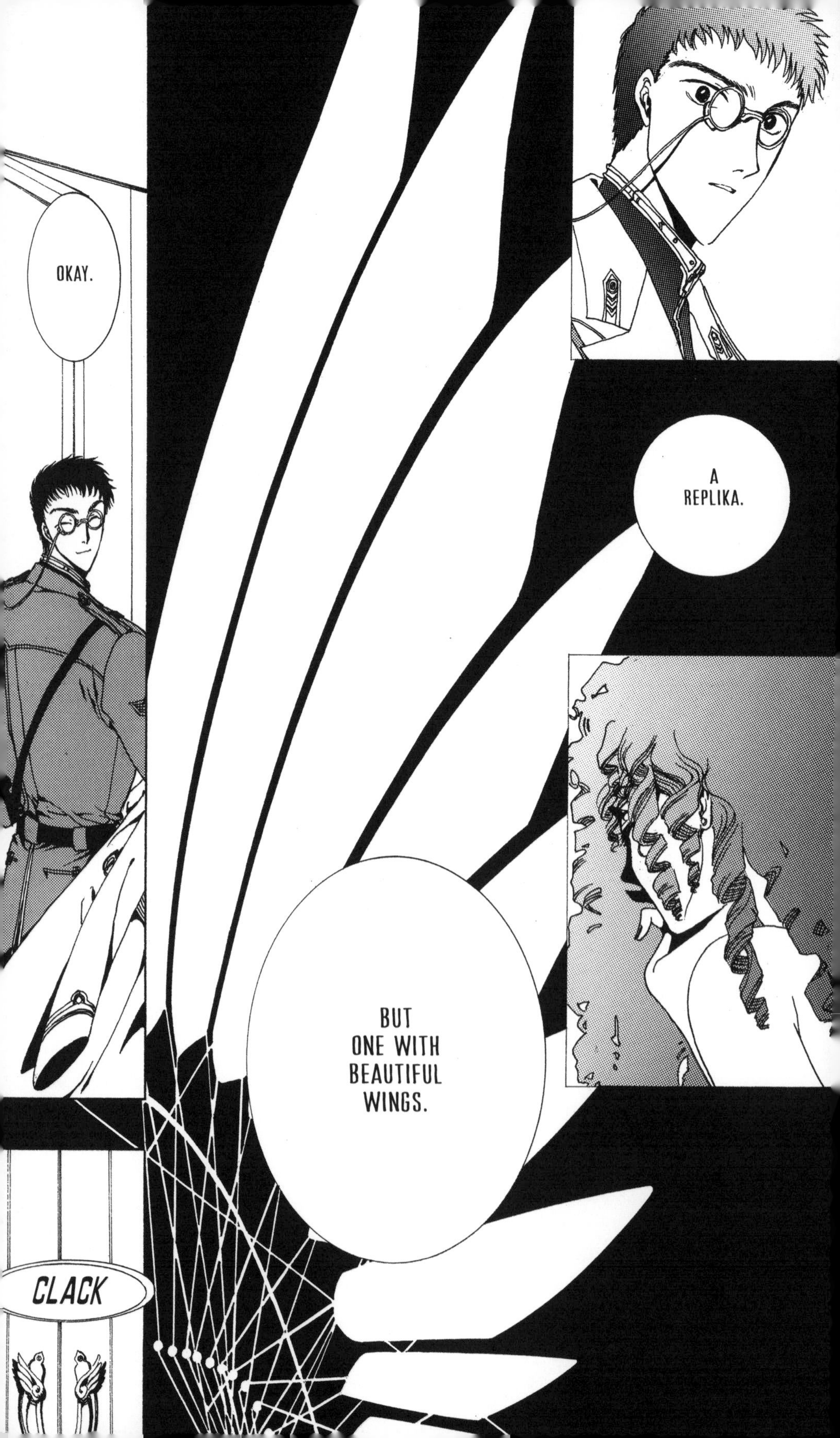
A REPLIKA.
BUT ONE WITH BEAUTIFUL WINGS.
OKAY.
CLACK

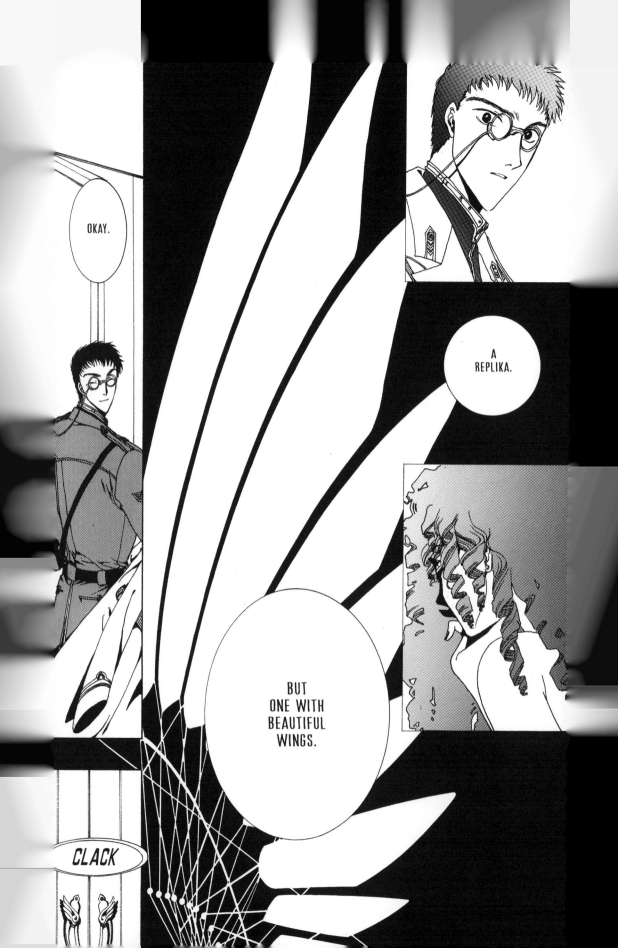

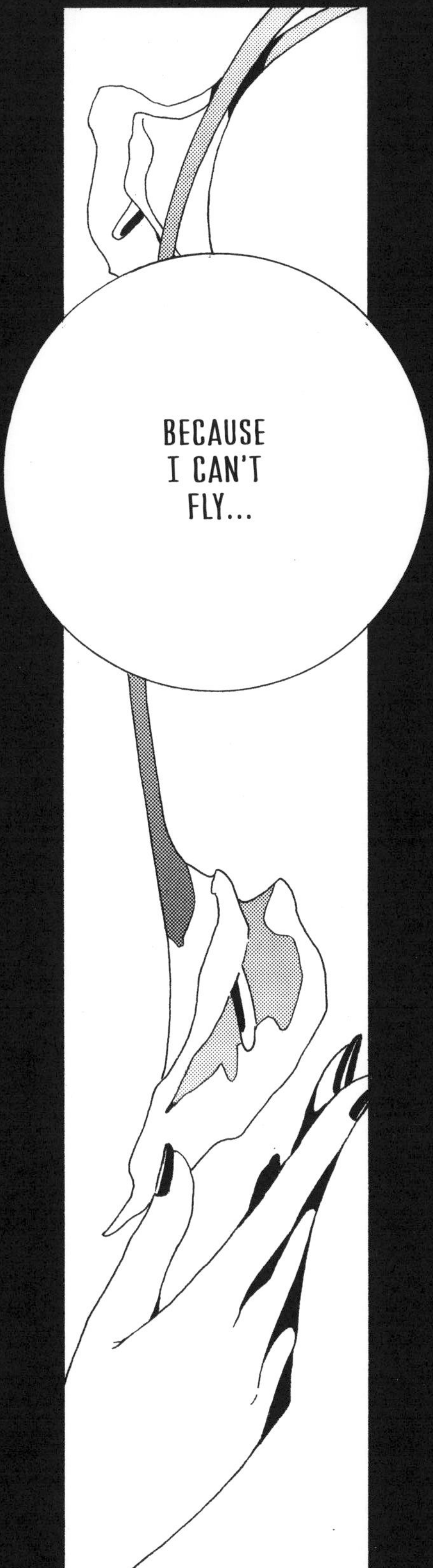
BECAUSE I CAN'T FLY...

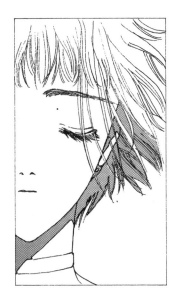

I CAN HEAR

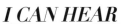

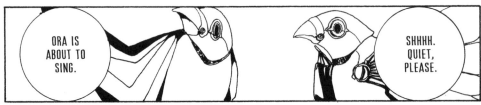

『きこえる』

SHHHH. QUIET, PLEASE.
ORA IS ABOUT TO SING.

THE BEGINNING

『はじまる』

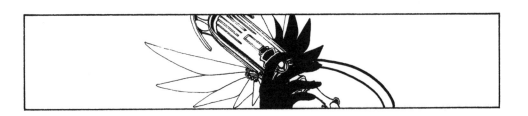

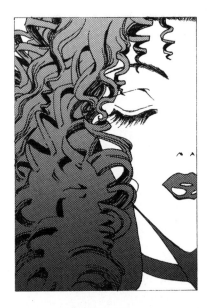

LOVE
It's my dream

A beautiful dream
Never before seen

A beautiful deceit
Never detected

A beautiful love
That no one can break

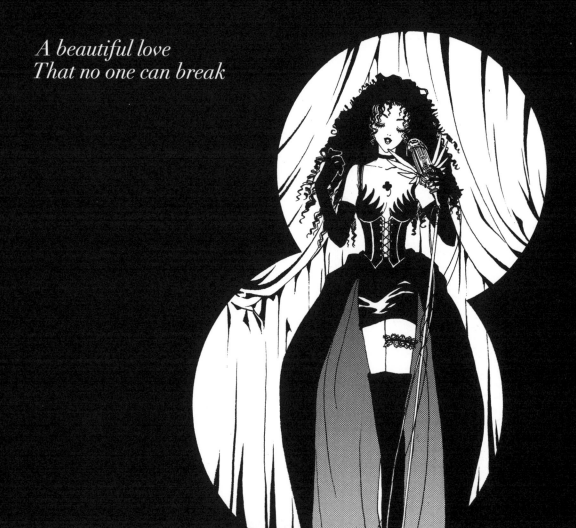

『誰も知らない二重唱』

A DUET NO ONE KNOWS

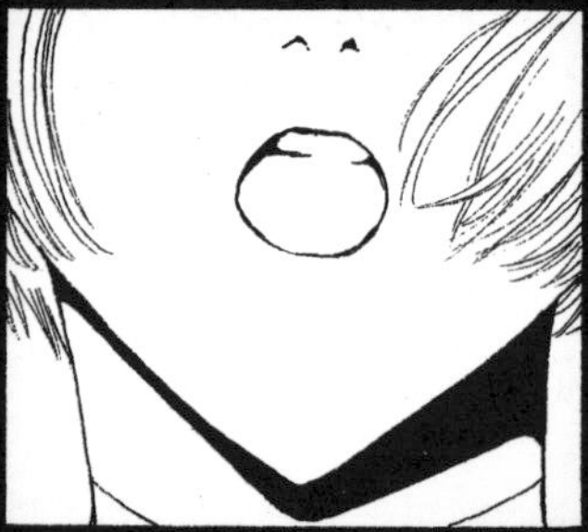

LOVE

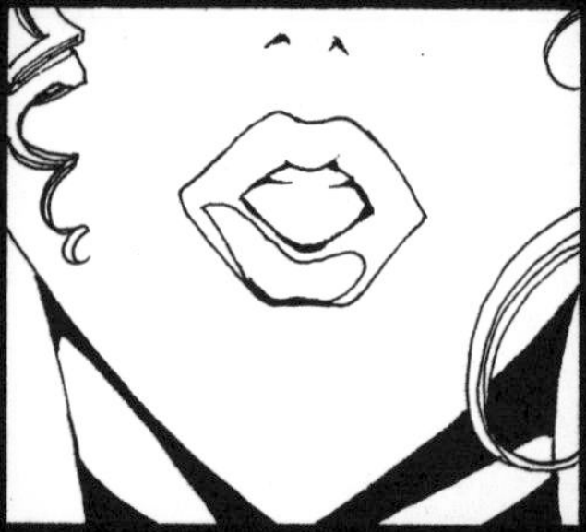

You might laugh
But it's the most
beautiful word

Now come close to me

I'll sing an endless song

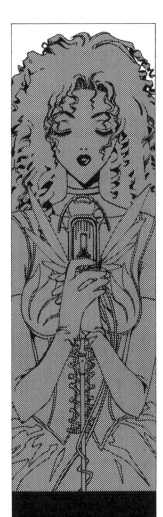

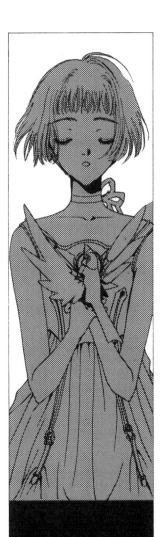

God, please show me

The truest love
Red deeper than red

LOVE

You might laugh
But it's the most important word

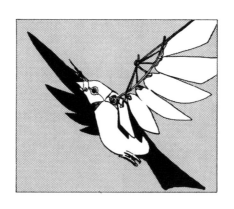

LOVE

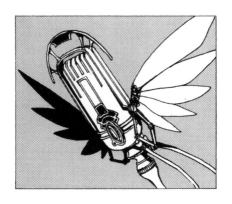

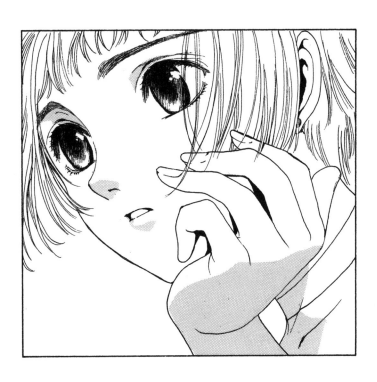

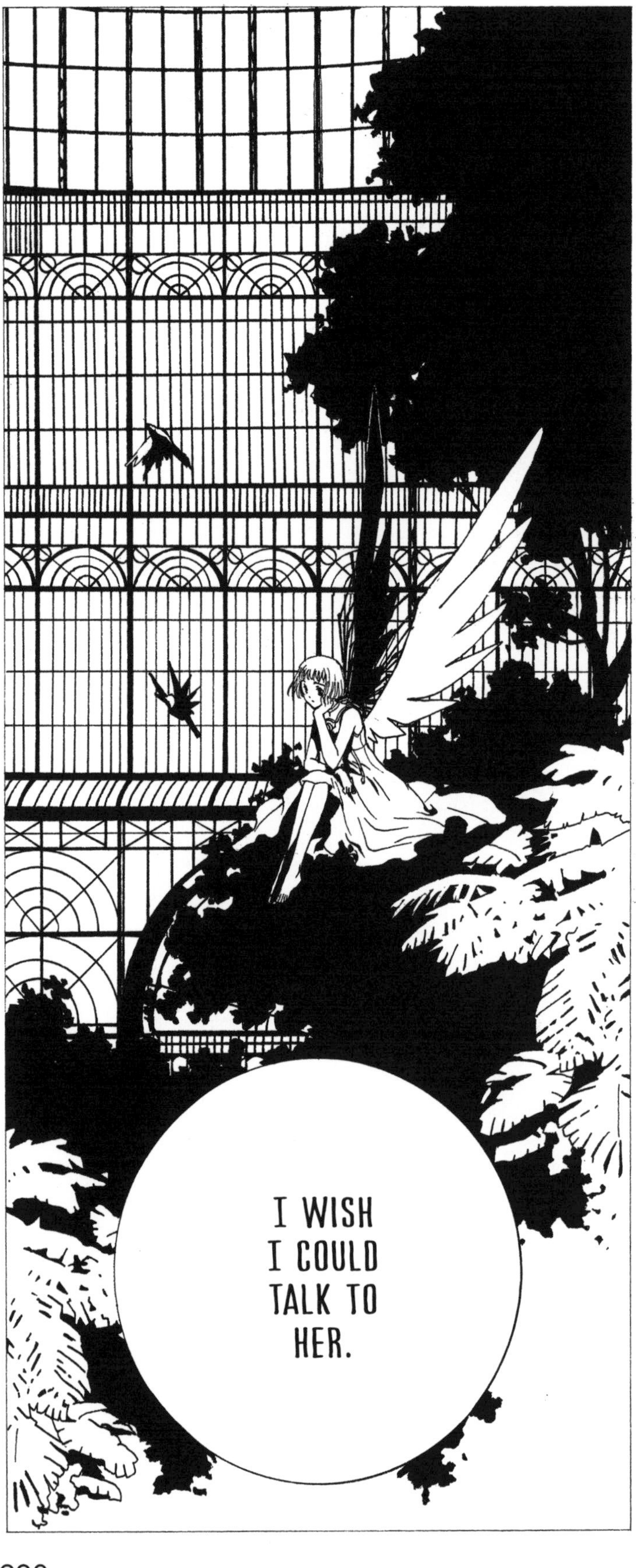
I WISH I COULD TALK TO HER.

FISH

『魚（さかな）

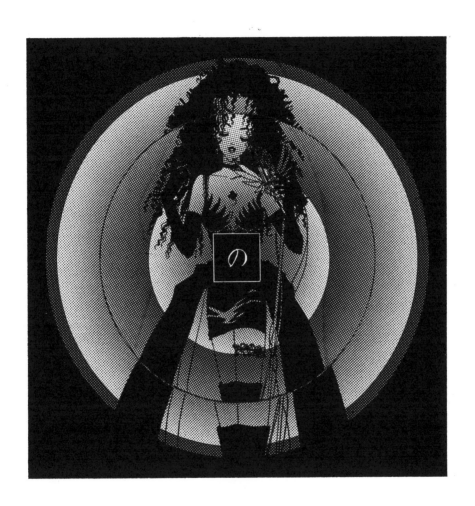

の

目（め）』

EYE

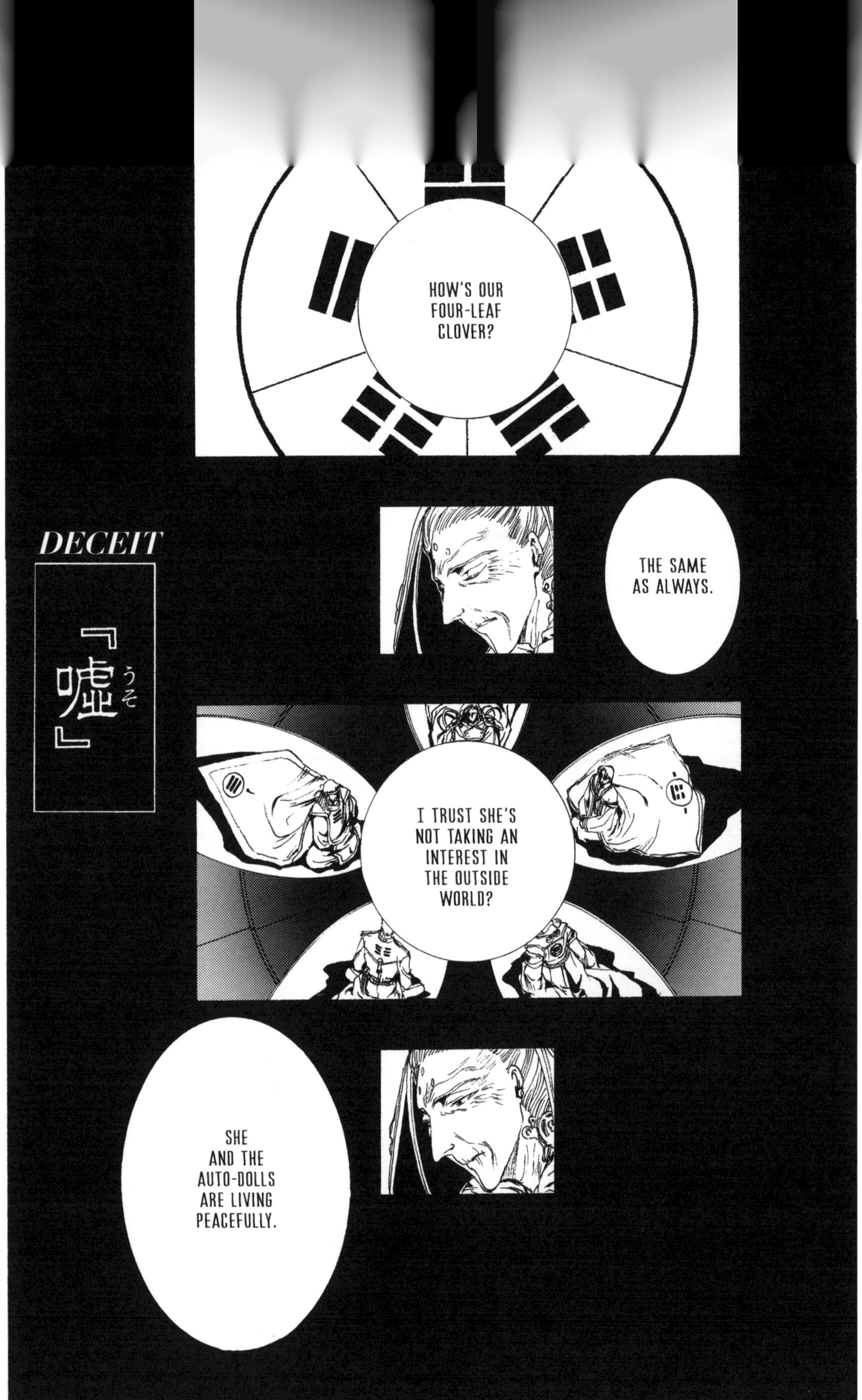
HOW'S OUR FOUR-LEAF CLOVER?
THE SAME AS ALWAYS.
DECEIT
『嘘』うそ
I TRUST SHE'S NOT TAKING AN INTEREST IN THE OUTSIDE WORLD?
SHE AND THE AUTO-DOLLS ARE LIVING PEACEFULLY.

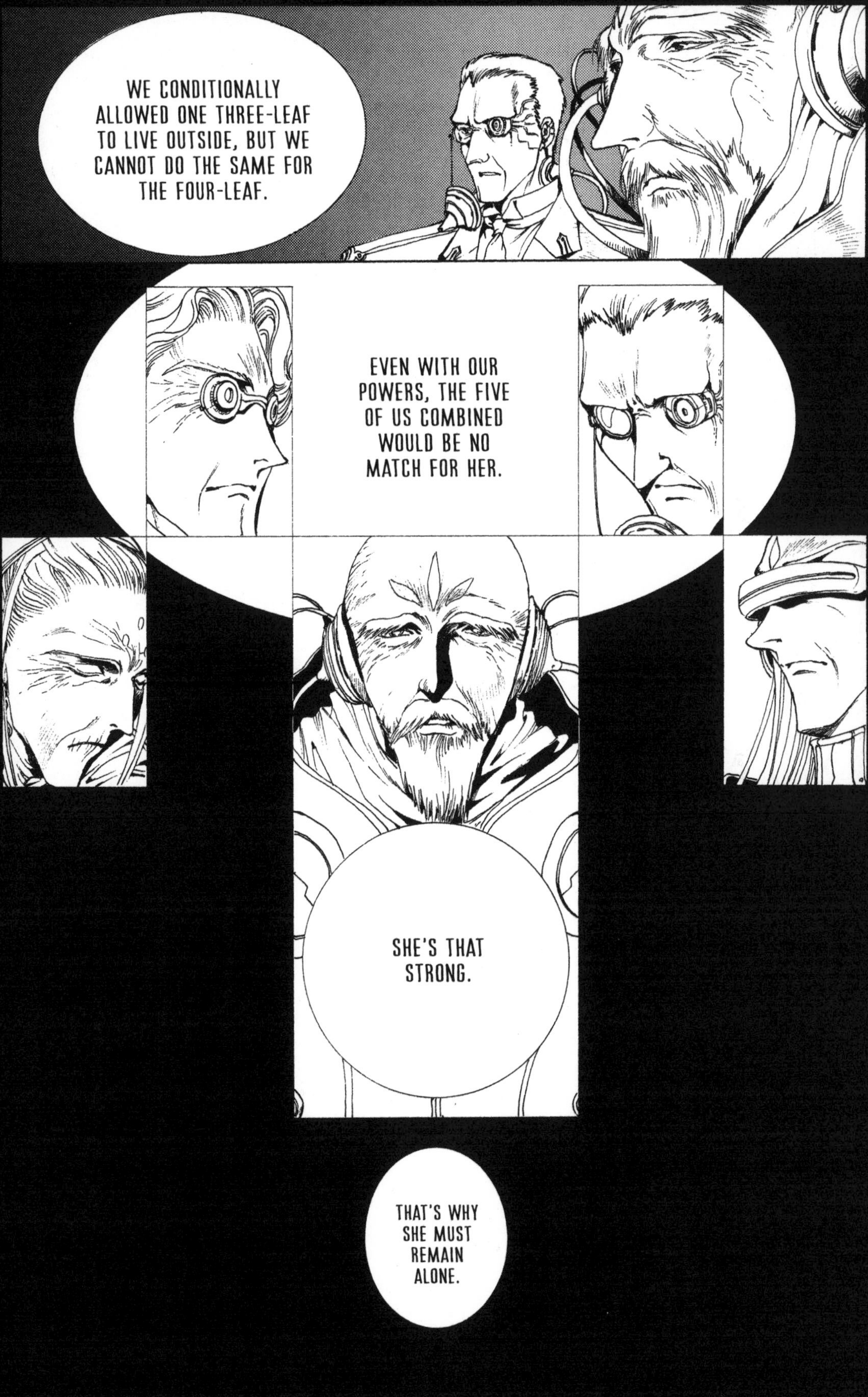
WE CONDITIONALLY ALLOWED ONE THREE-LEAF TO LIVE OUTSIDE, BUT WE CANNOT DO THE SAME FOR THE FOUR-LEAF.
EVEN WITH OUR POWERS, THE FIVE OF US COMBINED WOULD BE NO MATCH FOR HER.
SHE'S THAT STRONG.
THAT'S WHY SHE MUST REMAIN ALONE.

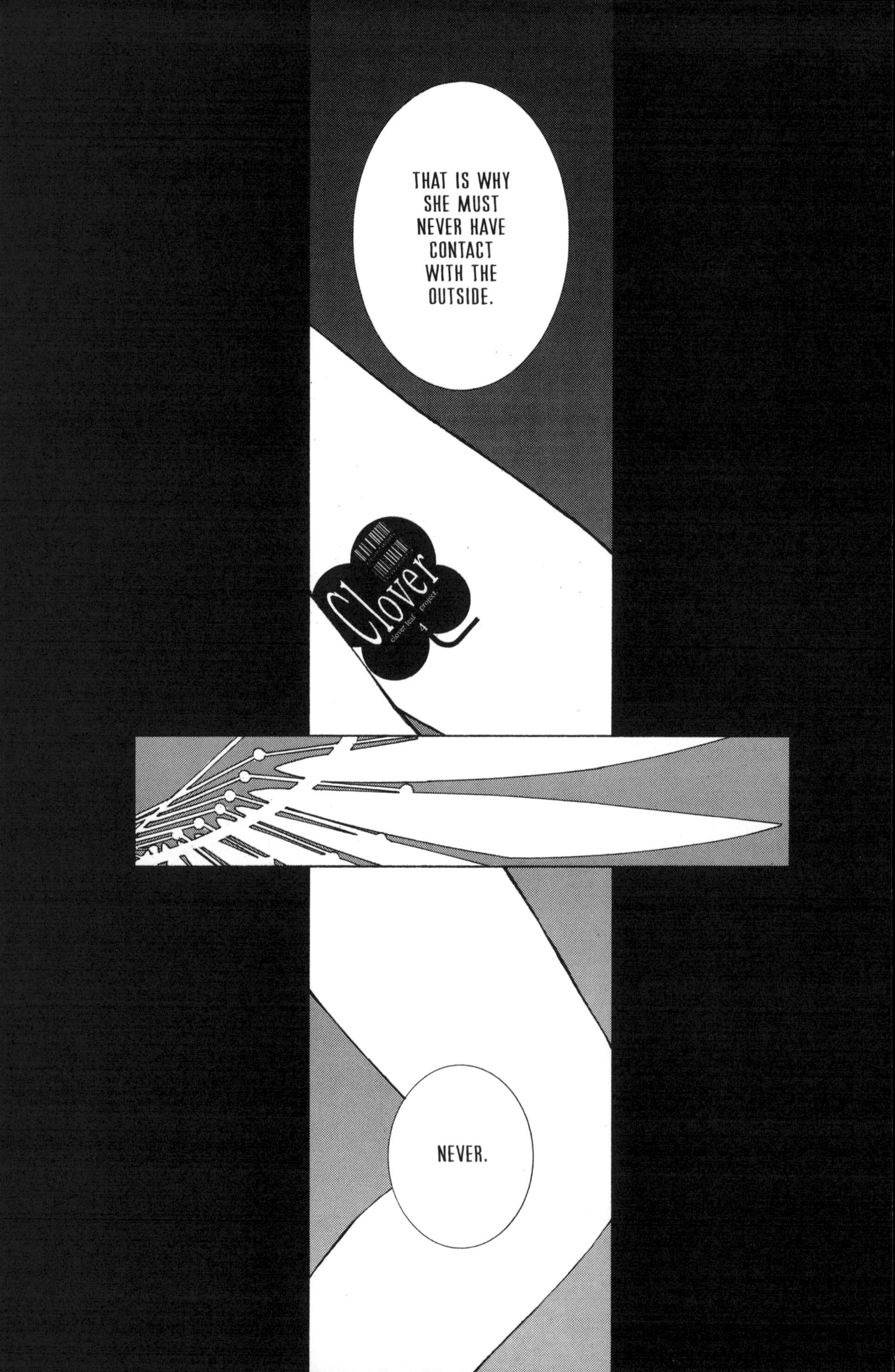
THAT IS WHY SHE MUST NEVER HAVE CONTACT WITH THE OUTSIDE.
Clover
clover leaf project.
4
NEVER.

『小鳥から小鳥への電話』

A CALL FROM BIRD TO BIRD

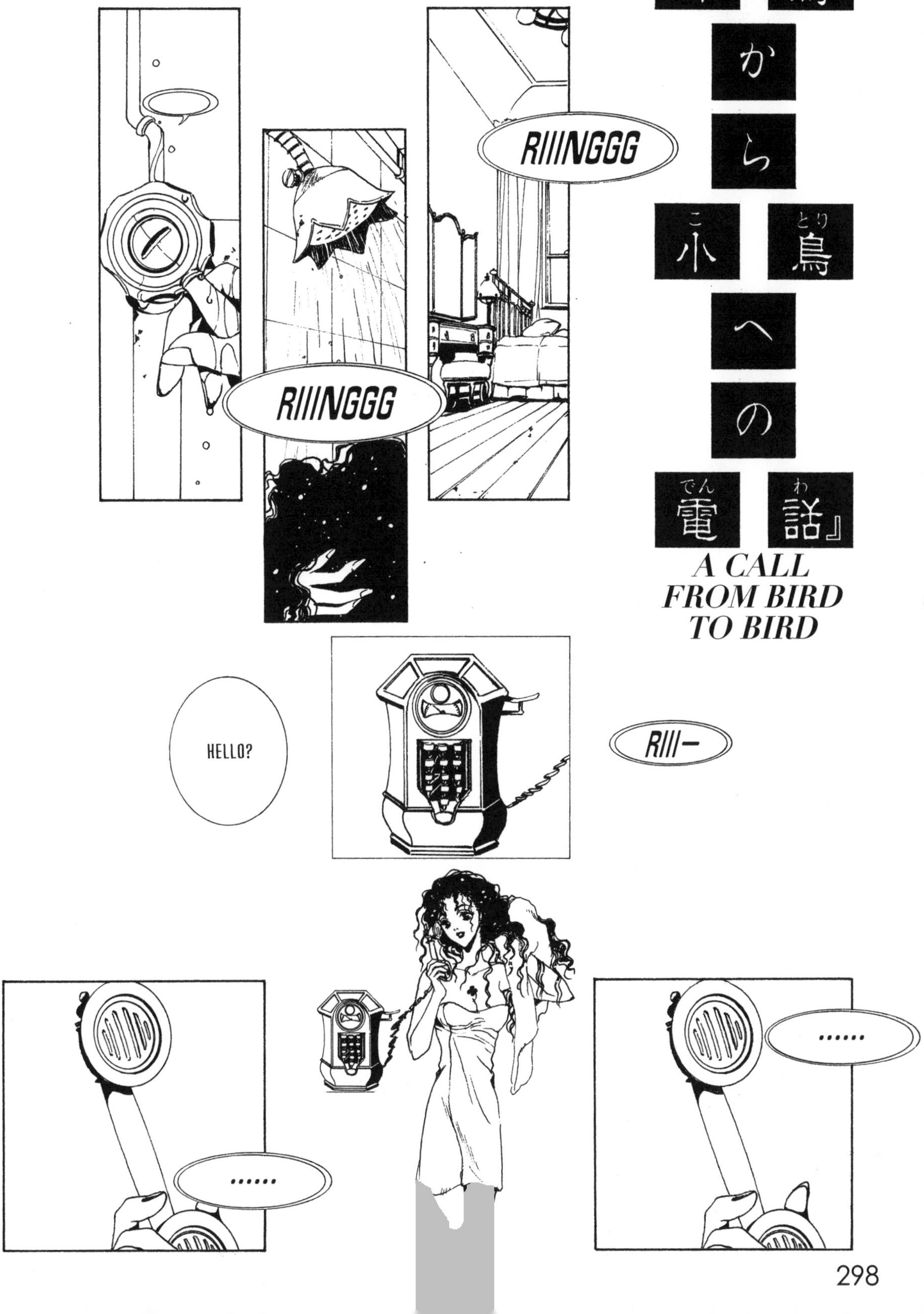

RIIINGGG
RIIINGGG
RIII—
HELLO?
....
....

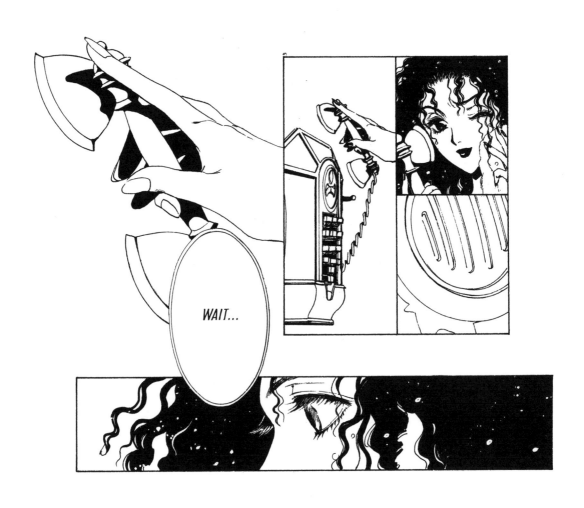

WAIT...

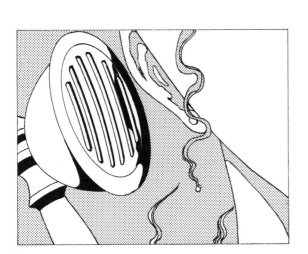

...I'M
A BIG FAN
OF YOURS.

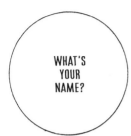

WHAT'S
YOUR
NAME?

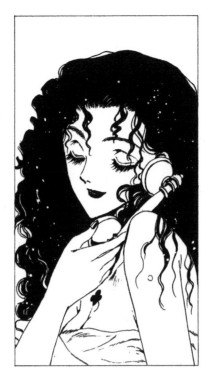

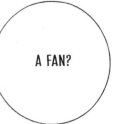

A FAN?

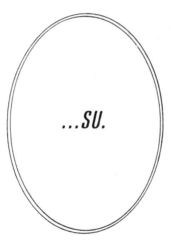

...SU.

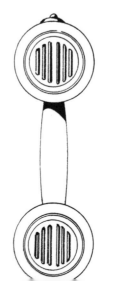

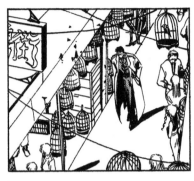

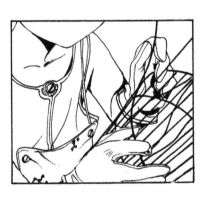

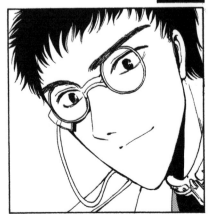

『小鳥に贈られる小鳥』

YOU'RE VERY GOOD AT THAT.

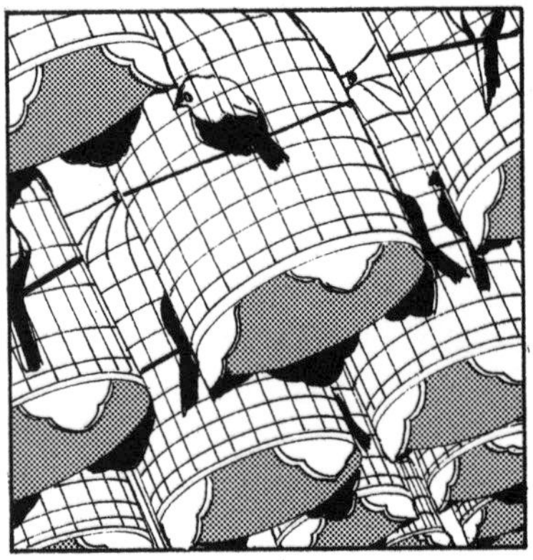

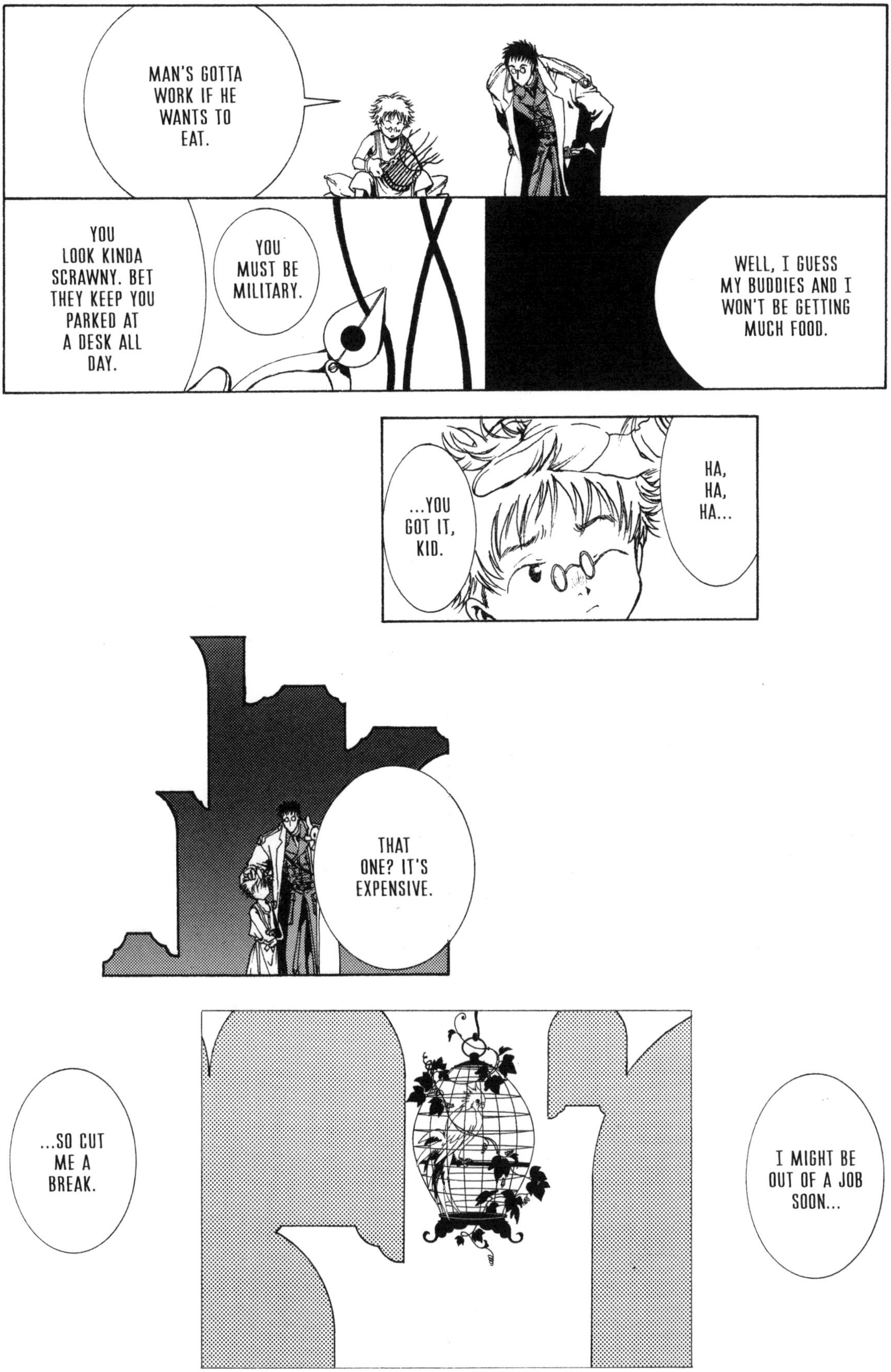
MAN'S GOTTA WORK IF HE WANTS TO EAT.
WELL, I GUESS MY BUDDIES AND I WON'T BE GETTING MUCH FOOD.
YOU MUST BE MILITARY.
YOU LOOK KINDA SCRAWNY. BET THEY KEEP YOU PARKED AT A DESK ALL DAY.
HA, HA, HA...
...YOU GOT IT, KID.
THAT ONE? IT'S EXPENSIVE.
I MIGHT BE OUT OF A JOB SOON...
...SO CUT ME A BREAK.

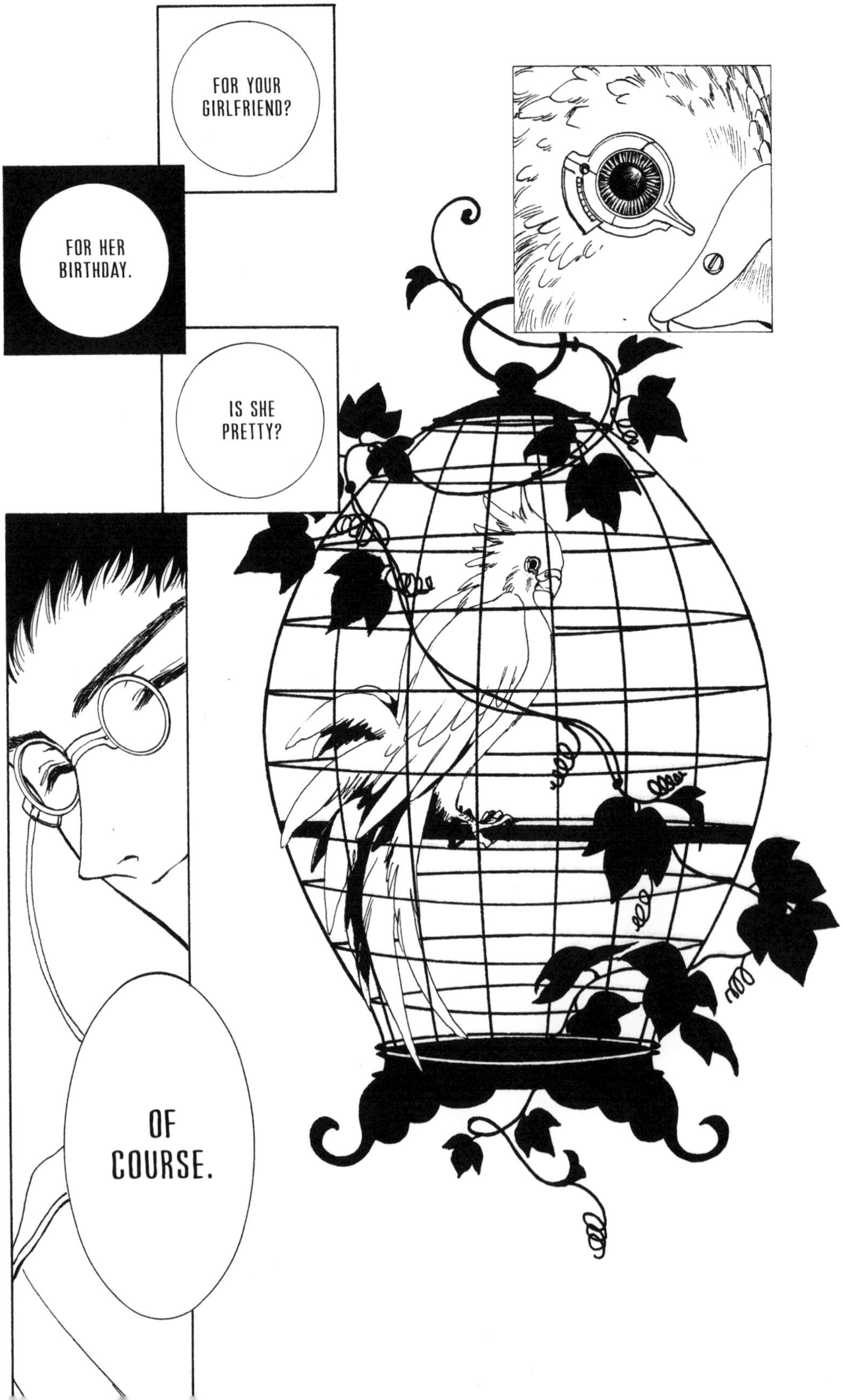
FOR YOUR GIRLFRIEND?
FOR HER BIRTHDAY.
IS SHE PRETTY?
OF COURSE.

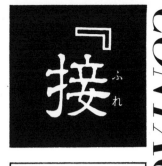

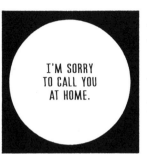

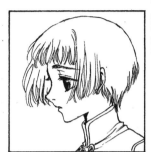

I'M SORRY TO CALL YOU AT HOME.

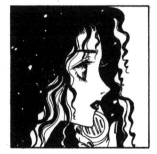

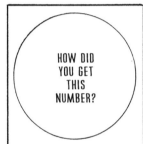

HOW DID YOU GET THIS NUMBER?

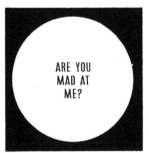

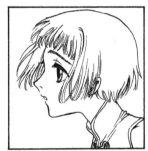

ARE YOU MAD AT ME?

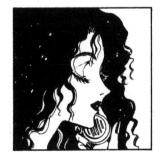

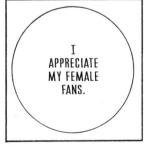

I APPRECIATE MY FEMALE FANS.

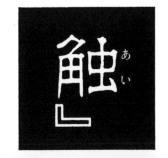

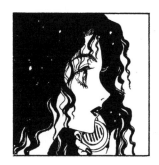

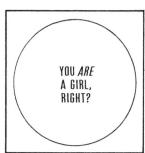

YOU *ARE*
A GIRL,
RIGHT?

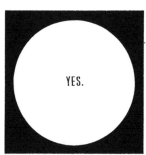

YES.

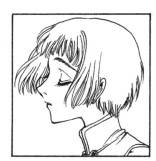

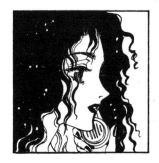

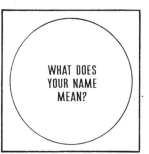

WHAT DOES
YOUR NAME
MEAN?

SU...
SÌ...
THE
NUMBER
FOUR.

CAT

『猫

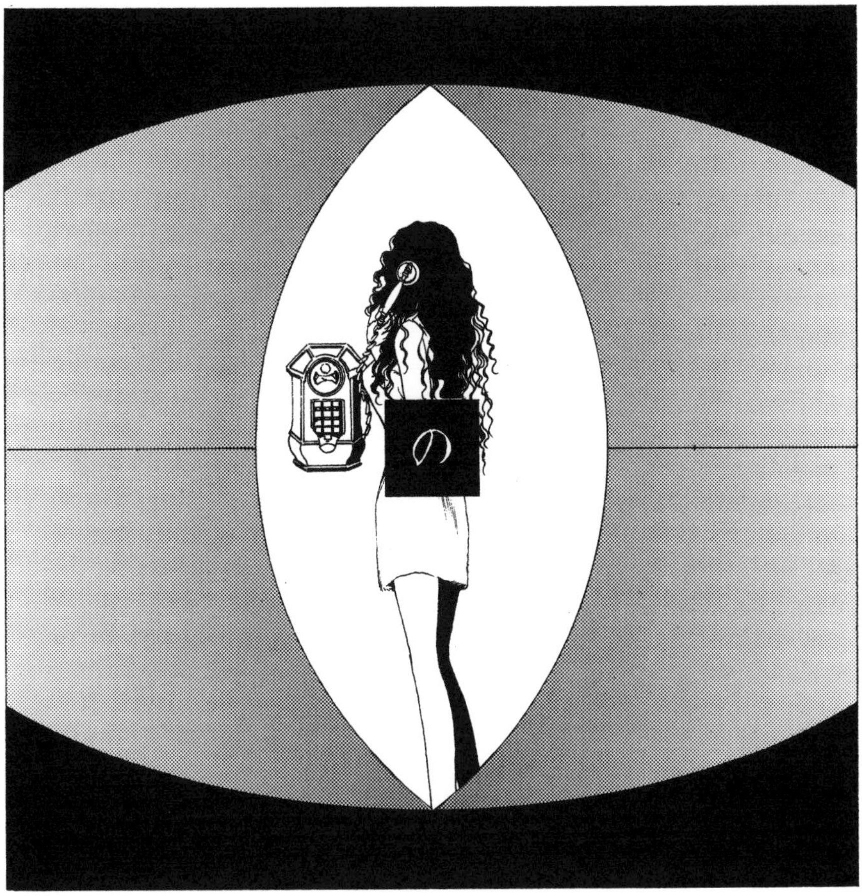
の

目』

EYE

CAN YOU...

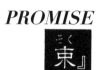

PROMISE

『約束』

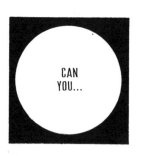

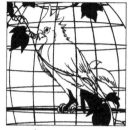

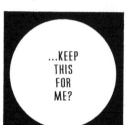

...KEEP THIS FOR ME?

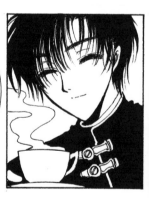

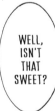

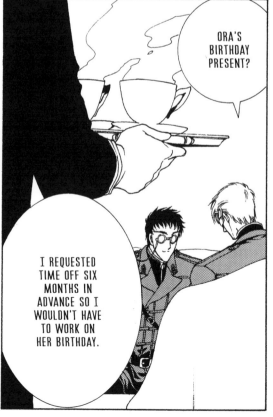

ORA'S BIRTHDAY PRESENT?
I REQUESTED TIME OFF SIX MONTHS IN ADVANCE SO I WOULDN'T HAVE TO WORK ON HER BIRTHDAY.

WELL, ISN'T THAT SWEET?

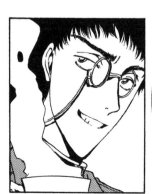

MAKE SURE YOU DON'T EAT IT.

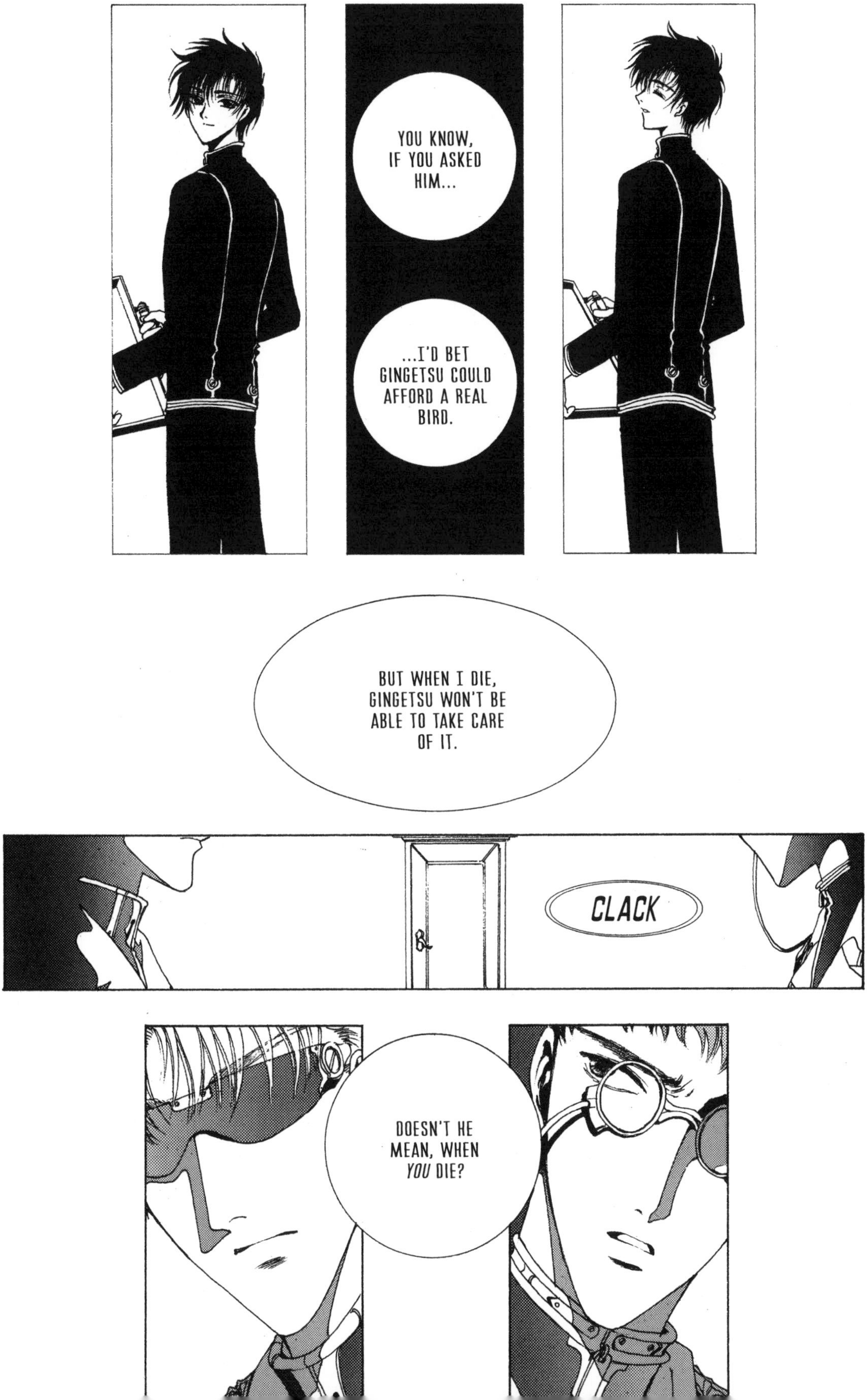
YOU KNOW, IF YOU ASKED HIM...
...I'D BET GINGETSU COULD AFFORD A REAL BIRD.
BUT WHEN I DIE, GINGETSU WON'T BE ABLE TO TAKE CARE OF IT.
CLACK
DOESN'T HE MEAN, WHEN *YOU* DIE?

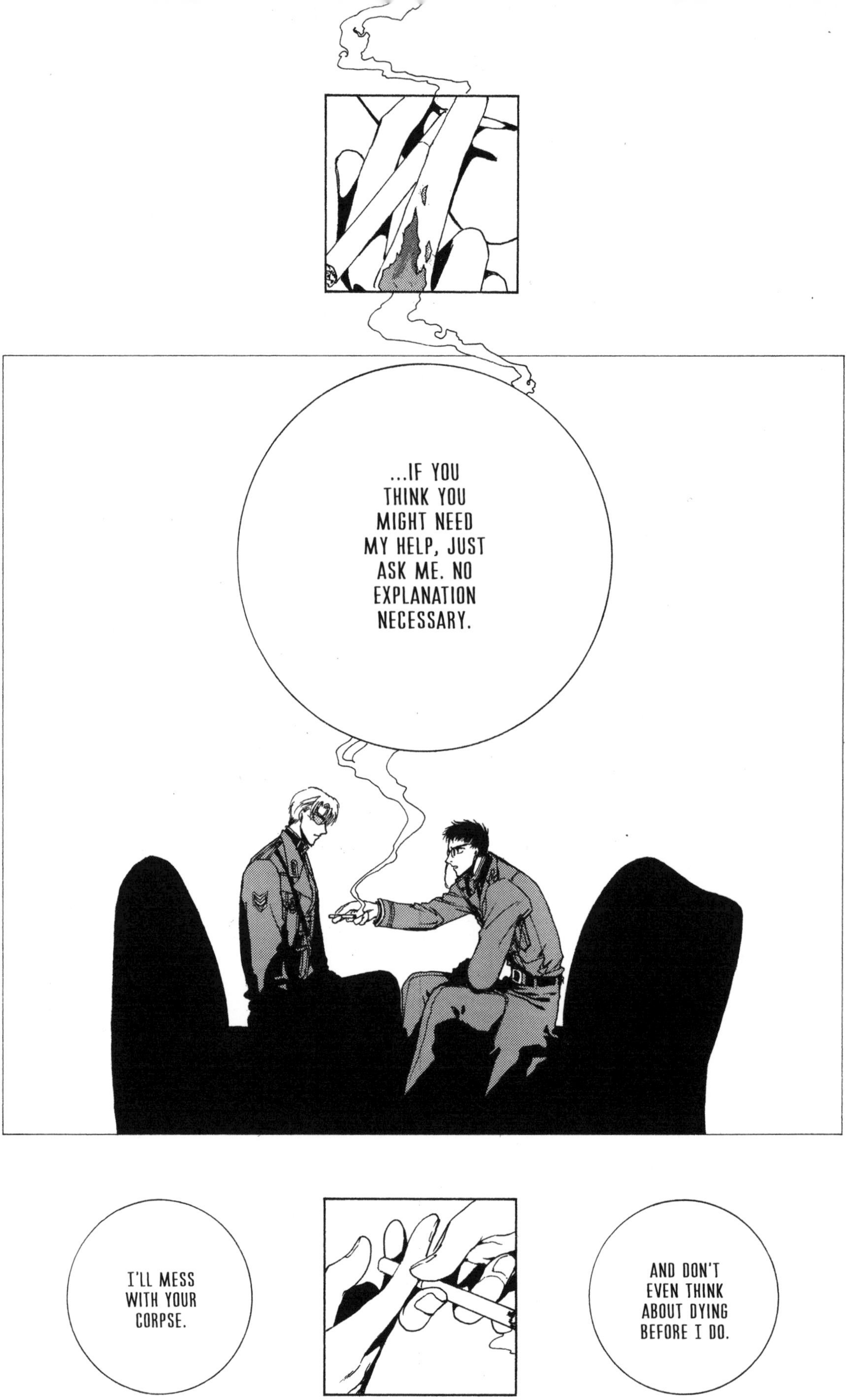
...IF YOU THINK YOU MIGHT NEED MY HELP, JUST ASK ME. NO EXPLANATION NECESSARY.
AND DON'T EVEN THINK ABOUT DYING BEFORE I DO.
I'LL MESS WITH YOUR CORPSE.

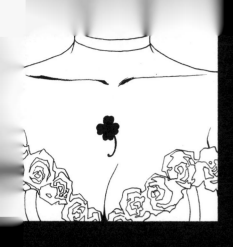

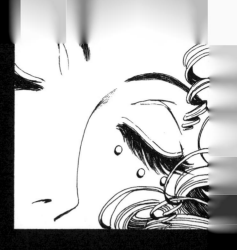

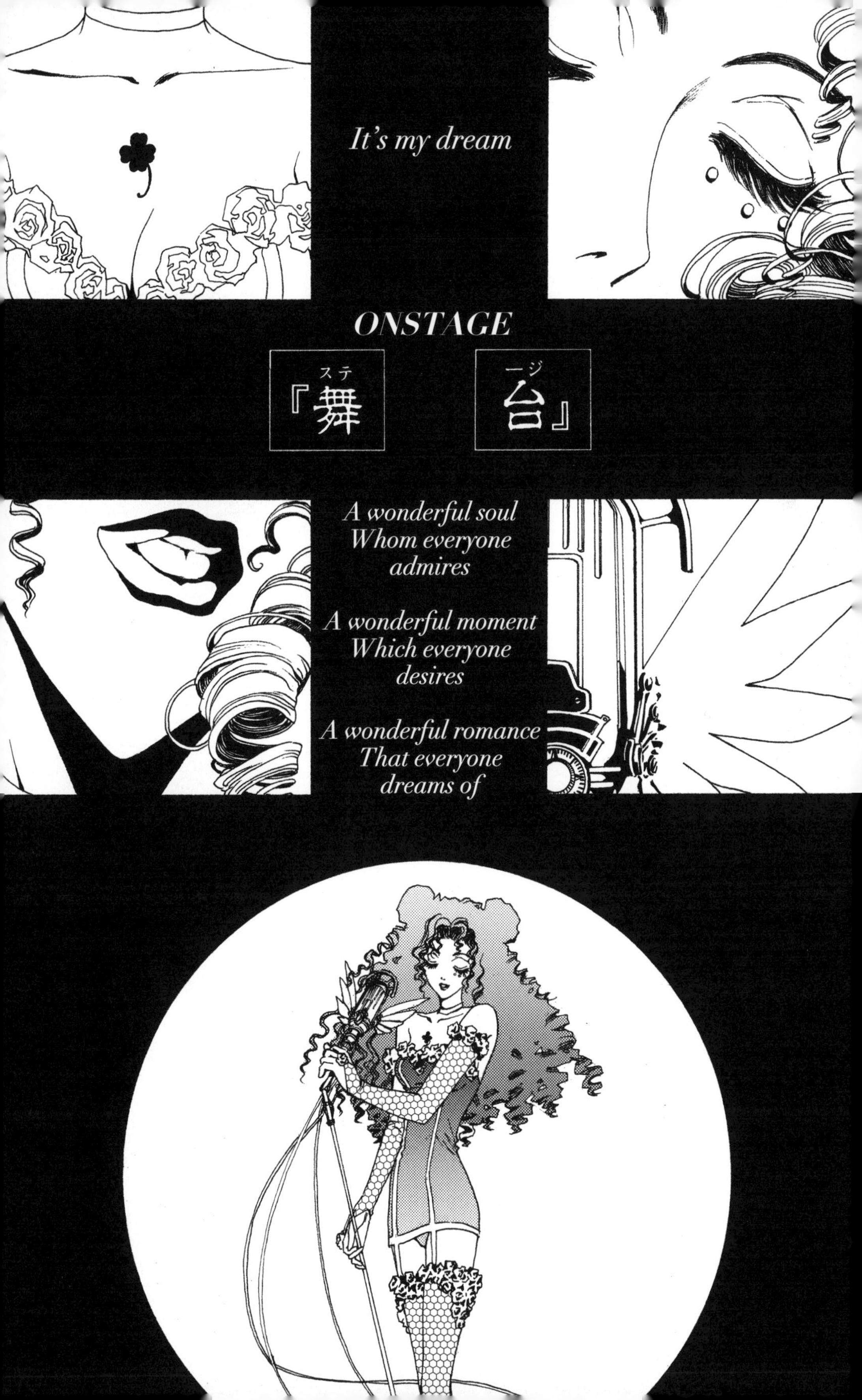
It's my dream
ONSTAGE
ステージ
『舞台』
A wonderful soul
Whom everyone
admires
A wonderful moment
Which everyone
desires
A wonderful romance
That everyone
dreams of

LOVE

True love is
unmatched

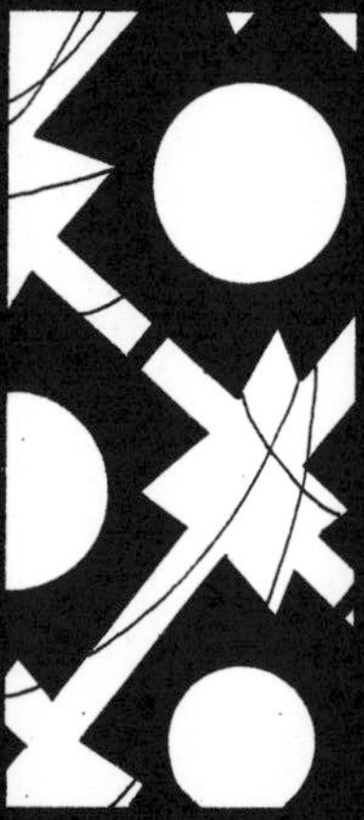

LOVE
You might laugh
But once lost, it never returns

LOVE
You might laugh
But to us, it's the
most important
word

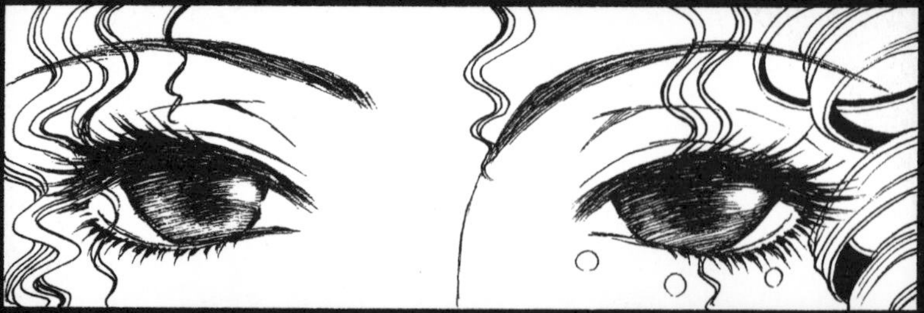

LOVE

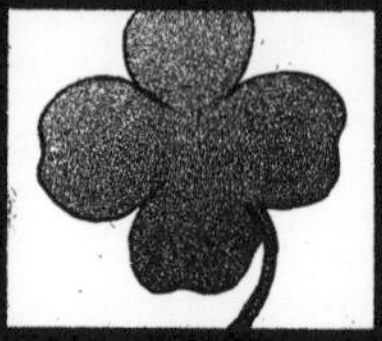

『小鳥の内緒話』

A BIRD'S SECRET

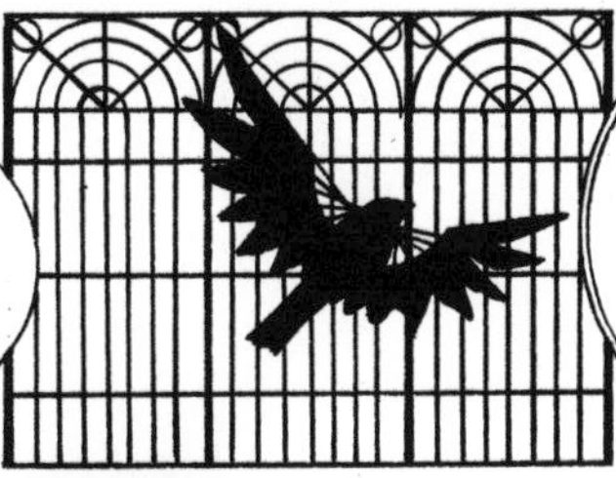

I HAVEN'T SEEN YOU AT THE CLUB.
I KNOW.

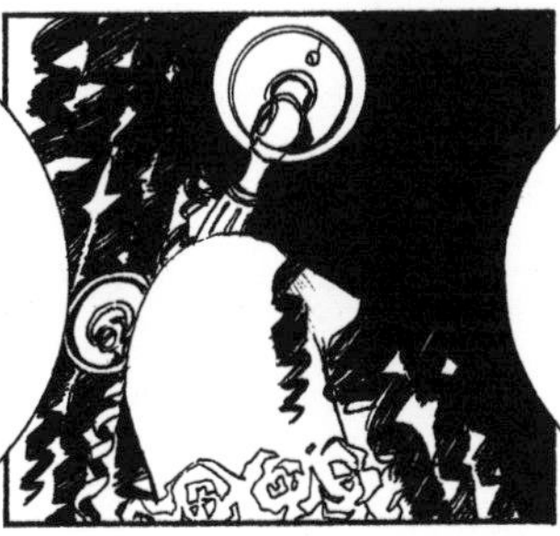

THEN HOW CAN YOU HEAR ME?
MY SONGS AREN'T PLAYED ON ANY OF THE MAJOR STATIONS.

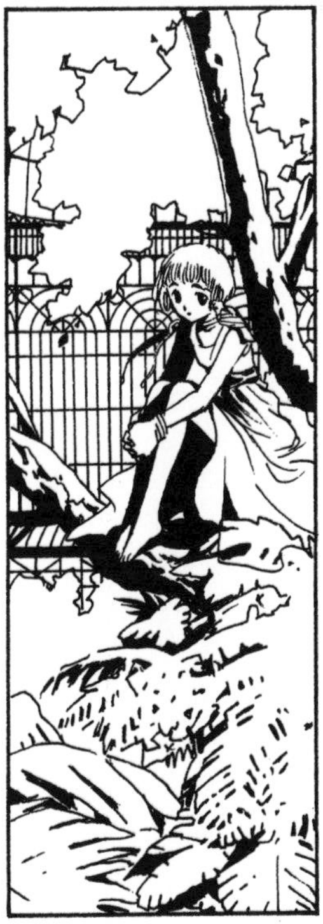

DO I HAVE TO TELL YOU?

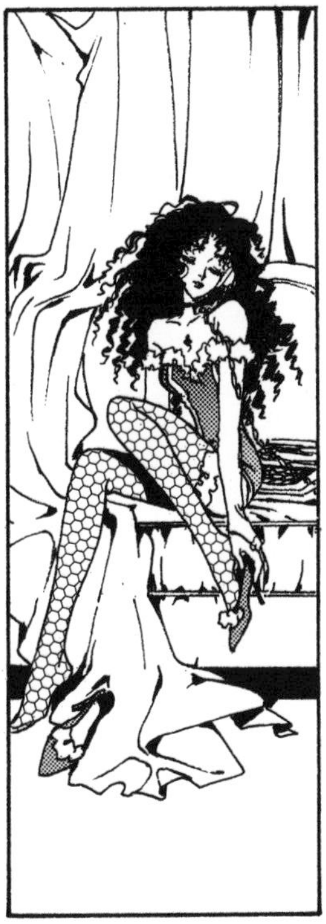

NO. EVERYONE HAS THEIR SECRETS.

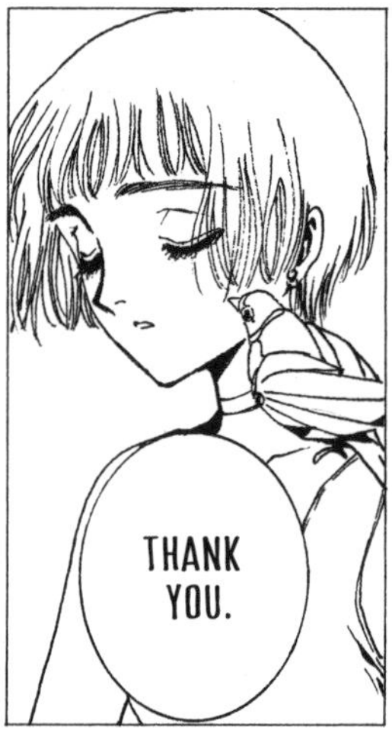
THANK YOU.

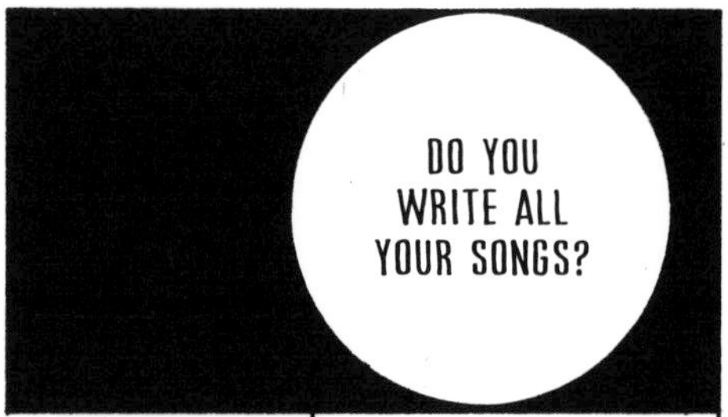
DO YOU WRITE ALL YOUR SONGS?

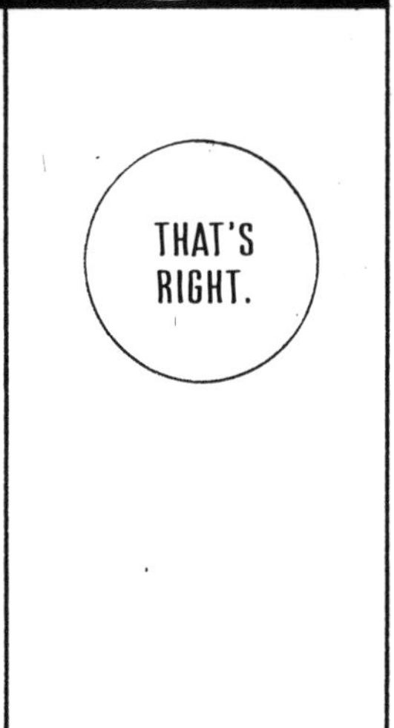
THAT'S RIGHT.

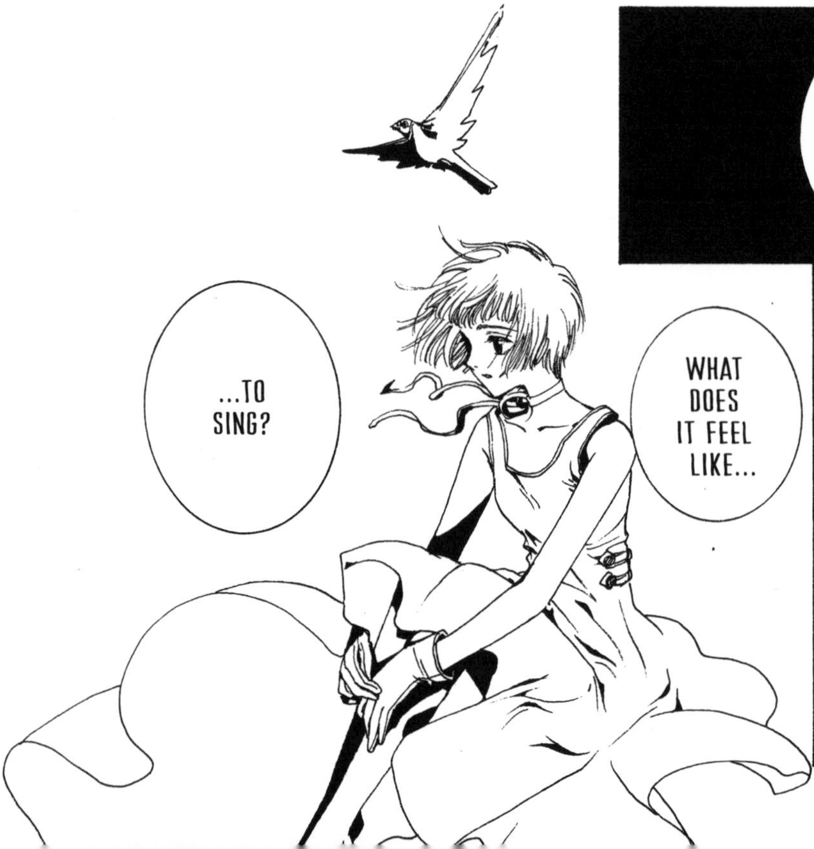
WHAT DOES IT FEEL LIKE...
...TO SING?

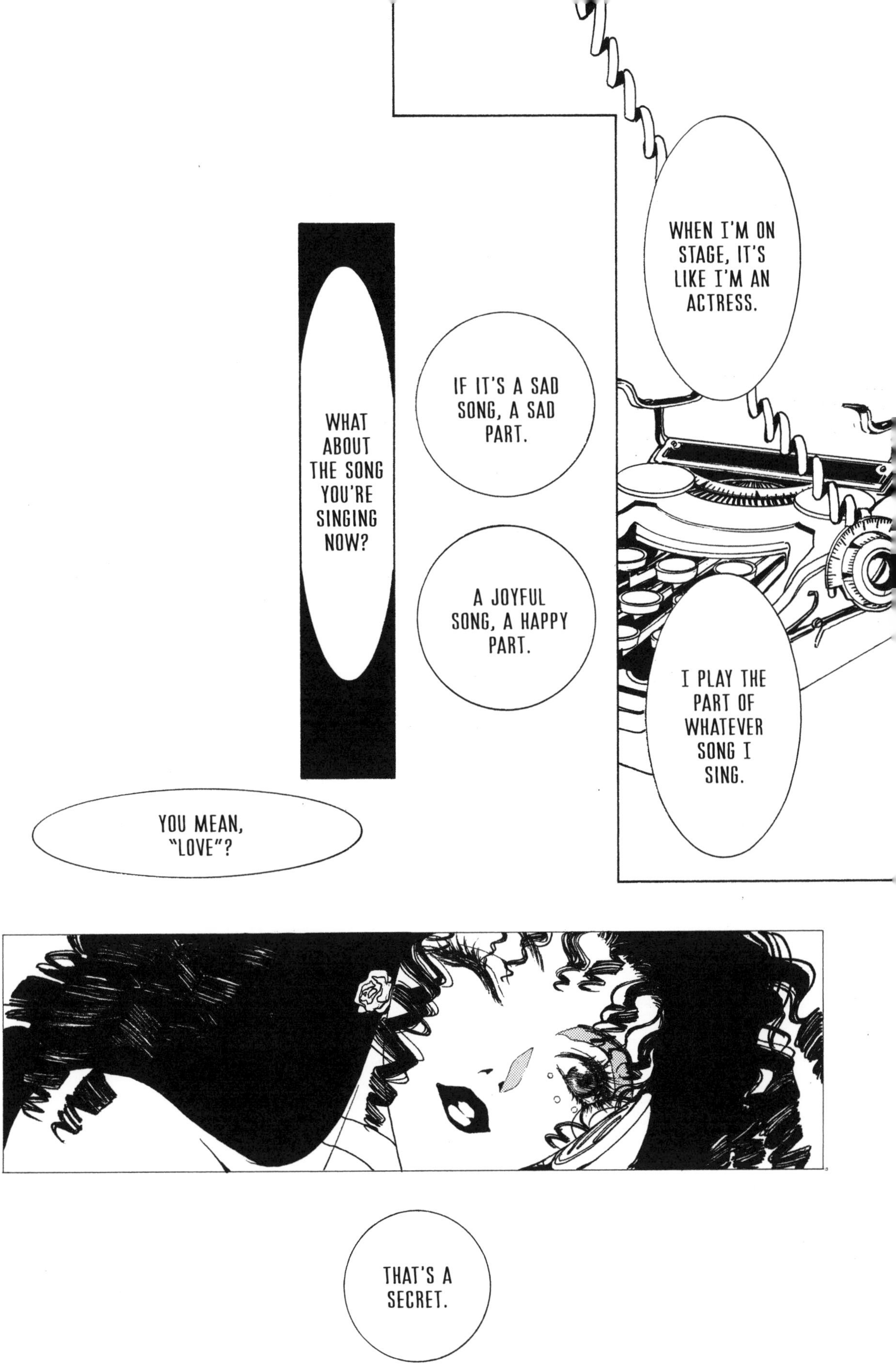
WHEN I'M ON STAGE, IT'S LIKE I'M AN ACTRESS.
IF IT'S A SAD SONG, A SAD PART.
A JOYFUL SONG, A HAPPY PART.
I PLAY THE PART OF WHATEVER SONG I SING.
WHAT ABOUT THE SONG YOU'RE SINGING NOW?
YOU MEAN, "LOVE"?
THAT'S A SECRET.

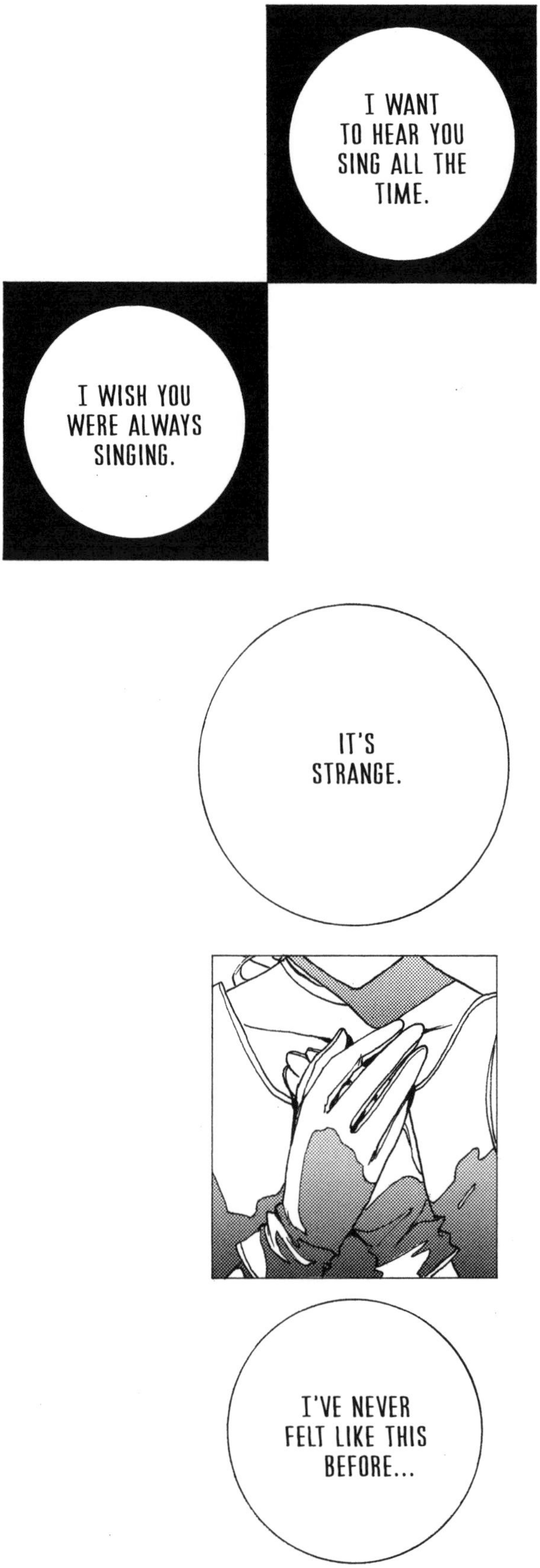

I WANT
TO HEAR YOU
SING ALL THE
TIME.

I WISH YOU
WERE ALWAYS
SINGING.

IT'S
STRANGE.

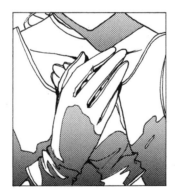

I'VE NEVER
FELT LIKE THIS
BEFORE...

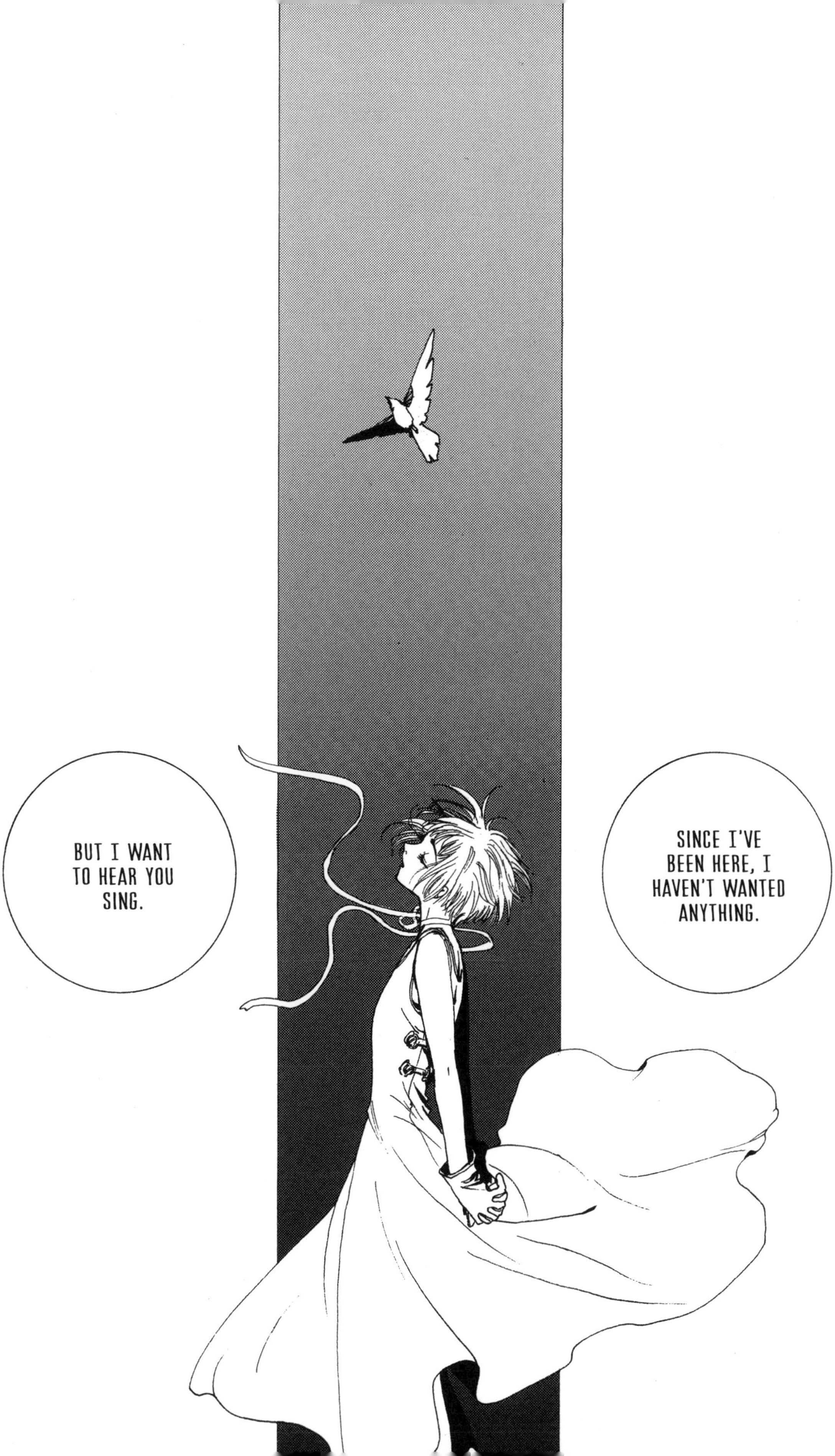
SINCE I'VE BEEN HERE, I HAVEN'T WANTED ANYTHING.
BUT I WANT TO HEAR YOU SING.

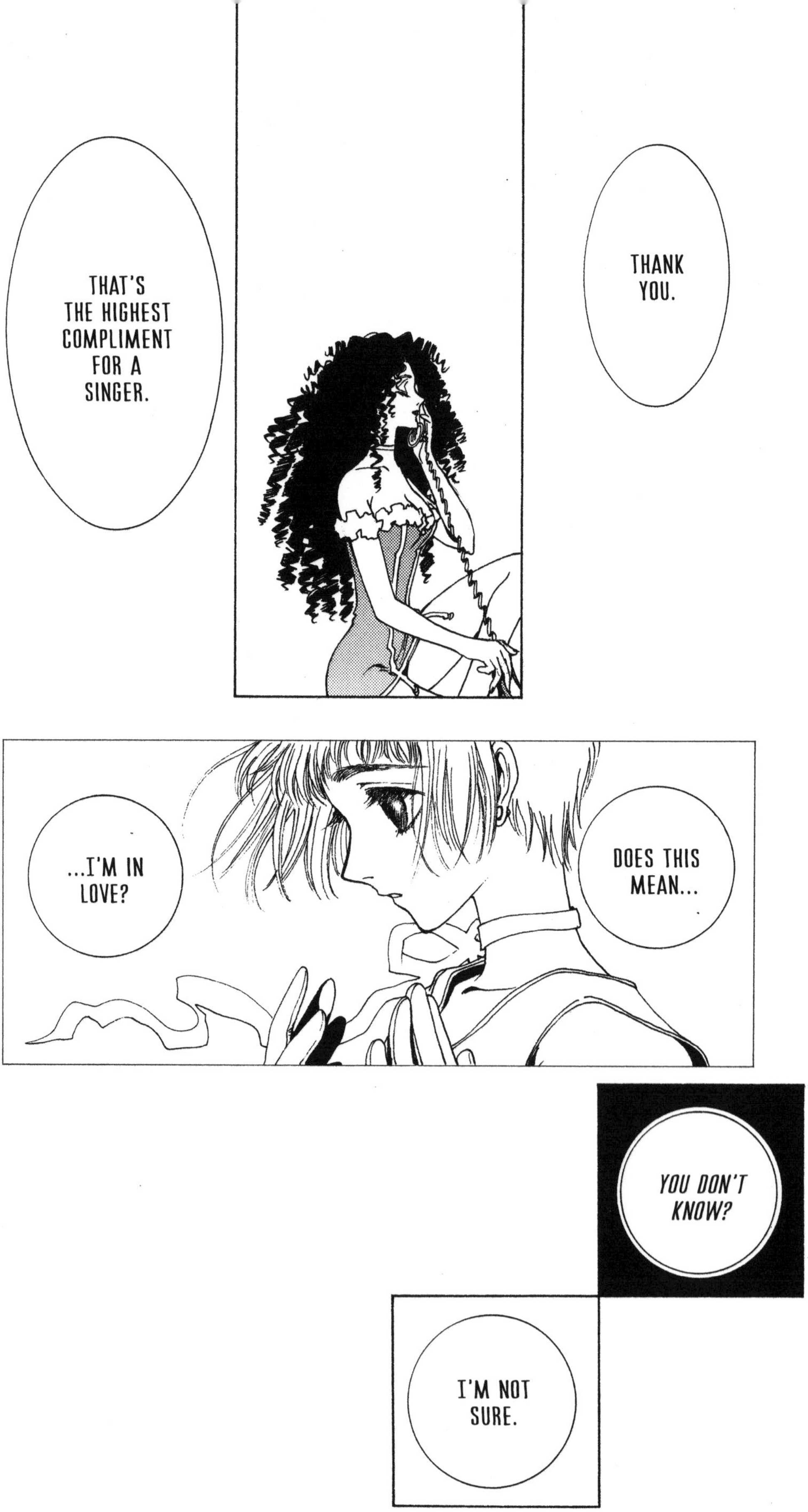
THANK YOU.
THAT'S THE HIGHEST COMPLIMENT FOR A SINGER.
DOES THIS MEAN...
...I'M IN LOVE?
YOU DON'T KNOW?
I'M NOT SURE.

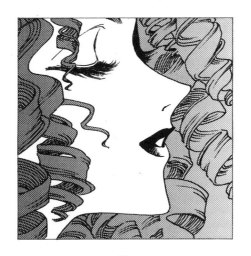

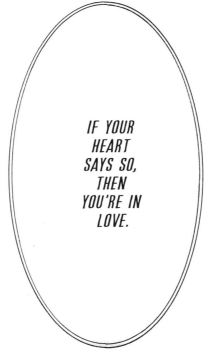

IF YOUR
HEART
SAYS SO,
THEN
YOU'RE IN
LOVE.

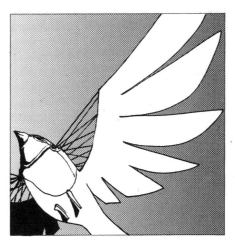

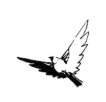

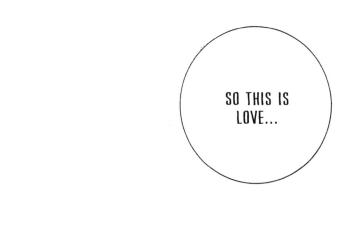

SO THIS IS
LOVE...

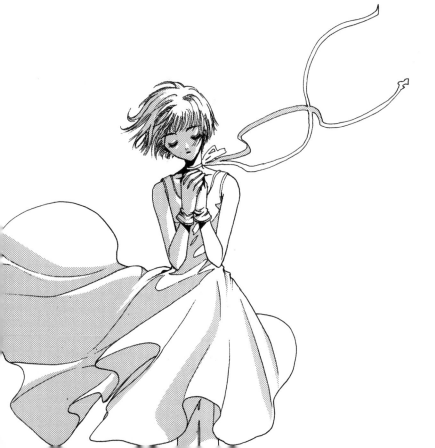

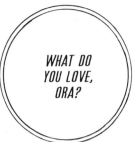

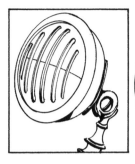

WHAT DO YOU LOVE, ORA?

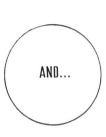

AND...

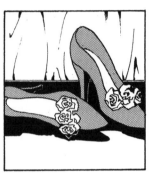

TO SING.

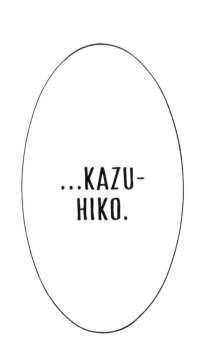

...KAZU-HIKO.

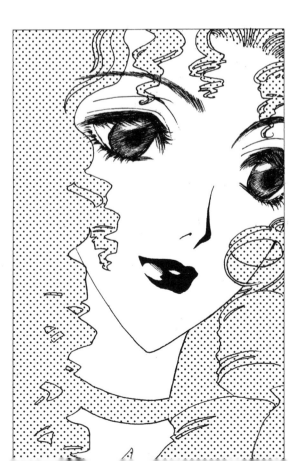

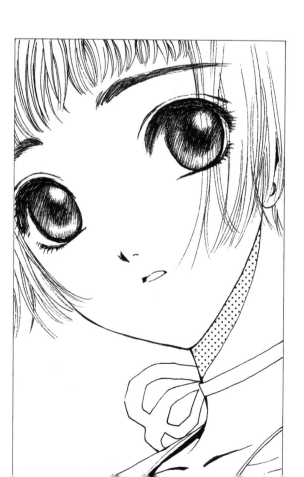

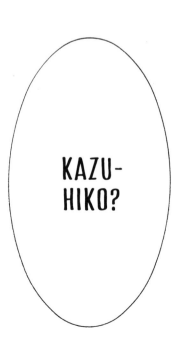

KAZU-
HIKO?

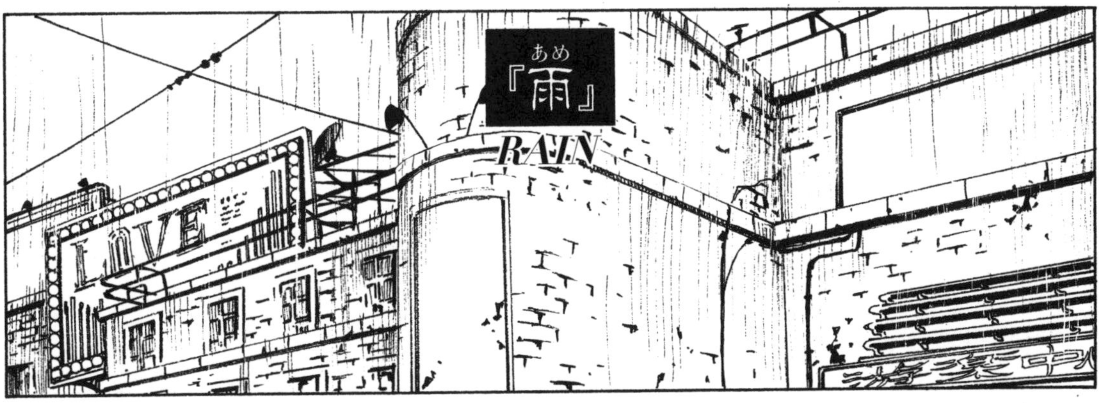
『雨』(あめ)
RAIN
LOVE

LOVE

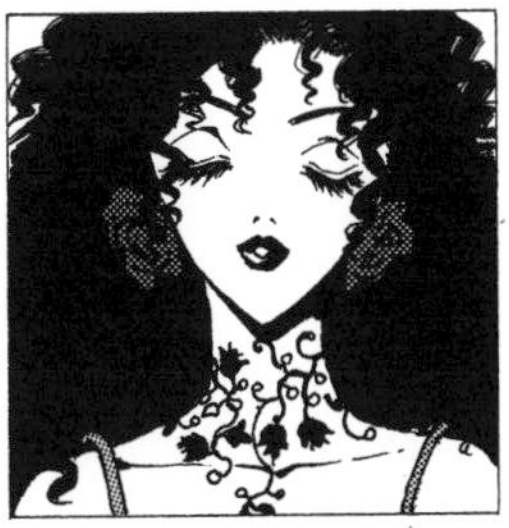

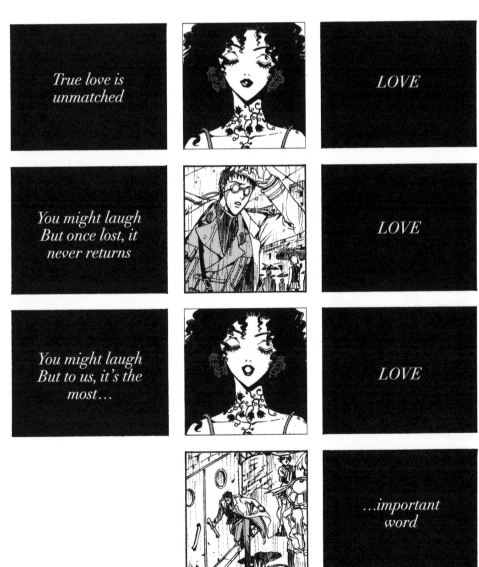

True love is unmatched

LOVE

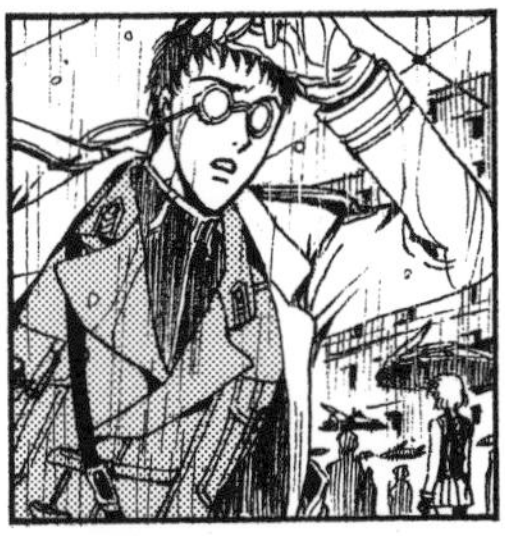

You might laugh
But once lost, it never returns

LOVE

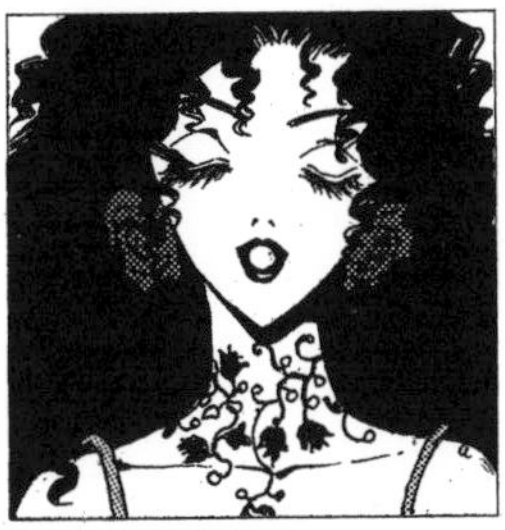

You might laugh
But to us, it's the most…

…important word

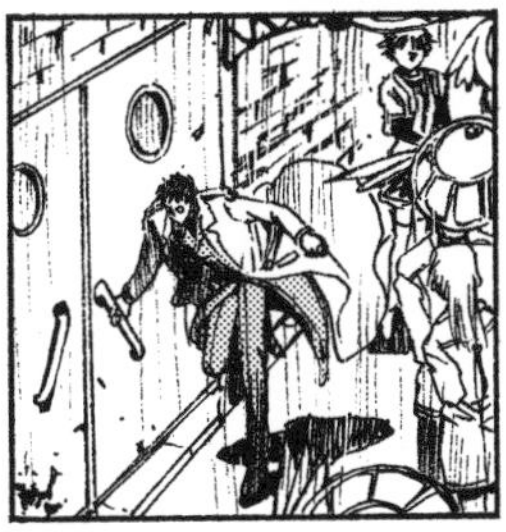

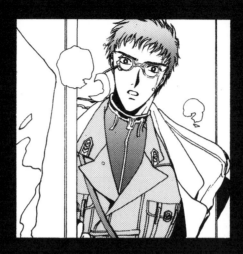

LOVE

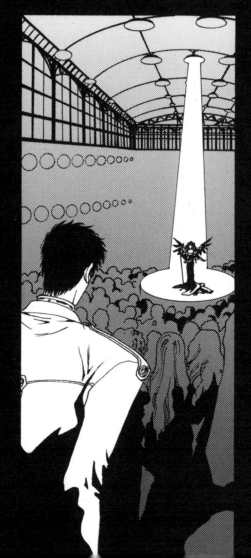

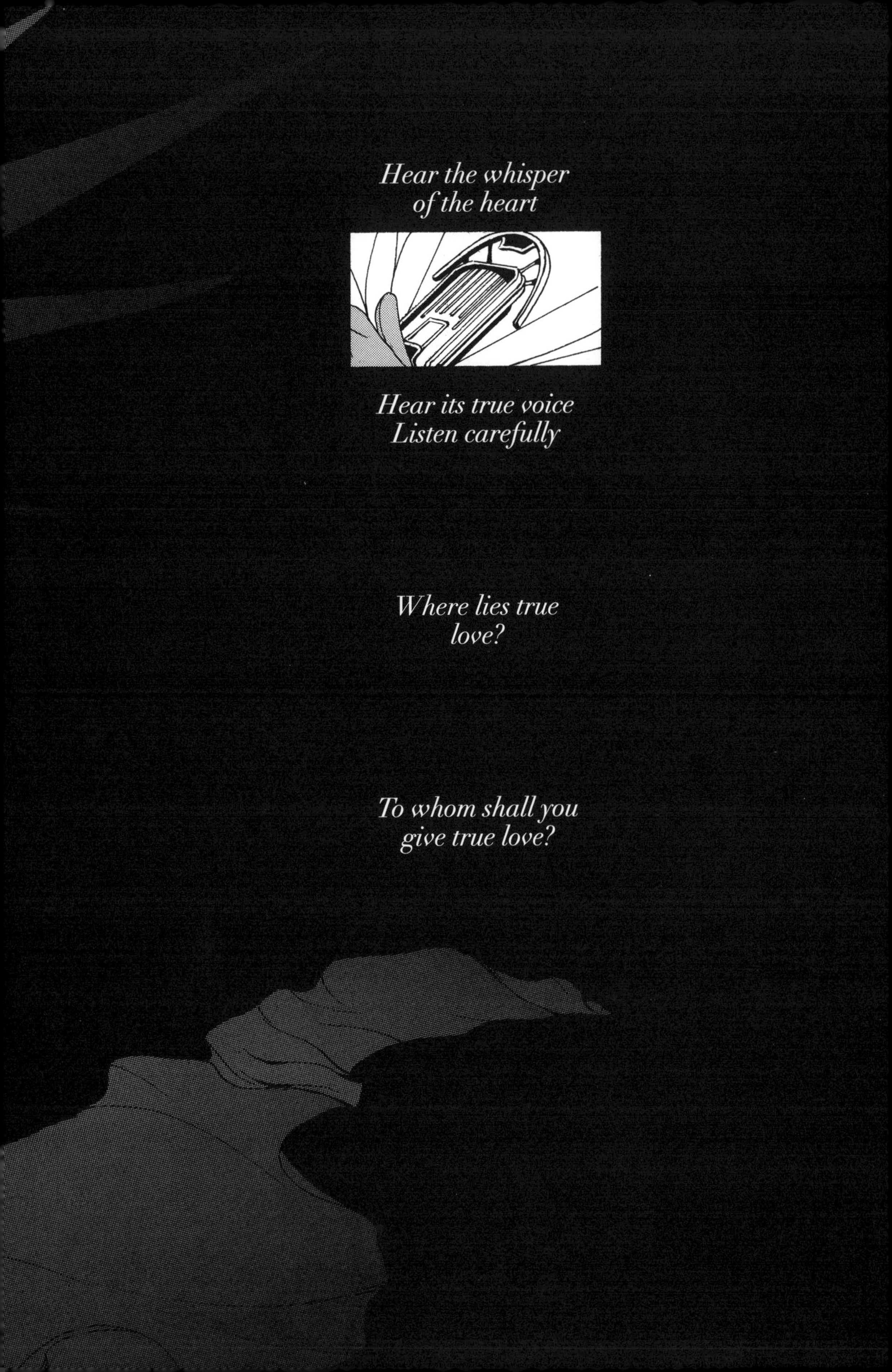
Hear the whisper of the heart
Hear its true voice Listen carefully
Where lies true love?
To whom shall you give true love?

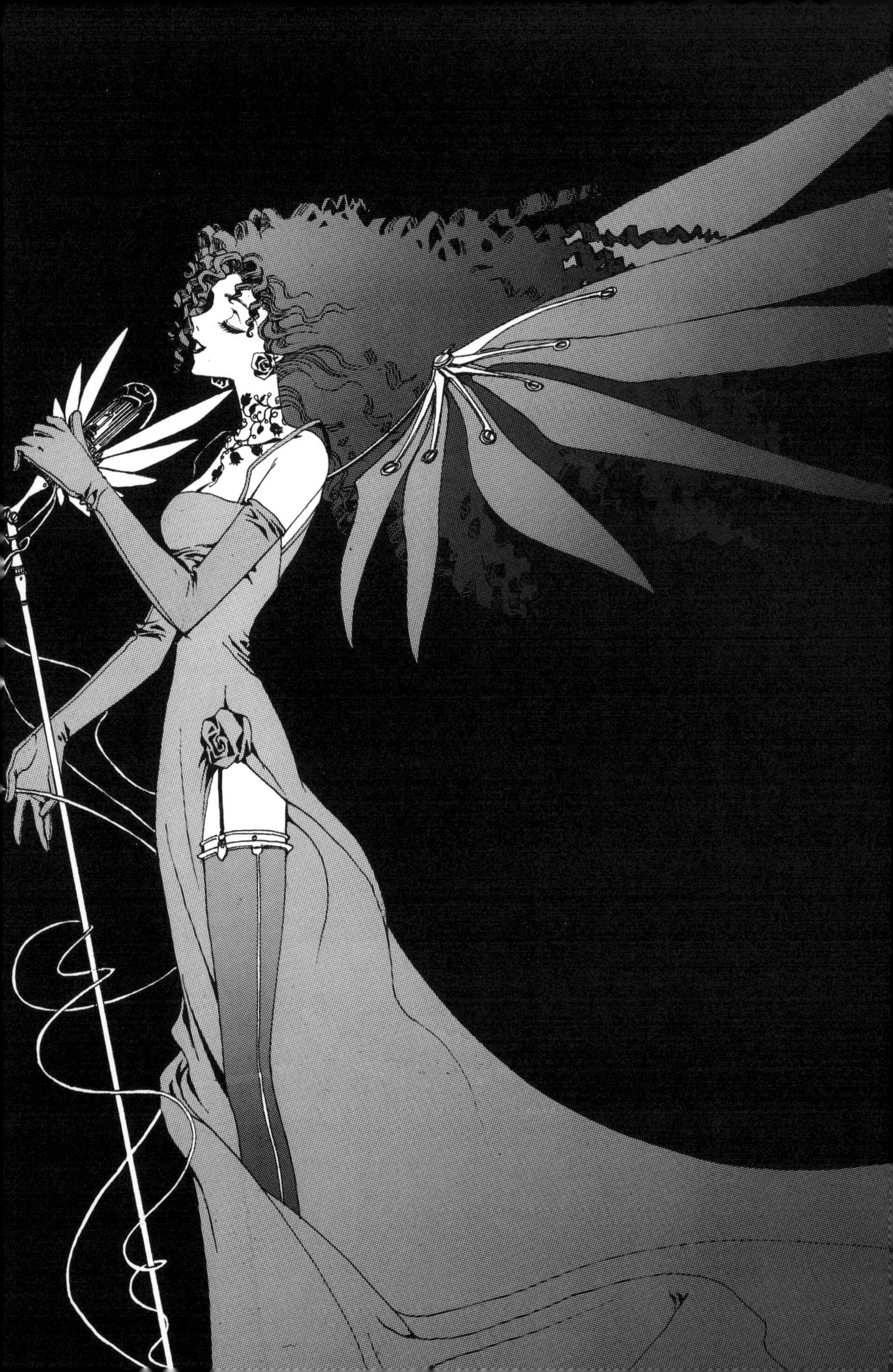

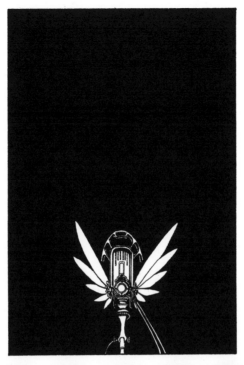

『たった一人のために

A SONG FOR ONE うたう歌』

DID YOU
CHANGE
THE LYRICS
TODAY?

LOVE

Hear the whisper

of the heart

Hear its true voice

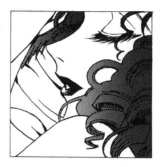

Listen carefully

Where lies true love?

To whom shall

you give true love?

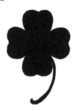

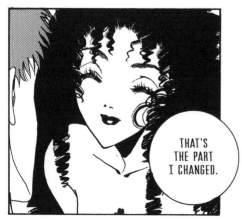

THAT'S THE PART I CHANGED.

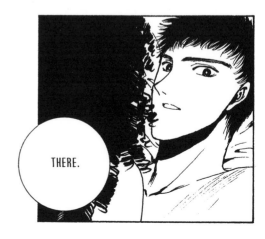

THERE.

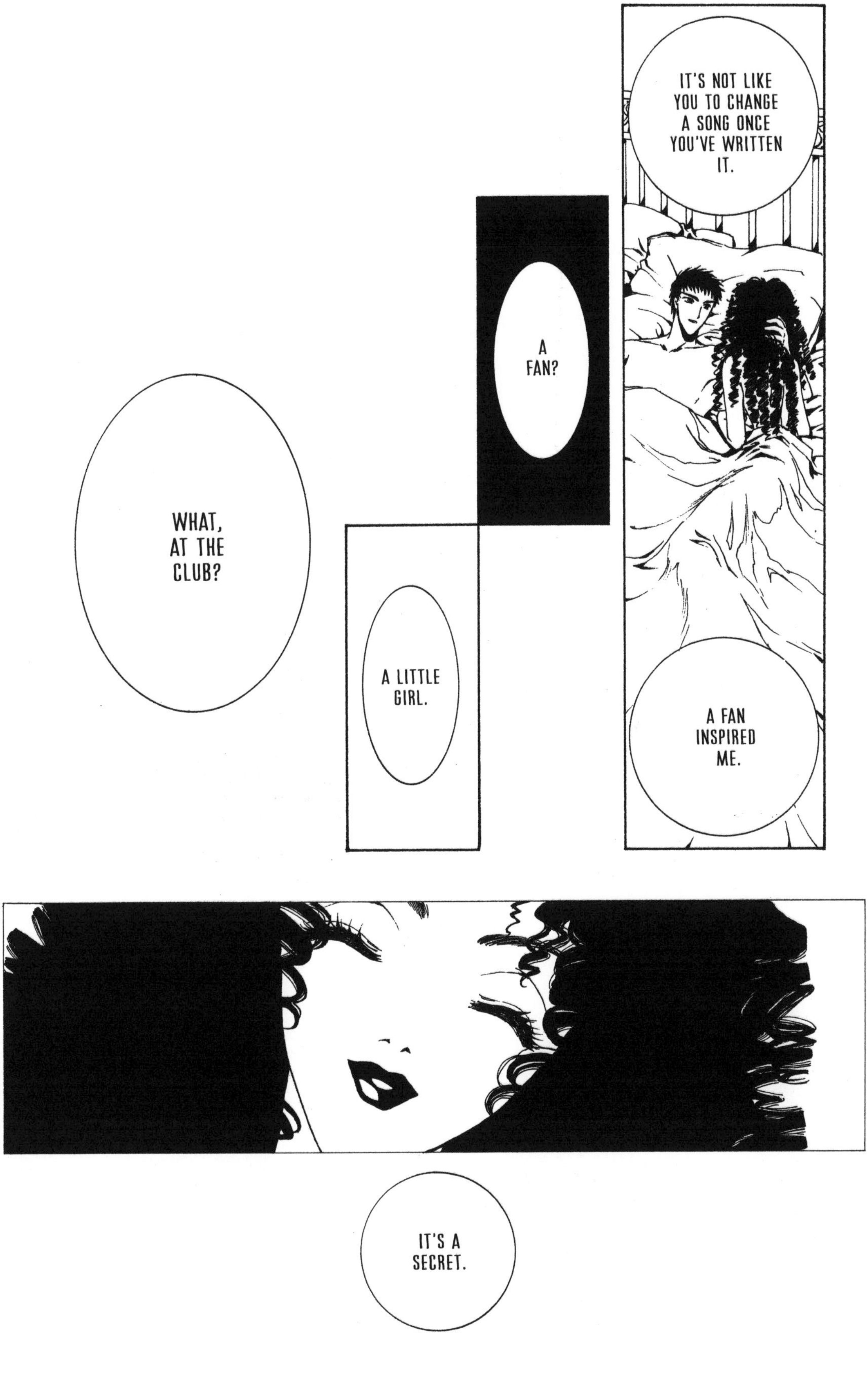
IT'S NOT LIKE YOU TO CHANGE A SONG ONCE YOU'VE WRITTEN IT.
A FAN INSPIRED ME.
A FAN?
A LITTLE GIRL.
WHAT, AT THE CLUB?
IT'S A SECRET.

BIRD

『鳥（とり）の目（め）』

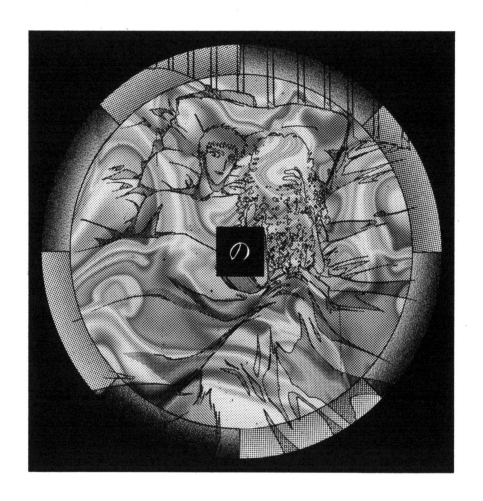

EYE

『小鳥の 心の 小鳥』

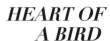

A BIRD IN THE HEART OF A BIRD

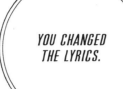

YOU CHANGED THE LYRICS.

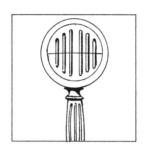

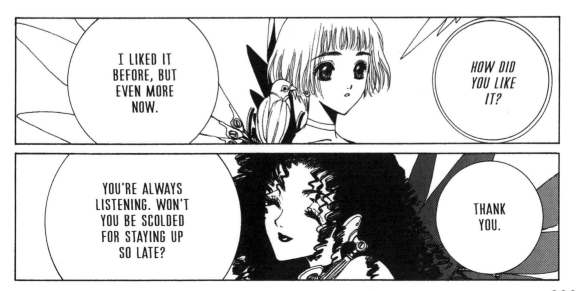

HOW DID YOU LIKE IT?

I LIKED IT BEFORE, BUT EVEN MORE NOW.

THANK YOU.

YOU'RE ALWAYS LISTENING. WON'T YOU BE SCOLDED FOR STAYING UP SO LATE?

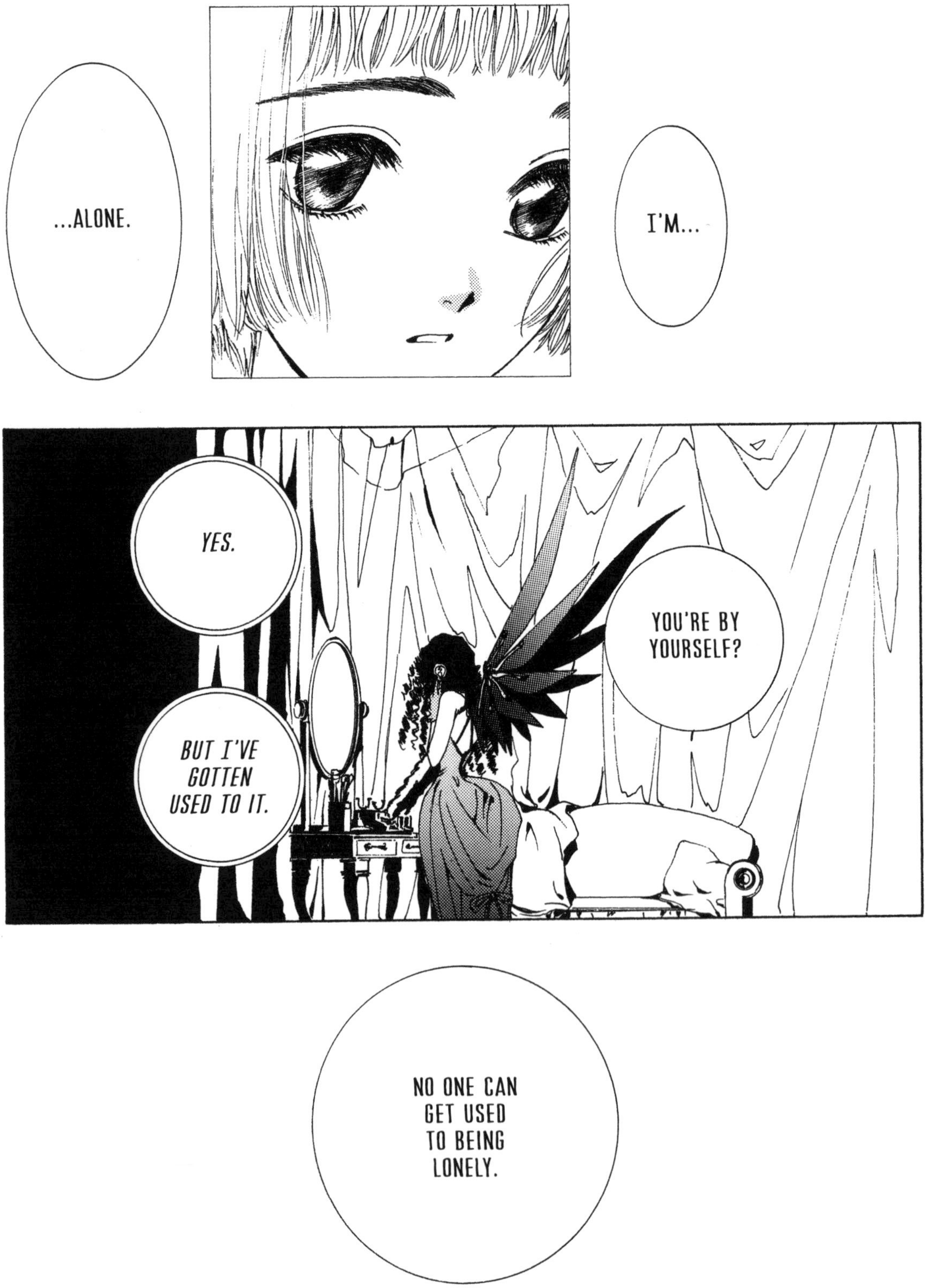
I'M...
...ALONE.
YOU'RE BY YOURSELF?
YES.
BUT I'VE GOTTEN USED TO IT.
NO ONE CAN GET USED TO BEING LONELY.

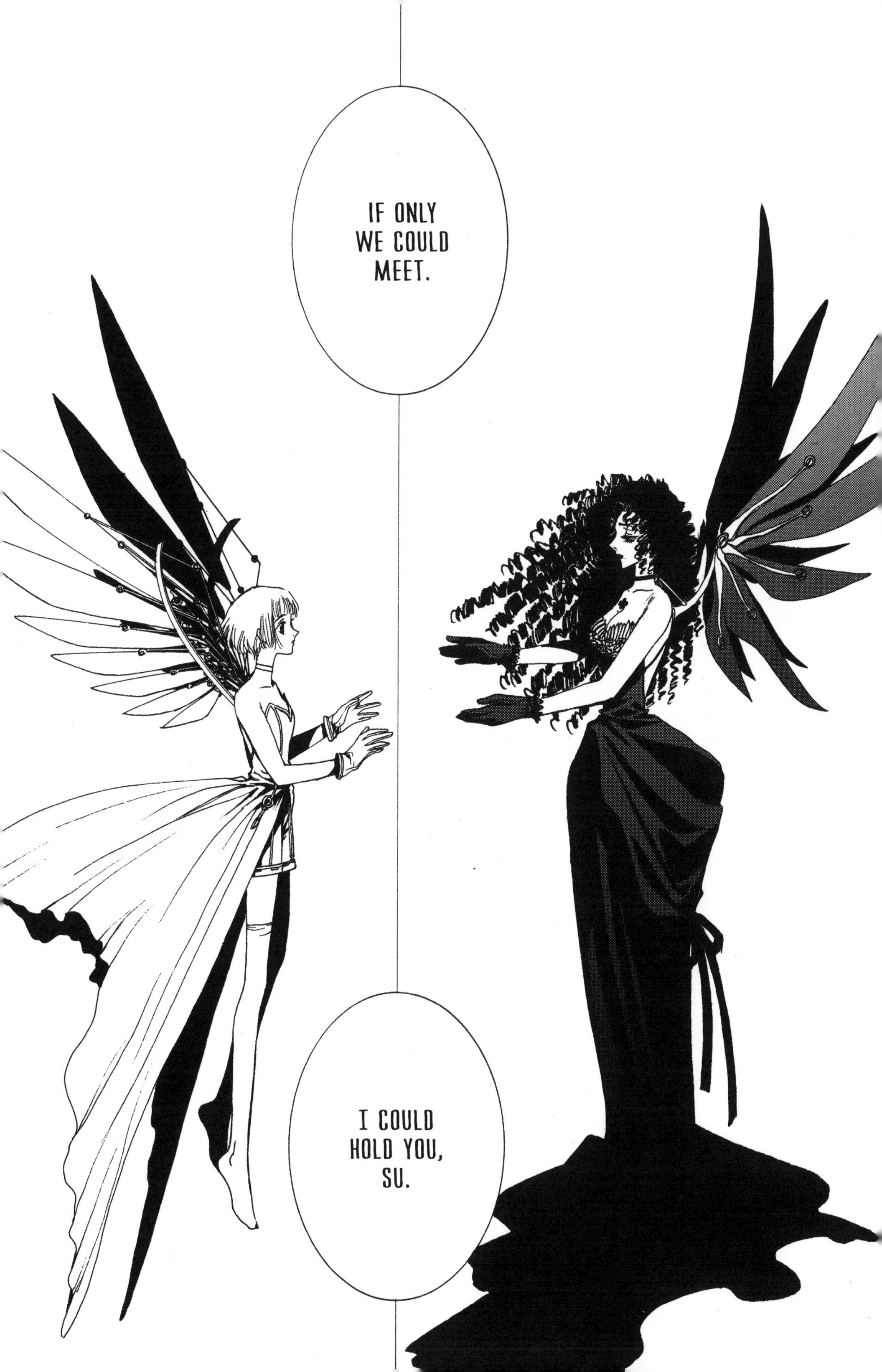
IF ONLY WE COULD MEET.
I COULD HOLD YOU, SU.

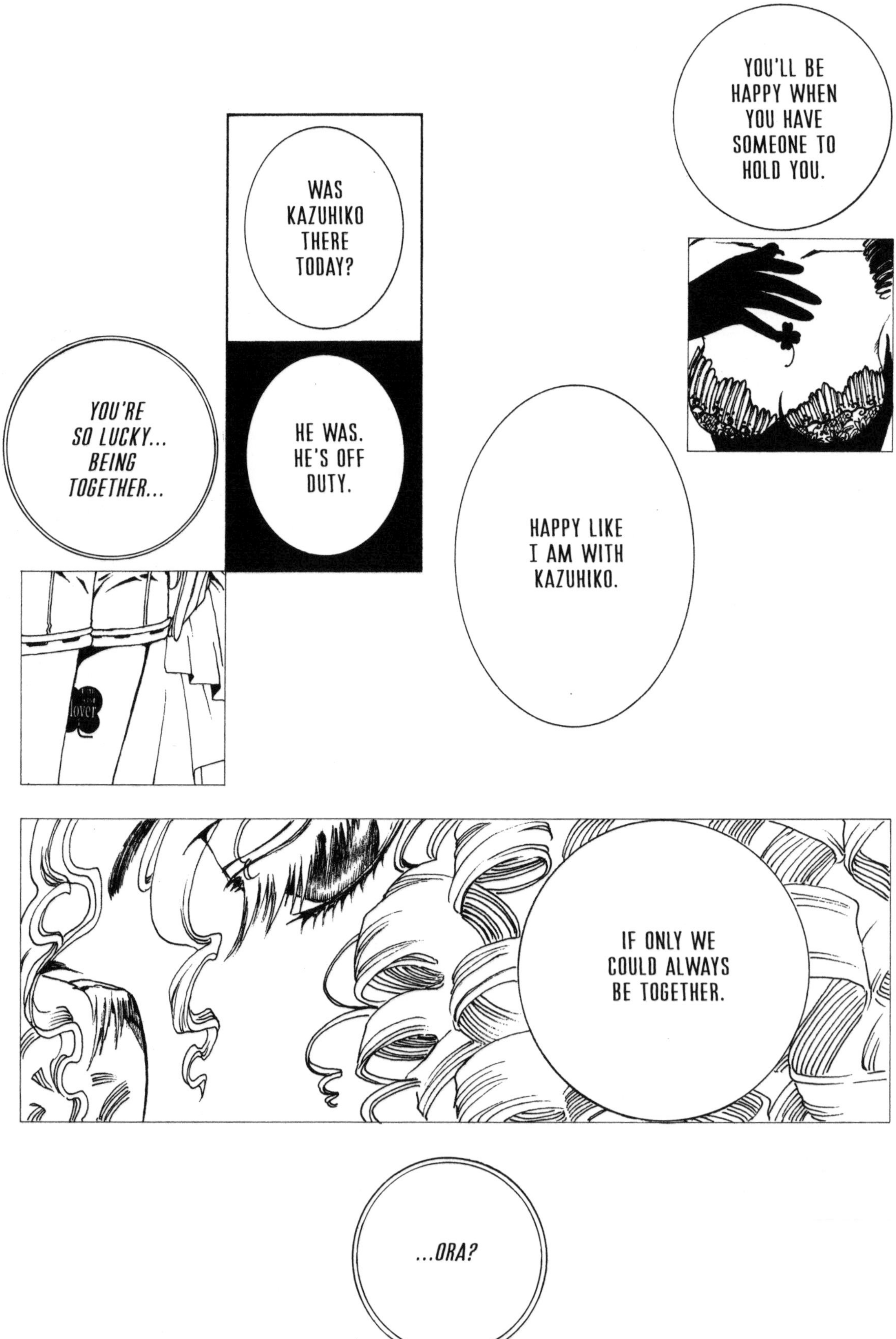
YOU'LL BE HAPPY WHEN YOU HAVE SOMEONE TO HOLD YOU.
HAPPY LIKE I AM WITH KAZUHIKO.
WAS KAZUHIKO THERE TODAY?
HE WAS. HE'S OFF DUTY.
YOU'RE SO LUCKY... BEING TOGETHER...
IF ONLY WE COULD ALWAYS BE TOGETHER.
...ORA?

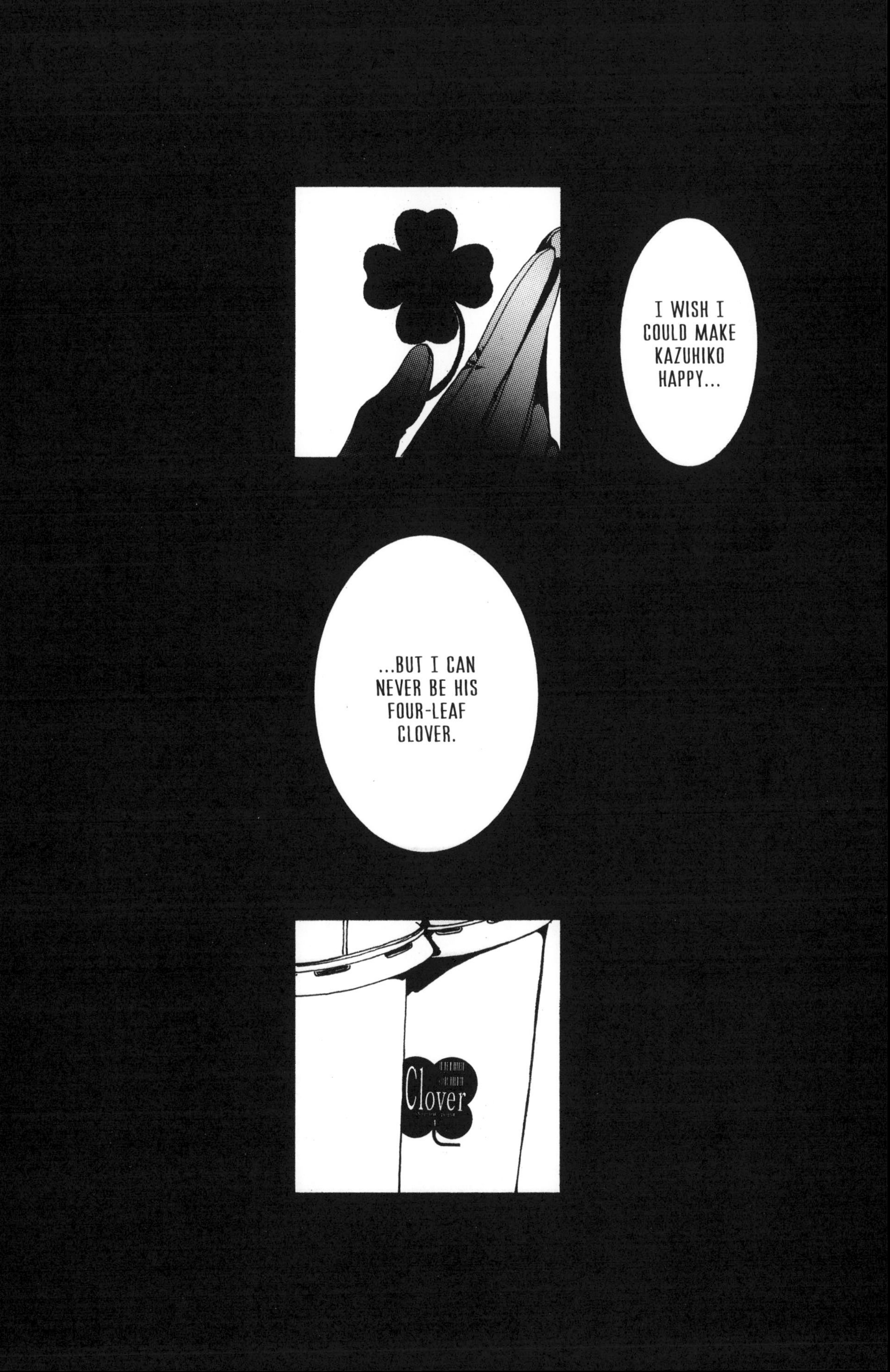
I WISH I COULD MAKE KAZUHIKO HAPPY...
...BUT I CAN NEVER BE HIS FOUR-LEAF CLOVER.
Clover

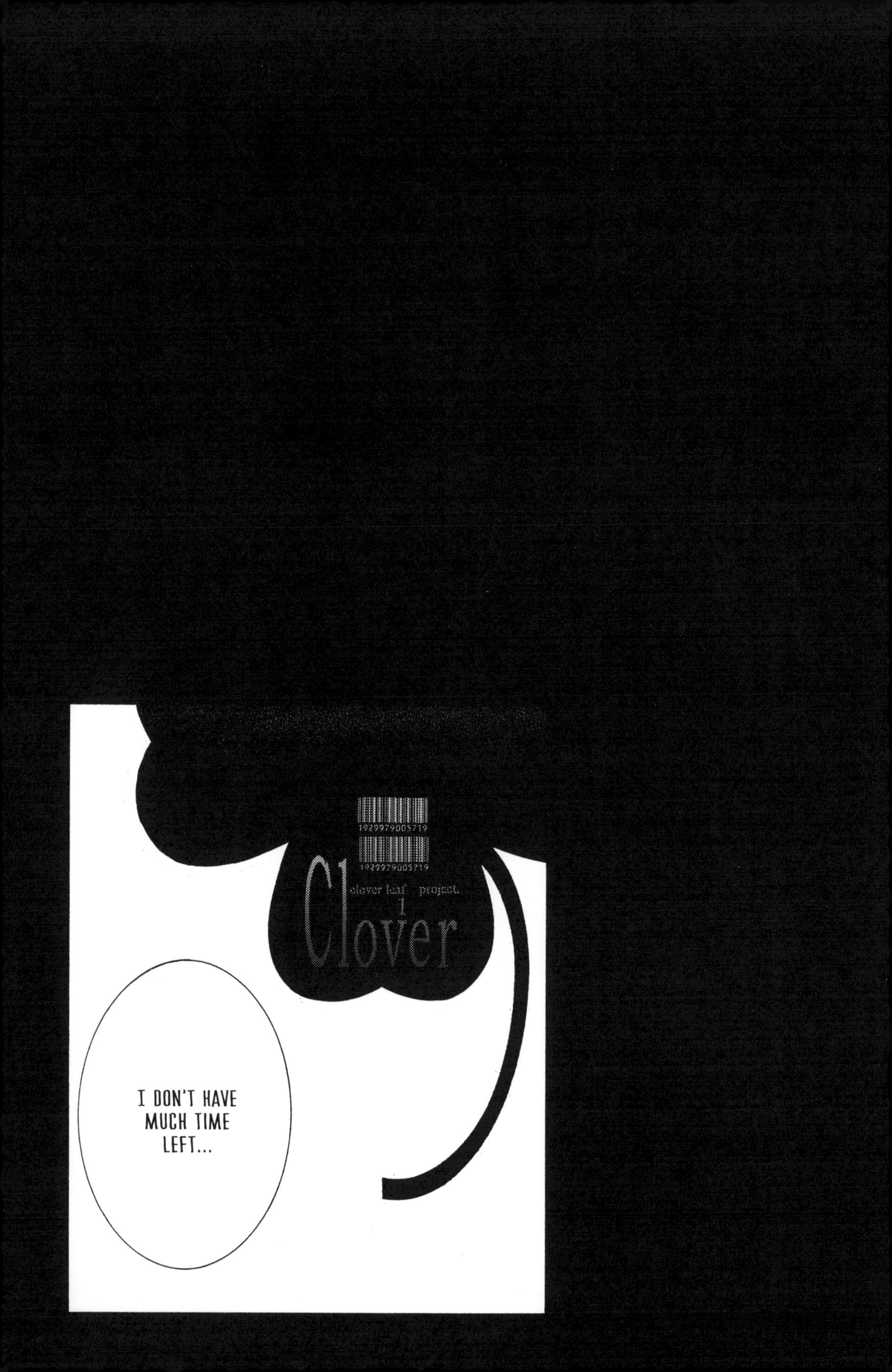
clover leaf project.
1
Clover
I DON'T HAVE MUCH TIME LEFT...

IS FLEETING HAPPINESS...
...TRUE, OR JUST DESPAIR?
AREN'T YOU HAPPY?

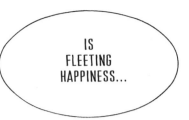

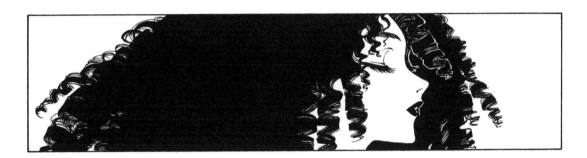

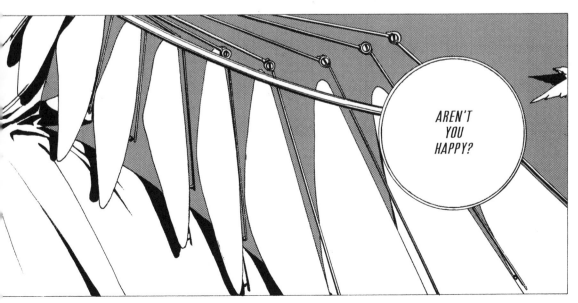

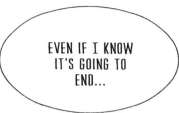

EVEN IF I KNOW
IT'S GOING TO
END...

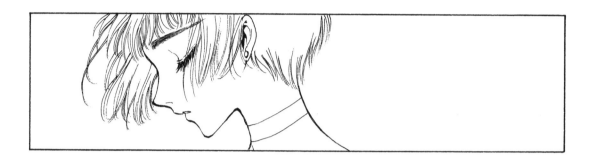

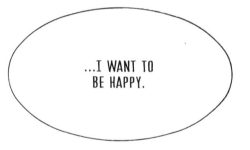

...I WANT TO
BE HAPPY.

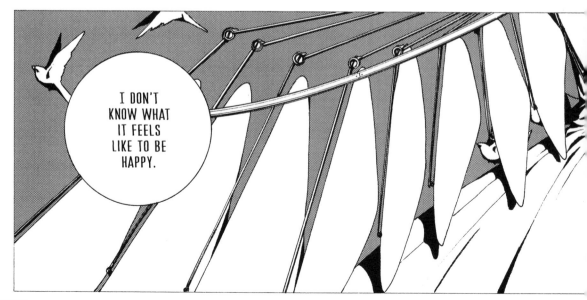

I DON'T
KNOW WHAT
IT FEELS
LIKE TO BE
HAPPY.

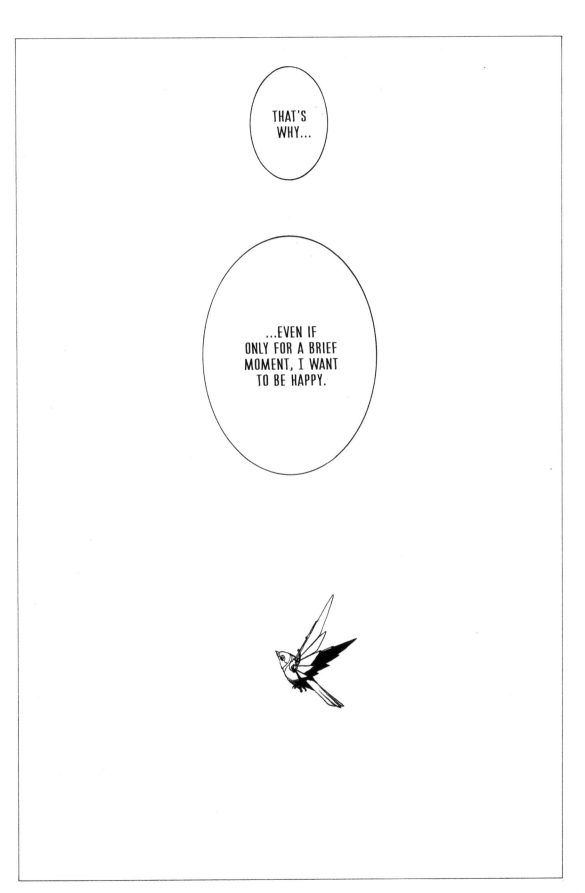

THAT'S
WHY...

...EVEN IF
ONLY FOR A BRIEF
MOMENT, I WANT
TO BE HAPPY.

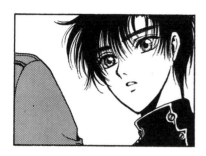

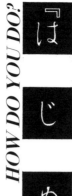

NICE TO MEET YOU.

『はじめまして』

HOW DO YOU DO?

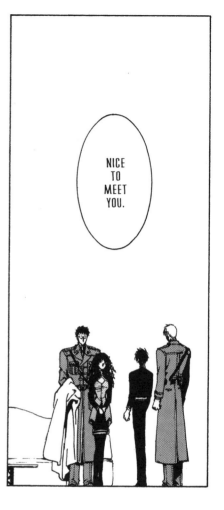

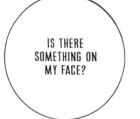

IS THERE SOMETHING ON MY FACE?

Clover

YOU'RE BEAUTIFUL.
ISN'T SHE?

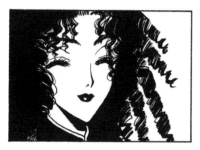

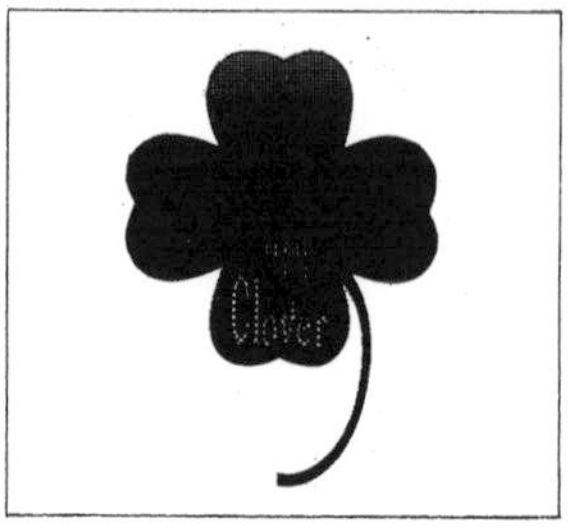

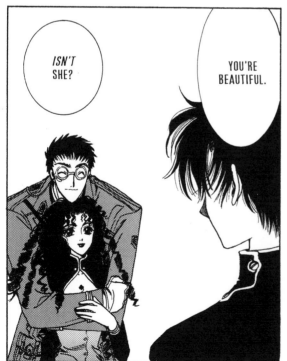

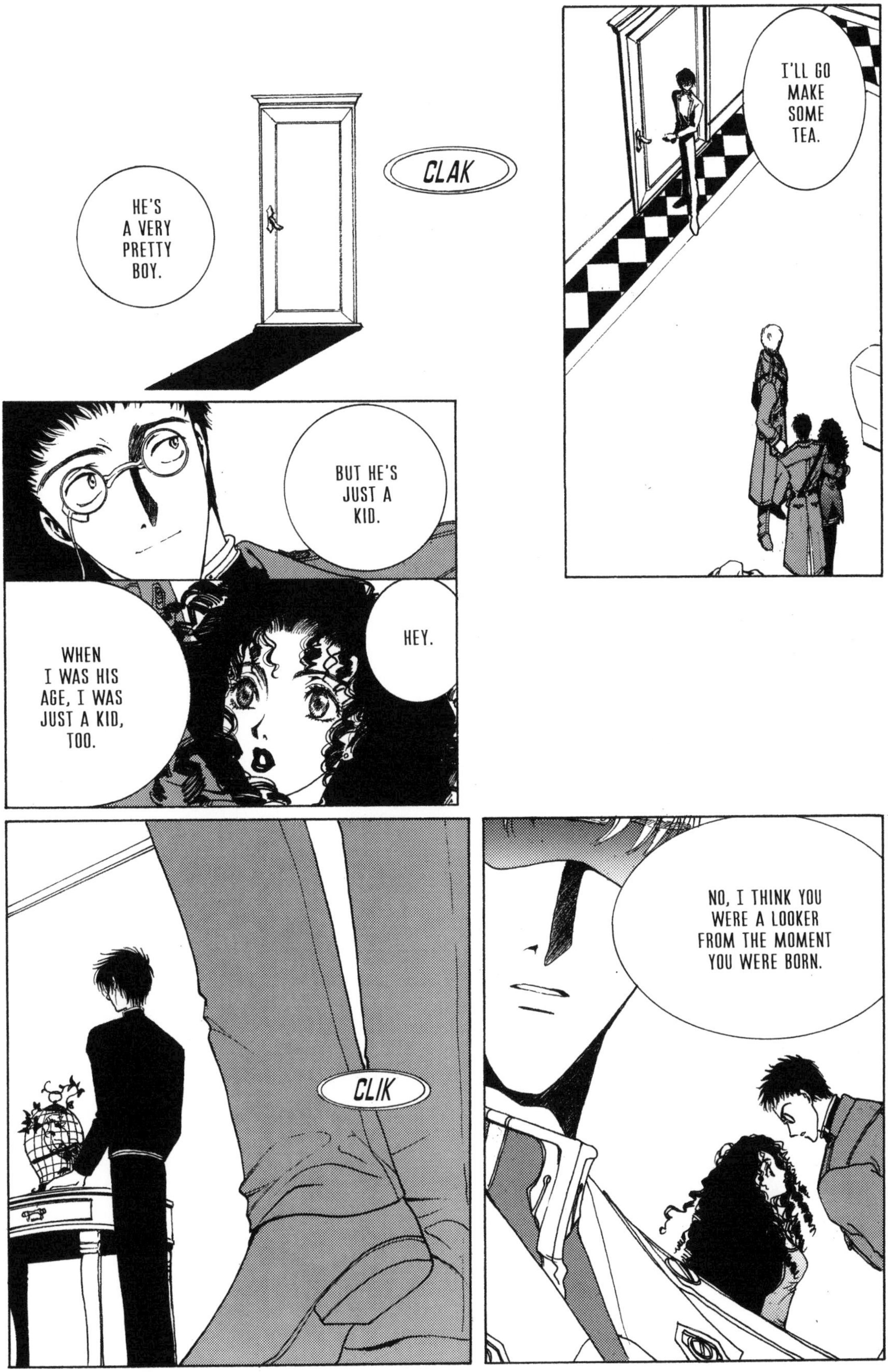
I'LL GO MAKE SOME TEA.
CLAK
HE'S A VERY PRETTY BOY.
BUT HE'S JUST A KID.
HEY.
WHEN I WAS HIS AGE, I WAS JUST A KID, TOO.
NO, I THINK YOU WERE A LOOKER FROM THE MOMENT YOU WERE BORN.
CLIK

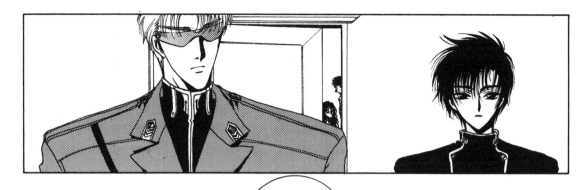

SHE
SEEMS
VERY
HAPPY.

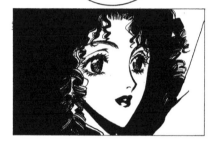

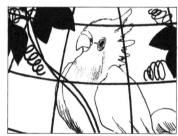

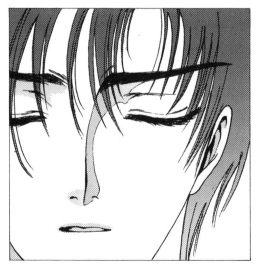

...I'M
GLAD.

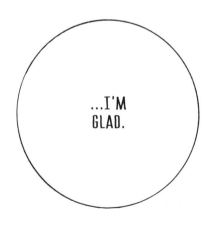

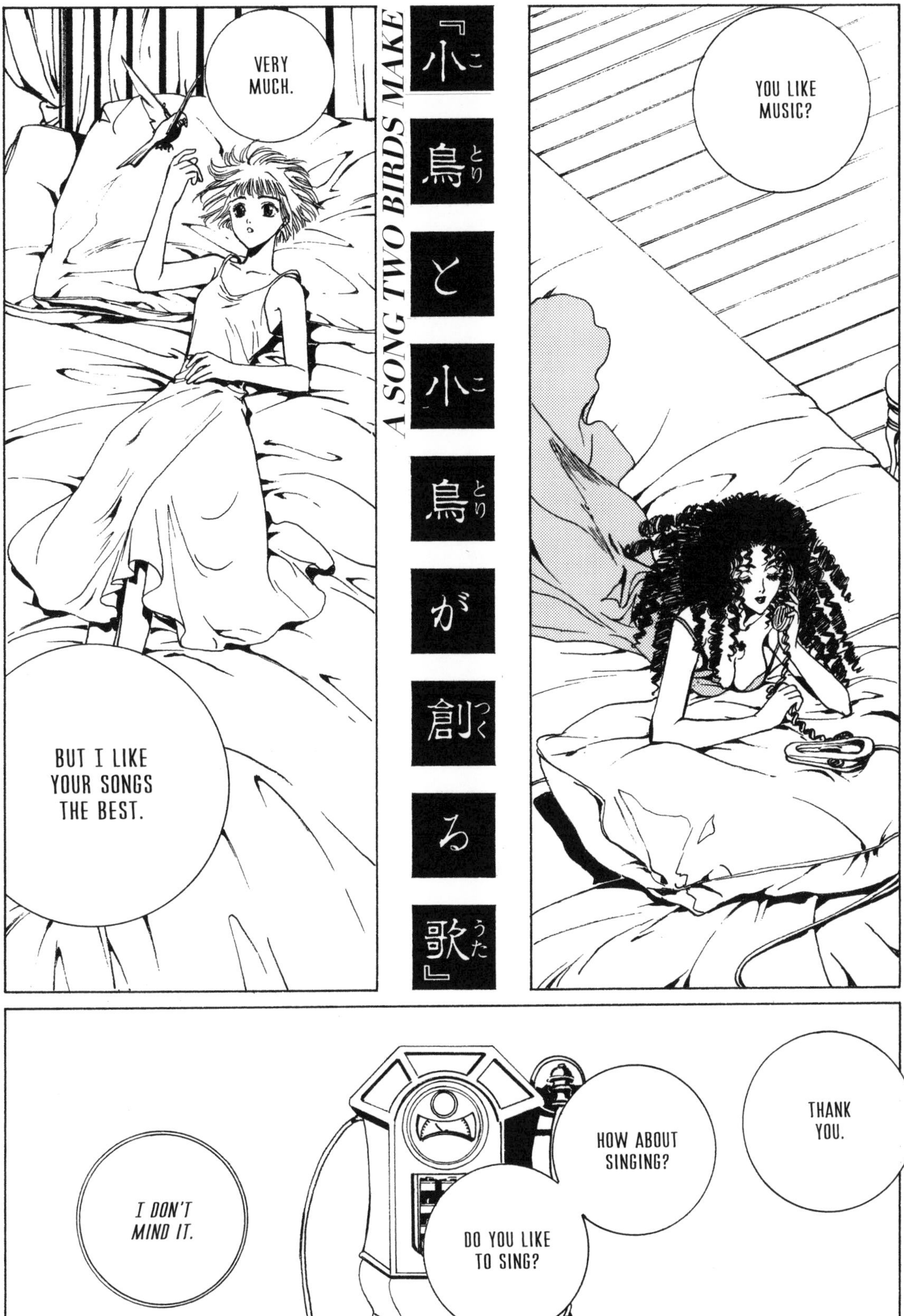
YOU LIKE MUSIC?
『小鳥と小鳥が創る歌』
A SONG TWO BIRDS MAKE
VERY MUCH.
BUT I LIKE YOUR SONGS THE BEST.
THANK YOU.
HOW ABOUT SINGING?
DO YOU LIKE TO SING?
I DON'T MIND IT.

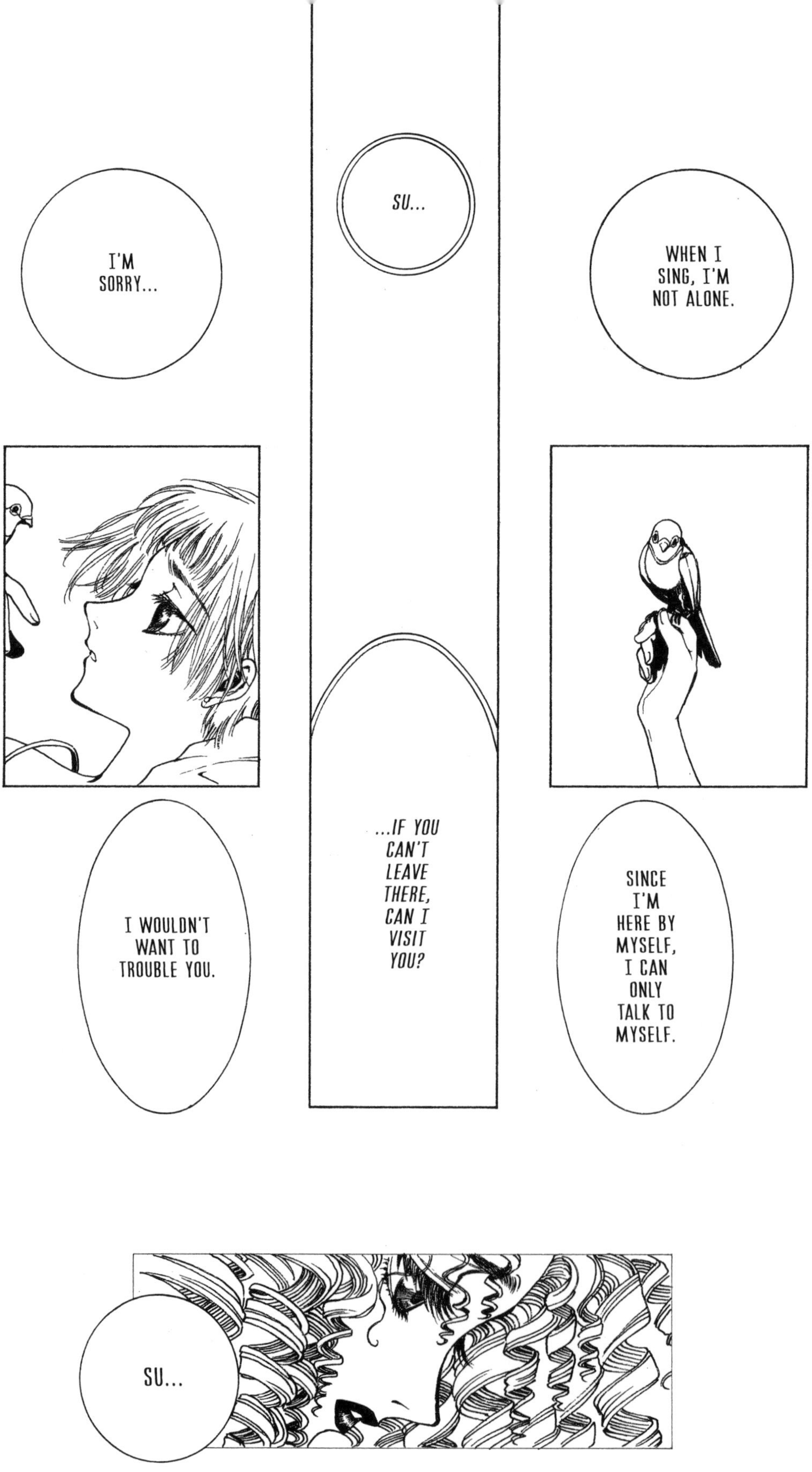
WHEN I SING, I'M NOT ALONE.
SINCE I'M HERE BY MYSELF, I CAN ONLY TALK TO MYSELF.
SU...
...IF YOU CAN'T LEAVE THERE, CAN I VISIT YOU?
I'M SORRY...
I WOULDN'T WANT TO TROUBLE YOU.
SU...

WHEN I DIE, NO ONE WILL CRY FOR ME.
SINCE I'M ALONE, NOTHING WILL CHANGE WHEN I'M GONE.
I'D CRY FOR YOU.
WHY?

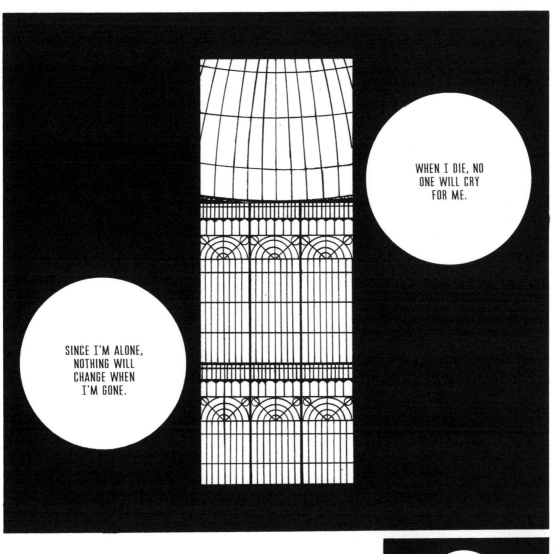

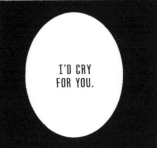

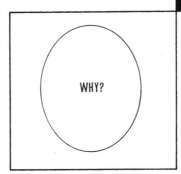

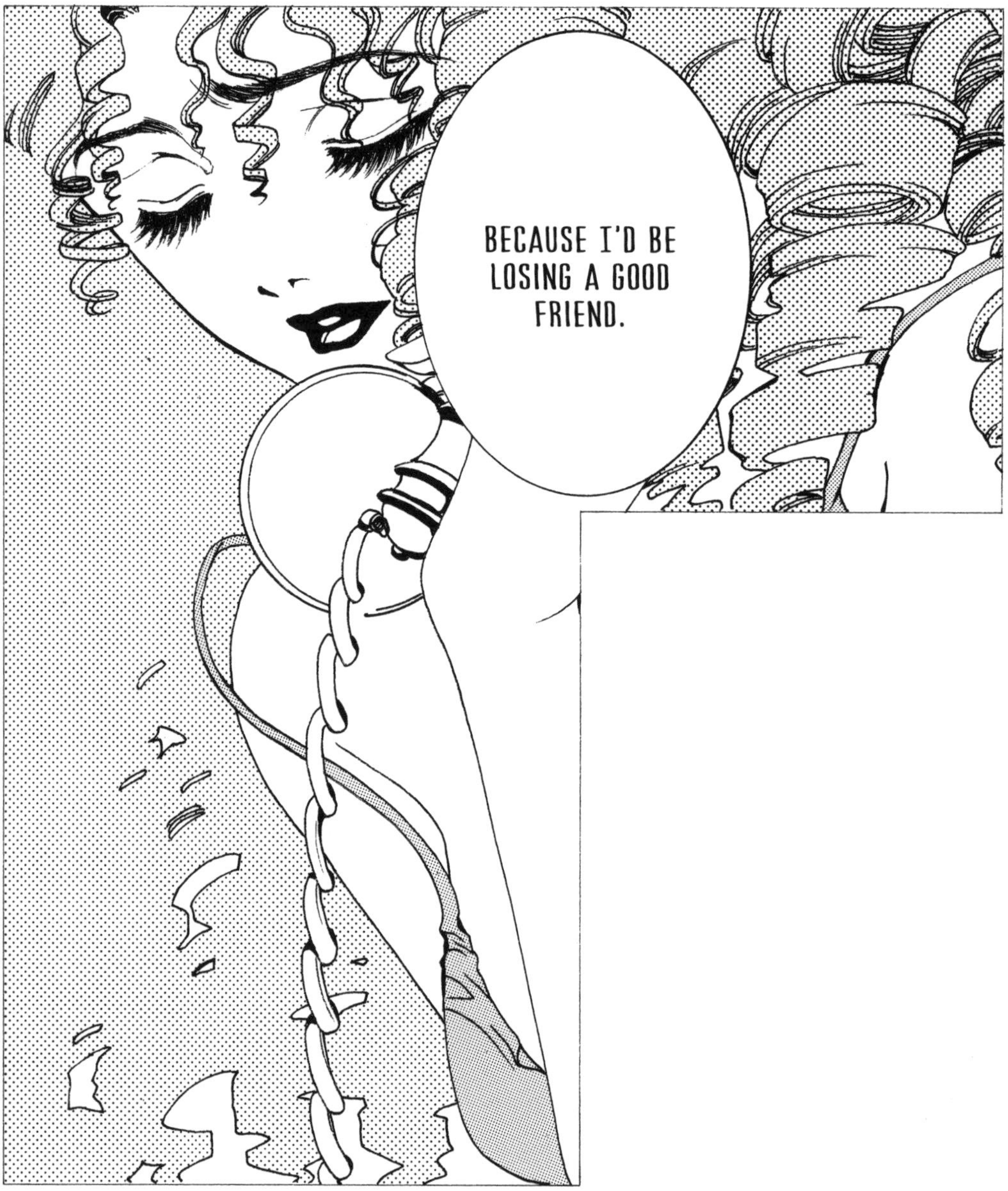
BECAUSE I'D BE LOSING A GOOD FRIEND.

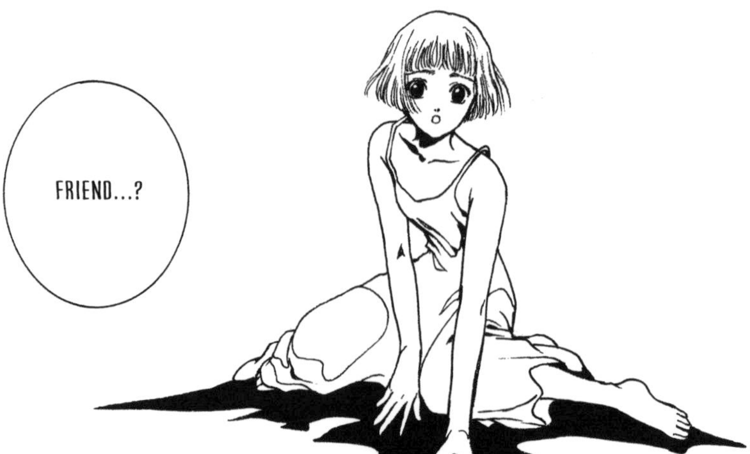
FRIEND...?

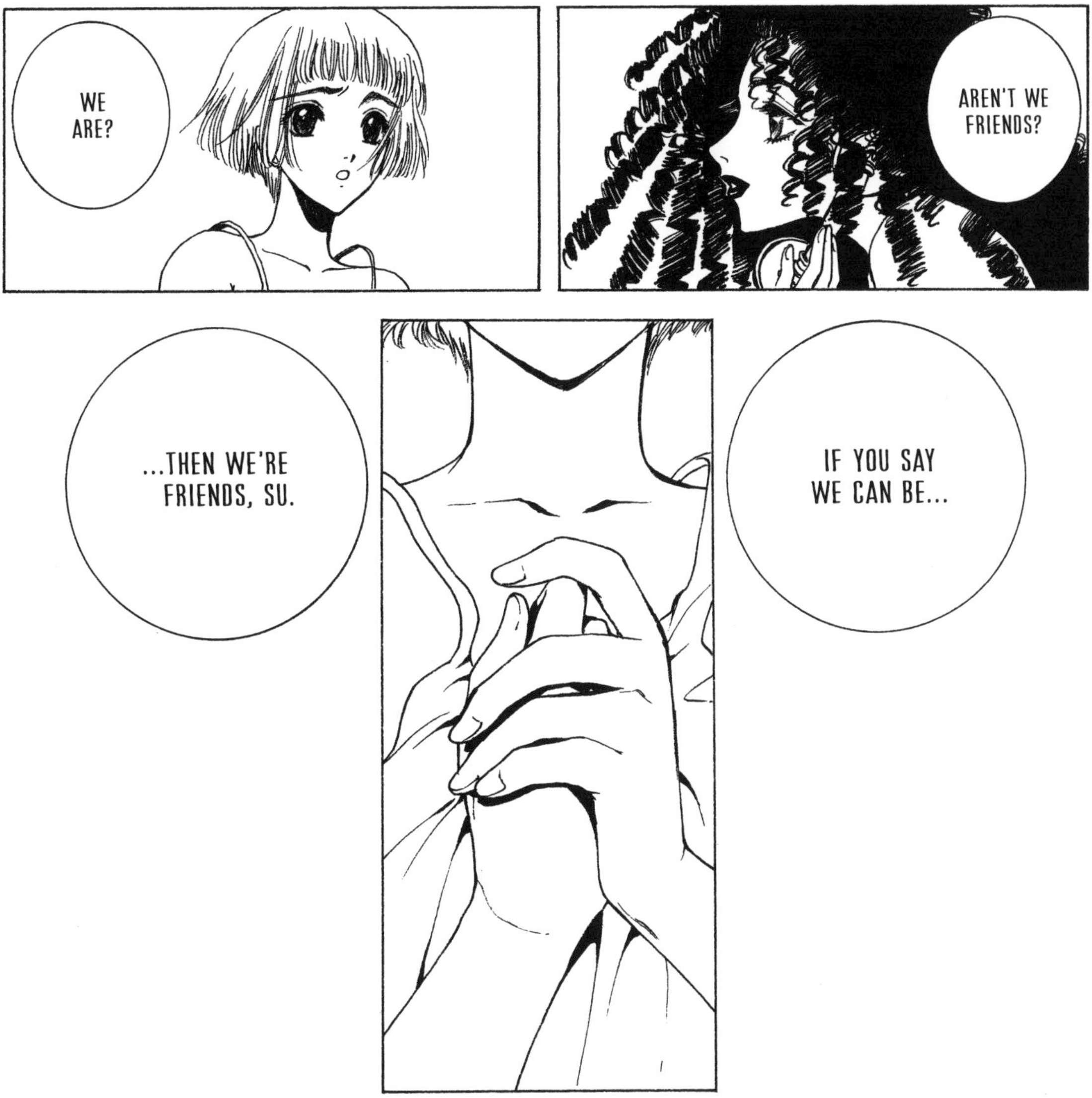
AREN'T WE FRIENDS?
WE ARE?
IF YOU SAY WE CAN BE...
...THEN WE'RE FRIENDS, SU.

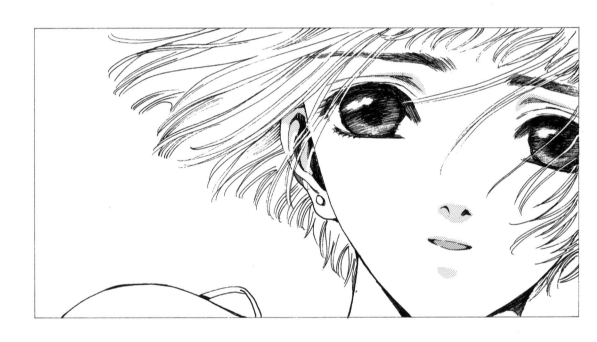

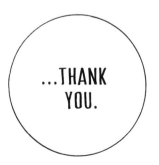

...THANK
YOU.

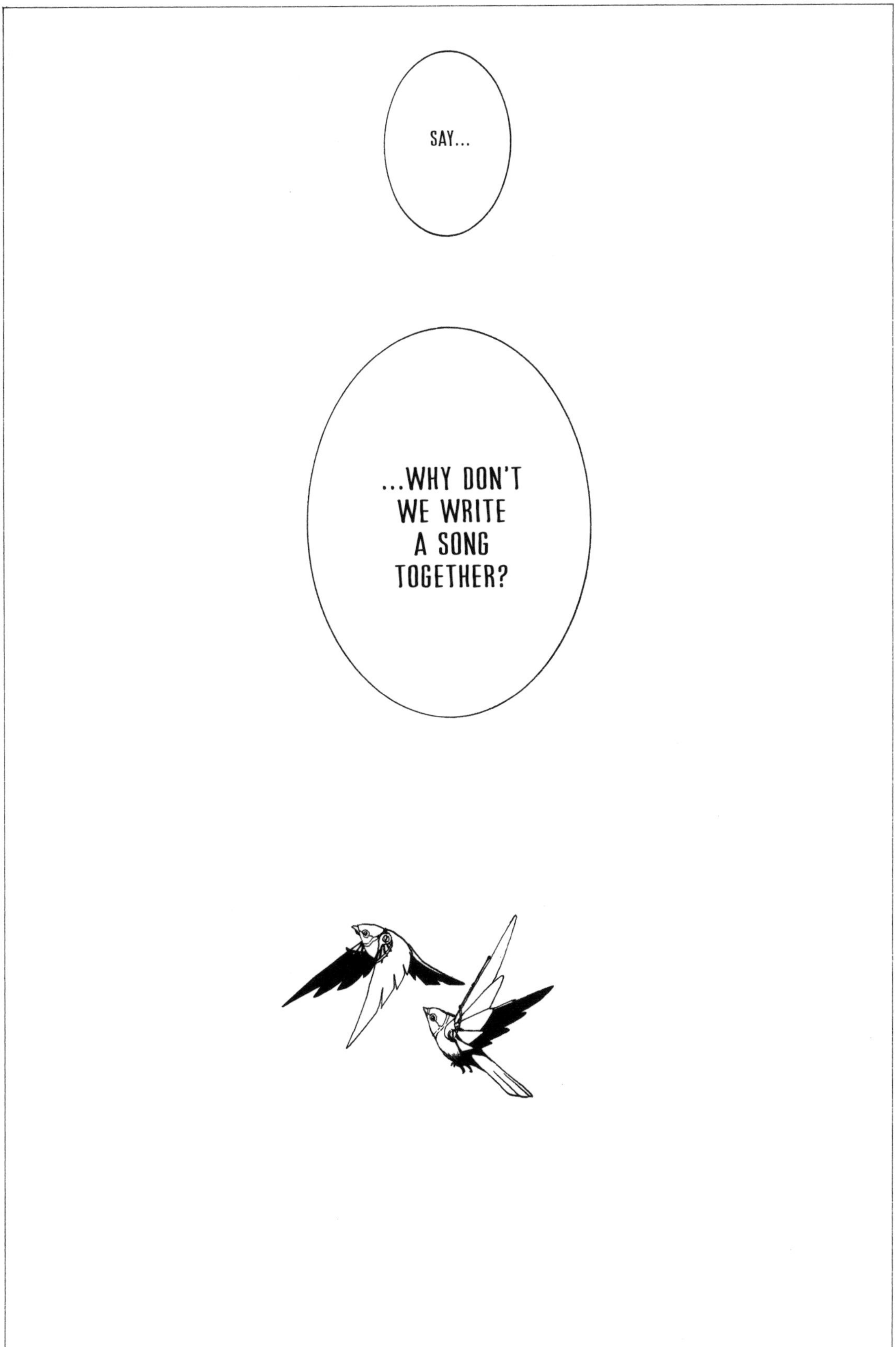
SAY...
...WHY DON'T WE WRITE A SONG TOGETHER?

『小鳥たちの内緒の歌』

THE SECRET SONG OF THE BIRDS

…I seek happiness
To find happiness with you

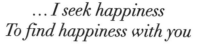

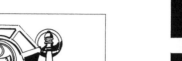

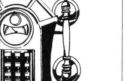

…So take me
Somewhere far away
To a true Elsewhere

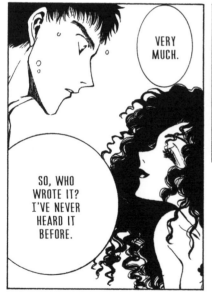

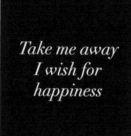

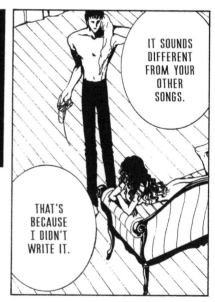

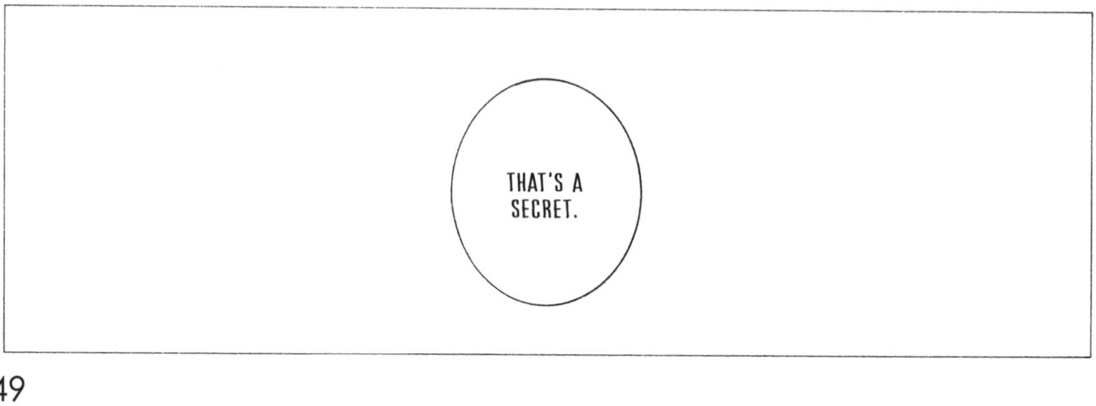

IT SOUNDS DIFFERENT FROM YOUR OTHER SONGS.
THAT'S BECAUSE I DIDN'T WRITE IT.

Take me away
I wish for
happiness

YOU LIKE IT?

VERY MUCH.
SO, WHO WROTE IT? I'VE NEVER HEARD IT BEFORE.

THAT'S A SECRET.

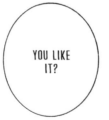

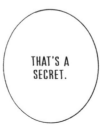

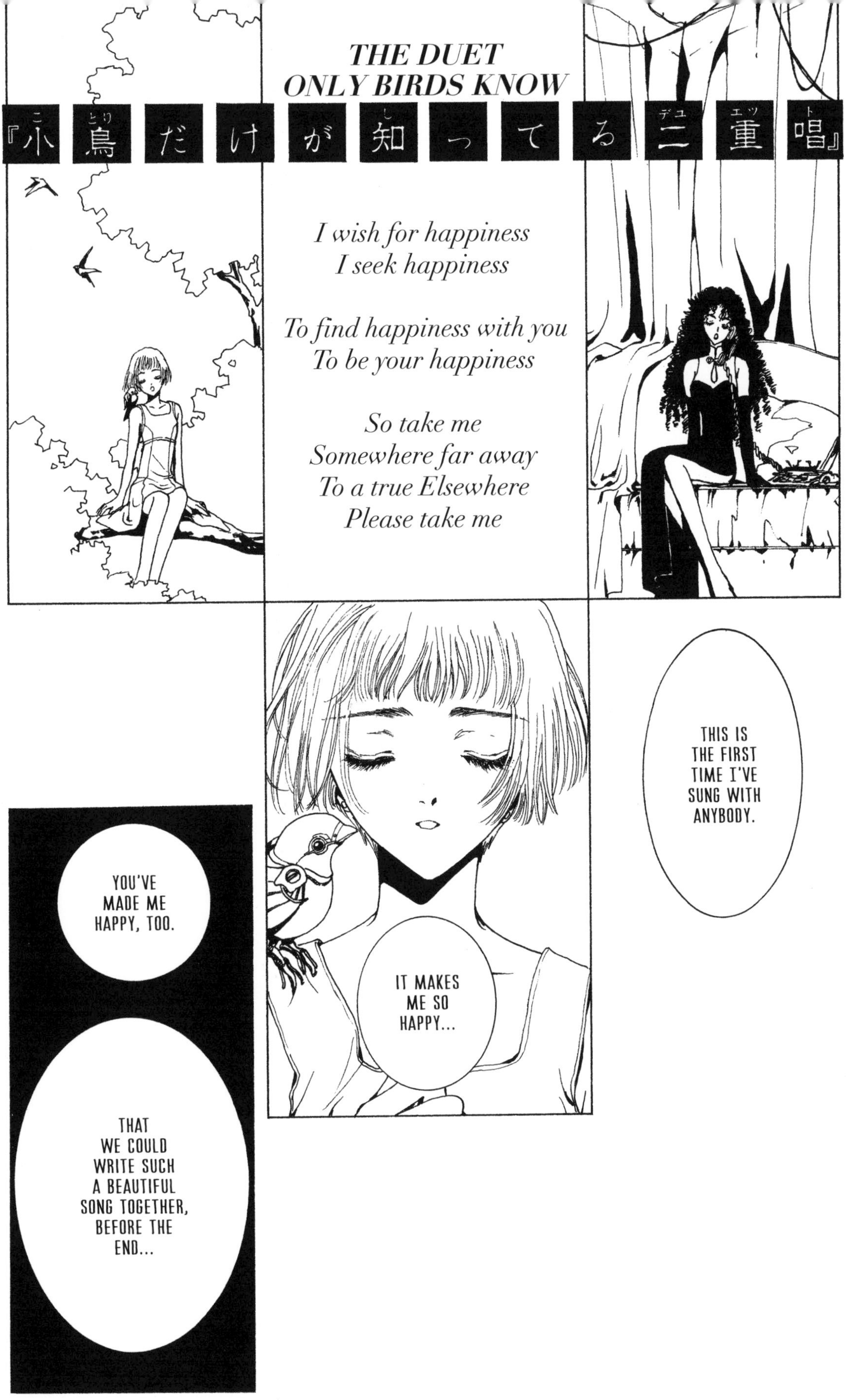
THE DUET ONLY BIRDS KNOW
『小鳥だけが知ってる二重唱』
I wish for happiness
I seek happiness
To find happiness with you
To be your happiness
So take me
Somewhere far away
To a true Elsewhere
Please take me
THIS IS THE FIRST TIME I'VE SUNG WITH ANYBODY.
IT MAKES ME SO HAPPY...
YOU'VE MADE ME HAPPY, TOO.
THAT WE COULD WRITE SUCH A BEAUTIFUL SONG TOGETHER, BEFORE THE END...

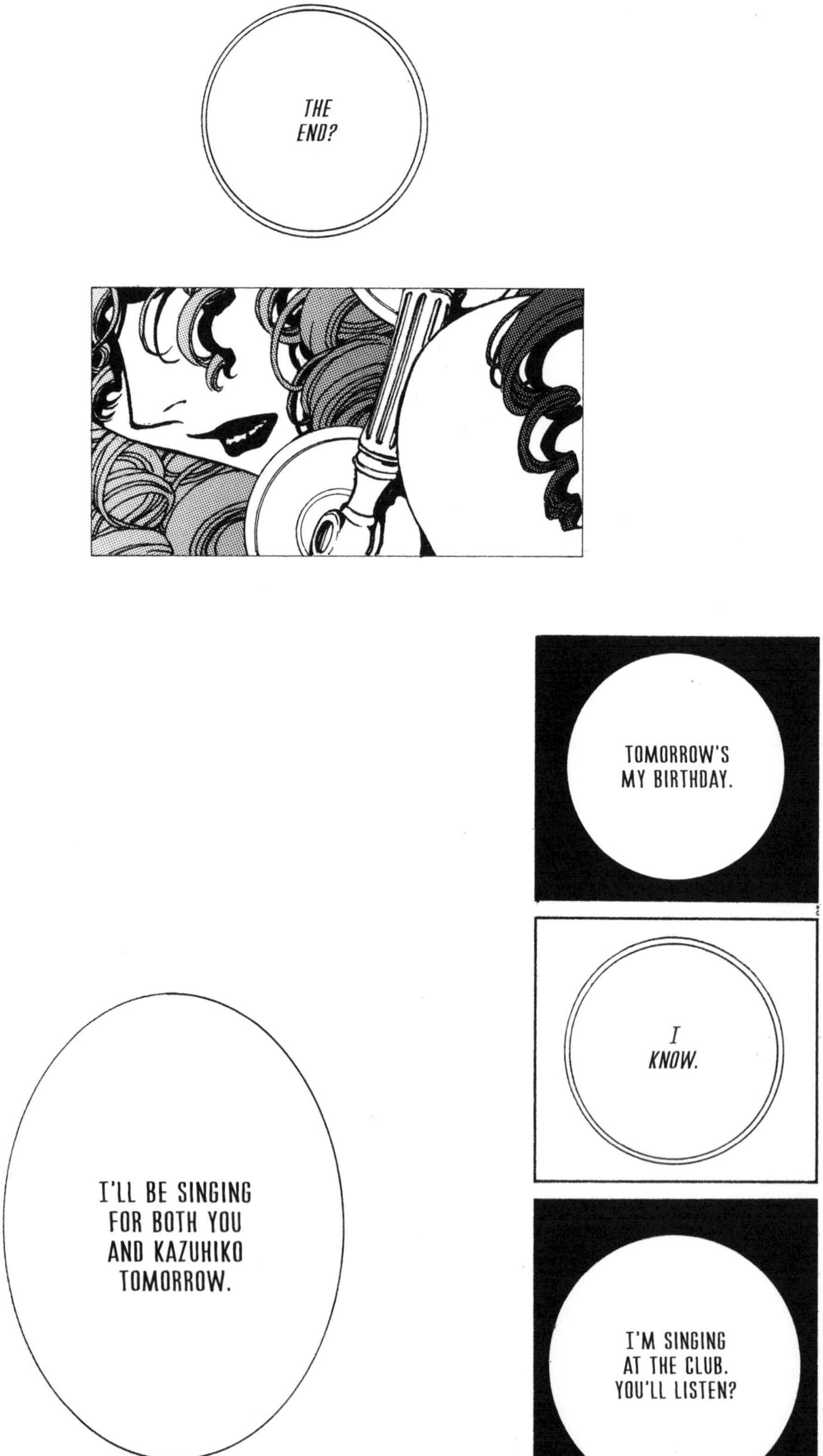
THE END?
TOMORROW'S MY BIRTHDAY.
I KNOW.
I'M SINGING AT THE CLUB. YOU'LL LISTEN?
I'LL BE SINGING FOR BOTH YOU AND KAZUHIKO TOMORROW.

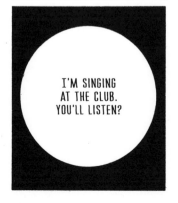

AN UNFADING NIGHT

『消え ない 夜』

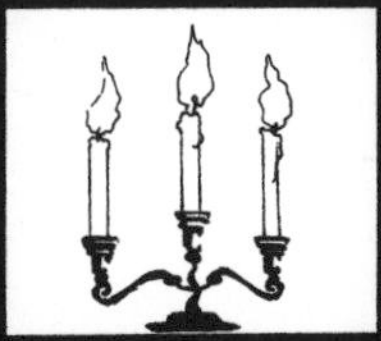

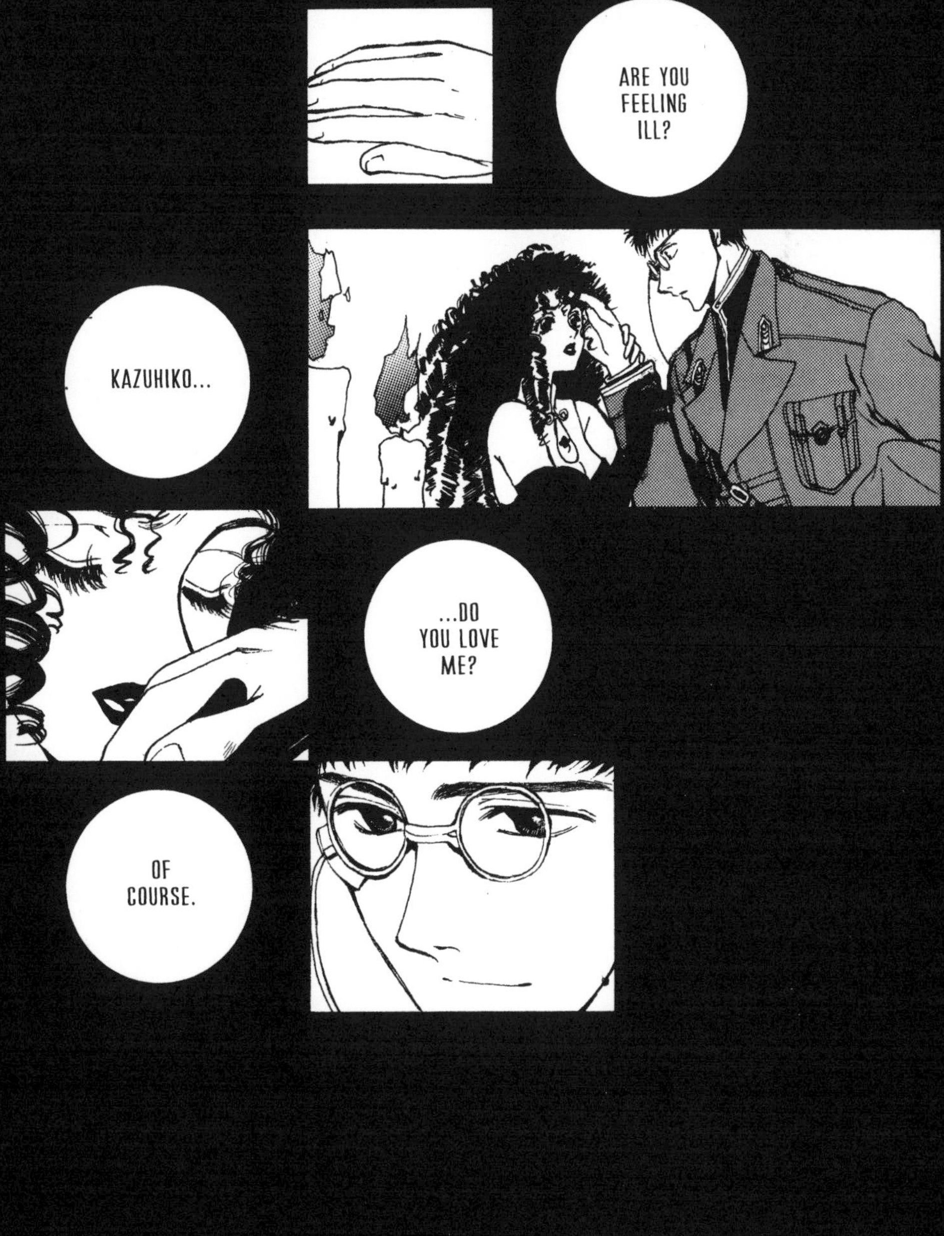
ARE YOU FEELING ILL?
KAZUHIKO...
...DO YOU LOVE ME?
OF COURSE.

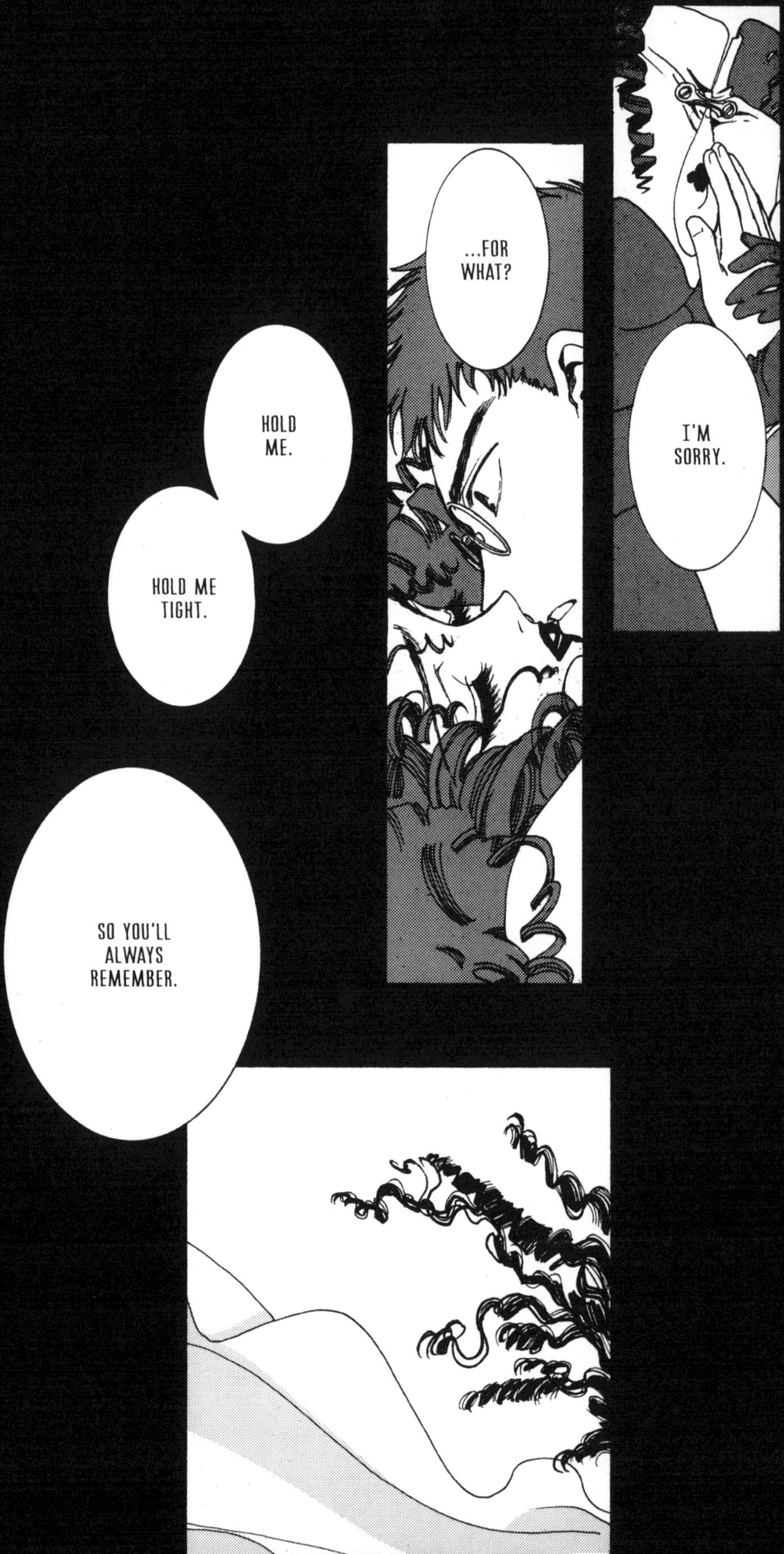
I'M SORRY.
...FOR WHAT?
HOLD ME.
HOLD ME TIGHT.
SO YOU'LL ALWAYS REMEMBER.

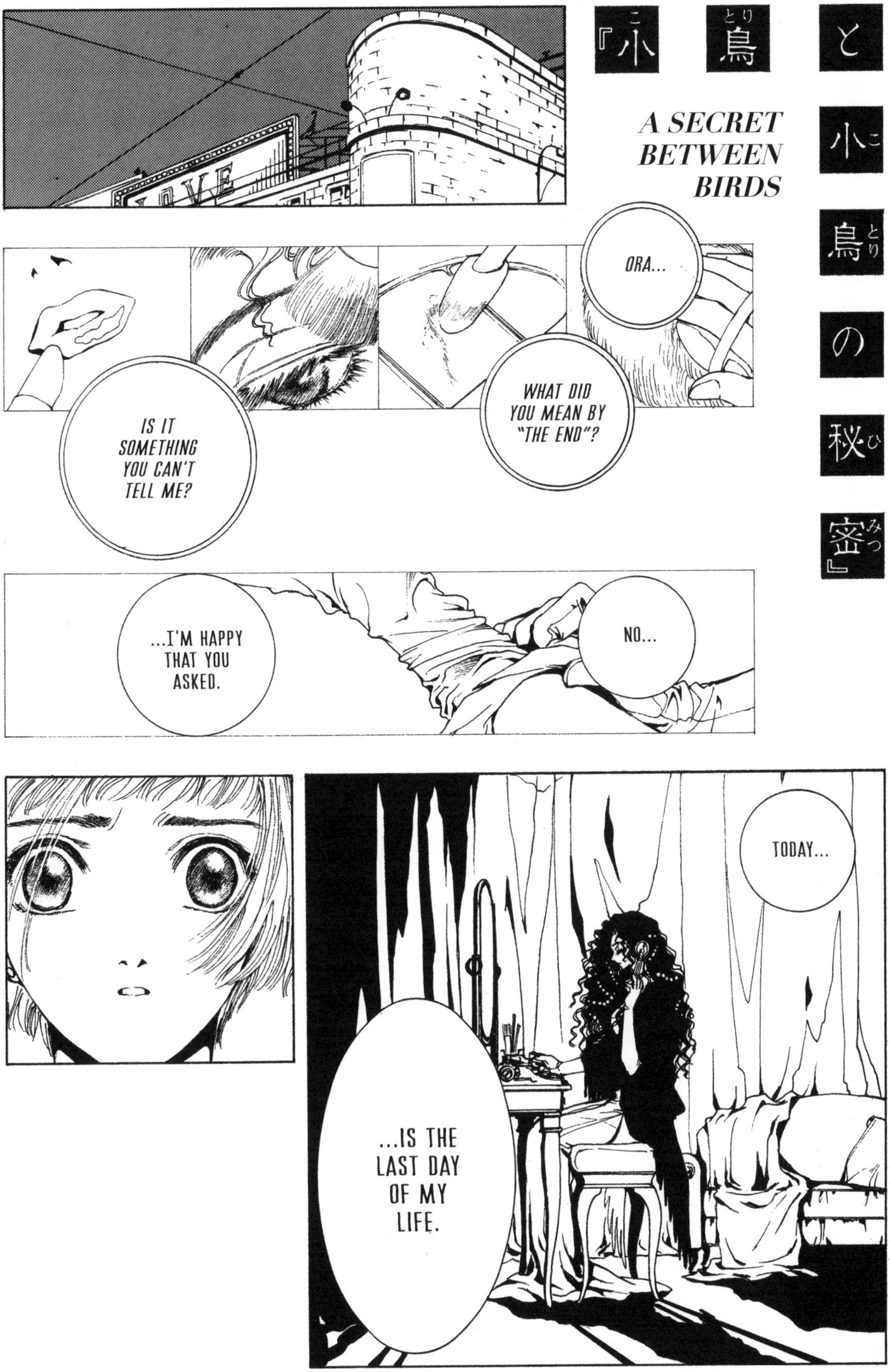
『小鳥と小鳥の秘密』
A SECRET BETWEEN BIRDS
ORA...
WHAT DID YOU MEAN BY "THE END"?
IS IT SOMETHING YOU CAN'T TELL ME?
NO...
...I'M HAPPY THAT YOU ASKED.
TODAY...
...IS THE LAST DAY OF MY LIFE.

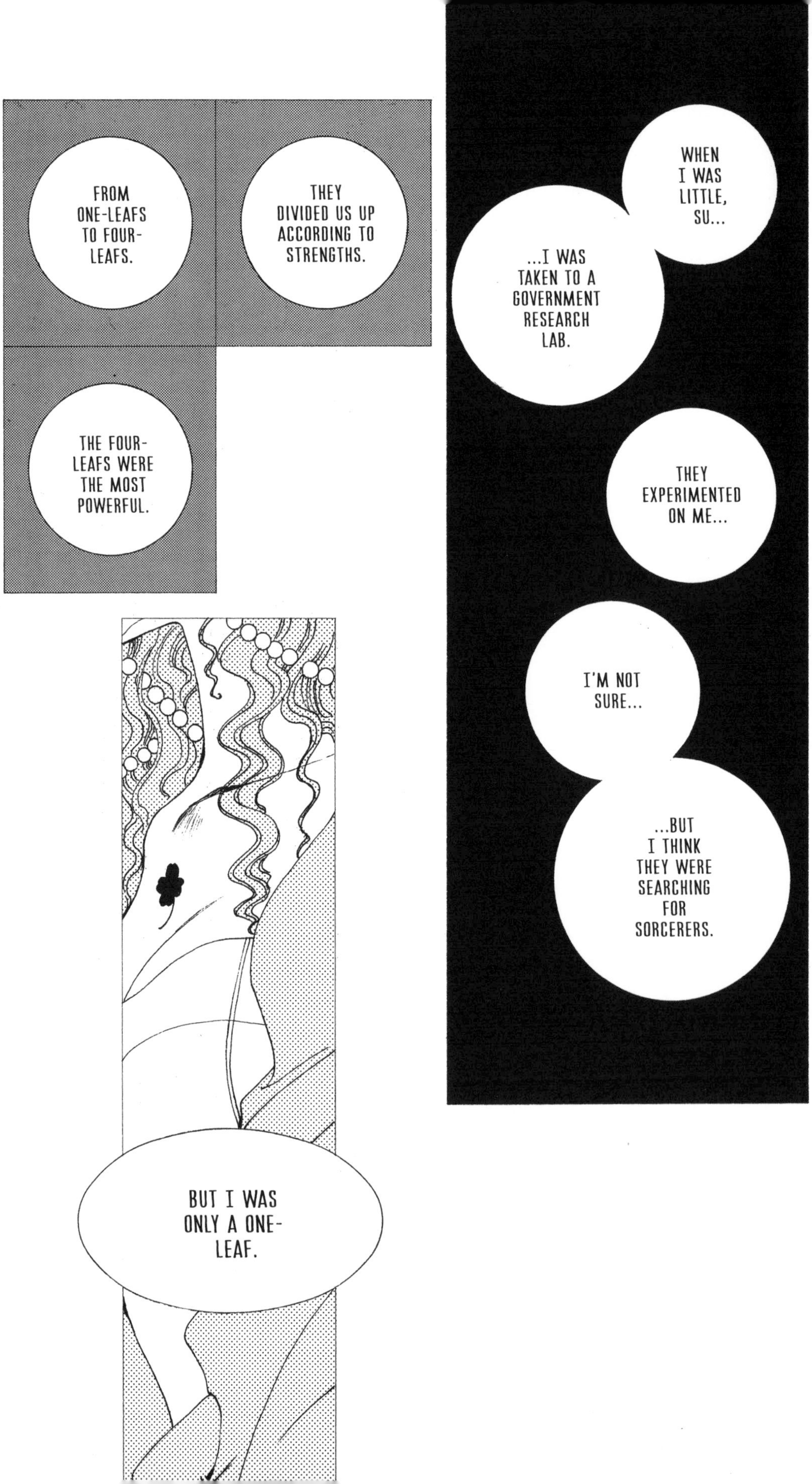
WHEN I WAS LITTLE, SU...
...I WAS TAKEN TO A GOVERNMENT RESEARCH LAB.
THEY EXPERIMENTED ON ME...
I'M NOT SURE...
...BUT I THINK THEY WERE SEARCHING FOR SORCERERS.
THEY DIVIDED US UP ACCORDING TO STRENGTHS.
FROM ONE-LEAFS TO FOUR-LEAFS.
THE FOUR-LEAFS WERE THE MOST POWERFUL.
BUT I WAS ONLY A ONE-LEAF.

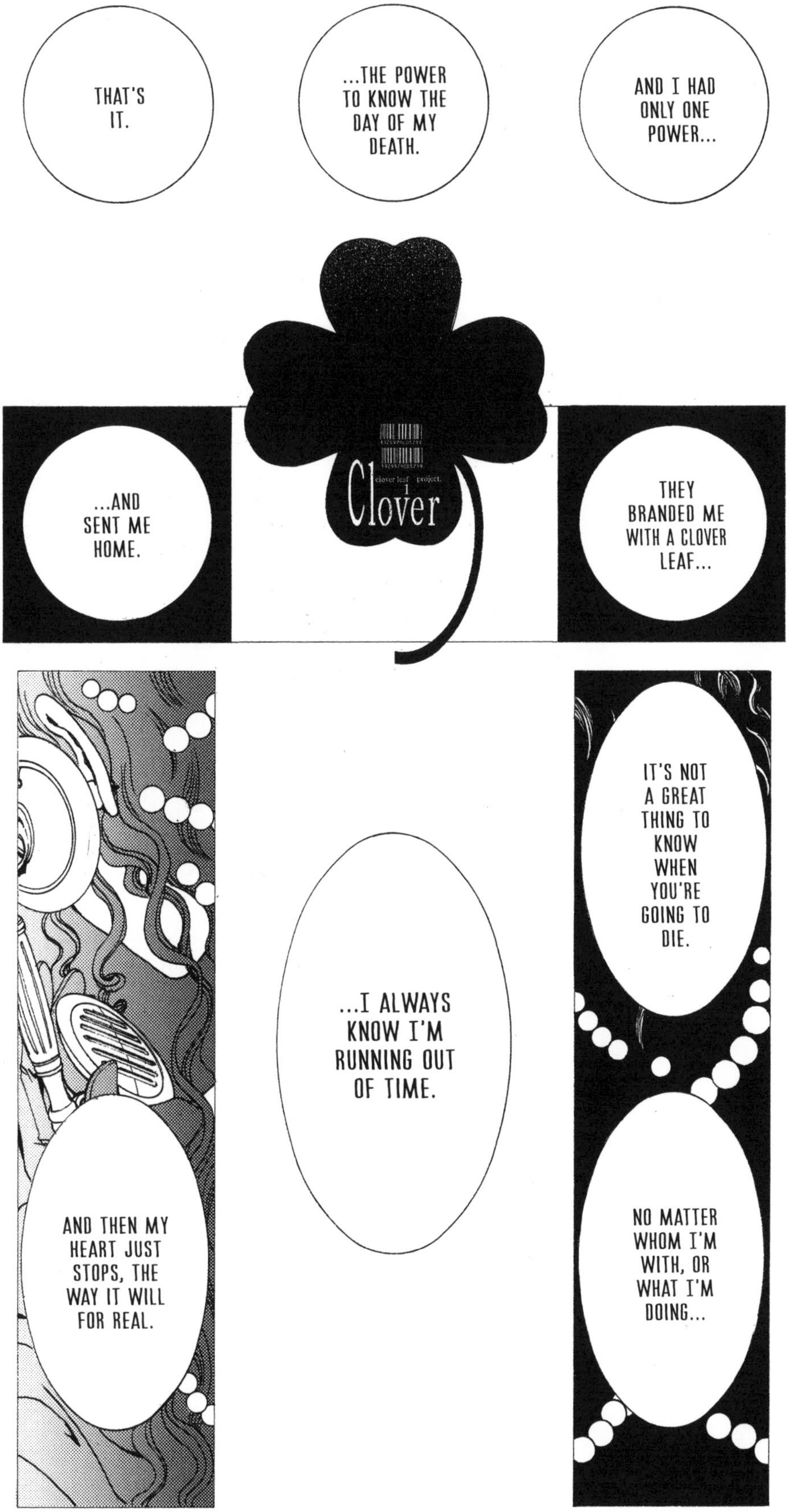
AND I HAD ONLY ONE POWER...
...THE POWER TO KNOW THE DAY OF MY DEATH.
THAT'S IT.
THEY BRANDED ME WITH A CLOVER LEAF...
clover leaf project. 1
Clover
...AND SENT ME HOME.
IT'S NOT A GREAT THING TO KNOW WHEN YOU'RE GOING TO DIE.
NO MATTER WHOM I'M WITH, OR WHAT I'M DOING...
...I ALWAYS KNOW I'M RUNNING OUT OF TIME.
AND THEN MY HEART JUST STOPS, THE WAY IT WILL FOR REAL.

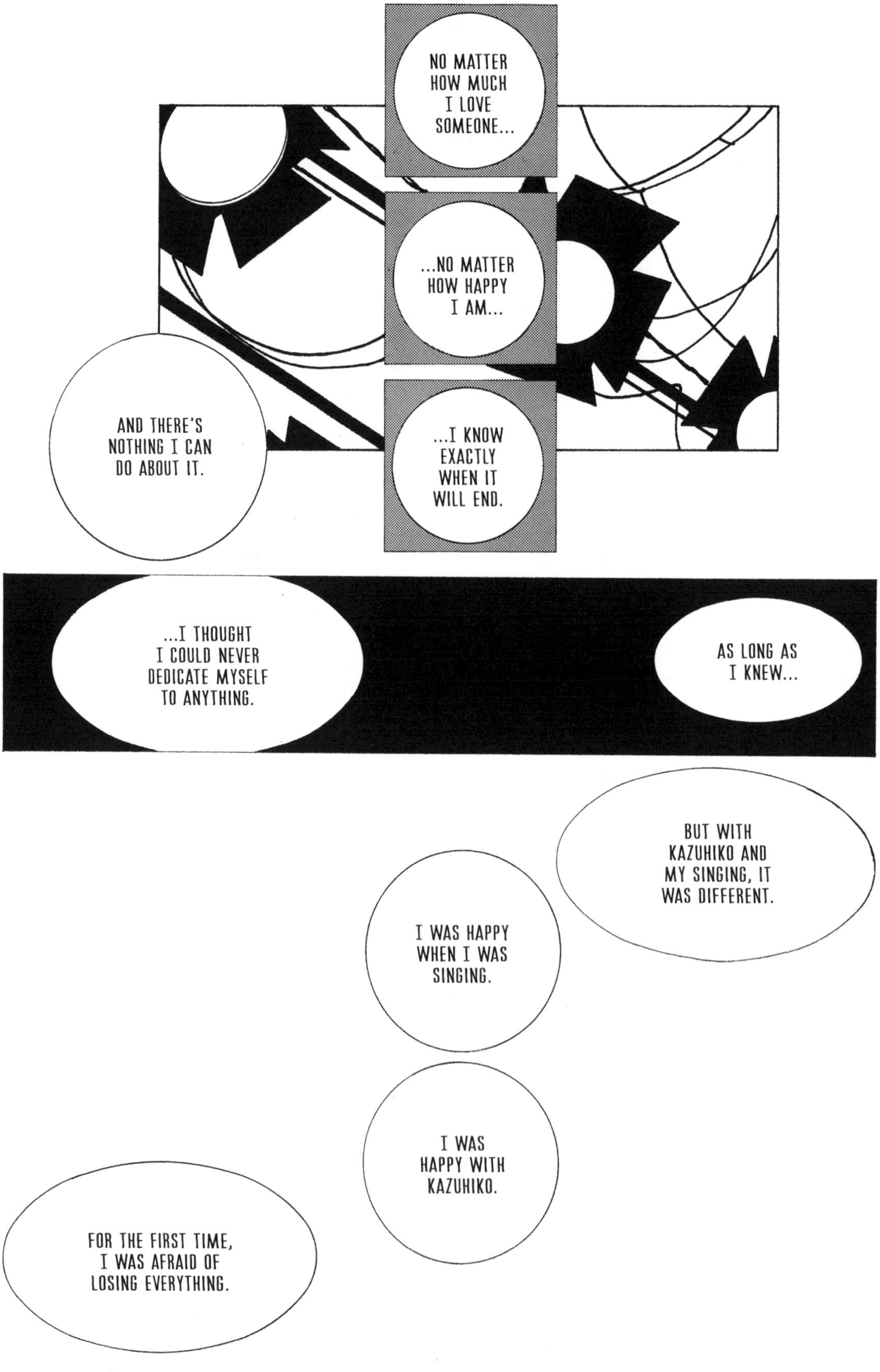
NO MATTER HOW MUCH I LOVE SOMEONE...
...NO MATTER HOW HAPPY I AM...
...I KNOW EXACTLY WHEN IT WILL END.
AND THERE'S NOTHING I CAN DO ABOUT IT.
AS LONG AS I KNEW...
...I THOUGHT I COULD NEVER DEDICATE MYSELF TO ANYTHING.
BUT WITH KAZUHIKO AND MY SINGING, IT WAS DIFFERENT.
I WAS HAPPY WHEN I WAS SINGING.
I WAS HAPPY WITH KAZUHIKO.
FOR THE FIRST TIME, I WAS AFRAID OF LOSING EVERYTHING.

I WANTED TO MAKE KAZUHIKO HAPPY, YOU SEE.
BUT I COULD NEVER BE HIS FOUR-LEAF CLOVER.
I COULD NEVER DO ANYTHING FOR HIM.
AND NOW I'M GOING TO DIE TODAY.

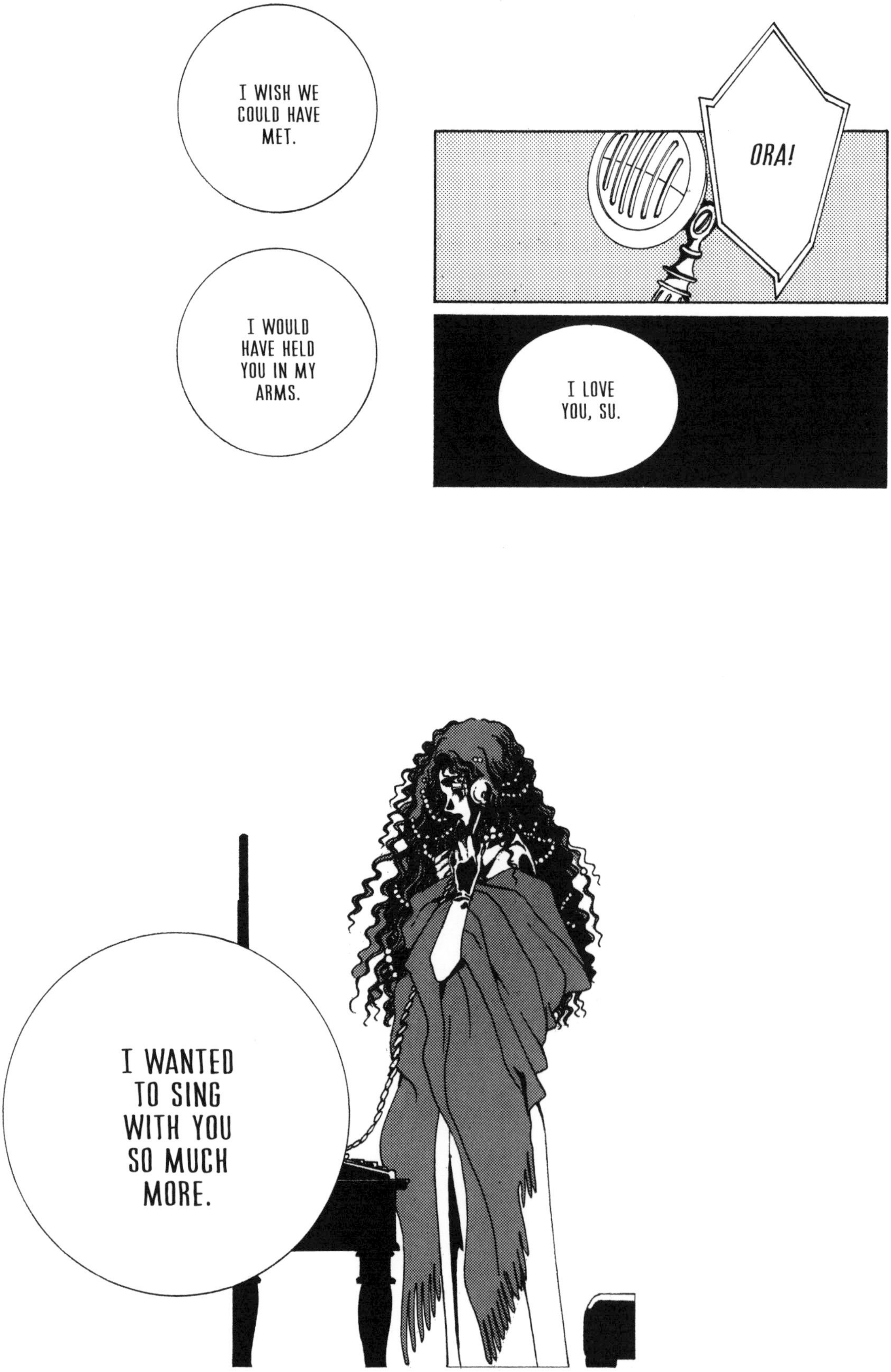
ORA!
I LOVE YOU, SU.
I WISH WE COULD HAVE MET.
I WOULD HAVE HELD YOU IN MY ARMS.
I WANTED TO SING WITH YOU SO MUCH MORE.

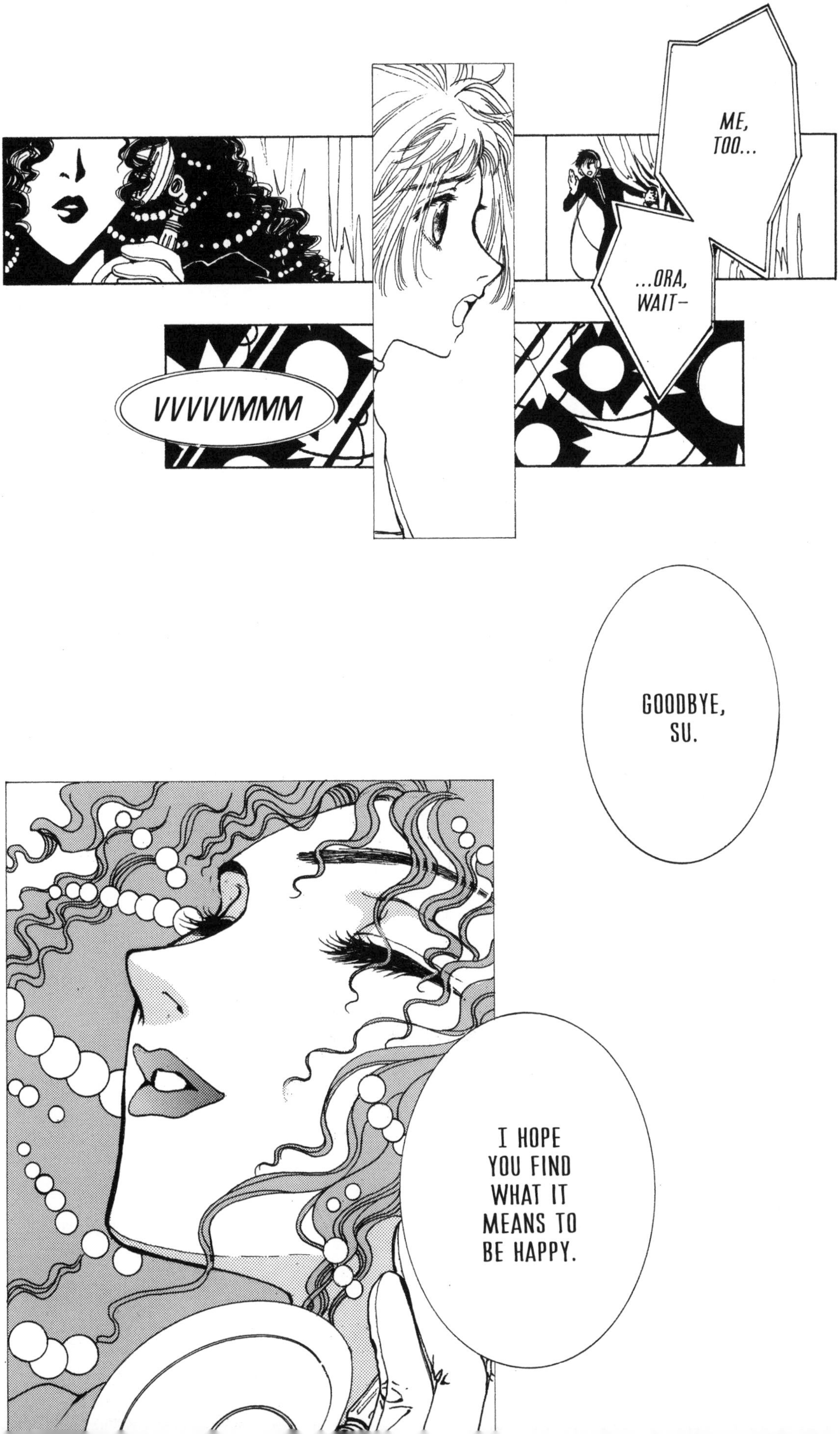
ME, TOO...
...ORA, WAIT–
VVVVVMMM
GOODBYE, SU.
I HOPE YOU FIND WHAT IT MEANS TO BE HAPPY.

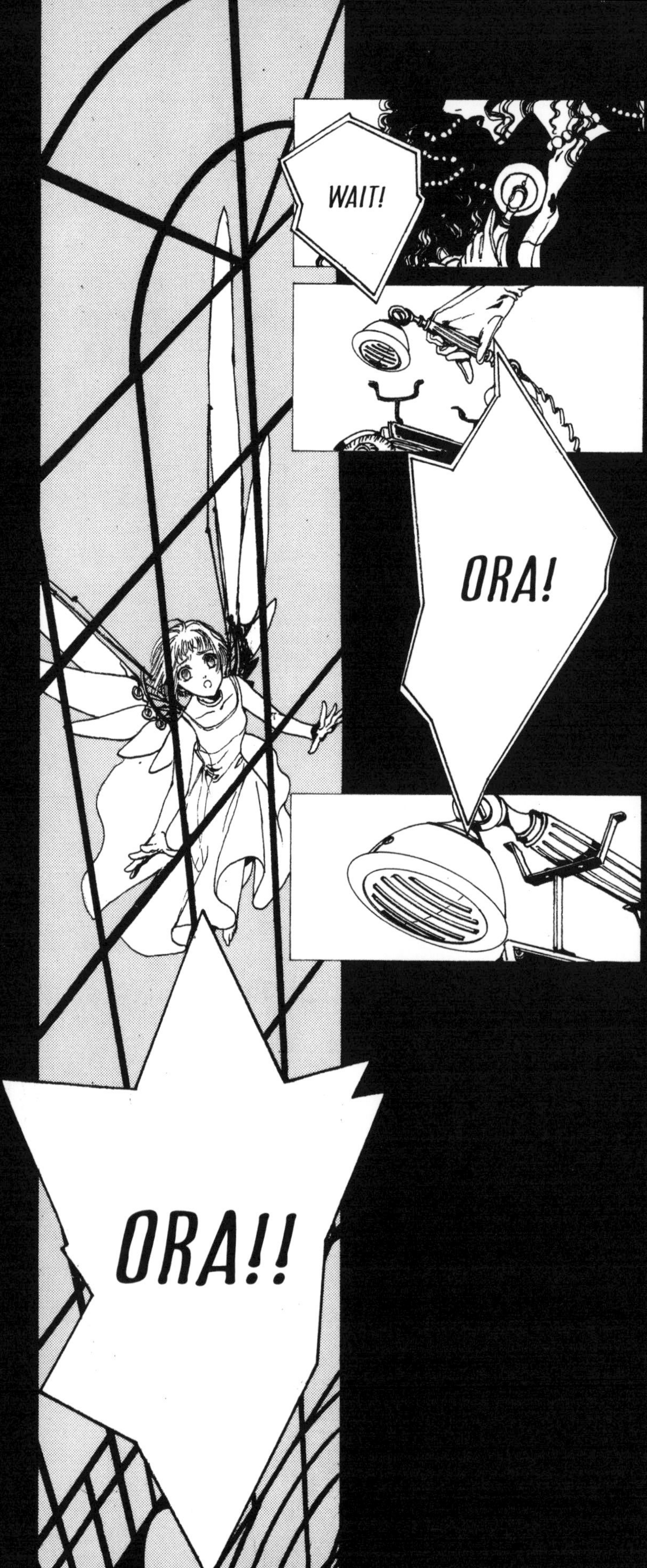
WAIT!
ORA!
ORA!!

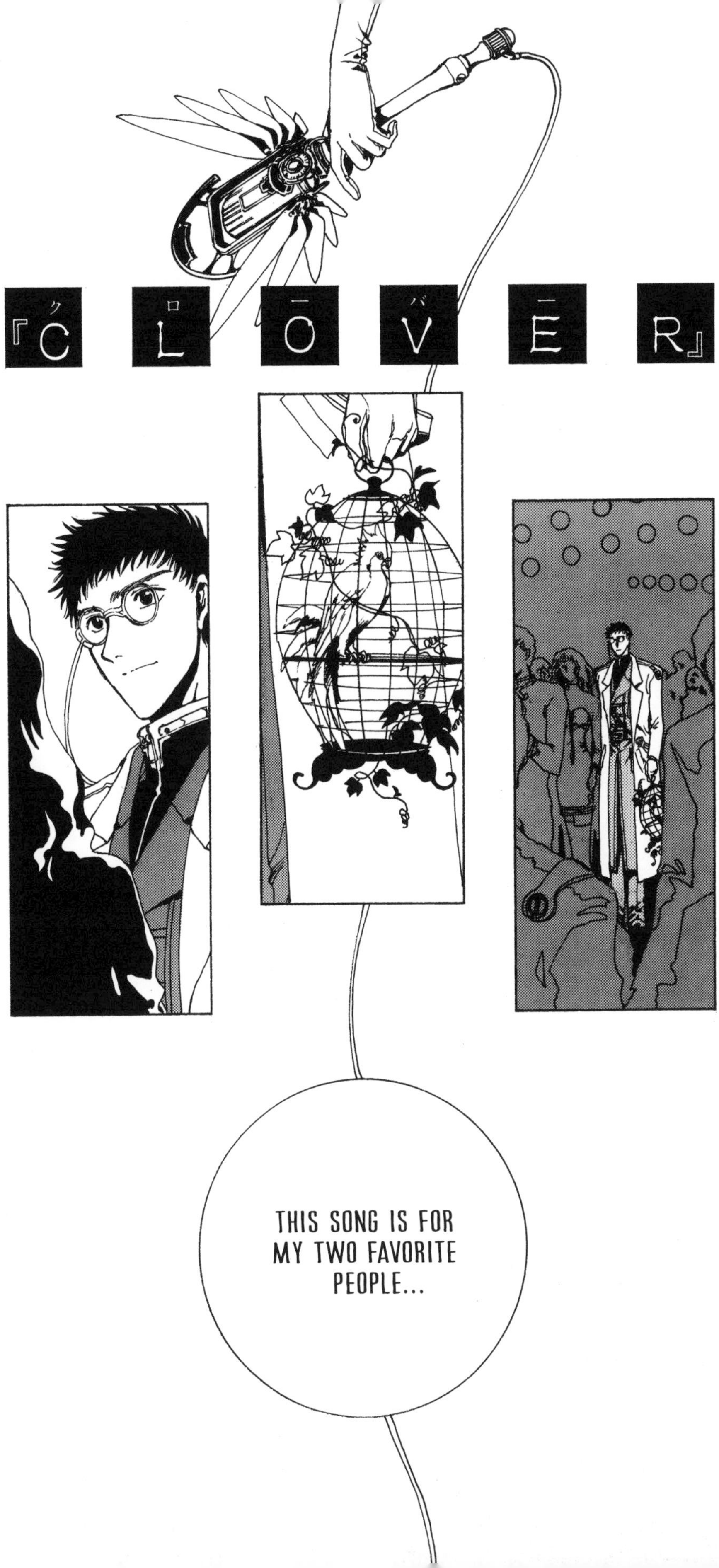
『CLOVER』
クローバー
THIS SONG IS FOR MY TWO FAVORITE PEOPLE...

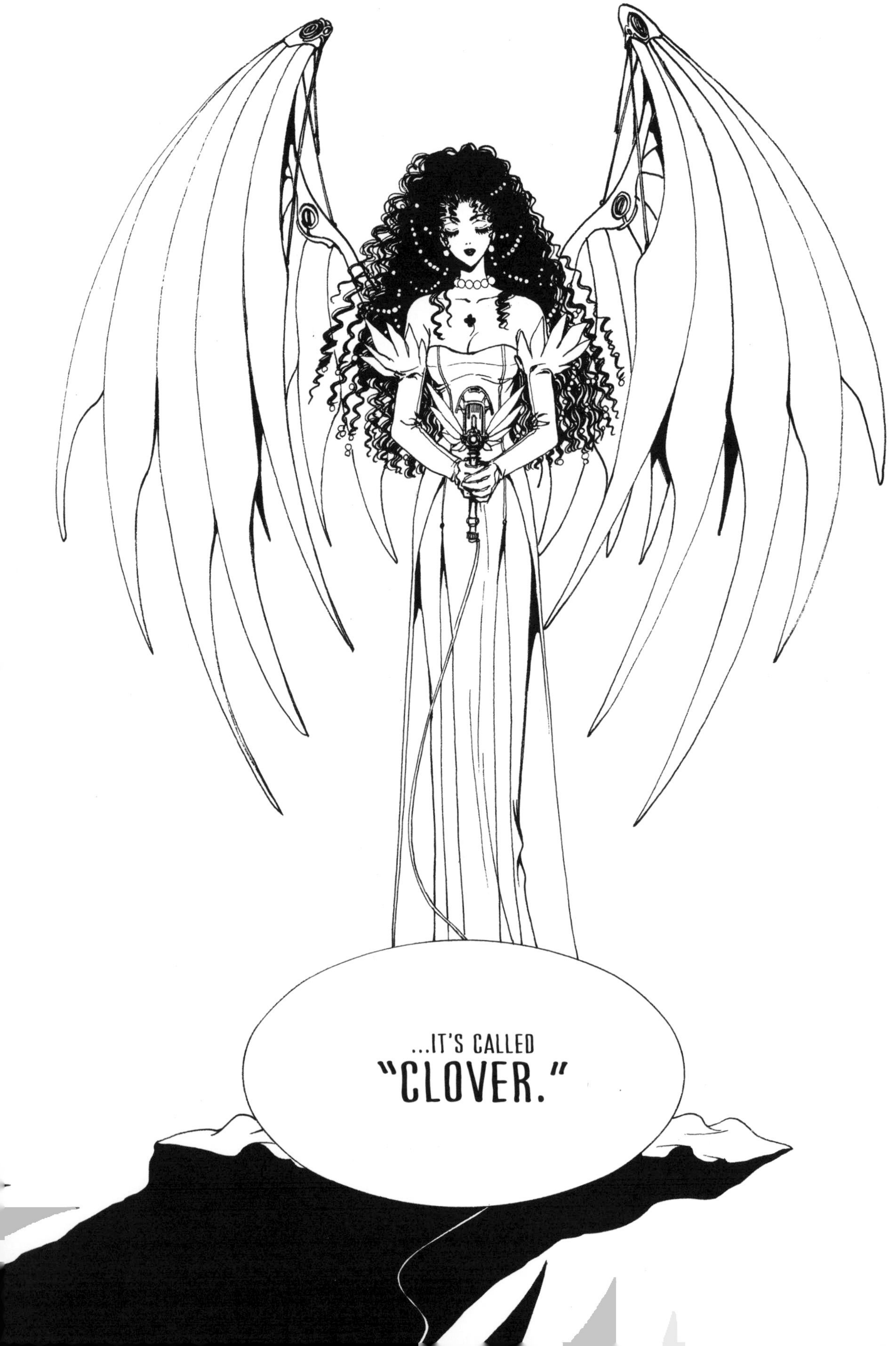
...IT'S CALLED
"CLOVER."

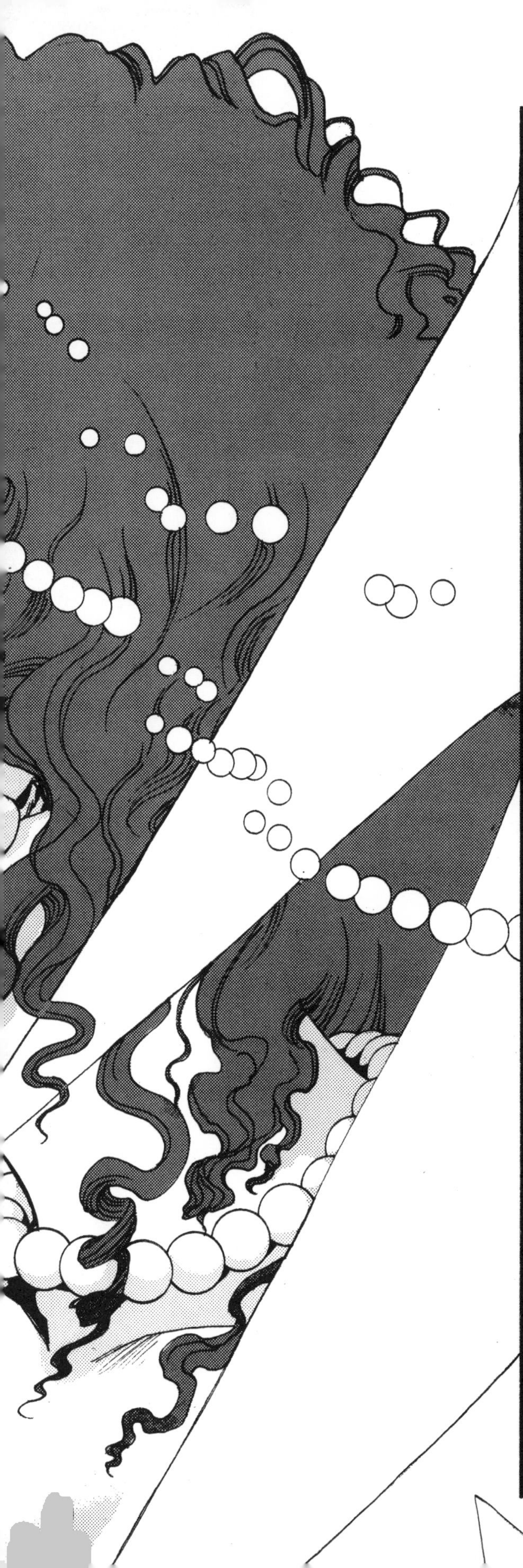

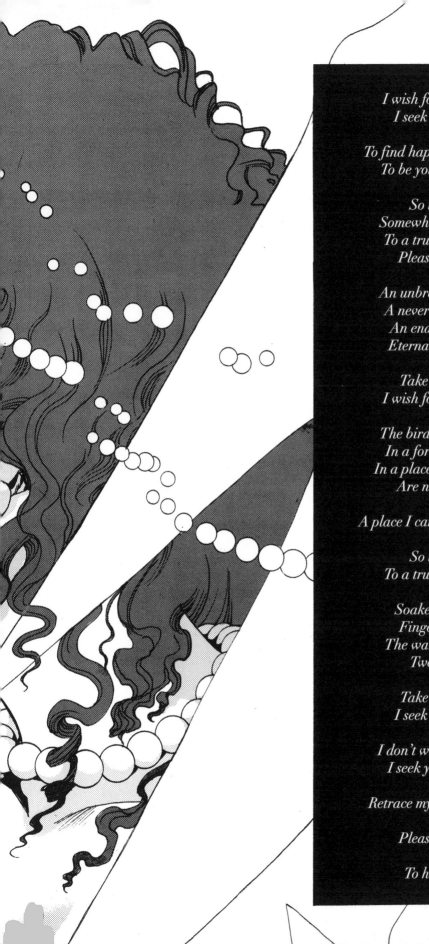

I wish for happiness
I seek happiness

To find happiness with you
To be your happiness

So take me
Somewhere far away
To a true Elsewhere
Please take me

An unbreakable spell
A never-ending kiss
An endless dream
Eternal happiness

Take me away
I wish for happiness

The birds sing a song
In a foreign tongue
In a place where wings
Are not enough

A place I cannot reach alone

So take me
To a true Elsewhere

Soaked feathers
Fingers locked
The warmth of skin
Two hearts

Take me away
I seek happiness

I don't want your past
I seek your present

Retrace my broken future

Please take me

To happiness

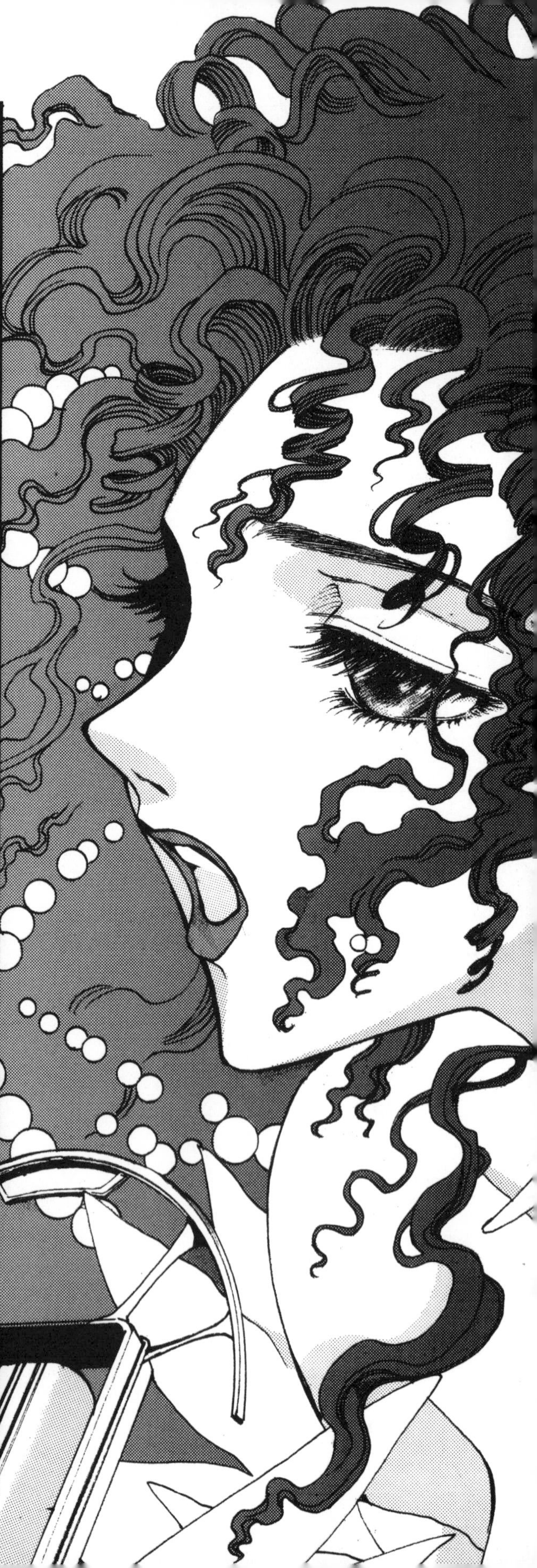

I wish for happiness
I seek happiness

To find happiness with you
To be your happiness

Take me
To a true Elsewhere
Please take me

A bird in a cage
A bird without wings
A bird without a voice
A lonely bird

So take me
I wish for happiness

I'm happy just to be with you
Happy just to see your smile

So take me
To a true Elsewhere

Take me away
I seek happiness

My first thought is of you
My last wish is for you

A promised land where fairies wait
With room just enough for two

So take me there

I want to forget reality
To be in my dreams with you
Where I can be thinking of you forever

Take me

To happiness

HUMAN『人の目』EYE

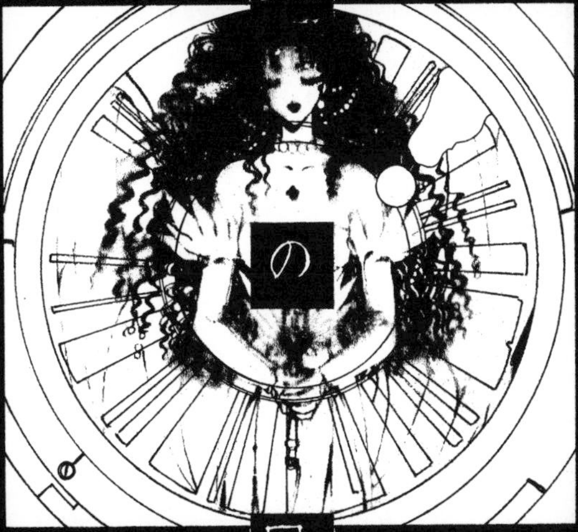

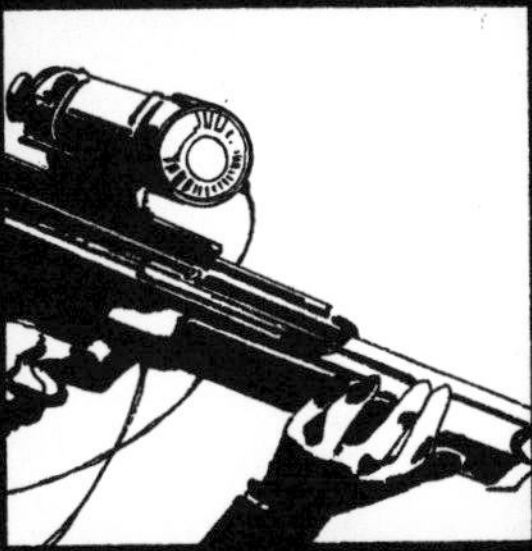

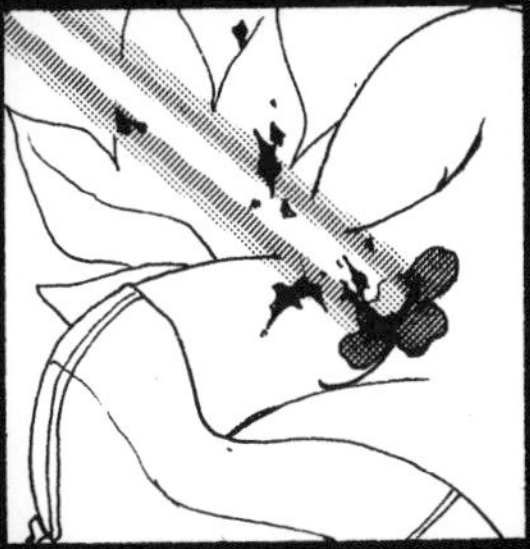

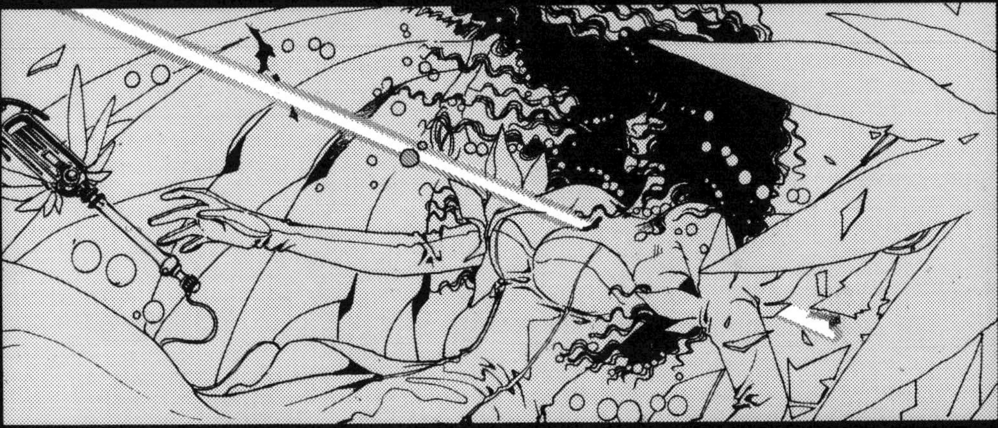

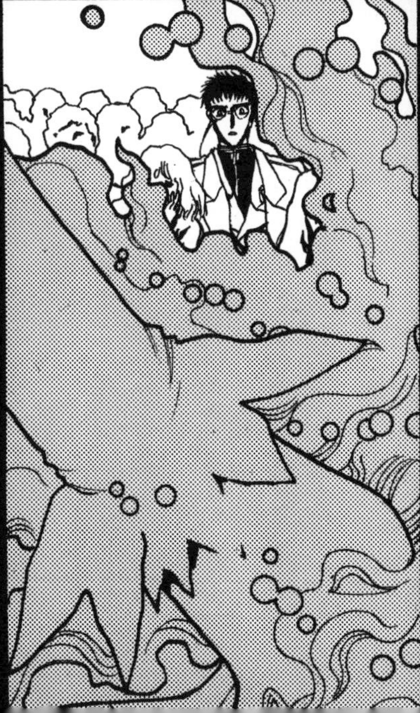

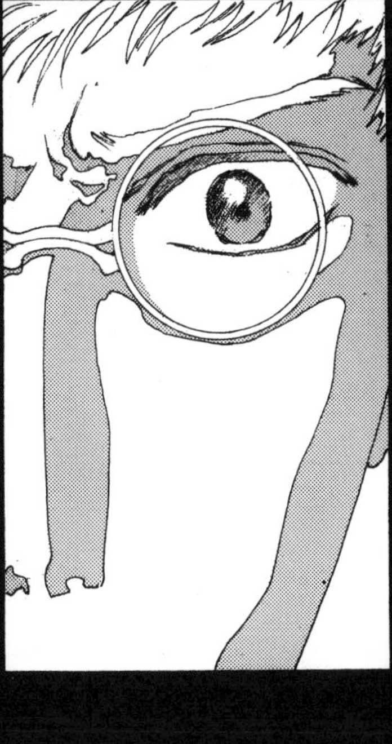

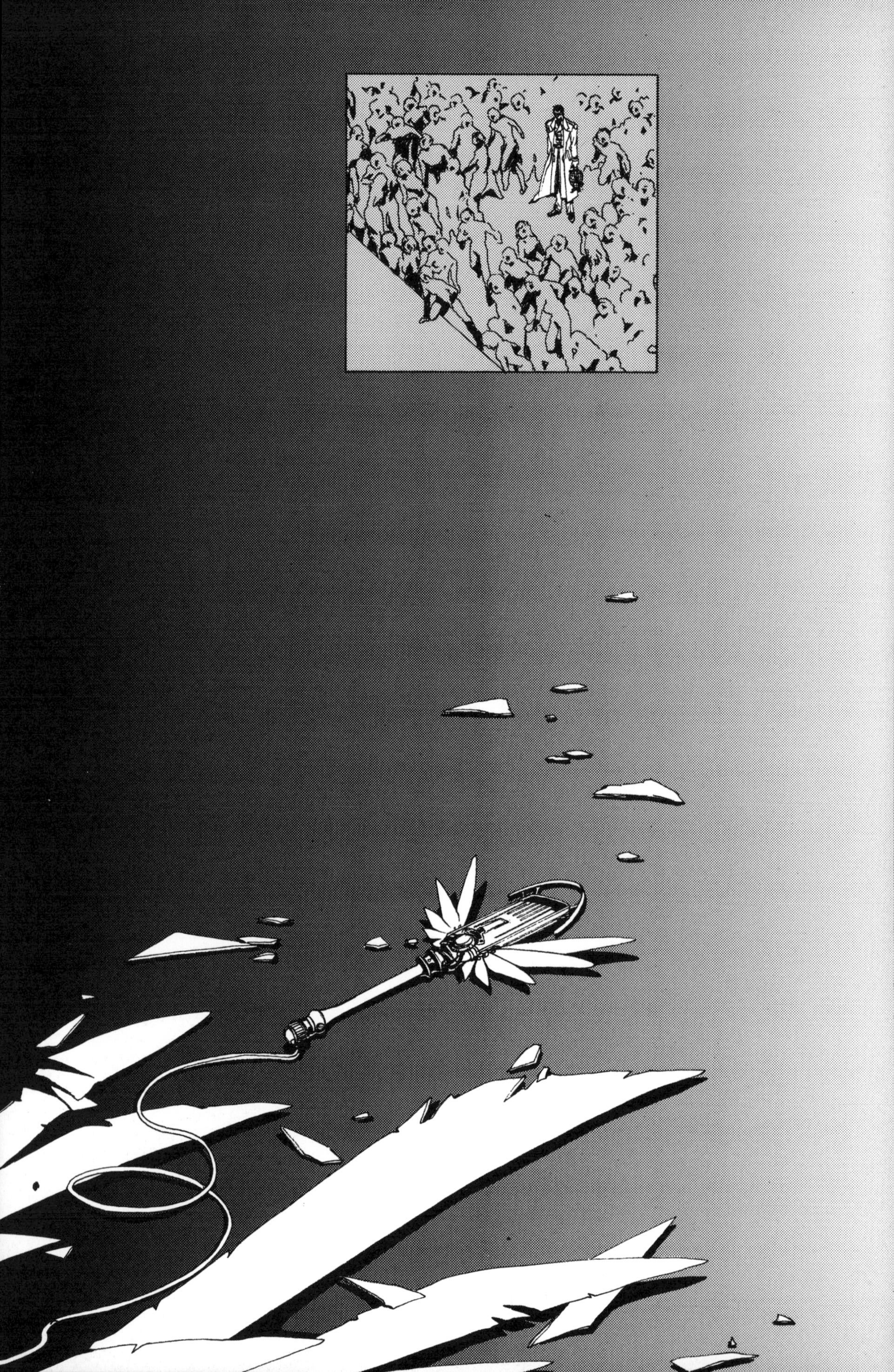

『小鳥の涙』
A BIRD'S TEAR

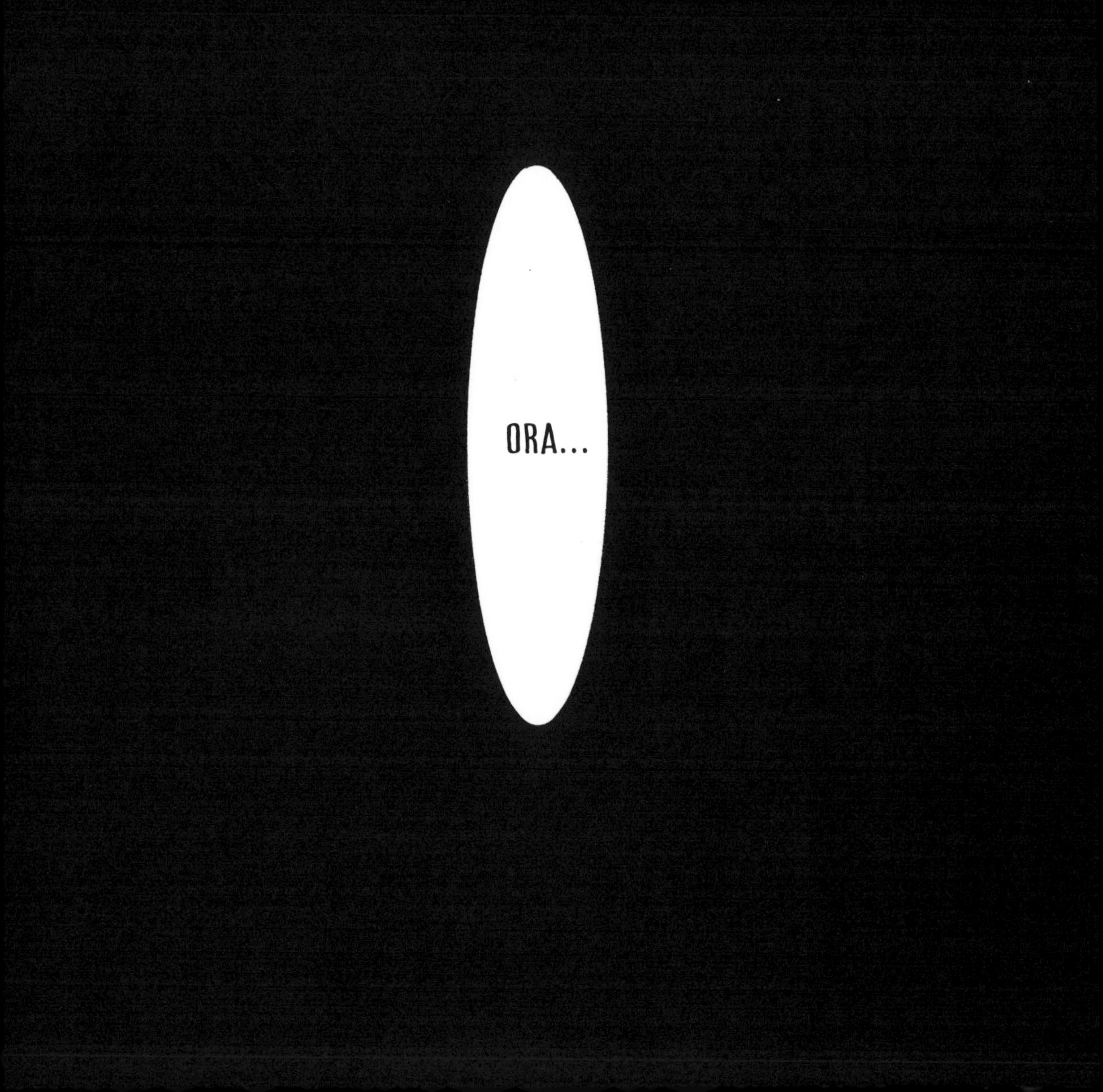
ORA...

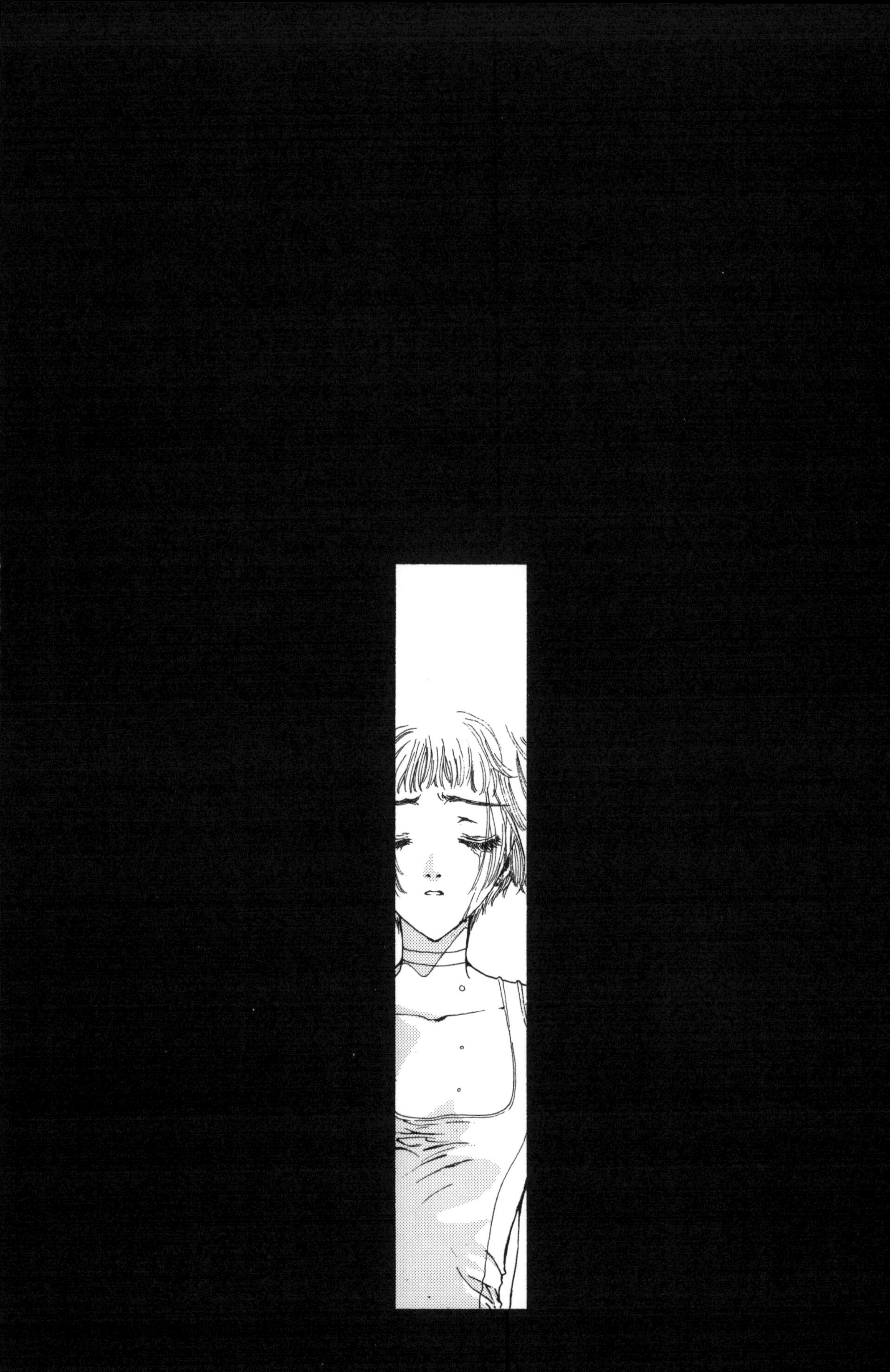

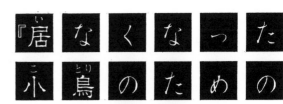

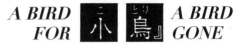

『居なくなった小鳥のための小鳥』
A BIRD FOR A BIRD GONE

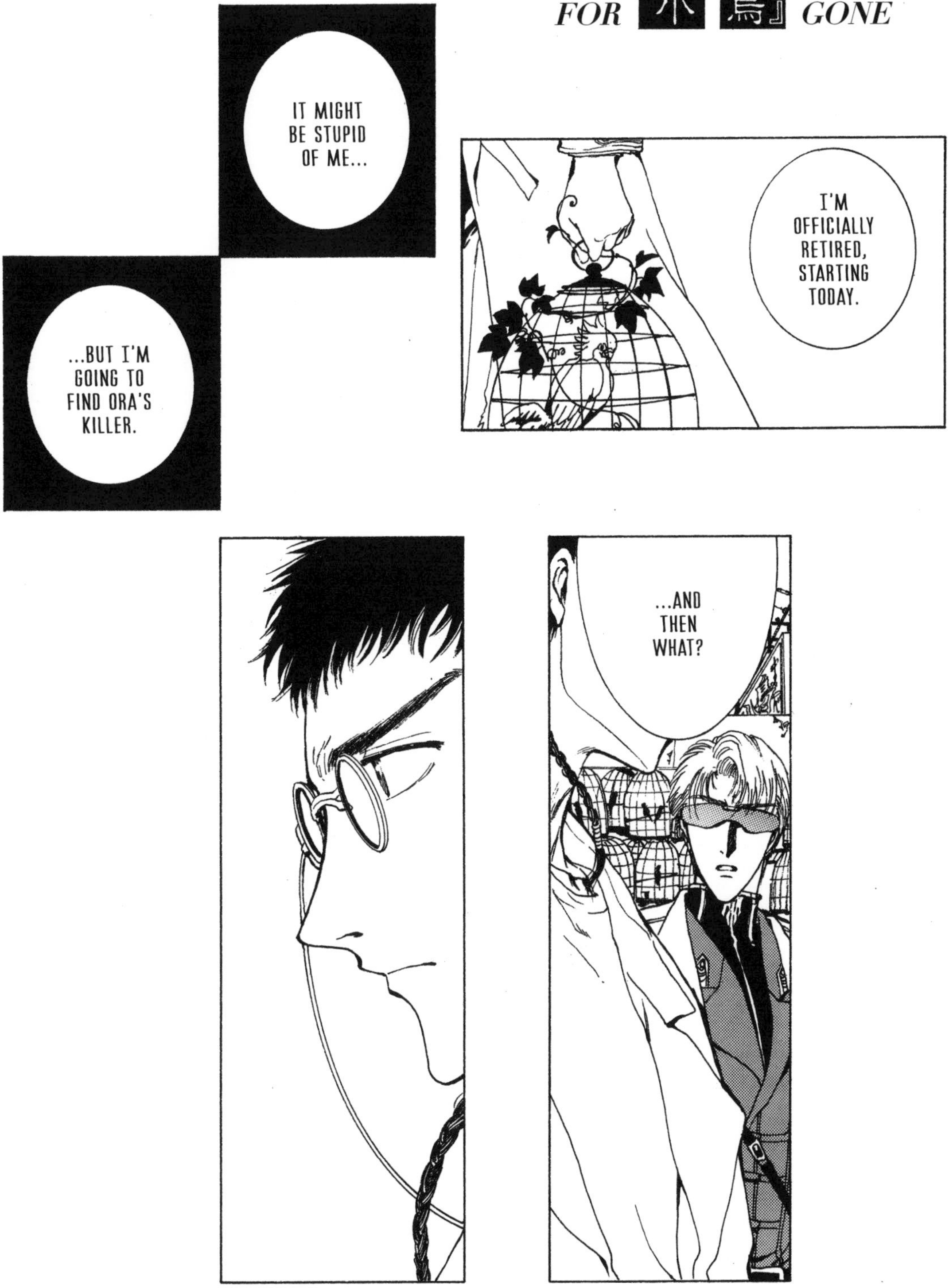
I'M OFFICIALLY RETIRED, STARTING TODAY.
IT MIGHT BE STUPID OF ME...
...BUT I'M GOING TO FIND ORA'S KILLER.
...AND THEN WHAT?

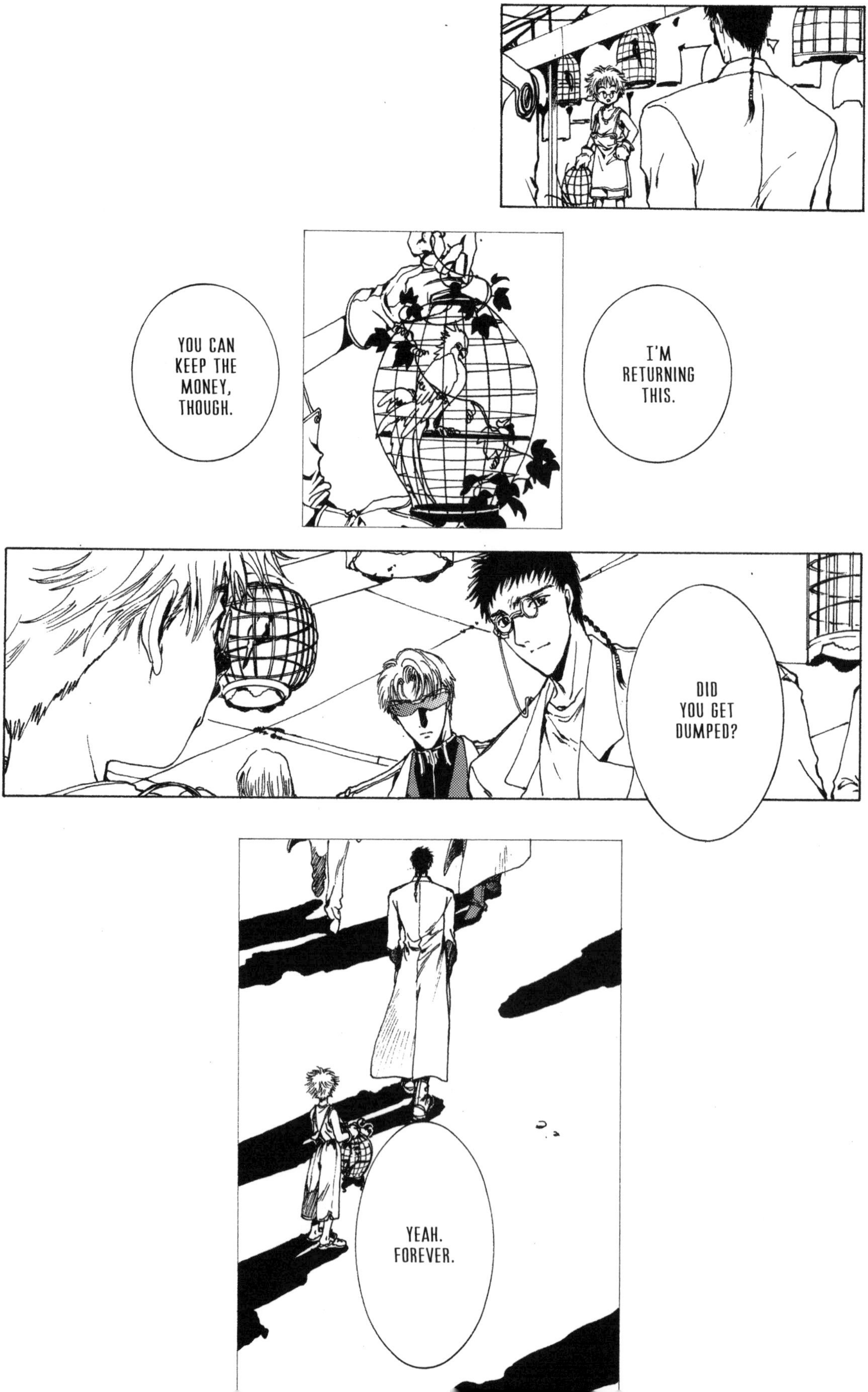
I'M RETURNING THIS.
YOU CAN KEEP THE MONEY, THOUGH.
DID YOU GET DUMPED?
YEAH. FOREVER.

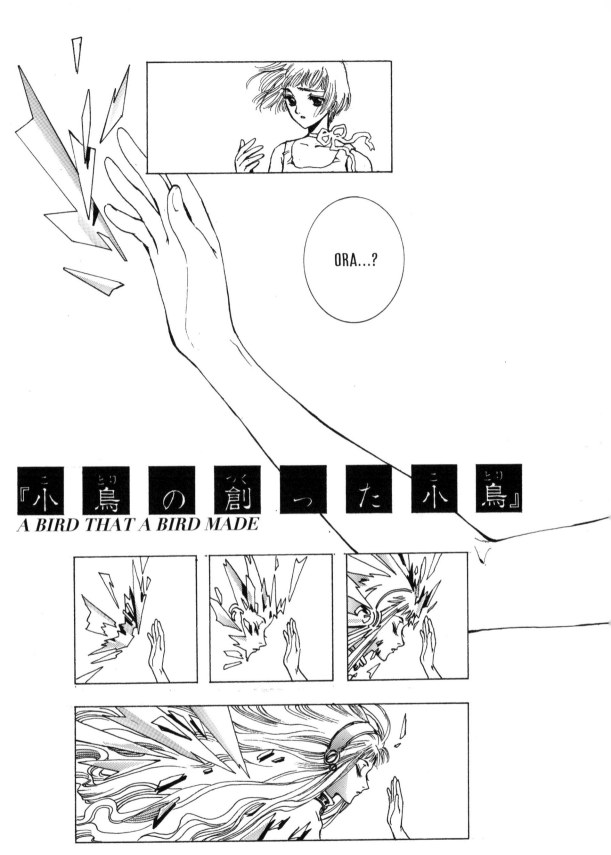

ORA...?

『小鳥の創った小鳥』
A BIRD THAT A BIRD MADE

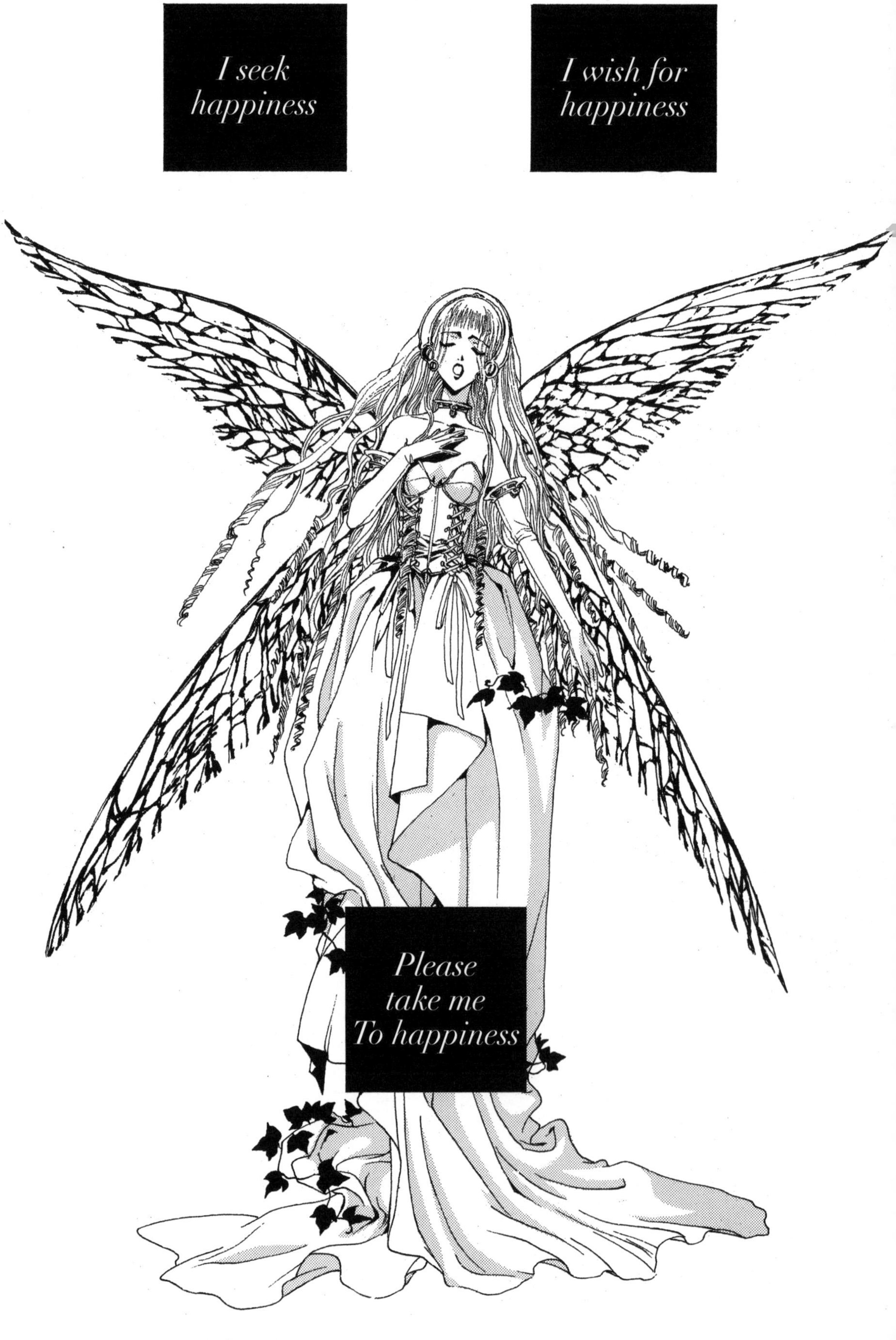
I wish for happiness
I seek happiness
Please take me To happiness

*If you find a
four-leaf clover
It will bring you
happiness*

*But it can
Never be found*

*Happiness lies inside
A secret cage*

*No one can possess
The four-leaf clover*

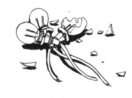

*But then,
what of the three-leaf clover?*

FOUR-LEAF 『四つ葉のクローバー』CLOVER

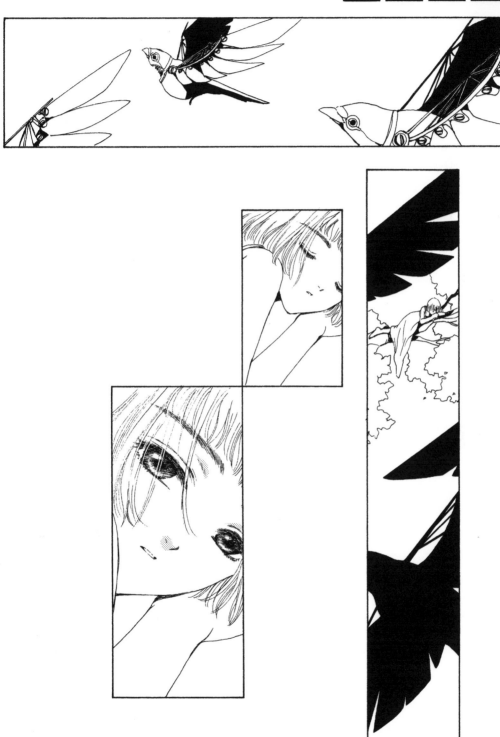

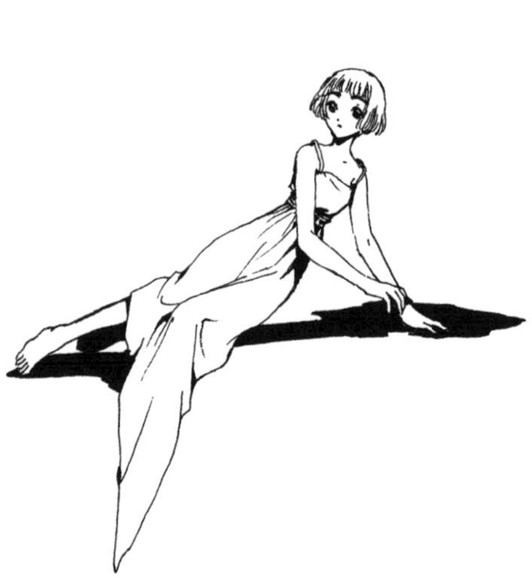

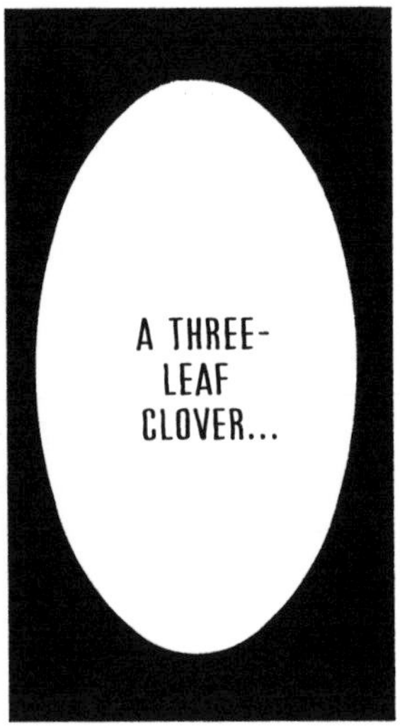
A THREE-LEAF CLOVER...

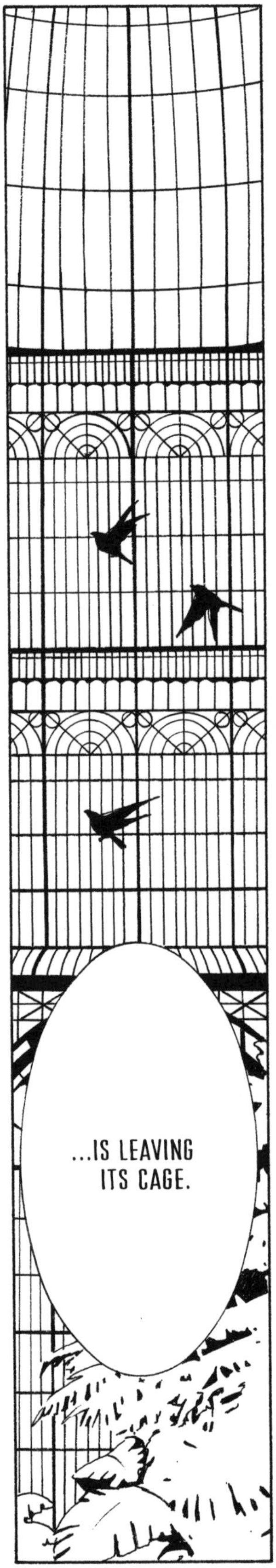
...IS LEAVING ITS CAGE.

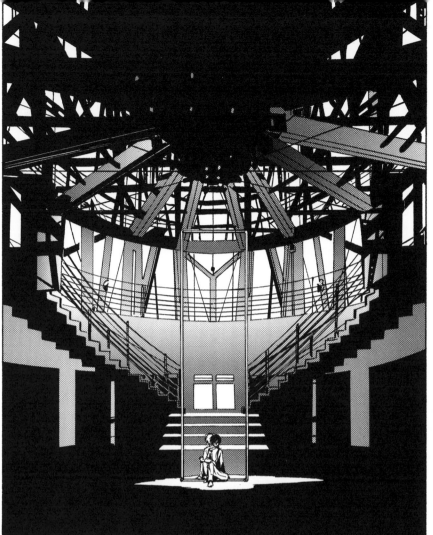

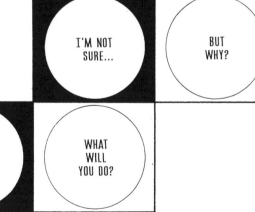

THREE-LEAF CLOVER

『三つ葉のクローバー』

BUT WHY?

I'M NOT SURE...

WHAT WILL YOU DO?

I'M NOT SURE.

BUT YOU'RE LEAVING?

I AM.

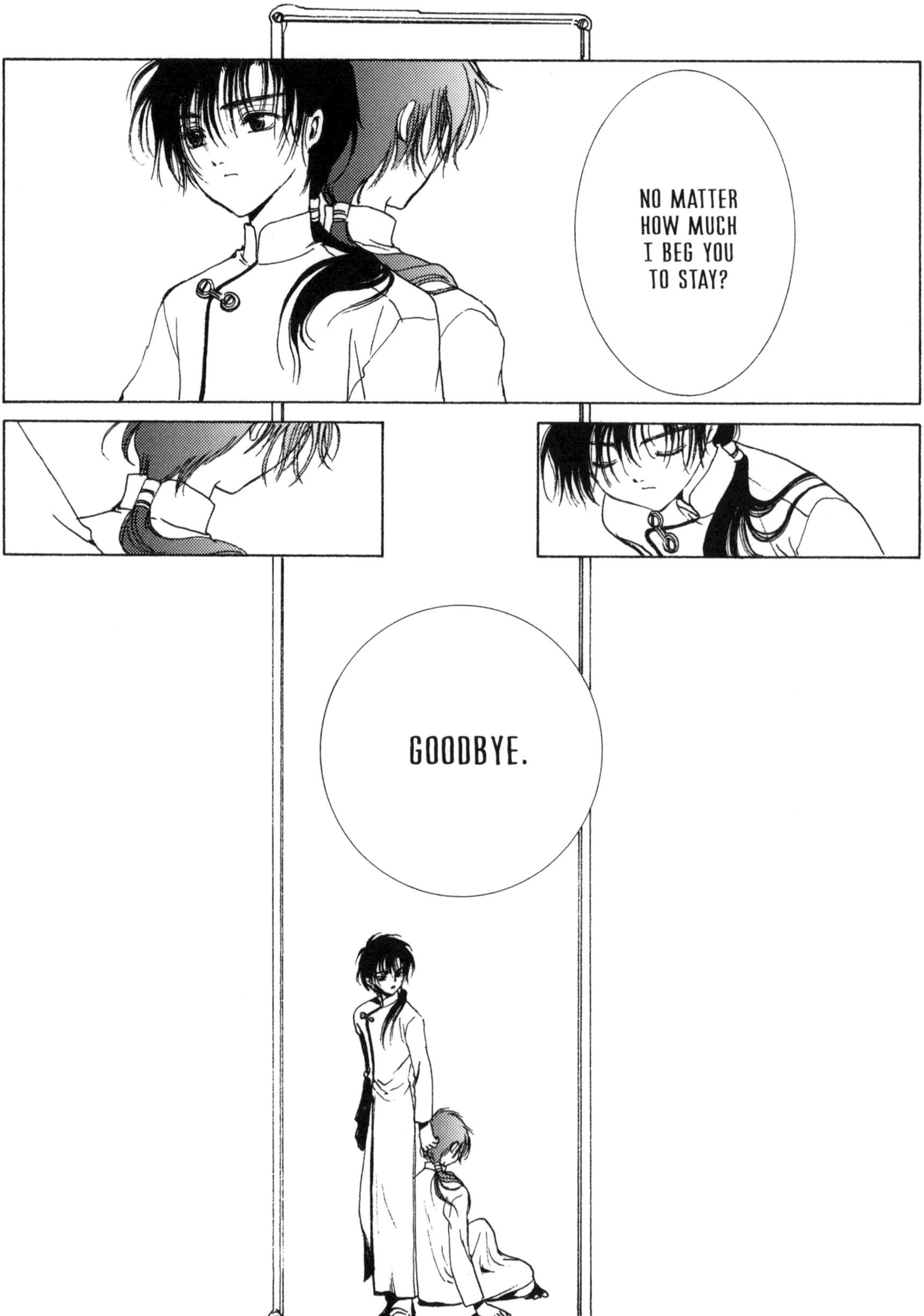
NO MATTER HOW MUCH I BEG YOU TO STAY?
GOODBYE.

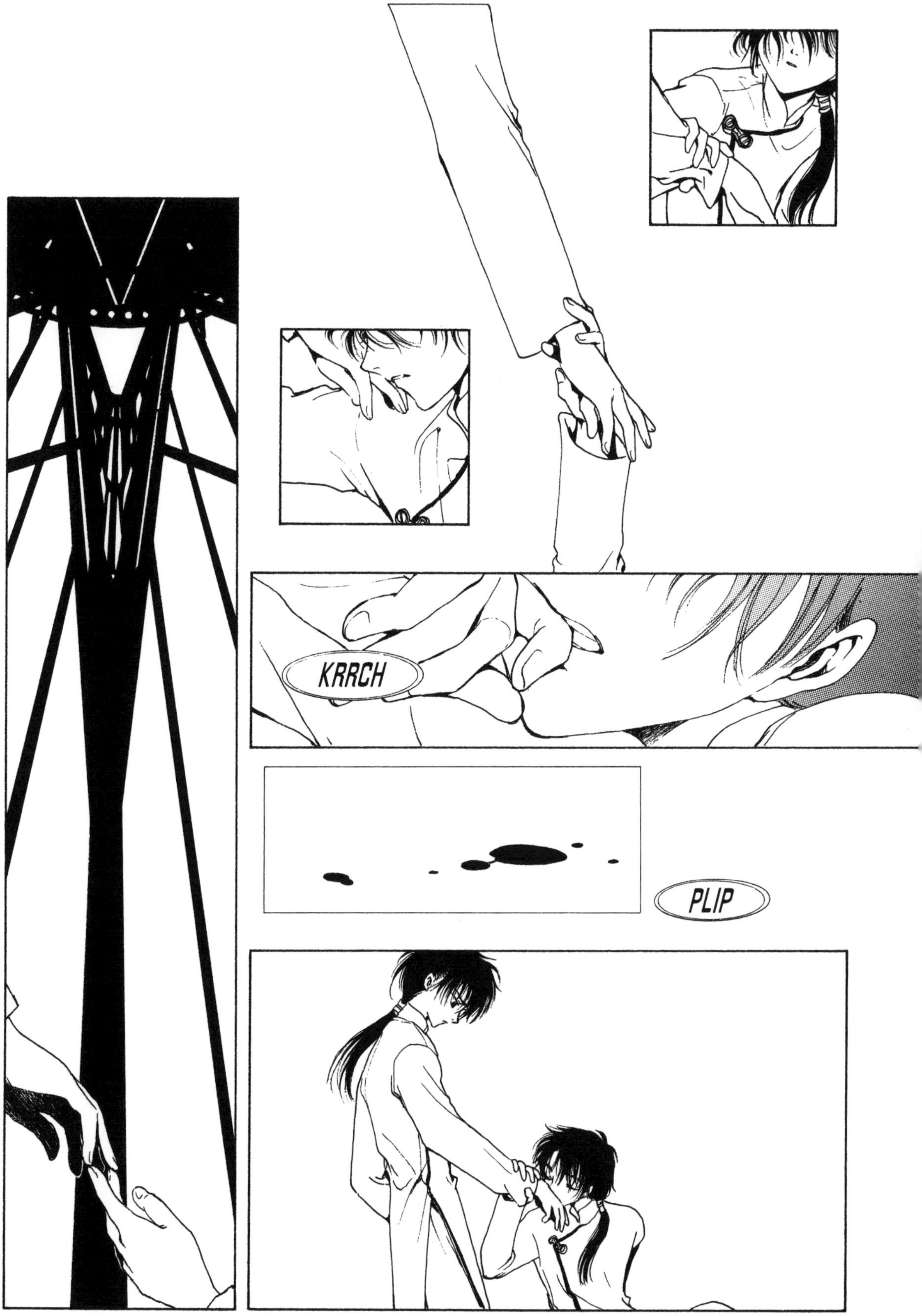
KRRCH
PLIP

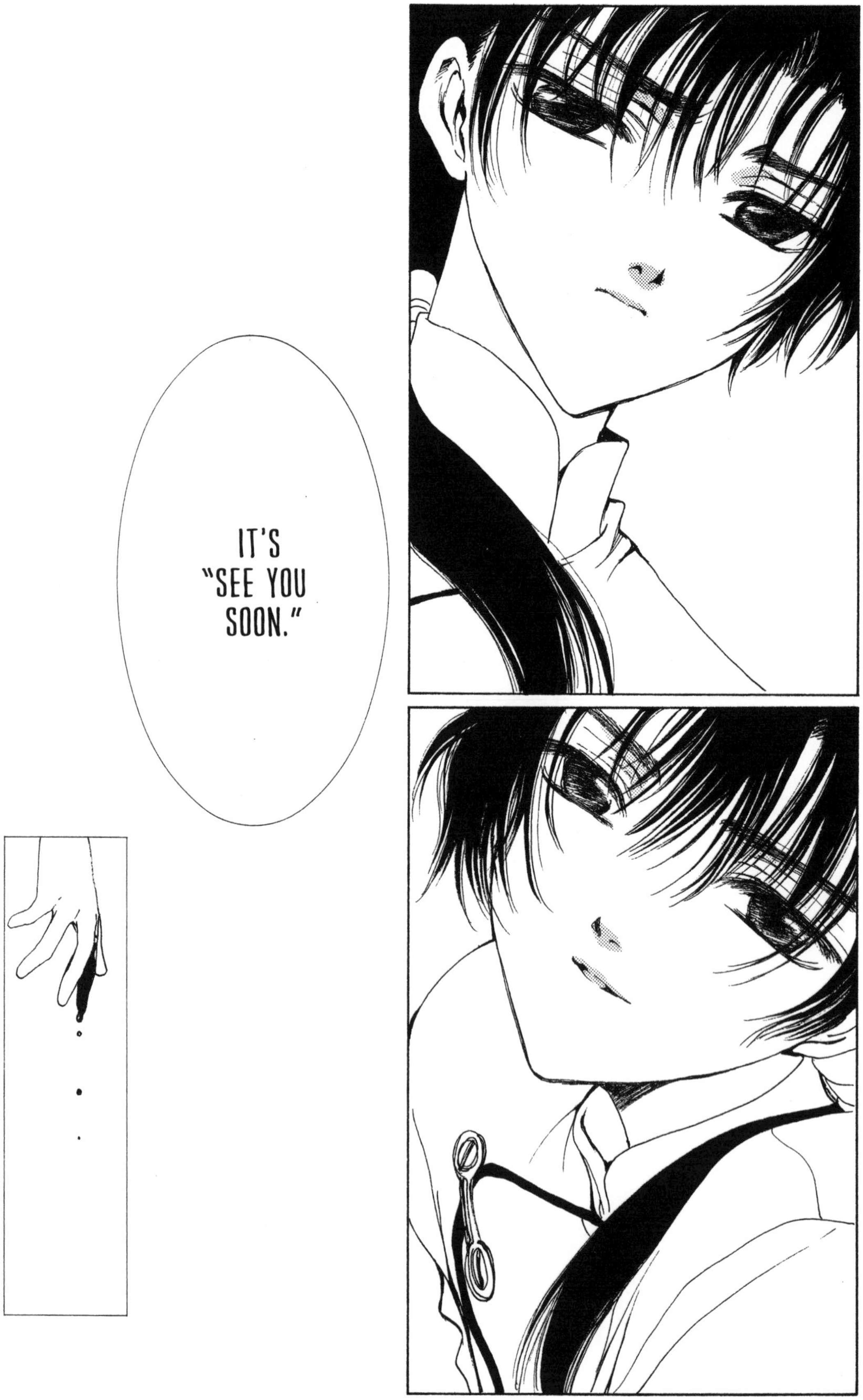
IT'S "SEE YOU SOON."

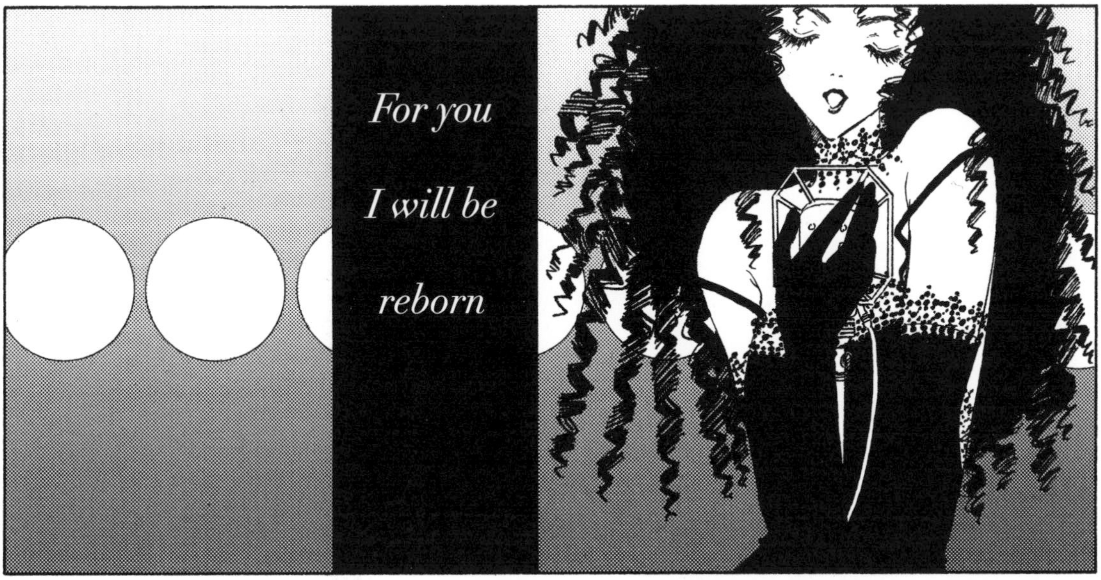
For you
I will be
reborn

SINGING VOICE 『歌う声』

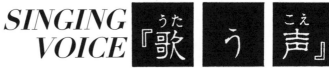

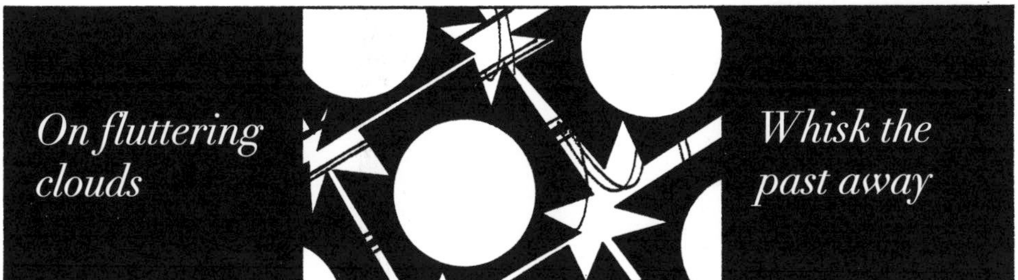
On fluttering clouds
Whisk the past away

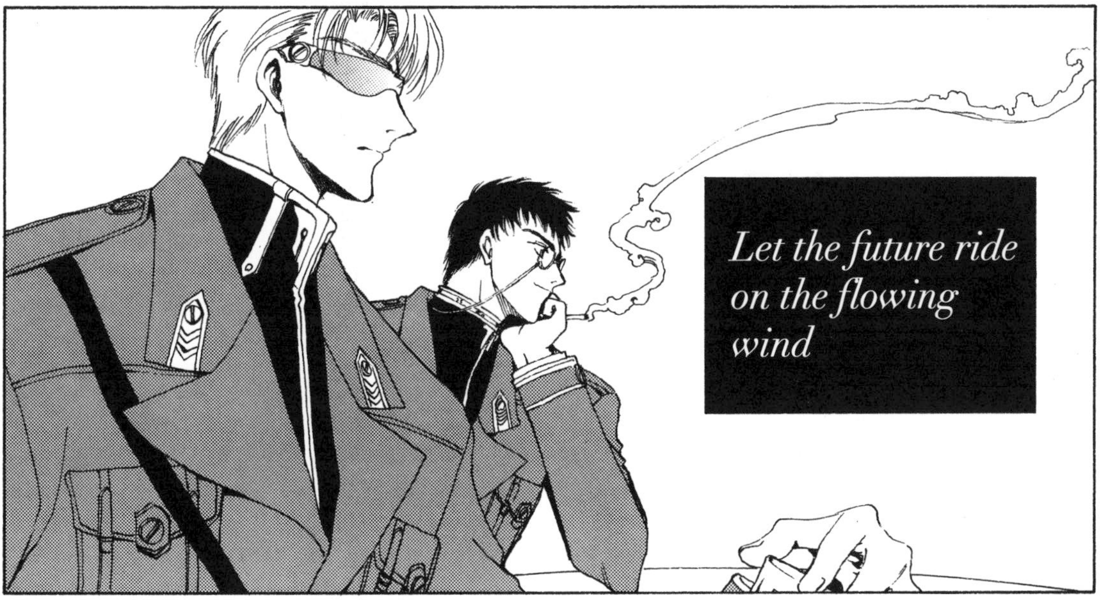
Let the future ride on the flowing wind

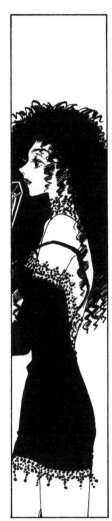

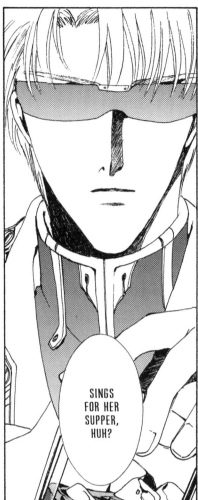

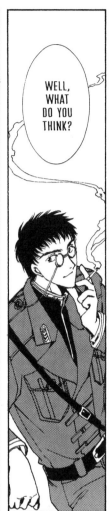

WELL, WHAT DO YOU THINK?
SINGS FOR HER SUPPER, HUH?

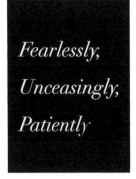

Fearlessly, Unceasingly, Patiently

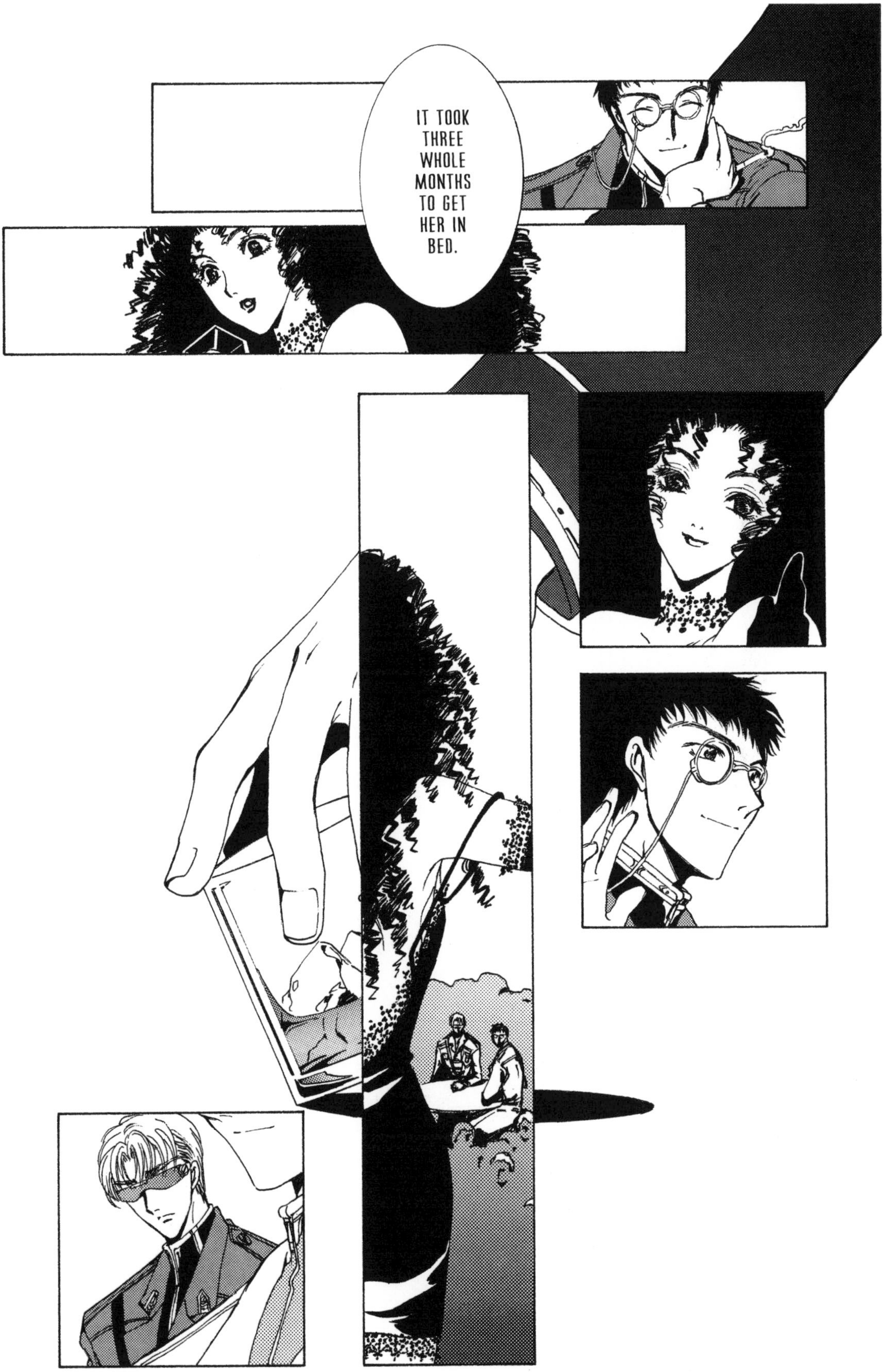
IT TOOK THREE WHOLE MONTHS TO GET HER IN BED.

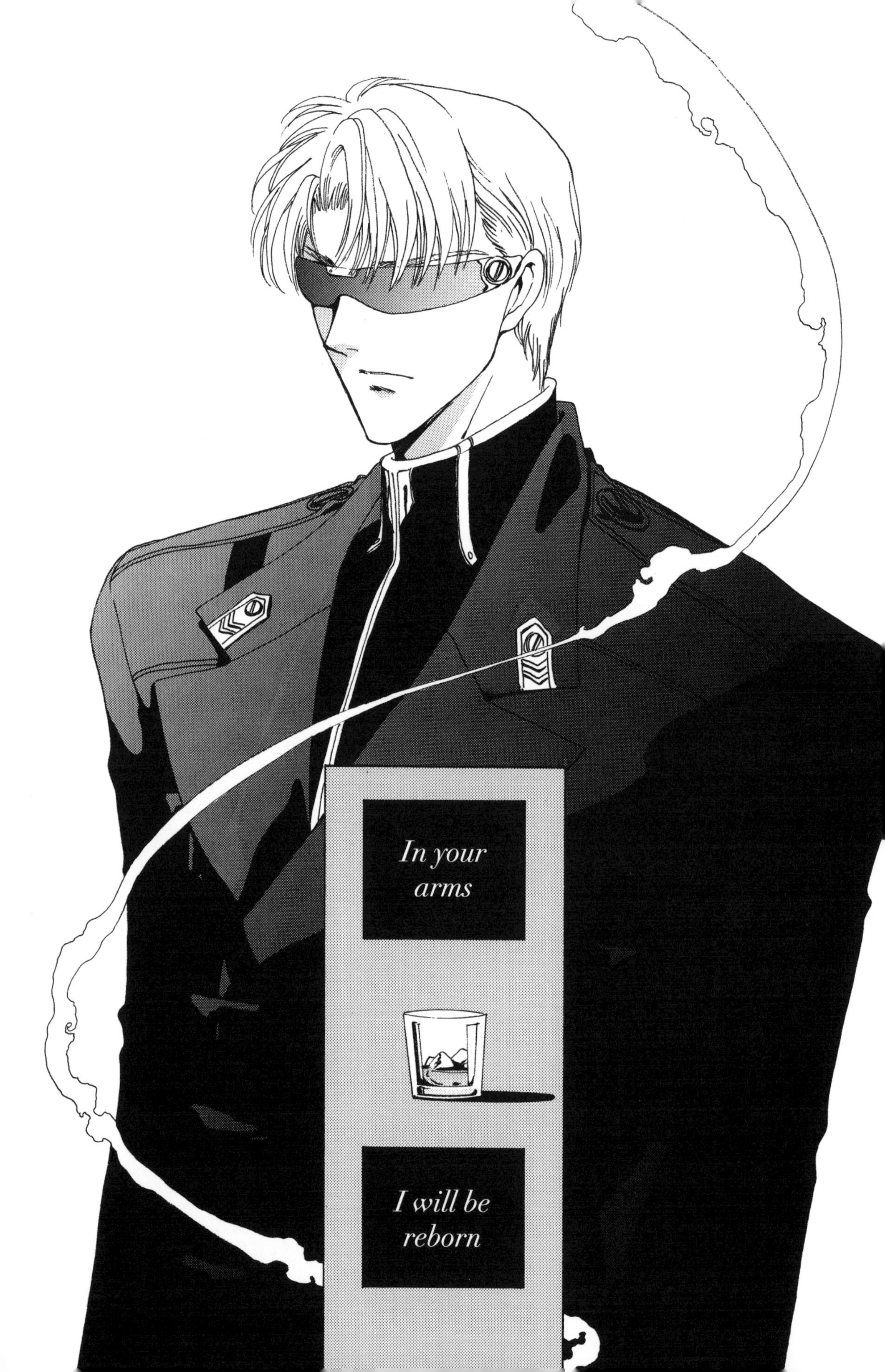
In your arms
I will be reborn

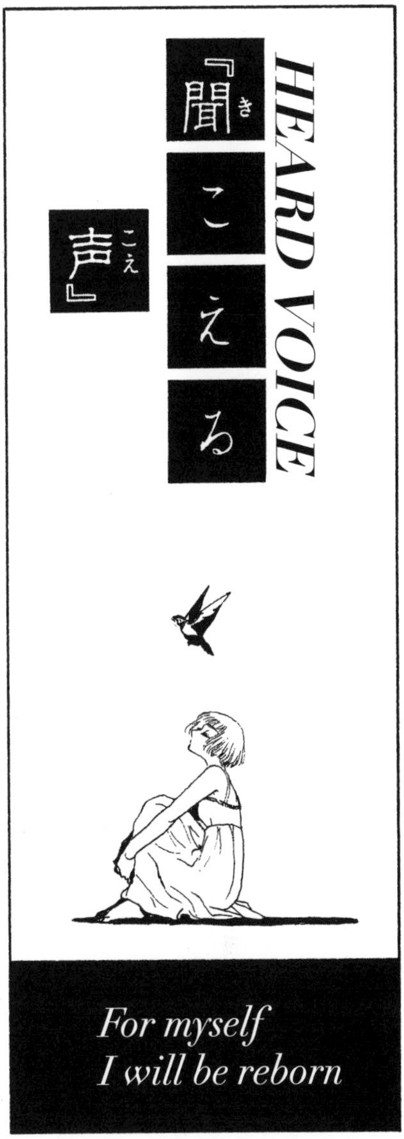
HEARD VOICE
『聞こえる声』
For myself
I will be reborn

Once again
I await my
birth in a
golden egg

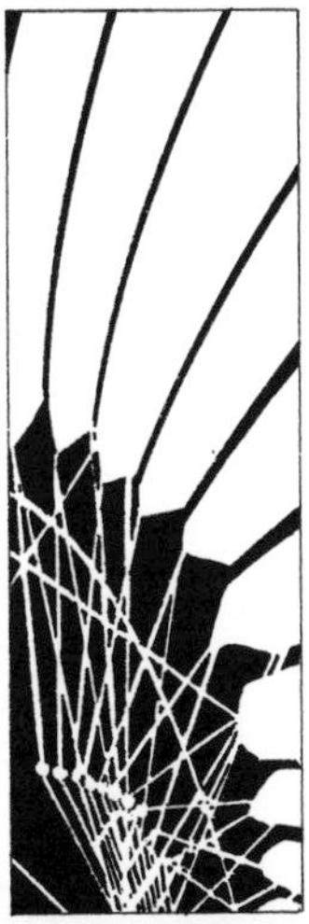

Once again
to fly with
silver wings

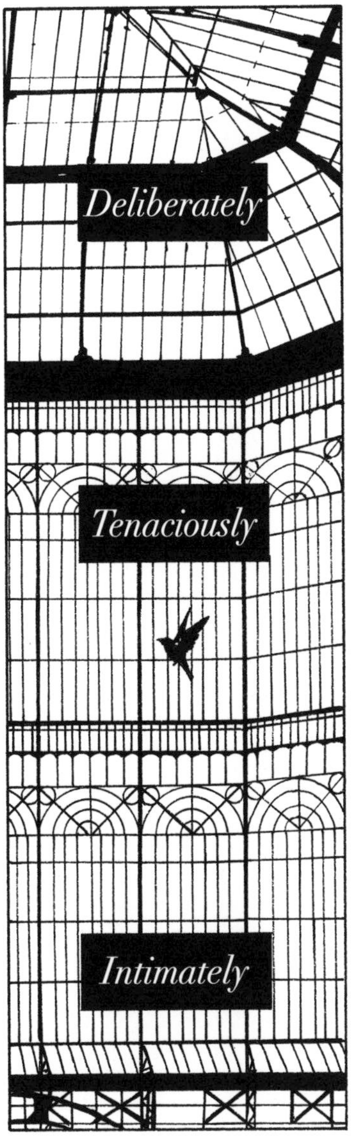
Deliberately
Tenaciously
Intimately

In your arms

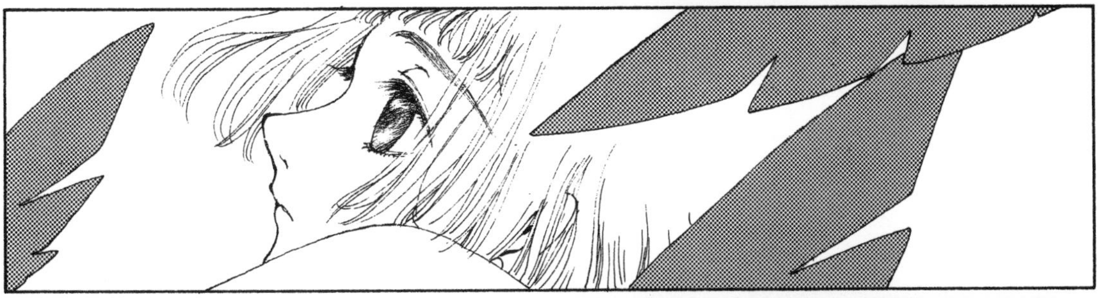

I will be reborn

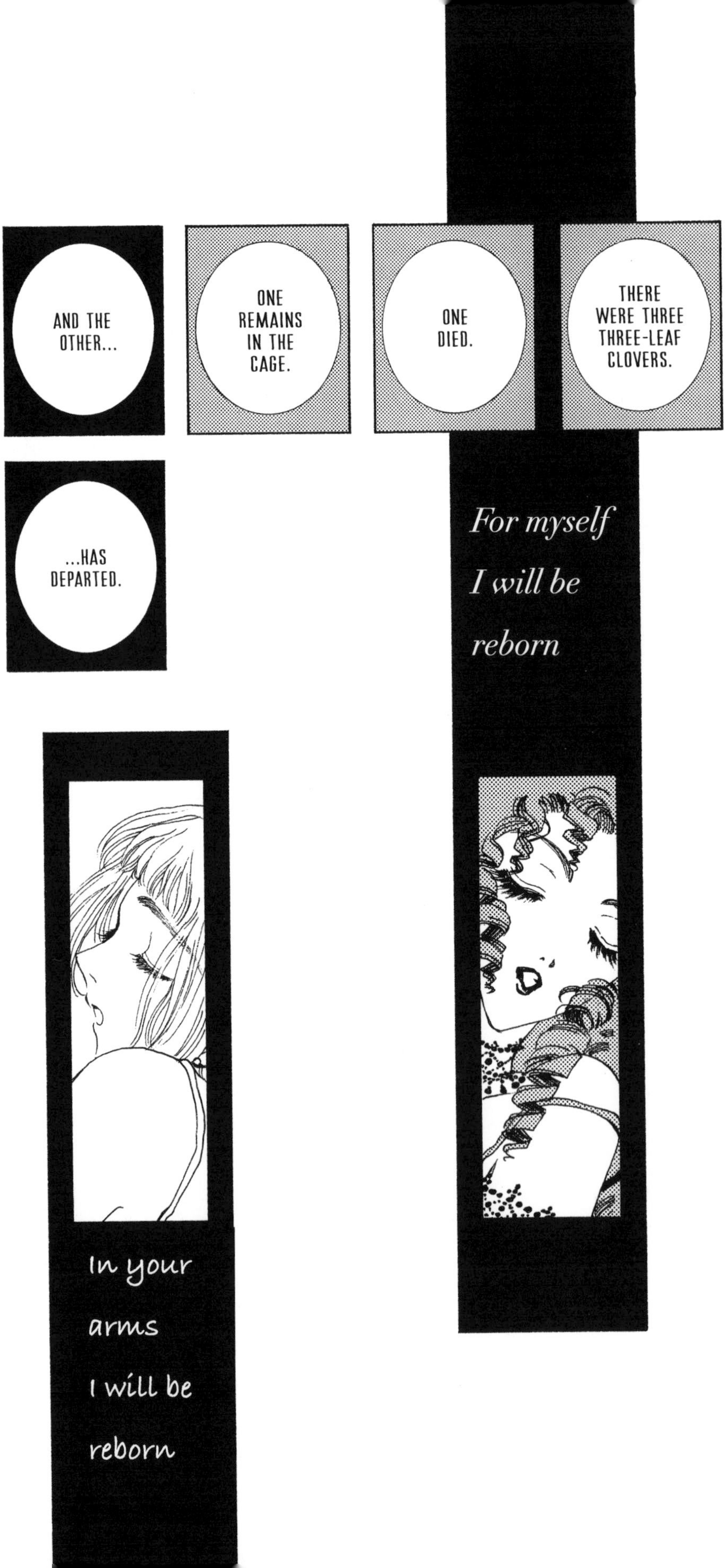
THERE WERE THREE THREE-LEAF CLOVERS.
ONE DIED.
ONE REMAINS IN THE CAGE.
AND THE OTHER...
...HAS DEPARTED.
For myself I will be reborn
In your arms I will be reborn

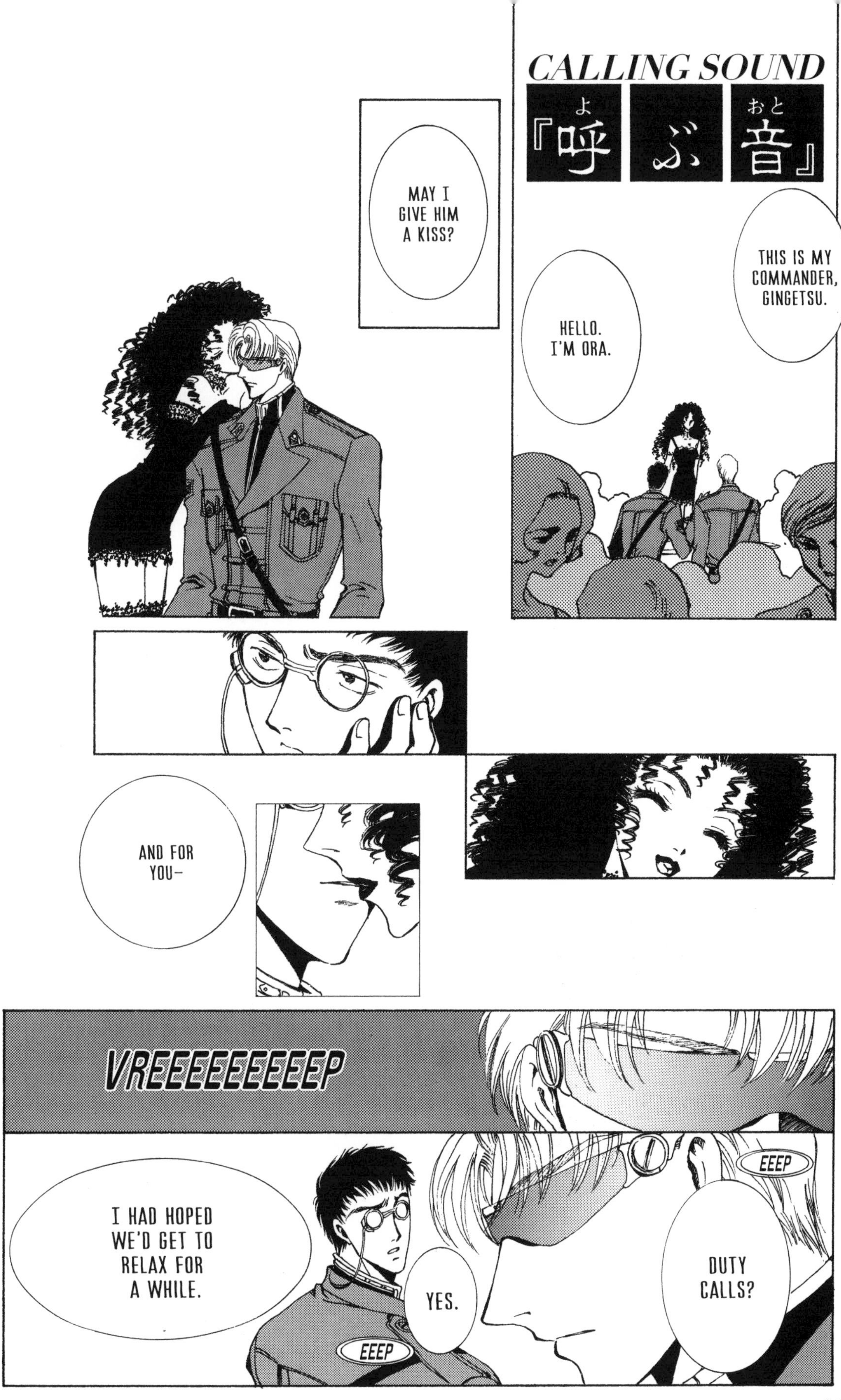
CALLING SOUND
『呼ぶ音』
THIS IS MY COMMANDER, GINGETSU.
HELLO. I'M ORA.
MAY I GIVE HIM A KISS?
AND FOR YOU–
VREEEEEEEEEEP
EEEP
DUTY CALLS?
YES.
EEEP
I HAD HOPED WE'D GET TO RELAX FOR A WHILE.

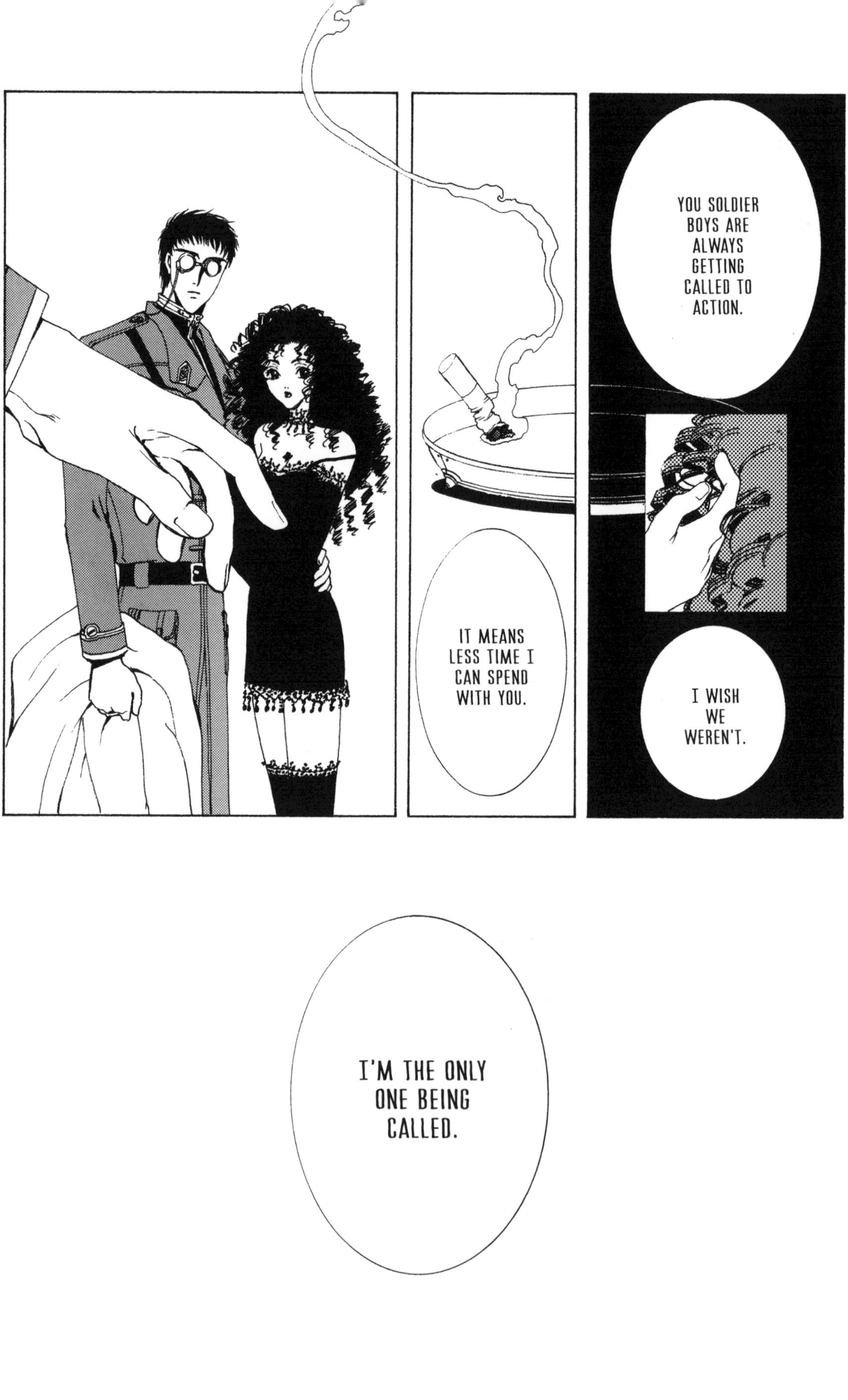
YOU SOLDIER BOYS ARE ALWAYS GETTING CALLED TO ACTION.
IT MEANS LESS TIME I CAN SPEND WITH YOU.
I WISH WE WEREN'T.
I'M THE ONLY ONE BEING CALLED.

COMMUNICATION

『通信』

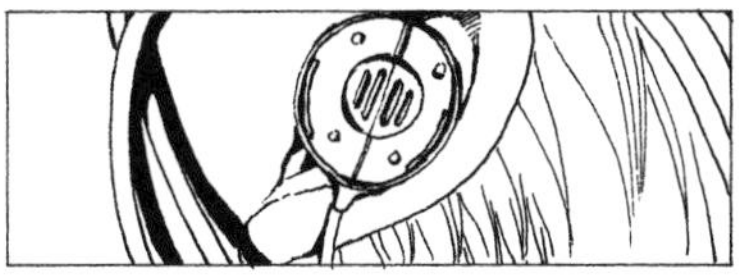

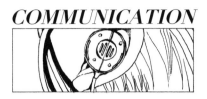

A THREE-LEAF HAS ESCAPED.

ONE OF THEM HAS LEFT THE CAGE.

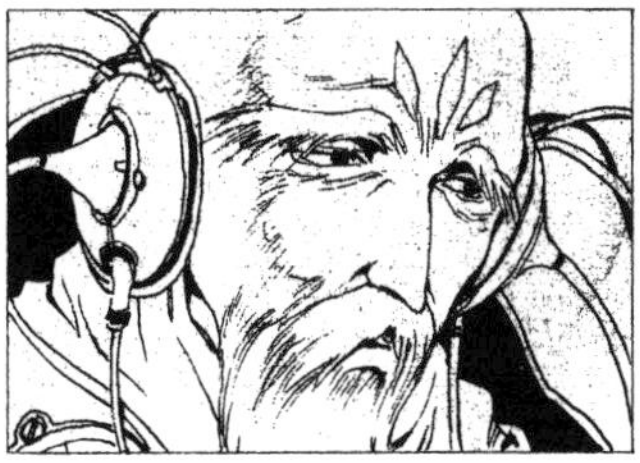

AT LEAST THEY DIDN'T BOTH LEAVE.

AZAIEA HASN'T FOUND OUT YET...

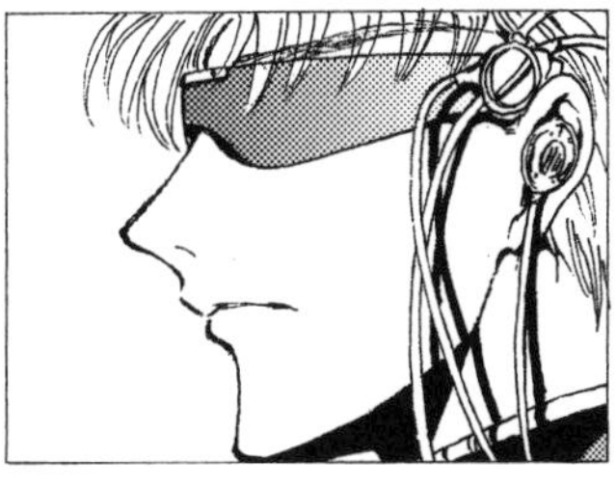

...BUT THE REAL PROBLEM IS THE COUNCIL.

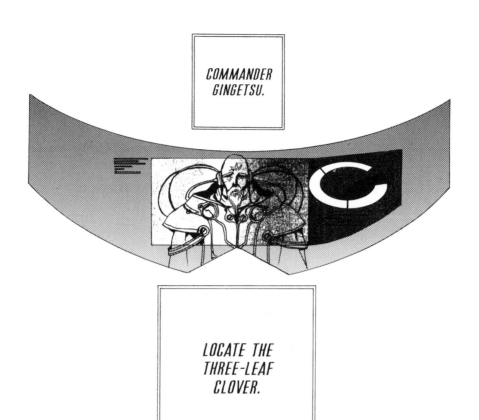

COMMANDER GINGETSU.

LOCATE THE THREE-LEAF CLOVER.

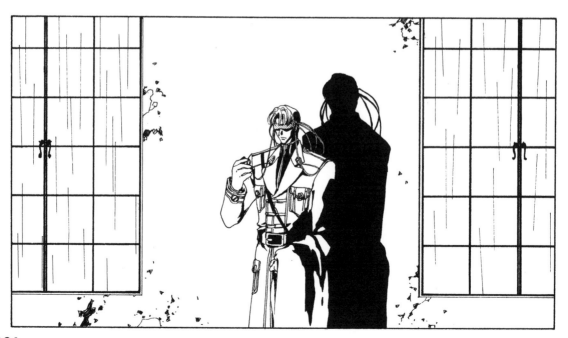

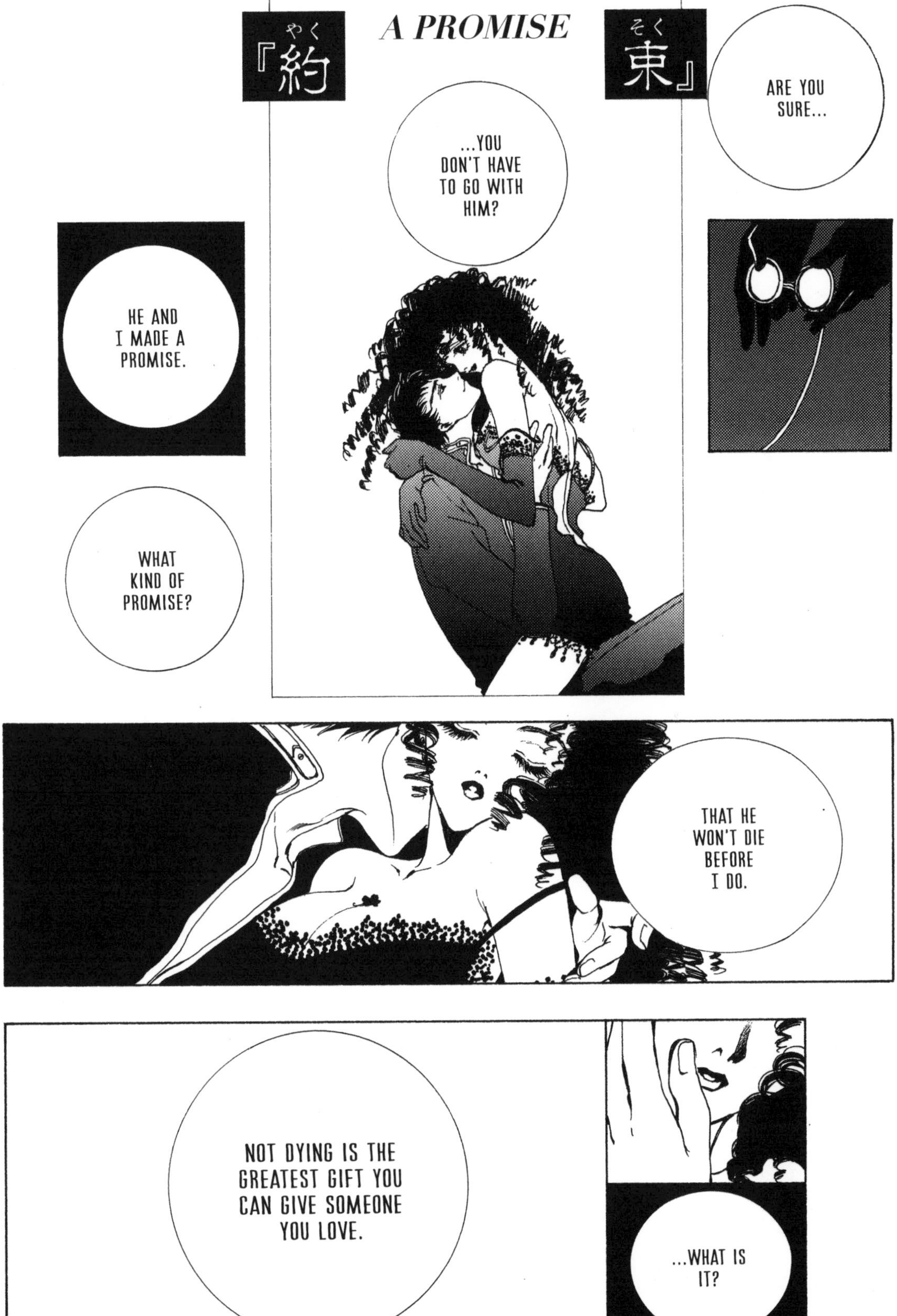
『約束』
A PROMISE
ARE YOU SURE...
...YOU DON'T HAVE TO GO WITH HIM?
HE AND I MADE A PROMISE.
WHAT KIND OF PROMISE?
THAT HE WON'T DIE BEFORE I DO.
...WHAT IS IT?
NOT DYING IS THE GREATEST GIFT YOU CAN GIVE SOMEONE YOU LOVE.

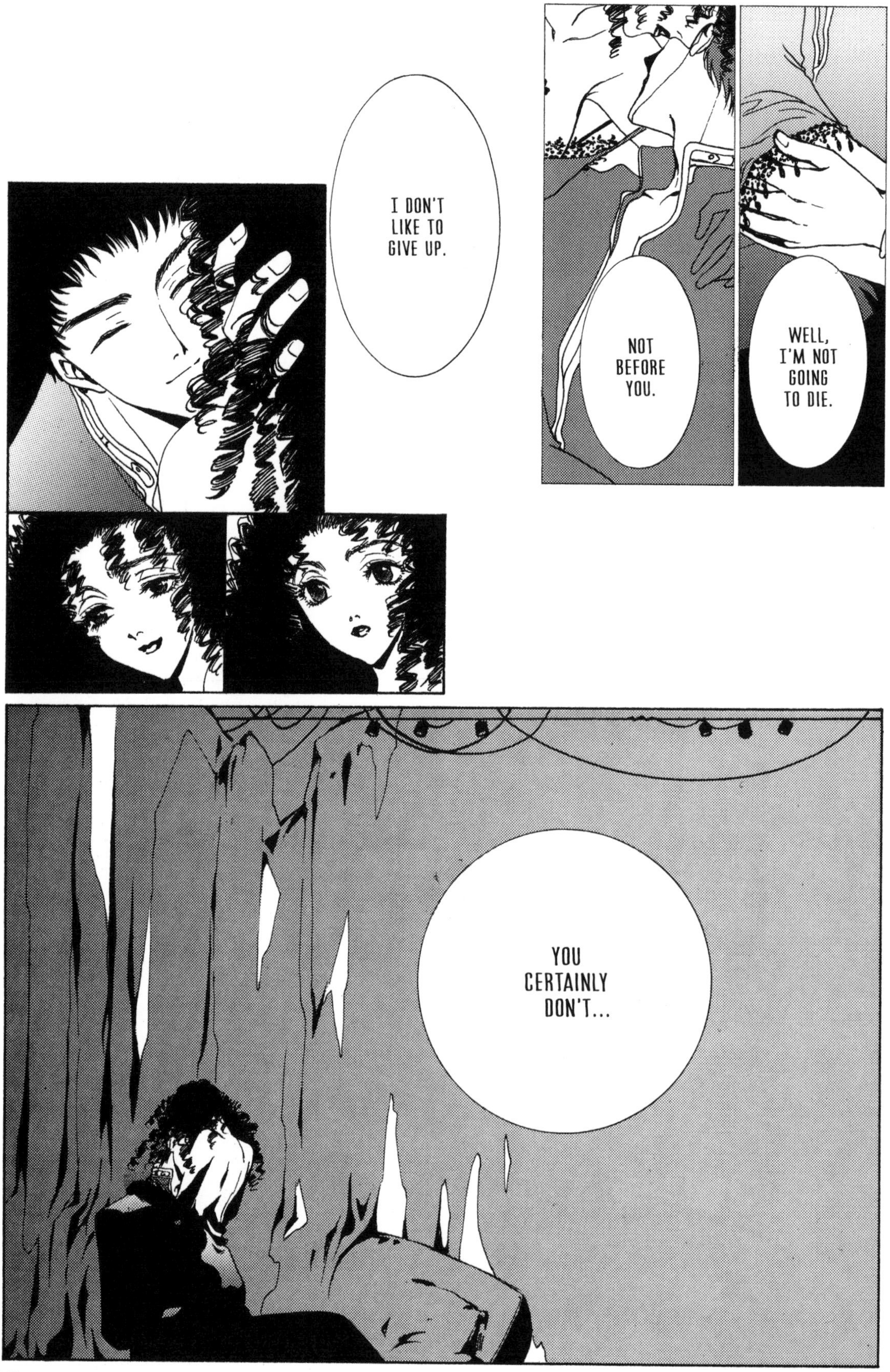
WELL, I'M NOT GOING TO DIE.
NOT BEFORE YOU.
I DON'T LIKE TO GIVE UP.
YOU CERTAINLY DON'T...

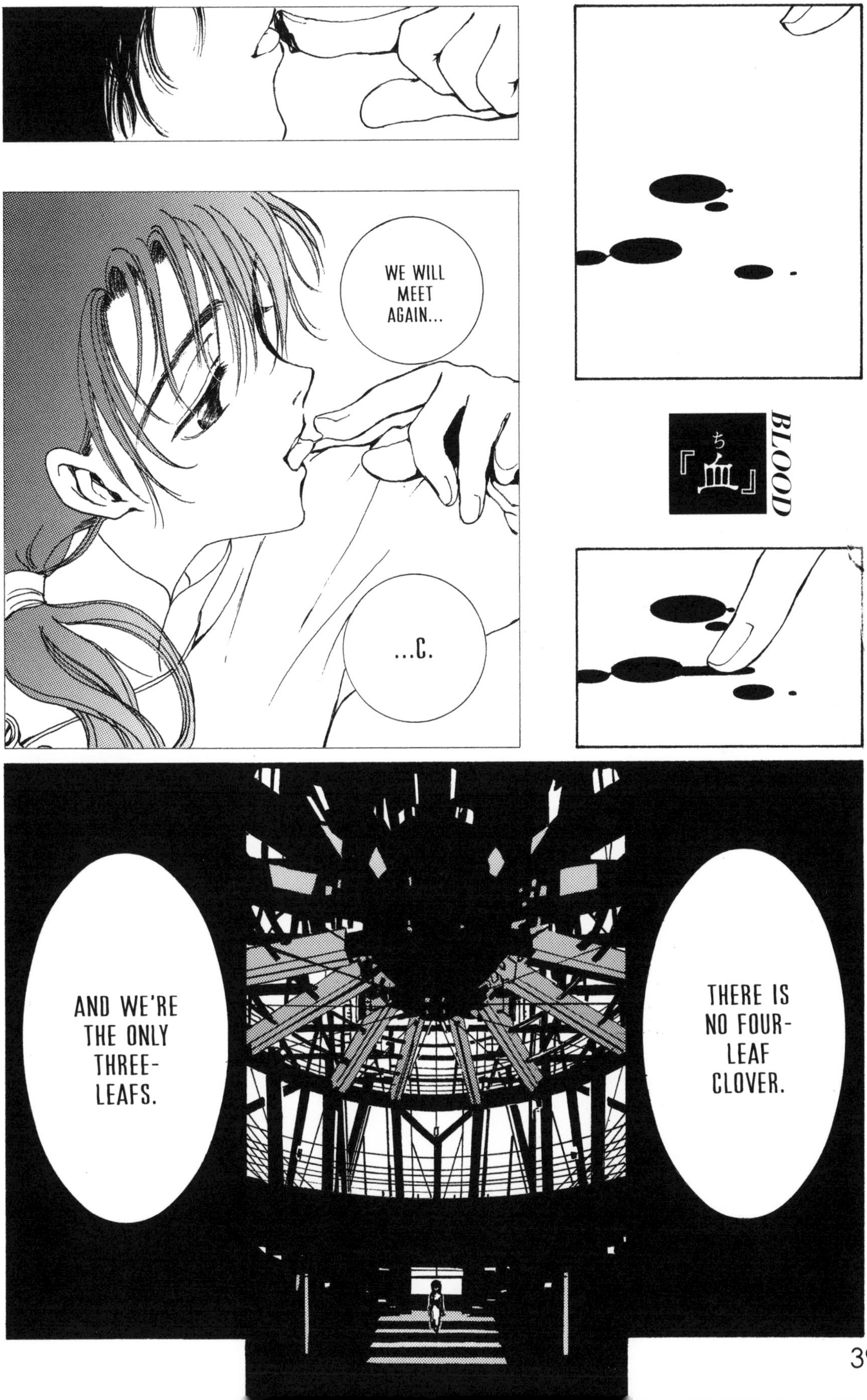

『血』
ち
BLOOD
WE WILL MEET AGAIN...
...C.
THERE IS NO FOUR-LEAF CLOVER.
AND WE'RE THE ONLY THREE-LEAFS.

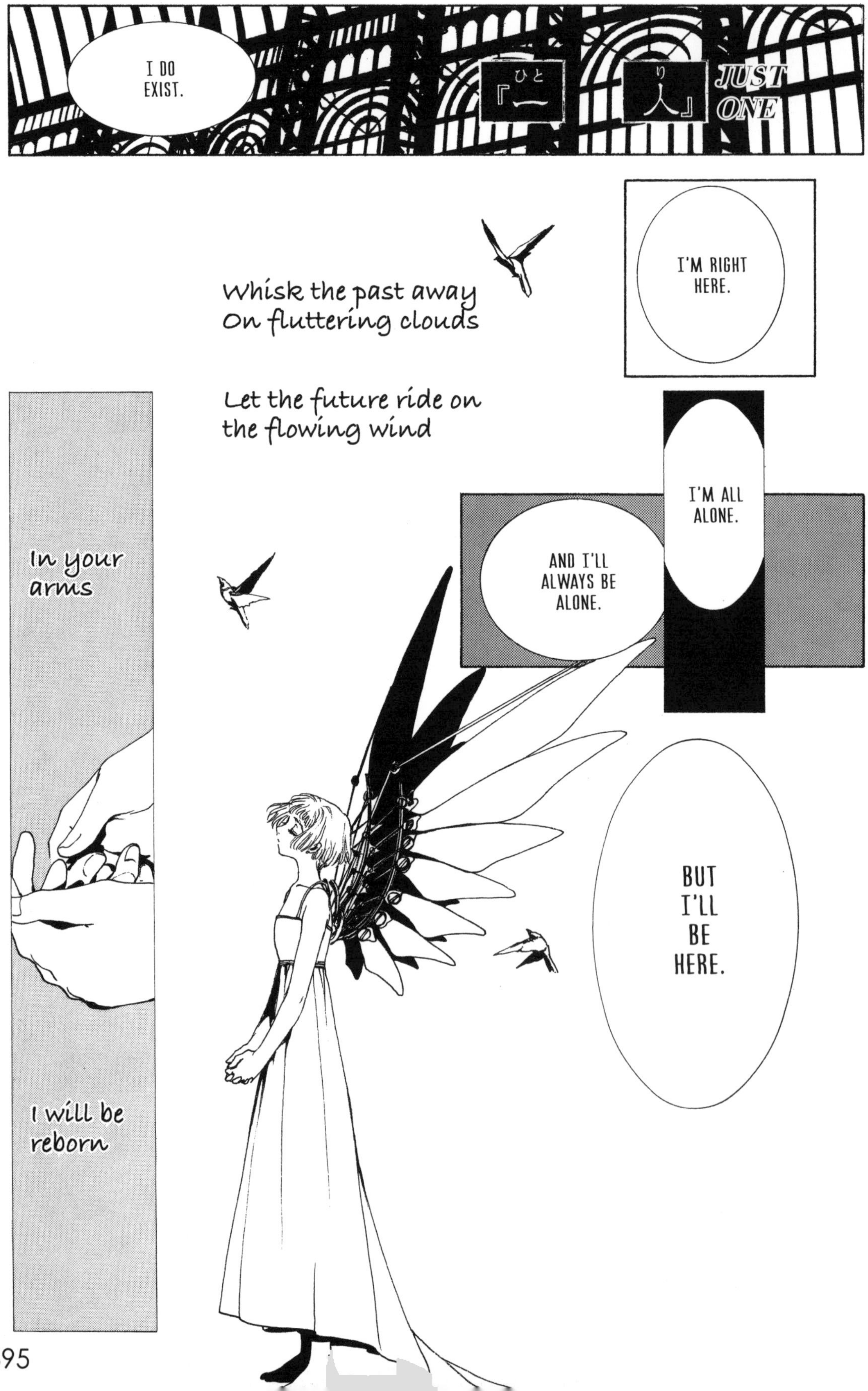
『一人』
JUST ONE
I DO EXIST.
I'M RIGHT HERE.
Whisk the past away On fluttering clouds
Let the future ride on the flowing wind
I'M ALL ALONE.
AND I'LL ALWAYS BE ALONE.
BUT I'LL BE HERE.
In your arms
I will be reborn

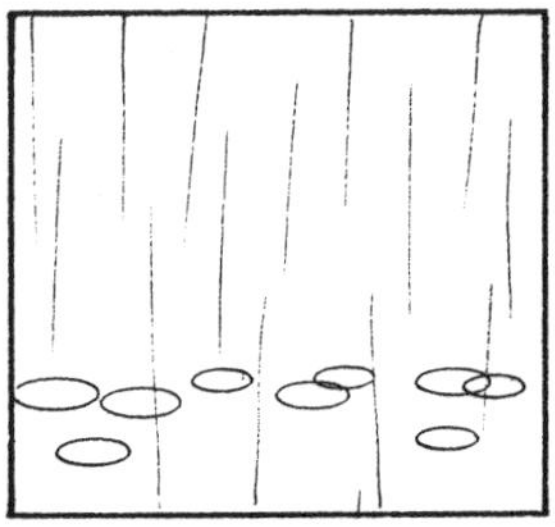
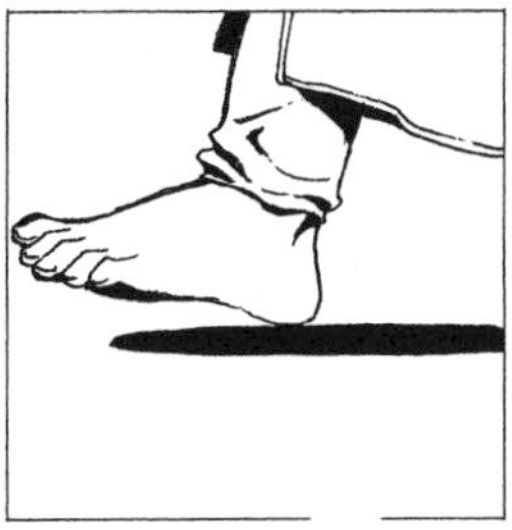
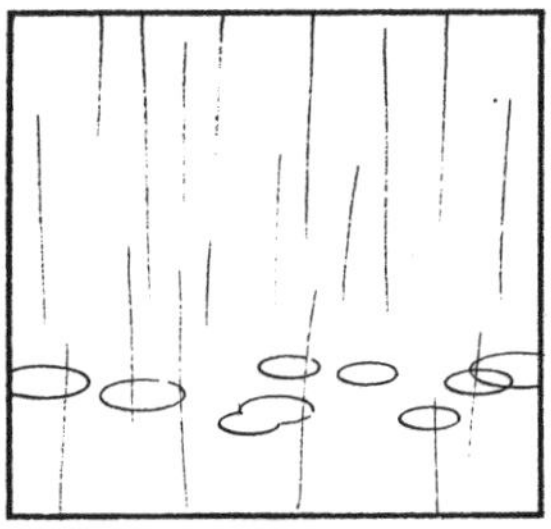

『追われる者』 THE HUNTED

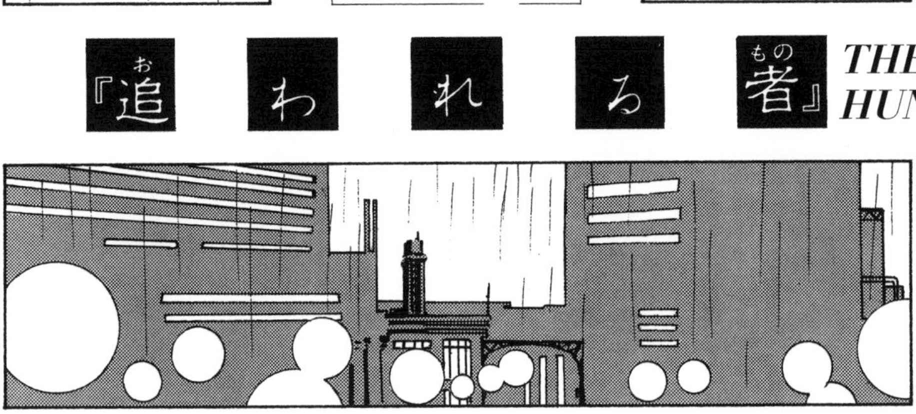
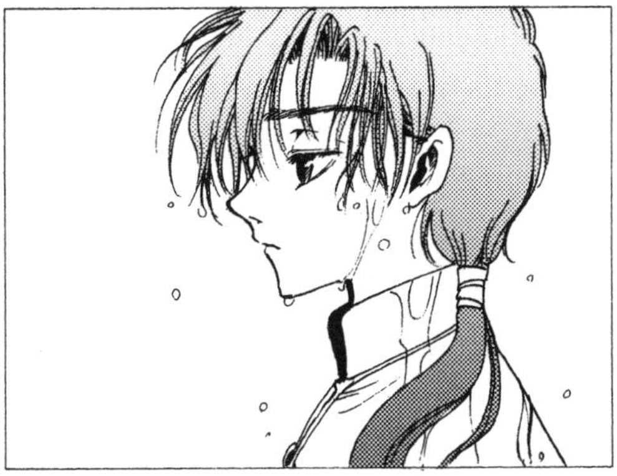
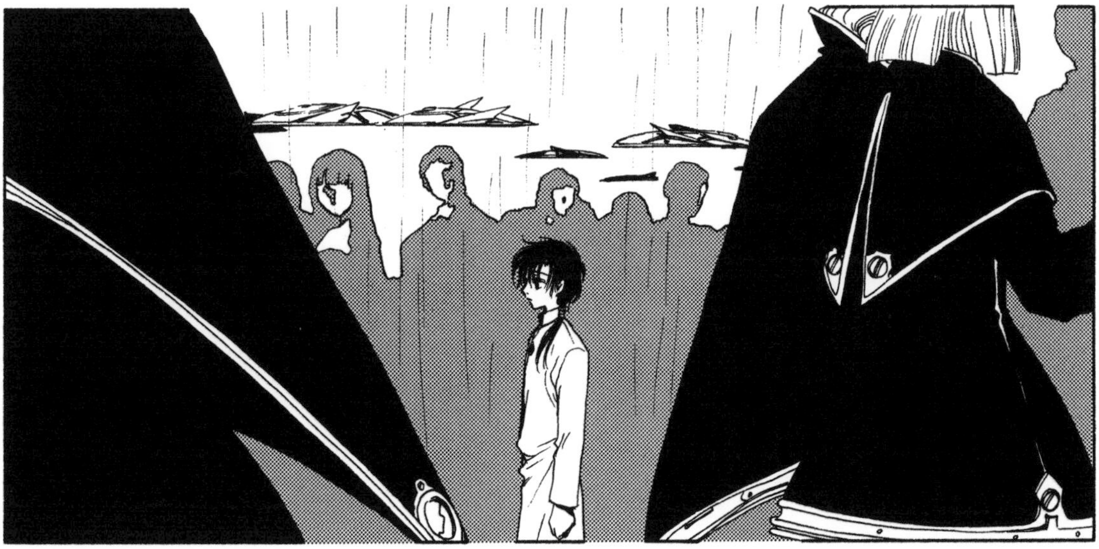

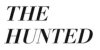

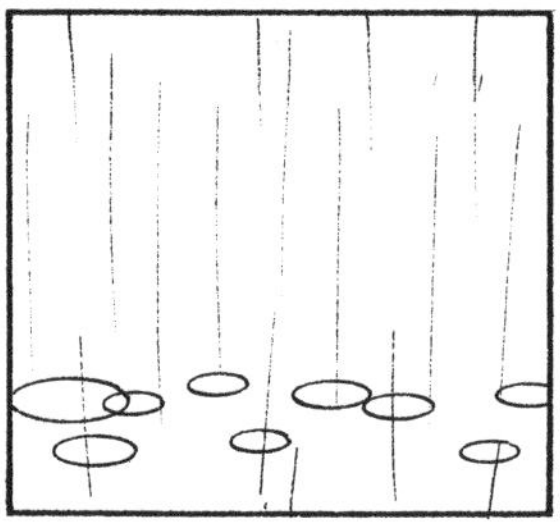
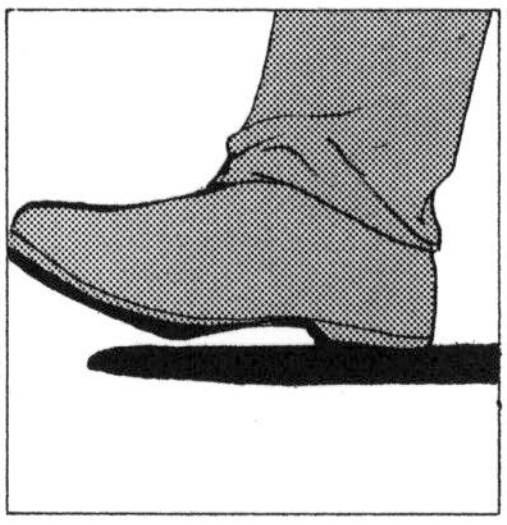
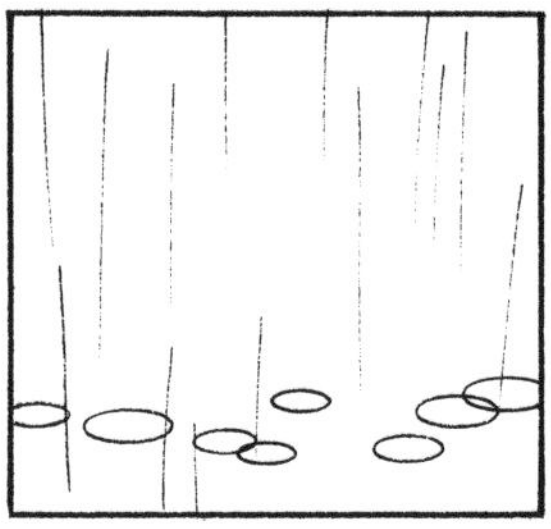

THE HUNTER『追う者』

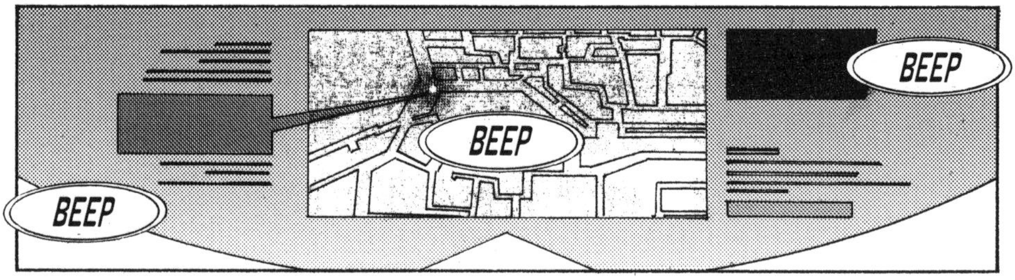
BEEP
BEEP
BEEP

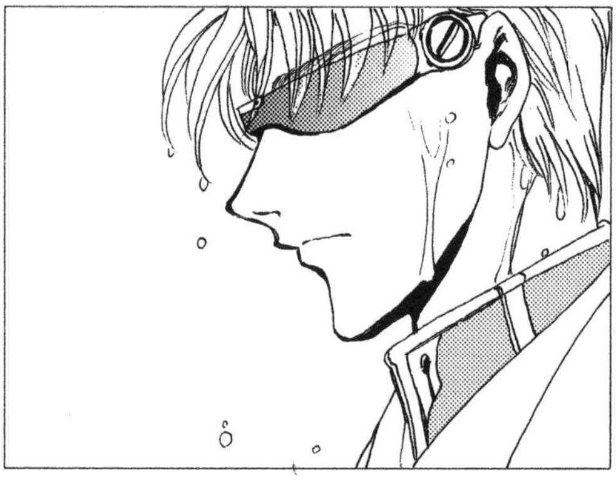
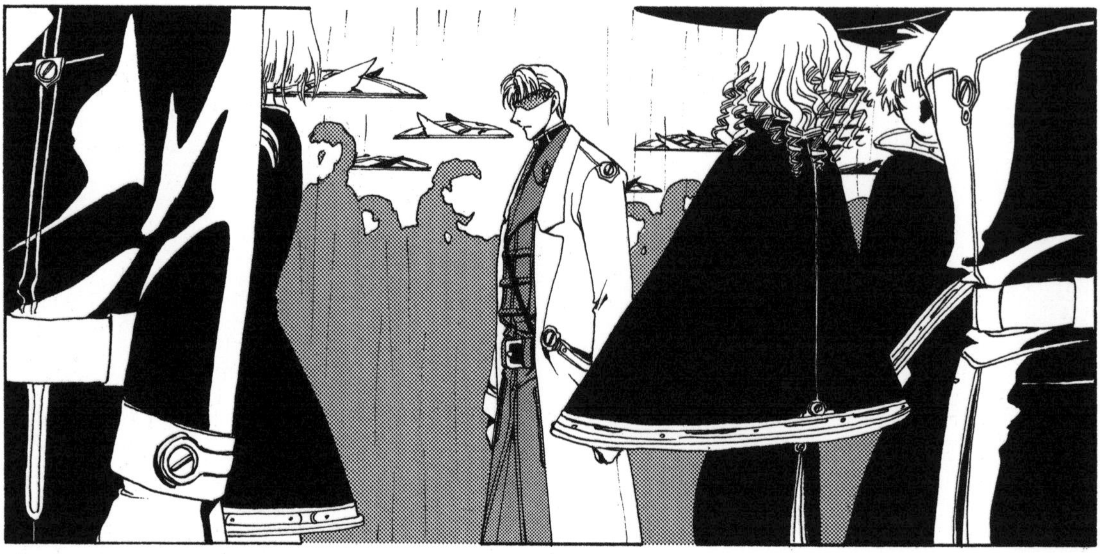

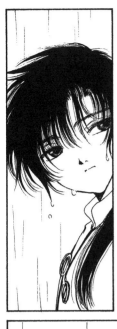

YOU
MUST
BE C.

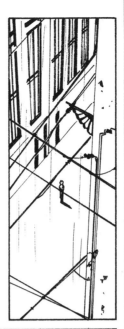

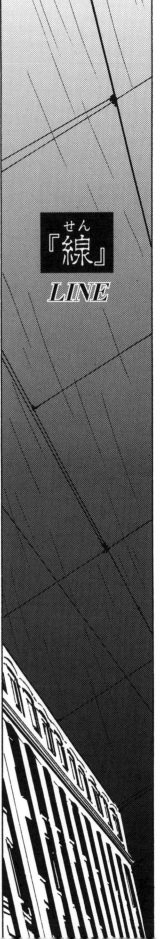

『線』
LINE

COME
WITH
US.

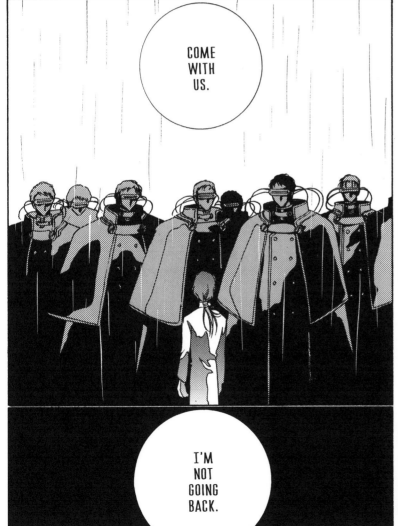

I'M
NOT
GOING
BACK.

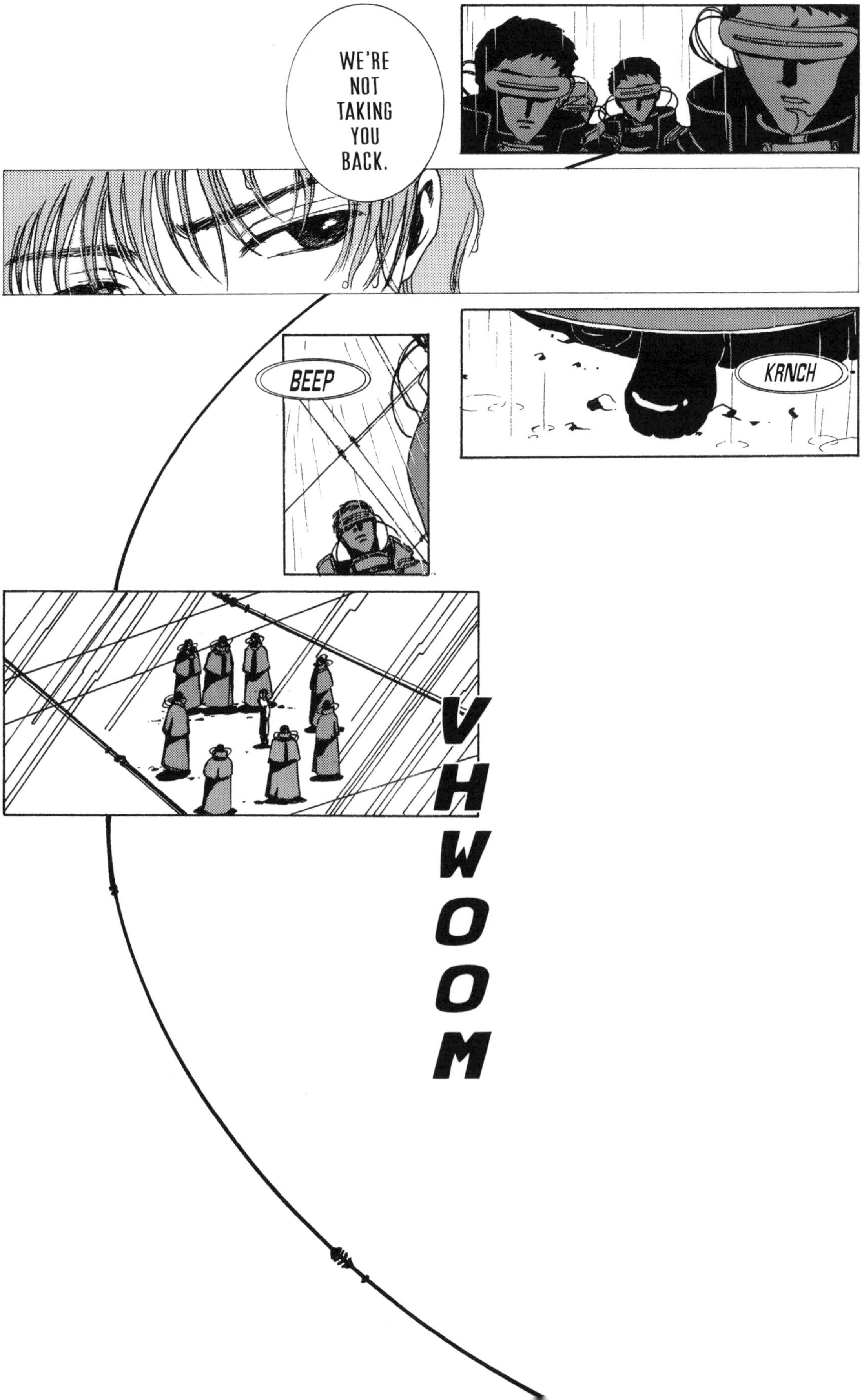
WE'RE NOT TAKING YOU BACK.
KRNCH
BEEP
VHWOOM

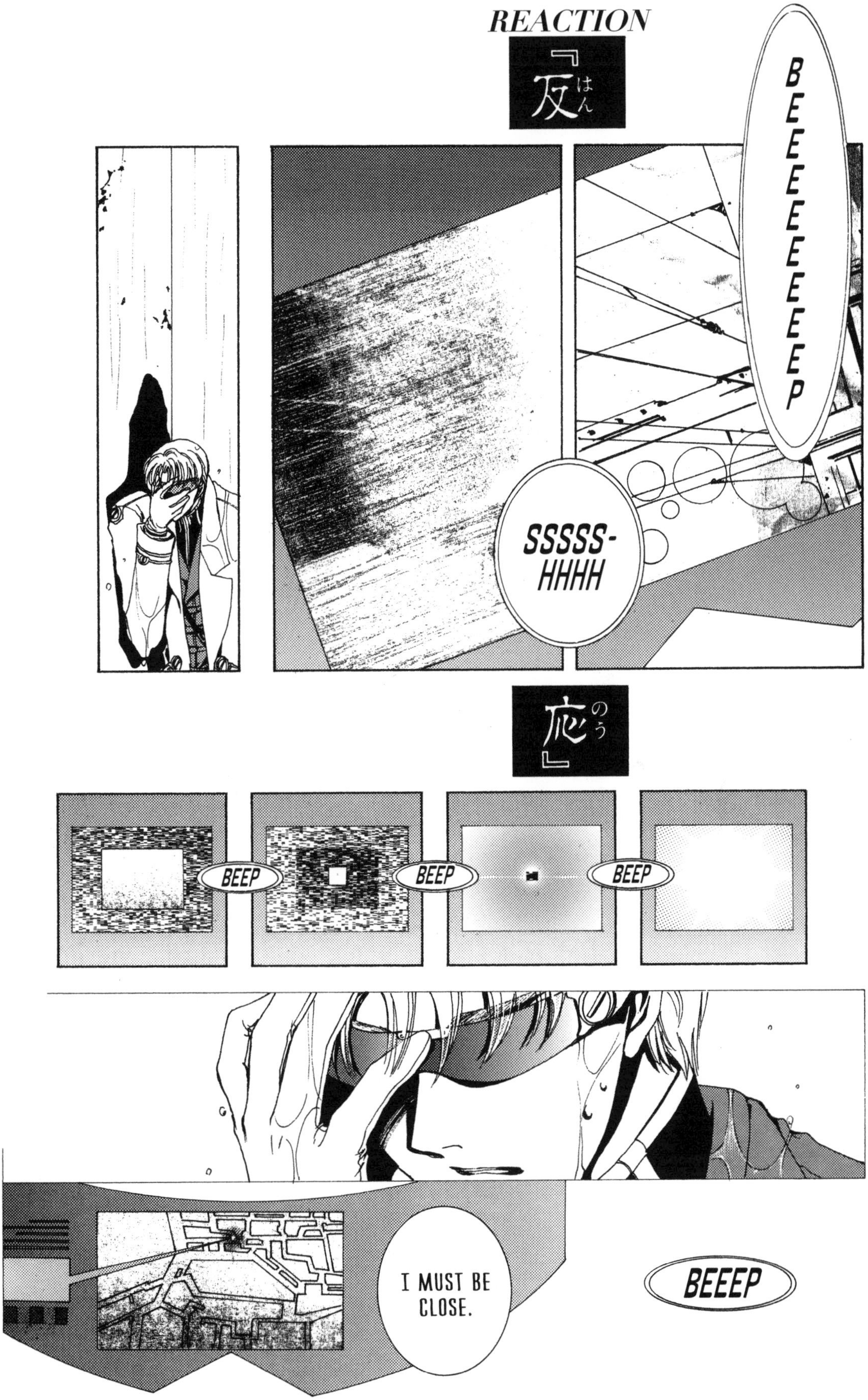

REACTION
『反はん
BEEEEEEEEEP
SSSSS-HHHH
応のう』
BEEP
BEEP
BEEP
BEEEP
I MUST BE CLOSE.

SPIDERWEB

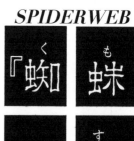

『蜘蛛の巣』

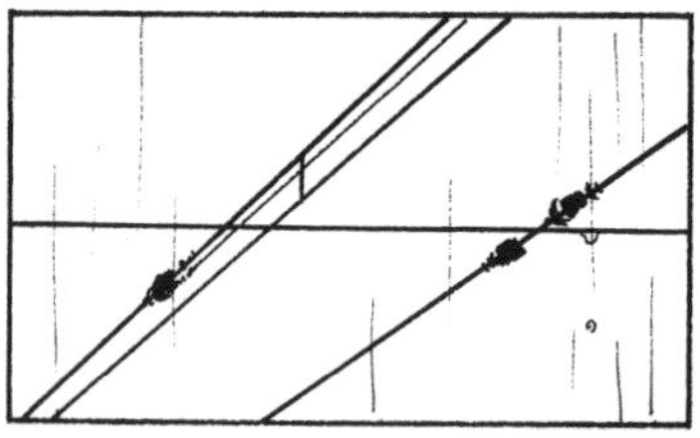

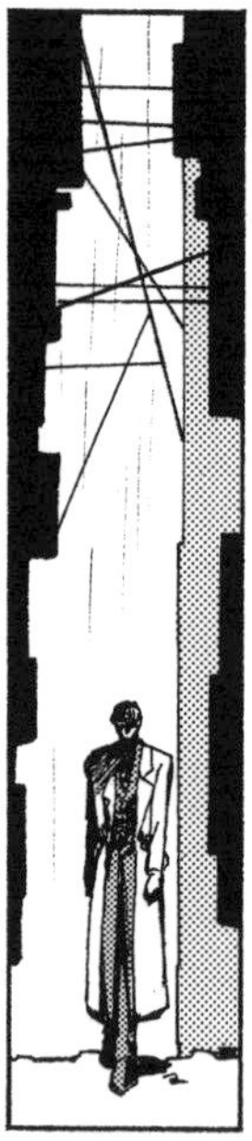

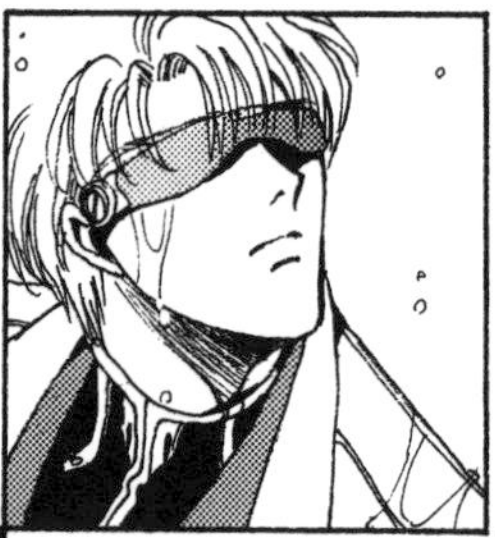

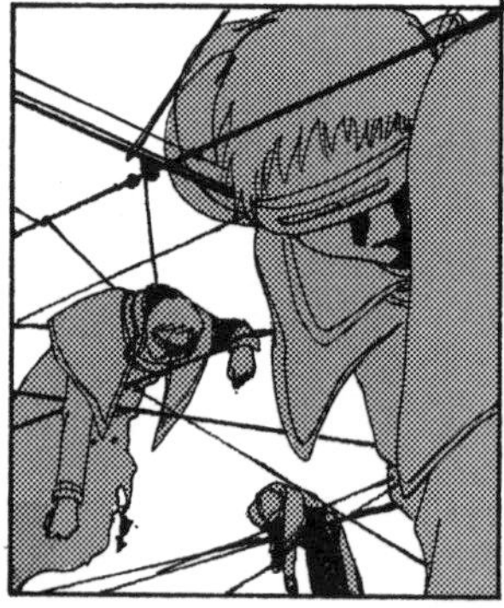

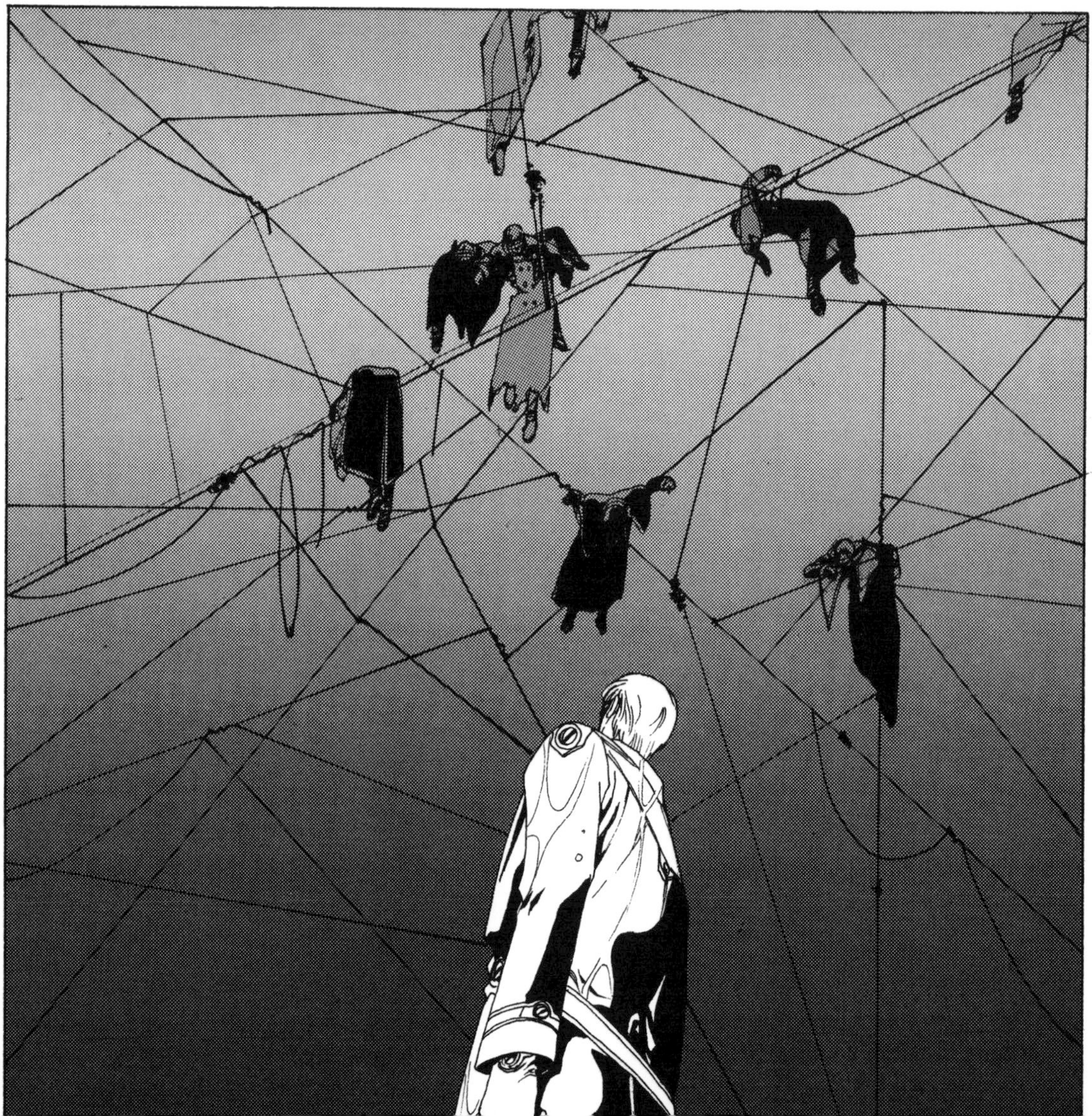

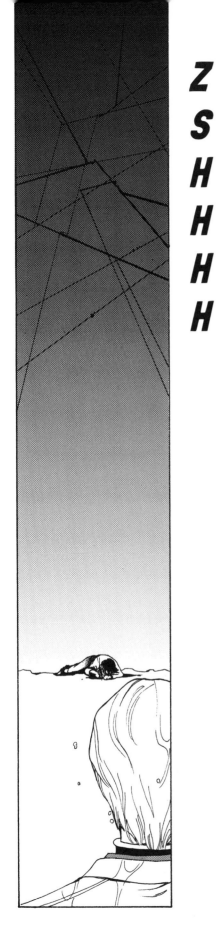
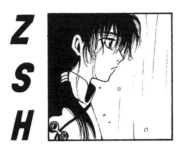
Z
S
H
H
H
H
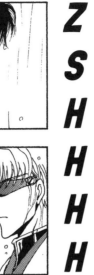
Z
S
H
H
H
H
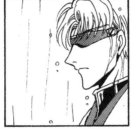

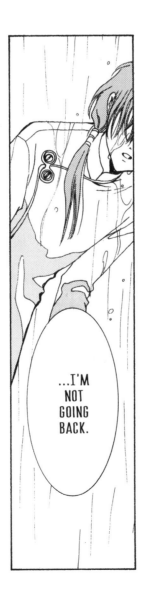

...I'M
NOT
GOING
BACK.

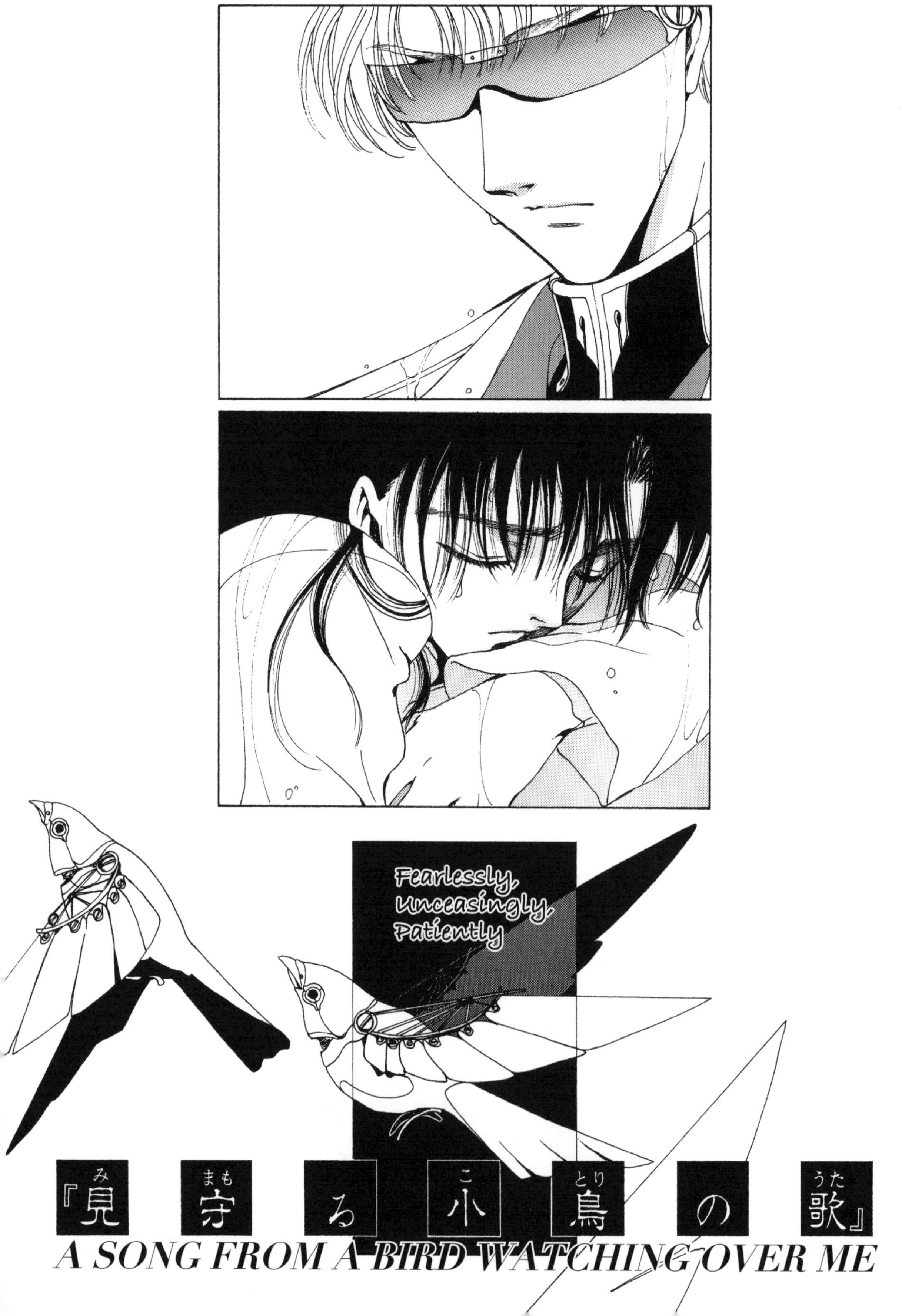
Fearlessly,
Unceasingly,
Patiently
『見守る小鳥の歌』
A SONG FROM A BIRD WATCHING OVER ME

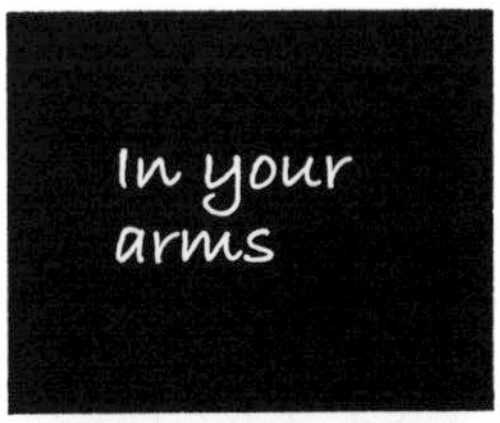
In your arms
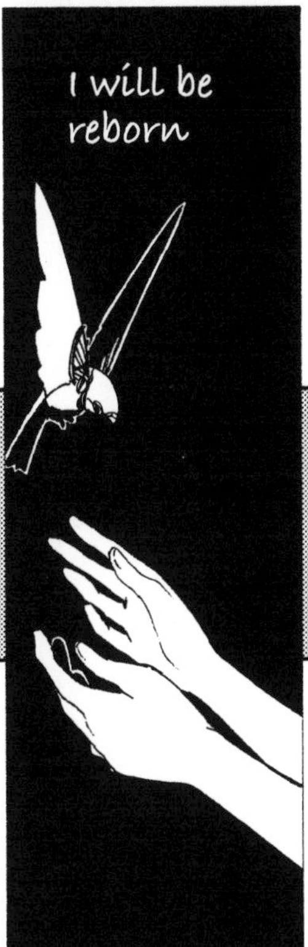
I will be reborn
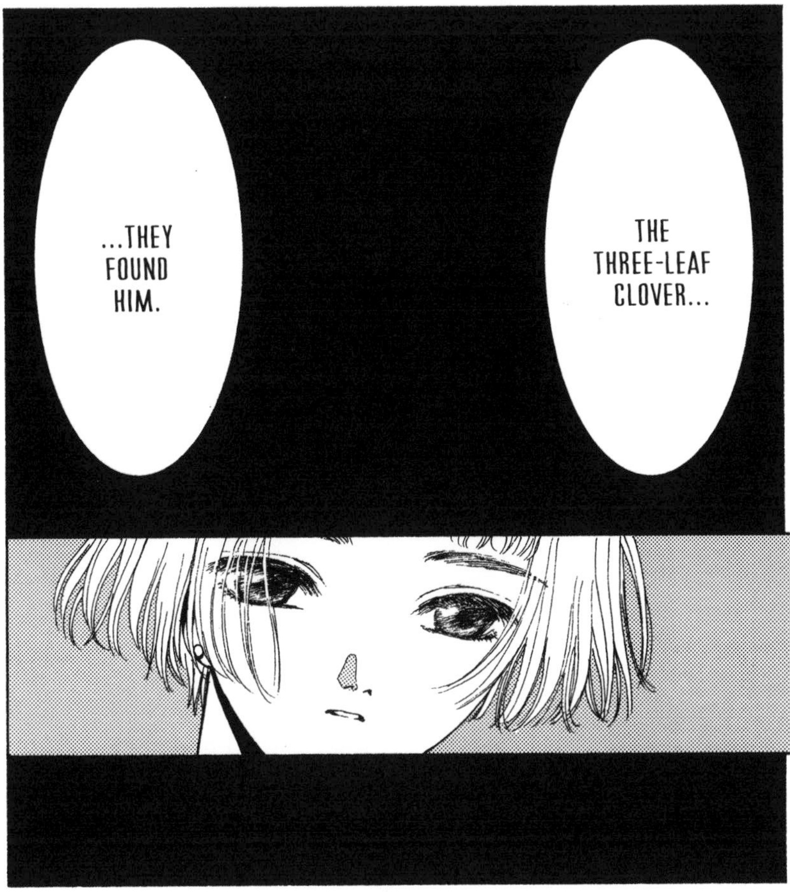
THE THREE-LEAF CLOVER...
...THEY FOUND HIM.
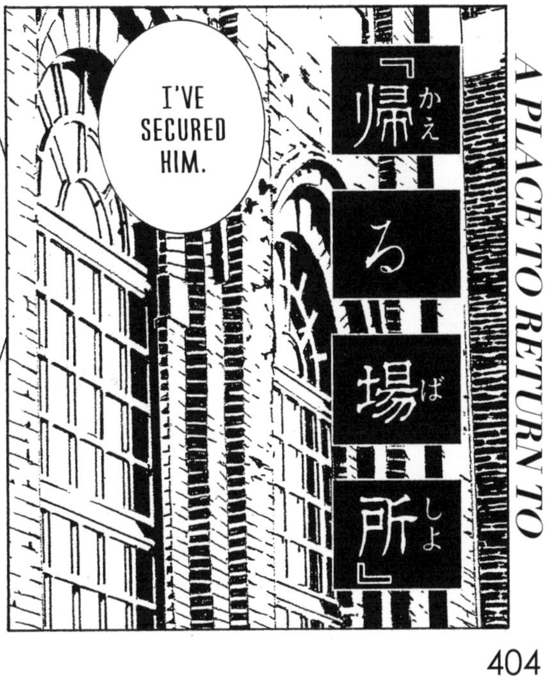
A PLACE TO RETURN TO
『帰る場所』
I'VE SECURED HIM.
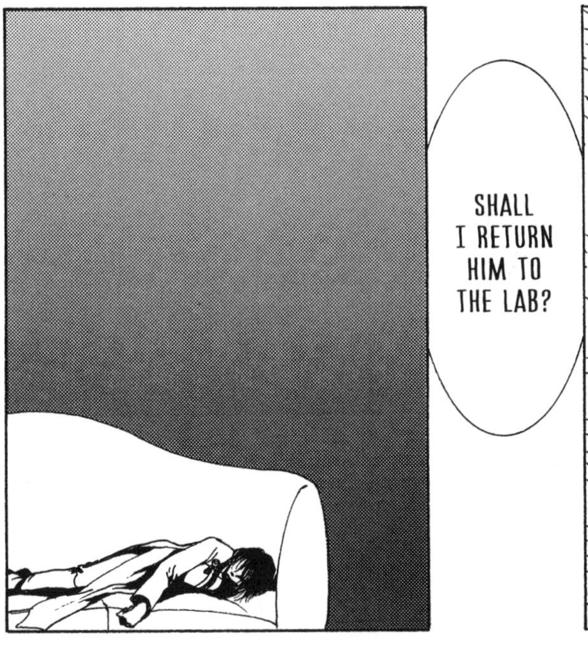
SHALL I RETURN HIM TO THE LAB?

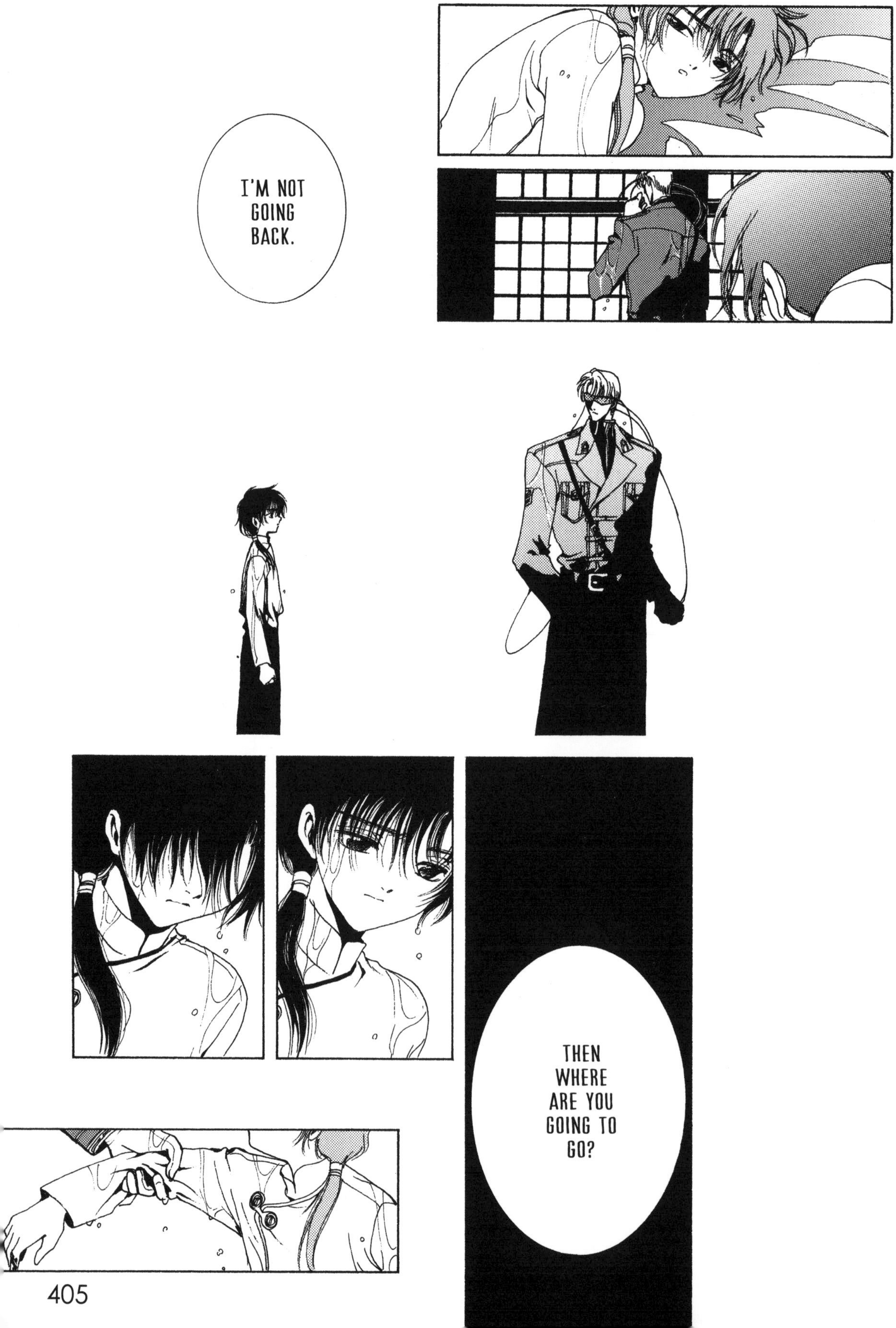
I'M NOT GOING BACK.
THEN WHERE ARE YOU GOING TO GO?

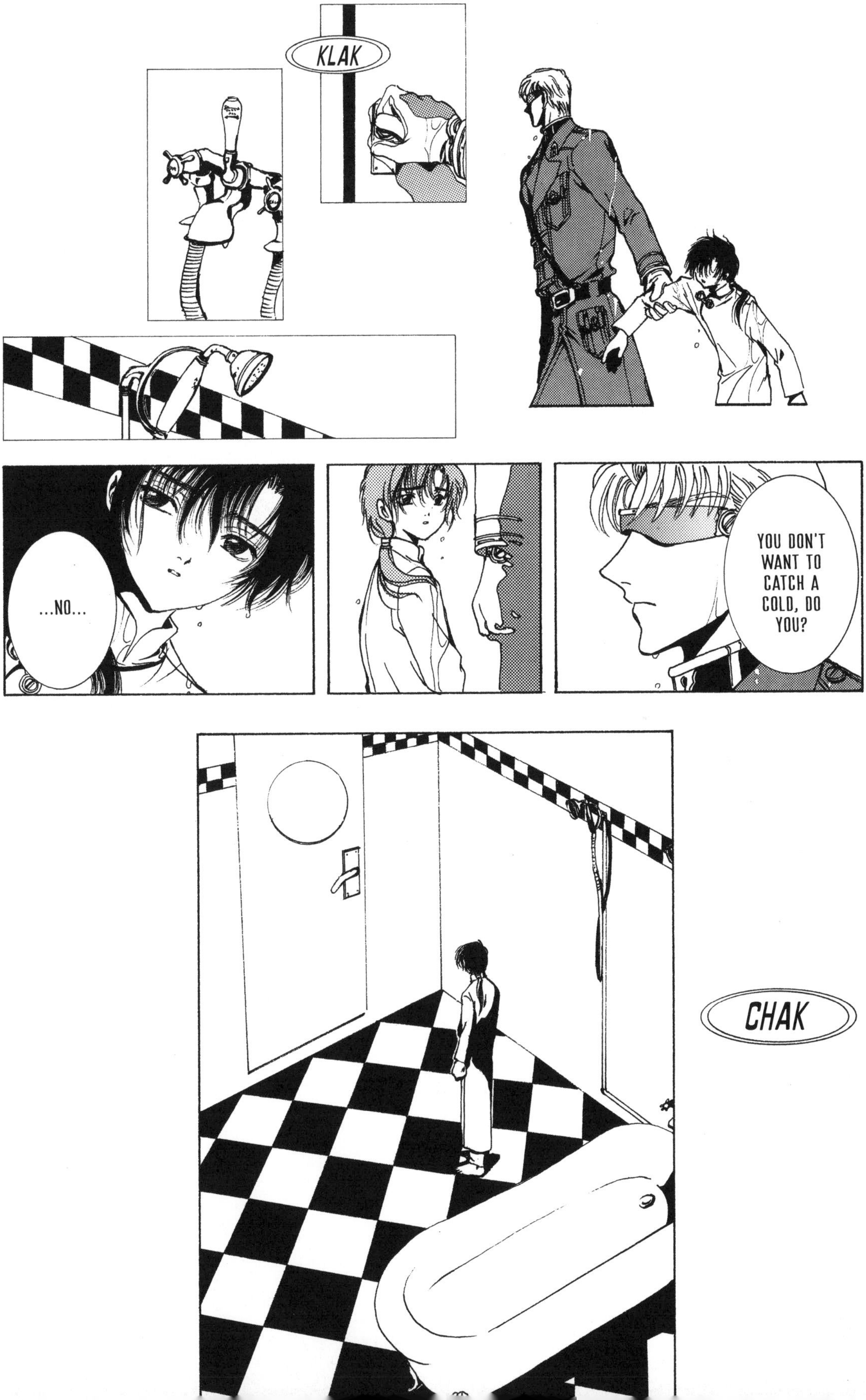
KLAK
YOU DON'T WANT TO CATCH A COLD, DO YOU?
...NO...
CHAK

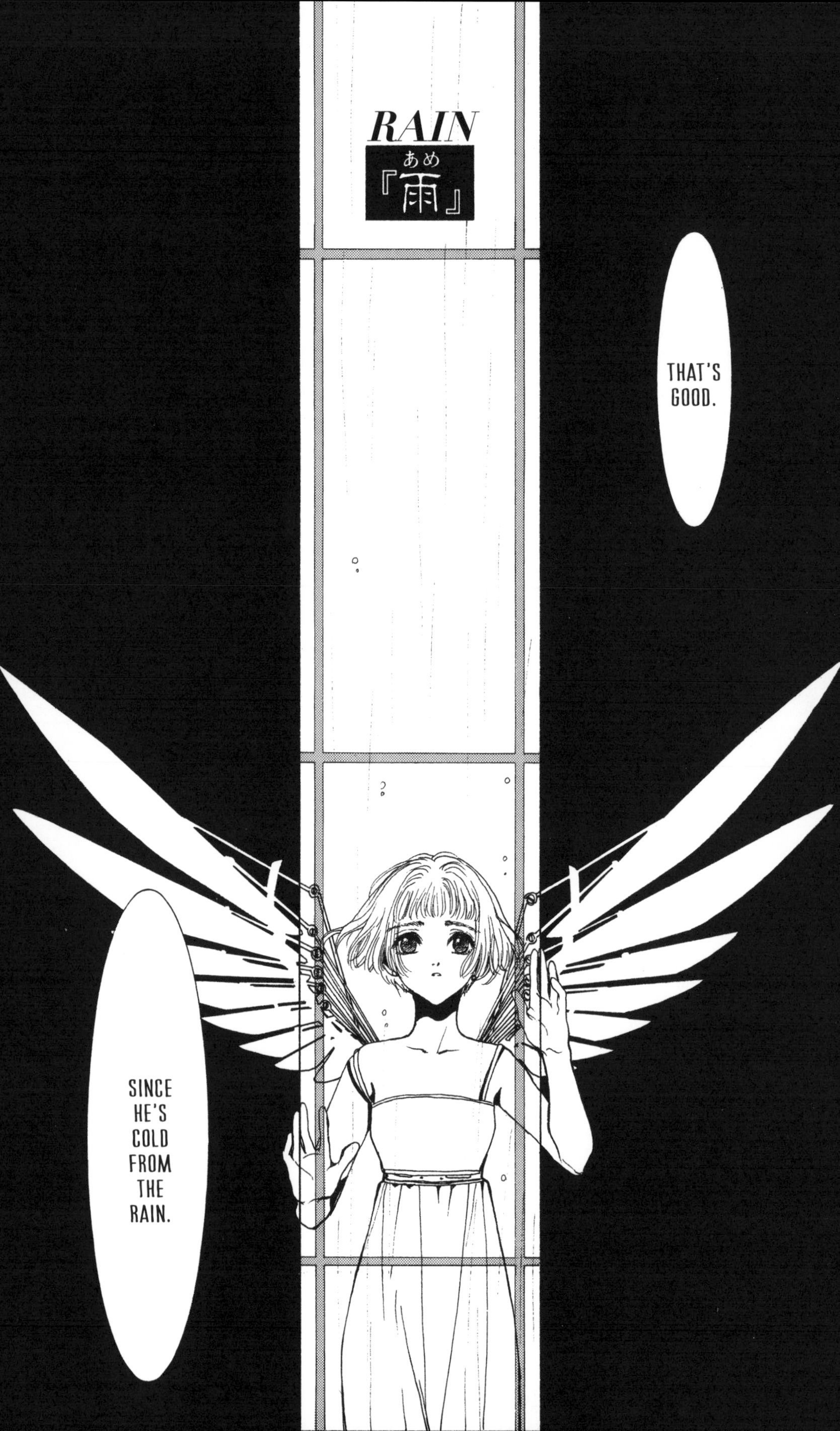
RAIN
あめ
『雨』
THAT'S GOOD.
SINCE HE'S COLD FROM THE RAIN.

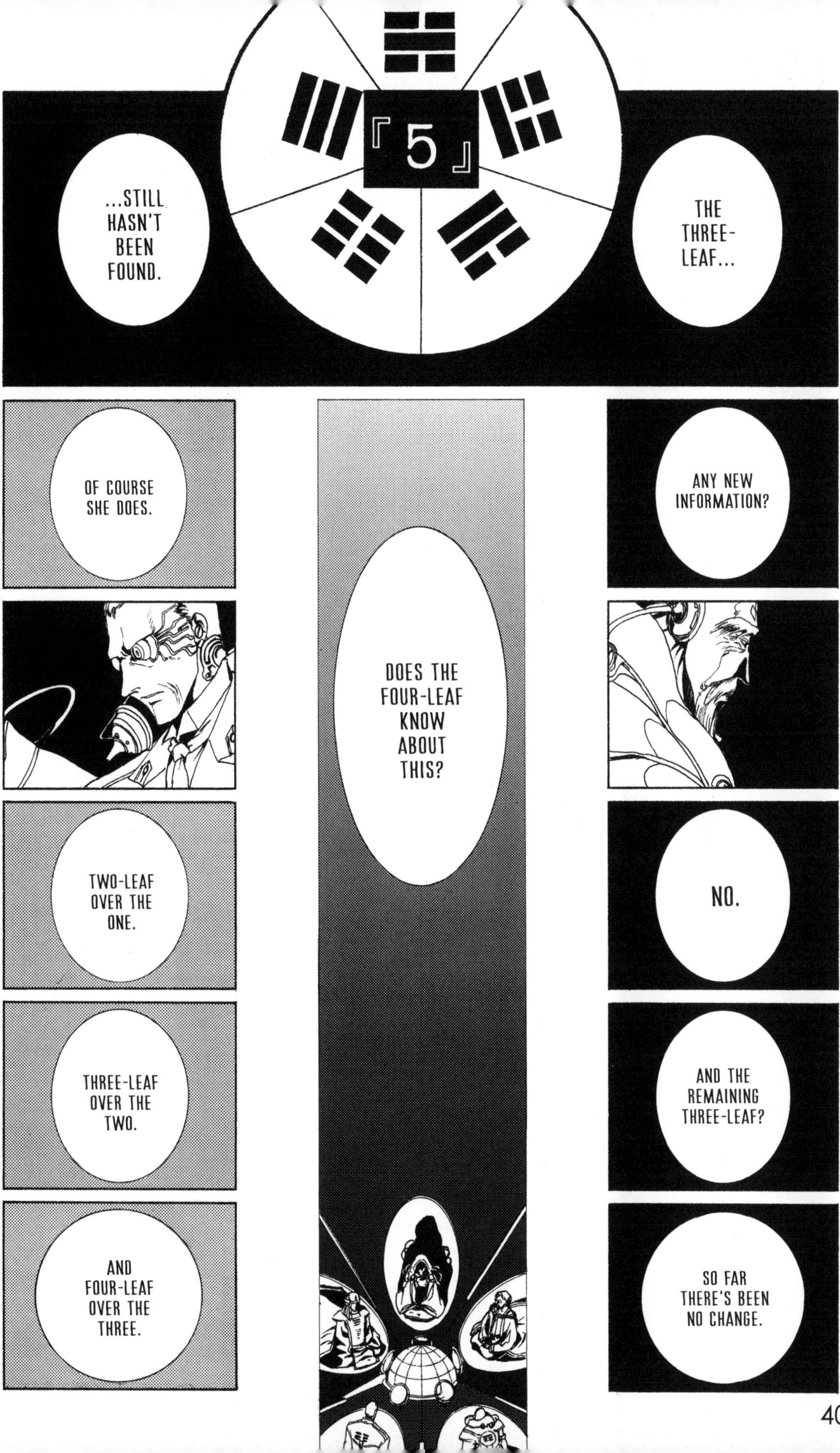
『5』
THE THREE-LEAF...
...STILL HASN'T BEEN FOUND.
ANY NEW INFORMATION?
NO.
AND THE REMAINING THREE-LEAF?
SO FAR THERE'S BEEN NO CHANGE.
DOES THE FOUR-LEAF KNOW ABOUT THIS?
OF COURSE SHE DOES.
TWO-LEAF OVER THE ONE.
THREE-LEAF OVER THE TWO.
AND FOUR-LEAF OVER THE THREE.

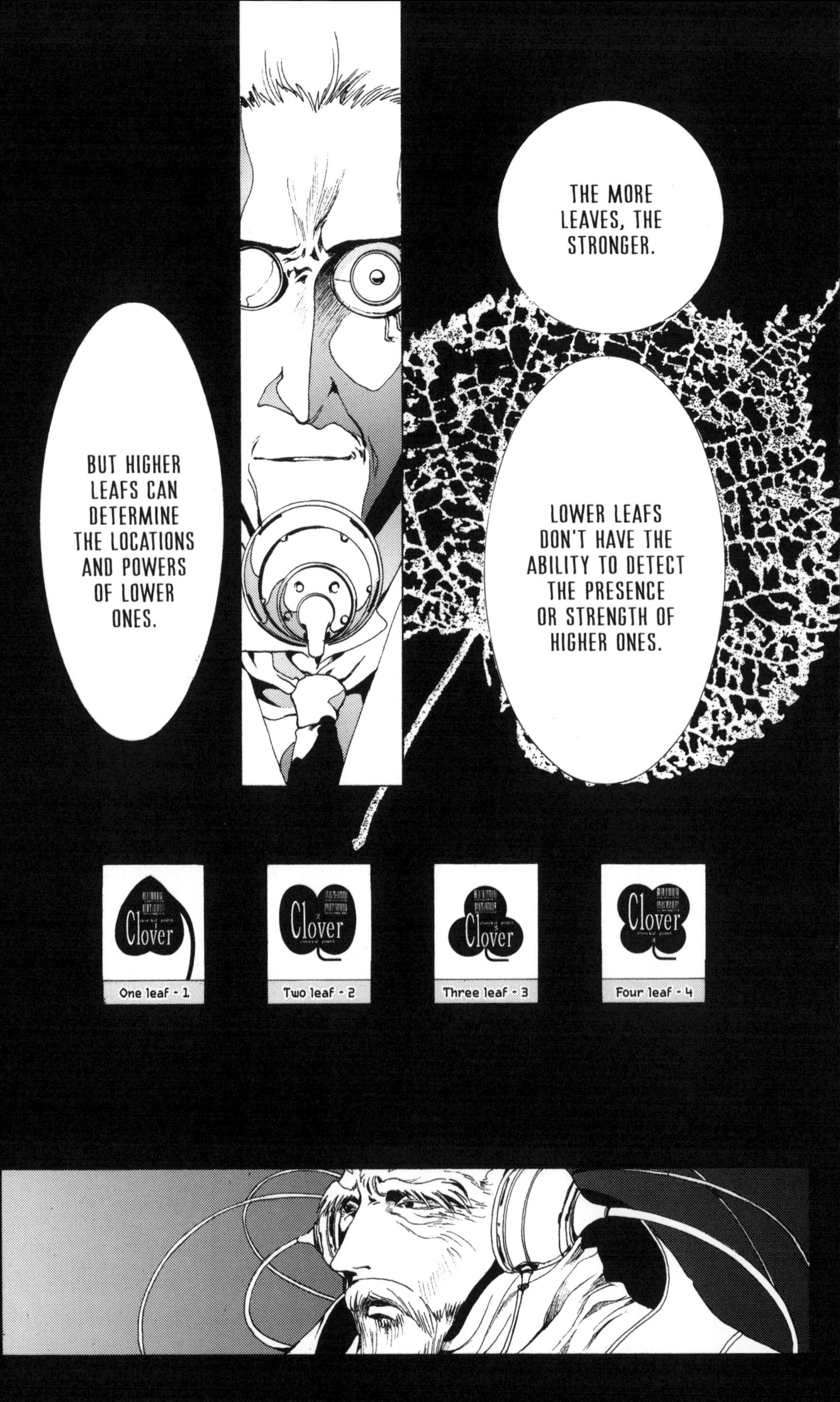
THE MORE LEAVES, THE STRONGER.
LOWER LEAFS DON'T HAVE THE ABILITY TO DETECT THE PRESENCE OR STRENGTH OF HIGHER ONES.
BUT HIGHER LEAFS CAN DETERMINE THE LOCATIONS AND POWERS OF LOWER ONES.
Clover
One leaf - 1
Clover
Two leaf - 2
Clover
Three leaf - 3
Clover
Four leaf - 4

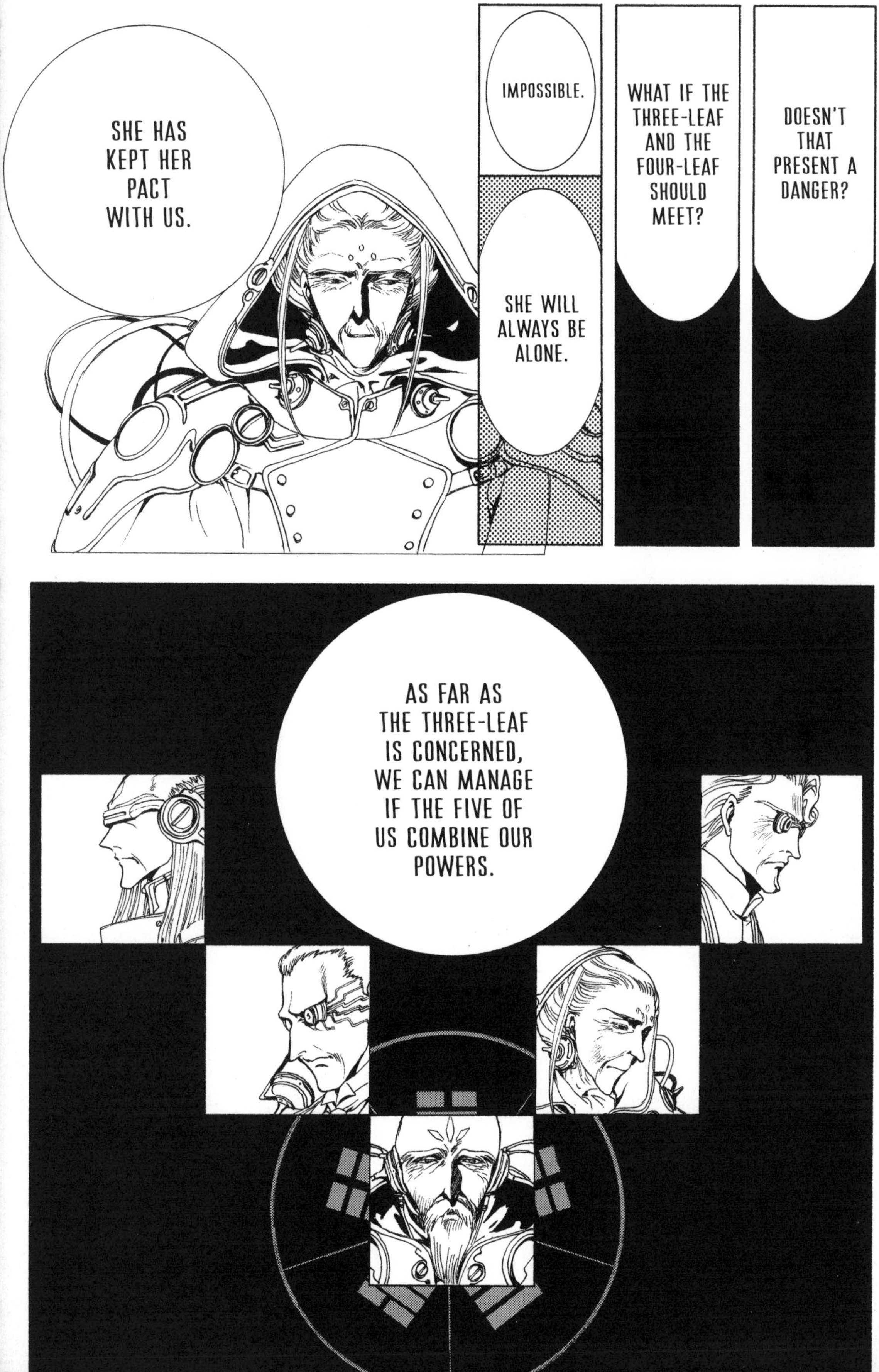
DOESN'T THAT PRESENT A DANGER?
WHAT IF THE THREE-LEAF AND THE FOUR-LEAF SHOULD MEET?
IMPOSSIBLE.
SHE WILL ALWAYS BE ALONE.
SHE HAS KEPT HER PACT WITH US.
AS FAR AS THE THREE-LEAF IS CONCERNED, WE CAN MANAGE IF THE FIVE OF US COMBINE OUR POWERS.

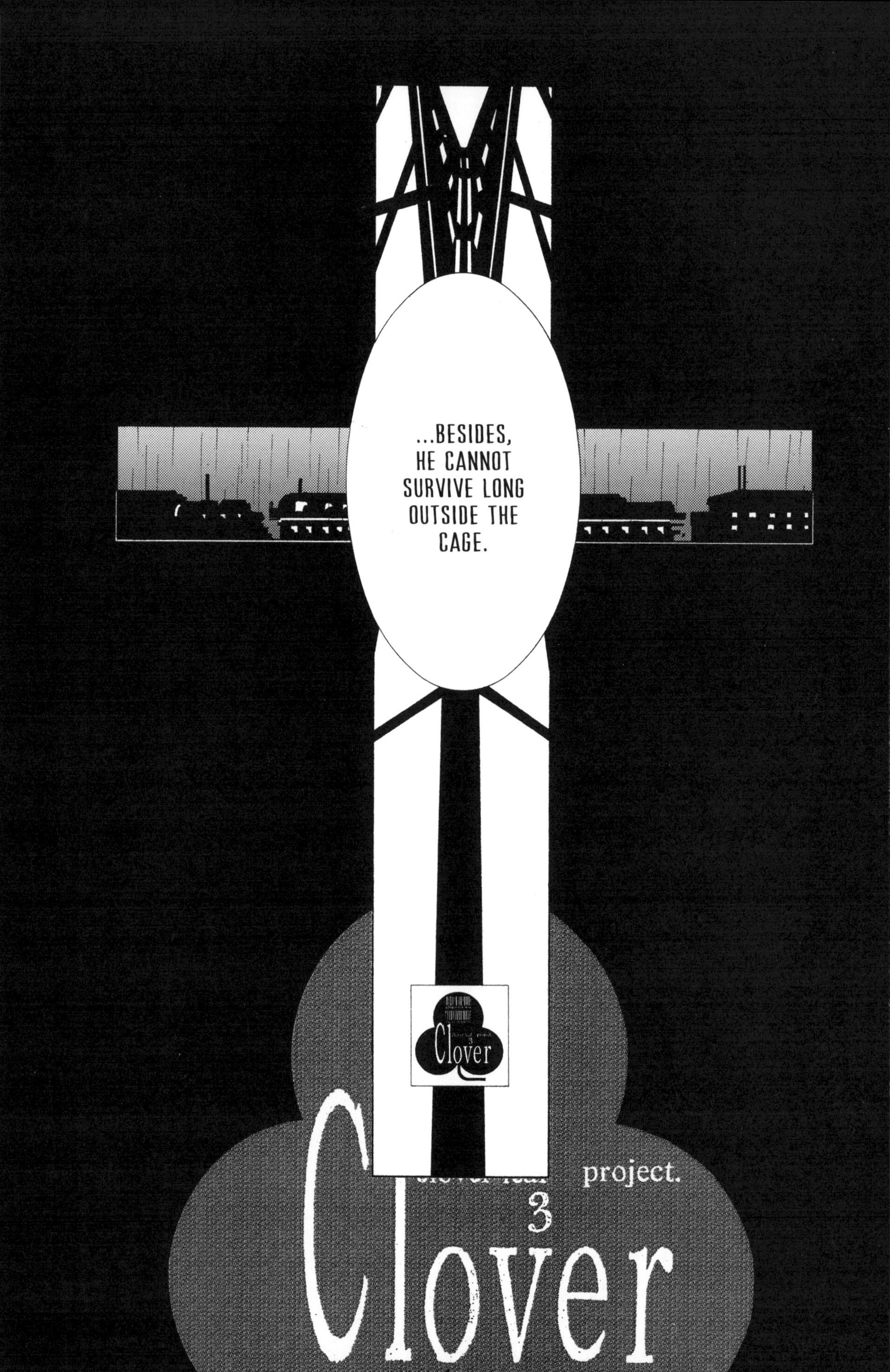
...BESIDES, HE CANNOT SURVIVE LONG OUTSIDE THE CAGE.
project.
3
Clover

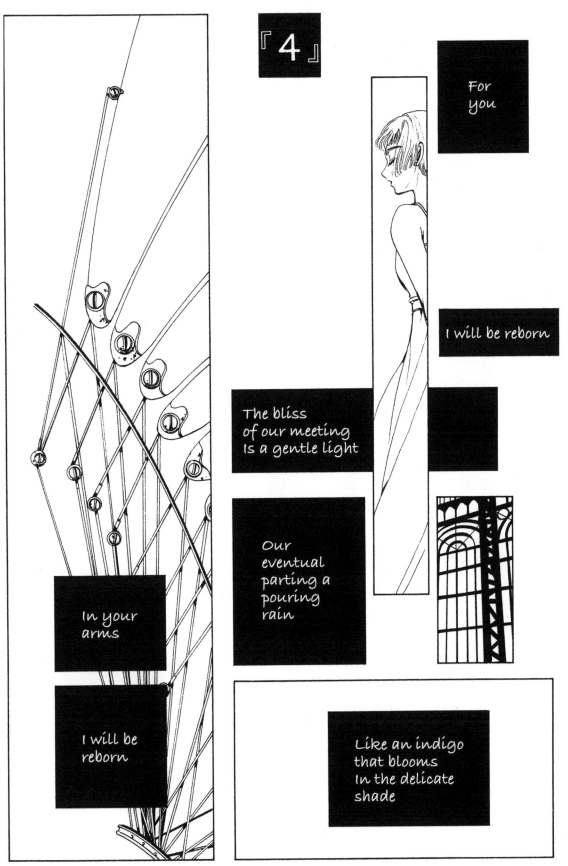

『4』

For
you

I will be reborn

The bliss
of our meeting
Is a gentle light

Our
eventual
parting a
pouring
rain

In your
arms

I will be
reborn

Like an indigo
that blooms
In the delicate
shade

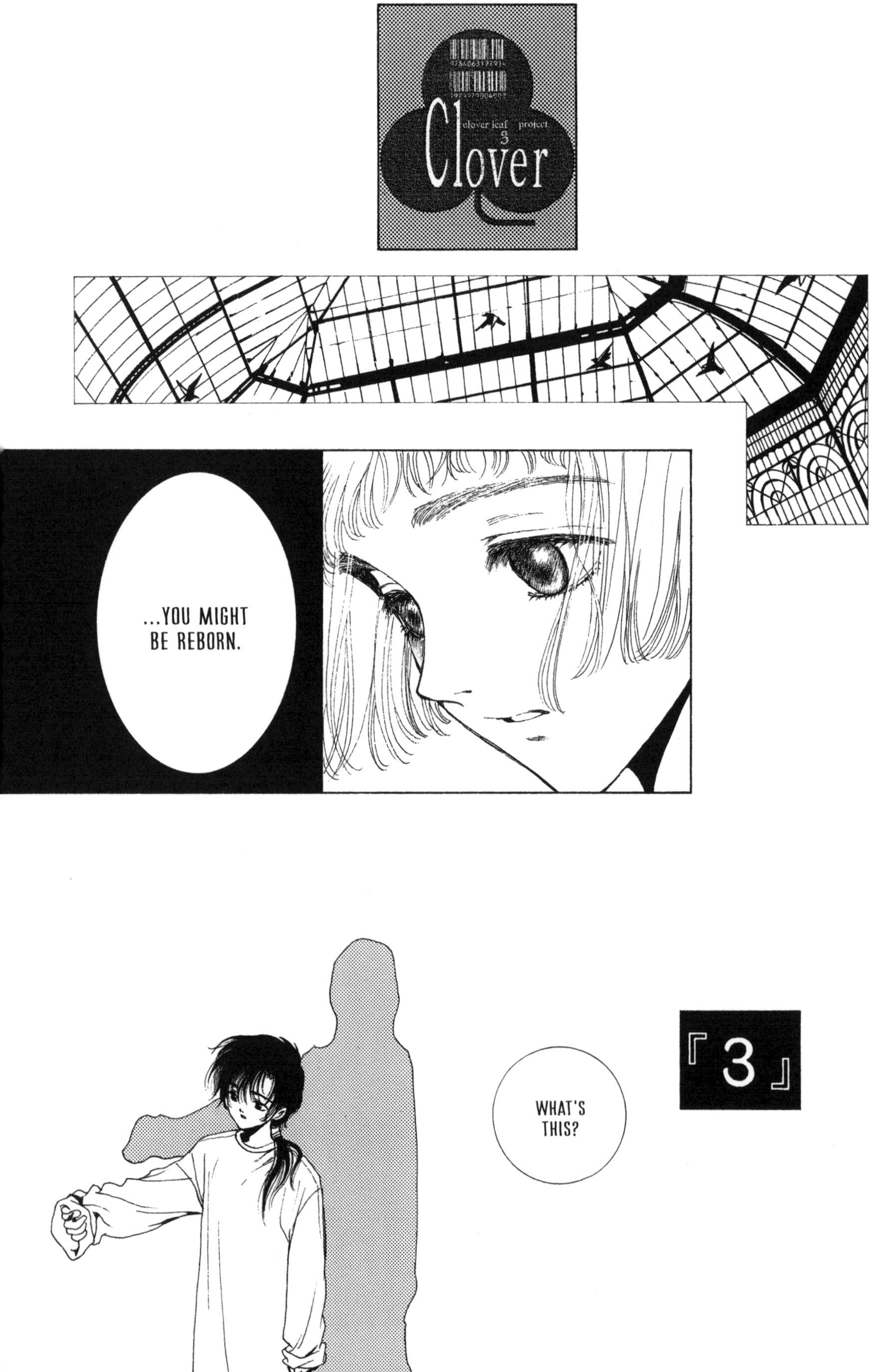
clover leaf project.
3
Clover
...YOU MIGHT BE REBORN.
『3』
WHAT'S THIS?

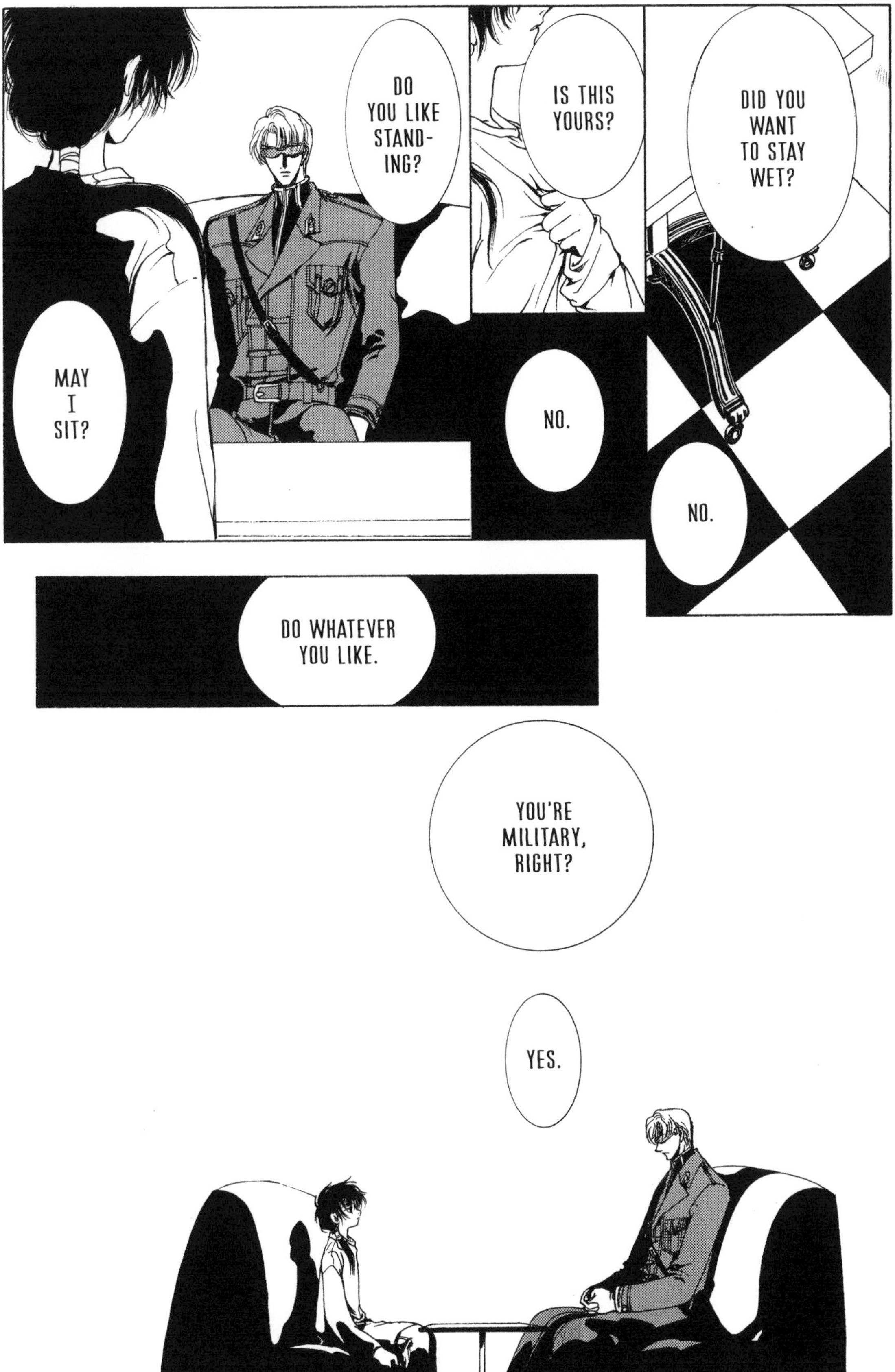
DID YOU WANT TO STAY WET?
NO.
IS THIS YOURS?
NO.
DO YOU LIKE STANDING?
MAY I SIT?
DO WHATEVER YOU LIKE.
YOU'RE MILITARY, RIGHT?
YES.

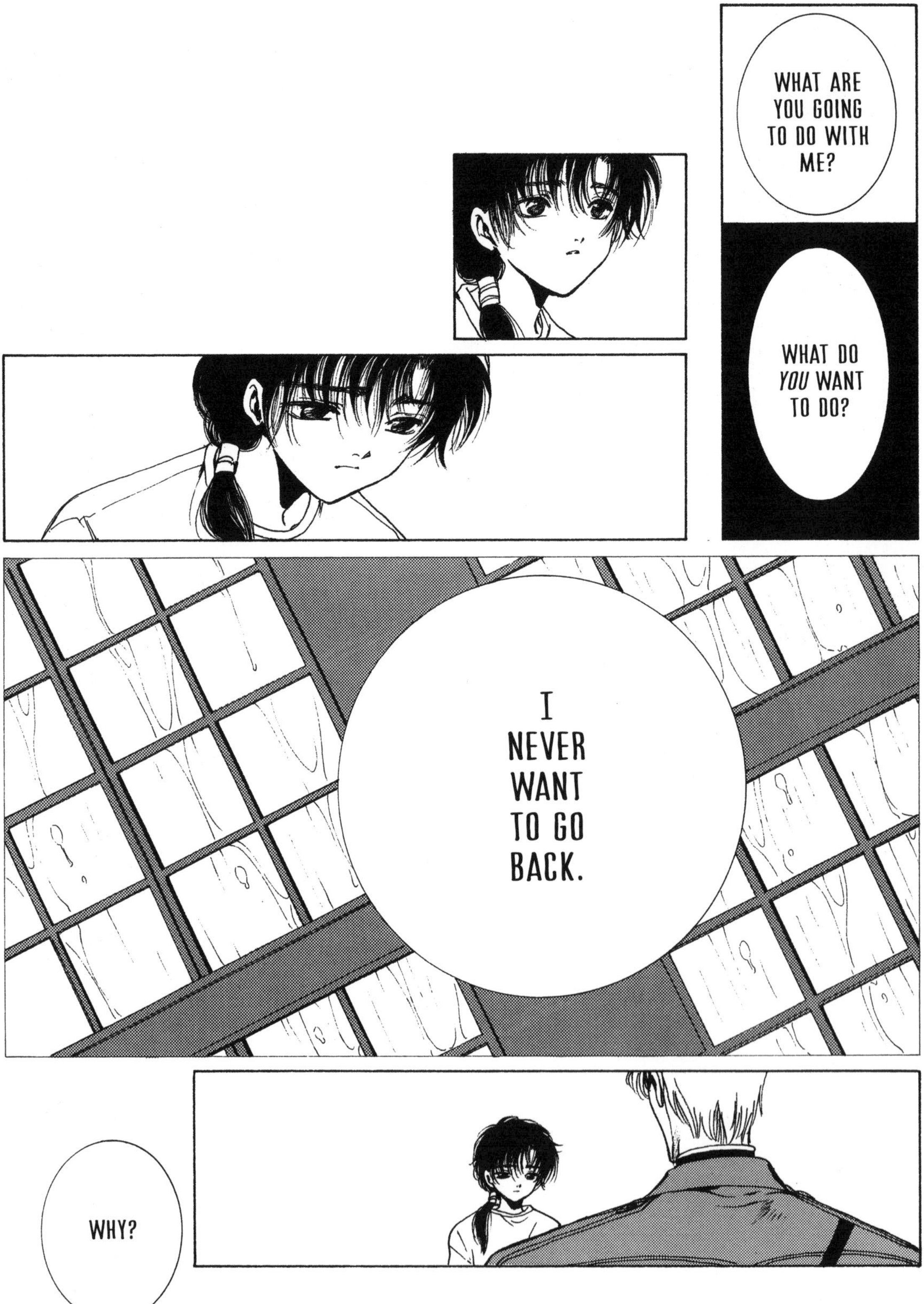
WHAT ARE YOU GOING TO DO WITH ME?
WHAT DO *YOU* WANT TO DO?
I NEVER WANT TO GO BACK.
WHY?

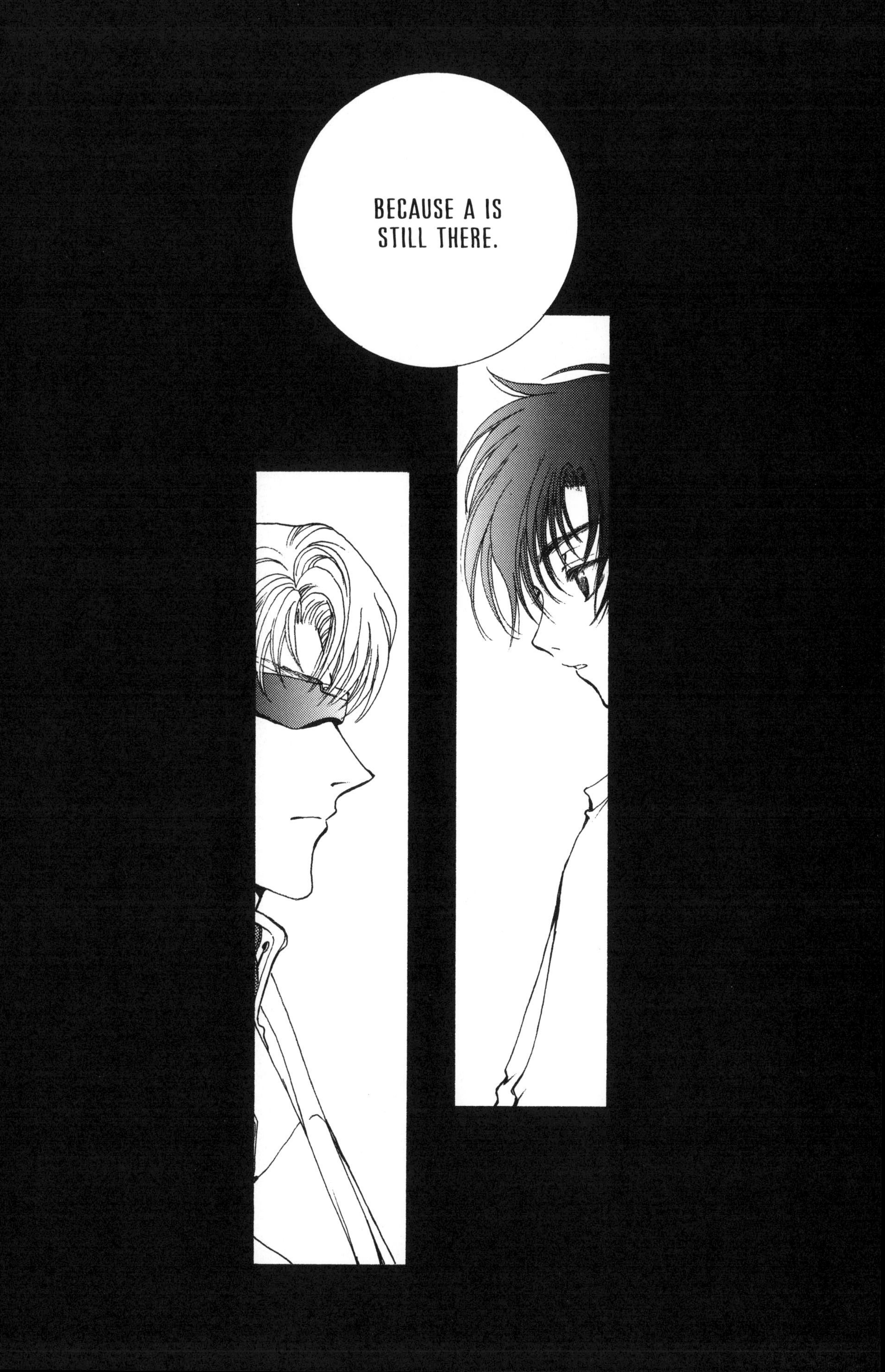
BECAUSE A IS STILL THERE.

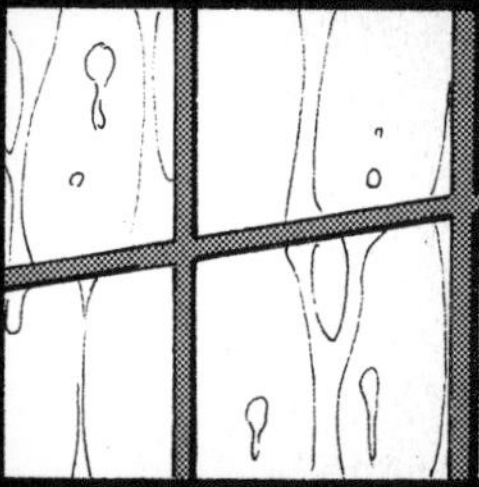

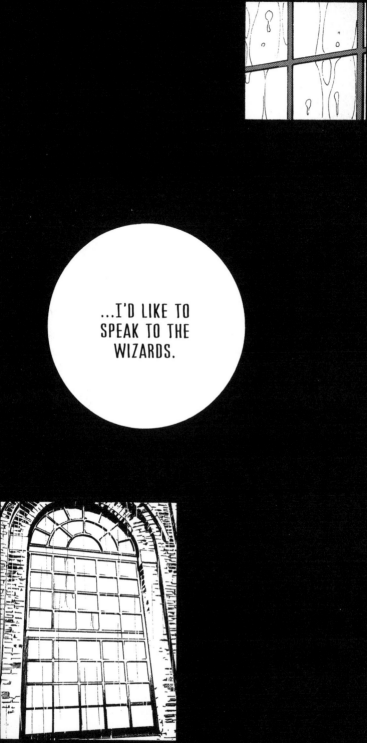

...I'D LIKE TO SPEAK TO THE WIZARDS.

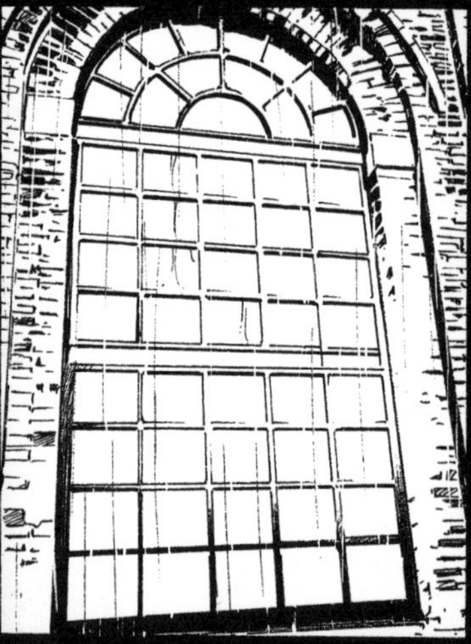

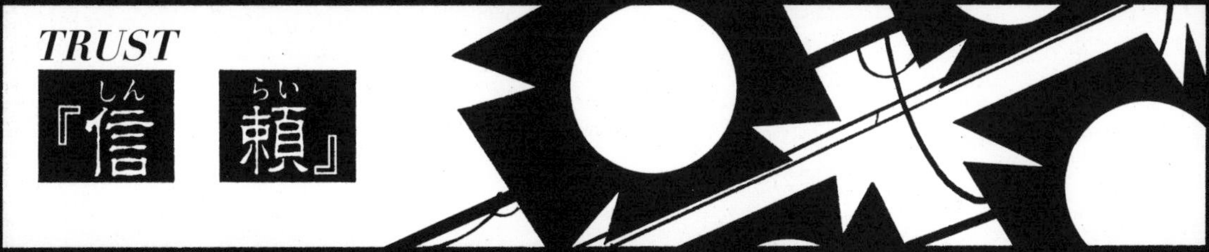

TRUST

『信頼』

The bliss of our meeting
Is a gentle light
Our eventual parting a
pouring rain

Like an indigo that blooms
In the delicate shade

In your arms
I will be reborn

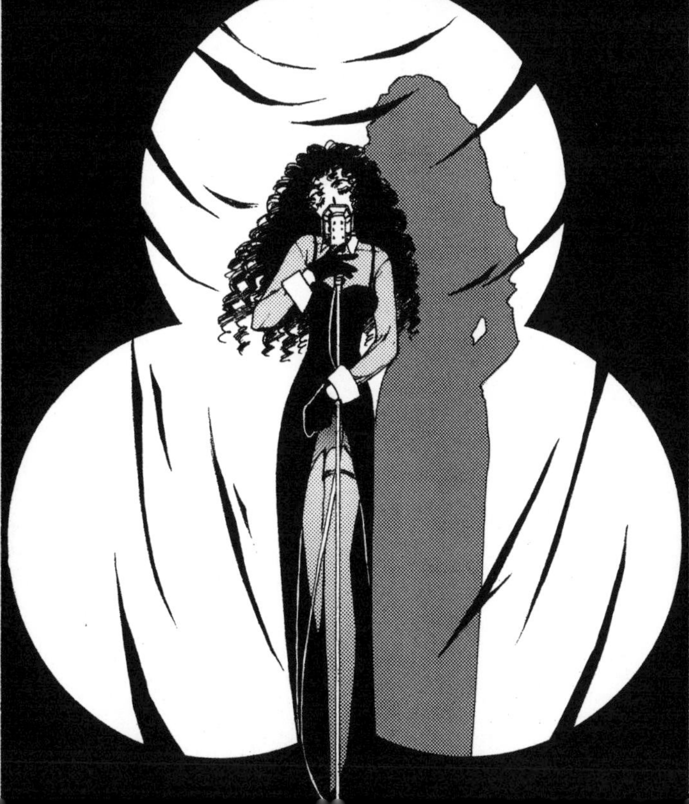

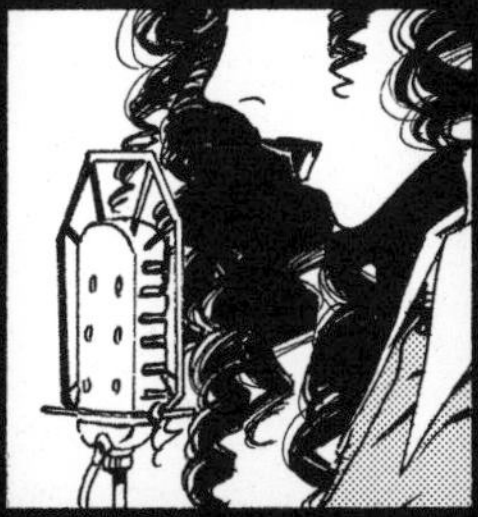

For you

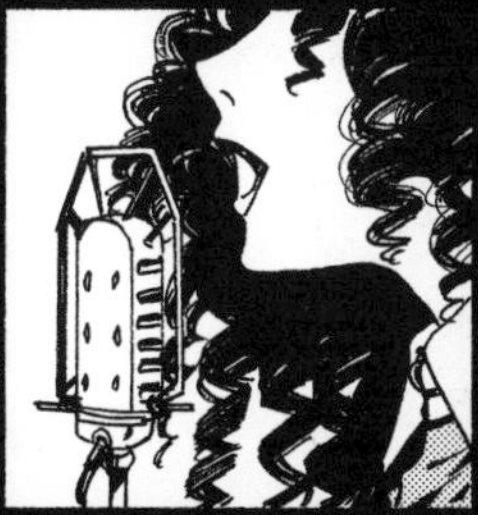

I will be reborn

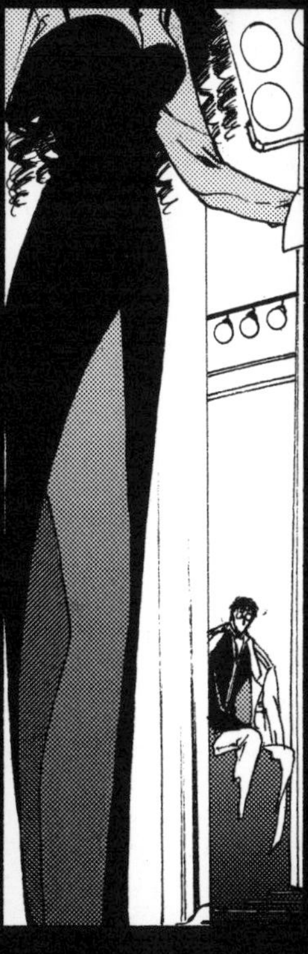

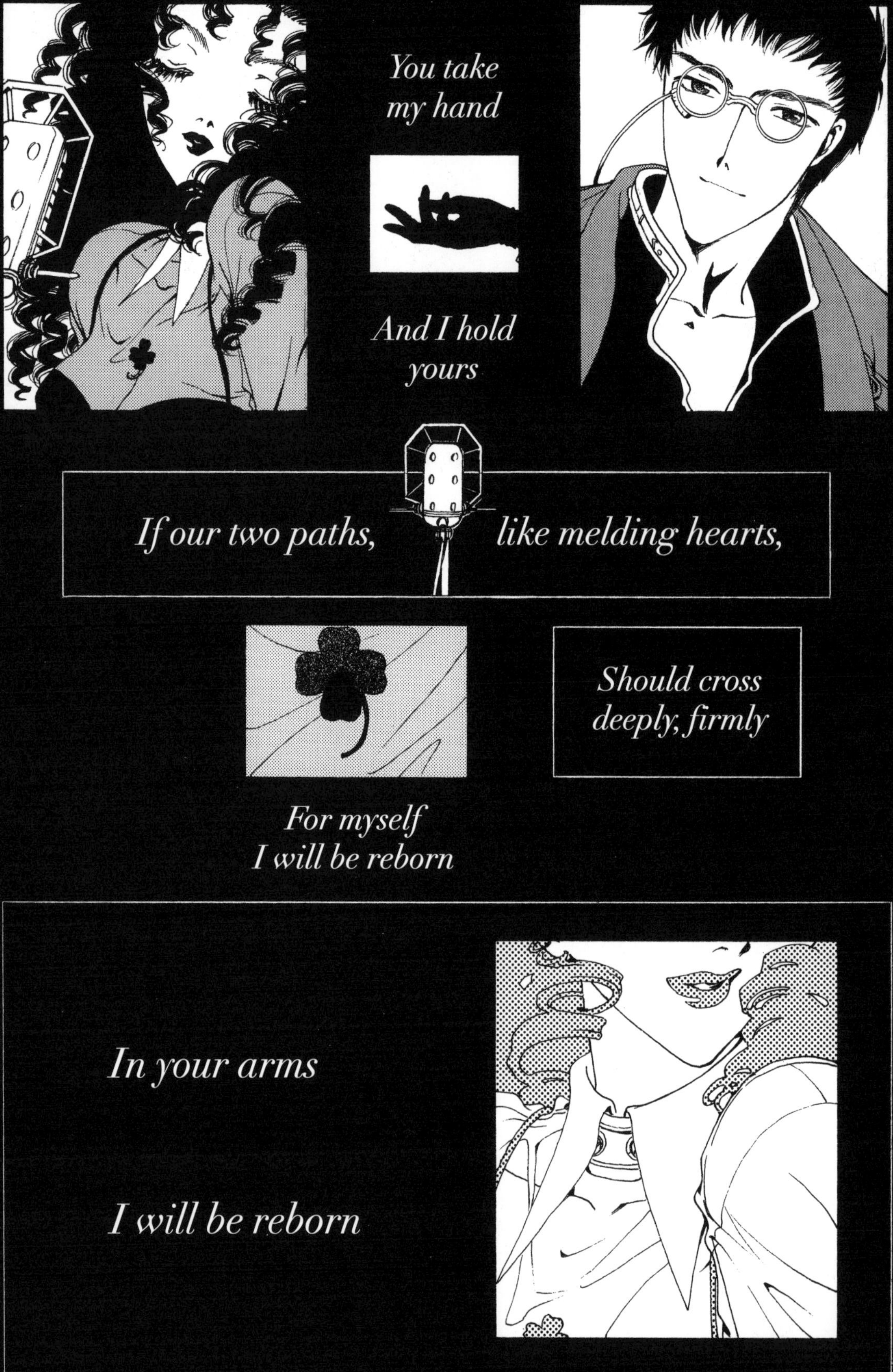
You take my hand
And I hold yours
If our two paths, like melding hearts,
Should cross deeply, firmly
For myself I will be reborn
In your arms
I will be reborn

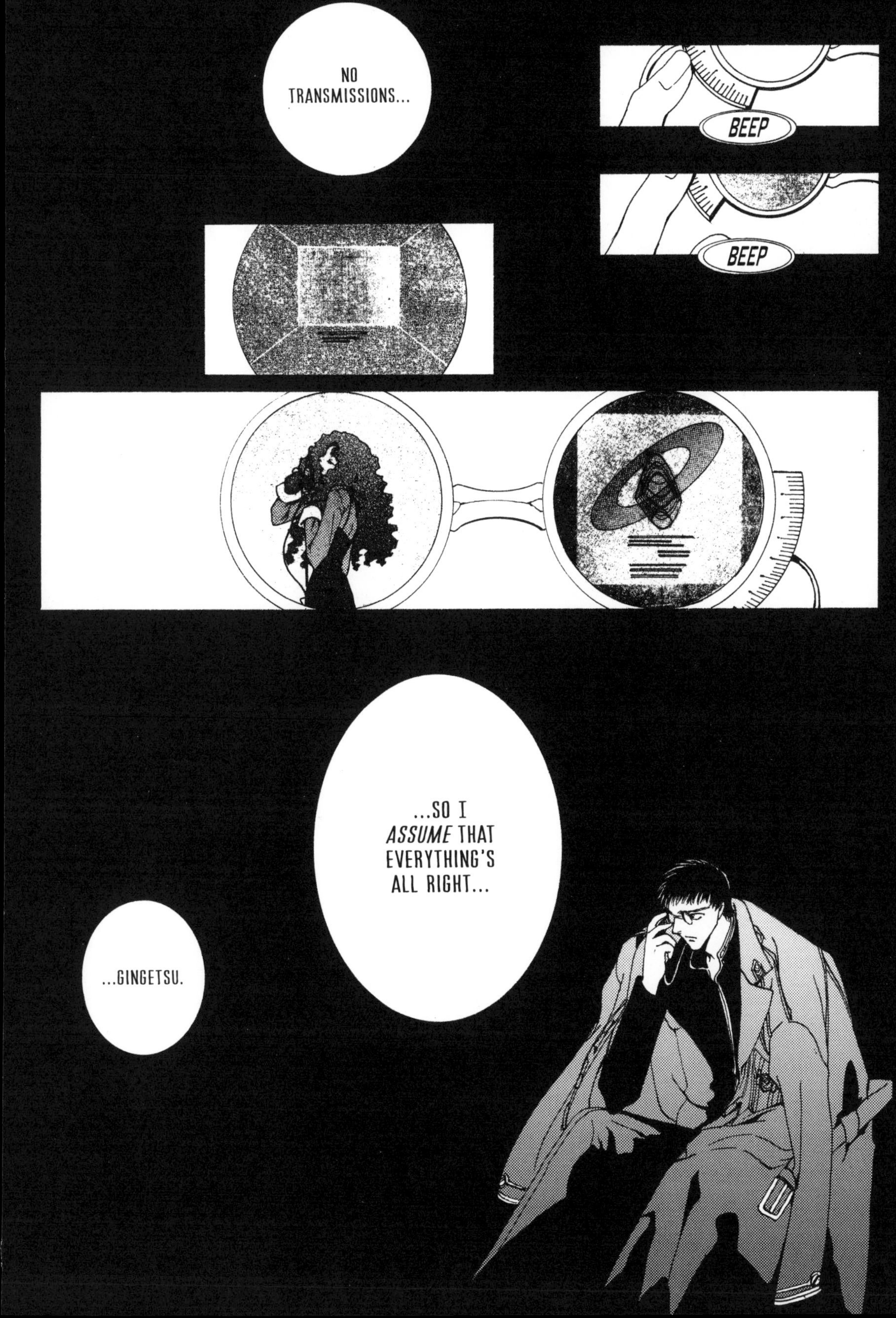
BEEP
BEEP
NO TRANSMISSIONS...
...SO I ASSUME THAT EVERYTHING'S ALL RIGHT...
...GINGETSU.

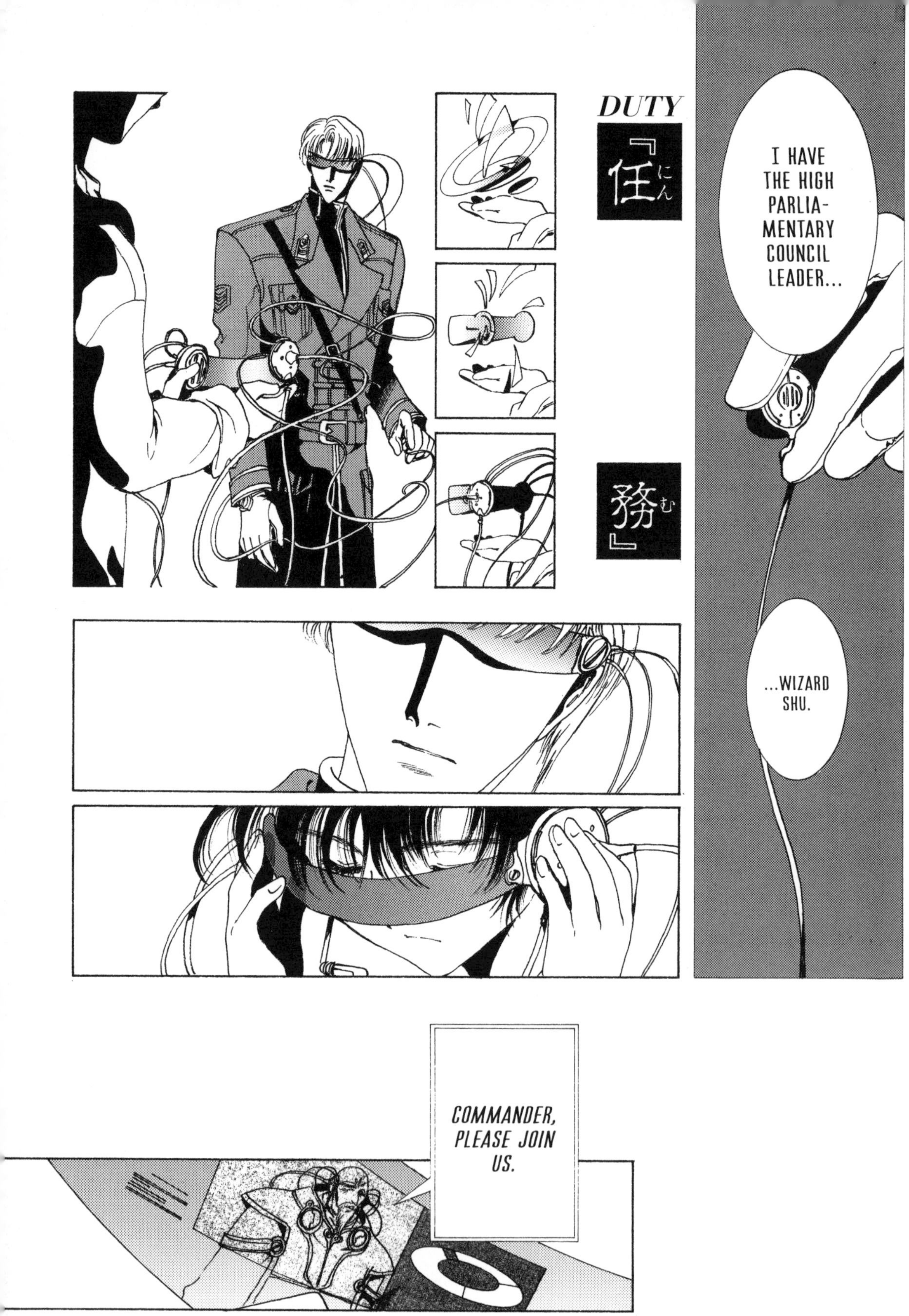
I HAVE THE HIGH PARLIA-MENTARY COUNCIL LEADER...
...WIZARD SHU.
DUTY
『任務』
COMMANDER, PLEASE JOIN US.

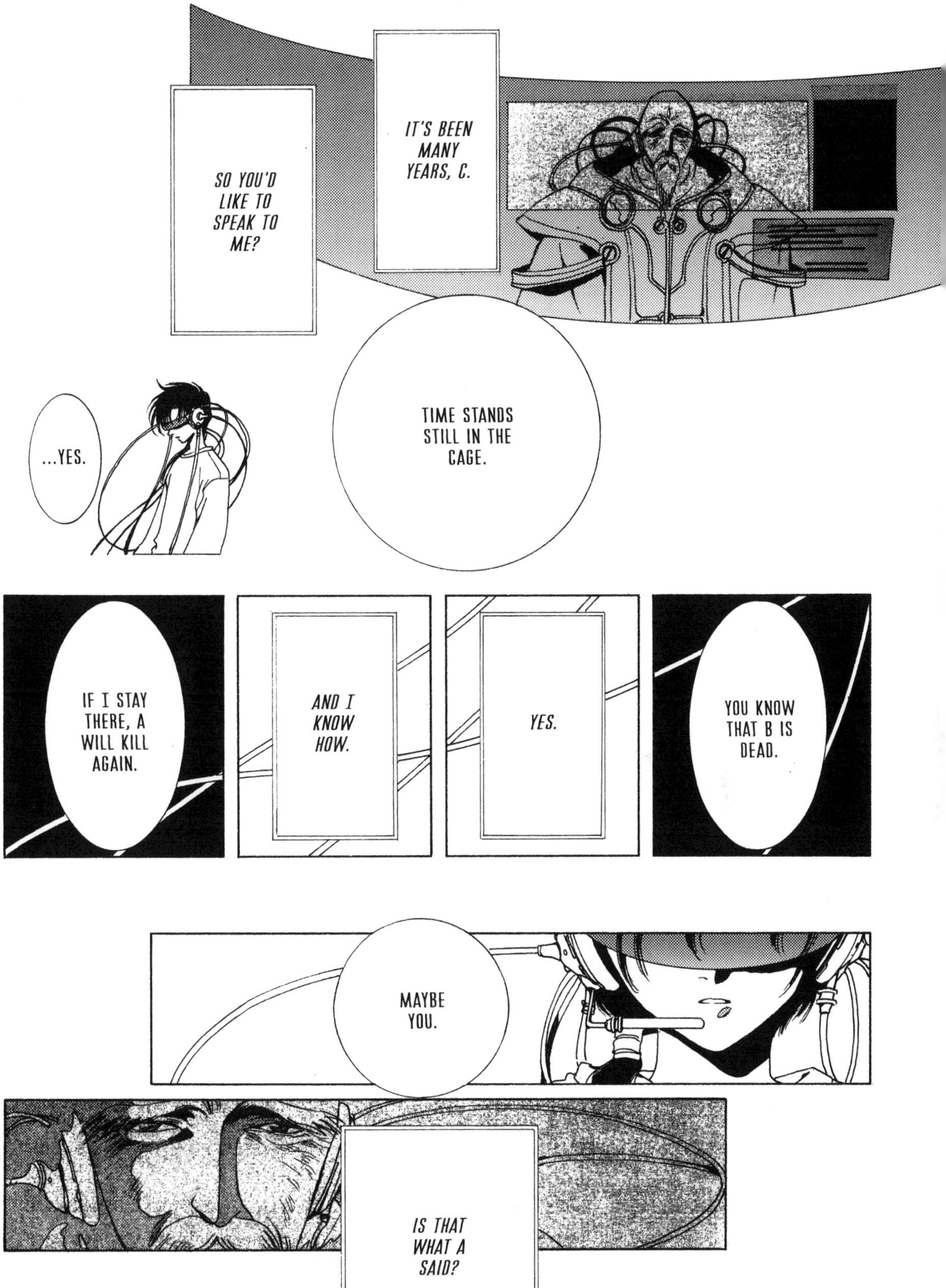
IT'S BEEN MANY YEARS, C.
SO YOU'D LIKE TO SPEAK TO ME?
TIME STANDS STILL IN THE CAGE.
...YES.
YOU KNOW THAT B IS DEAD.
YES.
AND I KNOW HOW.
IF I STAY THERE, A WILL KILL AGAIN.
MAYBE YOU.
IS THAT WHAT A SAID?

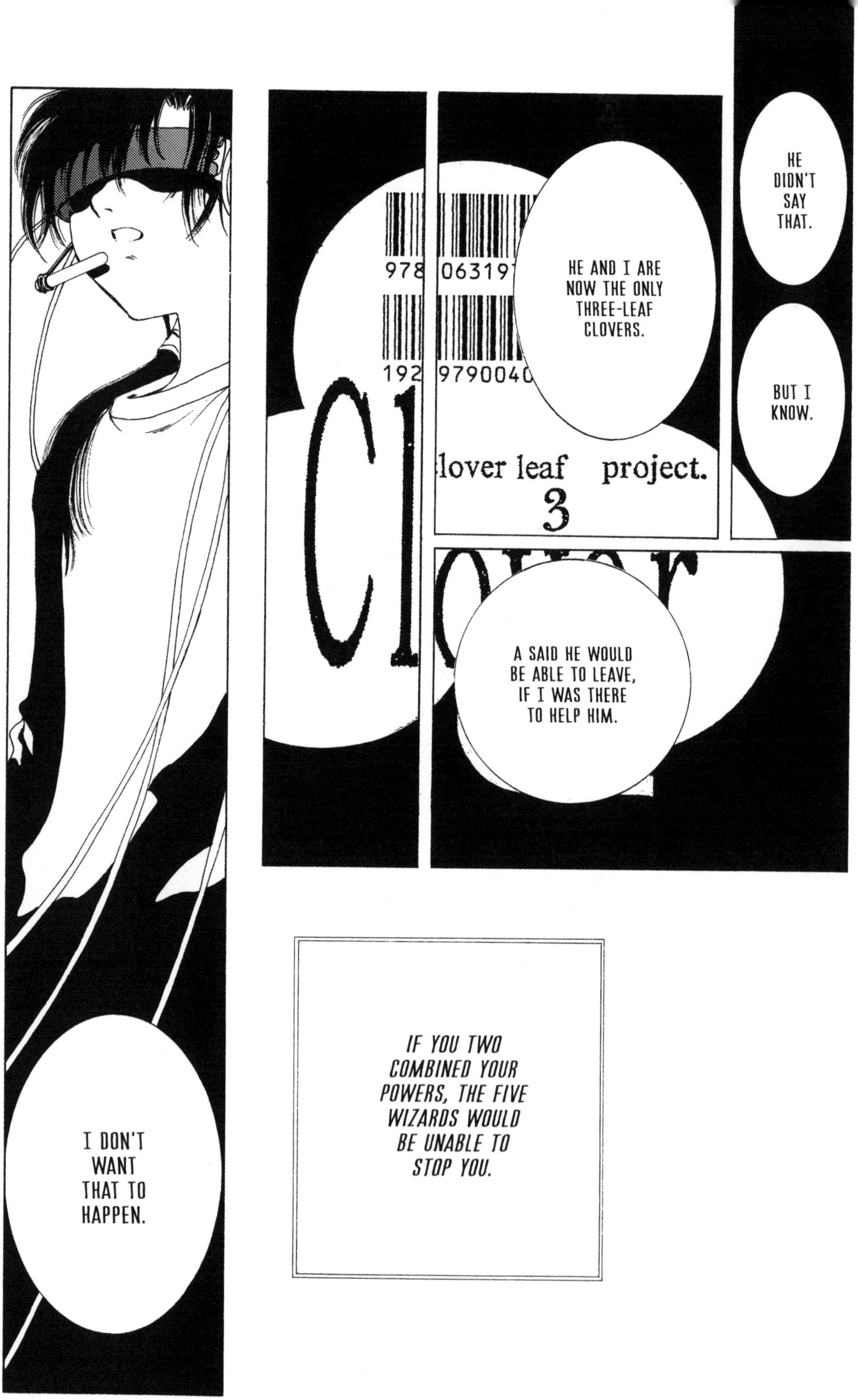
HE DIDN'T SAY THAT.
BUT I KNOW.
HE AND I ARE NOW THE ONLY THREE-LEAF CLOVERS.
lover leaf project.
3
A SAID HE WOULD BE ABLE TO LEAVE, IF I WAS THERE TO HELP HIM.
IF YOU TWO COMBINED YOUR POWERS, THE FIVE WIZARDS WOULD BE UNABLE TO STOP YOU.
I DON'T WANT THAT TO HAPPEN.

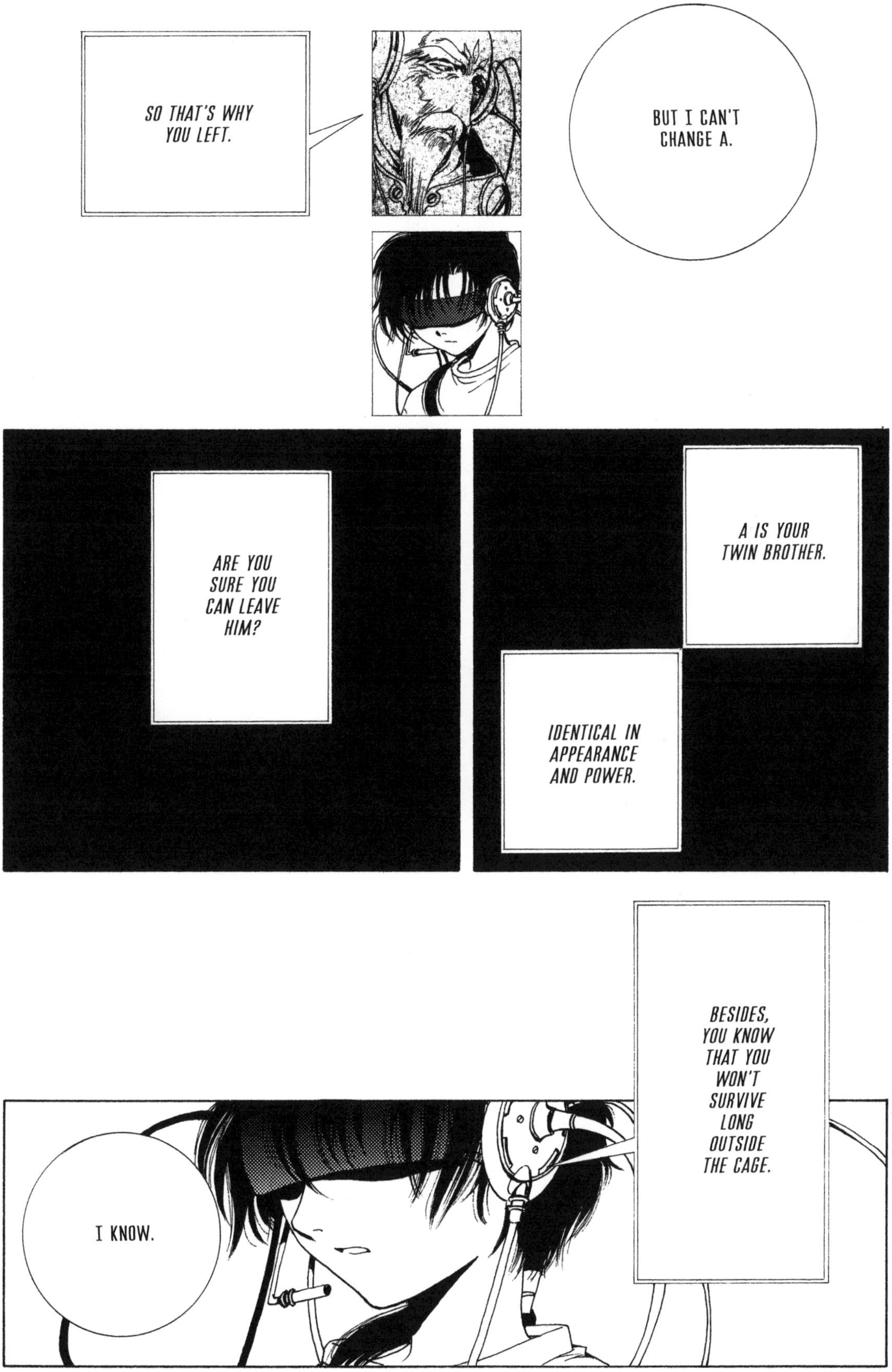
BUT I CAN'T CHANGE A.
SO THAT'S WHY YOU LEFT.
A IS YOUR TWIN BROTHER.
IDENTICAL IN APPEARANCE AND POWER.
ARE YOU SURE YOU CAN LEAVE HIM?
BESIDES, YOU KNOW THAT YOU WON'T SURVIVE LONG OUTSIDE THE CAGE.
I KNOW.

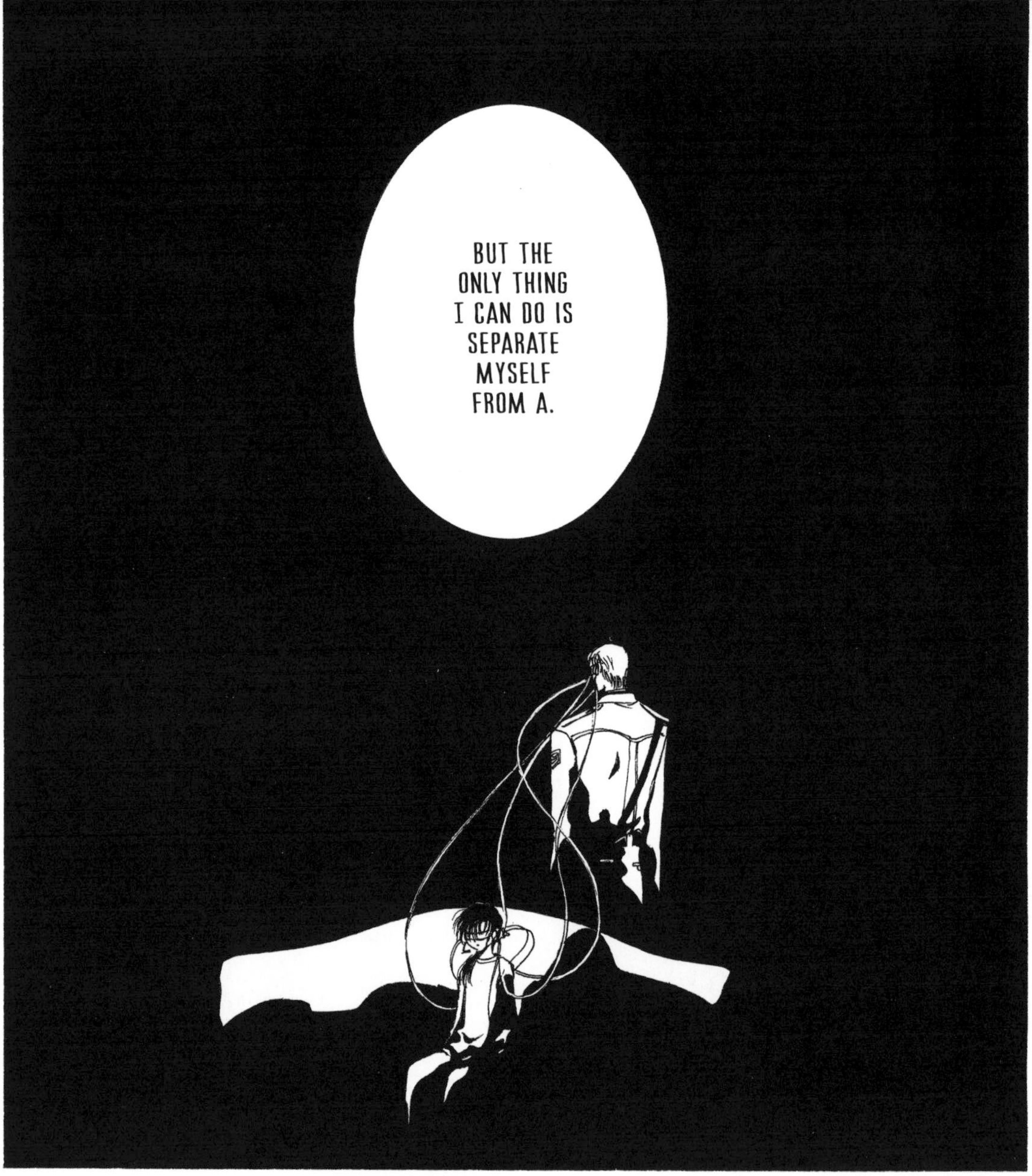
BUT THE ONLY THING I CAN DO IS SEPARATE MYSELF FROM A.

A'S EMOTIONS ARE UNSTABLE...

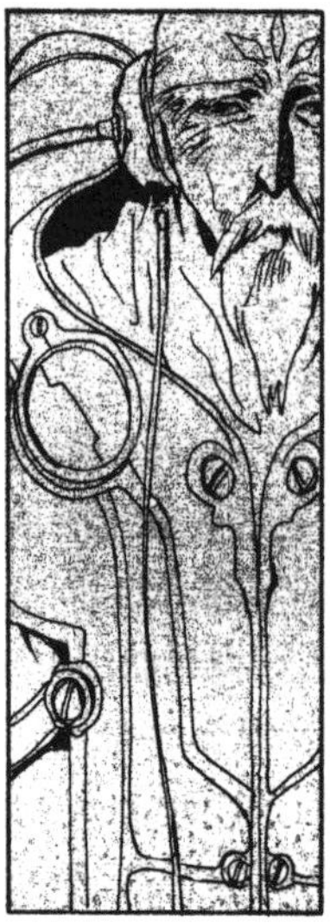

...IT PROBABLY IS DANGEROUS TO KEEP YOU TWO TOGETHER.

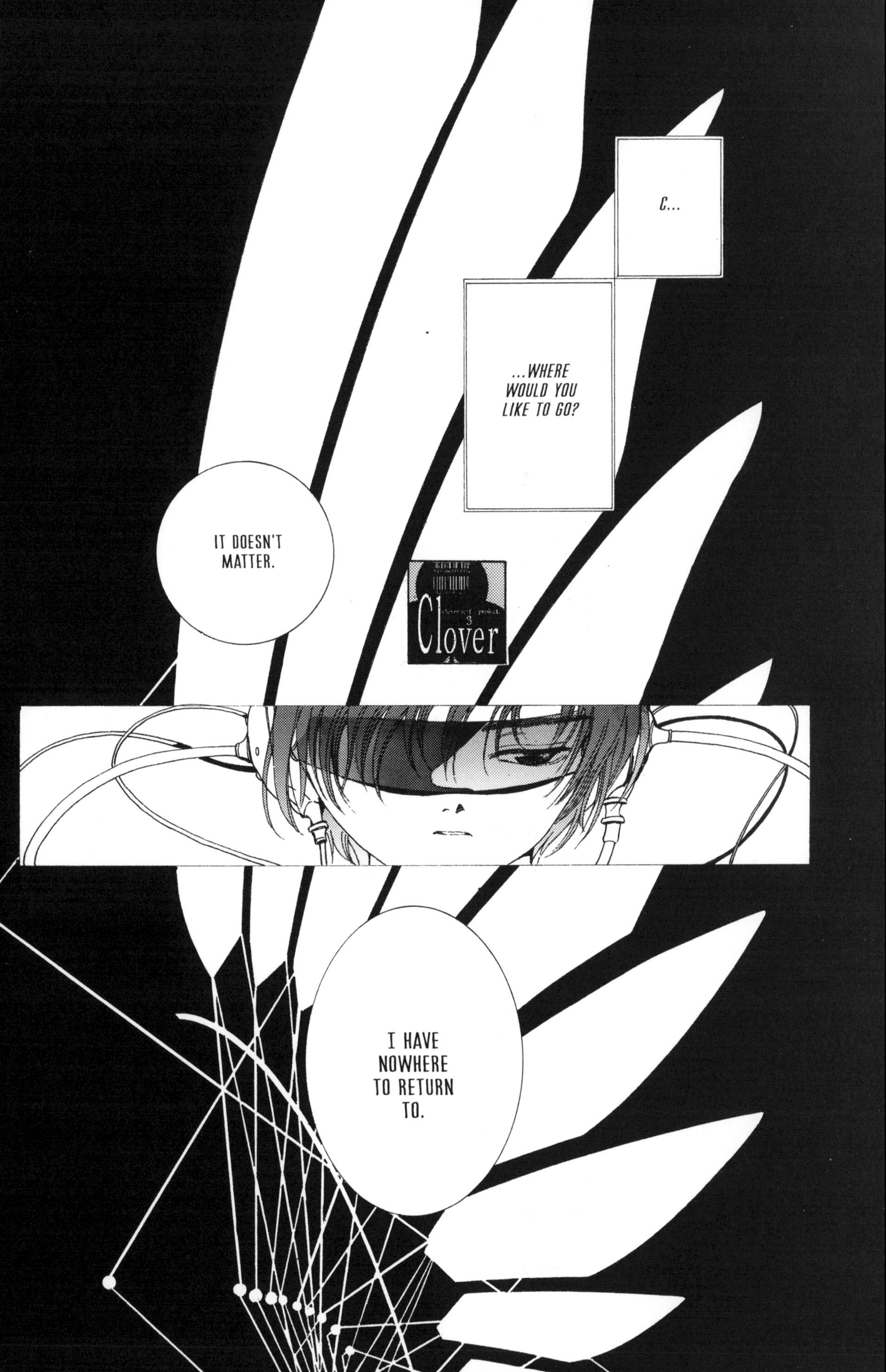
C...
...WHERE WOULD YOU LIKE TO GO?
IT DOESN'T MATTER.
Clover
I HAVE NOWHERE TO RETURN TO.

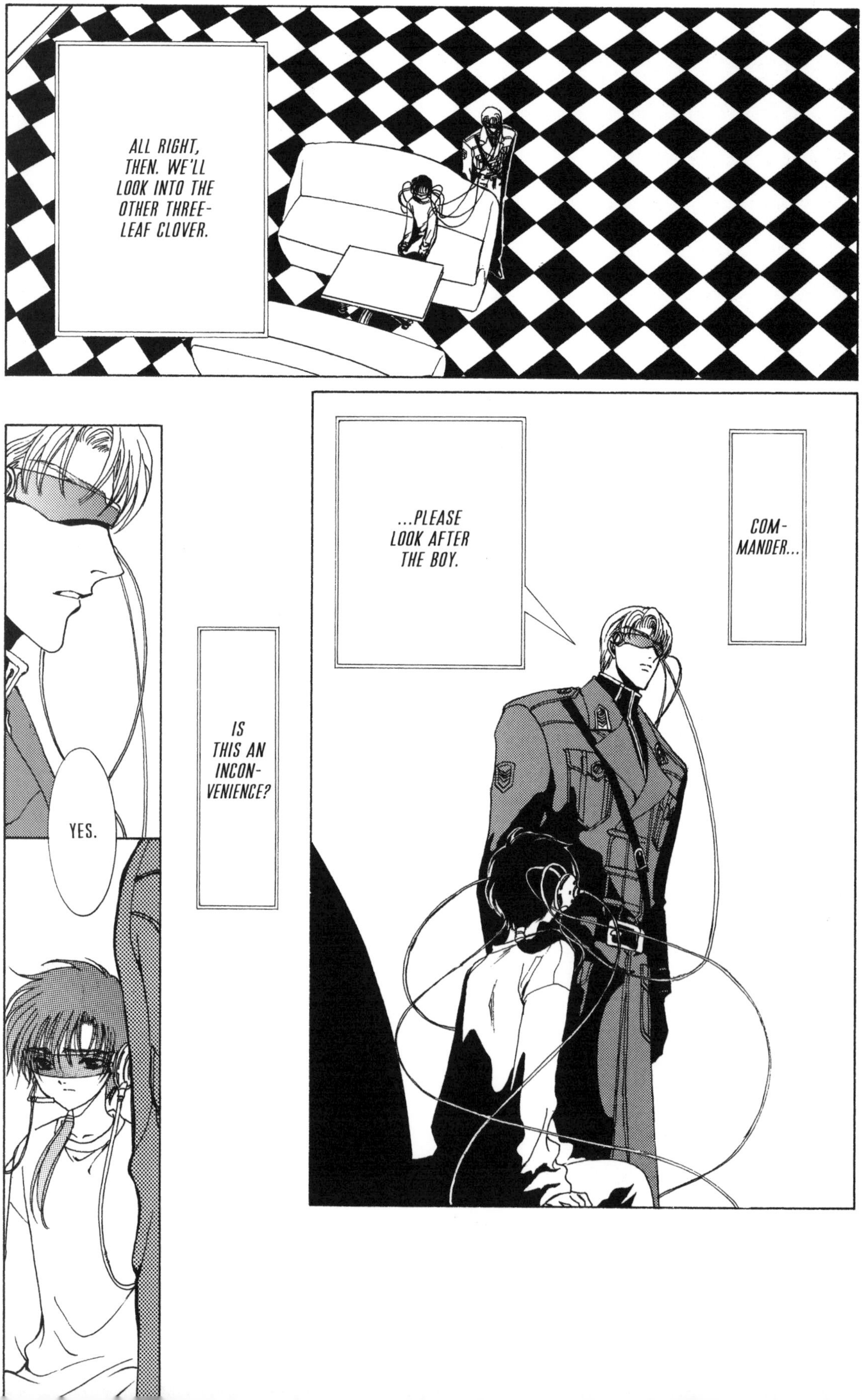
ALL RIGHT, THEN. WE'LL LOOK INTO THE OTHER THREE-LEAF CLOVER.
COM-MANDER...
...PLEASE LOOK AFTER THE BOY.
IS THIS AN INCON-VENIENCE?
YES.

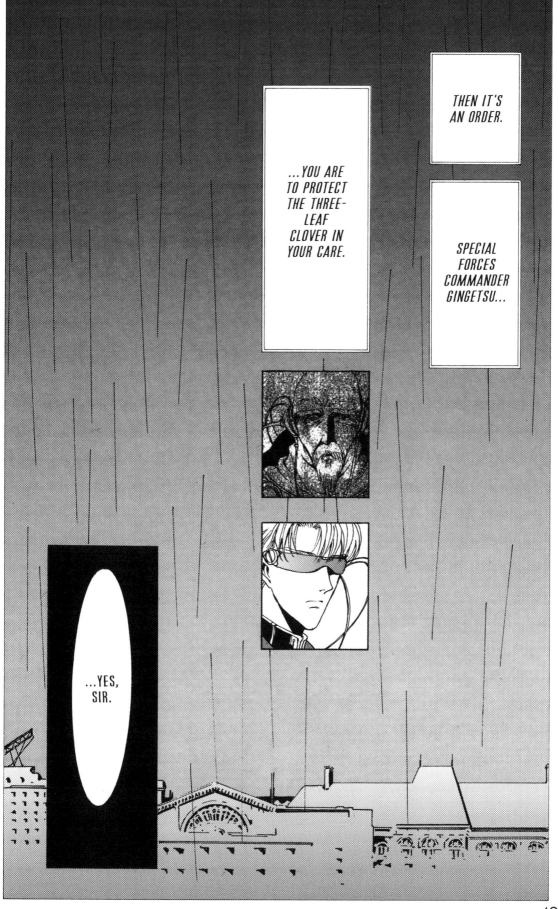

THEN IT'S AN ORDER.

SPECIAL FORCES COMMANDER GINGETSU...

...YOU ARE TO PROTECT THE THREE-LEAF CLOVER IN YOUR CARE.

...YES, SIR.

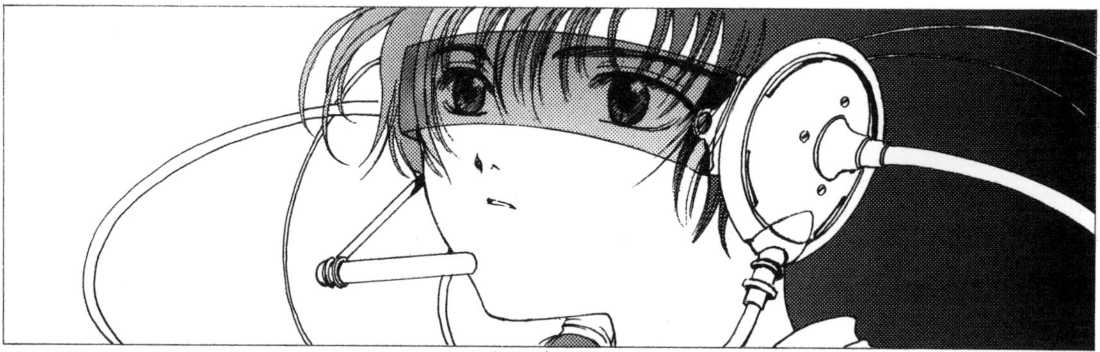

BRAND
『印』(しるし)

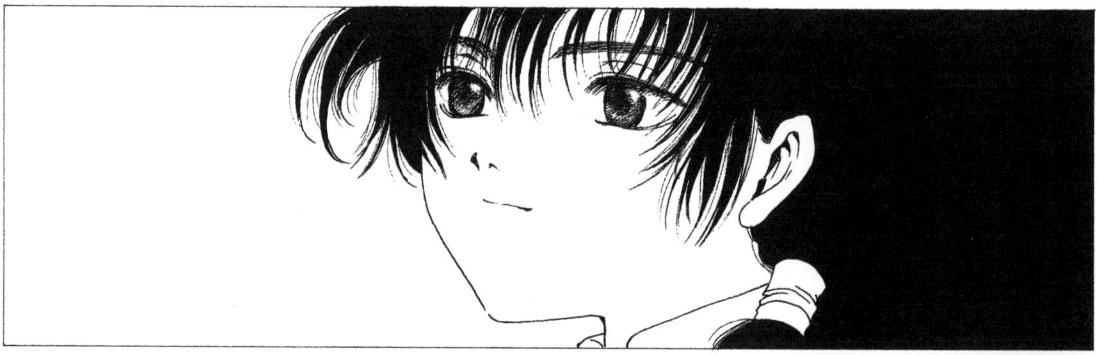

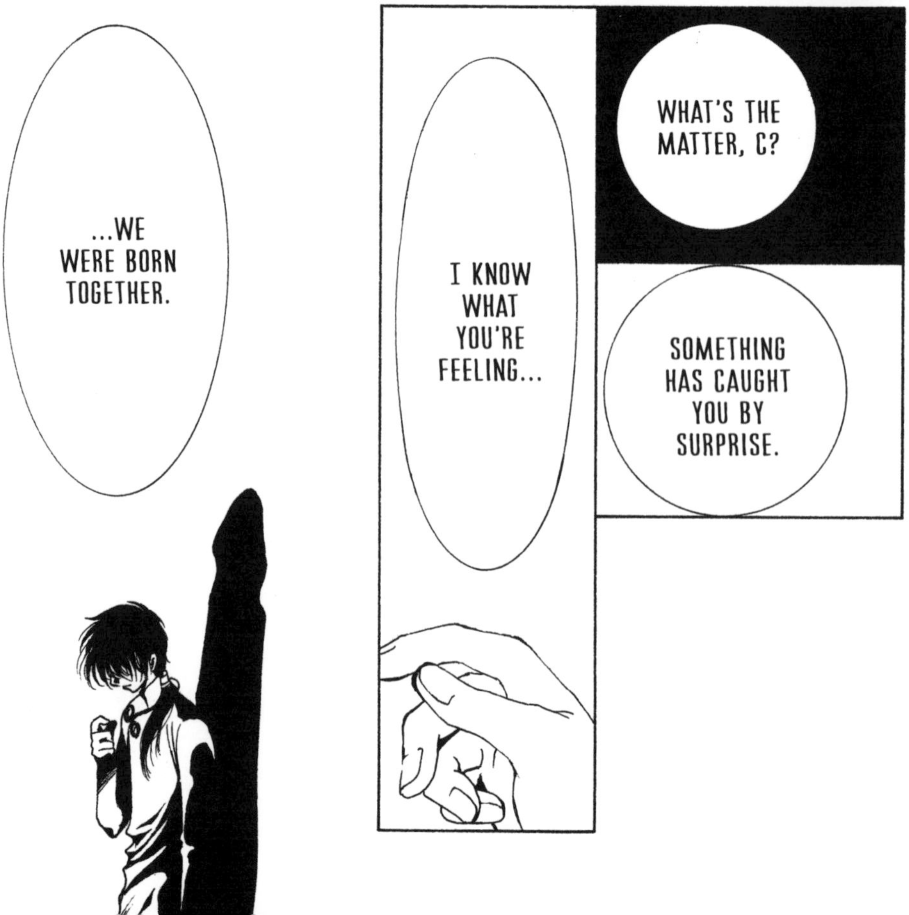
WHAT'S THE MATTER, C?
SOMETHING HAS CAUGHT YOU BY SURPRISE.
I KNOW WHAT YOU'RE FEELING...
...WE WERE BORN TOGETHER.

AND
WE WILL
ALWAYS BE
TOGETHER.

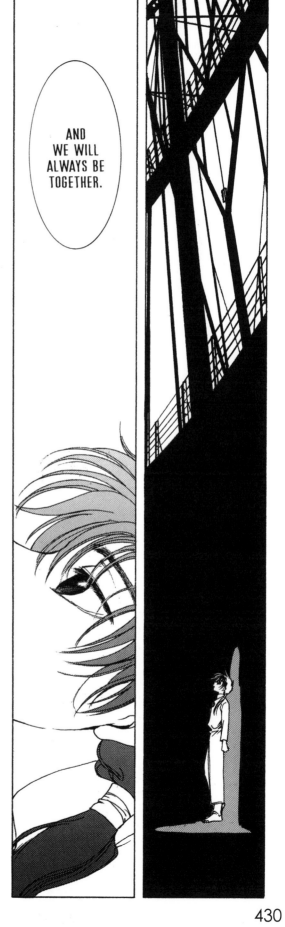

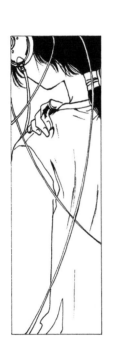

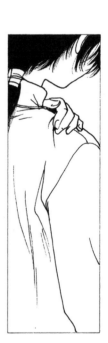

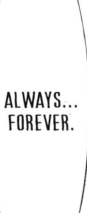

ALWAYS...
FOREVER.

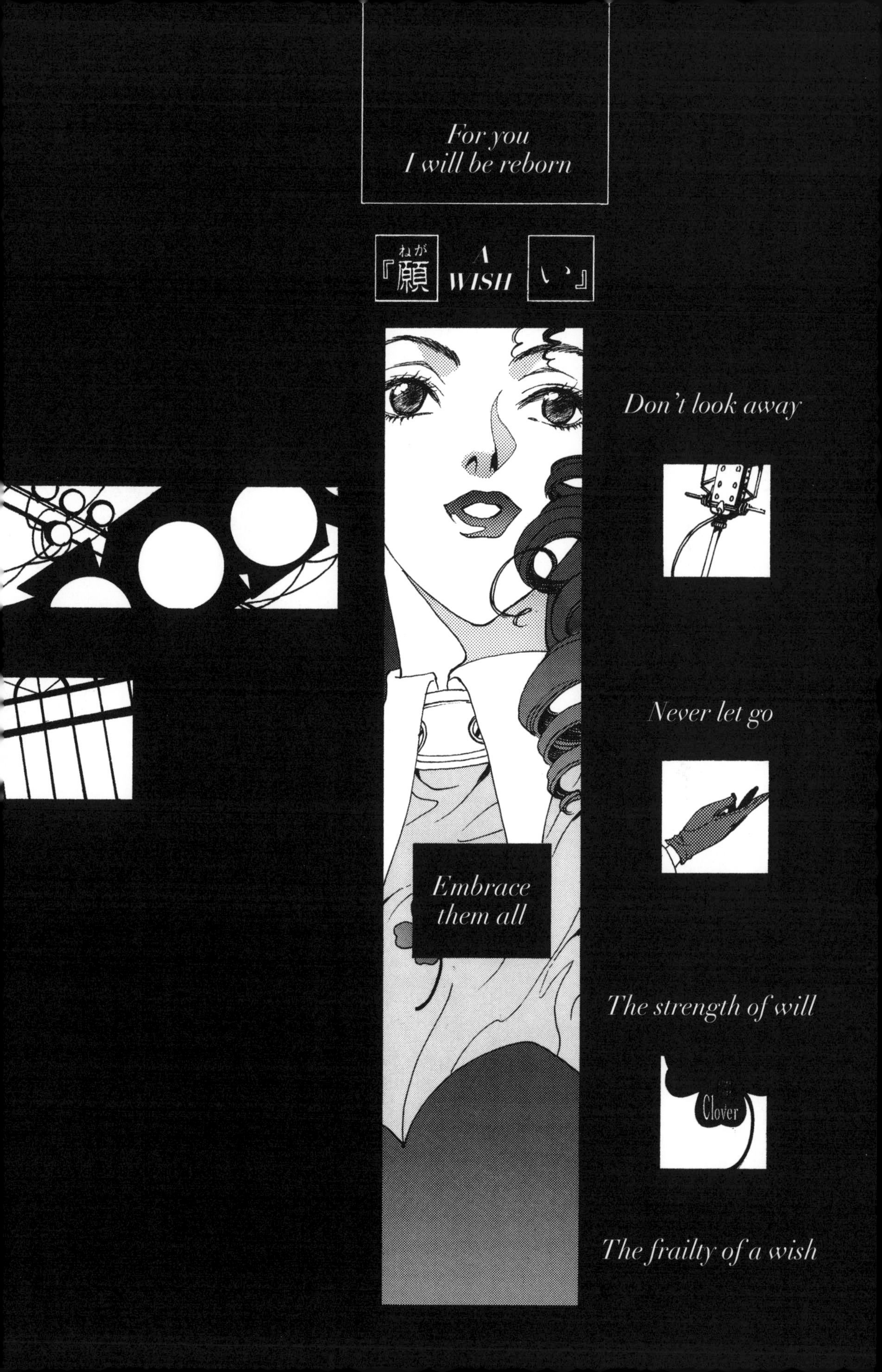
For you
I will be reborn
『願い』
A WISH
Don't look away
Never let go
Embrace them all
The strength of will
Clover
The frailty of a wish

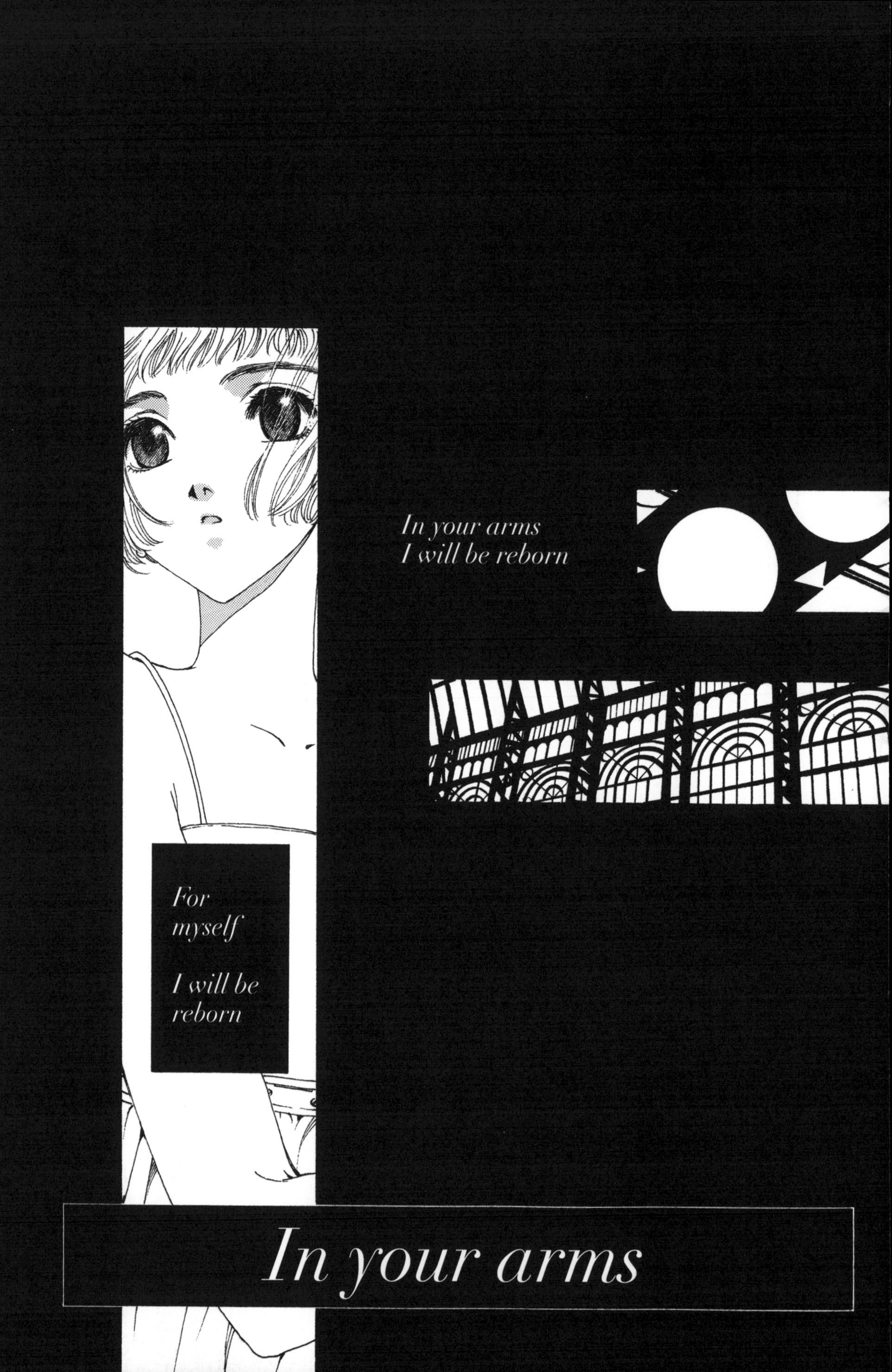
In your arms
I will be reborn
For myself
I will be reborn
In your arms

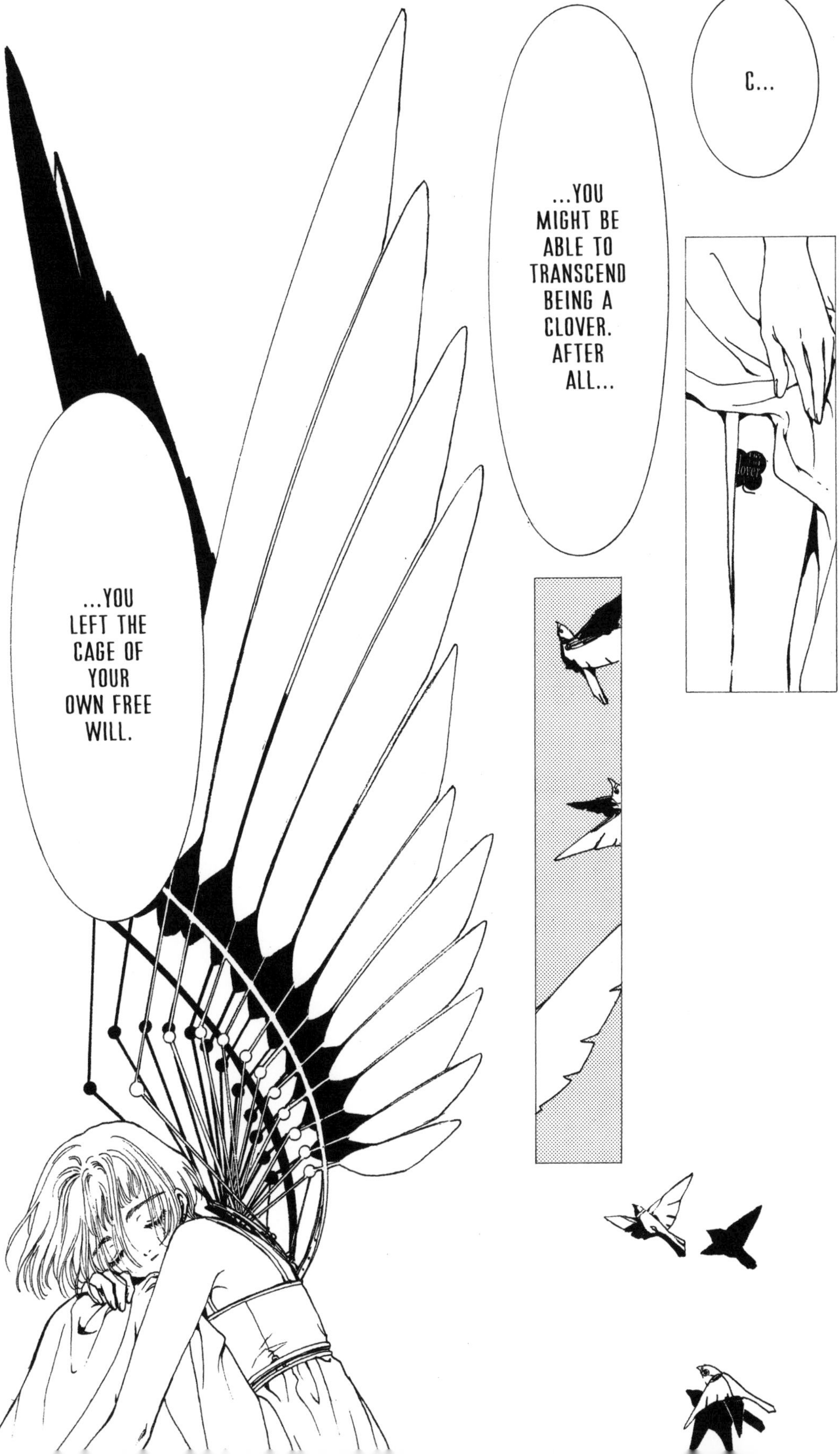
C...
...YOU MIGHT BE ABLE TO TRANSCEND BEING A CLOVER. AFTER ALL...
...YOU LEFT THE CAGE OF YOUR OWN FREE WILL.

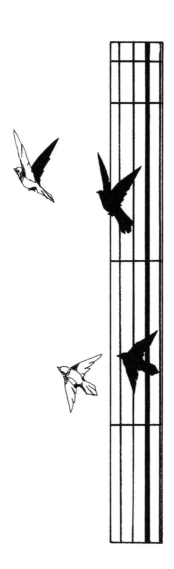
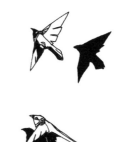

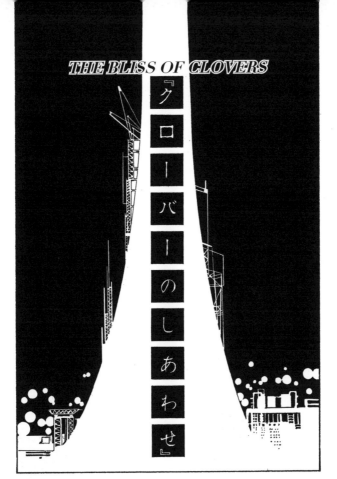

THE BLISS OF CLOVERS

『クローバーのしあわせ』

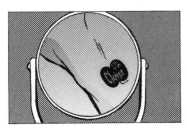 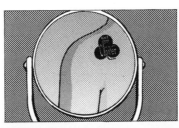 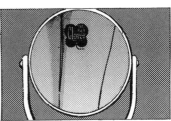

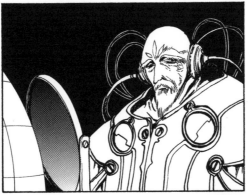

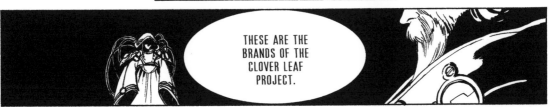

THESE ARE THE BRANDS OF THE CLOVER LEAF PROJECT.

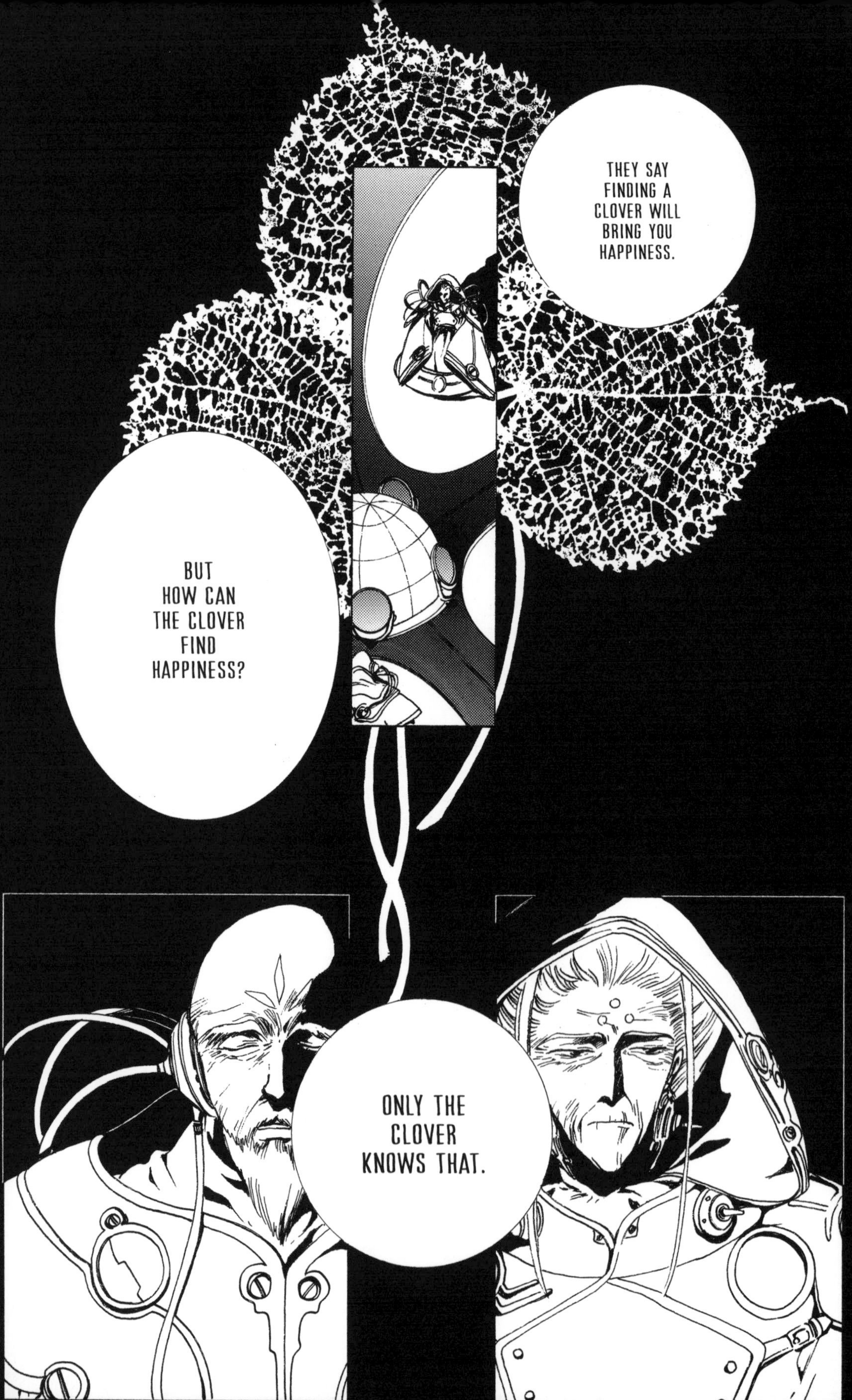
THEY SAY FINDING A CLOVER WILL BRING YOU HAPPINESS.
BUT HOW CAN THE CLOVER FIND HAPPINESS?
ONLY THE CLOVER KNOWS THAT.

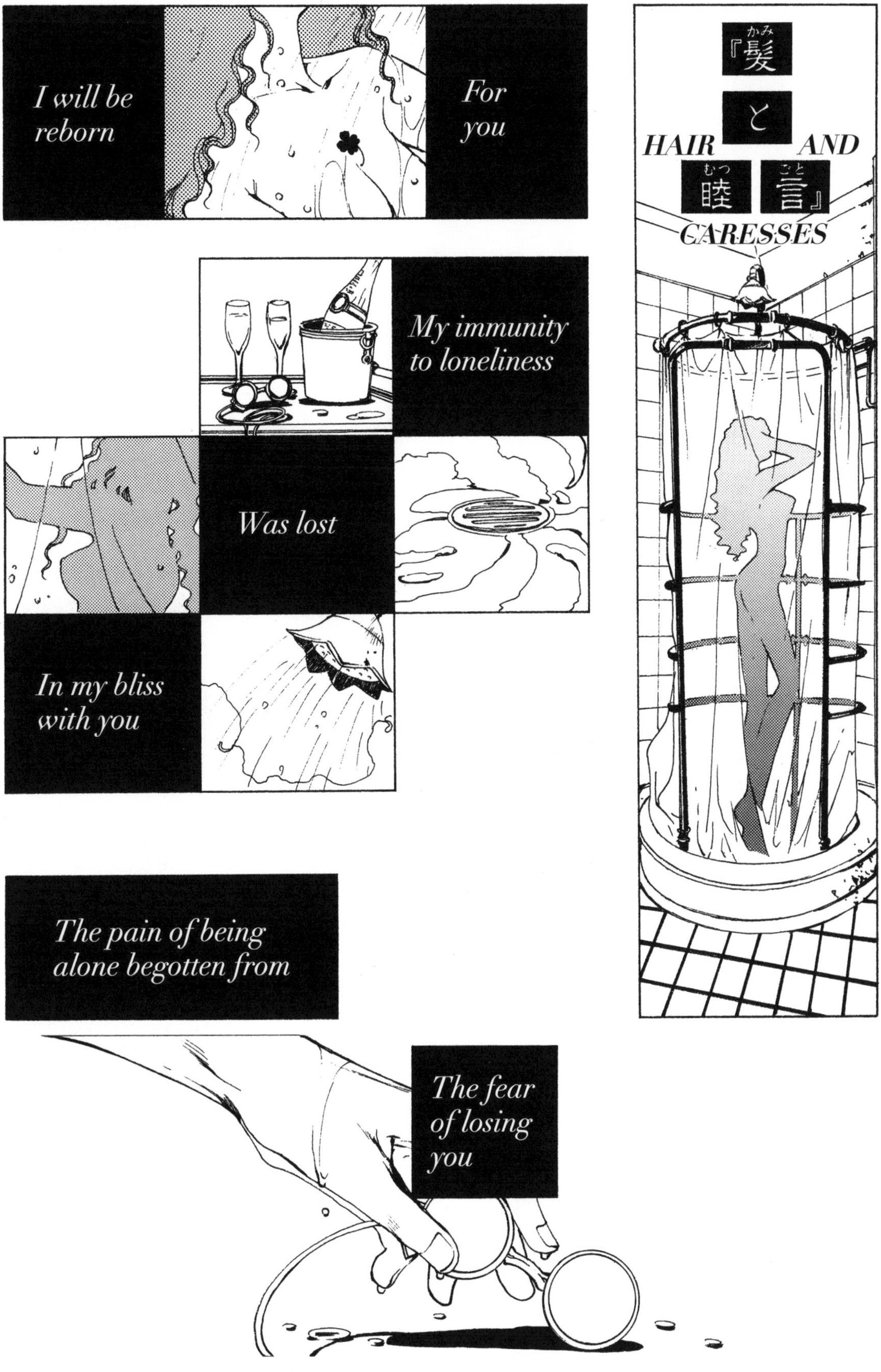
『髪と睦言』
HAIR AND CARESSES
For you
I will be reborn
My immunity to loneliness
Was lost
In my bliss with you
The pain of being alone begotten from
The fear of losing you

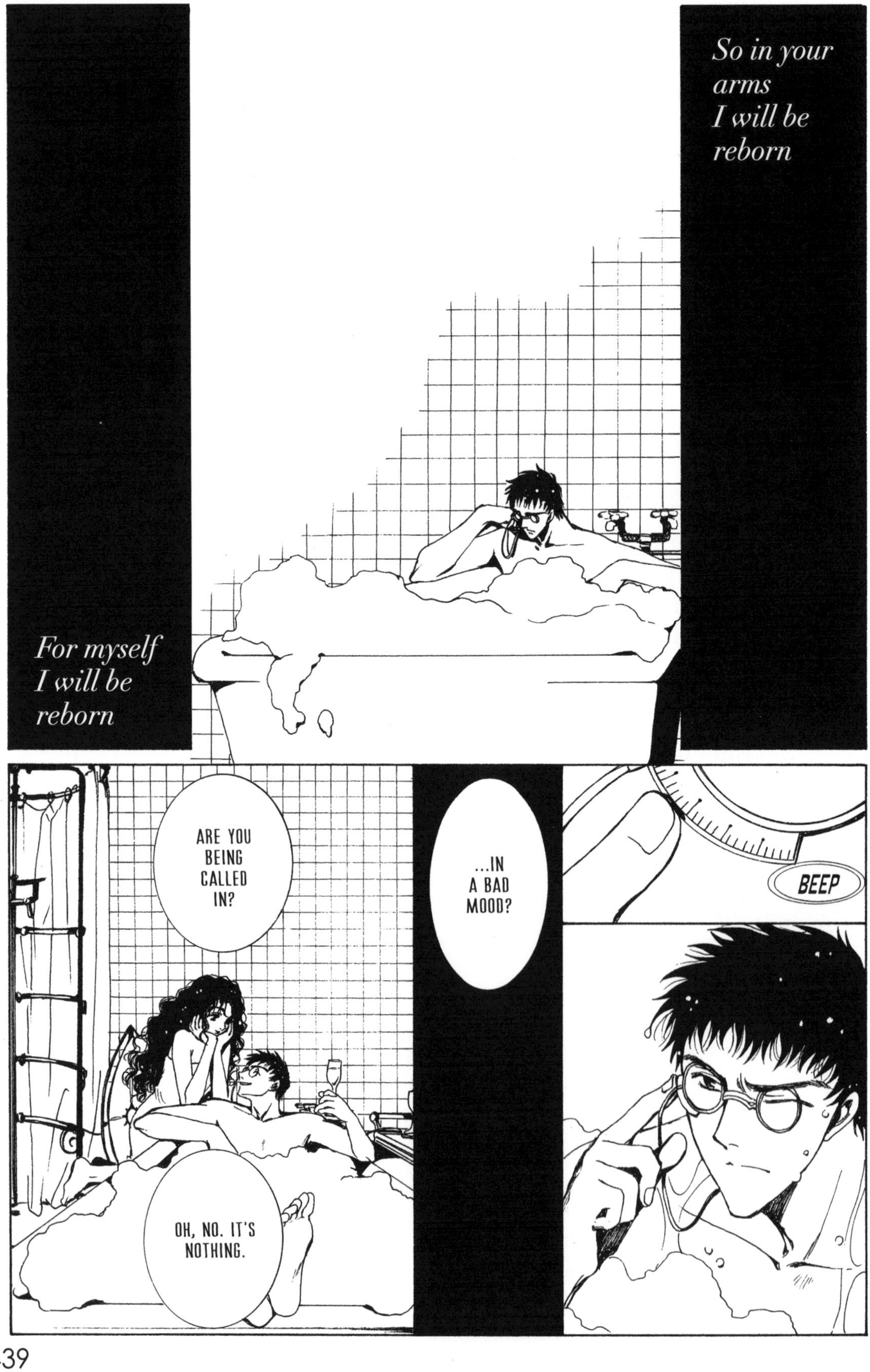

So in your arms I will be reborn
For myself I will be reborn
BEEP
ARE YOU BEING CALLED IN?
...IN A BAD MOOD?
OH, NO. IT'S NOTHING.

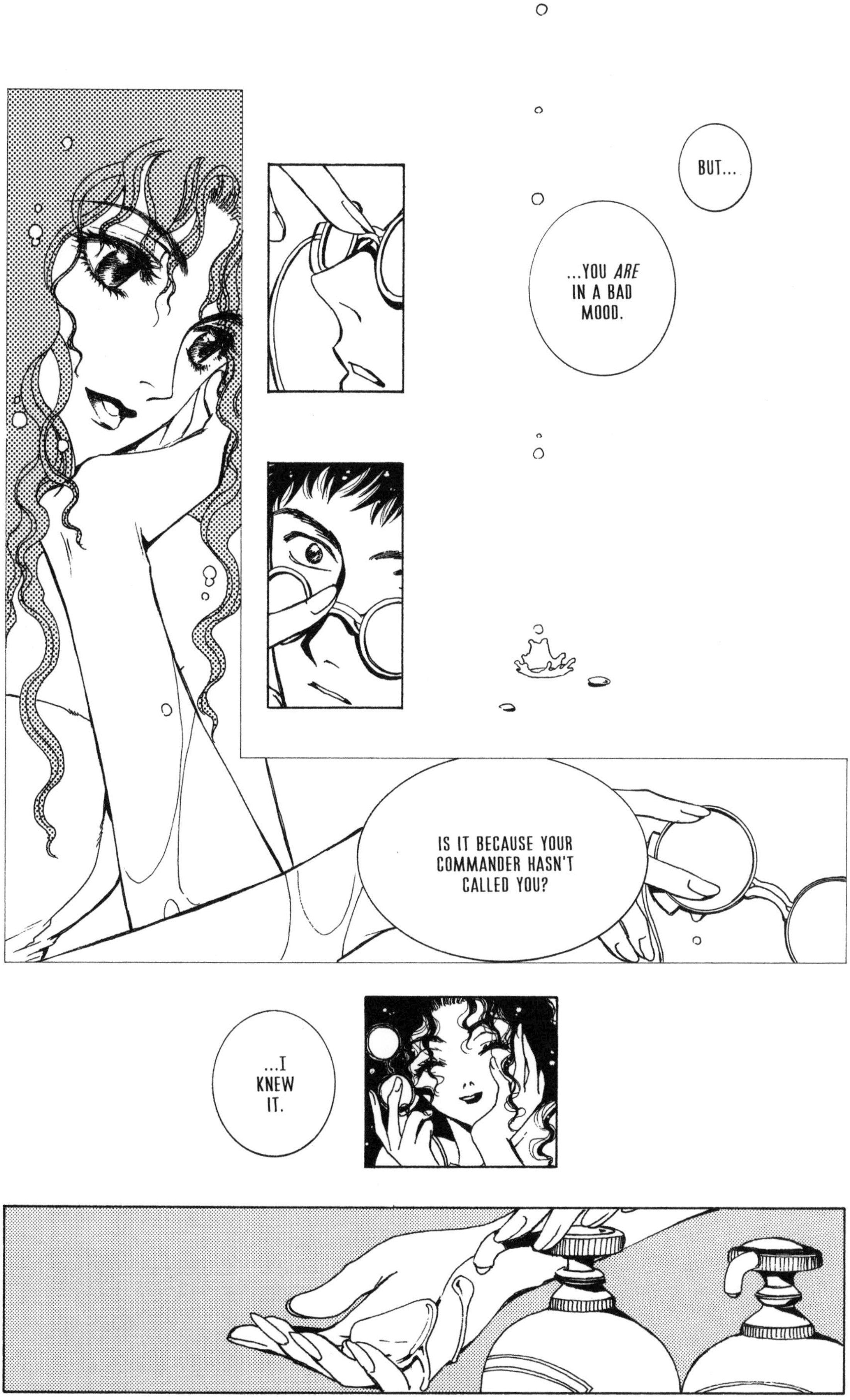
BUT...
...YOU *ARE* IN A BAD MOOD.
IS IT BECAUSE YOUR COMMANDER HASN'T CALLED YOU?
...I KNEW IT.

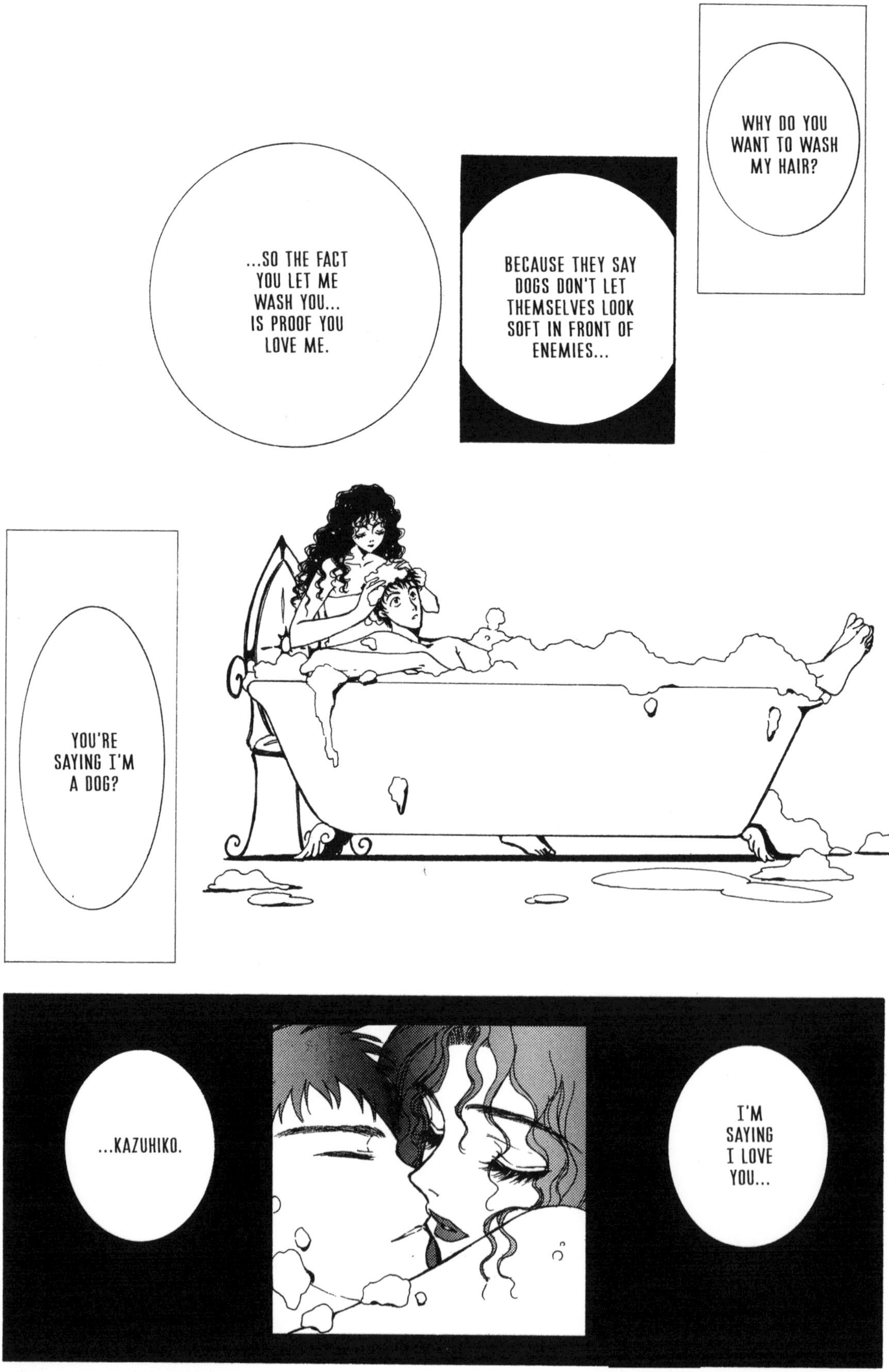
WHY DO YOU WANT TO WASH MY HAIR?
BECAUSE THEY SAY DOGS DON'T LET THEMSELVES LOOK SOFT IN FRONT OF ENEMIES...
...SO THE FACT YOU LET ME WASH YOU... IS PROOF YOU LOVE ME.
YOU'RE SAYING I'M A DOG?
I'M SAYING I LOVE YOU...
...KAZUHIKO.

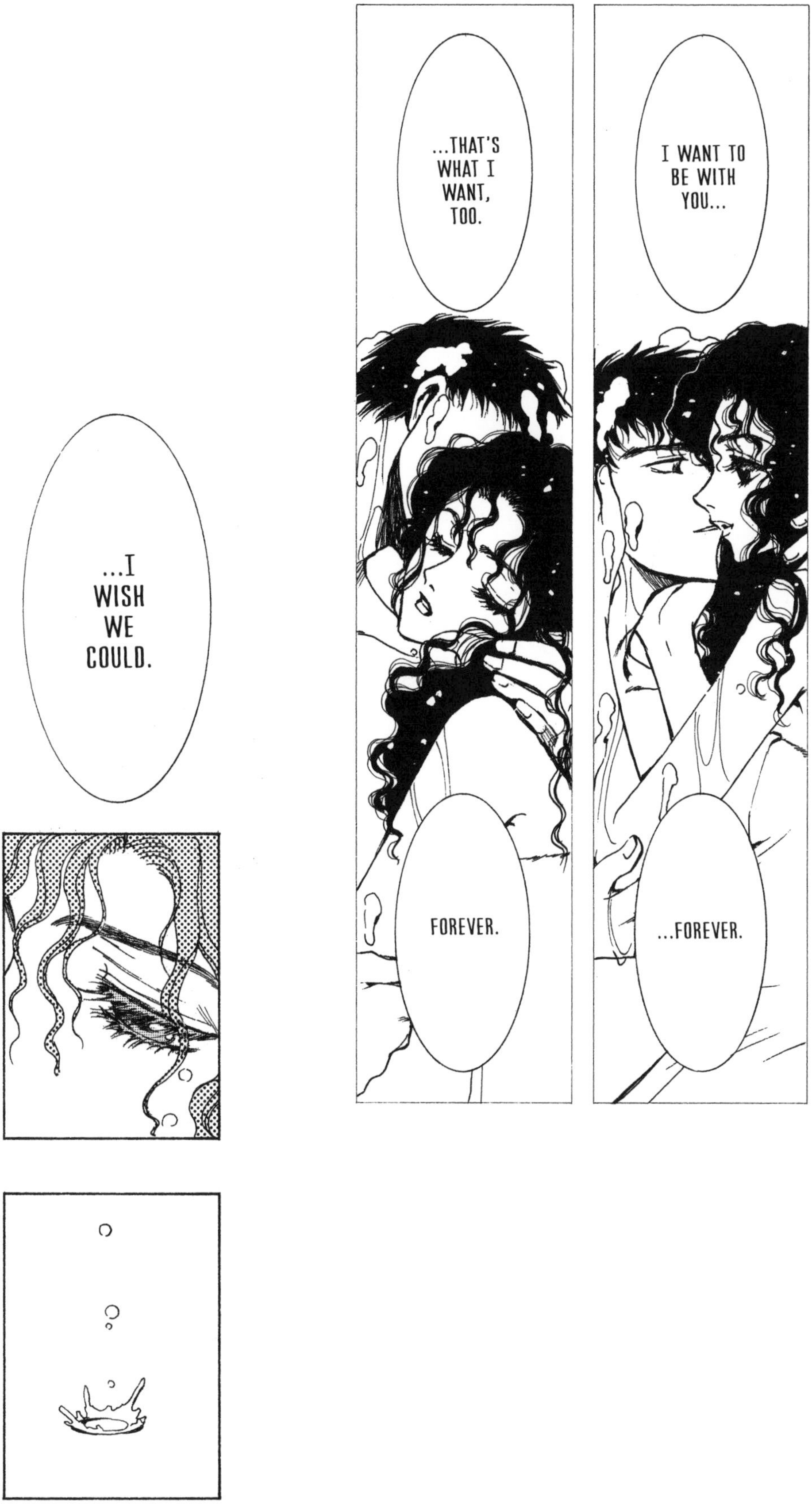
I WANT TO BE WITH YOU...
...FOREVER.
...THAT'S WHAT I WANT, TOO.
FOREVER.
...I WISH WE COULD.

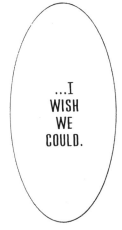

MIRROR AND TOUCH

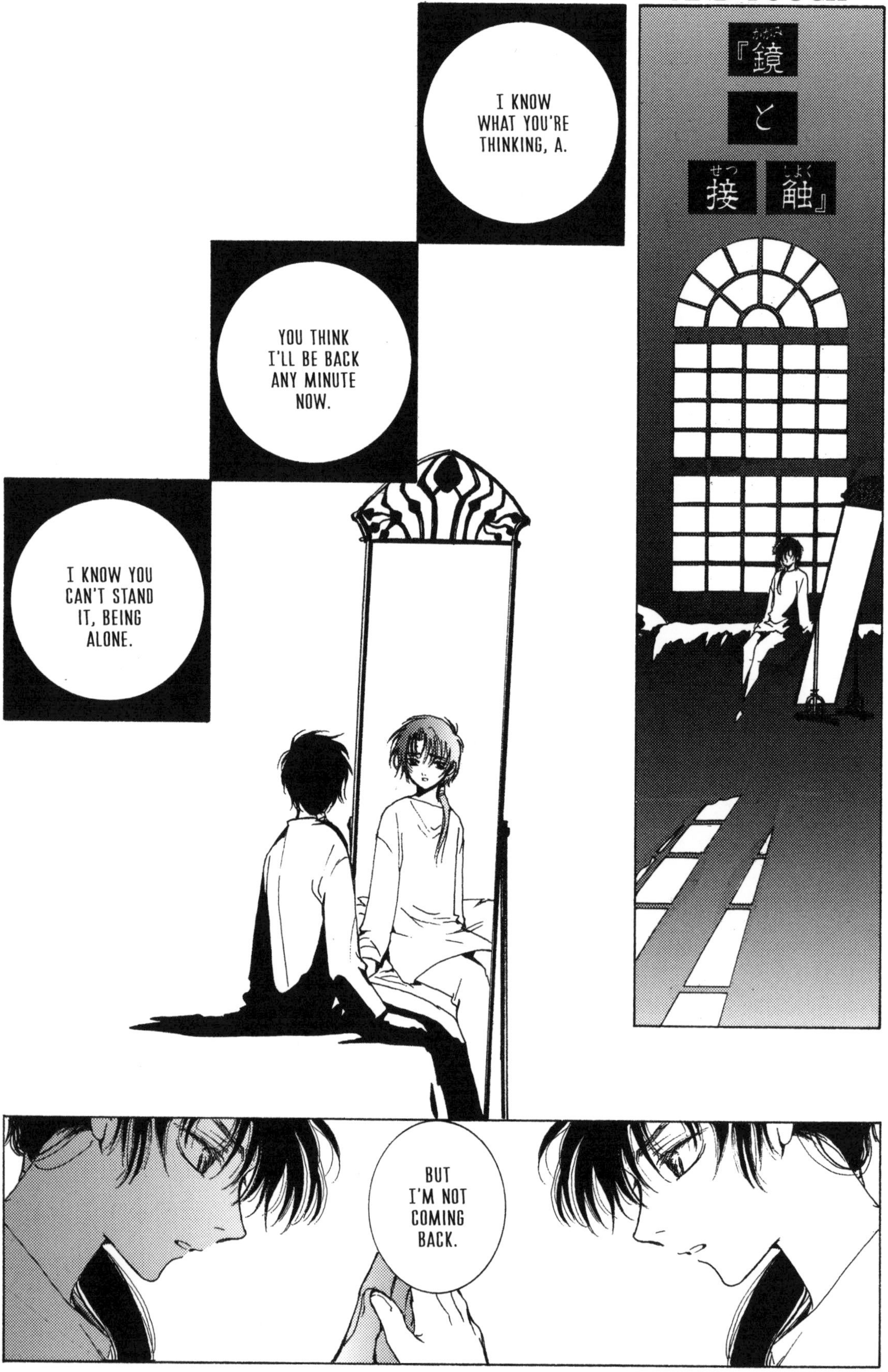
『鏡と接触』
I KNOW WHAT YOU'RE THINKING, A.
YOU THINK I'LL BE BACK ANY MINUTE NOW.
I KNOW YOU CAN'T STAND IT, BEING ALONE.
BUT I'M NOT COMING BACK.

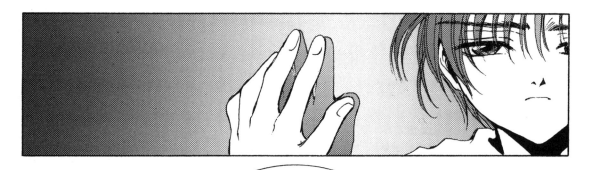

A, EVEN WHEN WE'RE TOGETHER, IT'S LIKE...

...I'M ALONE.

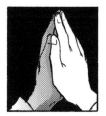

KRRAAASHH

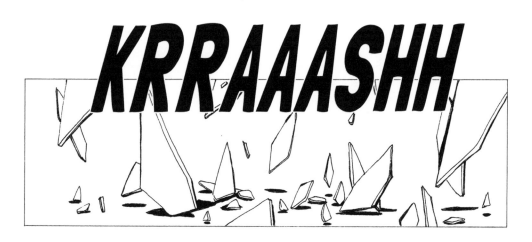

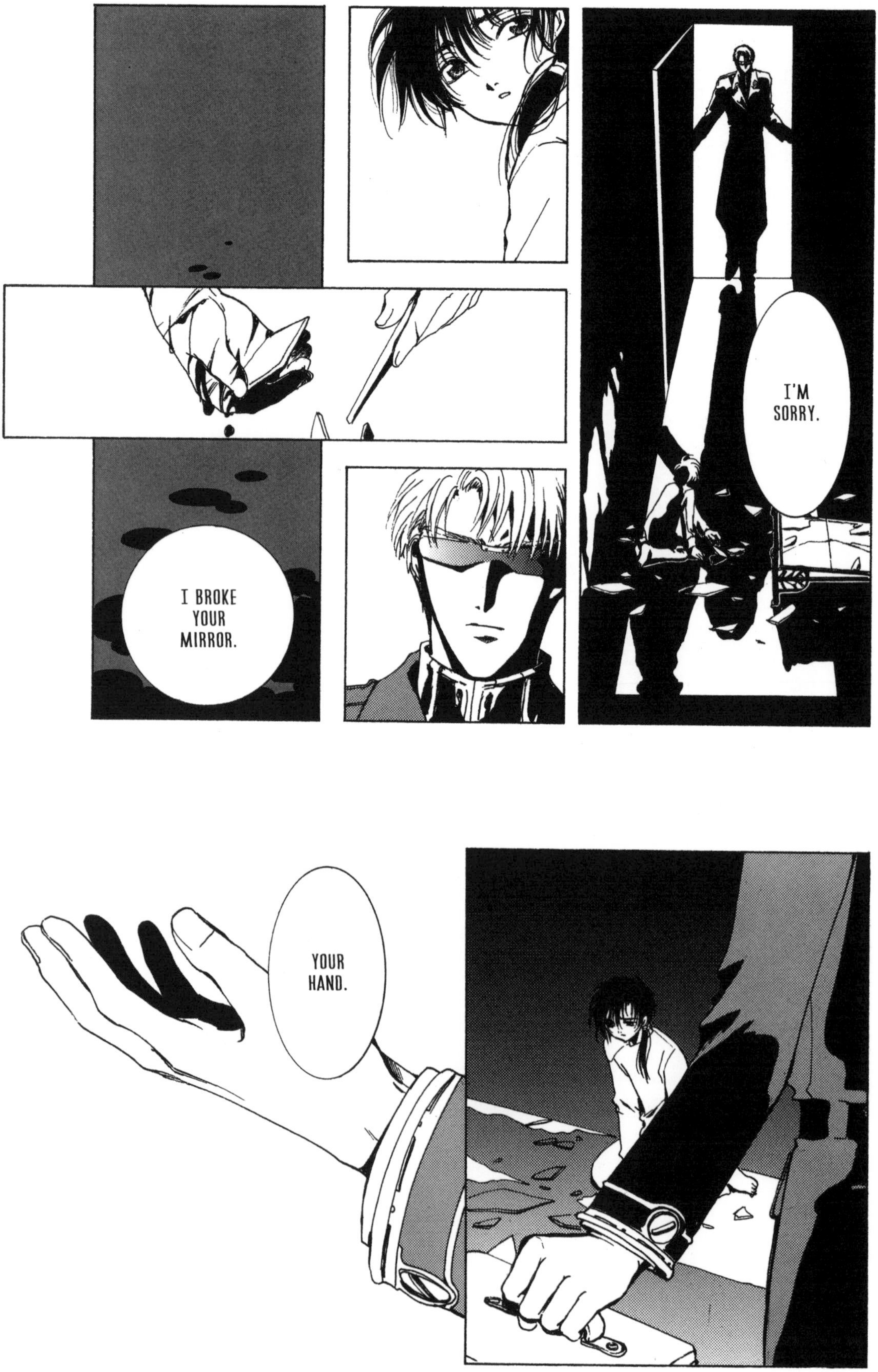
I'M SORRY.
I BROKE YOUR MIRROR.
YOUR HAND.

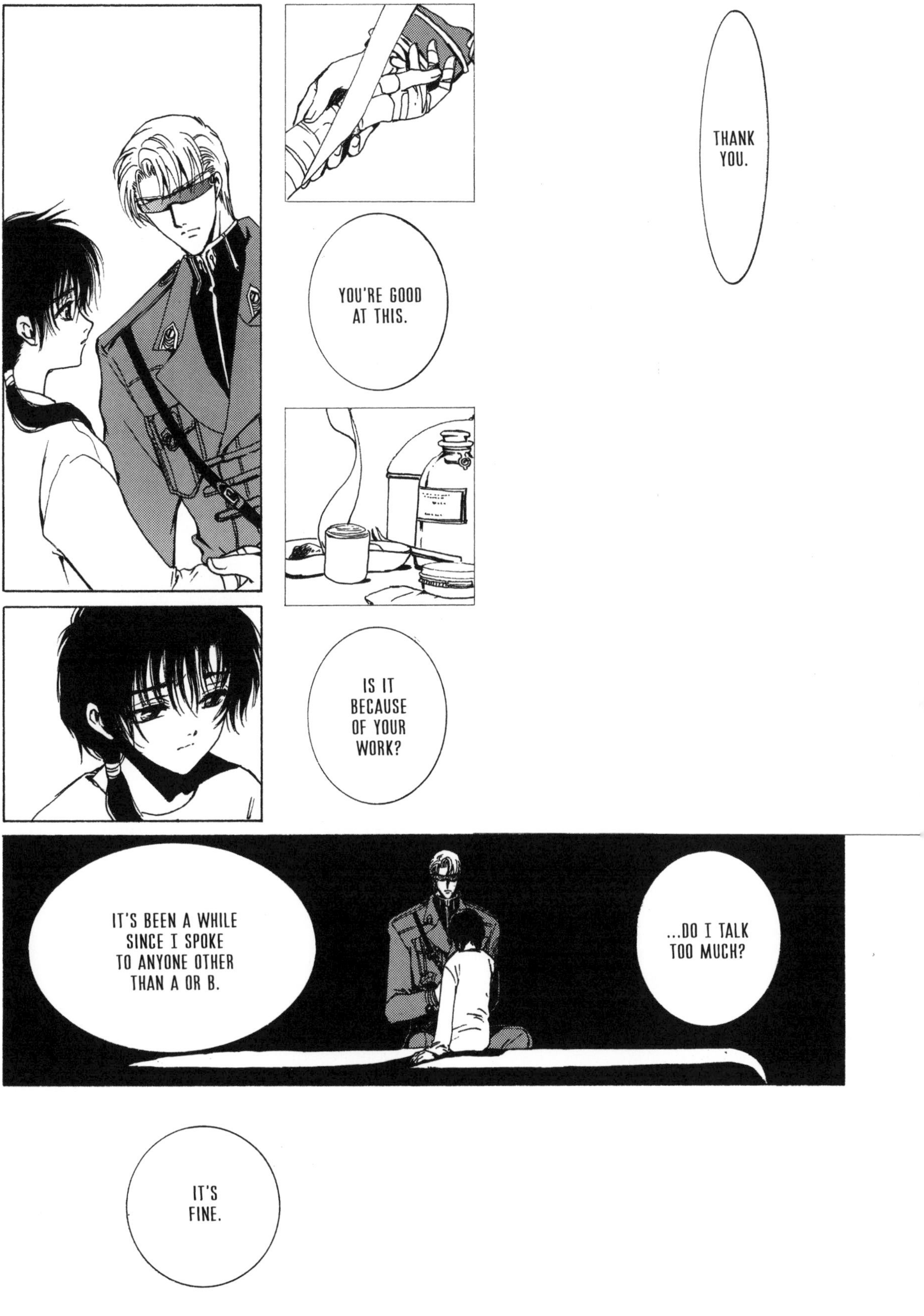
THANK YOU.
YOU'RE GOOD AT THIS.
IS IT BECAUSE OF YOUR WORK?
IT'S BEEN A WHILE SINCE I SPOKE TO ANYONE OTHER THAN A OR B.
...DO I TALK TOO MUCH?
IT'S FINE.

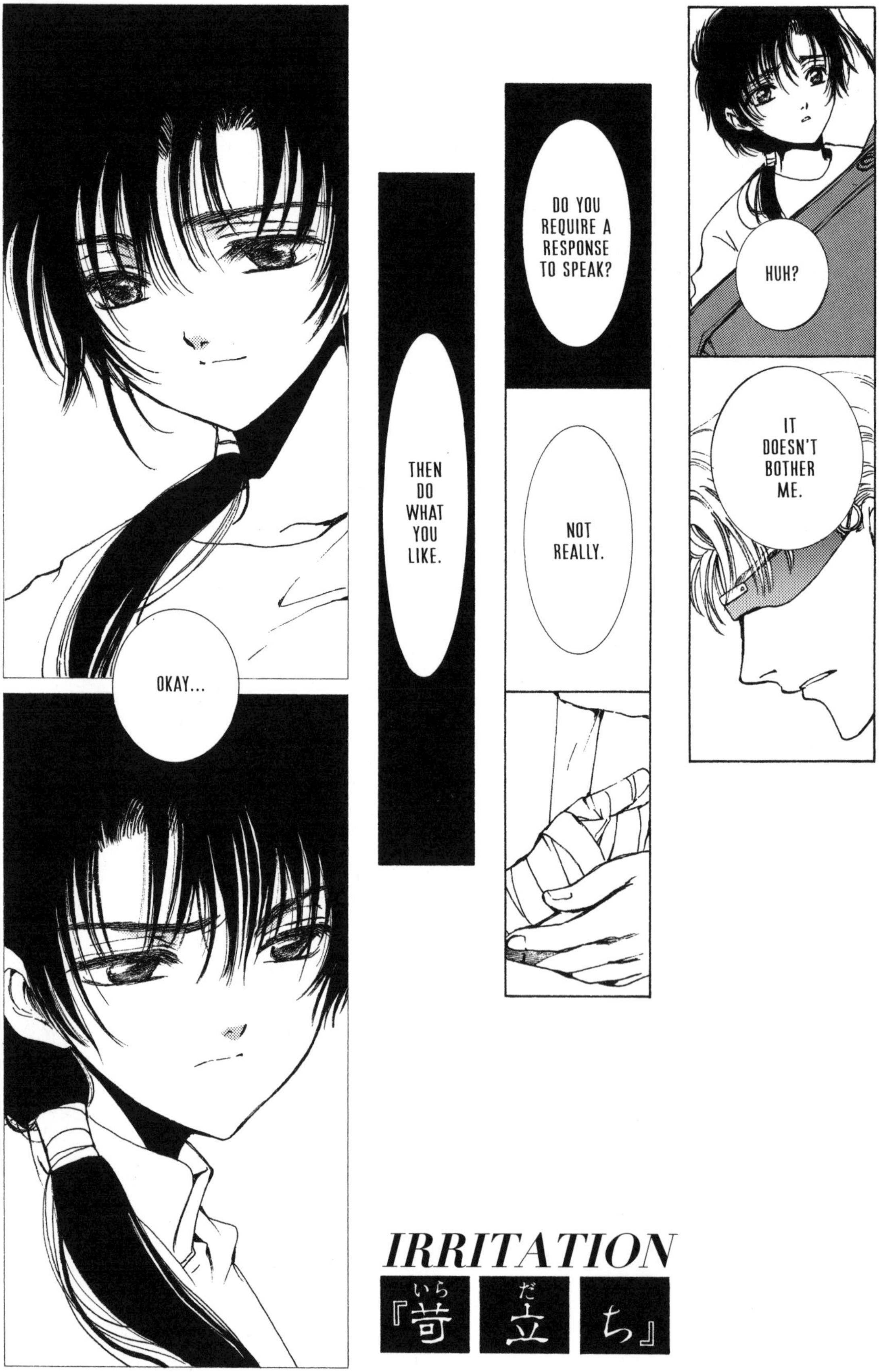
HUH?
IT DOESN'T BOTHER ME.
DO YOU REQUIRE A RESPONSE TO SPEAK?
NOT REALLY.
THEN DO WHAT YOU LIKE.
OKAY...
IRRITATION
『苛立ち』

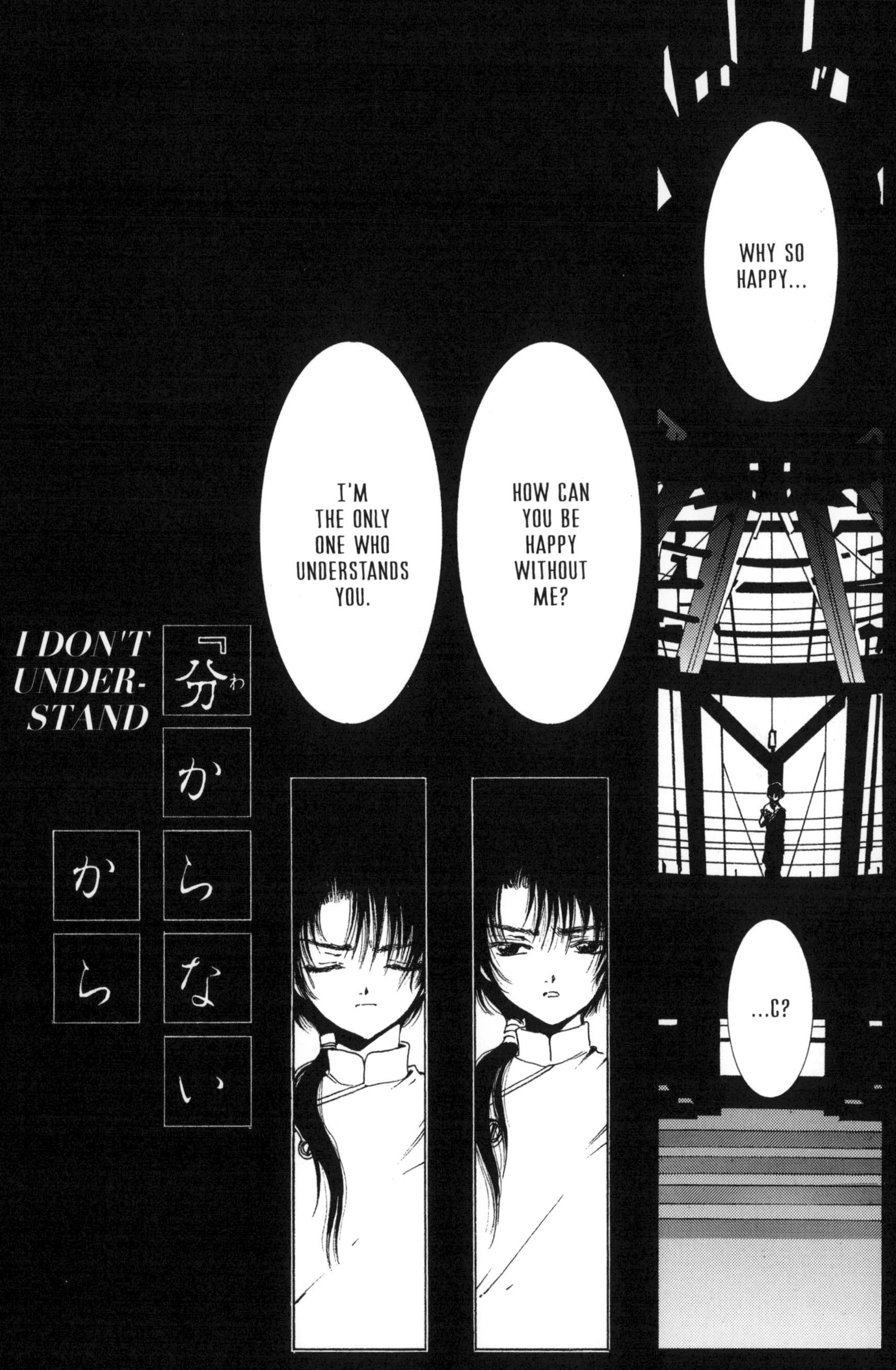
WHY SO HAPPY...
...C?
HOW CAN YOU BE HAPPY WITHOUT ME?
I'M THE ONLY ONE WHO UNDERSTANDS YOU.
I DON'T UNDERSTAND
『分からないから

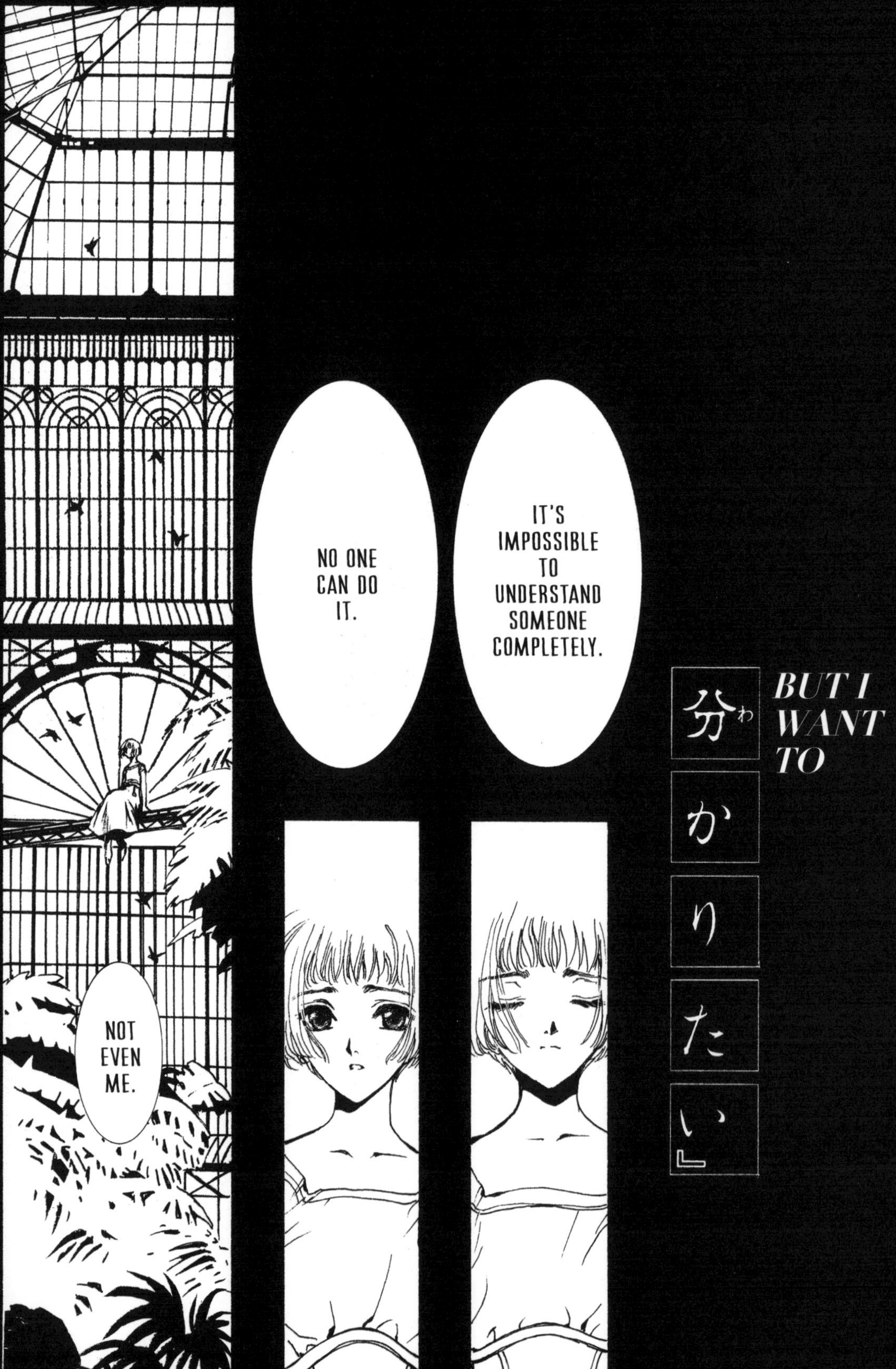
分かりたい」
BUT I WANT TO
IT'S IMPOSSIBLE TO UNDERSTAND SOMEONE COMPLETELY.
NO ONE CAN DO IT.
NOT EVEN ME.

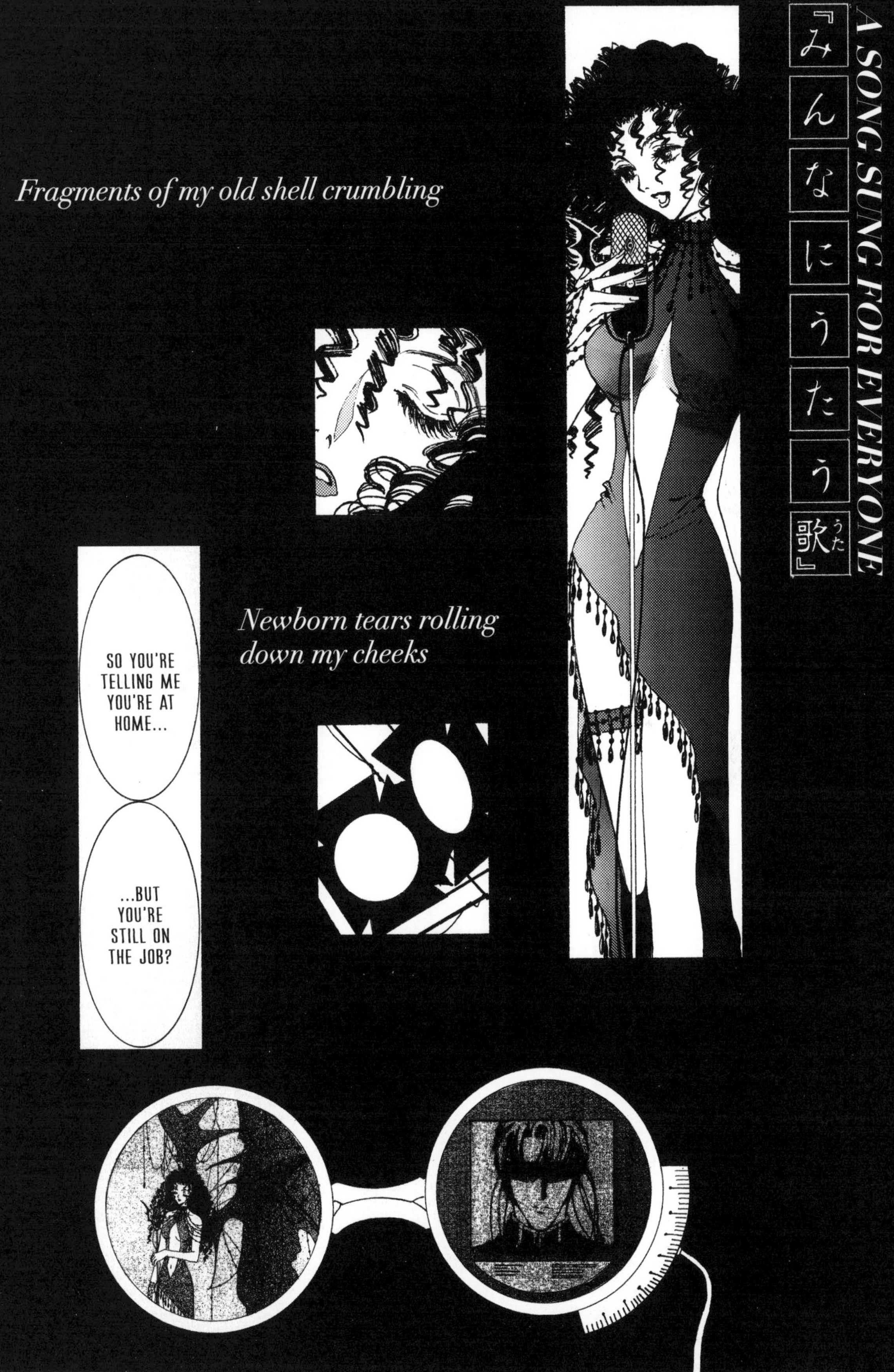
A SONG SUNG FOR EVERYONE
『みんなにうたう歌』
Fragments of my old shell crumbling
Newborn tears rolling down my cheeks
SO YOU'RE TELLING ME YOU'RE AT HOME...
...BUT YOU'RE STILL ON THE JOB?

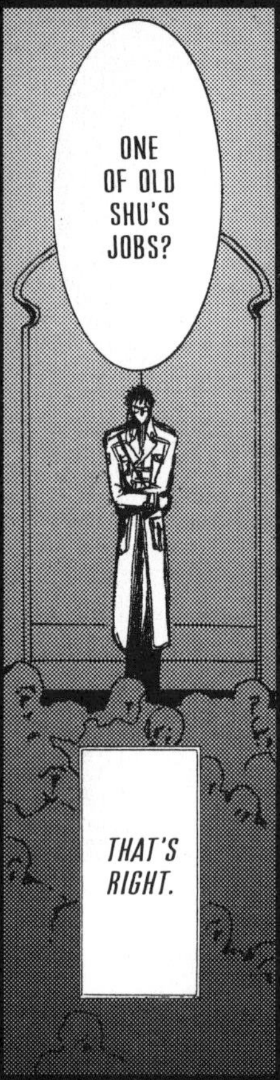
ONE OF OLD SHU'S JOBS?
THAT'S RIGHT.
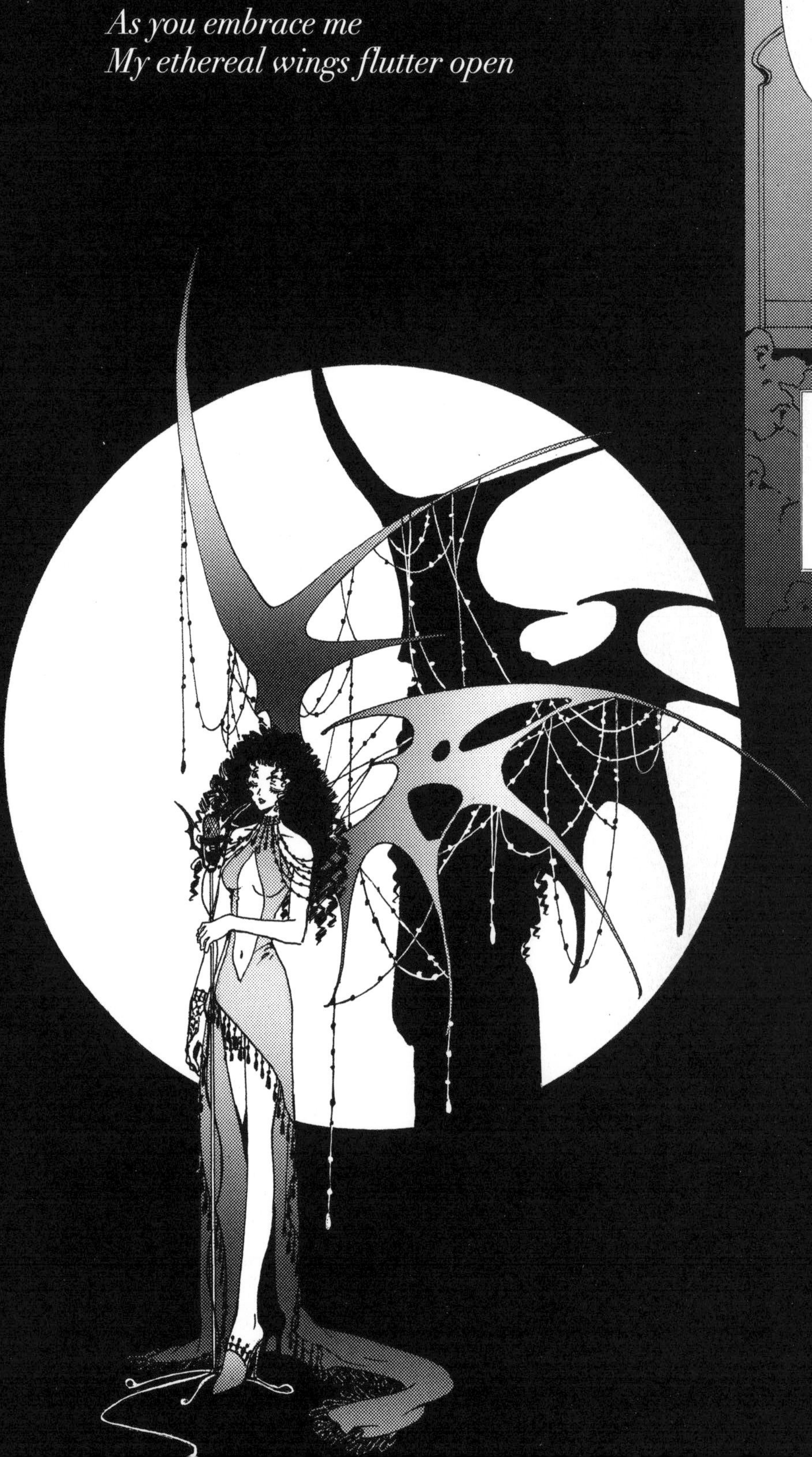
As you embrace me
My ethereal wings flutter open

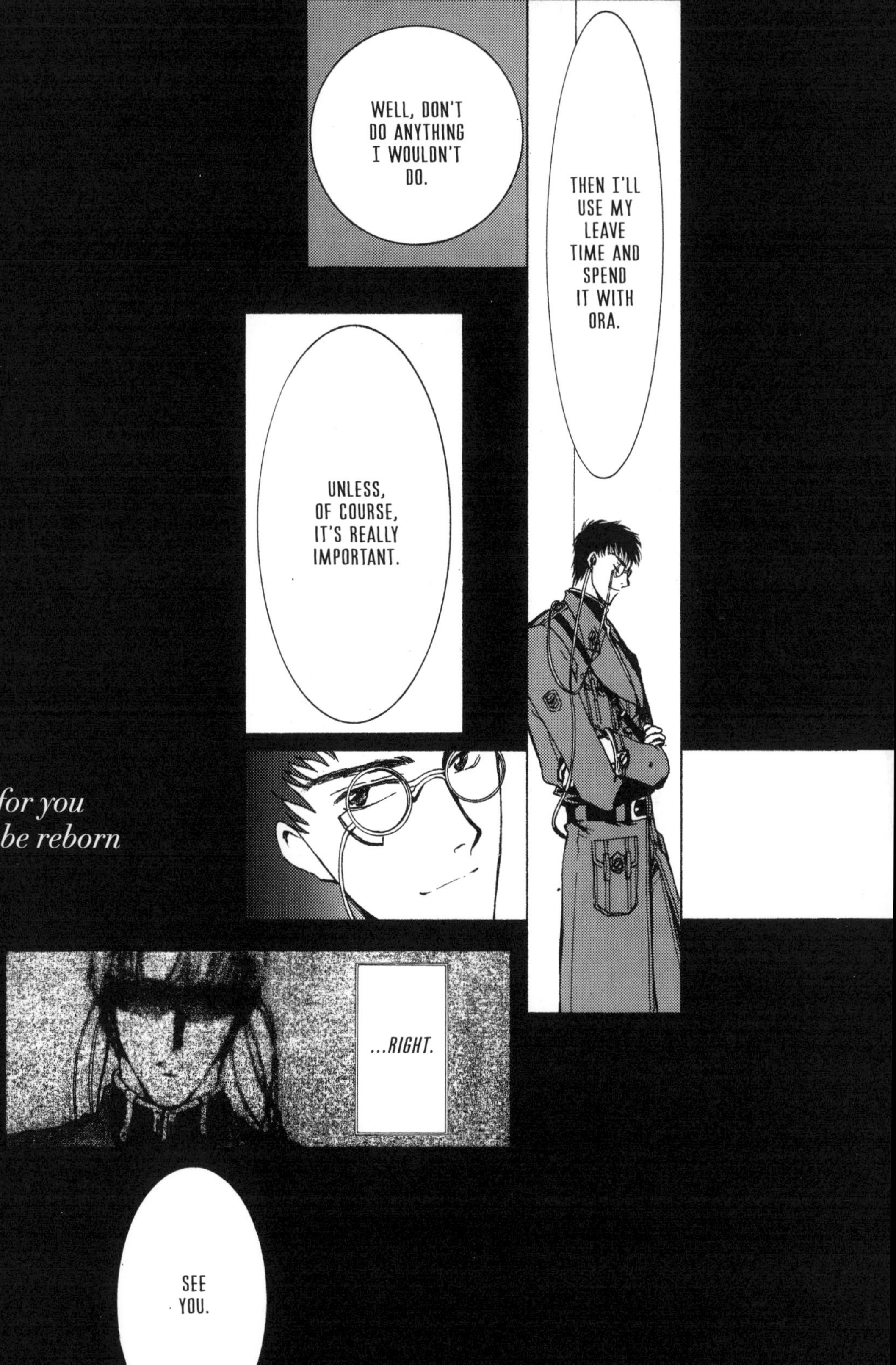
THEN I'LL USE MY LEAVE TIME AND SPEND IT WITH ORA.
WELL, DON'T DO ANYTHING I WOULDN'T DO.
UNLESS, OF COURSE, IT'S REALLY IMPORTANT.
...RIGHT.
SEE YOU.

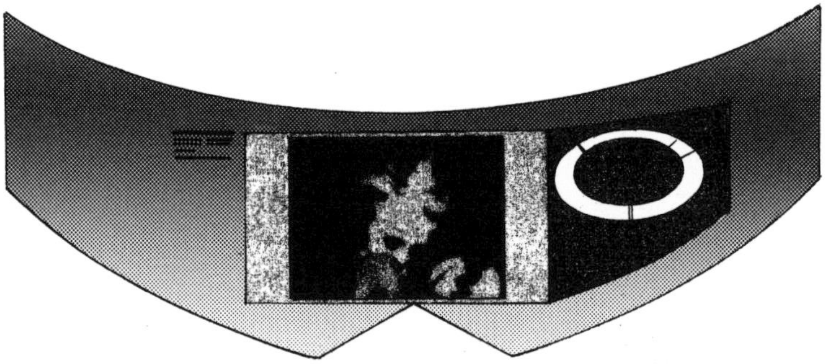

A SONG FOR A COUPLE

『ふたりできく歌』

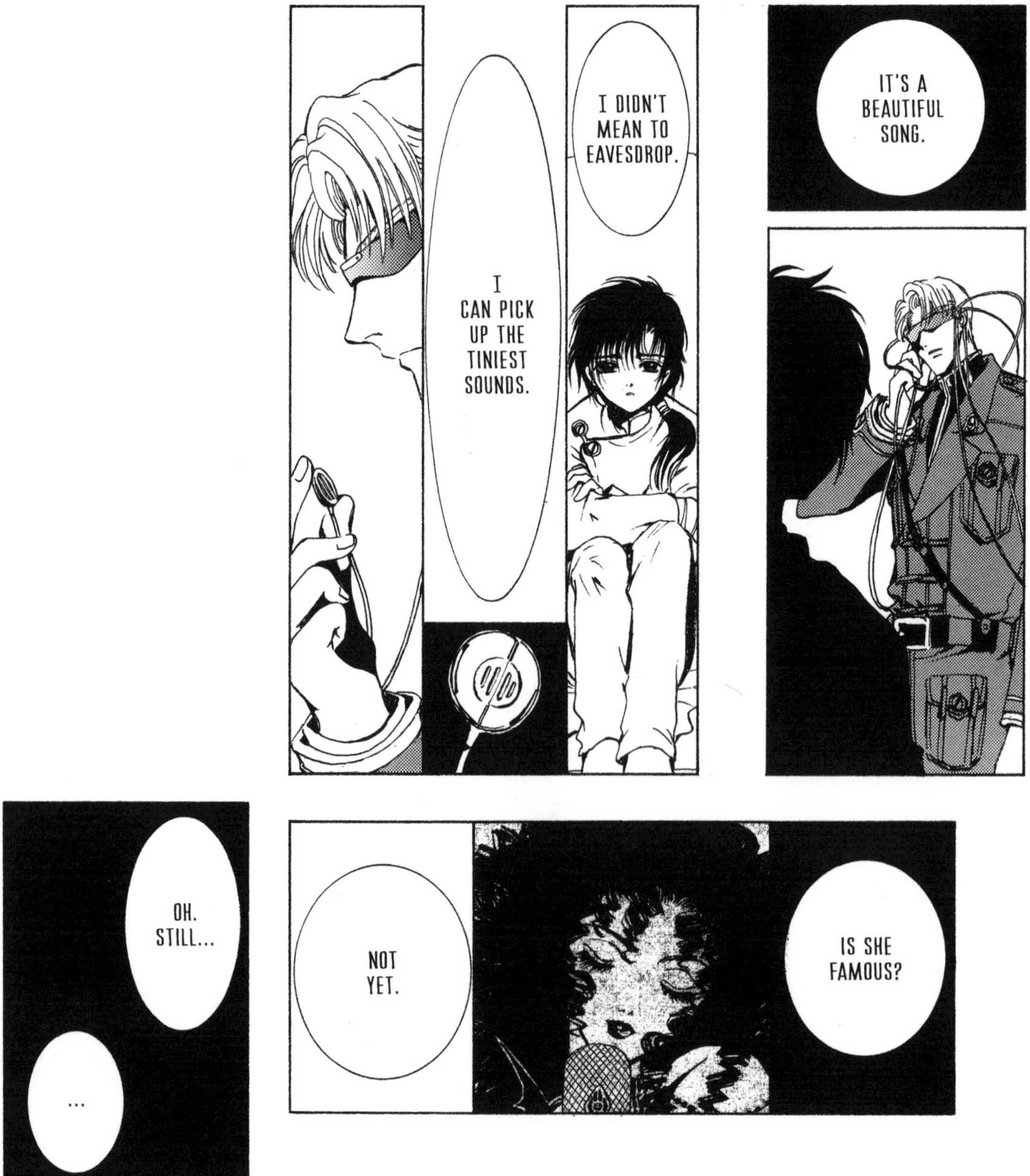

IT'S A BEAUTIFUL SONG.
I DIDN'T MEAN TO EAVESDROP.
I CAN PICK UP THE TINIEST SOUNDS.
IS SHE FAMOUS?
NOT YET.
OH. STILL...
...

...SHE SINGS BEAUTIFULLY.

In your arms

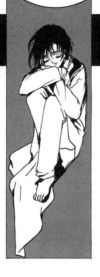

I will be reborn

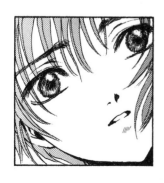

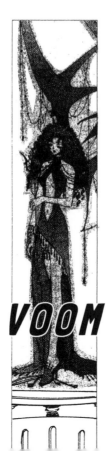

VOOM

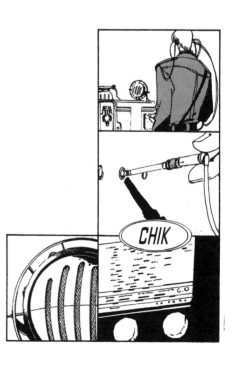

CHIK

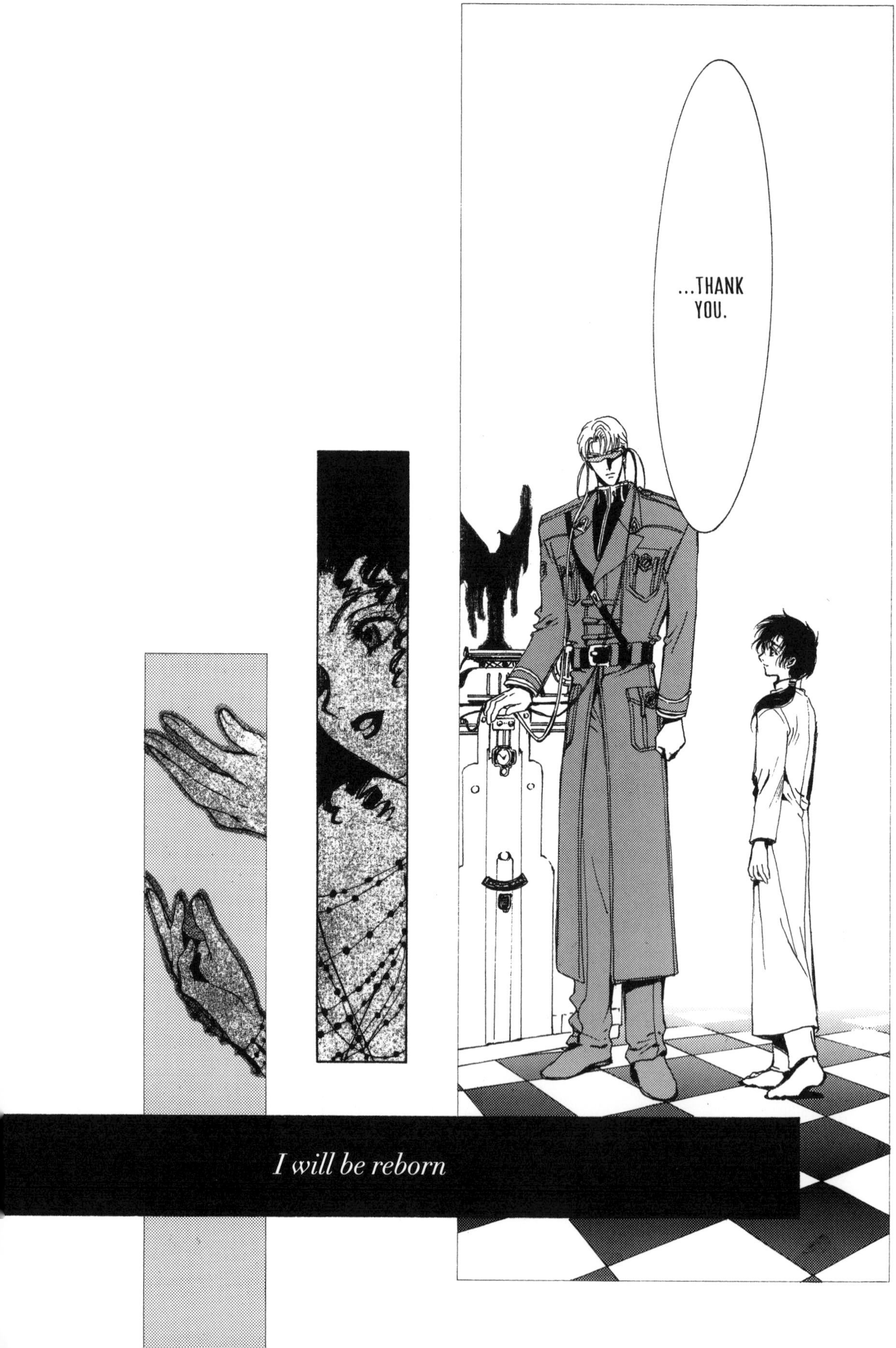
...THANK YOU.
I will be reborn

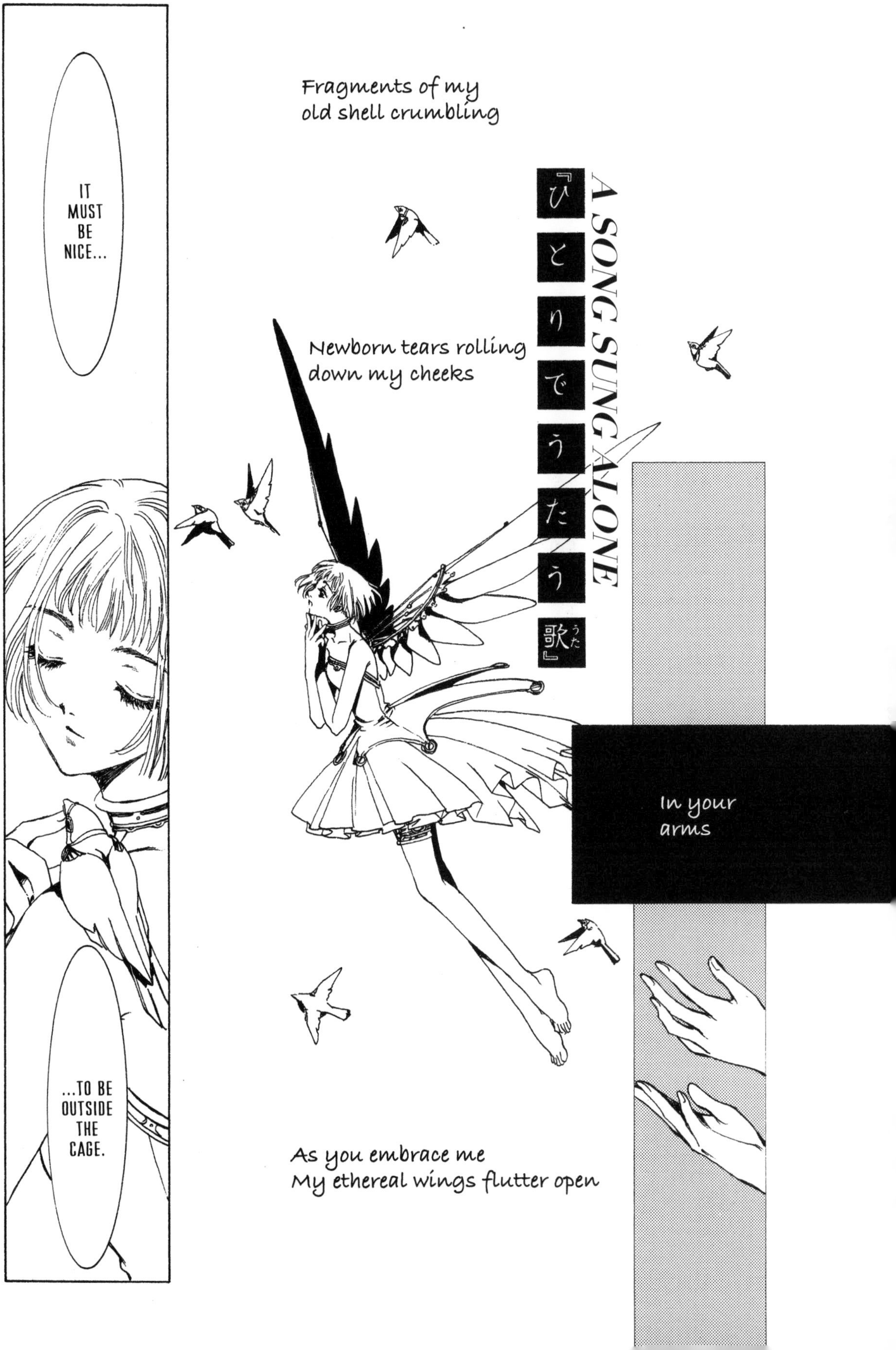
A SONG SUNG ALONE
『ひとりでうたう歌』
Fragments of my old shell crumbling
Newborn tears rolling down my cheeks
In your arms
As you embrace me My ethereal wings flutter open
IT MUST BE NICE...
...TO BE OUTSIDE THE CAGE.

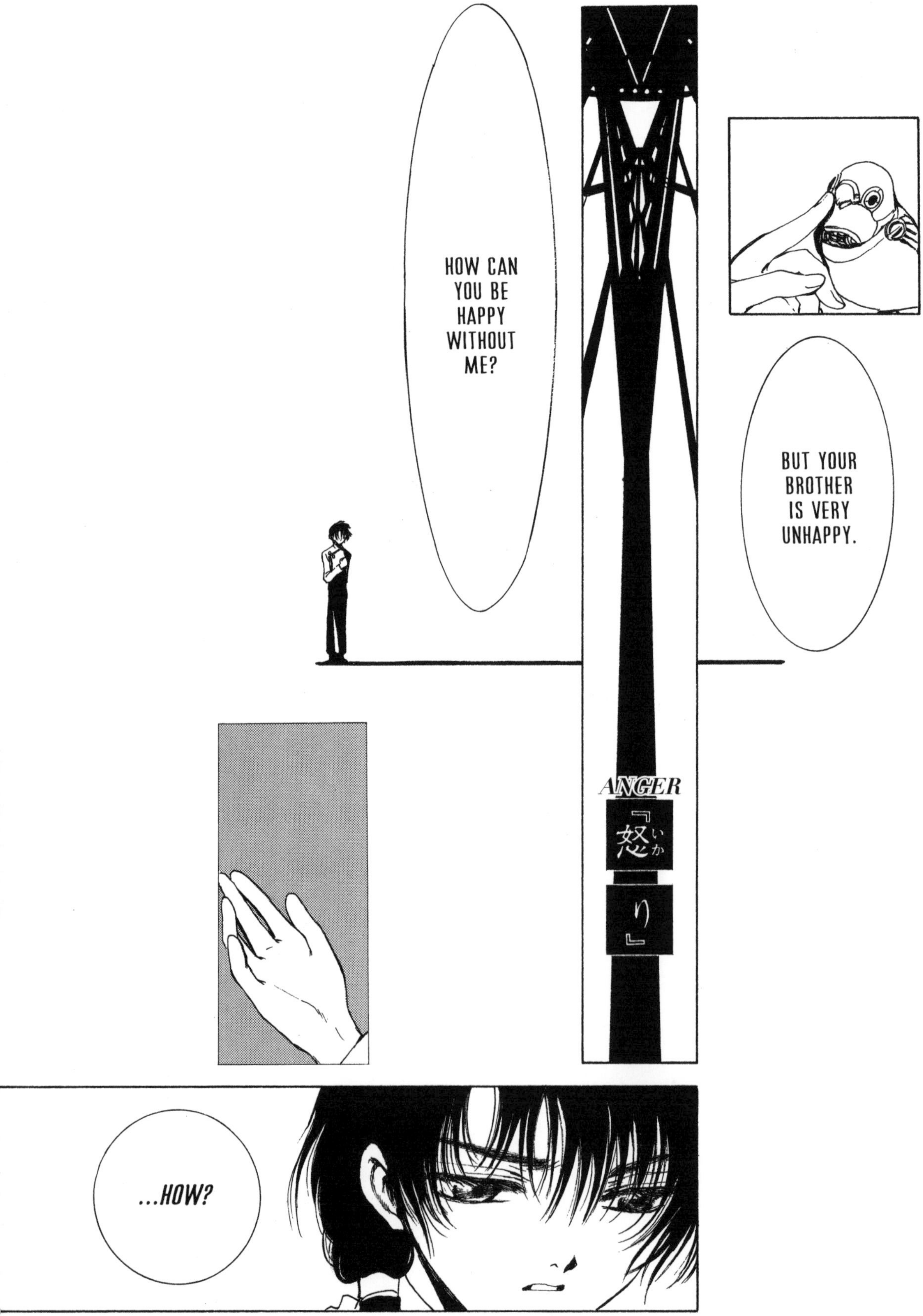

BUT YOUR BROTHER IS VERY UNHAPPY.
ANGER
『怒り』
HOW CAN YOU BE HAPPY WITHOUT ME?
...HOW?

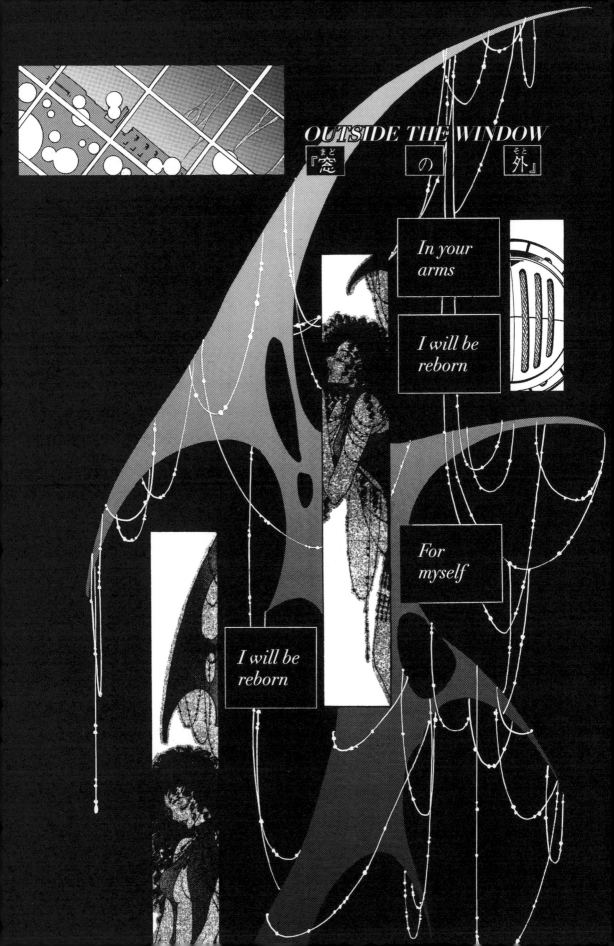

OUTSIDE THE WINDOW
『窓 の 外』

In your arms

I will be reborn

For myself

I will be reborn

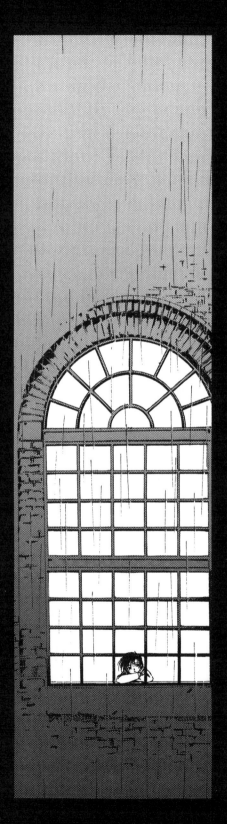

With your voice and your touch

Let me forget everything

Break off the chains that bind

My heart and feet

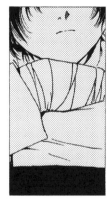

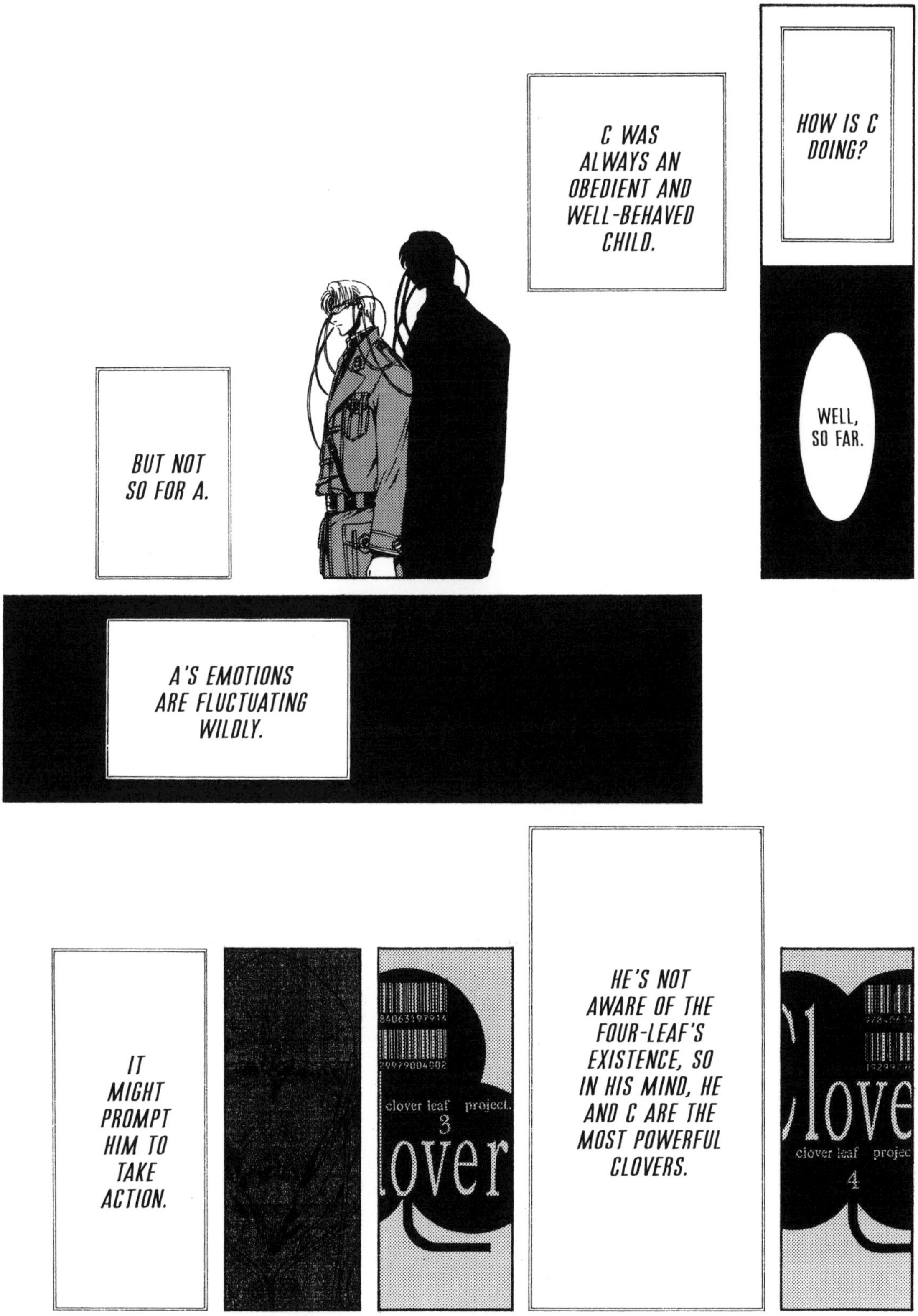
HOW IS C DOING?
WELL, SO FAR.
C WAS ALWAYS AN OBEDIENT AND WELL-BEHAVED CHILD.
BUT NOT SO FOR A.
A'S EMOTIONS ARE FLUCTUATING WILDLY.
HE'S NOT AWARE OF THE FOUR-LEAF'S EXISTENCE, SO IN HIS MIND, HE AND C ARE THE MOST POWERFUL CLOVERS.
IT MIGHT PROMPT HIM TO TAKE ACTION.

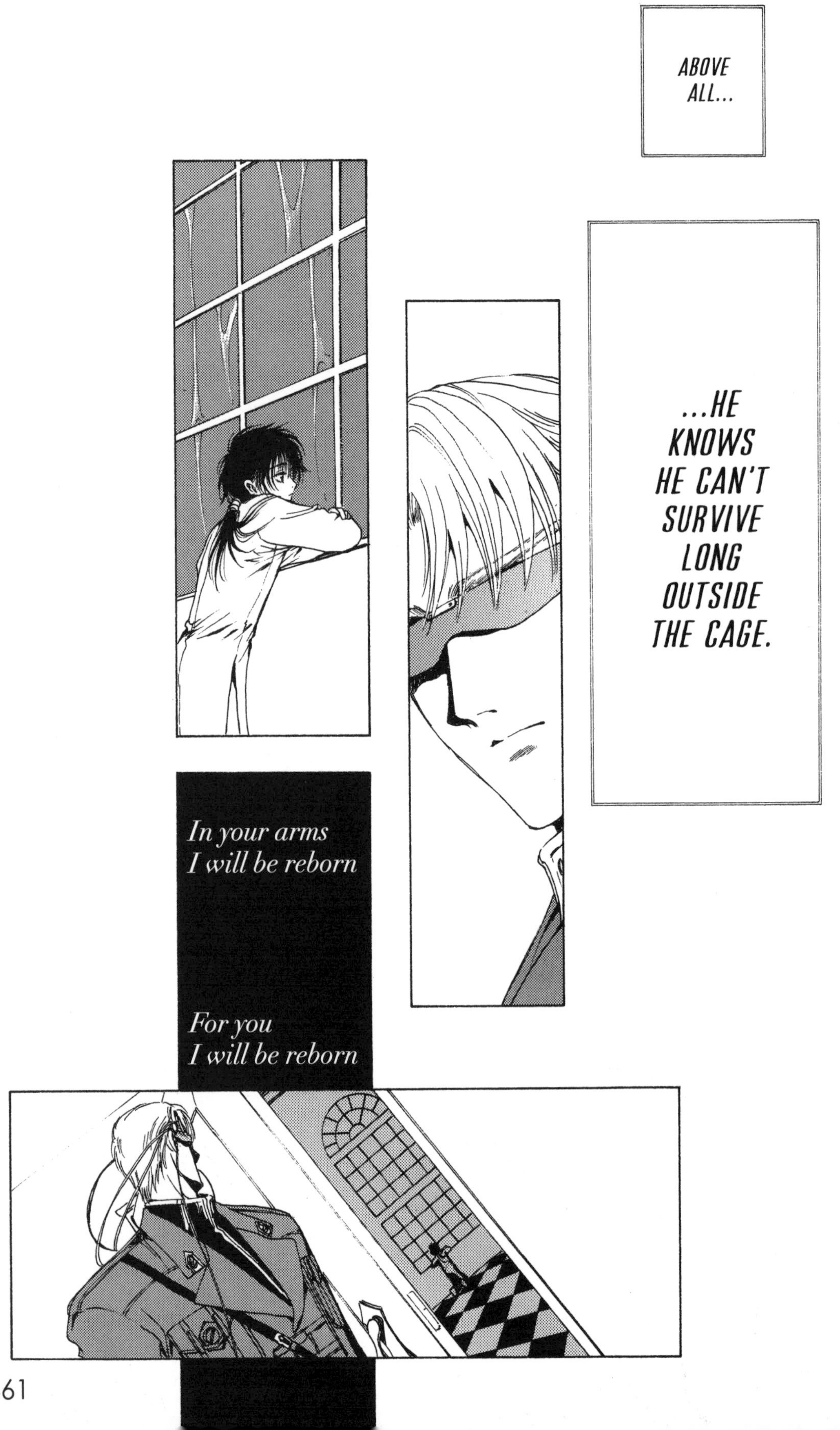
ABOVE ALL...
...HE KNOWS HE CAN'T SURVIVE LONG OUTSIDE THE CAGE.
In your arms
I will be reborn
For you
I will be reborn

DO YOU
WANT TO GO
OUTSIDE?

NO.

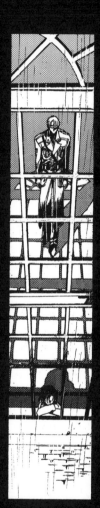

*In your arms
I will be reborn*

*For myself
I will be reborn*

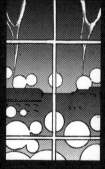

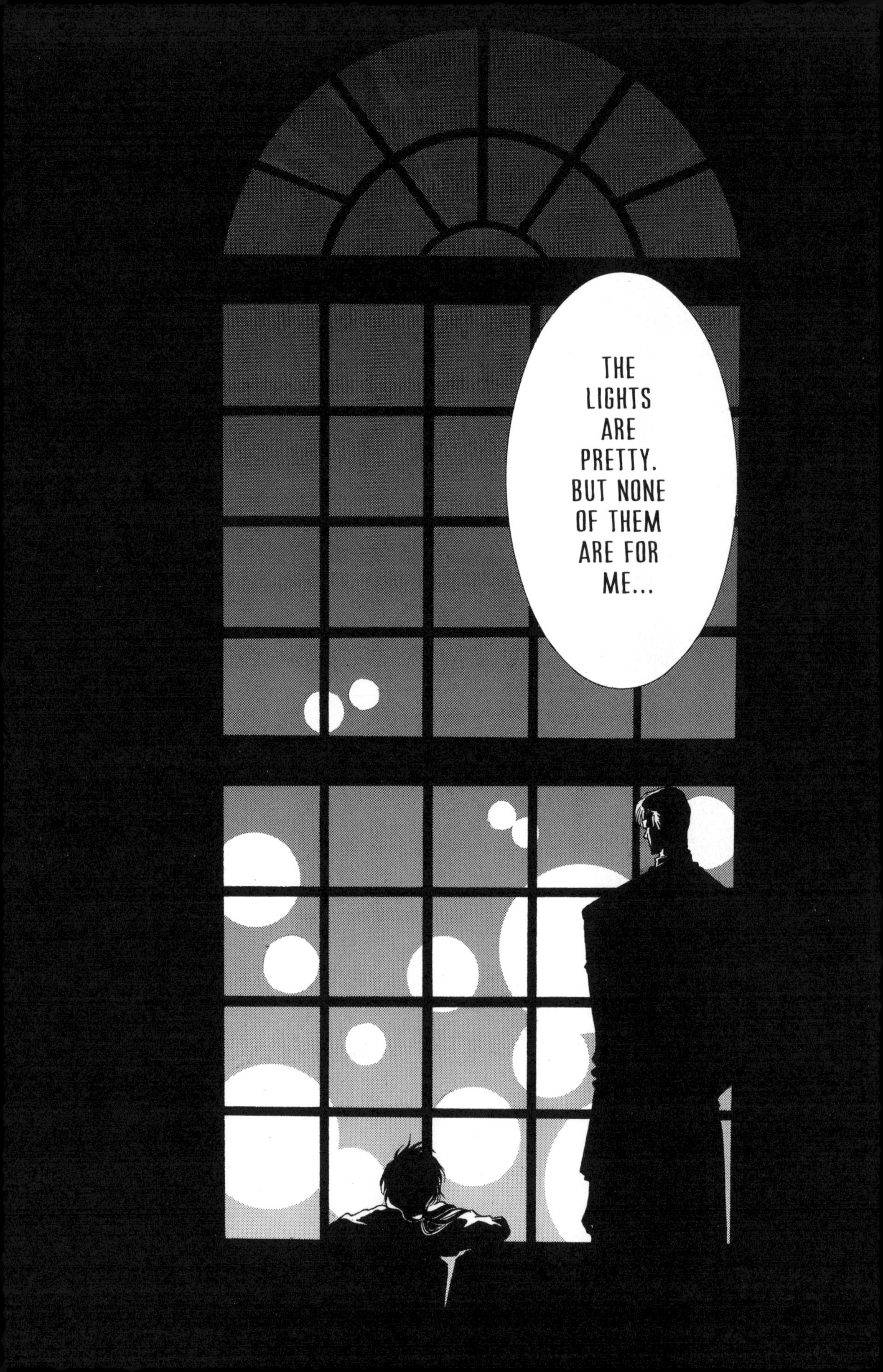
THE LIGHTS ARE PRETTY. BUT NONE OF THEM ARE FOR ME...

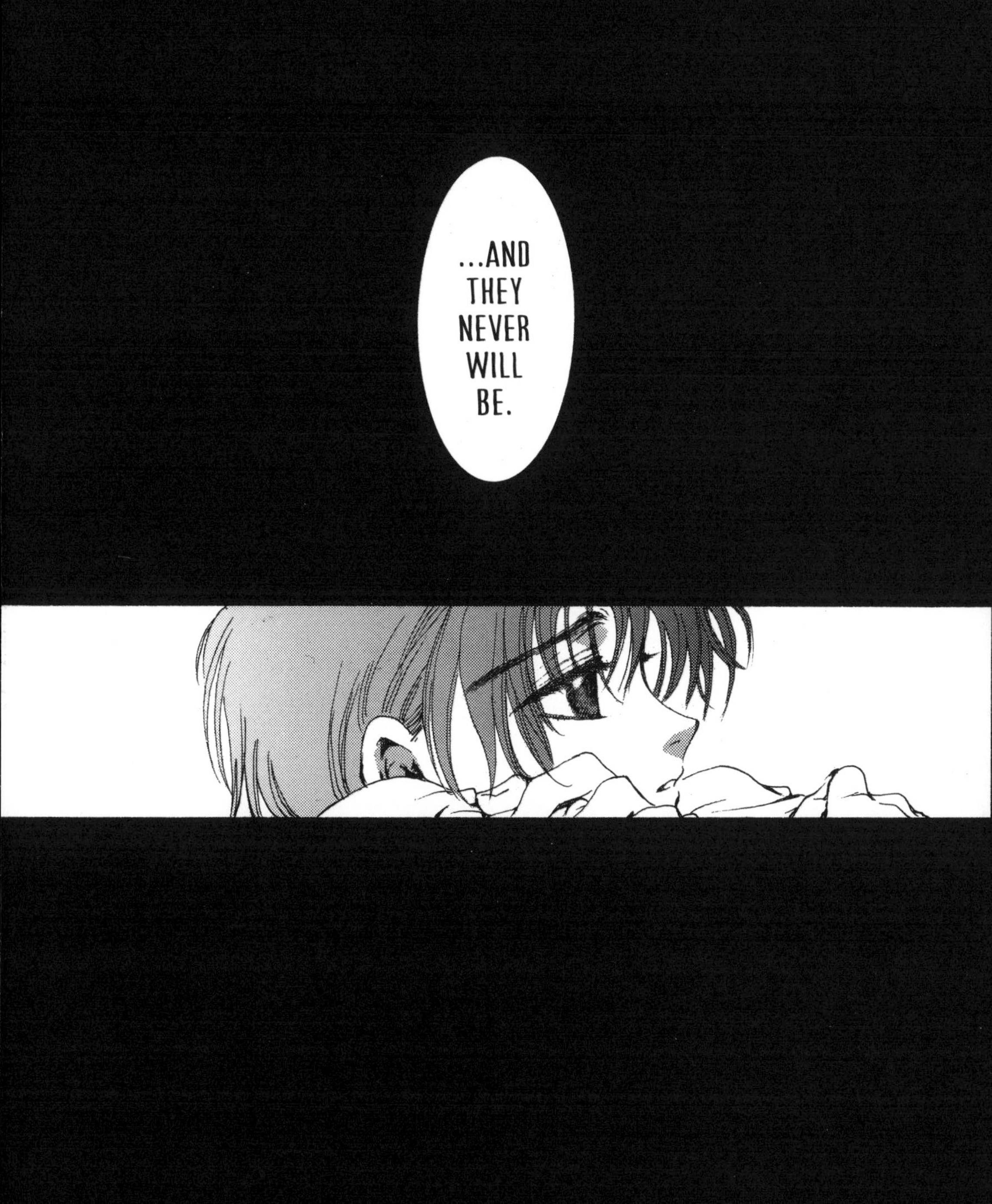
...AND THEY NEVER WILL BE.

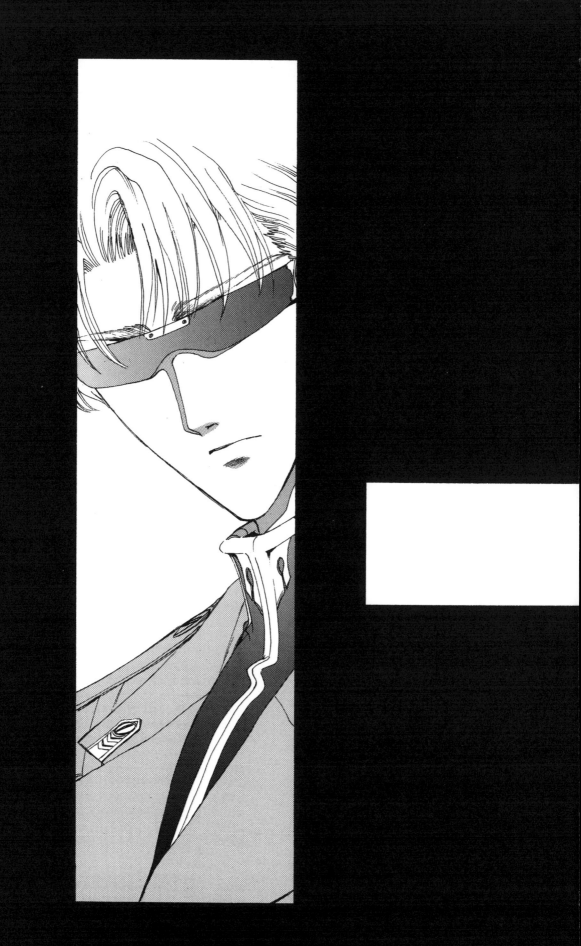

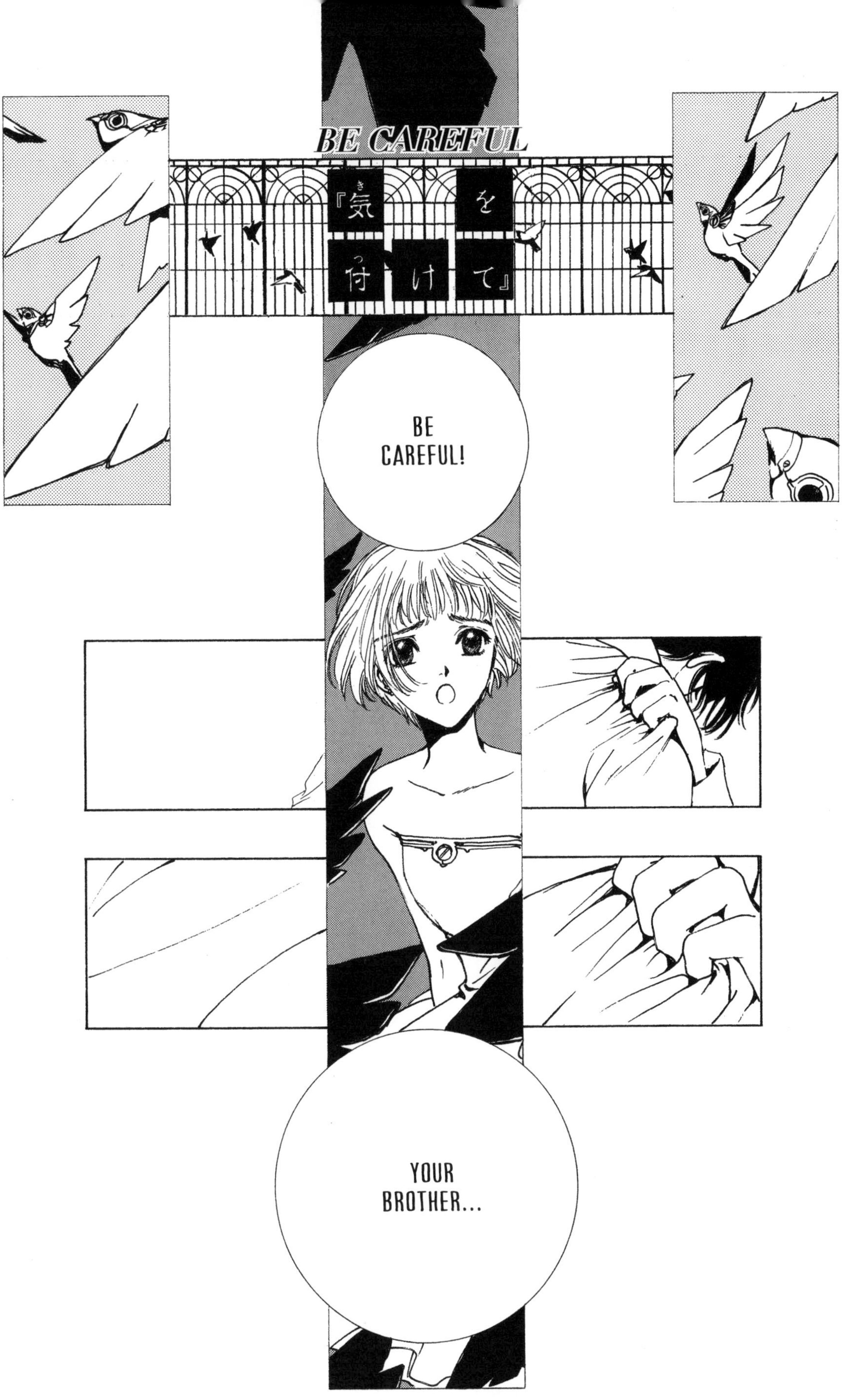
BE CAREFUL
『気を付けて』
BE CAREFUL!
YOUR BROTHER...

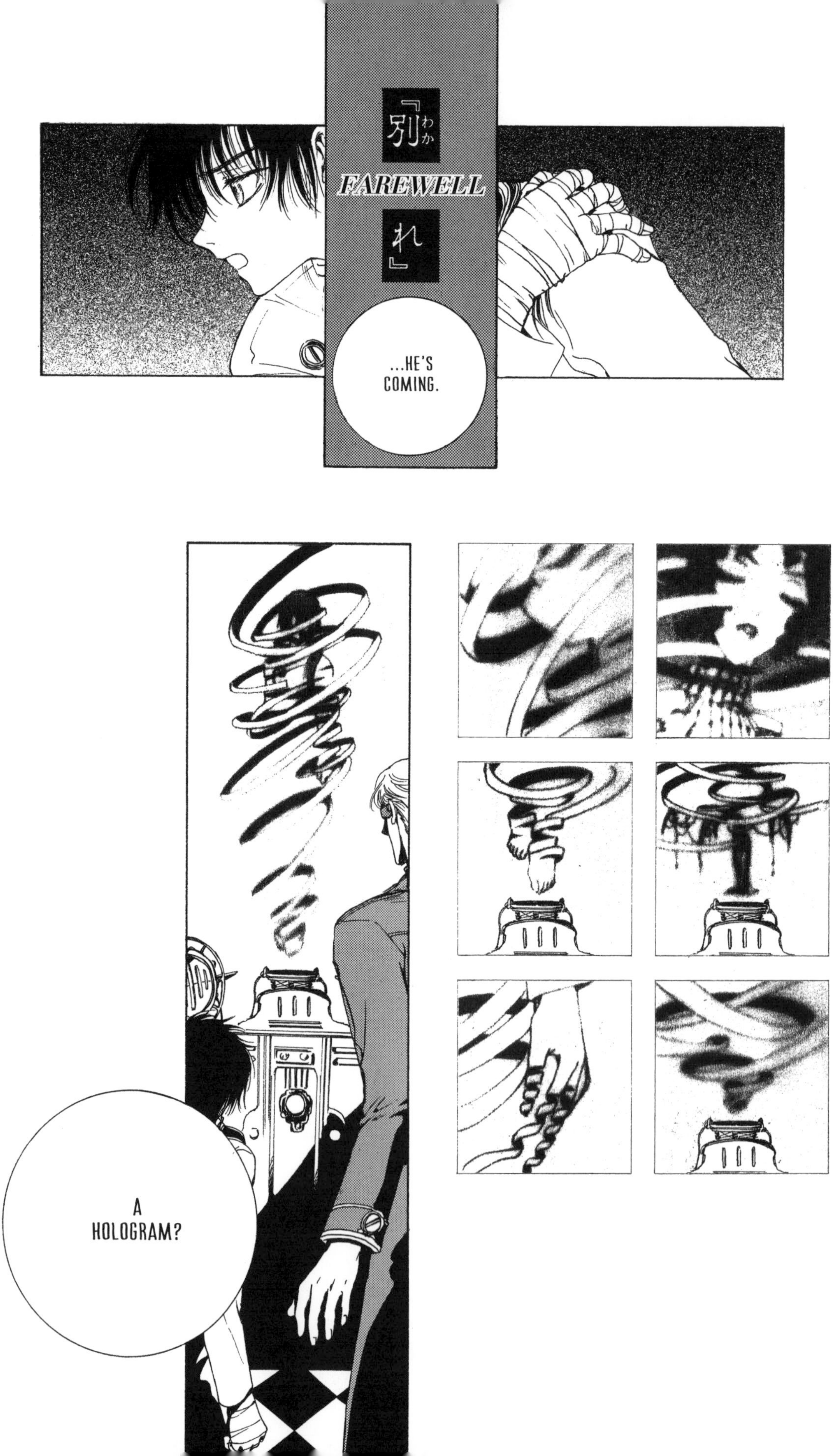
『別れ』
FAREWELL
...HE'S COMING.
A HOLOGRAM?

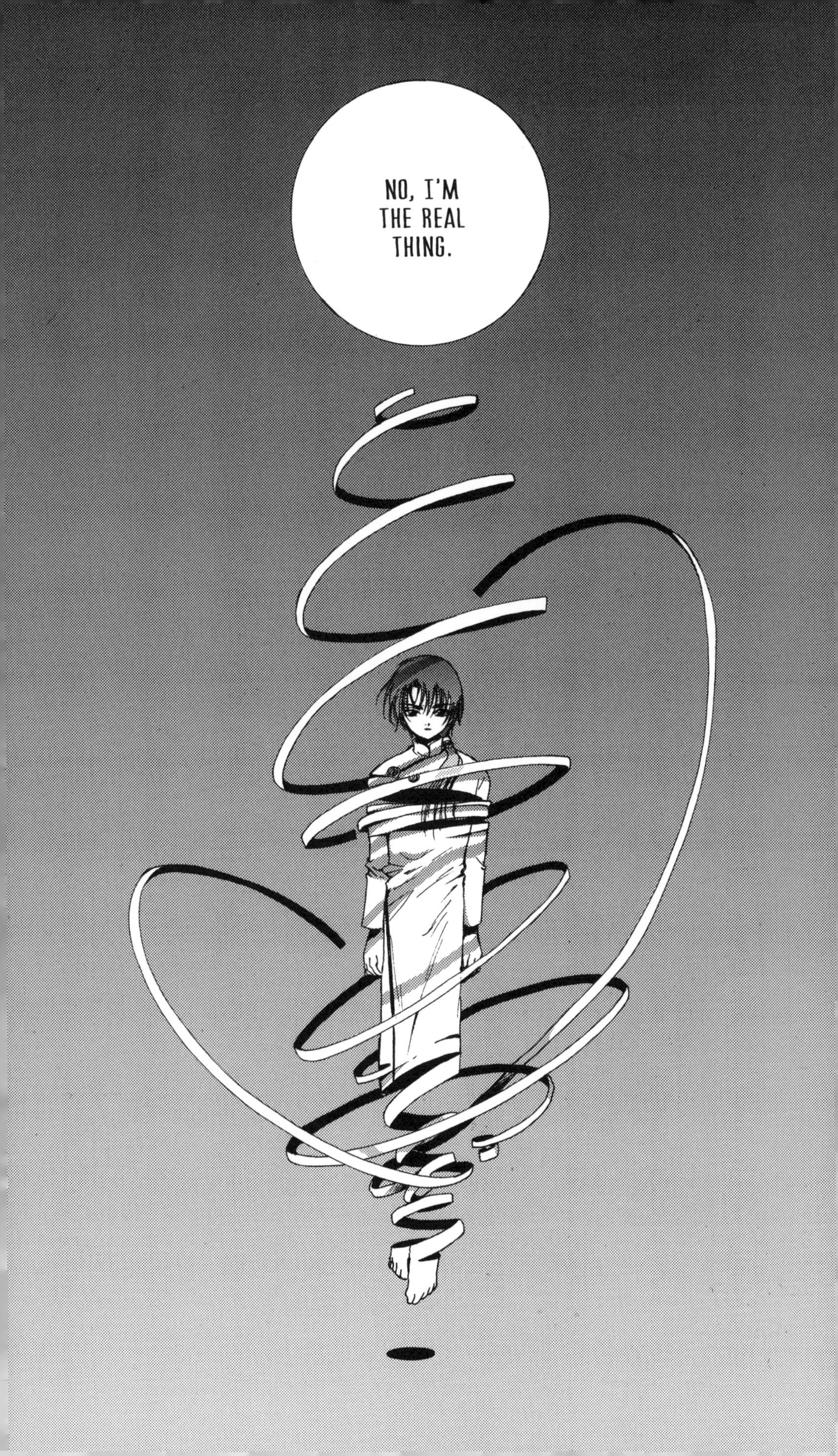
NO, I'M THE REAL THING.

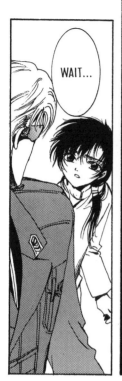

WAIT...

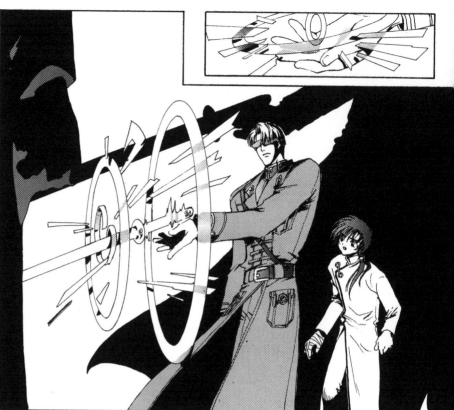

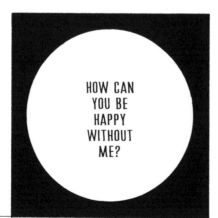

HOW CAN
YOU BE
HAPPY
WITHOUT
ME?

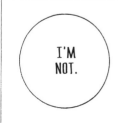

I'M
NOT.

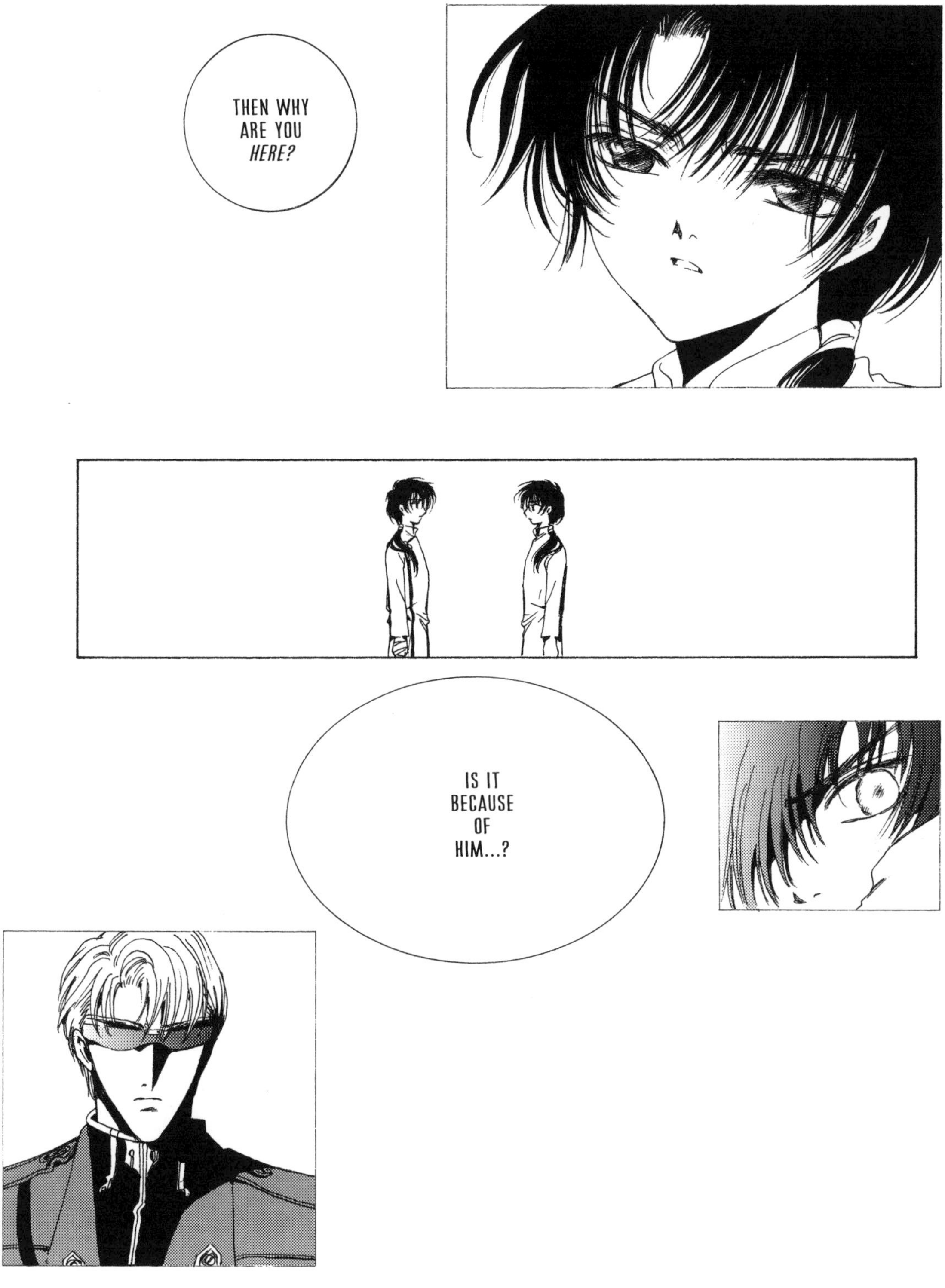
THEN WHY ARE YOU *HERE?*
IS IT BECAUSE OF HIM...?

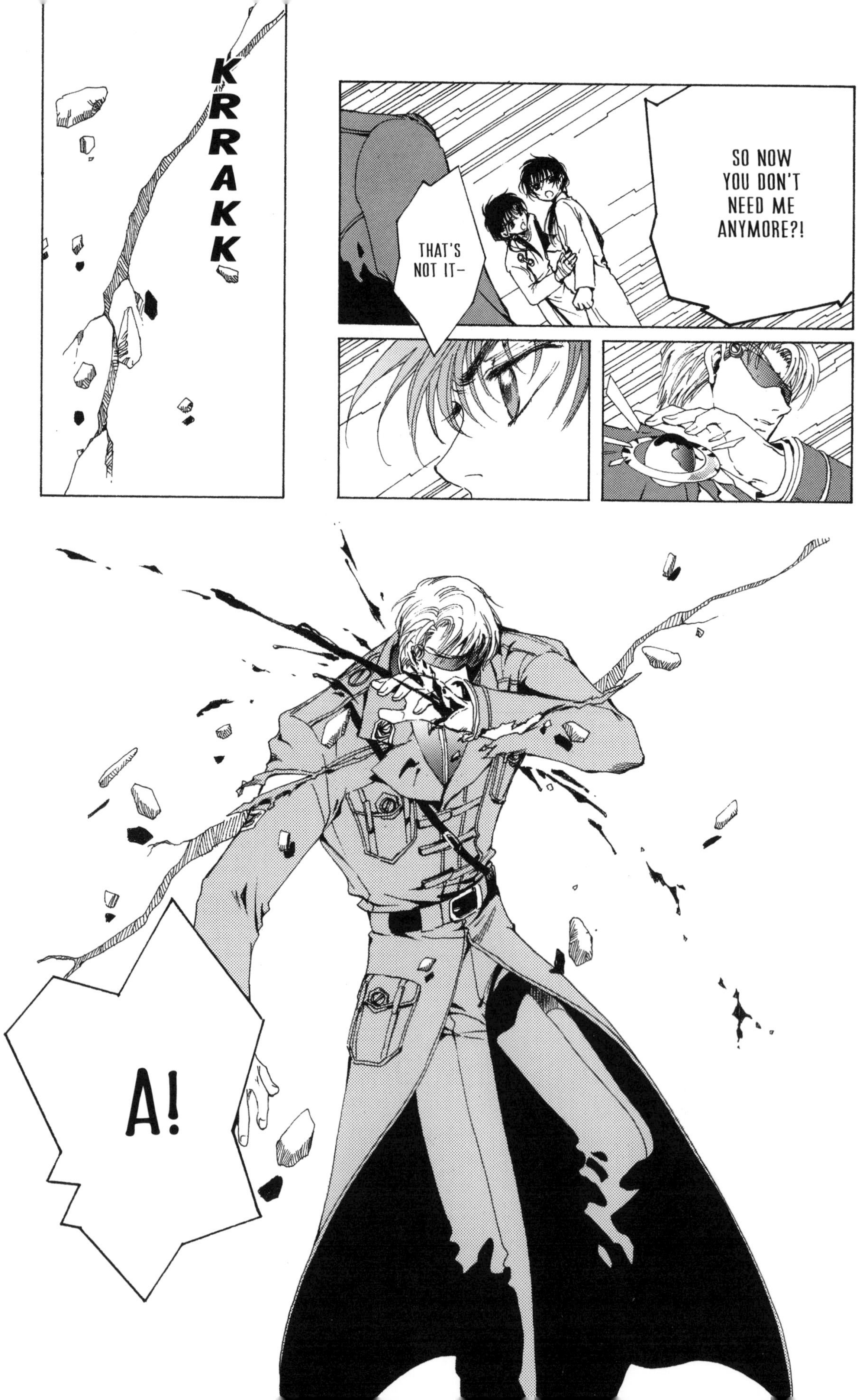
SO NOW YOU DON'T NEED ME ANYMORE?!
THAT'S NOT IT–
KRRAKK
A!

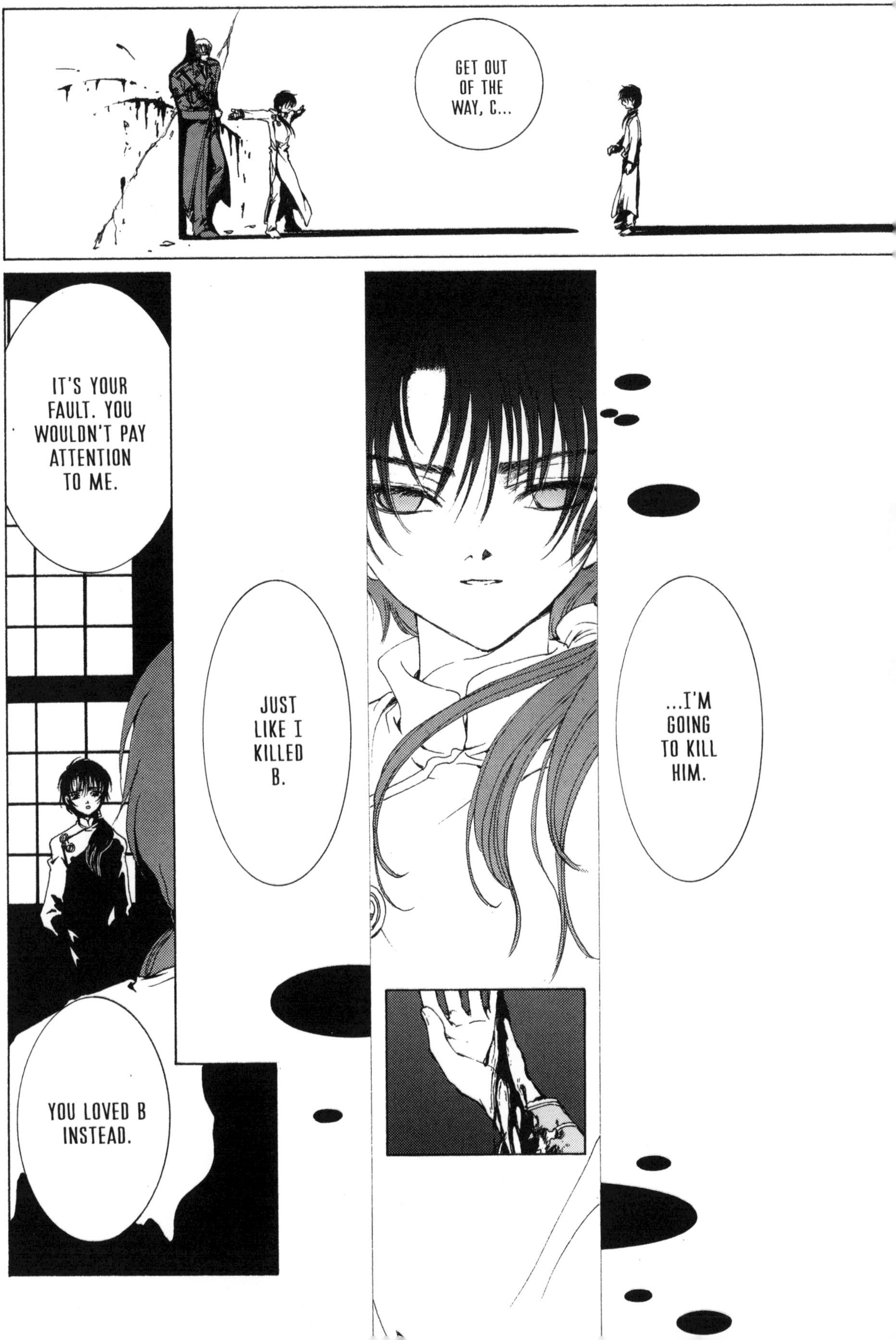
GET OUT OF THE WAY, C...
...I'M GOING TO KILL HIM.
JUST LIKE I KILLED B.
IT'S YOUR FAULT. YOU WOULDN'T PAY ATTENTION TO ME.
YOU LOVED B INSTEAD.

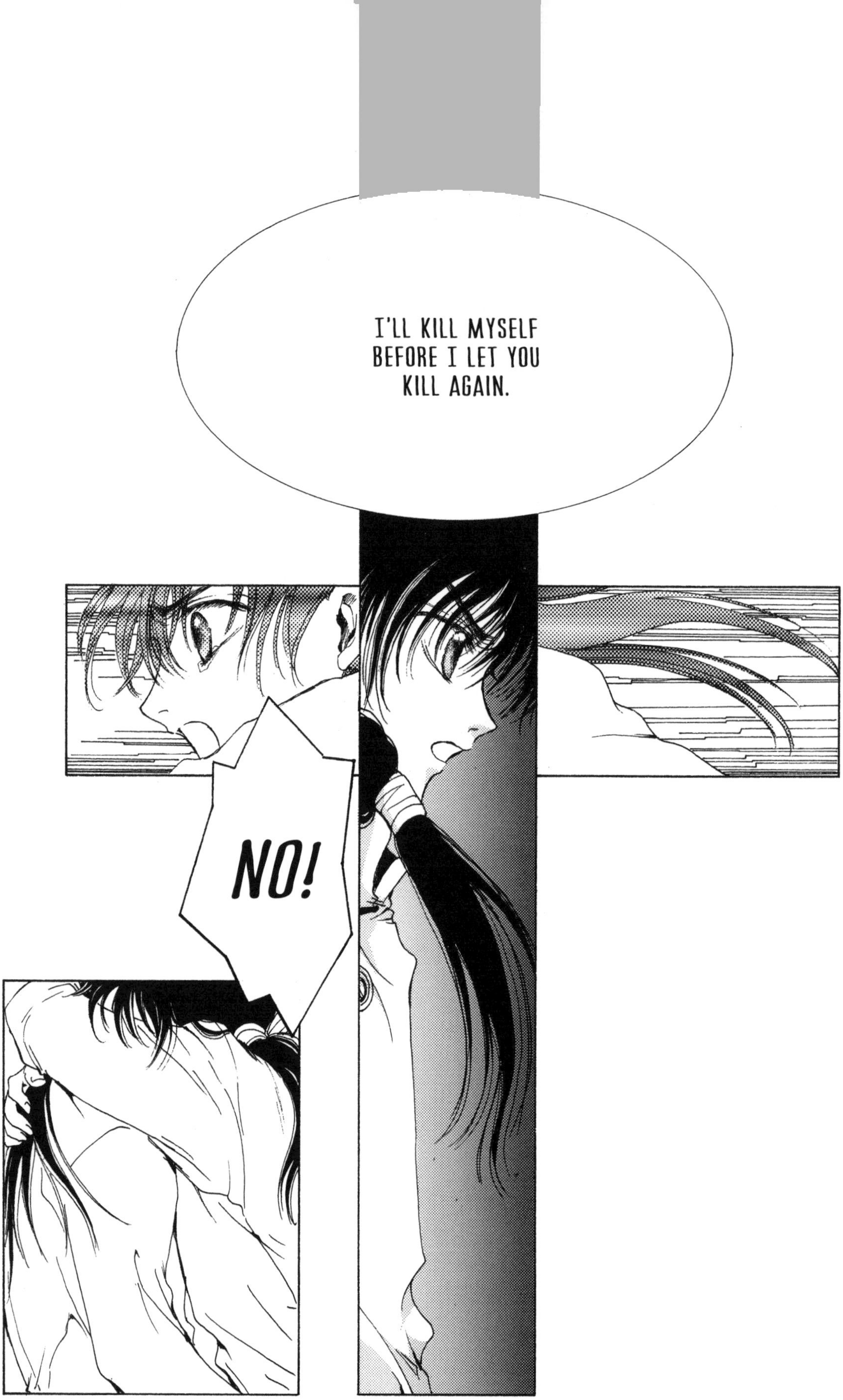
I'LL KILL MYSELF BEFORE I LET YOU KILL AGAIN.
NO!

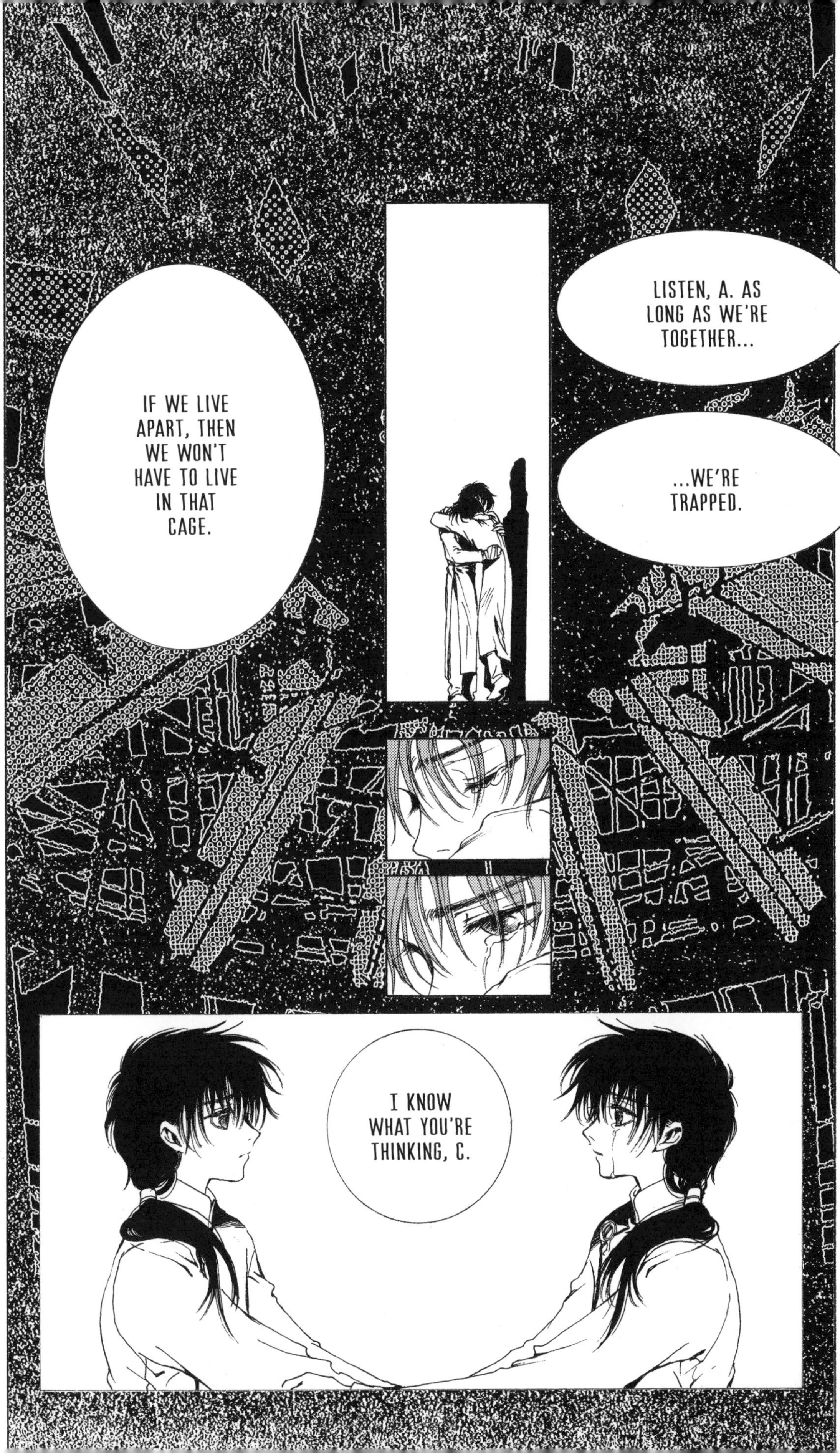
LISTEN, A. AS LONG AS WE'RE TOGETHER...
...WE'RE TRAPPED.
IF WE LIVE APART, THEN WE WON'T HAVE TO LIVE IN THAT CAGE.
I KNOW WHAT YOU'RE THINKING, C.

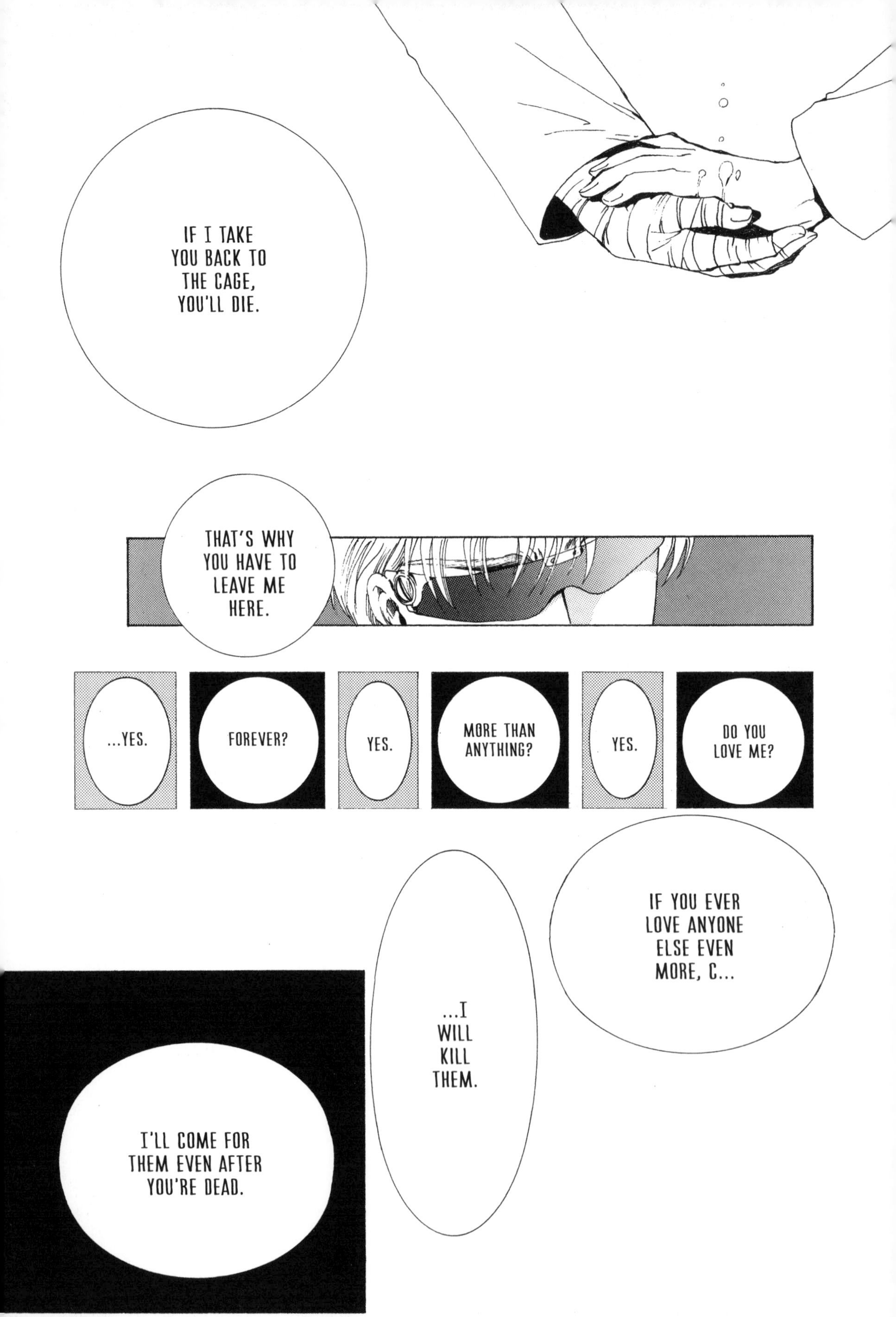
IF I TAKE YOU BACK TO THE CAGE, YOU'LL DIE.
THAT'S WHY YOU HAVE TO LEAVE ME HERE.
DO YOU LOVE ME?
YES.
MORE THAN ANYTHING?
YES.
FOREVER?
...YES.
IF YOU EVER LOVE ANYONE ELSE EVEN MORE, C...
...I WILL KILL THEM.
I'LL COME FOR THEM EVEN AFTER YOU'RE DEAD.

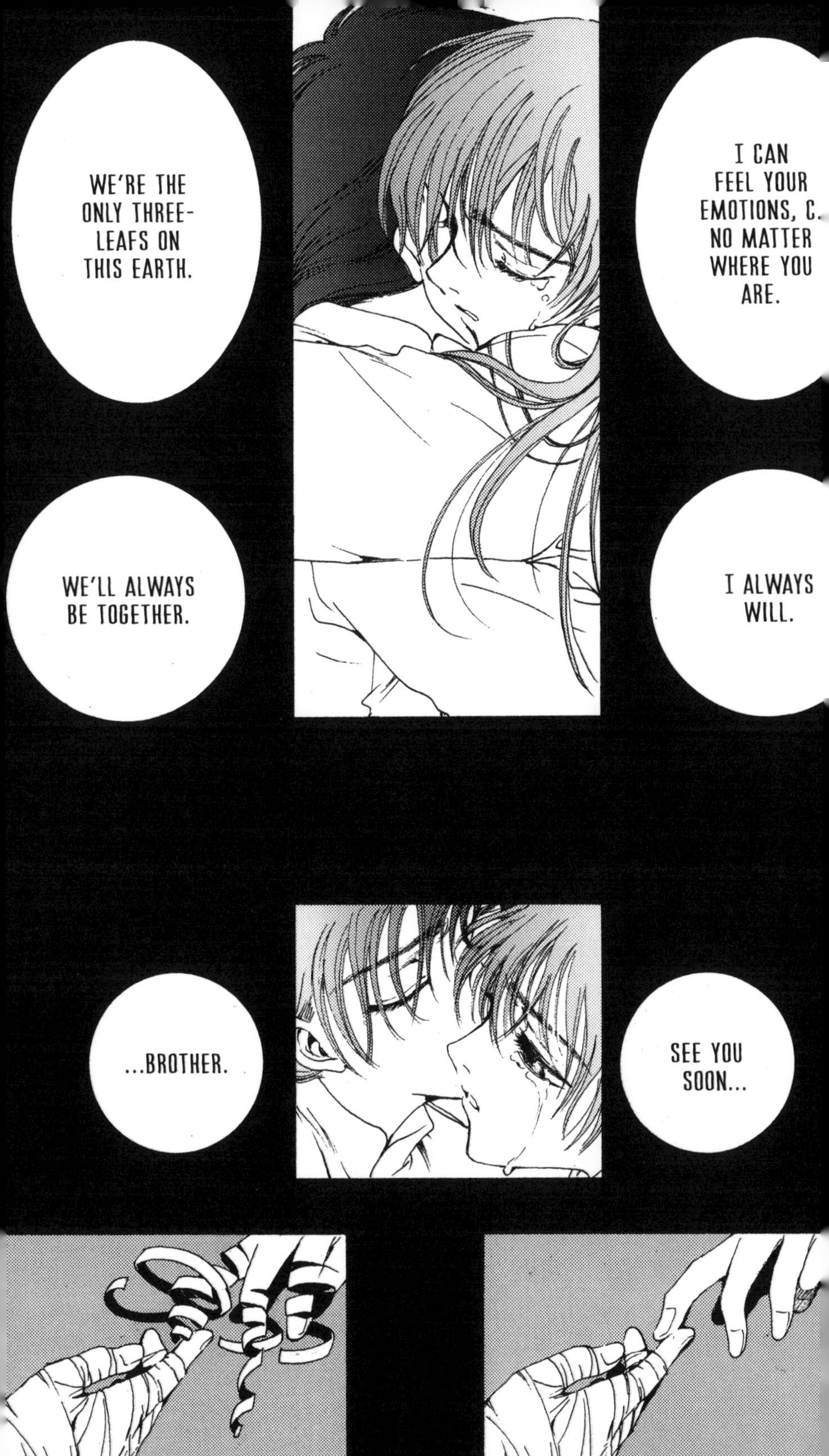
I CAN FEEL YOUR EMOTIONS, C. NO MATTER WHERE YOU ARE.
WE'RE THE ONLY THREE-LEAFS ON THIS EARTH.
I ALWAYS WILL.
WE'LL ALWAYS BE TOGETHER.
SEE YOU SOON...
...BROTHER.

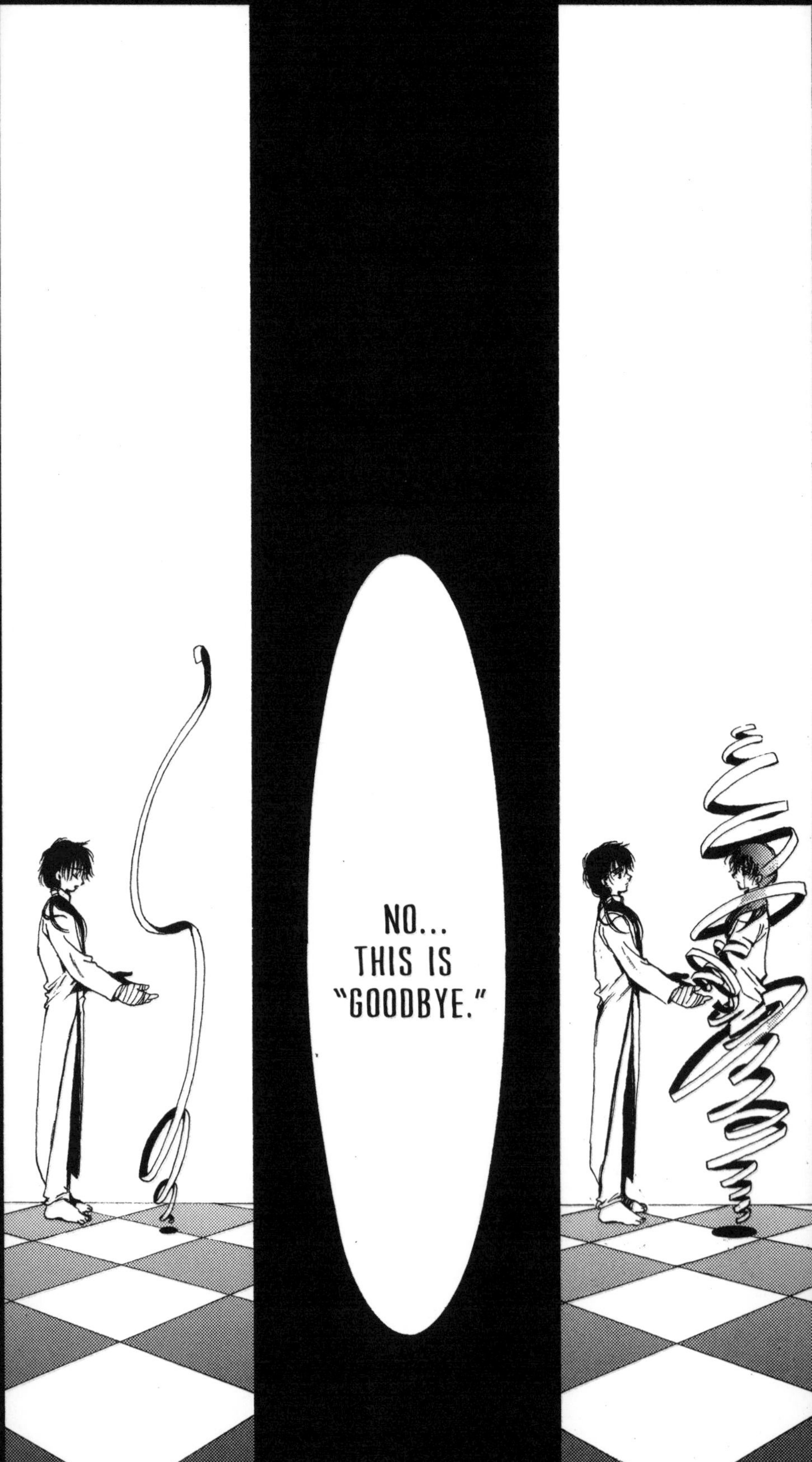
NO...
THIS IS
"GOODBYE."

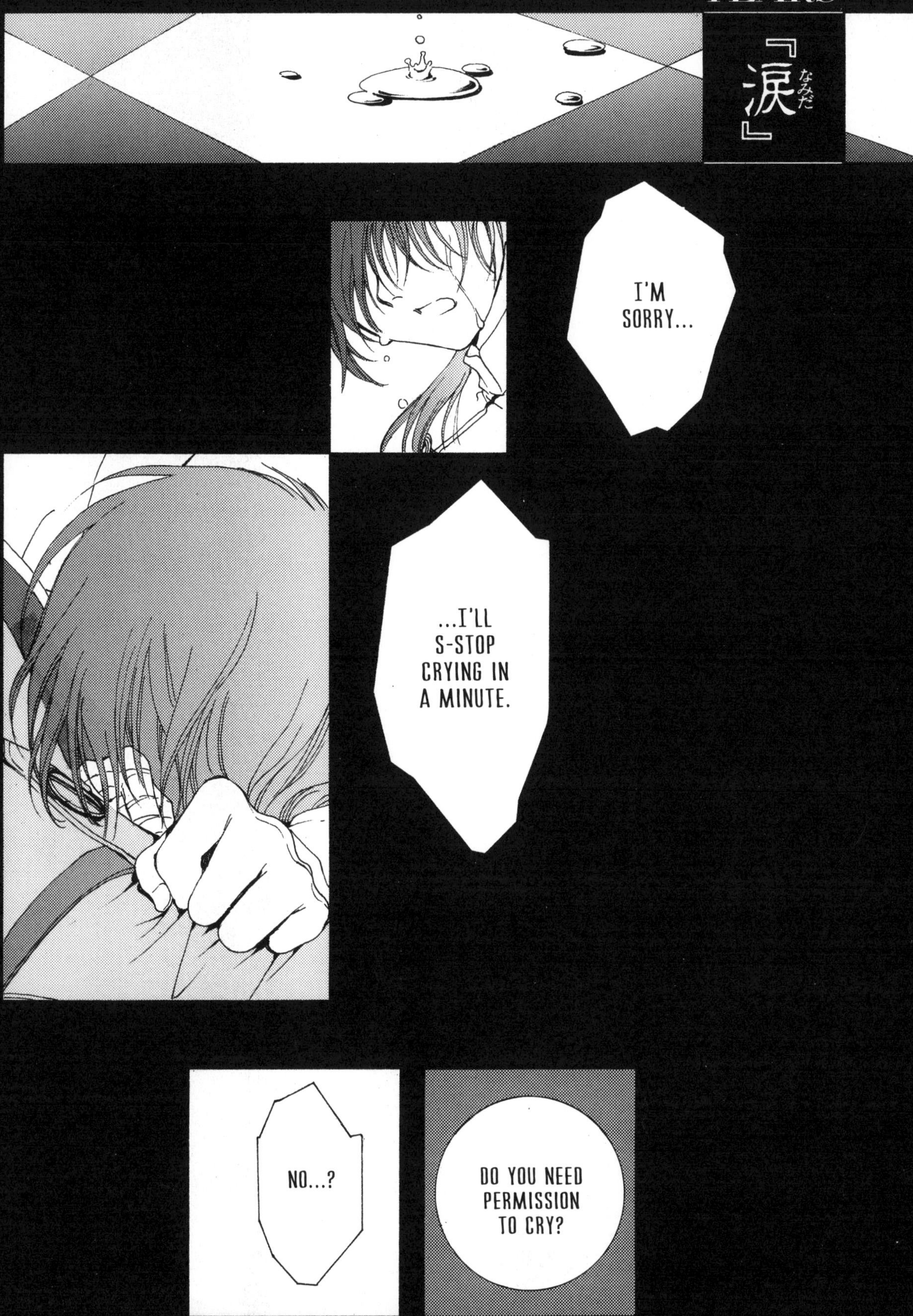
『涙』
なみだ
I'M SORRY...
...I'LL S-STOP CRYING IN A MINUTE.
DO YOU NEED PERMISSION TO CRY?
NO...?

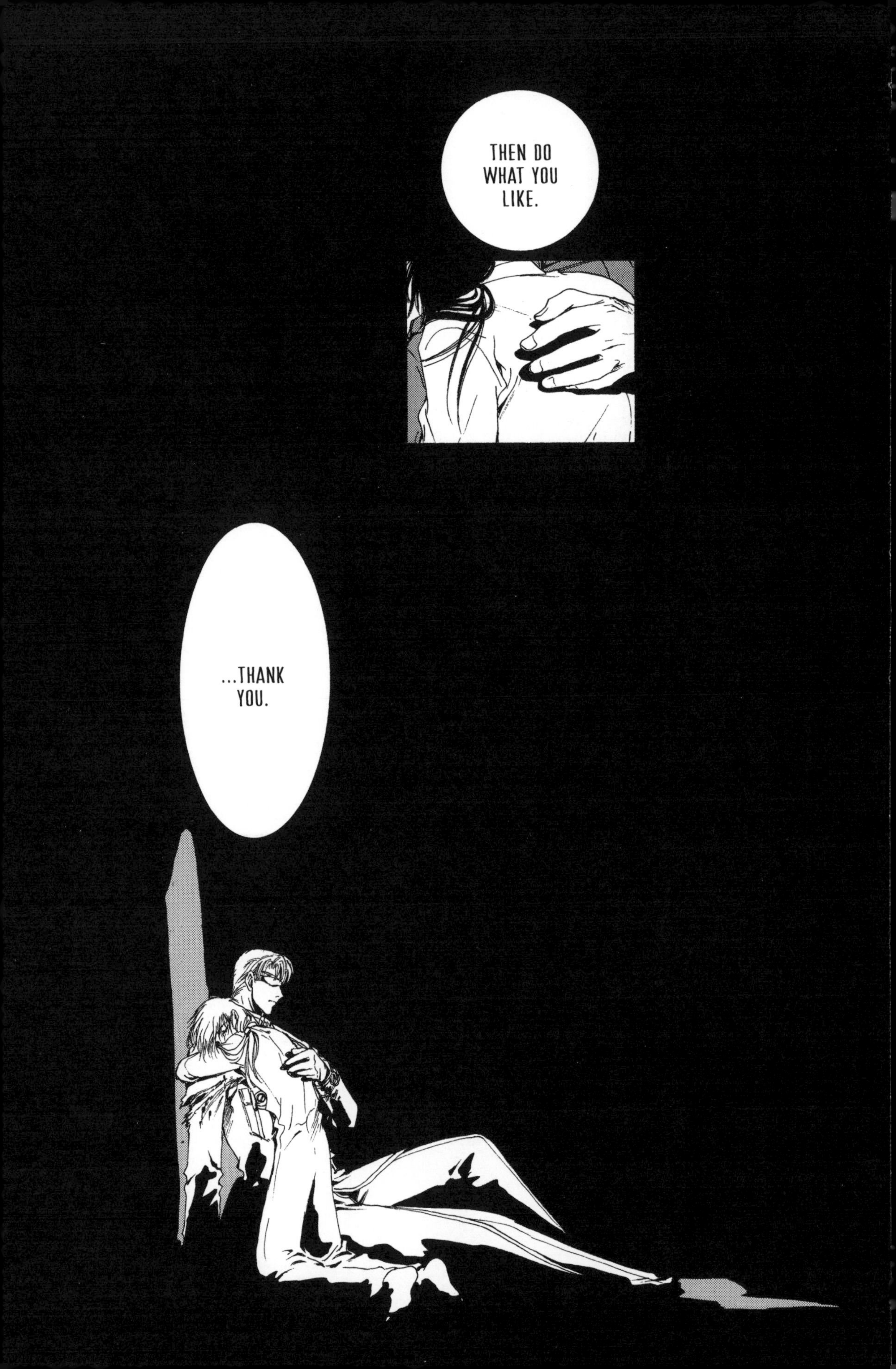
THEN DO WHAT YOU LIKE.
...THANK YOU.

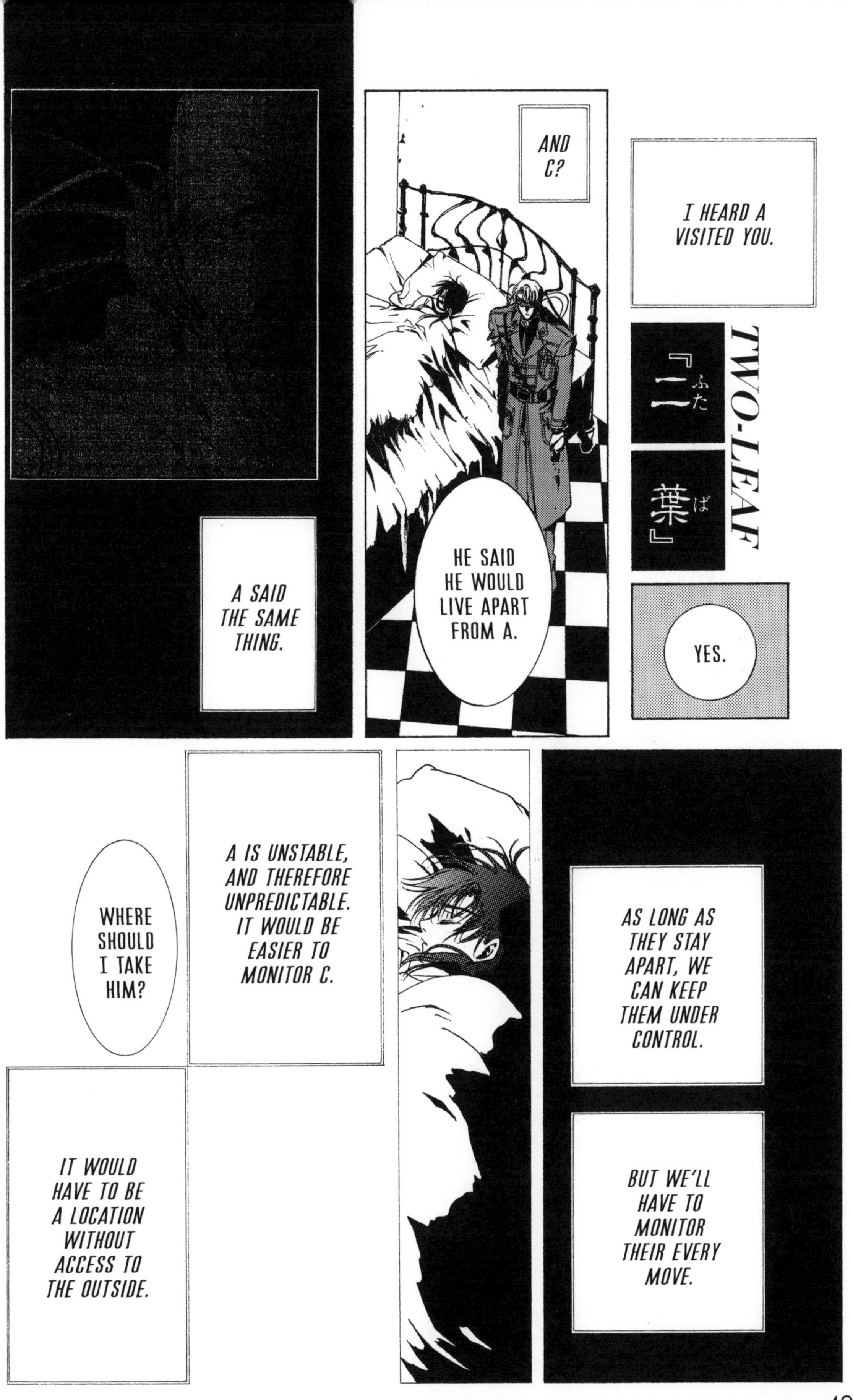
I HEARD A VISITED YOU.
TWO-LEAF
『二葉』
YES.
AND C?
HE SAID HE WOULD LIVE APART FROM A.
A SAID THE SAME THING.
AS LONG AS THEY STAY APART, WE CAN KEEP THEM UNDER CONTROL.
BUT WE'LL HAVE TO MONITOR THEIR EVERY MOVE.
A IS UNSTABLE, AND THEREFORE UNPREDICTABLE. IT WOULD BE EASIER TO MONITOR C.
WHERE SHOULD I TAKE HIM?
IT WOULD HAVE TO BE A LOCATION WITHOUT ACCESS TO THE OUTSIDE.

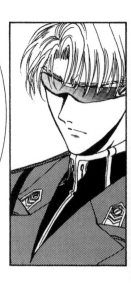

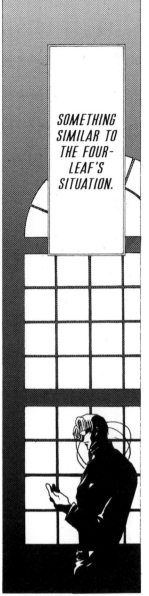

SOMETHING SIMILAR TO THE FOUR-LEAF'S SITUATION.
THEN AS LONG AS I RESTRICT HIS ACCESS...
...I CAN KEEP HIM HERE. IT'S COMPLETELY SECURE.
BUT... YOU'RE A TWO-LEAF, GINGETSU.
THERE IS NO WAY THAT I CAN ALLOW YOU TO BE TOGETHER.

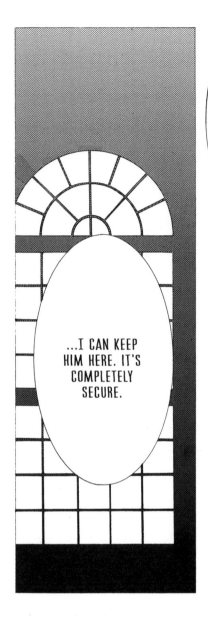

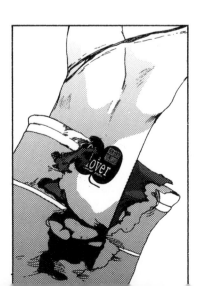

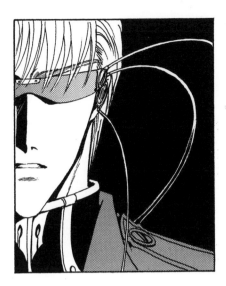

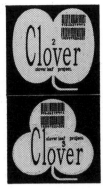

TWO PLUS THREE EQUALS FIVE.

COMBINED, YOU TWO COULD OVERPOWER THE COUNCIL.

THEN I WILL IMPLANT A KILL DEVICE IN MY BODY.

WE WOULD
NEED TO
ENSURE THAT
YOU COULDN'T
BE REVIVED.

...IT WOULD
HAVE TO BE
IMPLANTED
IN YOUR
BRAIN.

THE COUNCIL
WILL CONTROL
THE SWITCH.

IF ANY SITUATION
ARISES INVOLVING
THE THREE-LEAFS OR
MYSELF, YOU CAN
ACTIVATE IT.

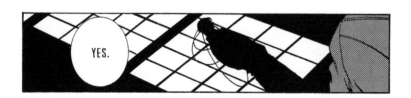

YES.

WHY
ARE YOU
DOING
THIS...?

...IS IT
BECAUSE
YOU WERE
A PRODUCT
OF THE
CLOVER LEAF
PROJECT?

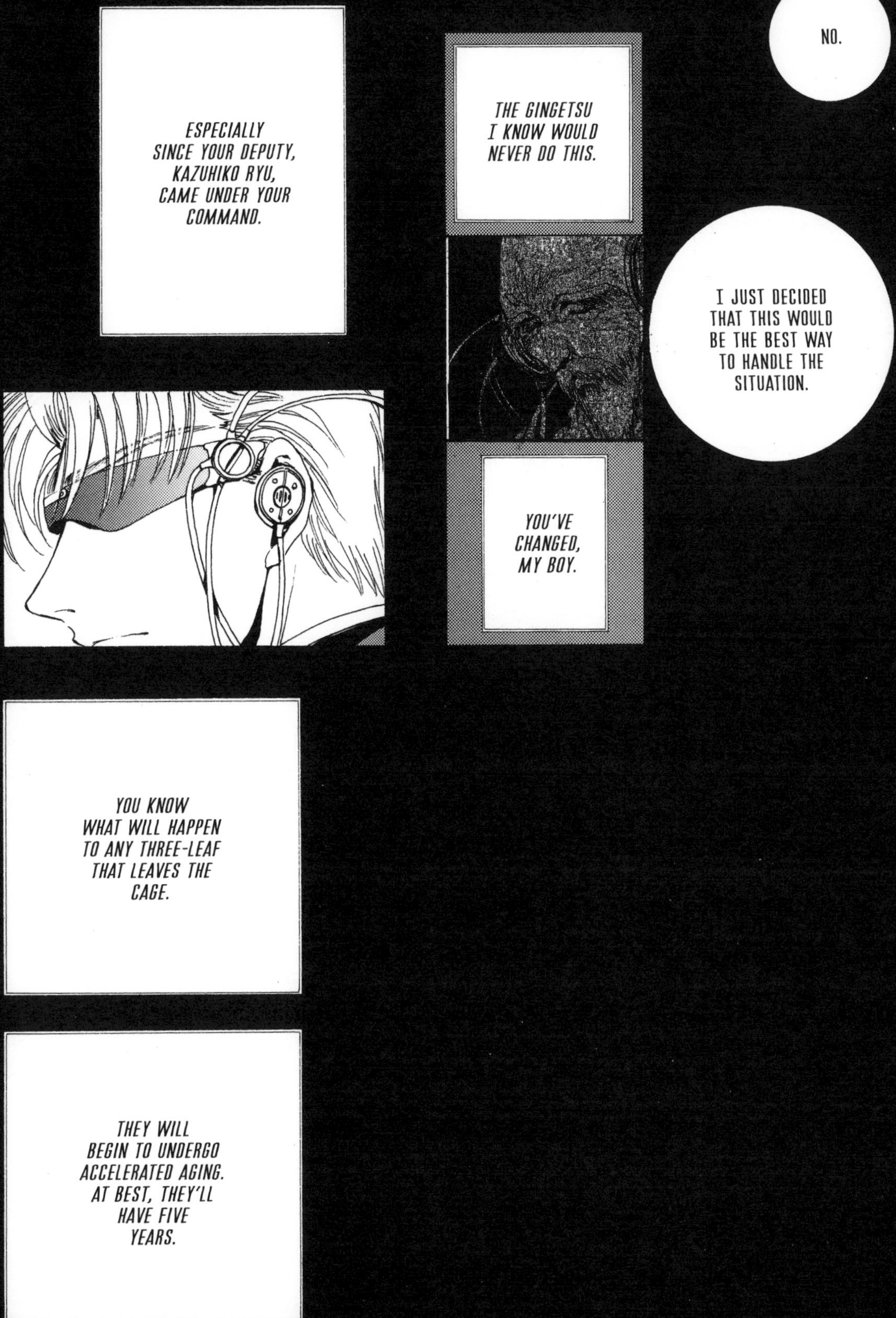
NO.
I JUST DECIDED THAT THIS WOULD BE THE BEST WAY TO HANDLE THE SITUATION.
THE GINGETSU I KNOW WOULD NEVER DO THIS.
YOU'VE CHANGED, MY BOY.
ESPECIALLY SINCE YOUR DEPUTY, KAZUHIKO RYU, CAME UNDER YOUR COMMAND.
YOU KNOW WHAT WILL HAPPEN TO ANY THREE-LEAF THAT LEAVES THE CAGE.
THEY WILL BEGIN TO UNDERGO ACCELERATED AGING. AT BEST, THEY'LL HAVE FIVE YEARS.

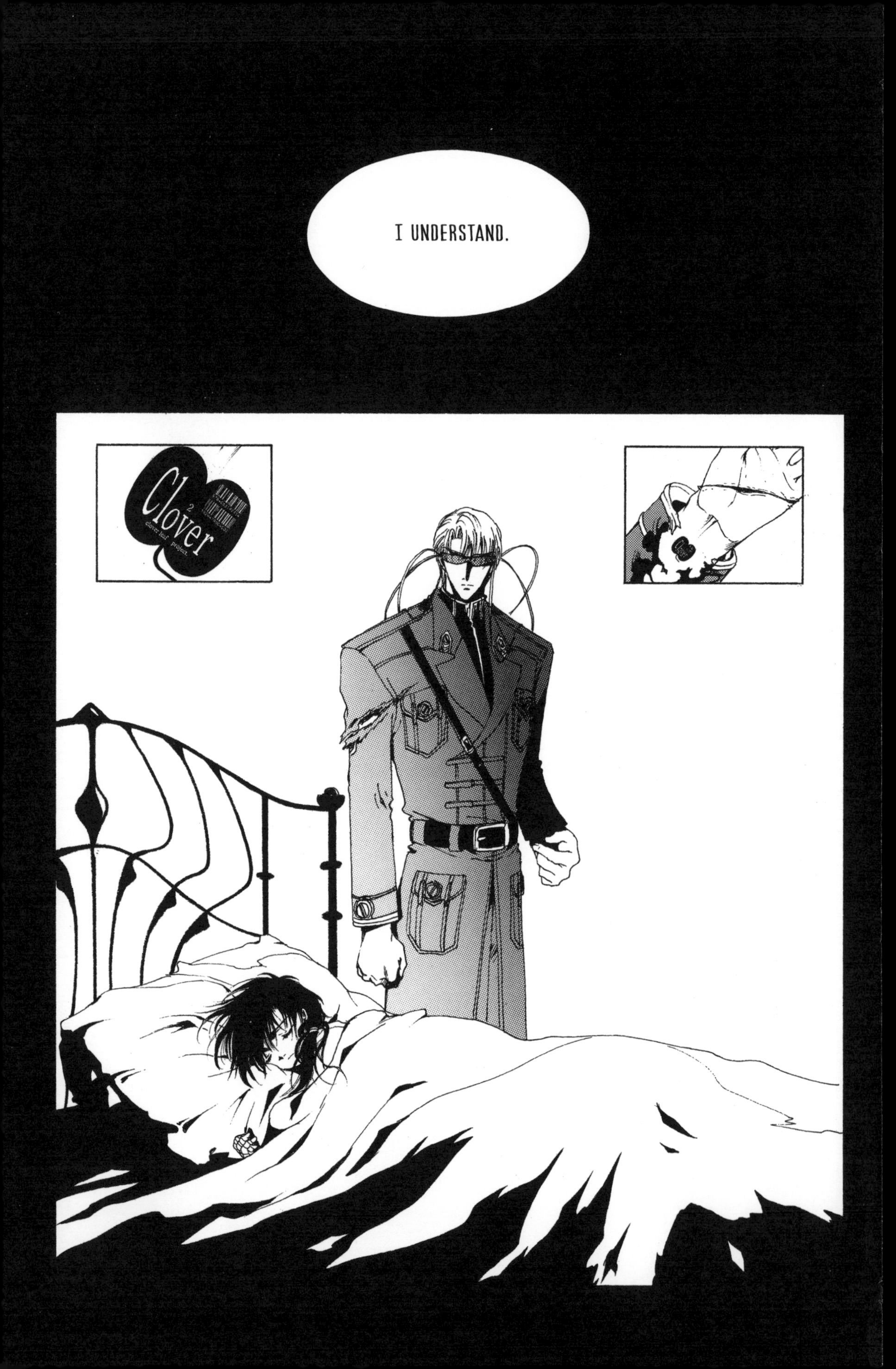
I UNDERSTAND.
Clover
2
clover leaf project

『生まれ変わる』
BEING REBORN

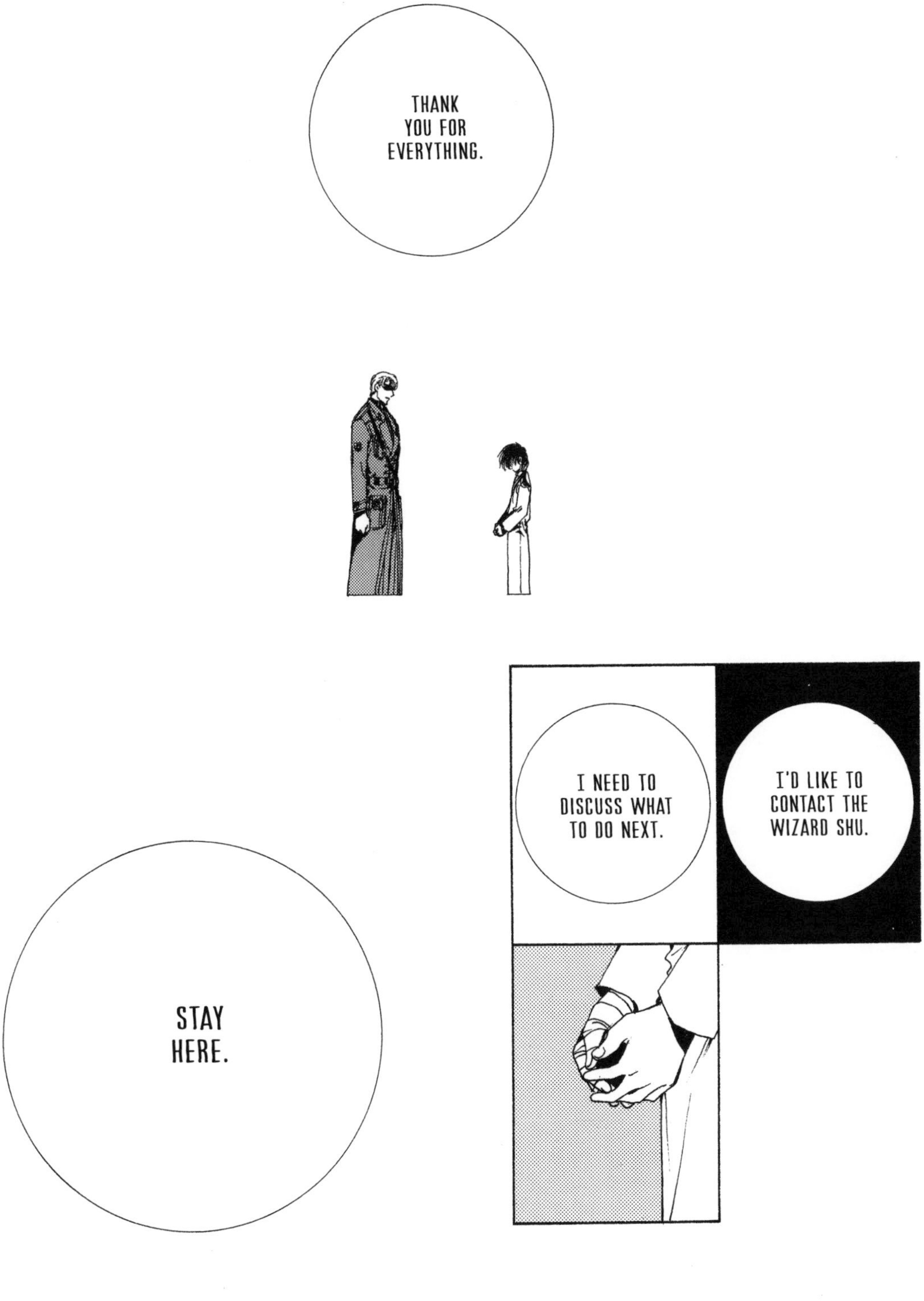
THANK YOU FOR EVERYTHING.
I'D LIKE TO CONTACT THE WIZARD SHU.
I NEED TO DISCUSS WHAT TO DO NEXT.
STAY HERE.

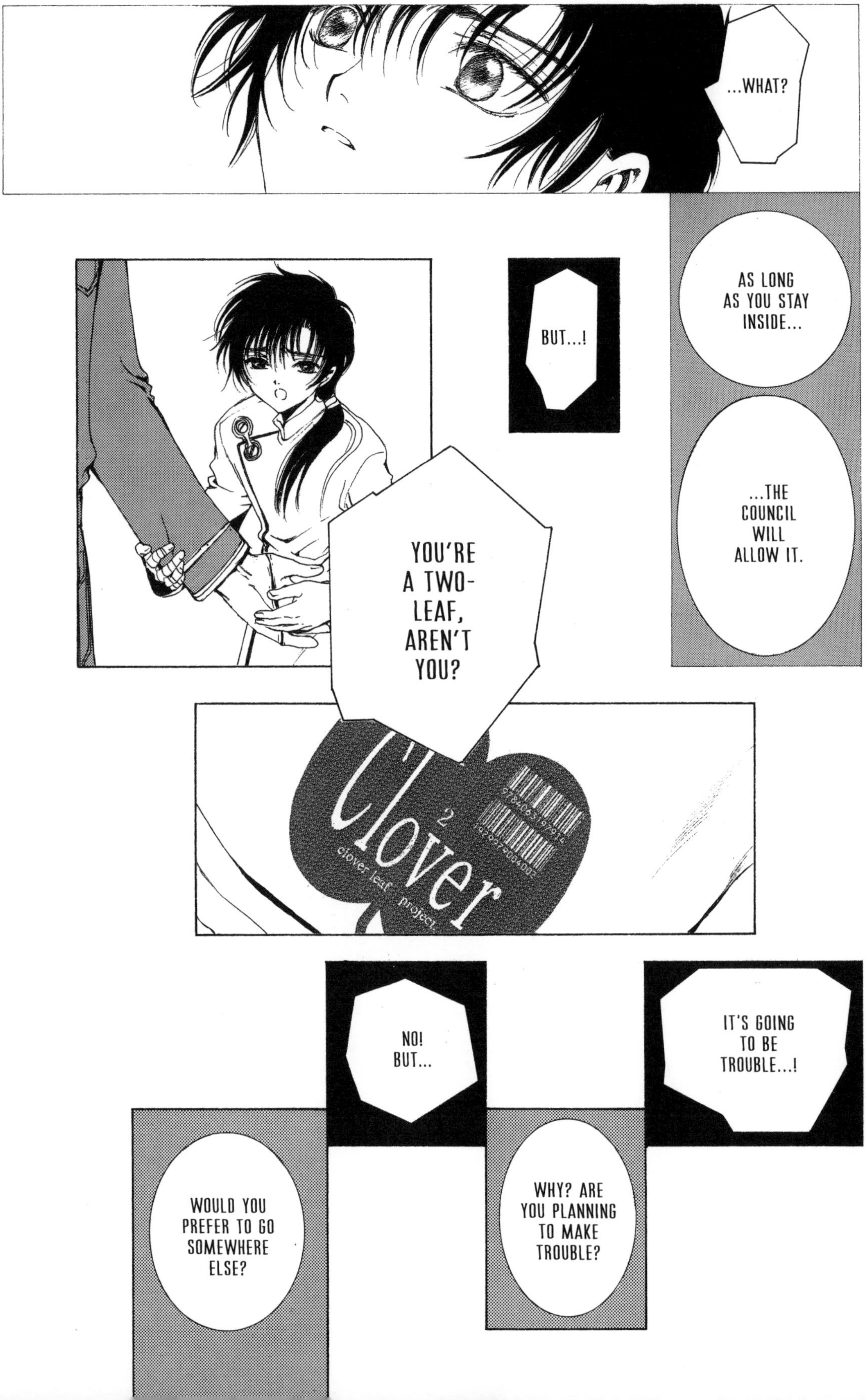
...WHAT?
AS LONG AS YOU STAY INSIDE...
...THE COUNCIL WILL ALLOW IT.
BUT...!
YOU'RE A TWO-LEAF, AREN'T YOU?
Clover
2
clover leaf project.
IT'S GOING TO BE TROUBLE...!
WHY? ARE YOU PLANNING TO MAKE TROUBLE?
NO! BUT...
WOULD YOU PREFER TO GO SOMEWHERE ELSE?

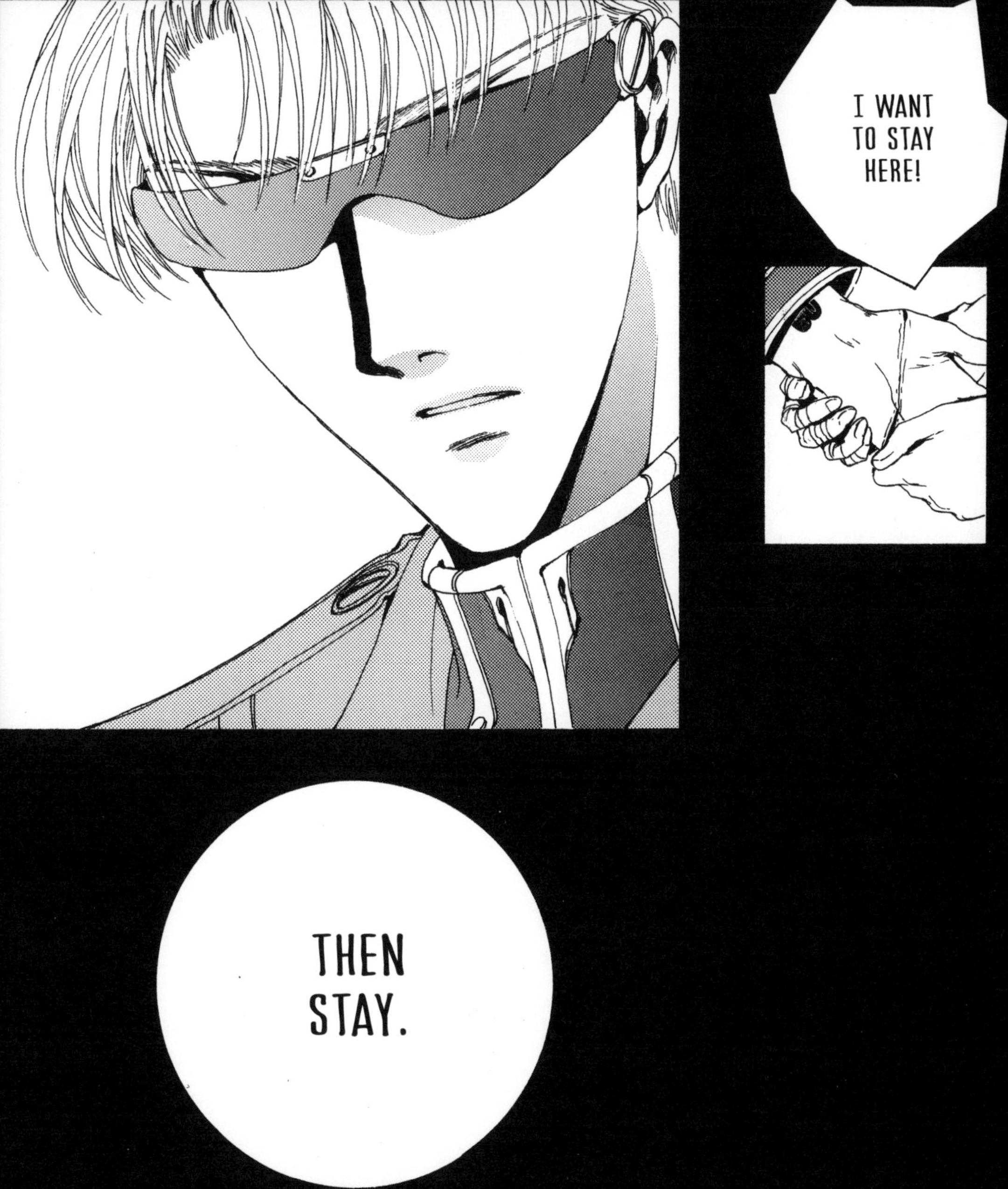
I WANT TO STAY HERE!
THEN STAY.

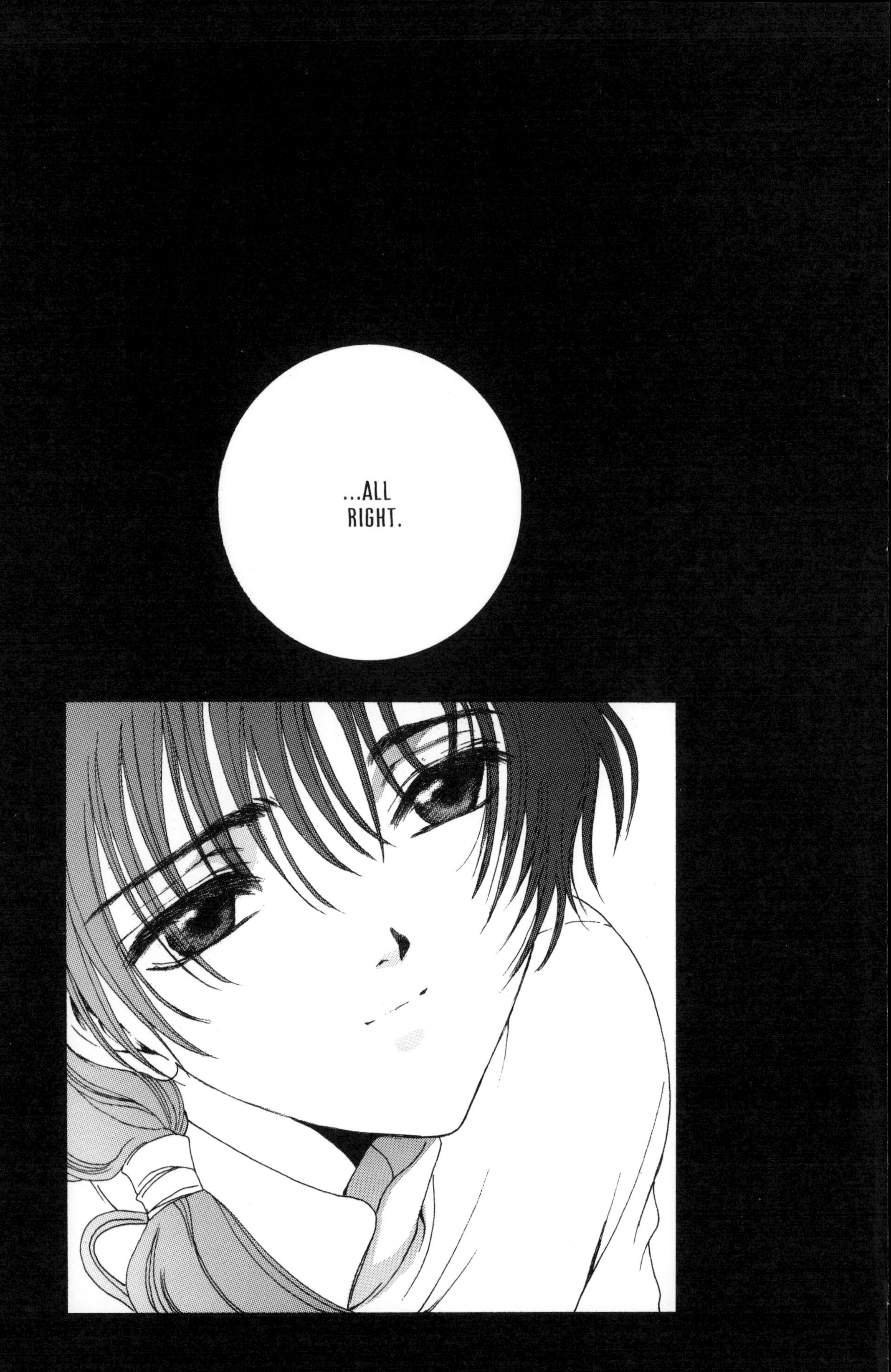
...ALL RIGHT.

C → R

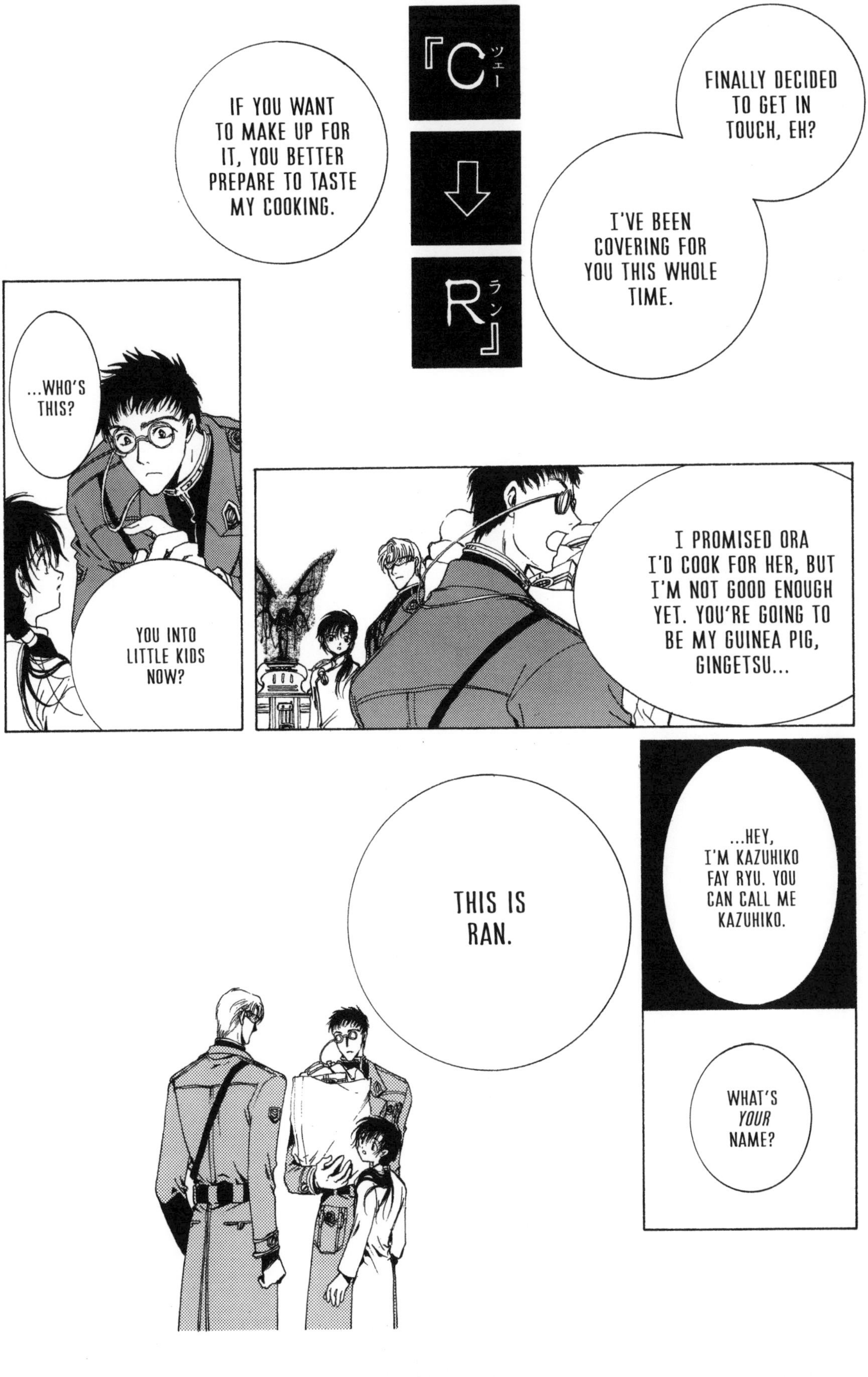
『C ツェー
R ラン』
FINALLY DECIDED TO GET IN TOUCH, EH?
I'VE BEEN COVERING FOR YOU THIS WHOLE TIME.
IF YOU WANT TO MAKE UP FOR IT, YOU BETTER PREPARE TO TASTE MY COOKING.
I PROMISED ORA I'D COOK FOR HER, BUT I'M NOT GOOD ENOUGH YET. YOU'RE GOING TO BE MY GUINEA PIG, GINGETSU...
...WHO'S THIS?
YOU INTO LITTLE KIDS NOW?
...HEY, I'M KAZUHIKO FAY RYU. YOU CAN CALL ME KAZUHIKO.
WHAT'S *YOUR* NAME?
THIS IS RAN.

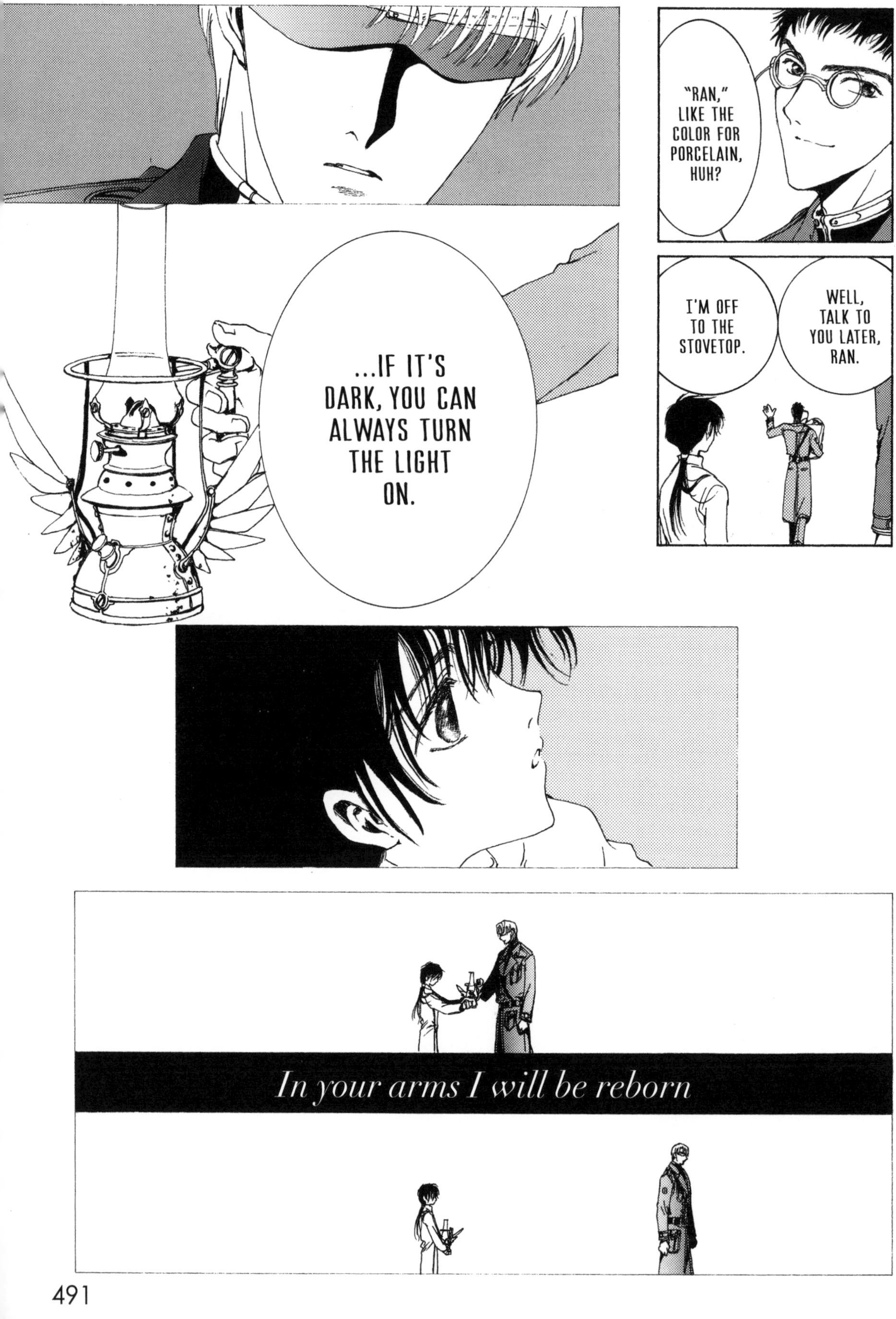
"RAN," LIKE THE COLOR FOR PORCELAIN, HUH?
WELL, TALK TO YOU LATER, RAN.
I'M OFF TO THE STOVETOP.
...IF IT'S DARK, YOU CAN ALWAYS TURN THE LIGHT ON.
In your arms I will be reborn

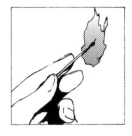

A crimson ember
Just catching light
Let it not be put out
Let it not vanish

My thoughts
Newly born
Let them not ebb
Let them not fracture

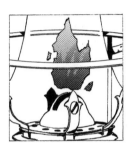

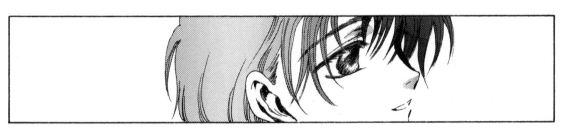

Within this cradle you tend
I will begin again
For myself I will be reborn

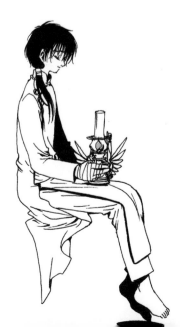

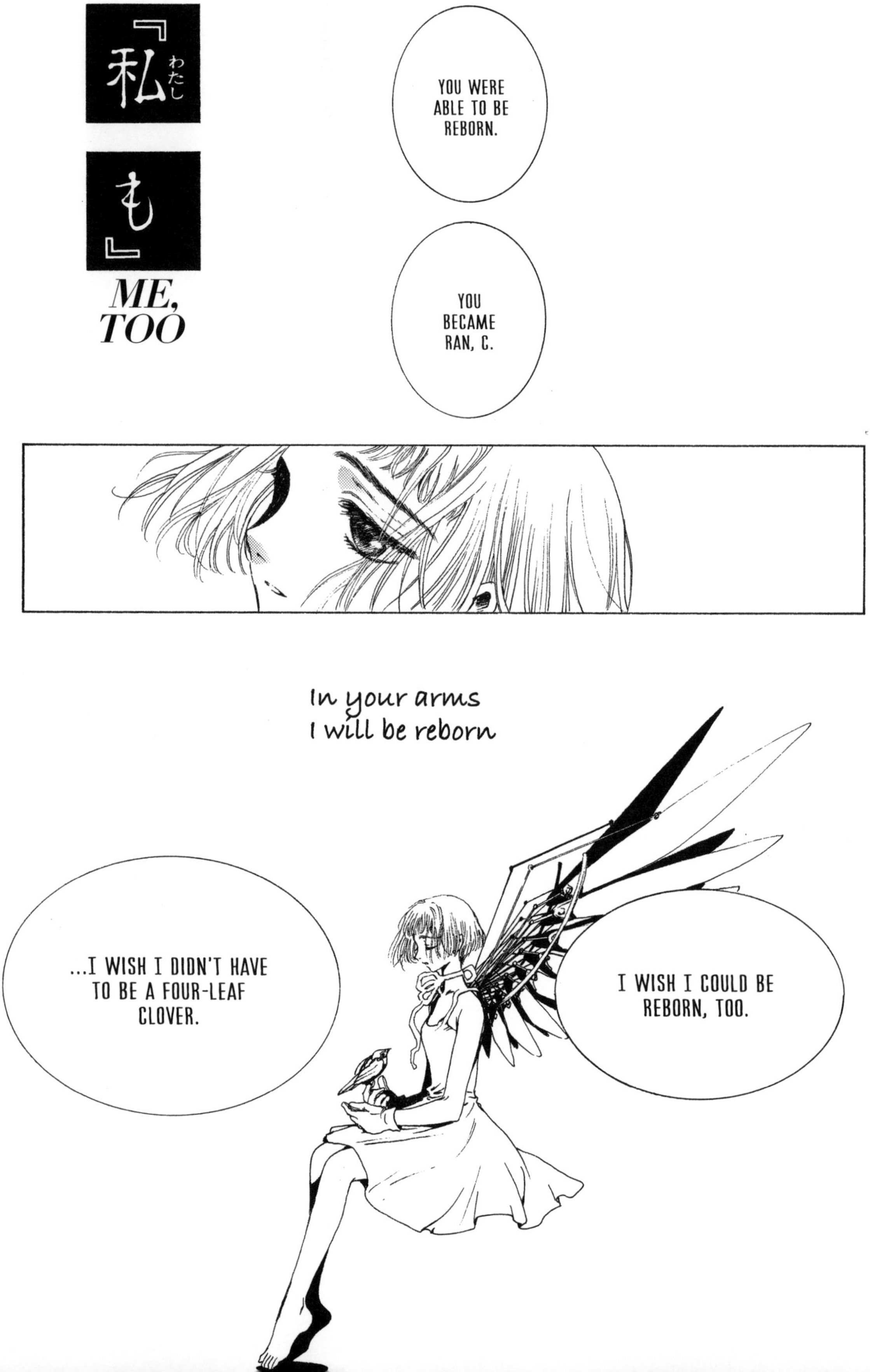
YOU WERE ABLE TO BE REBORN.
YOU BECAME RAN, C.
『私(わたし)も』
ME, TOO
In your arms I will be reborn
I WISH I COULD BE REBORN, TOO.
...I WISH I DIDN'T HAVE TO BE A FOUR-LEAF CLOVER.

C·L·O·V·E·R

For you I will be reborn
Whisk the past away on fluttering clouds
Letting the future ride on flowing winds
Fearlessly, unceasingly, patiently

In your arms I will be reborn

For myself I will be reborn
Once again I await my birth in a golden egg
Once again to fly with silver wings
Deliberately, tenaciously, intimately

In your arms I will be reborn

For you I will be reborn
The bliss of our meeting is a gentle light
Our eventual parting a pouring rain
Like an indigo that blooms in the delicate shade

In your arms I will be reborn

You take my hand, I hold yours
If our two paths, like melding hearts, should cross deeply, firmly
For myself I will be reborn

In your arms I will be reborn

Don't look away, never let go
The strength of will, the frailty of a wish—embrace them all

In your arms I will be reborn

For myself I will be reborn
My immunity to loneliness
Was lost in my bliss with you
The pain of being alone begotten from
The fear of losing you

So in your arms I will be reborn

For myself I will be reborn
Fragments of my old shell crumbling, newborn tears rolling down my cheeks
As you embrace me, my ethereal wings flutter open
Only for you will I be reborn

In your arms I will be reborn

With your voice and your touch, let me forget everything
Break off the chains that bind my heart and feet

In your arms I will be reborn

For you I will be reborn
A crimson ember just catching light—let it not be put out, let it not vanish
My thoughts, newly born—let them not ebb, let them not fracture
Within this cradle you tend
I will begin again

For myself I will be reborn
In your arms I will be reborn

THE END

CLOVER

BONUS GALLERY

CLAMP

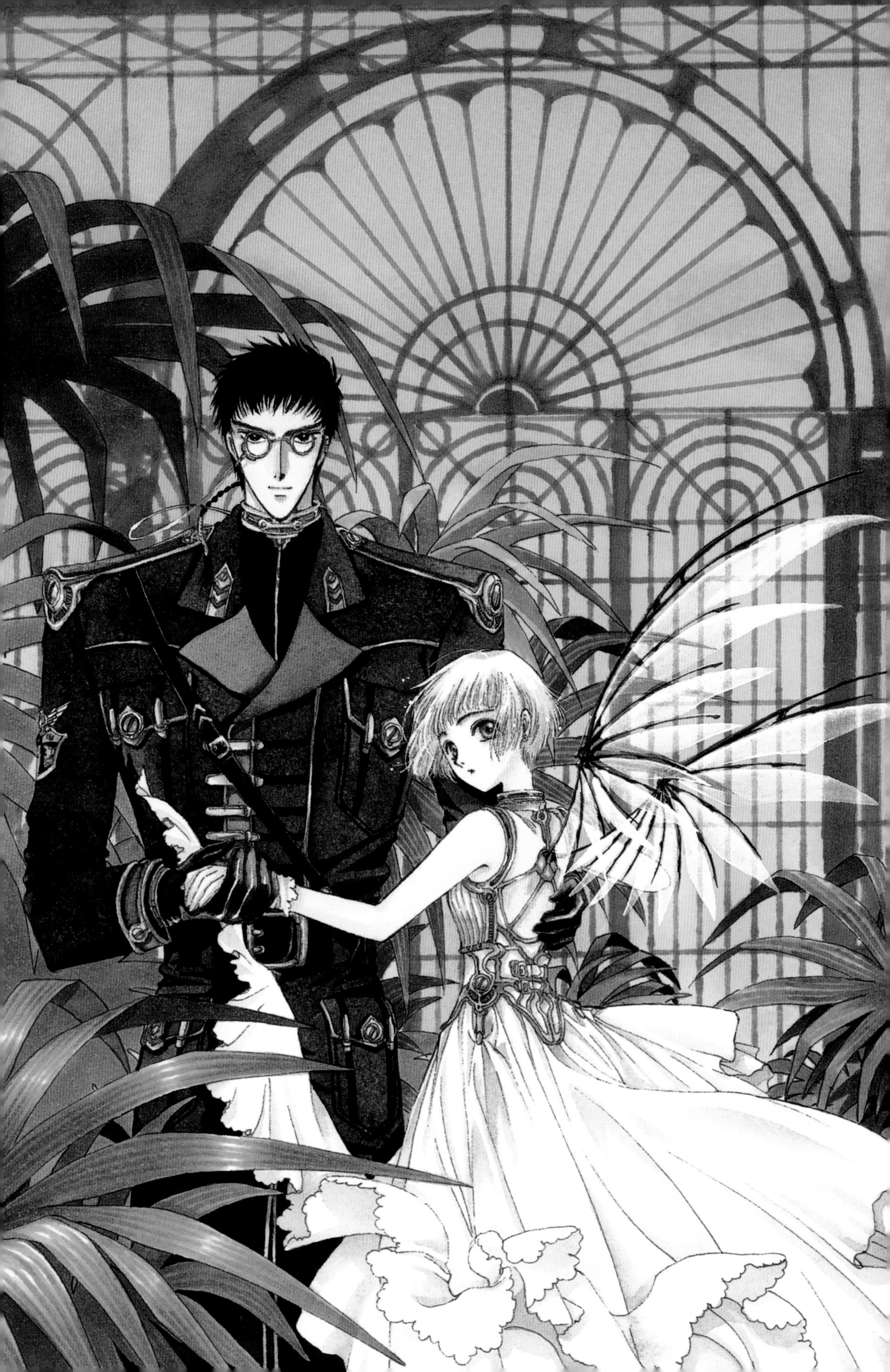

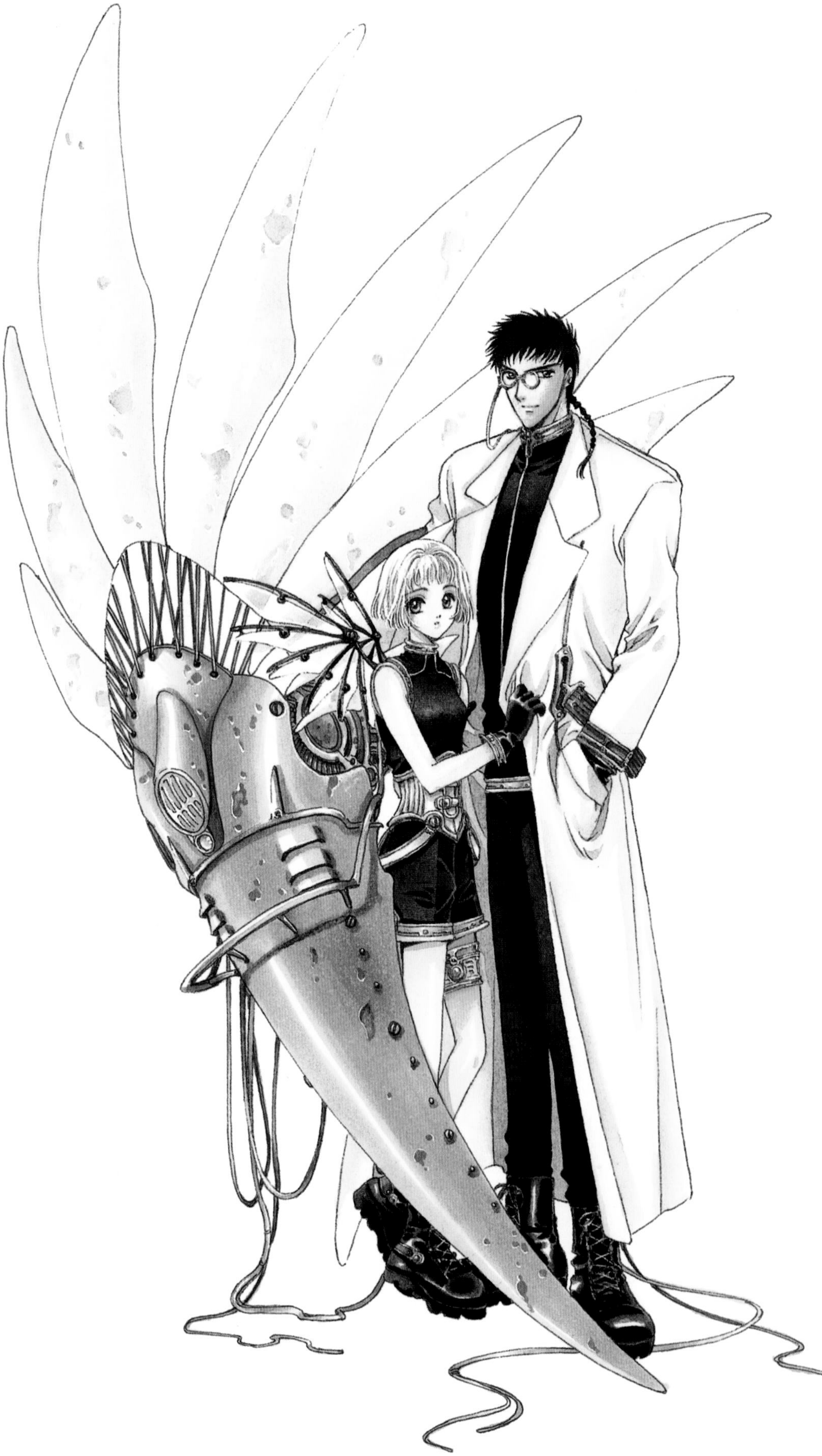

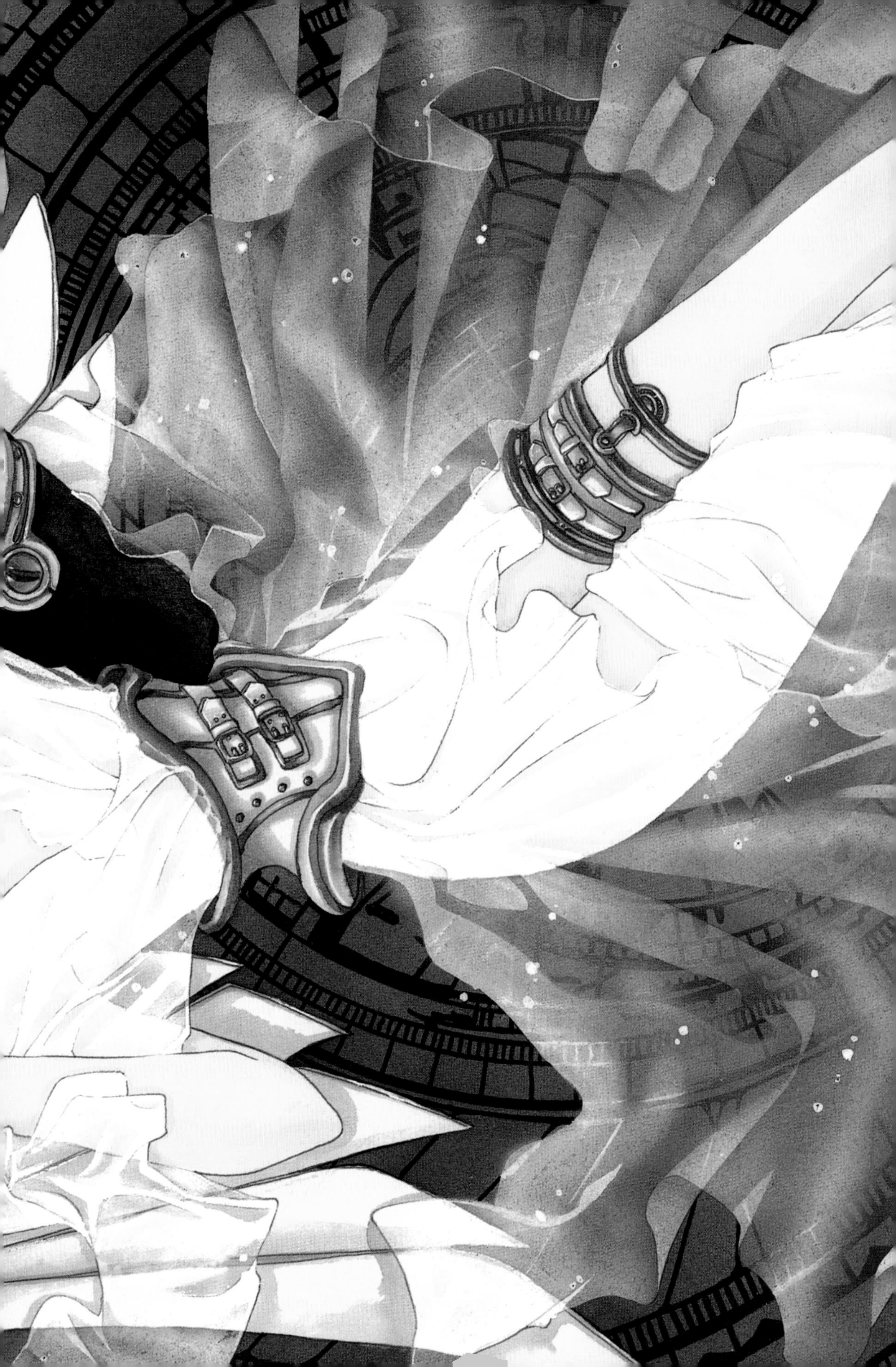

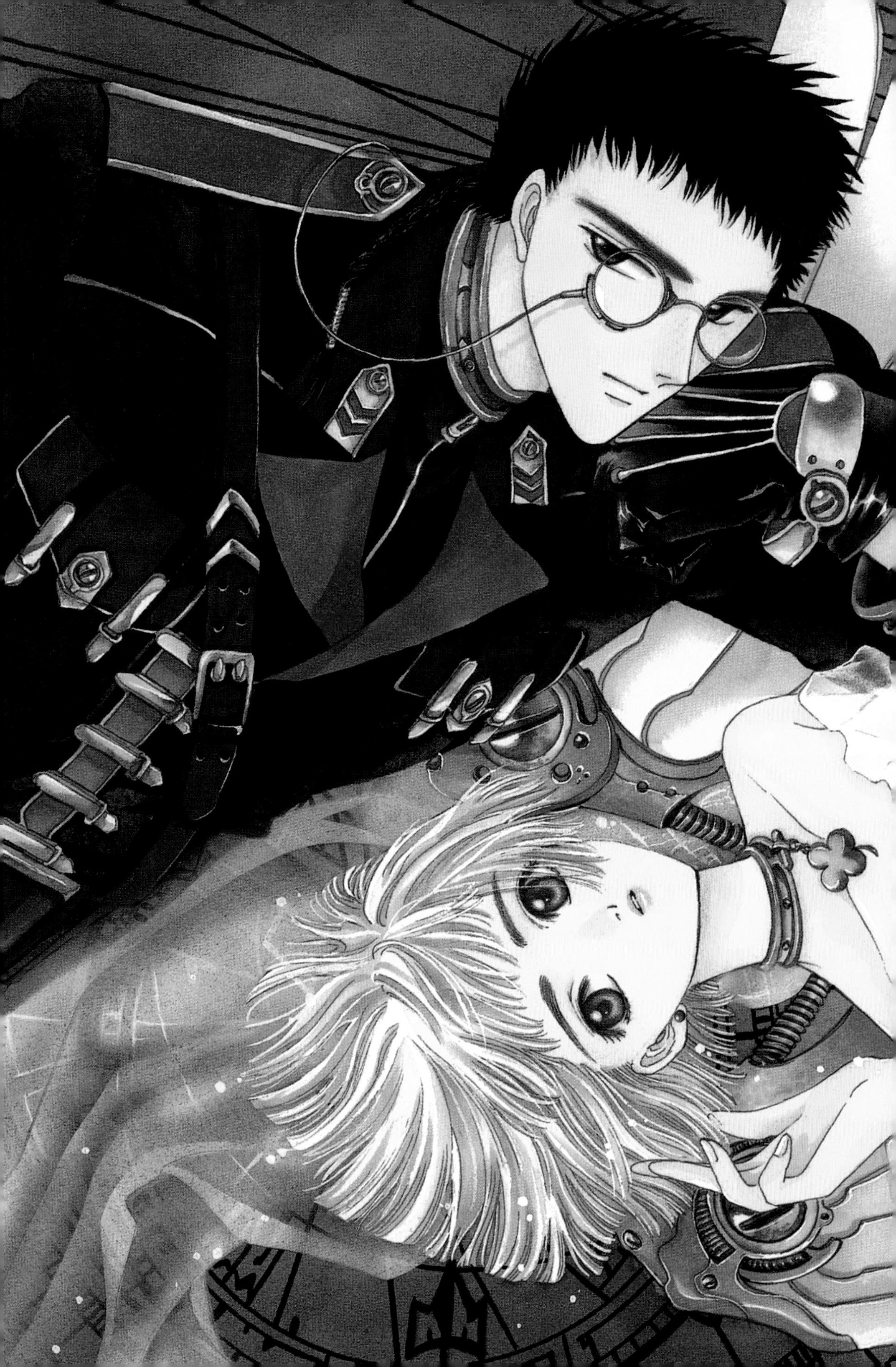

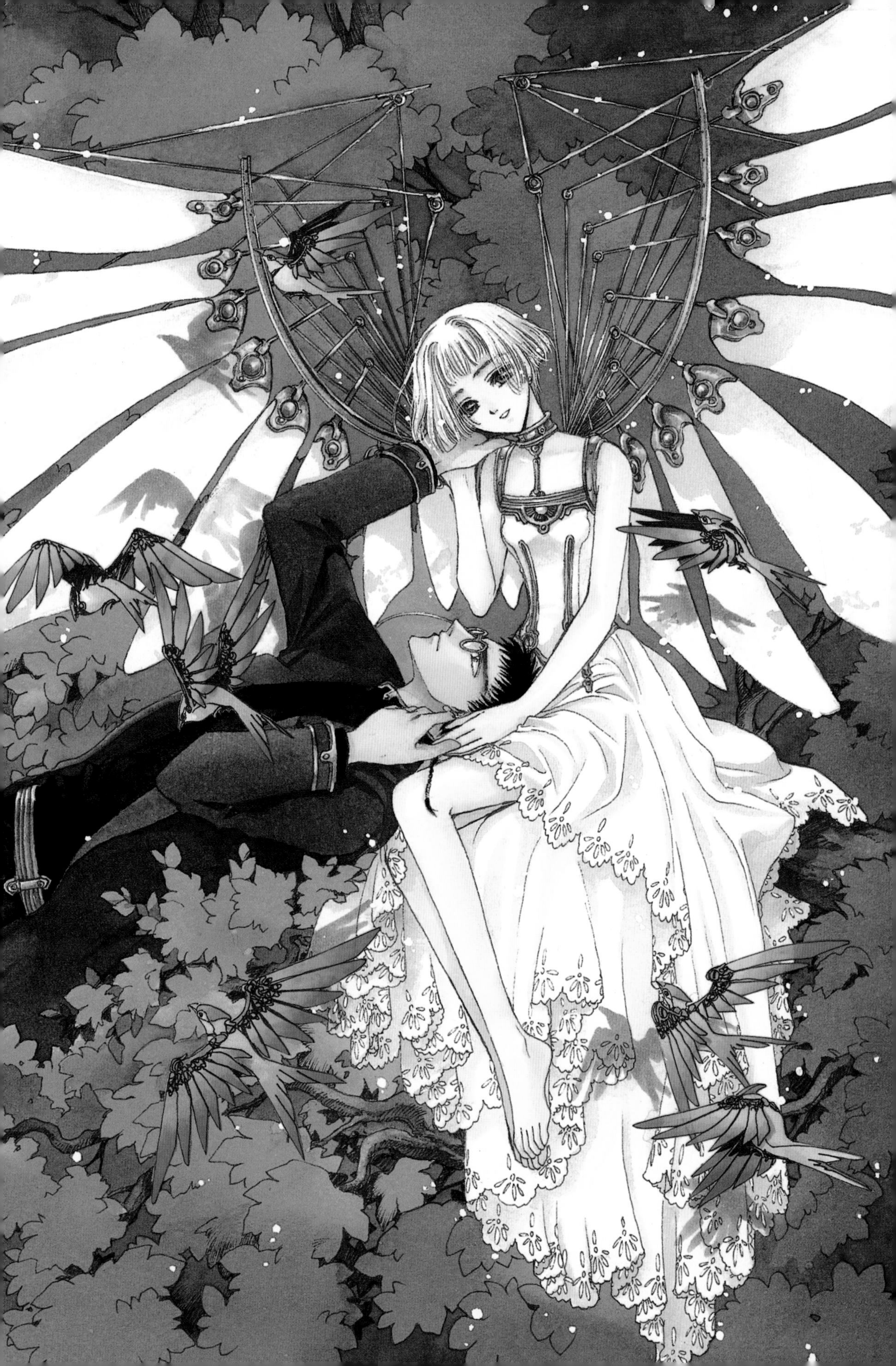

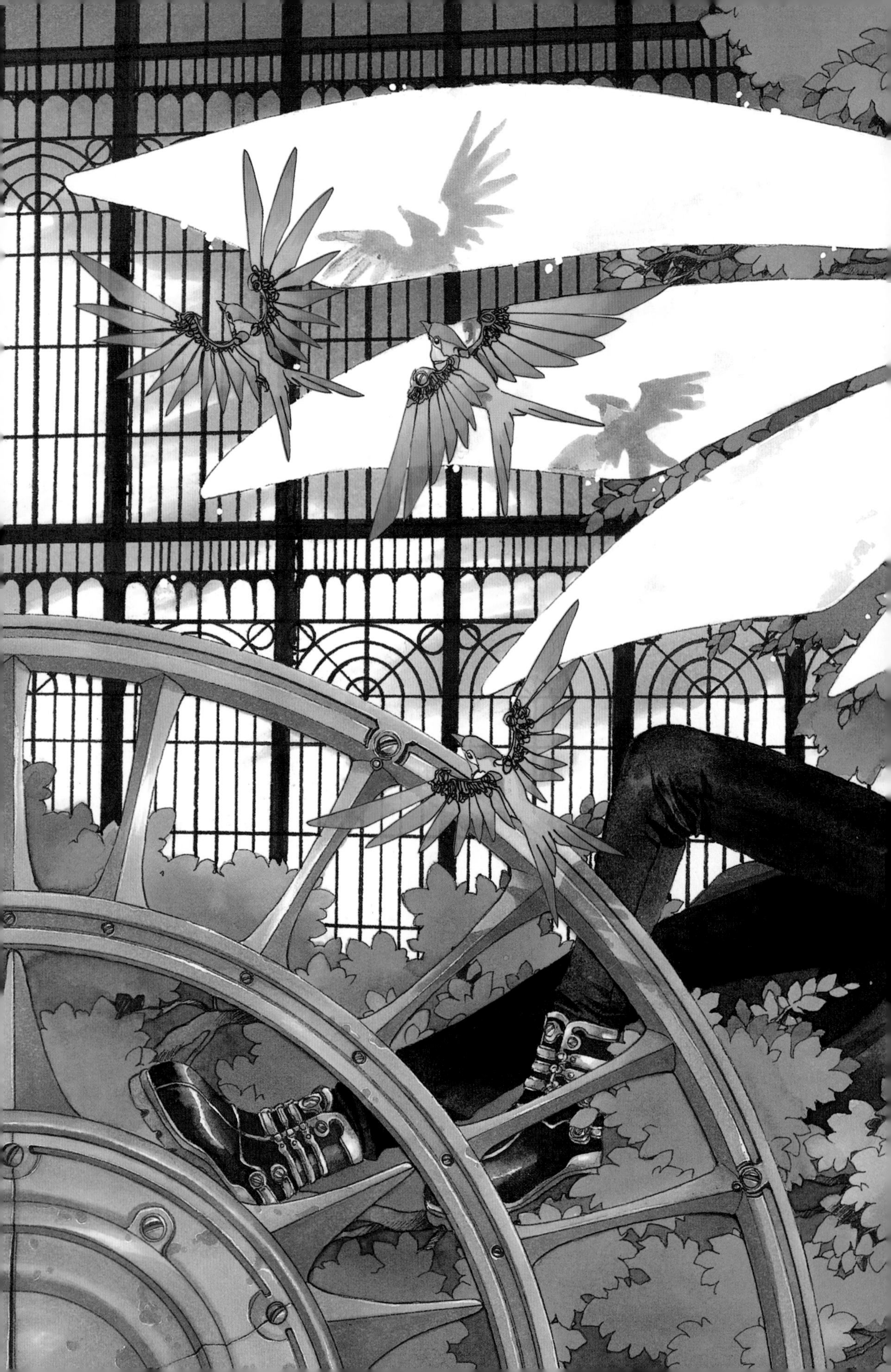

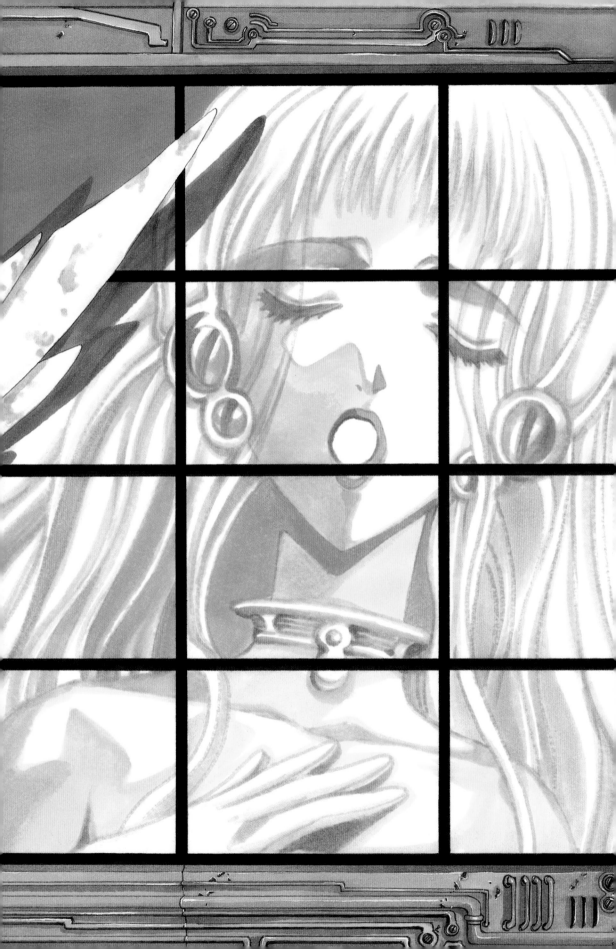

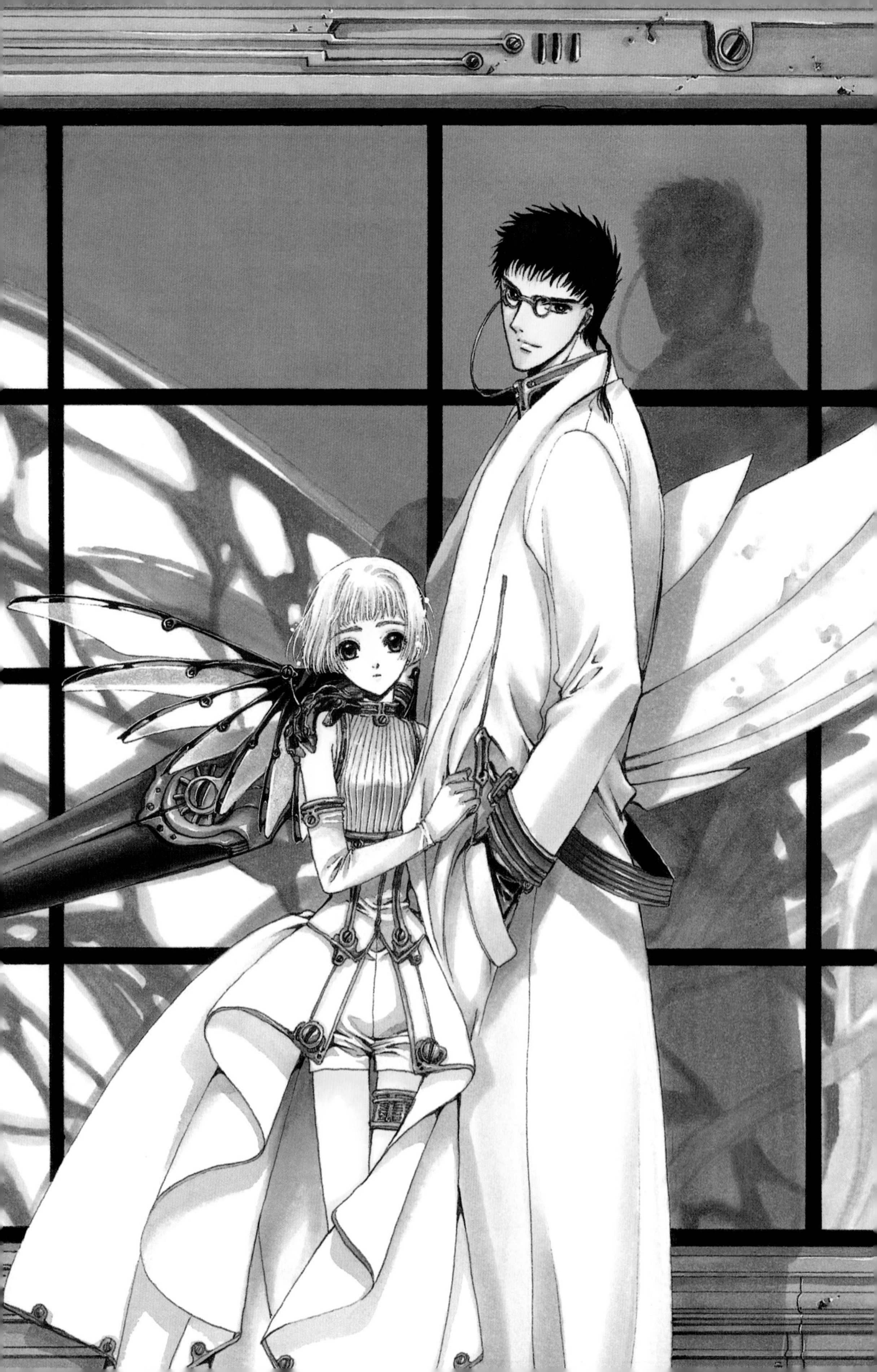

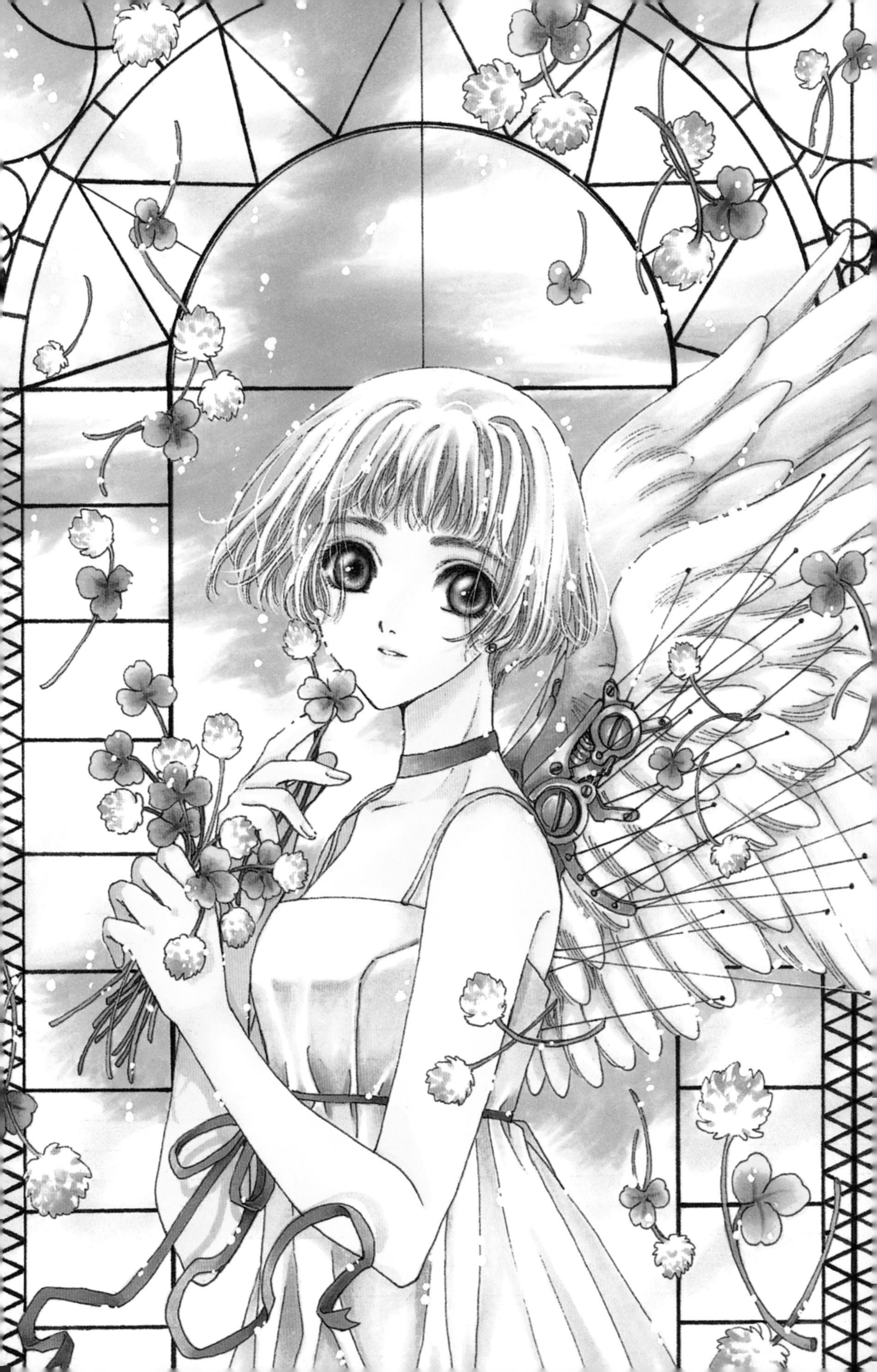

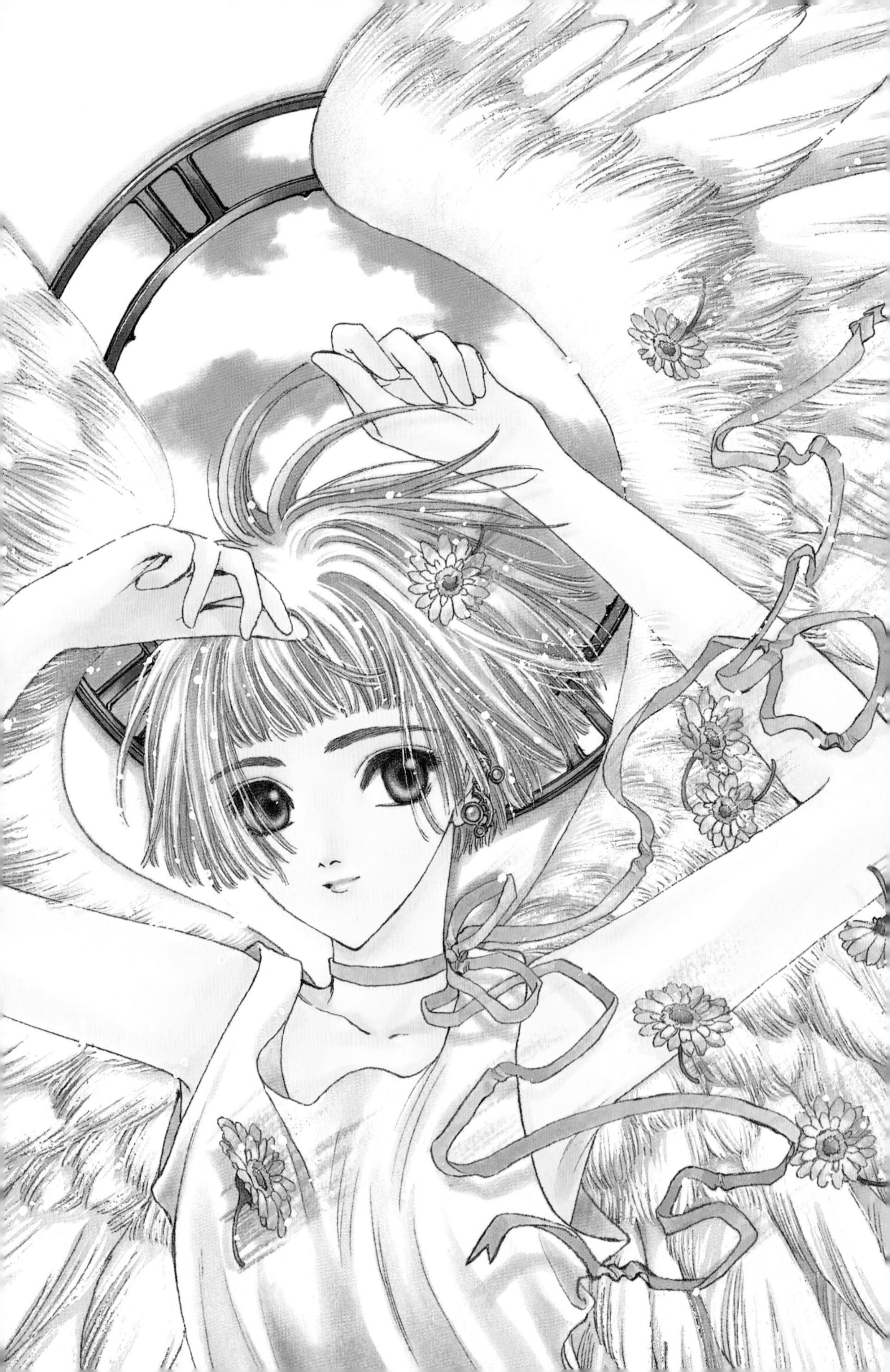

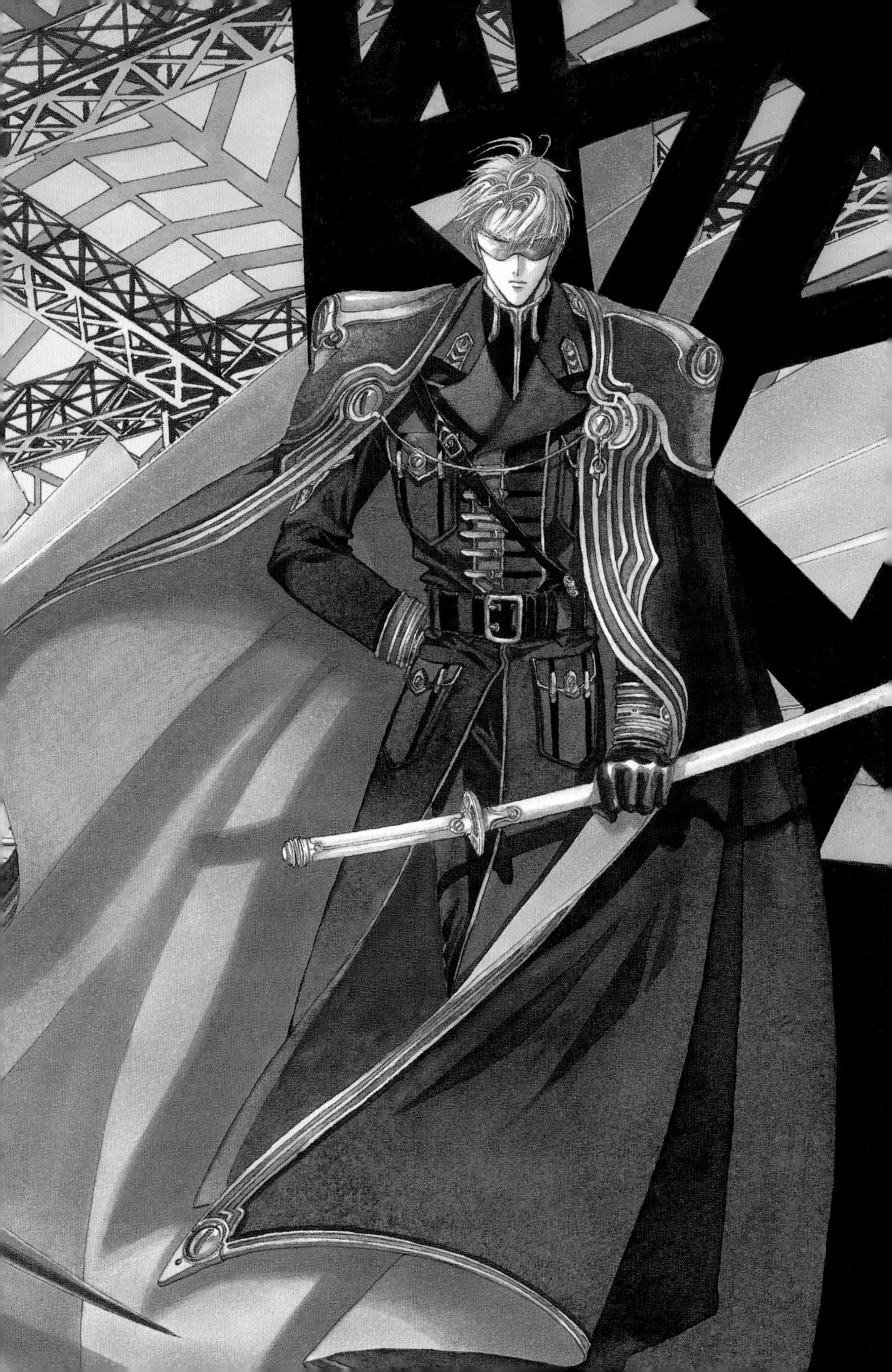

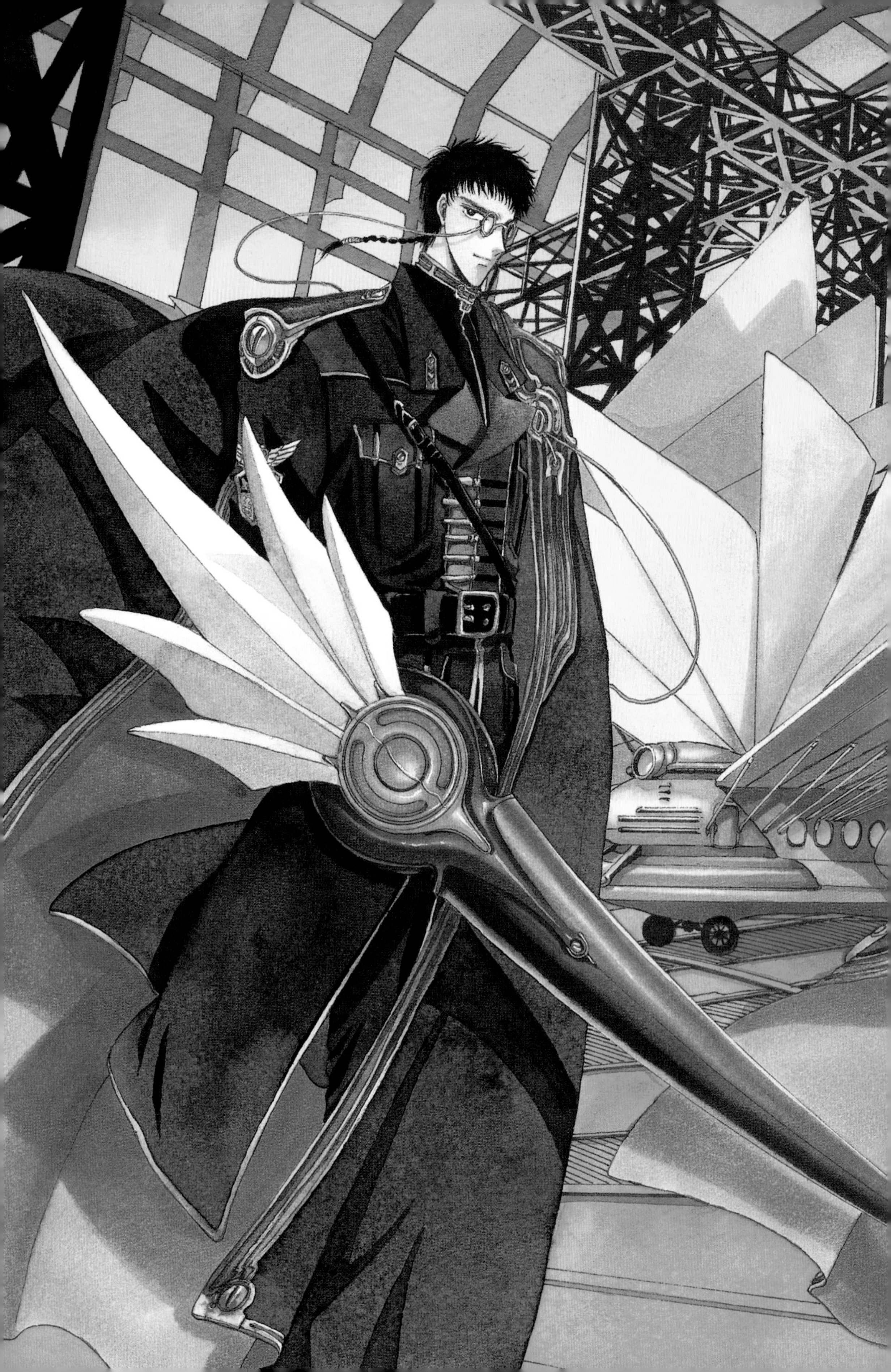

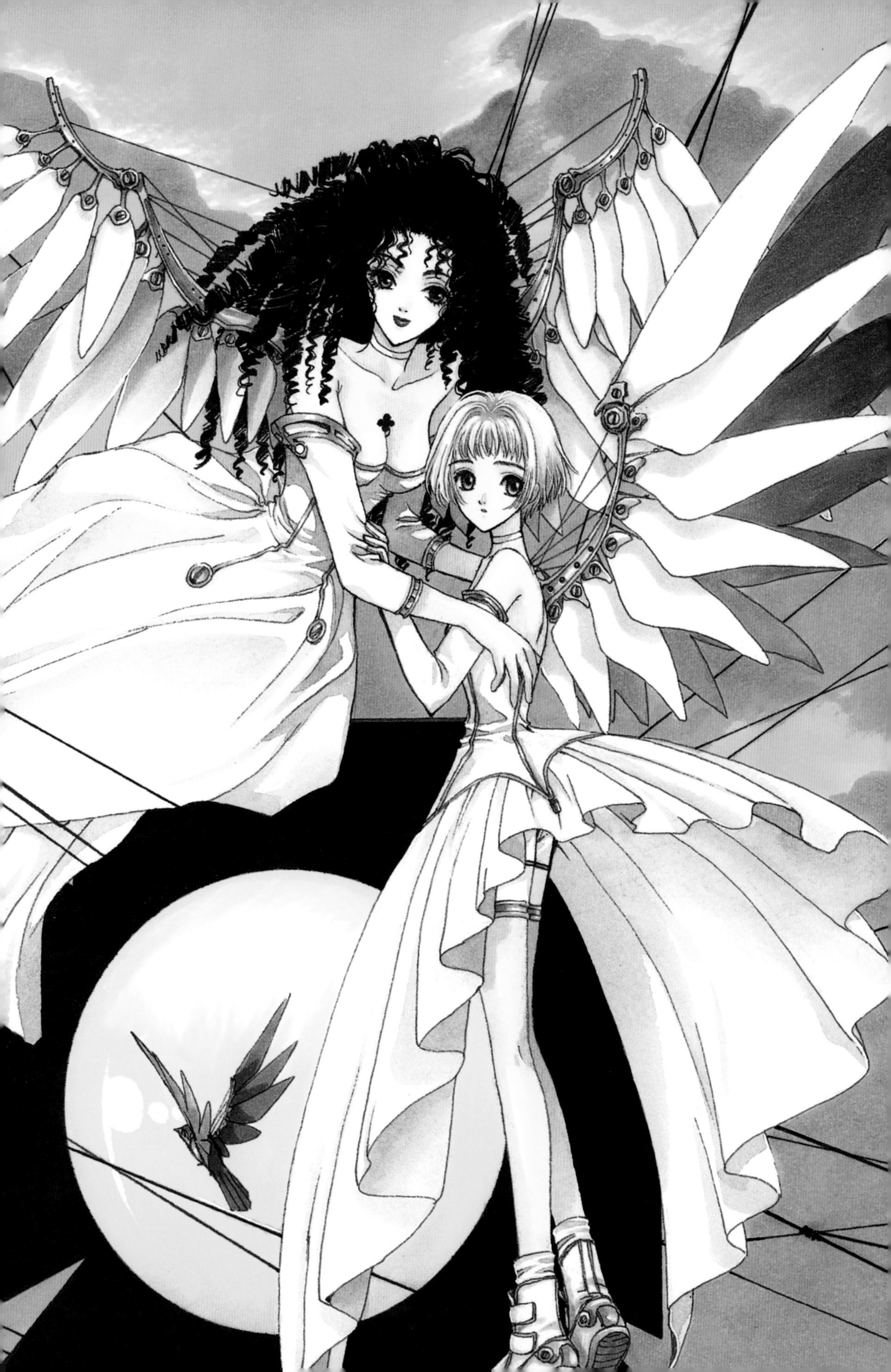

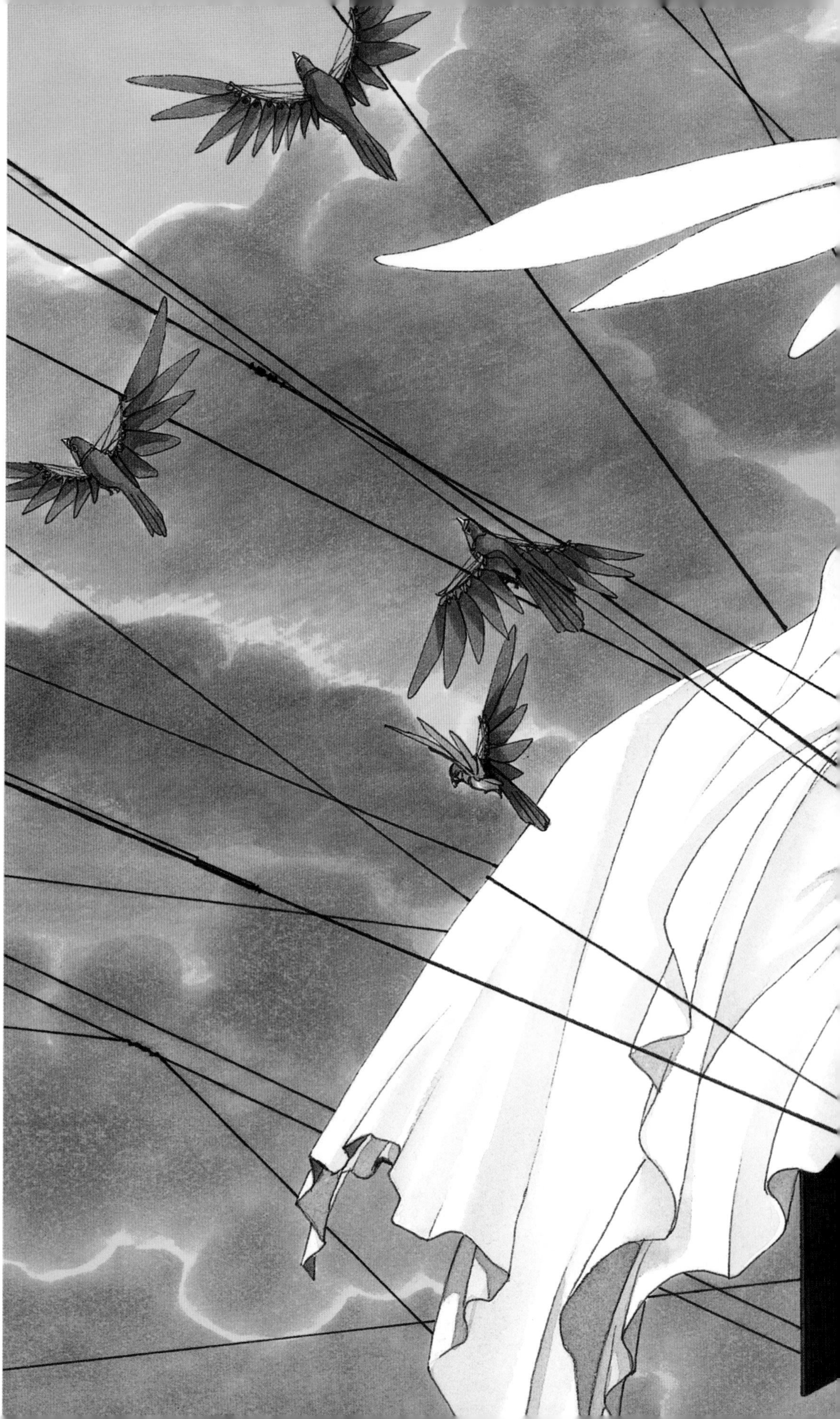

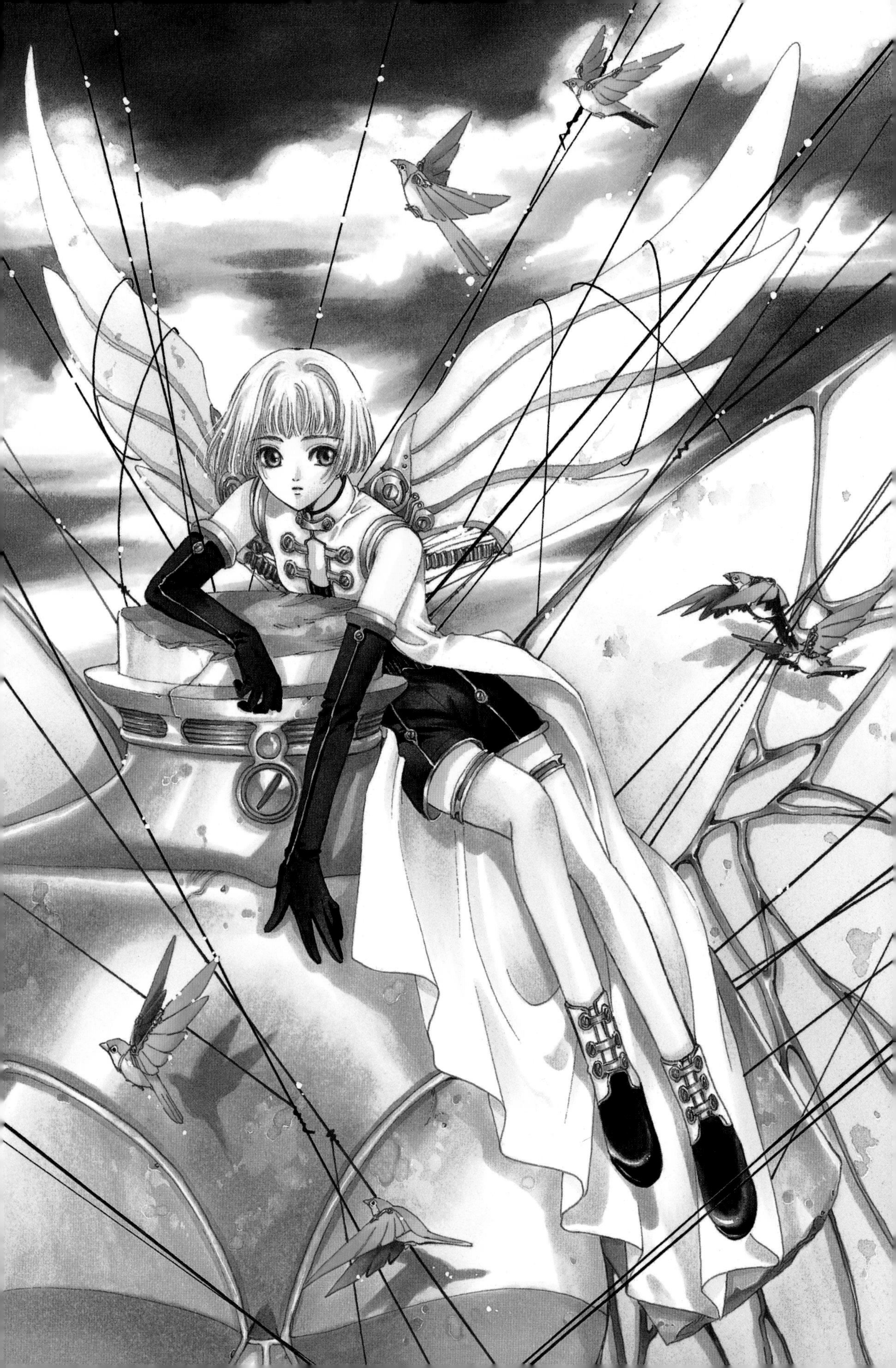

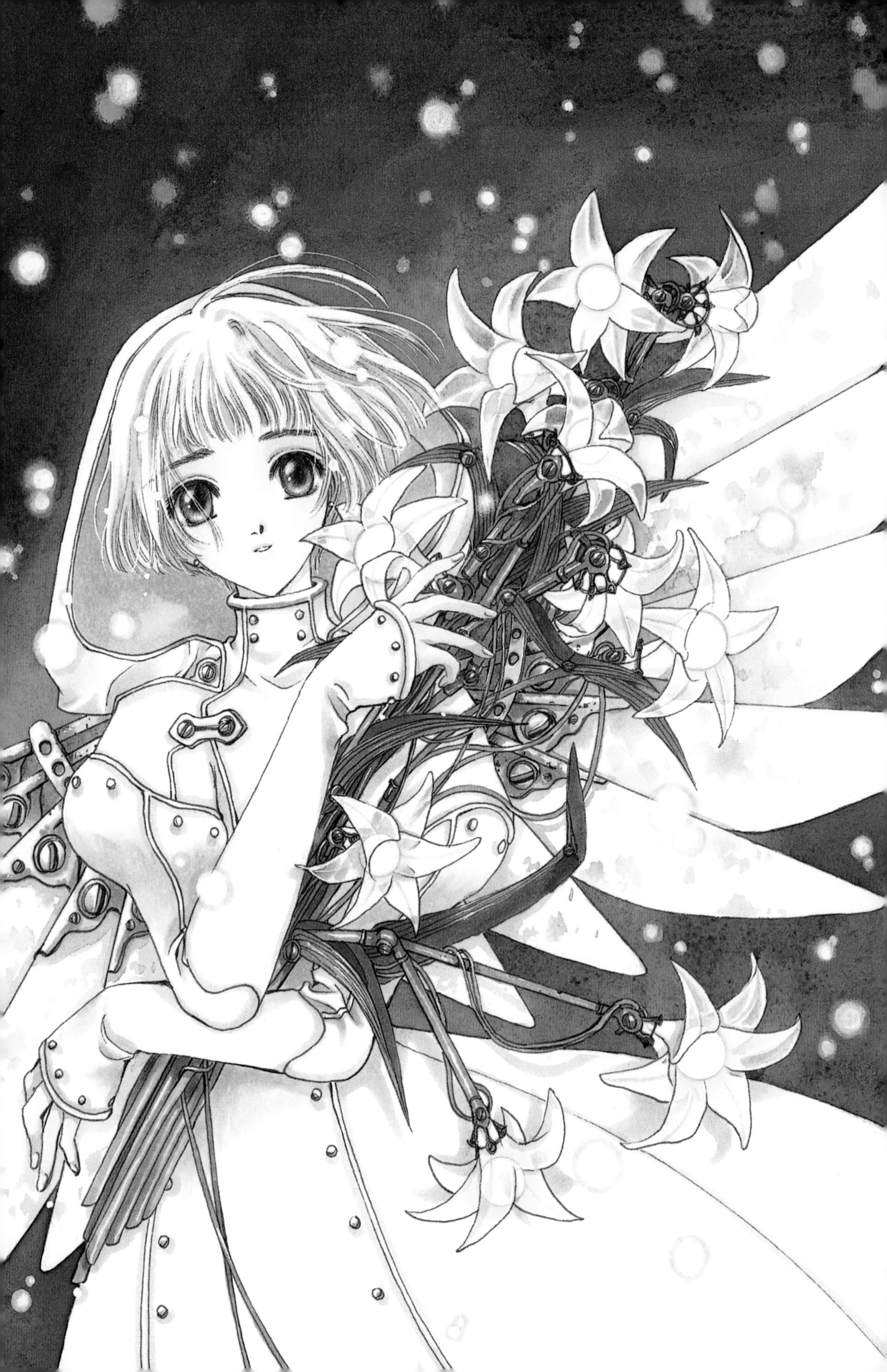

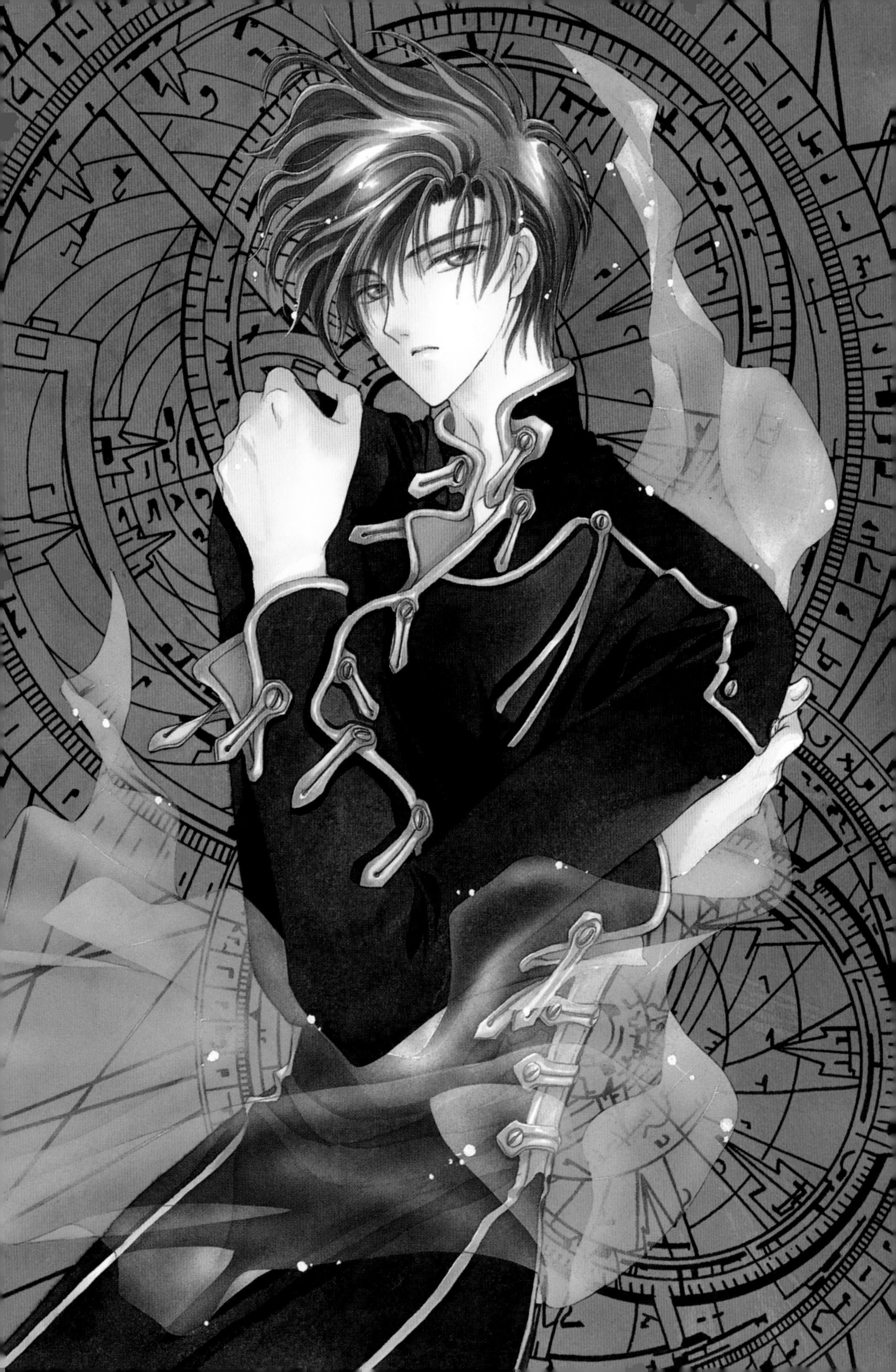

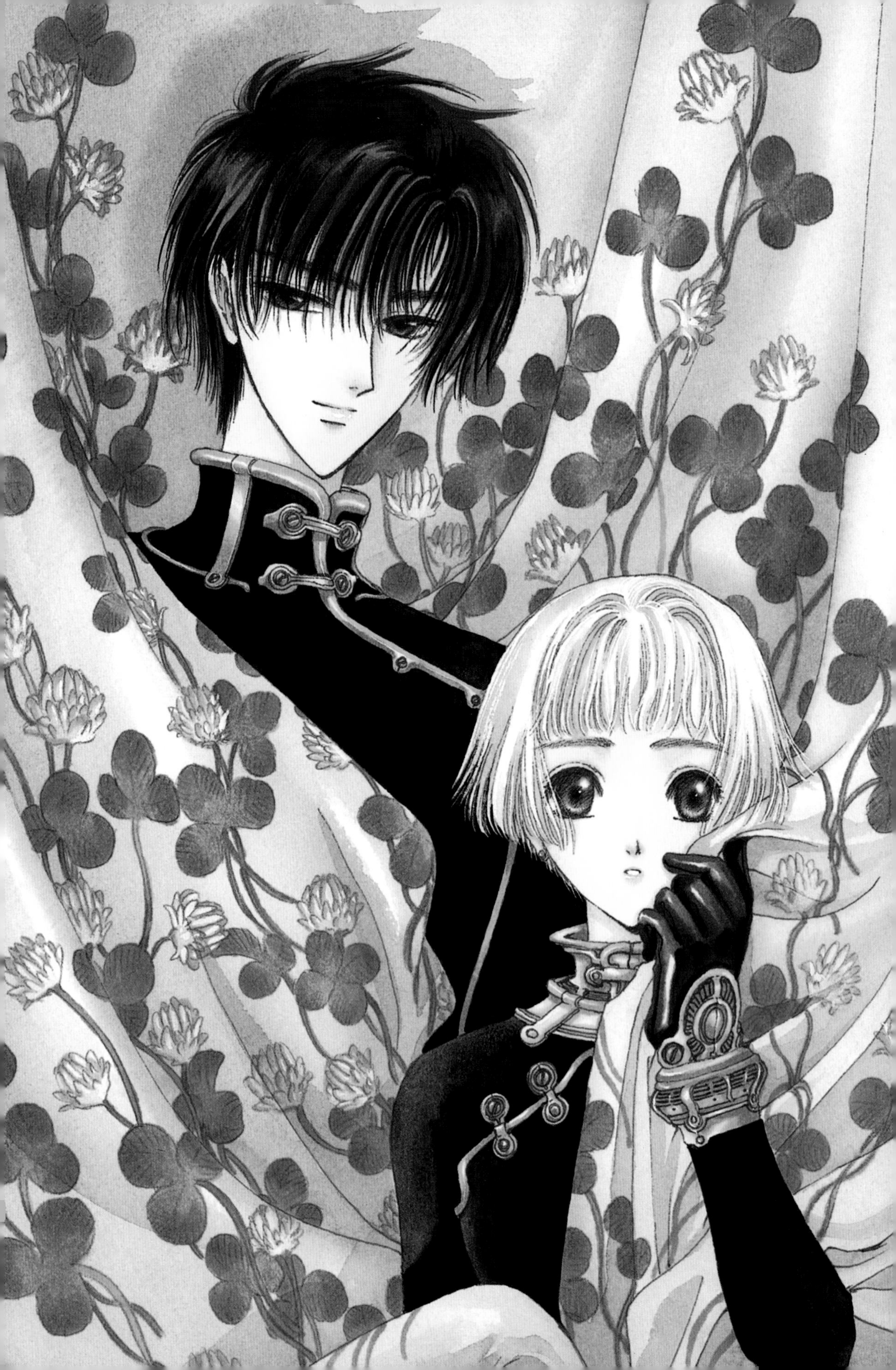

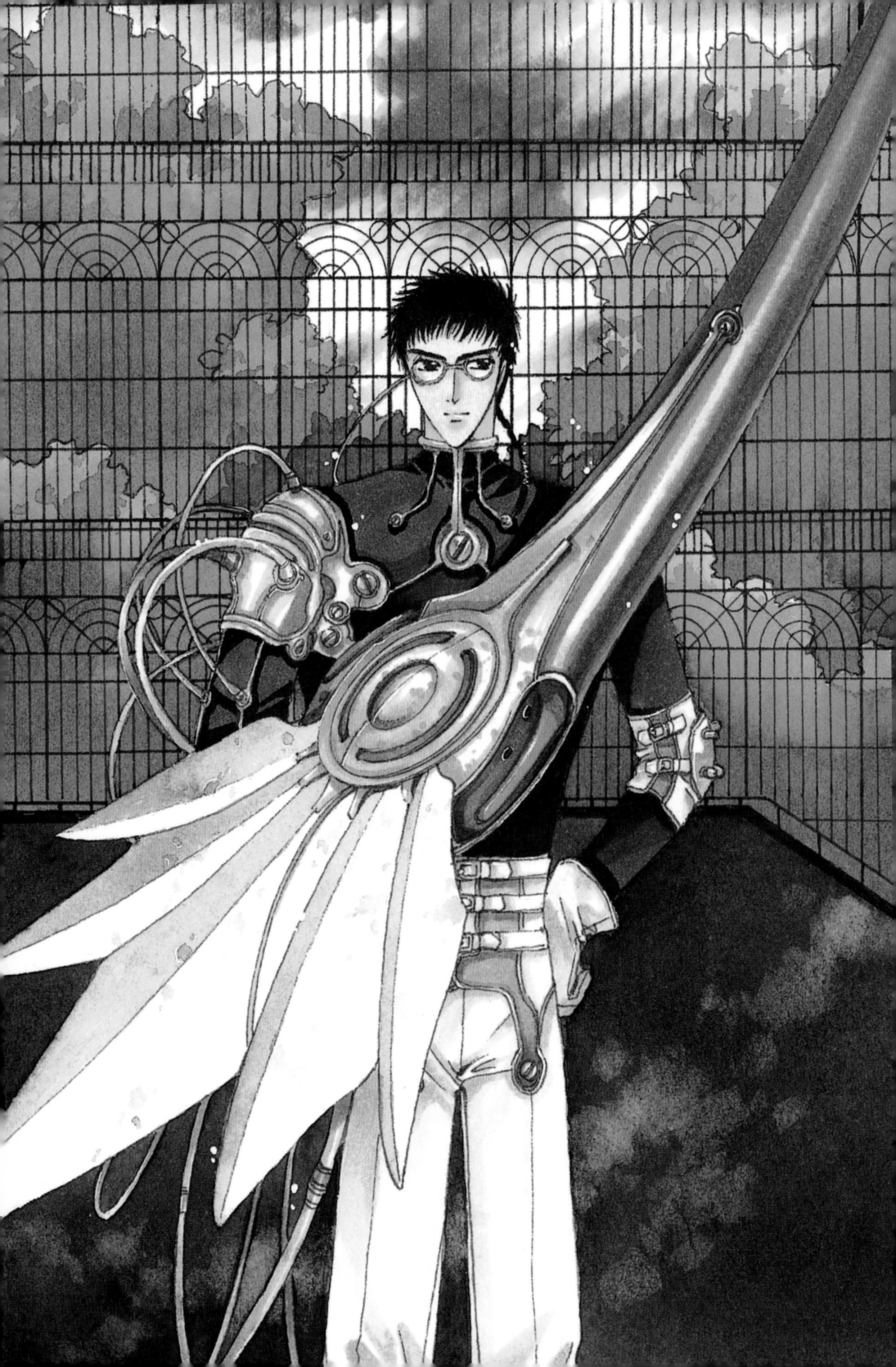

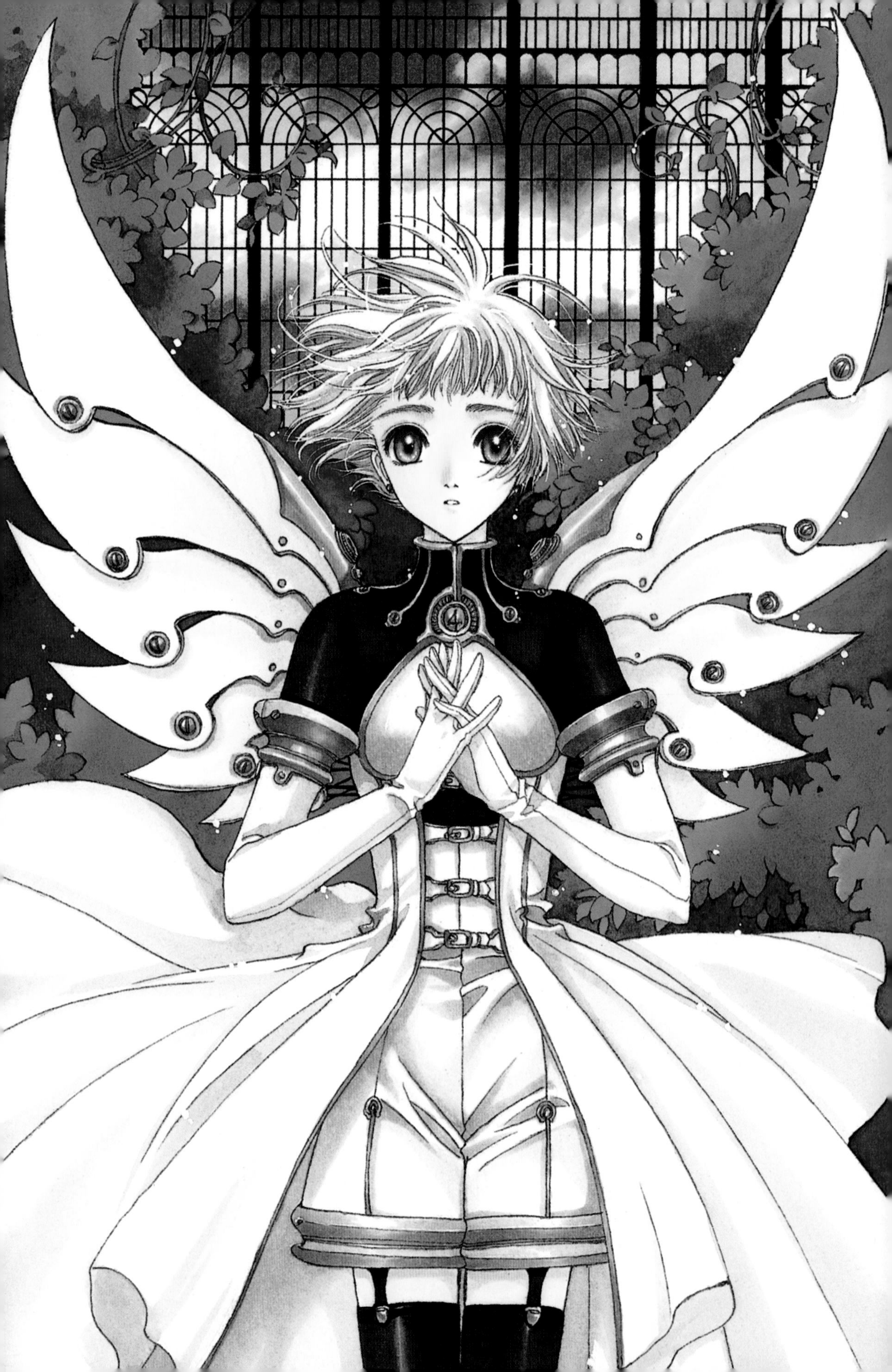

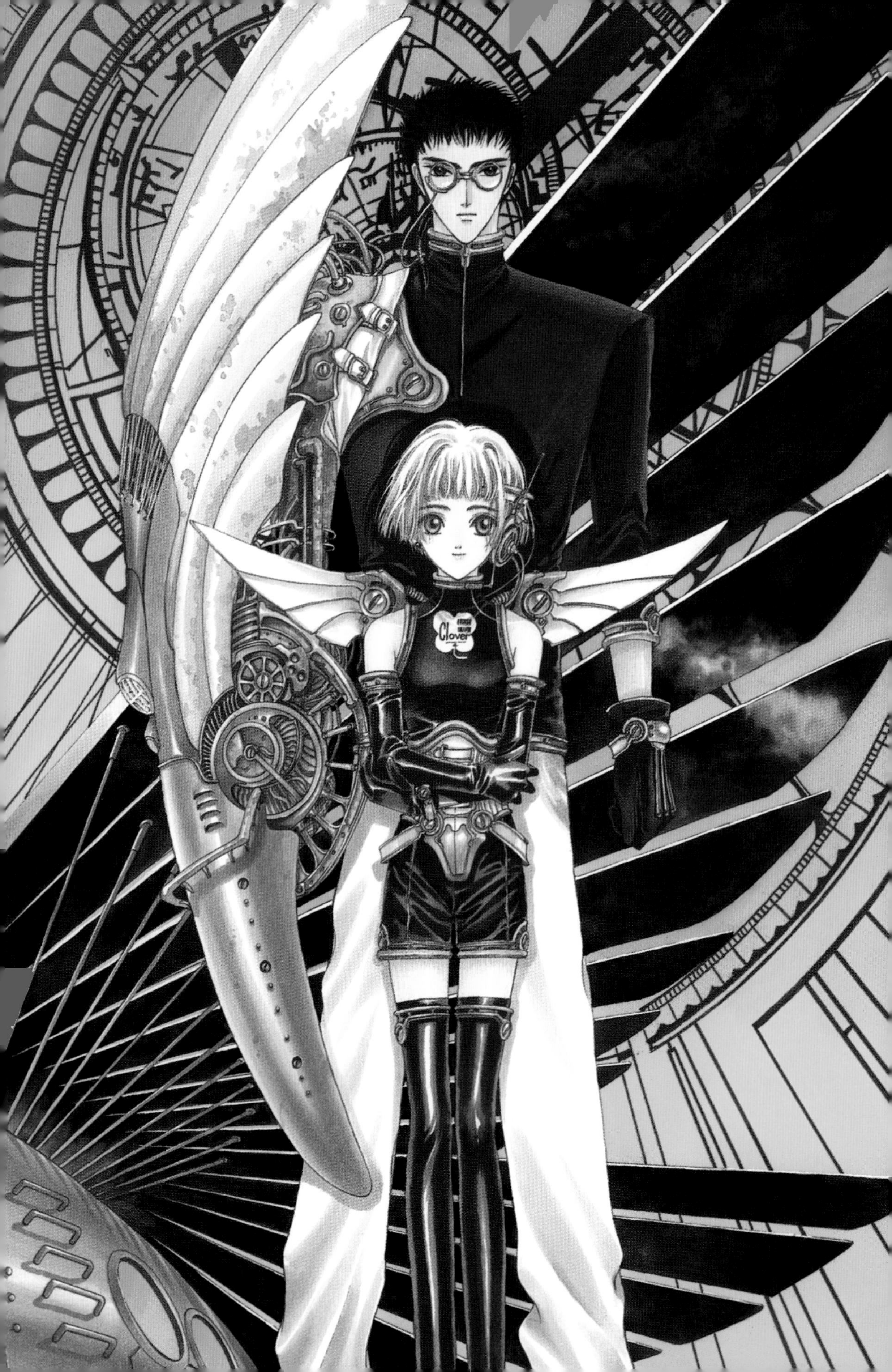
Clover

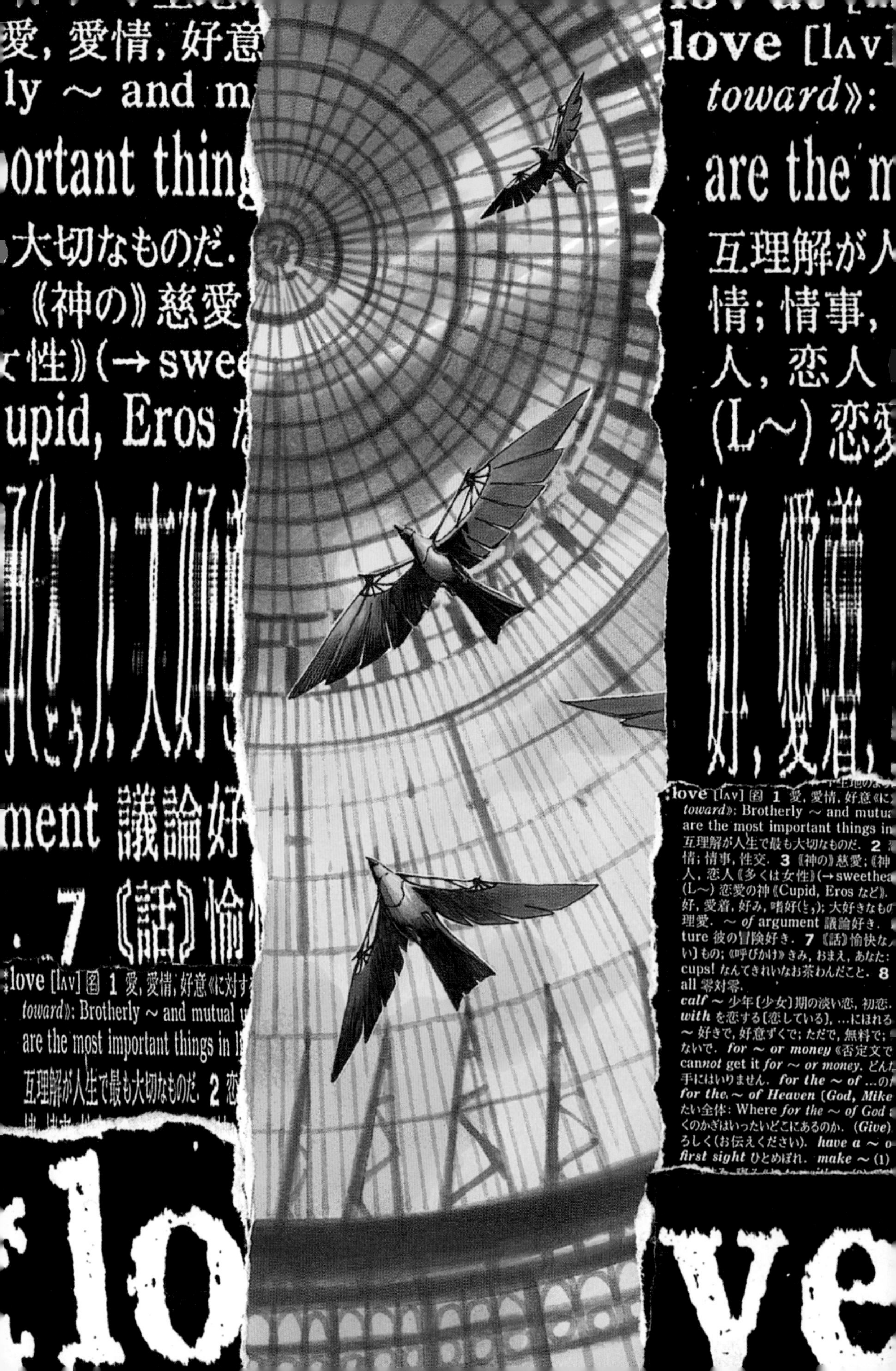

愛, 愛情, 好意
ly ~ and m
ortant thing
大切なものだ.
《神の》慈愛
upid, Eros
ment 議論好
7 《話》愉
love [lʌv] 图 1 愛, 愛情, 好意《に対す
toward》: Brotherly ~ and mutual
are the most important things in l
互理解が人生で最も大切なものだ. 2 恋
love [lʌv]
toward》:
are the m
互理解が人
情; 情事,
人, 恋人
(L~) 恋愛
love [lʌv] 图 1 愛, 愛情, 好意《に
toward》: Brotherly ~ and mutua
are the most important things in
互理解が人生で最も大切なものだ. 2
情; 情事, 性交. 3 《神の》慈愛; 《神
人, 恋人《多くは女性》(→sweethea
(L~) 恋愛の神《Cupid, Eros など》.
好, 愛着, 好み, 嗜好(しこう); 大好きなもの
理愛. ~ of argument 議論好き.
ture 彼の冒険好き. 7 《話》愉快な
い]もの; 《呼びかけ》きみ, おまえ, あなた:
cups! なんてきれいなお茶わんだこと. 8
all 零対零.
calf ~ 少年[少女]期の淡い恋, 初恋.
with を恋する[恋している], …にほれる
~ 好きで, 好意ずくで; ただで, 無料で;
ないで. for ~ or money 《否定文で
cannot get it for ~ or money. どん
手にはいりません. for the ~ of …の
for the ~ of Heaven [God, Mike
たい全体: Where for the ~ of God
くのかぎはいったいどこにあるのか. (Give)
ろしく(お伝えください). have a ~ o
first sight ひとめぼれ. make ~ (1)
lo
ve

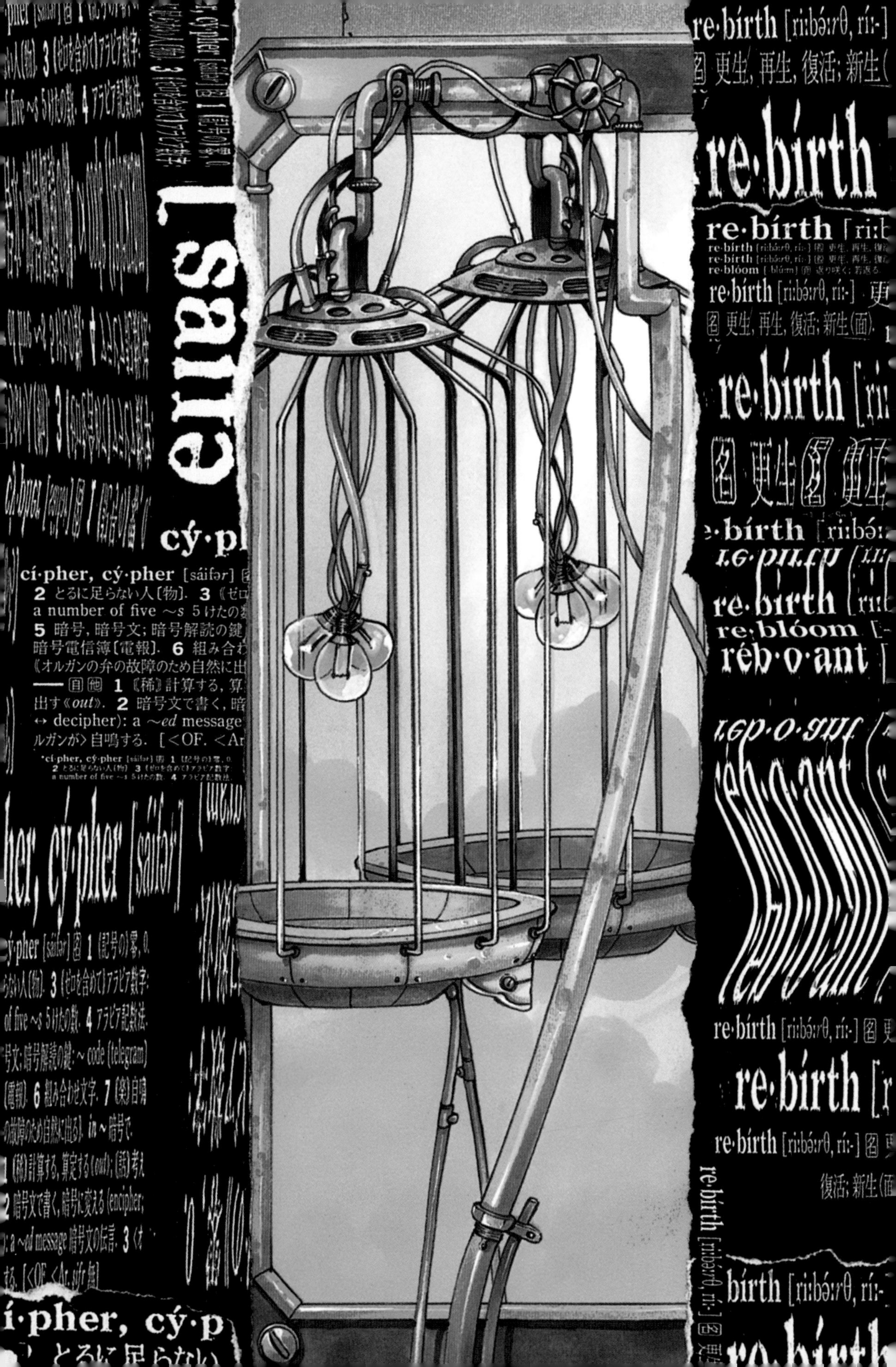

cý·ph
cí·pher, cý·pher [sáifər] 图
2 とるに足らない人〔物〕. 3《ゼロ
a number of five ～s 5けたの数
5 暗号, 暗号文; 暗号解読の鍵
暗号電信簿〔電報〕. 6 組み合わ
《オルガンの弁の故障のため自然に出
── 自 他 1《稀》計算する, 算
出す《out》. 2 暗号文で書く, 暗
↔ decipher): a ～ed message
ルガンが〉自鳴する. [＜OF. ＜Ar
her, cý·pher [sáifər]
ý·pher [sáifər] 图 1《記号の》零, 0.
らない人〔物〕. 3《ゼロを含めて》アラビア数字:
of five ～s 5けたの数. 4 アラビア記数法.
号文; 暗号解読の鍵: ～ code (telegram)
〔電報〕. 6 組み合わせ文字. 7《楽》自鳴
の故障のため自然に出る〉. in ～ 暗号で.
1《稀》計算する, 算定する《out》; 《話》考え
2 暗号文で書く, 暗号に変える (encipher;
): a ～ed message 暗号文の伝言. 3〈オ
る. [＜OF. ＜Ar. sifr 無]
í·pher, cý·p
2 とるに足らない
re·bírth [riːbə́ːrθ, ríː-]
图 更生, 再生, 復活; 新生
re·bírth
re·bírth [riː
re·bírth [riːbə́ːrθ, ríː-] 图 更生, 再生, 復活
re·bírth [riːbə́ːrθ, ríː-] 图 更生, 再生, 復活
re·blóom [-blúːm] 自 返り咲く; 若返る
re·bírth [riːbə́ːrθ, ríː-] 更
图 更生, 再生, 復活; 新生(面)
re·bírth [ri
图 更生
re·bírth [riːbə́
re·bírth [ri
re·blóom [-
réb·o·ant
re·bírth [riːbə́ːrθ, ríː-] 图 更
re·bírth [
re·bírth [riːbə́ːrθ, ríː-] 图
復活; 新生(面
re·bírth [riːbə́ːrθ, ríː-]
bírth [riːbə́ːrθ, ríː-

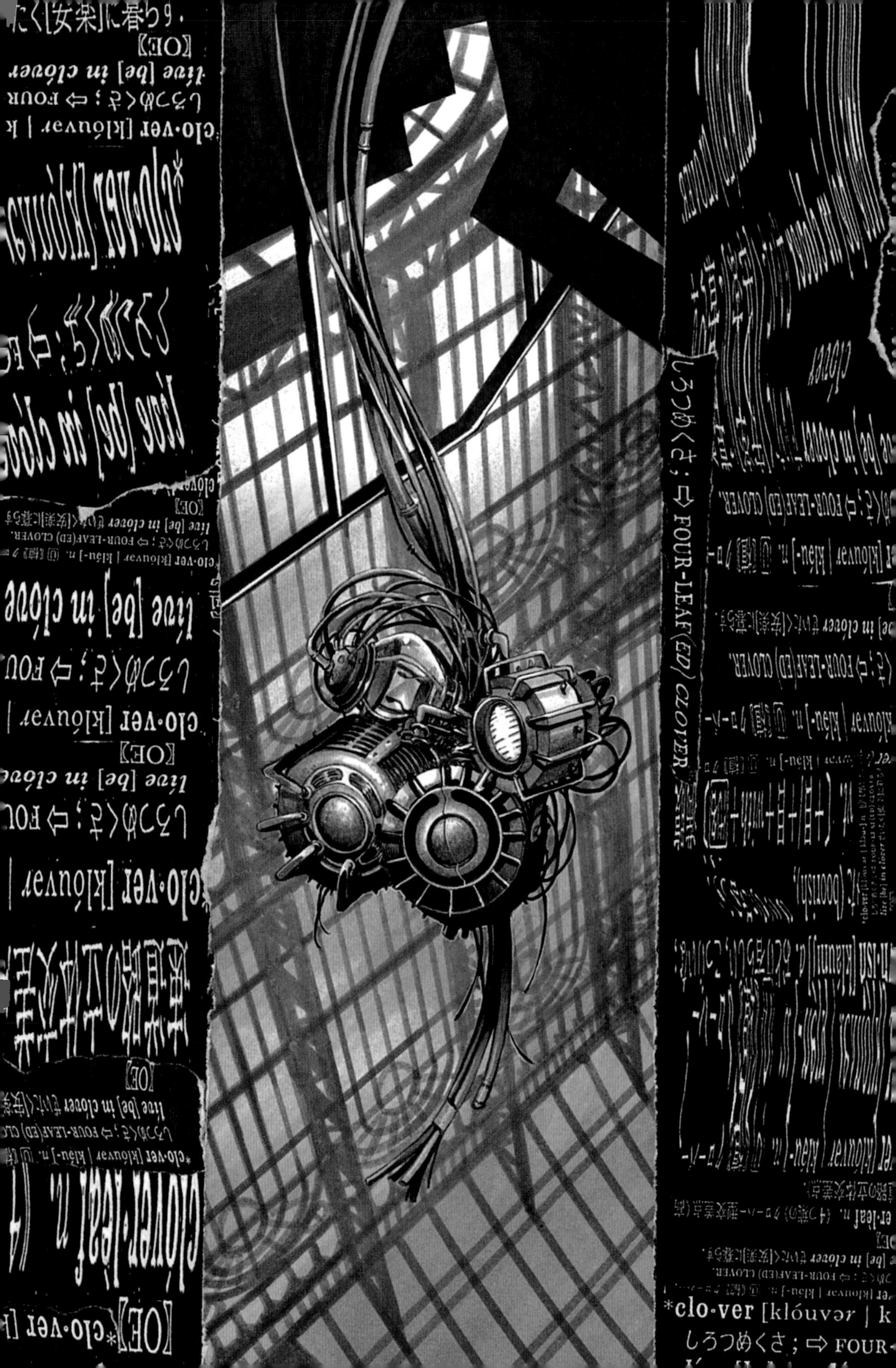

しろつめくさ；⇨ FOUR-LEAF(ED) CLOVER
*clo·ver [klóuvər | k
しろつめくさ；⇨ FOUR-

Take me to happiness 🍀

Date: 12/23/21

GRA 741.5 CLO
Clover /